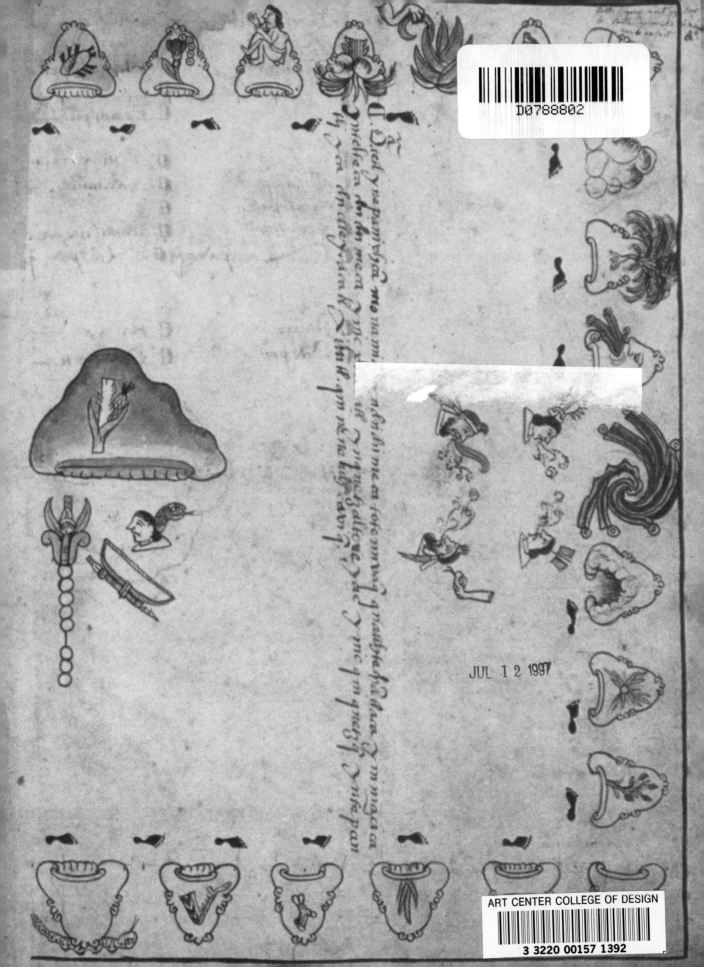

REFRAMING
THE RENAISSANCE

REFRAMING THE RENAISSANCE

Visual Culture in Europe and Latin America 1450–1650

Edited with an Introduction by

CLAIRE FARAGO

Yale University Press
New Haven and London

Designed by Miranda Harrison

Set in Bembo by Best-set Typesetter Ltd., Hong Kong
Printed in Hong Kong through World Print Ltd

Library of Congress Cataloging-in-Publication Data

Reframing the Renaissance: visual culture in Europe and Latin America, 1450–1650 / edited with and introduction by Claire Farago.   p.   cm.
Includes bibliographical references and index.
ISBN 0-300-06295-8   (hardback)
1. Art, Renaissance.   2. Art, Colonial – Latin America-Foreign influences.
3. Art, Renaissance – Influence.   4. Intercultural communication.
I. Farago, Claire J.
N6370.R36   1995   95-12148
709′.02′4 – dc20   CIP

Permission has been granted from:
Routledge, to cite text from Gayatri Chakravorti Spivak, *In Other Worlds*;
Columbia University Press, to cite text from P.O. Kristeller, *Renaissance Thought and Its Sources*;
University of Chicago Press, to include a portion of the first chapter of W.J.T. Mitchell, *Picture Theory*, as part of his contribution to this volume.

Frontispiece: Saltcellar, Sapi-Portuguese, ivory, *c*.1490–1530. Rome, Museo Preistorico e Etnografico, Luigi Pigorini. (Photo: Sergio Rossini, courtesy of the museum.)

CONTENTS

ACKNOWLEDGMENTS

This project germinated in a conference session, entitled "Reevaluating the Eurocentrism of Italian Renaissance Art History," that Gail Geiger and I organized for the College Art Association Annual Conference in Chicago in February 1992. Eloise Quiñones Keber and Cecelia Klein, who encouraged this project since its conception, generously contributed their papers from that session in revised and expanded form. Thomas Cummins, who acted as discussant for the CAA session, has contributed his own paper here. I would like to take note of another conference, entitled "Cross-Cultural Encounters," co-sponsored by the National Renaissance Society of America and the Northern California Renaissance Society at Stanford University in March 1992, which has been a stimulating source of ideas for this volume. Claudia Lazzaro and Jonathan Riess contributed articles based on papers presented at Stanford. Thomas DaCosta Kaufmann and Alessandro Nova participated in this volume on the basis of conversations we began at the same event.

My contribution to the volume has been enriched by ongoing conversations with all my contributors, whose collaboration on the Introduction made a world of difference (in all senses). I owe them individual thanks for their devotion to this project, and I am also grateful to other friends and colleagues who acted as valuable sounding boards at various points along the way: Janis Bell, Christopher Braider, Aline Brandauer, Tom Cummins, Anthony Cutler, Steven Epstein, Margaret Ferguson, Werner Gundersheimer, Ken Iwamasa, Thomas DaCosta Kaufmann, Martin Kemp, Cecelia Klein, Pamela Jones, Claudia Lazzaro, Dana Leibsohn, Keith Moxey, Alessandro Nova, Eloise Quiñones Keber, Donald Preziosi, Yvonne Reineke, Jonathan Riess, Joyce Robinson, Antonette Rosato, Pauline Watts, and Kathleen Weil-Garris Brandt all read earlier drafts at crucial junctures. Melanie McHugh and Shanna Waddell contributed in many essential ways as my research assistants. Randi Jenne prepared the manuscript for press.

I am also pleased to record accumulated debts to institutions that have encouraged this work. My initial interest in exchanges between Europe and the Americas was supported by a National Endowment for the Humanities Fellowship at The John Carter Brown Library in 1991–92. Generous support from the Graduate Committee on the Arts and Humanities at the University of Colorado supported the expense of illustrations. Of course, in every institution, real people give it life. At the JCB, Norman Fiering and his staff made their exceptional resources exceptionally available. At CU, the Steering Committee for Critical Studies of the Americas gave this project a home in its formative stages: I am particularly grateful to Manning Marable, William Wei, and Raymond L. Williams for their encouragement and excellent advice. Thanks to my editors at Yale University Press, Gillian Malpass and Miranda Harrison, for expertly shepherding the manuscript through press with great alacrity.

Anyone who studies human activities considered liminal by the dominant culture is contributing to the reformation of the canon. Before this project took shape as an anthology, I developed the main outlines for a critical study of Italian Renaissance art viewed in terms of cultural exchange by taking my research into the classroom.[1] It is almost needless to say that this experience made an important difference to the critical framing of these collected essays. As this book is going to press, I have become aware of an insightful and forthright contribution to the embattled topic of canon reform, John Guillory's *Cultural Capital: The Problem of Literary Canon Formation* (1993), to which this volume is a readymade response. Like Henry Louis Gates Jr., Guillory observes that the relationship between our critical postures and the social struggles they reflect is highly mediated. If I had known of Guillory's argument for considering the history of aesthetic judgment as "a privileged site for re-imagining the relation between the cultural and the economic in social life," I would have discussed it in the Introduction. At this point I would just like to note that Guillory's concern with the need to historicize the concept of value should encompass the fifteen and sixteenth centuries. What Guillory and others (Raymond Williams and Terry Eagleton, for two) describe as the eighteenth-century struggle to distinguish works of art from commodities is, undeniably, significant. But this explanatory model does not acknowledge that the concept of a work of art as an object intended for individual aesthetic contemplation is also a historical, culturally specific formation. A responsible account of the history of canon formation cannot neglect this significant aspect of its own development.

That is what much of this book is about – crossing and recrossing the boundaries of the concept that a work of art is an object intended for individual aesthetic contemplation. There are no timeless categories and there is no knowledge that is not a product of its own time. For this reason, and to honor the significant contributions that research and dialogue in the classroom made to revisioning the Renaissance for me, I dedicate this volume to all students, past, present, and future, of Renaissance art "out of the canon."

C.F.
Boulder, Colorado
April 18, 1995

Janis Bell is an associate professor of art history at Kenyon College. She has published on Raphael's coloring and its reception, on Caravaggio's coloring, and on the color theories of Leonardo da Vinci and Matteo Zaccolini in the *Art Bulletin, Journal of the Warburg and Courtauld Institutes, Achademia Leonardi Vinci*, and elsewhere. She is currently preparing an edition of Zaccolini's *Prospettiva del Colore*.

Tom Cummins is an assistant professor in the Art Department at the University of Chicago. He works in Latin American art and has published articles on Pre-Columbian Ecuadorian ceramics and colonial Peruvian painting. He is co-editor with Elizabeth Boone of *Native Traditions in the Postcolonial World* (forthcoming).

Anthony Cutler is Research Professor of Art History at Pennsylvania State University. His most recent publications are *The Hand of the Master. Craftsmanship, Ivory and Society in Byzantium* (1994), and articles in the *Art Bulletin, Journal of the Warburg and Courtauld Institutes, Burlington Magazine*, and *Dumbarton Oaks Papers*.

Claire Farago is an associate professor of art history at the University of Colorado at Boulder. She is the author of *Leonardo da Vinci's 'Paragone'* (1992) and articles on Renaissance art theory published in the *Art Bulletin* and elsewhere. She is currently completing a book, *Art as Institution*, on the history of the category "visual art," and writing on the ethnic complexity of devotional images produced in colonial New Mexico.

Pamela Jones is an associate professor of art history at the University of Massachusetts at Boston and a specialist in Italian Baroque art and religious thought. She is the author of *Federico Borromeo and the Ambrosiana. Art Patronage and Reform in Seventeenth-Century Milan* (1993) and articles appearing in the *Art Bulletin, Studies in the History of Art*, the *Leids Kunsthistorisch Jaarboek*, and elsewhere. She is currently writing on Caravaggio, and researching genre, audience, and display in Italian religious art from 1550 to 1650.

Thomas DaCosta Kaufmann is Professor in the Department of Art and Archaeology, Princeton University. A recent recipient of a Guggenheim Fellowship, his books include *The Mastery of Nature: Aspects of Art, Science and Humanism in the Renaissance* (1993); *Central European Drawings 1680–1800* (1989), and *The School of Prague: Painting at the Court of Rudolf II* (1988), which won the Mitchell Prize for art history. His *Court, Cloister, and City: The Art and Culture of Central Europe, 1450–1800*, is being published in 1995.

Eloise Quiñones Keber is Professor of Art History at Baruch College and The Graduate Center of the City University of New York, where she teaches pre-columbian art and the art of colonial and modern Mexico. Her most recent book, *Codex Telleriano-Remensis: Ritual, Divination, and History in a Pictorial Aztec Manuscript*, 1995, is a facsimile edition and commentary. She has published and lectured extensively on ancient Mexican manuscripts, Aztec art before and after the Spanish conquest, and on issues surrounding the encounter between indigenous and European traditions in sixteenth-century Mexico.

Martin Kemp is British Academy Wolfson Research Professor at the University of St Andrews, Scotland. In October 1995 he takes up the Professorship in the History of Art at the University of Oxford. He studied Natural Sciences and Art History at Cambridge, and at the Courtauld Institute of Art, London. He is the author of *Leonardo da Vinci, The Marvellous Works of Nature and Man* (1981, winner of the Mitchell Prize), and *The Science of Art, Optical Themes in Western Art from Brunelleschi to Seurat* (1990). He is currently researching issues in scientific representation and writing a book on anatomical, physiognomic, and natural themes in art from the Renaissance to the nineteenth century.

Cecelia F. Klein is Professor of Pre-Columbian/Colonial Art History at UCLA where she is currently writing a book on Mesoamerican art as seen through the lens of colonial writers and artists. She is the author of numerous articles on Aztec art and religion, including several on Aztec women and female deities.

Claudia Lazzaro, Professor and Chair of the Department of the History of Art at Cornell University, is the author of *The Italian Renaissance Garden* (1990) and several articles on villas and gardens. She is currently working on two projects involving visual representations of cultural identity – that of Italy in the three centuries of the Italian garden tradition and that of Florence under the sixteenth-century Medici.

Dana Leibsohn is an assistant professor at Smith College where she teaches art history. She has written articles on literacy, colonial studies in Latin America, and indigenous maps and manuscript paintings from New Spain. Her current research focuses on Pueblo and Spanish histories from seventeenth-century New Mexico, and on Nahua books and images created in Mexico.

W. J. T. Mitchell is Gaylord Donnelley Distinguished Service Professor of Art and English at the University of Chicago, and editor of *Critical Inquiry*. His recent books include *Iconology: Image, Text, Ideology* (1986) and *Picture Theory* (1994), and he has edited two recent collections of essays, *Art and the Public Sphere* (1993) and *Landscape and Power* (1994).

Alessandro Nova is Professor of Art History at the Kunstgeschichtliches Institut of J. W. Goethe Universität in Frankfurt. His most recent book is a monograph on Girolamo Romanino (1995), and he has published widely on art and patronge in Rome, Florence, and Northern Italy. Editor of a forthcoming volume of essays on Velasquez's *Las Meninas*, he is currently writing a book on the Franciscan Osservanta movement in fifteenth-century Italy.

Jonathan B. Riess, Professor of Art History at the University of Cincinnati, is, most recently, author of *The Renaissance Antichrist: Luca Signorelli's Orvieto Frescoes* (1995). He publishes on political aspects of medieval and Renaissance art in Central Italy.

Pauline Moffitt Watts is a member of the European history faculty at Sarah Lawrence College. She is the author and editor of books and articles in medieval and early modern religious and intellectual history, including several studies dealing with cross-cultural contacts in sixteenth-century Mexico. Her publications include *Nicolas Cusanus* (1982), and she is currently writing a book on the evangelization of Mexico, entitled *From the Desert to the New World: Monasticism, Resistance, and Reform in Sixteenth-Century Mexico*.

Modern scholarship has been far too much influenced by all kinds of prejudices, against the use of Latin, against the medieval church, and also by the unwarranted effort to read later developments, such as the German Reformation, or French libertinism, or nineteenth-century liberalism or nationalism, back into the Renaissance. The only way to understand the Renaissance is a direct and, possibly, an objective study of the original sources. We have no real justification to take sides in the controversies of the Renaissance, and to play up humanism against scholasticism, or scholasticism against humanism, or modern science against both of them. Instead of trying to reduce everything to one or two issues, which is the privilege and curse of political controversy, we should try to develop a kind of historical pluralism.

Paul Oskar Kristeller,
"Humanism and Scholasticism in the Italian Renaissance," 1945

Our intelligent and conscientious moderator seemed constantly to summarize me out of the group. After hearing us make our preliminary statements, he said that we were all interested in culture as process rather than object of study. No, I would not privilege process. After the next batch of short speeches, he said that it was evident that we wanted to formulate a coherent notion of explanation and culture that would accommodate all of us. No, I would not find unity in diversity; sometimes confrontation rather than integration seemed preferable.

Gayatri Chakravorti Spivak,
"Explanation and Culture: Marginalia," 1979

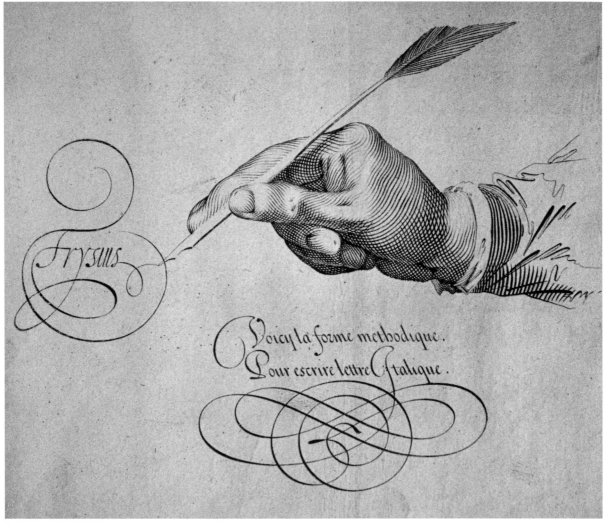

Jan van den Velde, *Instruction in the writing of the Italic Hand*. Engraved by Simon Frysius, from *Spieghel der Schrijfkonste*, Rotterdam, 1605. London, Victoria & Albert Museum. (Photo: Martin Kemp.) See Chapter 9 for full discussion.

Reframing the Renaissance

CLAIRE FARAGO

The initial idea for this collection of essays arose out of my own interest in the sixteenth-century change in status of the visual arts in Italy. I wanted to learn whether and how extensive global commerce affected sixteenth-century Italian discussions of art. I soon realized that existing accounts of the history of western aesthetic theory do not consider contact with non-European societies to have been a contributing factor before the nineteenth century, so I began to wonder how complete our historical understanding really was. It never occurred to academicians discussing the problem of the arts at the seventeenth-century Académie Royale de Peinture et de Sculpture, or to writers who popularized systematic classifications of the *beaux arts* in the eighteenth century, to include nonwestern styles of artistic production.[1] Yet the history of the classification of the arts and categories for judging artistic excellence deserves to be studied from a point of view broad enough to take into account the extensive migration of visual culture long before global contact was initiated at the end of the fifteenth century, and even more so during the era we still call the Renaissance.[2] Non-European art and artifacts were present in Europe throughout the Middle Ages and, after the Ottoman Turks captured Constantinople in 1453, great quantities of new material began arriving from the eastern Mediterranean basin, then Africa, the Americas, Asia, and elsewhere. During this period, the appreciation of art increased dramatically in Italy and elsewhere in Europe. A few extraordinary records – such as Albrecht Dürer's frequently cited admiration for Aztec gold- and silverwork – even attest to the appreciation of non-European objects as products of extraordinary artistic ingenuity.[3] At the same time, the value of certain kinds of artifice became the subject of violent controversy. What did new awareness of other cultures contribute to European conceptions of the arts during this initial period of global contact? And how did the exportation of Renaissance ideals and material culture, from Italy to other parts of Europe and worldwide, fare in this environment of intensified cultural interaction?

I also had to ask why the contribution of non-European cultures to western aesthetics and to the theoretical literature on art that preceded it was not widely acknowledged when the discipline of art history was professionalized in the nineteenth century. The hierarchy of the fine arts, of course, but also the organization of the discipline in terms of national cultures suggest some preliminary answers. It is a complex matter, however, to examine the history of our modern categories of artistic production and aesthetic appreciation. The recorded wonders of architecture and portable artifacts, even live specimens, that reached Europe during the Renaissance were classified in a variety of ways. My initial investigation of the history of the sixteenth-century status of the arts viewed in historiographical *and* crosscultural terms opened up a vast interdisciplinary field of research that invited a collaborative approach. This volume, which pools the resources of specialists in many subfields of sixteenth-century studies, is the result of that collaboration.

Reframing the Renaissance tries to define a new program for the study of Renaissance visual culture focused on cultural exchange. The essays throughout are addressed to Renaissance specialists and the subjects will, we hope, interest an interdisciplinary audience concerned with the early modern period. The collection grew out of the awareness that any attempt to reimagine Renaissance art as a culturally and historically specific style that originated in Central Italy and was disseminated around the globe should carefully *reexamine* the function, reception, and power of specific kinds of images and other objects of human manufacture. The first, historiographical section of *Reframing the Renaissance*, entitled "New Problems, New Paradigms: Revising the Humanist Model," identifies significant problems of ethnocentrism in past conceptualizations of Renaissance art. The second section, entitled "Renaissance Theories of the Image," presents specialized studies of various conceptual frameworks in which visual representation functioned. The third section, "Early Collecting Practices," treats an important source of information about sixteenth-century cultural exchange. The individual studies throughout the volume emphasize the essentially heterogeneous character of the many kinds of objects and activities we now loosely call art. The final section, entitled "Mediating Images: Developing an Intercultural Perspective," presents case studies of culturally hybrid images – of unruly women, colonial maps of Central Mexico, and a negative ethnic stereotype prominently depicted in an Italian Renaissance religious fresco. The authors adapt traditional techniques of art history – formal analysis, iconography, connoisseurship – to study the asymmetrical process of cultural exchange. An Epilogue relating the central issues explored in this volume to contemporary discussions of how we construct the human subject completes the study.

The quincentennial observance of Columbus's fateful first voyage encouraged many scholars with interests in crosscultural studies to focus on exchanges between "Old" and "New World" cultures. I have retained this focus in *Reframing the Renaissance*, mainly for pragmatic reasons. First, in attempting to control a very large topic, it seemed prudent to restrict some of the parameters. Second, there already exists an interdisciplinary field of study concerned with cultural interaction in the Spanish colonial world. As the five contributions to this volume that treat relations between transplanted Europeans and indigenous Americans in Latin America demonstrate, crosscultural investigations of early modern visual culture in this area are able to draw upon an extensive, theoretically sophisticated foundation of recent scholarship. This is a great advantage in defining a new program for the study of Renaissance art focused on the migration of visual culture and the conditions of reception.

*   *   *

Whose Renaissance? Revisiting "The Renaissance Problem"

Nearly every reevaluation of the Renaissance – this one is no exception – begins by acknowledging Jacob Burckhardt's *The Civilization of the Renaissance in Italy/Die Kultur der Renaissance in Italien*, first published in 1860. Supplemented by Burckhardt's historical guide to the visual arts in Italy and his other writings on art and architecture, this study – and writings by his immediate contemporaries including Michelet, Ruskin, and Taine – established the concept of the Renaissance as central to the discipline of art history. More than any other scholar, Burckhardt also established a role for visual evidence in the writing of cultural history.[4] As a result of extensive interest in the social and intellectual history of the visual arts over the past thirty years, we have become increasingly aware that our modern distinctions of art matured out of the particular historical and cultural circumstances in which Burckhardt lived and wrote.[5] Realizing that art defined as the object of individual aesthetic contemplation is a relatively recent construct, Peter Burke, in his own reassessment of the Italian Renaissance, recommends a shift in the focus of our attention to a wider range of "communicative events," such as popular songs, sermons, graffiti, and rituals.[6] Burke's revisionist approach to cultural history retains the spirit of Burckhardt's *Civilization*: both historians examine ritual, popular images, and other cultural activities with regard to a wider range of purposes than the category usually implied by "work of art."

Reframing the Renaissance also examines a broad range of communicative events. The present collection of essays tries to suggest, however, that much more is involved in reassessing the history of Renaissance art than trading one modern category for another, presumably less restrictive, one. The aesthetic system of the "fine arts" that designates the triad of painting, sculpture, and architecture emerged gradually over several hundred years. The system of classification that distinguishes the "fine arts" from the liberal arts and from the sciences was codified only in the eighteenth century, on the foundation of an extensive body of theoretical and critical literature in French, German, Italian, and English, and institutionalized artistic instruction at the professional level.[7] Burckhardt's writings are firmly grounded in this humanist model of culture. Yet his inclusion of popular culture to characterize the Italian national spirit in the early modern period, together with his famous characterization of the state as a "work of art," presents a much broader concept of what constitutes a work of art than his predecessors in aesthetic theory had envisioned. The terms of his argument about the state as the product of reflection and deliberation would take us far afield from the present discussion. Yet it is worth noting in the present context that Burckhardt constructed a generalized concept of art by borrowing a metaphor from political theory and analytical philosophy.[8]

The concept that a work of art can be something produced for individual contemplation in any medium or style by any culture or period is even more recent. At the beginning of the nineteenth century, Amerindian art was considered only to be of historical interest.[9] Some of Burckhardt's contemporaries challenged existing artistic norms associated with the revival of classical antiquity, being the first to suggest that the entire human race was engaged in the spiritual activity of making "visual art." It has been widely claimed, however, that nineteenth-century art historians and theorists such as Semper, Riegl, and Fiedler (who claimed that a work of art is the product of perception, regardless of its stylistic conventions) merely naturalized the Renaissance metaphor that art imitates nature. Most of the criticism has come from art historians who, justifiably, point to the untenability of this scheme. Yet they have considered the problems of privileging representational art only within the narrowly circumscribed limits of European art.[10]

In light of all the attention that art historians have paid to the history of our formal categories of art, it is surprising that no one has drawn a connection to the issues raised by Henry Louis Gates, Jr., and others, such as Samir Amin, concerned with the history of Eurocentrism. When Burckhardt's conception of the Italian Renaissance first became the "Renaissance problem" in historiography fifty years after the publication of *The Civilization of the Renaissance*, justification for his concept of periodization gravitated to the center of discussion. Then it was argued, largely on the basis of early humanist histories, that Burckhardt's scheme was justified because early humanists like Alberti and Vasari had used metaphors of revival and rebirth to define their historical position as separate from the past.[11] Today Vasari's humanist model of culture should make us ask different questions. Vasari's famous account of the birth of modern art (the "*buona maniera moderna*"), the most complete history written during the Renaissance, follows the established humanist model of historical change as a process of cultural decline and revival: the revival of the ancient art of imitating nature arrested a long decline instigated by "barbarians" who practiced the Byzantine manner (*maniera greca* or *maniera vecchia* "e *non* antichi") in painting and the German manner (*maniera tedesca*) in architecture.[12] No one would wish to dispute the historical influence of Vasari's humanist scheme, or deny the popularity of metaphors of rebirth during the period we still call the Renaissance. What counts as historical truth has, however, shifted considerably since the first contributions to the "Renaissance problem" nearly a century ago.

Vasari's praise of Italian artists at the expense of "barbarian" others could once be unselfconsciously used as evidence justifying the concept of periodization. Gates and other critics like Edward Said have charged that contemporary scholarship keeps itself pure by not taking certain kinds of contexts into account.[13] Said himself has been criticized for imposing his own binary oppositions (such as the oversimplistic concept of cultural domination and subordination). Yet his critique of the conflictual self–other relationship embedded in the European construction of the Orient provoked a richly conceived field of theorizing about the complexities of cultural interaction. Writers like Said who adopt the position of the formerly colonized subject are entirely new voices in the discursive space of cultural history writing – and their ongoing contributions are radically changing our understanding.

This collection of essays accepts Said's challenge of examining the assumptions on which "Renaissance" art history is conventionally based, not by rejecting historical schemes like Vasari's *arti del disegno*, but by making the history of our categories part of our subject of study. As the following specialized studies individually and collectively make clear, the mechanisms by which we discern differences in other cultures and the values we attach to these differences are not linked in any stable union. Samir Amin, the author of a leading study on Eurocentrism, defines Eurocentrism as a phenomenon that emerged fully in the nineteenth century.[14] According to its most sophisticated critics, the term Eurocentrism describes a complex set of dominant ideas associated with the rise of modern national identity, colonialism, and capitalism.[15] Said, Amin, and other critics regard the academic practices they associate with Eurocentrism as misleading because they are based on the flawed assumption that "internal factors peculiar to each society are decisive for their comparative evolution" culminating in the achievements of European civilization.[16] The Renaissance is regularly charged with providing the roots of these nineteenth-century practices.[17] Emerging interest in the institutional history of the discipline is beginning to reintegrate art history into a broader field of discussion centered on issues of methodology.[18] To open a discussion of methodology here is not meant to discredit the vigorous scholarship that goes on within the established perimeters of Renaissance art history, but rather to ask whether the categories into which our discipline is currently subdivided are really well suited to analyzing questions of intercultural exchange – significant historical questions that Said and many others have been pursuing and asking others to pursue in recent years. There already exists an established field of historical study, greatly envigorated by the Columbian Quincentenary, that examines the global expansion of Europe in the early contact period of the late fifteenth and sixteenth centuries. As might be expected, however, historians like Lewis Hanke, John Elliott, Edmundo O'Gorman, Anthony Pagden, and others have grounded their studies in texts, not visual images.[19]

It is not an easy matter to explain why Renaissance art historians have remained isolated from these debates and from interdisciplinary attempts to recognize Eurocentric practices and institute a more pluralistic historical vision. No doubt part of the answer lies with the polarizing effects of the "Eurocentrism" and "western canon" debates themselves. One of the major obstacles to revision is the nationalistic concern at the foundations of the scholarship. Perhaps another partial answer is embedded in our formal procedures of stylistic analysis, which are still closely associated with the typological thinking of the nineteenth century.[20]

Our understanding of Renaissance culture, fundamentally shaped by Burckhardt's study of Italy, has been changed and enriched by generations of debate over his characterization of historical periods, of individuality, of the Middle Ages and, most recently, of his treatment of gender.[21] Yet we still need integrated accounts that allow the disparate voices that have contributed to European conceptions of art to be heard. Parallel accounts that represent the same events from mutually exclusive points of view do not offer this perspective – the narratives presented by Paul Oskar Kristeller and Gates, respectively, can serve as examples. Kristeller examines only the dominant intellectual tradition with its roots in classical antiquity, while Gates dismisses western aesthetic theory out of hand for its racist elements. What are still missing are integrated attempts to define the issues that produced mutually exclusive narratives in the first place.

Gates grimly reminds us that written language, historically speaking, has been a significant, ethnocentric marker of cultural difference: in his revised narrative of aesthetic theory, Kant was the first to posit differences with regard to mental capacities and aesthetic capabilities on the basis of skin color; Hegel added a new feature when he claimed that, because Africans had not mastered the European art of writing languages, they had no history, and what Africans presumably lacked collectively, they also lacked individually: the childlike nature of slaves was due to their absence of memory.[22] Yet written language (*written* in European terms – that is, by means of an alphabetic script) is not the only ethnocentric indication of cultural difference. In the western tradition, other important criteria have been social organization: that is, forms of government, civil codes and customs, educational system, and artifacts or productions, including ritual and utilitarian objects, drama, music, and dance – what we loosely call art. All of these areas – language, societal organization, and art – have been powerful indexes of humanness. Many of the Eurocentric practices that Gates and others associate with the rise of the slave trade and other economic conditions have a much longer history concerning the respective roles of mental operations such as reasoning, memory, and the imagination in defining humanness. It is well known that during the same period when European painting, sculpture, and architecture first came to be defined as "theoretical" pursuits that depend on intellect and imagination, European images were exported on a global scale and artifacts also entered European collections from other parts of the world. These circumstances provided a particularly rich setting for the development of new cultural boundaries (inside and outside Europe) in which artistic production played an important role. We are, however, only beginning to formulate strategies for studying the contribution of fluctuating sixteenth-century senses of "art" to later ideas about cultural identity and aesthetic sensibility.[23]

The essays in this volume suggest some avenues for undercutting anachronistic cultural and aesthetic boundaries that interfere with our ability to see the complexity of artistic interactions during the sixteenth century. The history of the category "work of art" is a significant part of our subject of inquiry. Considered as a whole, this volume "reframes" the geographical, cultural, chronological, and conceptual boundaries of the Renaissance as it is usually defined. Part of the challenge of redefining the Renaissance in terms of cultural interaction is the manner in which newly emerging nations in the nineteenth century imagined themselves as antique. Why, asks Benedict Anderson, "[was] supposing 'antiquity' at a certain historical juncture, the necessary consequence of novelty?" – why should awareness of a radically changed form of consciousness in the nineteenth century lead to the construction of a "nationalist memory" reaching back in time?[24] Utilizing a "double vision" – to borrow a term from Joan Kelly – our essays individually and collectively look "inside" *and* "outside" the frameworks traditionally associated with the Renaissance.[25] The "inside and outside" that the problem of "national identity" poses for the study of Renaissance art is this: the history of the concept of national identity emerged along with the history that national identity frames. Considering nationalism in this light, scholars have helped to construct the modern idea of a nation as an enduring collective. A significant aspect of the problem of nationalism for historians of Renaissance culture, therefore, is to take into account the role of scholars who produced histories of "national culture."

Theorizing Cultural Interaction

The 1990–92 seasons offered an unprecedented number of museum exhibitions concerned with the early phase of European expansionism in a revisionist framework. Blockbuster exhibition formats were both diachronic (the "splendors" of Mexico spanned thirty centuries) and synchronic (the theme "1492" suggested reasons to survey artistic production around the globe).[26] As even the most spectacular of these exhibitions demonstrated, however, political and ideological issues that had been on the table of discussion in other fields, such as history, anthropology, literary and film criticism, for two and three decades have not made a major impact on museum practice. It is worth pondering the negative implications of a display strategy, conventionally regarded as neutral, for exhibitions which claim to represent all cultures on equal footing. To give just one example, for the sake of introducing broader methodological concerns, cultural bias on what might be called the performative level of *Circa 1492: Art in the Age of Exploration*, organized at the National Gallery in Washington, D.C., becomes apparent when we compare the presentation of the Asian section with the European Renaissance section of the same exhibition. The selection and presentation of the European objects invited specific visual comparisons from the audience – an audience informed, moreover, by text panels giving the public access to the specialized scholarship in the catalogue. The Chinese objects, however, displayed in the manner of many older museums of Asian art, were encased in large glass vitrines accompanied by the barest of labels, leaving viewers uninformed about the original cultural significance of the diverse materials gathered for aesthetic contemplation.[27]

I do not wish to lay blame for standard museum practices at the feet of any individual, or to deny the extraordinary visual experience that *Circa 1492* and other Quincentennial exhibitions presented, nor to discount the important scholarly contribution that these exhibitions and their monumental catalogues made. My point is that there is a pressing need to revise disciplinary practices at a fundamental, epistemological level. The short-coming of the collaboration among different subdisciplines of art history (or rather, lack of *real* collaboration) for *Circa 1492* as a whole was that it encouraged viewing practices rooted in European cultural imperialism. For did not American viewers learn a great deal about Renaissance Europe, about which they were already relatively well informed, while the decontextualized presentation of objects categorized by national culture as "Chinese" reinforced longstanding stereotypes of the exotic east in western eyes?

These problematic ideological implications were not lost on reviewers – even those as different from one another as Simon Schama and Homi Bhabha registered similar responses to the exhibition.[28] Bhabha charged that the major narrative message, namely the creation of a global culture around 1492, while it avoided the idea of progress by presenting a horizontal survey, failed to develop a "useful critical response" to cultural difference.[29] Cultural parallelism as an exhibition strategy, Bhabha elaborated, promotes "spectatorship" and, therefore, the parallels begin to look "distinctly circular" when they are framed within a relatively uncomplicated western aesthetic realm. Why, he asked, has this exhibition failed to problematize the notion of the human?

Schama reached a similar conclusion concerning the failure of the exhibition to theorize cultural interaction: he charged the National Gallery exhibition organizers with refusing to consider the phenomenon of Columbus and the historical experience of his four voyages as a European encounter with other cultures.[30] It is now commonplace, chided Schama, that many syncretistic societies "have managed to mutate into forms that reflect the possibility of a shared historical evolution," so why could the *mingling of destinies* not have been the focus of more Columbian commemoratives?[31]

These are good questions – but they have no ready answers. In the terms used by Thomas Kuhn to discuss the nature of scientific revolution, we find ourselves writing at a time when our inherited paradigms cannot be taken for granted because they do not seem to assimilate the phenomena that need explanation.[32] Some readers may disagree, but I think that the activity of paradigm formation does not usually fall to large museums, which always have to please their sponsors by pleasing the public, or to reviewers whose suggestions, however insightful, are still limited to a few pages of criticism on someone else's project. Scholars conceiving of research programs, on the other hand, have the academic freedom (at least in theory) and the intellectual responsibility to assess, revise, and propose paradigms – those fundamental intellectual armatures that determine what data to seek and how to organize the material on which conclusions are based.

What would the questions posed by Schama, Bhabha, and other critics sound like if art historians were providing extended answers? *Reframing the Renaissance* takes up the challenge of *theorizing* the human complexity of visual culture during the initial period of extensive interaction on a global scale. As editor, I initially framed the main areas of inquiry around epistemological issues raised by changing definitions and functions of art in the last four centuries. The conceptual skeleton of the volume was greatly enriched by ongoing exchanges with *all* the collaborators, who raised many more issues, grounded in diverse kinds of historical evidence. The wide variety of our interests and critical approaches allows *Reframing the Renaissance* to sustain a broad metacritical perspective *and* simultaneously to present a rich body of primary source material.

What would the history of Renaissance art look like if cultural interaction and exchange, and the conditions of reception, became our primary concerns? How can we change our existing paradigm to define this new puzzle? These are the overriding questions that circulate throughout the individual essays. Acknowledging the difference between the actual effects of emerging nationalistic practices and idealized European notions of cultural integrity and discreteness is central to the revisionist enterprise of *Reframing the Renaissance*. To historians of art – and especially to historians of Renaissance art – I hope that the organization of the volume appears as a systematic attempt to reground the discipline in the historical circumstances of its own making. Yet I do not want to make unjustified claims for the unity of what is, after all, an anthology. This volume is still an eclectic representation of the shifting of fields and frameworks that are currently under way in a number of academic disciplines. The format of an anthology is well suited to our interdisciplinary effort of reconceptualizing the Renaissance because anthologies, by their nature, avoid the impression of a unified narrative. At this preliminary stage of defining new analytical categories, it would be misleading to claim that the specialized papers included in this volume frame all the significant issues.

Visible symbols are prominent indicators of cultural identity yet, as Francis Haskell emphasized in *History and its Images*, it is notoriously difficult to establish the value of art as historical evidence. A potentially important contribution that this volume hopes to make to interdisciplinary discussions about cultural interaction grows out of the authors' overriding concern with interpretations of visual representation. In the following section of the Introduction I have tried to suggest how the contributors' shared interest in methodology intersects conceptually with the book's focus on the migration and reception of visual culture, by drawing a concrete example from my own research.

The Grotesque in the Mirror of European Theories of the Imagination

From the mid fourteenth to the mid seventeenth century – the period broadly designated by the term Renaissance – as painting, sculpture, and architecture "rose" from their medieval association with the mechanical arts and productive sciences, they became associated with other theoretical branches of knowledge, such as optics, anatomy, and the arts of discourse.[33] Whether the "nobility" of painting and the other two *arti del disegno*, sculpture and architecture, depended on their association with the mathematical sciences or with letters, however, their intellectualization was granted by a neo-Aristotelian model of cognition that privileges the role of vision above all the other special senses. In the course of the Renaissance, European writers put increasing emphasis on the distinctly human ability to think abstractly and to involve the visualizing powers of sight in combination with the imagination in the process of gaining a rational understanding of the created world and revealed knowledge of God.[34]

Transformations in a neo-Aristotelian theory of the imagination that granted increasingly rational powers to the artist's mental deliberations, together with the classification of human knowledge in a hierarchical scheme that had always subordinated fiction and fantasy to rational thought and divine revelation, are two very important factors in the historical notion of a hierarchy of the arts. Renaissance painting, sculpture, and architecture – defined as theoretically grounded pursuits associated with poetry or perspective, or both, and based on experience – provided the normative standards against which nonwestern cultural products were measured by Europeans for hundreds of years.

It is important to bear in mind that the word art did not yet mean what it does today. In the sixteenth century, art most often signified skill, as defined by the rhetorical tradition, or procedures, and as such it was the equivalent of terms like method or compendium.[35] Both skill and procedures were associated with artists' mental activity, their ability to invent new things out of their imaginations. The evolving definition of art is only one thread in a complex weave of changing attitudes towards human knowledge during this period, but perhaps a concrete example can clarify the negative implications glimpsed in the new sixteenth-century understanding of art for non-European cultures. To anticipate a point raised by W. J. T. Mitchell in the Epilogue about the relevance of an African spoon to the Sistine Ceiling, what would have been the appeal for European audiences of the late fifteenth- or early sixteenth-century ivory Sapi–Portuguese saltcellar with an Italian provenance reproduced in the Frontispiece?

Certainly, a sixteenth-century Italian (or any humanist) collector would have appreciated this magnificent object, commissioned from Sapi artists by Portuguese traders, for its precious material, skillful carving, and especially the figures as products of the artist's fertile imagination. But at the same time, the figures' elongated proportions and disproportionately large heads may have signified the artist's deficient knowledge of anatomy and ignorance of classicizing principles of proportion. Consequently, the maker of this object, should the Sapi carver's identity have been considered at all, might have been characterized as possessing an active but irrational imagination, unaccompanied by the rational powers exemplified in contemporary Italian and Italianate productions, where evidence of scientific knowledge in anatomy and perspective was manifested in the work.

For European audiences, the value of African–Portuguese ivories and similar objects might even have diminished had the amusing, grotesquely proportioned figures (amusing and grotesque in European eyes, that is) become vehicles of crosscultural communication instead of decontextualized signs of otherness and of universal artistic ingenuity. For the native inhabitants of Sierra Leone, as Suzanne Blier has recently shown, such carved images belonged to an entirely different conceptual framework.[36] The large seated figure at the top, despite its negroid physiognomy, was probably meant to represent an ancestral spirit incarnated in the form of a Portuguese trader (since both were white in the Sapi imaginary), made by artists who may not have had access to a living Portuguese model. The function of this hybrid object as a container of salt was foreign to the Sapi culture, but the severed heads and the main figure's seated position can be connected specifically with Sapi burial traditions. By contrast, the same scene is likely to have encouraged European fantasies of decapitation and cannibalism among "savages" – to judge from the popularity of such stories in sixteenth-century travel literature. Sensationalizing fantasies may even have prompted the commission of the object, although we are likely never to know because no records survive. This lack of documentation – which is characteristic of the entire class of fifteenth- and sixteenth-century African–Portuguese ivories – further suggests that these hybrid cultural products were valued primarily as exotic collectors' items, not as representations of Sapi beliefs, by the Europeans who sought them and assimilated them to their own frames of reference.

Taking part in a complex cultural exchange, exotic objects did not carry just one set of connotative meanings. A wide range of artifacts, regardless of their origins, may have evoked similar responses from European audiences. It seems to me that we have not considered the complex discursive field about artistic invention that may have encouraged such generalizations. The artifice of any work of art was most often evaluated as part of a contest between nature and art but, whatever the narrative framework, the artist's invention was always conceptually conjoined with the needs of both the subject and the particular viewing audience. In this three-way relationship among subject, artist, and audience, the intentions of the artificer were considered manifest in the work of art.[37]

That is, as early as the sixteenth century (and much earlier, in fact), European viewers thought it was possible to read the mentality of the artist out of his artistic productions. Artistic invention, conceived in sixteenth-century terms as any kind of artifice invented by the artist, is a historical, culturally specific category for assessing the epistemological status of a work of art as well as its maker. *Grotteschi* – the word refers literally to a kind of pictorial embellishment composed of playful, monstrous figures in ancient painting and architectural ornament – had long been associated with the active powers of the imagination. In the circle of Michelangelo, *grotteschi* were regarded as emblematic of the procedure of invention in architecture, where the parts are composed in a way not to be found in nature.[38] Such compounds, according to Vincenzo Danti, define an entirely new genius of the art of design, separate from painting, sculpture, and architecture, the arts that can "imitate or truly portray all things that can be seen."[39]

Grotteschi and similar artistic inventions signified in a doublehanded way, however. On one hand, they stood for artists' freedom and capacity to invent images out of their imaginations that nature could never create; on the other hand, and for the same reasons, *grotteschi* were associated with irrational mental activity, the active imagination unrestrained by human reason. The centrality of pure artifice to discussions of artistic invention is suggested by the circumstance that in 1563 the Council of Trent adopted a theory of images which effectively censured all unnecessary embellishments in sacred images.[40] The religious decorum of sacred images decreed by the post-Tridentine Church redirected previous appreciations of artistic license: too much artistic freedom manifested as too great a display of art was perceived as a threat to ecclesiastical authority. Reformed styles of optical naturalism were often considered outward signs of the truth-telling power of images.[41]

In the sober religious climate of the latter part of the sixteenth century, the subject of *grotteschi* gravitated to the center of discussions about art in Italy.[42] Under pressure to justify and reform devotional practices, writers who once might have praised *grotteschi*, *capricii*, and other pure *fantasie* as inventions intended solely to delight and amaze the viewer, emphasized other possibilities in the age-old European contrast between the fictions of human imagination and the mysteries of divine revelation. One interesting exchange which suggests that non-European objects directly affected these considerations took place in 1582 between Archbishop Gabriele Paleotti, author of a famous treatise to reform contemporary painting (discussed in another context in Chapter 6 of this volume by Pamela Jones), and his close friend Ulisse Aldrovandi, renowned natural scientist and collector of American material, a professor at the University of Bologna.[43] Paleotti's discussion of *grotteschi* (some fifty pages in the modern edition of his treatise) points to a crisis in representation that led to the creation of new cultural boundaries and new discussions of art.

In observing how old categories stretched to fit new situations, we can begin to understand how non-European art may have contributed to theoretical and critical discussions of western art which never directly mentioned their existence. Paleotti and Aldrovandi cast their discussions of *grotteschi* in terms of the Platonic problem of distinguishing between truth and the semblance of truth in artistic representations.[44] Their greatest challenge lay in defining the limits of artistic license, based on the premise that capricious fantasies which have no counterpart in the real world are inadmissible. But what if the capricious fictions of poets and painters actually existed? How is one to distinguish between inappropriate fantastic *grotteschi* and such virtuous naturalistic representations, visually or ontologically? The standard authorities Paleotti summoned to define inappropriate ornament could not have imagined the world that the prelate faced at the end of the sixteenth century. Paleotti, apparently heeding Aldrovandi's arguments, tried to make room for representations that *could* be capricious fantasies, but should *not* be considered as such because they actually *do* exist in nature.[45]

The exchange of ideas about *grotteschi* and other *capricii* in Italy further suggests how unclassicizing images, regardless of their origin or significance for the cultures that produced them, became emblematic of the opposition built into the western definition of image as likeness. It is difficult to imagine that Aldrovandi's material collection of American artifacts and natural specimens did not contribute substantially to Paleotti's theoretical considerations. Aldrovandi countered Paleotti's arguments by offering that the painter, out of scientific necessity to document objects, like those in his own collection, sometimes employs vivid colors and other forms of artifice (that the Council of Trent explicitly rejected for their "sensuous charm"). These visual documents contribute to human knowledge, *sometimes they even revise written authority*.[46] The ideas that Paleotti and

Aldrovandi exchanged about the nature of representation, while exceptional in providing historians with direct connections between Amerindian artifacts and theoretical discussions of art in Italy, were not unique. These and many other such conduits of cultural transmission that wait to be assessed suggest that non-European art played an important role in the construction of European conceptions of the perception of art.[47] For texts can document how exotic objects, regardless of their cultural origins, resonated for European cultures in similar ways.

Visual homologies made it easy to project ideas specific to one culture on to another, as many of the contributors to this volume elaborate. Anthony Pagden has named the mechanism for translating varieties of experience under these circumstances in literary texts the "principle of attachment" that leads to (mis)recognition.[48] In the process of detaching a motif from its original cultural context, Pagden explains, expropriation also encourages positive belief in a universal category of humanity. At present, we need to learn more about the various ways that the so-called visual arts have contributed to this complex process of collective identity formation.

The term "hybrid image" used throughout this study to designate certain types of culturally complex objects is indebted to contemporary colonial discourse analysis. Homi Bhabha, who has developed a concept of hybridity as a "problematic of colonial representation," maintains that, when the colonial subject mimics the forms of the dominant culture, the resulting hybrid forms introduce slippages and excesses of meaning.[49] The doubled form or hybrid repeats the fixed and empty presence of authority by articulating it with differential knowledges and positionalities that take the form of multiple or contradictory beliefs.[50] These hybrids pose a threat to "normalized" knowledge and disciplinary power.[51] Bhabha shifts the study of cultural interaction away from deterministic frameworks of interpretation, and the discussions of hybrid images in this volume are indebted to his model. Yet there are also problems with Bhabha's description of cultural authority. Historically, hybridity is far from being a neutral concept. The possible effects of human hybridization were debated at length by nineteenth-century racial theorists.[52] The overdetermined language of polygenism is inscribed (inadvertently, to be sure) in Bhabha's negative view that the "mutation" (i.e., the hybrid) "weakens" and "deforms" cultural authority. The studies of hybrid images which follow here do not take issue with Bhabha's underlying critique of cultural *authority*, but they focus on a different problem: this collection of essays stresses the ability of the hybrid to revise and envigorate cultural *identity*. Consequently, our understanding of "hybridity" is different. To restate this difference in the nineteenth-century language of racial theory, the anti-evolutionist anthropologist Franz Boas introduced the concept of fertile hybridization at the turn of the twentieth century.[53] Fertile hybrid images, accordingly, produce a surplus of meanings – that is, the same image can be interpreted in multiple ways and no single interpretation is authoritative, just as is the case in Bhabha's model of hybridity – but they exemplify the notion of culture as a constantly emerging form of collective identity, always in a state of transformation. A hydraulic metaphor can illustrate the difference between the two representations of culture, Bhabha's critique of cultural *authority* and our critique of existing models of cultural *identity*: univocal authority is emptied out by hybridity, identity is overflowing for the same reason – it is multiple and contradictory.[54]

Critical Studies in the Migration and Reception of Visual Culture

A responsible history of the dramatic transformation in the status of painting, sculpture, and architecture in the early modern period – and a better understanding of why the arts were hierarchically classified at all – must take many factors into account: the formation of critical literary practices, the rise of academic artistic theory and training, the emergence of aesthetic theory, the institutionalization and professionalization of the discipline of art history, the origins of museums and the history of collecting, the changing function of images – from devotional icons, for example, to objects of aesthetic contemplation. As anthropologist James Clifford observes, the corpus of texts we produce and reproduce about culture constitutes what we call culture.[55] The following studies, some reconstructing forgotten European frameworks for the reception of visual culture, others reconstructing the contributions of dispossessed indigenous cultures to composite collective identities, acknowledge the powerful assimilative mechanisms of individuals and cultures. These mechanisms, Stephen Greenblatt quips, "work like enzymes to change the ideological composition of foreign bodies."[56] Our model of diversity is based less on autonomy and cultural "purity" and more on interrelations and the zones of contact and intersection.[57] The following subsections of the Introduction briefly introduce the principal arguments of the contributors and set them into the conceptual framework of the volume.

New Problems, New Paradigms: Revising the Humanist Model

The three historiographical contributions to this section continue the line of inquiry begun in the Introduction by addressing the manner in which Italian Renaissance art came to occupy a normative role in the history of art. The authors stress that the humanist model of cultural opposition was applied to a wide variety of historical situations. Anthony Cutler leads off with an examination of the humanist model of cultural opposition that made Byzantium into Europe's inferior other over a four-hundred year period of historical writing. In Chapter 1, "The Pathos of Distance: Byzantium in the Gaze of Renaissance Europe and Modern Scholarship," Cutler criticizes the attempt to treat the orthodox Christian East as emerging from the same classical mold as the "West," because this interpretative framework, initiated by early humanist writers, does not evaluate Byzantine culture on its own terms. Judging Byzantine cultural products by Renaissance standards has emphasized factors of minor significance over matters of central importance to Byzantium. Cutler calls for a better interpretative model, one that scrutinizes the "liminal position" attributed to qualities of Byzantine art that do *not* fit the classical mold.

The construction of East and West as antithetical subjects was considerably assisted by the process Cutler describes. What justifies this crude binarism today? The presence of Byzantine art in Europe, especially in Italy, is considerable. The contribution of Byzantine art (and Byzantine theories of images) to European art and western aesthetics urgently demands reexamination in light of the obvious fact that, when Italian humanist writers and artists associated themselves directly with their ancient Greco-Roman roots (hence the term "Renaissance"), they neglected to mention prolonged cultural inter-actions with Byzantium (and elsewhere) that had taken, and continued to take, place on home soil.

Thomas DaCosta Kaufmann makes a similar case for the manner in which the humanist model of cultural opposition has affected studies of Renaissance style outside Italy. In Chapter 2, "Italian Sculptors and Sculpture Outside of Italy (Chiefly in Central Europe): Problems of Approach, Possibilities of Reception," Kaufmann argues that the transformations of Renaissance style in central Europe and elsewhere outside Italy have been inadequately conceptualized, above all due to the nationalist interests of (initially, mostly German) art historians. Kaufmann presents evidence of similar transformations of Italianate forms that occurred in places widely separated by geography and culture. He proposes a modern anthropological model to track the diffusion of these forms through interaction and circulation, and to account for the mediating conditions of active reception, even rejection, of the imported style in differing local circumstances.

My own contribution, Chapter 3, "'Vision Itself Has Its Own History': 'Race,' Nation, and Renaissance Art History," also examines nationalistic categories constructed by nineteenth-century German-speaking art historians, but the focus of this study is the paradigmatic role played by Renaissance art in theories of artistic change. The argument develops the premise that Wölfflin, Riegl, and other art historians participated in an interdisciplinary dialogue centered on racial theories of cultural evolution that was disrupted by two world wars; in the interim, in the increasingly hostile nationalistic climate of social democracy, Panofsky and his peers reinstituted the Enlightenment concept of humanist culture that their immediate predecessors like Riegl questioned. By neglecting the broader cultural context in which theories of artistic change developed, we inadvertently reproduce the nationalistic biases of our predecessors without under-standing that their arguments were meant to counter prevailing ethnocentric assumptions of the day.

The next section of *Reframing the Renaissance* turns to the primary evidence for the function, reception, and power of specific kinds of visual representations in the sixteenth century.

Renaissance Theories of the Image

Sixteenth-century European appreciations of naturalistic images are grounded in an Aristotelian theory of the imagination which holds that the mind transforms sense impressions into internal images which are stored in the memory and become the basis for higher forms of thought.[58] The next five essays deal with the reception of various kinds of naturalistic images in the sixteenth century. All the authors emphasize that lifelike images were thought to be powerful mnemonic tools working on the imagination.

Since Burckhardt associated the Renaissance with the revival of optical naturalism culminating in Raphael's late work, it is only fitting to open this section with a reassessment of Raphael's pivotal role in defining Renaissance classicism. Janis Bell, in Chapter 4, "Revisioning Raphael as a 'Scientific Painter,'" compares four centuries of

Raphael criticism, arguing that modern aesthetic appreciations of classical style, cast in term of its formal order, are symptomatic of an epistemological break with Aristotelian theories of images that emerged in the latter part of the seventeenth century. Our understanding of naturalism should encompass a range of meaning consistent with its earlier historical use because (here Bell draws conclusions similar to Cutler and Kaufmann) visual qualities that fit the nineteenth-century stereotype of classicism over-emphasize certain qualities while neglecting the scientific innovations in Raphael's treatment of color, shadow, and atmospheric effects – visual effects that find support in recent physiological theories of perception.

The next two essays, by Alessandro Nova and Pamela Jones, examine ways in which "aesthetic" response (i.e., an appeal to the mind through the senses) was incorporated into sixteenth-century religious practices in Italy. In complementary studies dealing with institutional attitudes towards sacred images in Italy, both authors indicate that the modern category of "high art" is inadequate to circumscribe the functions of sixteenth-century images because our secular approach to style has obscured the manner in which naturalistic detail in devotional images was intended to elicit emotional reponses from the viewer. Their researches corroborate Cutler's view (in Chapter 1) that the kind of relationship between viewer and the Divine established through the medium of the icon indicates *fundamental* cultural differences.

In the western Church, contact with the Divine is mediated through human inter-cessors. Nova's Chapter 5, "'Popular' Art in Renaissance Italy: Early Response to the Holy Mountain at Varallo," studies documentation for the late fifteenth-century recon-struction of Jerusalem at Monte Varallo in the Piedmont, founded by the Franciscan Observants and a popular pilgrimage site throughout the sixteenth century. The narrative tableaux at Varallo featured lifesize figures embellished with "real" details such as actual hair, clothing, furniture, and candles that are conventionally regarded today as appealing to an uneducated audience. This interpetation, Nova argues, does not explain why Sacro Monte was patronized by a fashionable, sophisticated Milanese aristocracy. Current scholarship is missing the main point: pilgrimage sites document a sixteenth-century form of material culture that offered a participatory religious experience to all ranks of society, regardless of taste and education.

Nova cites the early sixteenth-century humanist Girolamo Morone's enthusiastic remark that the dramatic episodes at Varallo were completely artless (made "without art"). Does this mean that period writers could consider veristic representations in general to be artless, or that posed figures clothed with actual clothing and hair were "artless" in a way that painted representations could never be? Based on a close reading of the textual and material evidence for Varallo, Nova concludes the latter; but the following chapter, which examines slightly later statements about *painting*, makes one suspect that deeper issues about the nature of imitation were routinely implicated in sixteenth-century discussions of "art." Our modern, secular readings of Renaissance discussions of lifelike-ness in art need to be reconsidered carefully in light of the function of religious images. What constitutes the effective imitation of a living, divine presence was *always* a highly charged issue for the Church implicating both artist and audience – long before the Council of Trent in 1563 tried to legislate what kinds of artistic license exceeded the limits of religious decorum.

Pamela Jones' essay, Chapter 6, entitled "Art Theory as Ideology: Gabriele Paleotti's Hierarchical Notion of Painting's Universality and Reception," is significant for documenting the emergence of consciously aestheticizing attitudes and a hierarchy of viewing practices based on education (and, therefore, on class). In the tense atmosphere of discussion about the limitations of artistic license after 1563, a central problem that preoccupied Paleotti in his widely disseminated *Discourse on Sacred and Profane Images* (Italian edition, 1582; Latin edition, 1594) was how to justify aesthetic enjoyment of landscape and other non-religious elements. He argued that elite viewers, unlike the uneducated masses, would not be seduced by artistic embellishments designed to delight the senses. To what extent, Jones wants to know, did post-Tridentine theories of the image succeed in creating a category of designated "illiterate persons" at the bottom of the viewing hierarchy, a hierarchy that might have assimilated laborers, peasants, women, and perhaps all the native inhabitants of "new worlds," in a single category?

Styles of scientific naturalism were intended to communicate with viewers through the supposedly universal language of sight. But the actual reception of naturalistic images outside Italy presents a very different view of the negotiations circulating among patron, artist, and viewer in the early colonial period. The last two studies of this section, by Pauline Watts and Thomas Cummins, cross disciplinary, geographical, and cultural boundaries to ask how the same European theories of images were translated to Latin America. Both authors examine records of crosscultural exchanges by exploring the translation of classical and Christian values in Latin America at a time when visual communication was considered an absolutely necessary instrument to overcome the language barrier. In Chapter 7, "Languages of Gesture in Sixteenth-Century Mexico: Some Antecedents and Transmutations," Watts discusses a wide range of colonial texts to reconstruct performative aspects of a purportedly universal language of gesture and expression grounded in classical/Christian rhetorical theory. She finds that the negotiated Christianities of state spectacle and religious drama record an active process of indigenous reception and strong indications of European phobic reaction to native ritual customs.

Like Watts, Cummins investigates how the mimetic aspects of images with mnemonic functions were used to correlate two unrelated cultures. Chapter 8, "From Lies to Truth: Colonial Ekphrasis and the Act of Crosscultural Translation," examines primary source material for slippages between the western sign and its colonial significance. The single common thread among all the categories of visual evidence that Cummins examines – including indigenous colonial paintings used in legal cases and Mexican pictorial manuscripts – is unexpected: Cummins finds that, *regardless* of their conventions of representation, colonial images were judged to contain truthful information if they gave evidence of a prior oral dialogue.

It could be argued further that Mexican calendrical illustrations were judged to contain "truthful" information because astronomical calculations had scientific status in Europe. To state this in the broader terms of Cummins' argument, the relationship of the Mexican calendrical diagrams to prior evidence, and the relationship between the legal pictorial evidence and prior testimony, are based on the same assumption of demonstrability. Indeed, Cummins speculates that the mestizo writer Diego Valadés discussed the reliability of the Mexican calendar in his *Rhetorica Christiana* (1579), written in Rome and published three years before the institution of the Gregorian calendar, as an intentional allusion to the impending reform. In other words, Valadés defended the truth value of Mexican images in terms that could be recognized by Europeans. In this process of cultural exchange, Nahua pictorial traditons were resituated in a European frame of reference.

Early Collecting Practices

The third section continues to examine the construction of new epistemological categories and the tearing down of old ones as people and things migrated on an unprecedented scale. A rapidly growing field of publications on the history of collecting suggests that private museums constitute a distinct form of documentary culture that preserves a rich font of under-utilized information about the contributions that non-European cultures made to European conceptions of the visual arts.[59] The three essays included here discuss the theories that supported the practice of collecting in some unusual areas. The objects considered occupy a liminal position in the history of the visual arts in that they were initially sources of sensual and intellectual delight for European audiences, but were later excluded from the aesthetic systematization of the fine arts. Even the present great interest in the early history of collecting tends to marginalize these early collecting activities, treating the objects as mere curiosities of the "minor arts" or relegating them to the history of science – thus reproducing eighteenth- and nineteenth-century aesthetic categories and viewing practices that are anachronistically applied to the material under consideration.

One of the dominant themes to emerge from the three studies included here is the central role played by the Aristotelian parallel between nature and art across a broad spectrum of collecting activities. Martin Kemp, in Chapter 9, "'Wrought by no Artist's Hand': The Natural, the Artificial, the Exotic, and the Scientific in some Artifacts from the Renaissance," emphasizes the inadequacy of any *rigid* system of classification to account for contemporary motivations behind the making and viewing of objects. From his study of virtuoso examples of human craftsmanship that incorporate natural objects (such as coconut shells and deer antlers), Kemp argues that these "cultural migrators" intentionally defied stable classification and interpretation of meaning. As Kemp discusses hybrids of nature and art invented by Wentzel Jamnitzer, Bernard Palissy, and others in the context of the intellectualization of the crafts, he finds that their display pieces were meant to confer status on a wider range of patrons than we usually assume. These objects were originally ordered by princely rulers, university scientists, courtly craftsmen–engineers, even city councils (as the illustration of the Uppsala cabinet in Figure 9.18 attests), who displayed not only their power but also genuine piety before God's magnificent creations.

The process of expropriating objects from cultures sacked and colonized by European conquest, as Claudia Lazzaro and Eloise Quiñones Keber both discuss, also created new ways of thinking about culture. Lazzaro, who takes a semiotic approach to fifteenth- and sixteenth-century images of animals, finds that the display of wild and domestic creatures produced a new category of culture against which the familiar could be defined. In Chapter 10, "Animals as Cultural Signs: A Medici Menagerie in the Grotto at Castello,"

Lazzaro discusses in detail the grotto of Cosimo I de' Medici's garden, begun in 1537 and developed in the 1560s, as a conveyor of political messages beyond its ostensible constructions of humanist allegory. Paradoxically, imported natural specimens functioned (alongside their domestic counterparts) as cultural signs grounded in the humanist revival of classical antiquity: live animals and their pictorial representations were used to symbolize political dominion and power for European rulers in a variety of cultural settings. As sixteenth-century collections of exotica were formed, new information was incorporated within taxonomic frameworks inherited from classical antiquity, which were often stretched beyond recognition in the process. The classical framework of Renaissance culture translated alterity into terms that were in use for centuries.

Kemp and Lazzaro both focus on the European reception of foreign material completely decontextualized from its original cultural context. In Chapter 11, "Collecting Cultures: A Mexican Manuscript in the Vatican Library," Quiñones Keber addresses a different side of the asymmetrical cultural exchange when she examines a highly prized, sixteenth-century illustrated manuscript known as Codex Vaticanus A. This hybrid document preserves the record of a lost Aztec screenfold book as it was copied into a European-style codex and provided with an extensive Italian commentary. In the process of physically reframing the native book format, the compiler of Codex Vaticanus A also framed Aztec culture in European values. Quiñones Keber argues, however, that the codex is more than a record of cultural expropriation because it preserves an anonymous Italian patron's attempt to understand a completely foreign culture. In her view, the failure of this early effort to "get things right" is a good moral lesson for contemporary art historians because it shows how unrealistic it is to aim for a prejudice-free understanding: we always understand the other by analogies to ourselves.

Mediating Images: Developing an Intercultural Perspective

The preceding sections of the anthology as described here have already begun to consider how European artistic ideals fared in the semiologically complex environment of the sixteenth century. The case studies included in the final section of the book are concerned entirely with the multivalent signifying power of hybrid images. Linguists argue that the potentially endless process of reproduction and transformation of meaning in language is arrested by the consensus of a "community of native speakers."[60] One of the most basic problems with the linguistic paradigm of community consensus, however, is its under-conceptualization of what happens when there is no homogeneous audience of native speakers to arrest the potentially endless transformations of meaning. The conditions of reception and the strategies of interpretation are different in each of the following studies, but every case emphasizes that hybrid images signify in multiple, open-ended ways.

Cecelia Klein, like Quiñones Keber, recalibrates traditional techniques of formal and iconographic analysis to detect tensions between coexisting cultures manifested in hybrid colonial objects. Readers can decide whether these two authors really hold mutually exclusive points of view, or whether they focus on different aspects of the same situation. Quiñones Keber emphasizes the *limits* of true cultural exchange (while *praising* an early attempt to overcome ethnocentrism). In Chapter 12, "Wild Woman in Colonial Mexico: An Encounter of European and Aztec Concepts of the Other," Klein emphasizes the *extent* of crosscultural communication (while *criticizing* the ethnocentrism of European missionaries during the early contact period). Klein situates her argument against extreme deconstructionist readings like Stephen Greenblatt's *Marvelous Possessions* which deny the possibility of real epistemological exchanges across the cultural boundaries of completely unrelated societies. This attitude, Klein maintains, is yet another pernicious form of Eurocentrism because it dispenses with any serious attempt to understand the indigenous colonial experience – such writing dismisses the ways that representation actually operates in a colonizing context. Supporting her argument with extensive evidence from both European and Precolumbian sources, Klein documents the native tradition of Cihuacoatl as it converged with European ideas of wanton, demonic women under asymmetrical conditions of cultural exchange. As the Nahua supernatural was progressively forced into a Christian mold, the native Cihuacoatl, patroness of women in childbirth and guarantor of long life and prosperity as well as death, was reshaped in terms meaningful and familiar to Europeans.

The reception of hybrid visual symbols and its implications are also the focus of Dana Leibsohn's study of maps made by native painters in early colonial Mexico. In Chapter 13, "Colony and Cartography: Shifting Signs on Indigenous Maps of New Spain," Leibsohn argues that the ways in which signs are used on indigenous maps – their lack of homogeneity, the accommodation of European signs through doubling and/or substitution, and the resistance to European introductions – never supplied their viewers with an unambiguous image of the actual world. Her study emphasizes the complexity and indeterminacy of ties that bind forms of visual representation and colonial politics. Leibsohn recognizes that the way we read maps and other symbolic representations largely determines what we understand about colonization: yet it is equally important to bear in mind that the transformations of European and indigenous pictorial symbols are only partially sustained by political motives and events.

The extent to which the original conditions of reception can be reconstructed from the surviving documents is also central to Jonathan Riess's examination of the fundamental historical paradigm for the subordination of all other cultures during the Renaissance: the censure of Jews and Muslims within Europe. In Chapter 14, "Luca Signorelli's *Rule of Antichrist* and the Christian Encounter with the Infidel," Riess recovers asymmetrical cultural interactions with the traditional tools of iconographical analysis. This interpretative strategy enables him to draw connections between Signorelli's representation of a usurious Jew in the Cappella Nuova frescoes, Orvieto Cathedral, 1499–1504, and textual evidence of the pro-Spanish, anti-semitic views of Pope Alexander VI. Riess finds that Renaissance humanist culture created false and pernicious ethnic stereotypes – an aspect of Christian humanism that has been elided from previous art historical accounts.

The final essay is a challenging reflection on the manner in which western writers have constructed the human subject. In the Epilogue, entitled "Iconology, Ideology, and Cultural Encounter: Panofsky, Althusser, and the Scene of Recognition," W. J. T. Mitchell examines the process by which social and cultural hierarchies are naturalized by visual regimes. He compares Panofsky's iconological method with Louis Althusser's Marxist critique of ideology by constructing an imaginary encounter between them.

Mitchell finds that the problematic assumption, so familiar to the Renaissance, that there is a universal ("natural") form of representation still haunts us. The closing essay serves as a striking reminder that no interpretative paradigm is universally valid – however universal its claims might be, every theory is the product of specific historical circumstances.

*   *   *

In opening this collection of essays, I would like to remind our readers of another anthology, one that has been an inspiring model of scholarship for its *in*clusionary tactics. I think I can speak for all of my contributors in hoping that we live up to our chosen namesake at least in this one respect. In the Introduction to *Rewriting the Renaissance: The Discourses of Sexual Difference in Early Modern Europe*, editors Margaret Ferguson, Maureen Quilligan, and Nancy Vickers write that:

> Although the representations of Renaissance culture perceived and created in the present volume of essays are by no means complete or in perfect harmony with each other, they do represent a collective effort to see, and talk, across several sets of boundaries. These include the boundaries that inhibit communication between scholars of different generations, different academic disciplines, and different methodological schools within a single discipline.

Reframing the Renaissance also represents a collective effort to bridge generational, disciplinary, and methodological distances. Yet no matter how conscientiously we interrogate the field of our disciplinary knowledge, we still answer to a "finite system of constraints," as Derrida says.[61] It will be easy to criticize our anthology for being too ambitious, for neglecting Spain, over-emphasizing Central Mexico, ignoring the Irish, slighting cultural exchanges within Europe, not dealing with the Reformation – for any number of valid reasons that, as editor, I can defend only by saying, yes, write those chapters! To get stuck in such a debate at all, however, is to misunderstand this volume. It will take more to revise our histories of western art than eliminating an anachronistic term, enlarging the canon, or reducing the complexity of historical events to a few metacategories. Beyond the *objects* of visual culture are historical theories of human agency that the contributors to this volume emphasize throughout – problematic notions of how the human subject has been constructed that have traditionally been written out of the history of art history altogether. It is worth reconsidering whose Renaissance is at the foundation of the discipline. While the official observance of Columbus's landfall has passed, many questions that five hundred years of intensive cultural interaction raise still need to be addressed. The authors of *Reframing the Renaissance* join voices in encouraging our readers to define many additional subjects worthy of study.

PART I

New Problems, New Paradigms: Revising the Humanist Model

1.1 *Archangel Michael*. Thirteenth century. Pisa, Museo di S. Matteo. (Photo: author.)

CHAPTER 1

The Pathos of Distance: Byzantium in the Gaze of Renaissance Europe and Modern Scholarship

ANTHONY CUTLER

When young, Claude Lévi-Strauss was taught the importance of distance. He learned that ethnography, that quintessential European discipline, could be practiced only beyond the bounds of Europe – in the Brazilian Mato Grosso, in the bazaars of Karachi and Chittagong. But in his old age, reflecting on his journeys, he sensed that space was simply a metaphor for time, that other cultures are the "past," a past that could not be recovered. And therein lay the difficulty, a problem that he couched in terms of alternatives:

> In the last analysis, I am the prisoner of a dilemma: either, like the traveler of old, [I am] faced with a stupendous spectacle, all or mostly all of which escaped him – or, worse, inspired his scorn and disgust; or [like] the modern traveler who chases after the vestiges of a lost reality.[1]

In the forty years since he wrote these words the problem has not gone away: for the cultural historian, as for the poet, the past is a foreign country. No matter how reflective our *voyages philosophiques* may be, they are self-reflexive. So it was in the case of Europeans of the fifteenth and sixteenth centuries when they looked at Byzantium; so it is, I shall suggest, with modern scholars when they look at this same slice of space and time. If, in and after the Quattrocento, Italians for the most part disdained the Christian East because their needs lay elsewhere, they at least gave voice to those needs, treating Byzantium first as an alien culture and, after its demise, as an irrelevance. Modern historiography, on the other hand, while claiming that somehow Byzantine art still has a lien on our concern, has treated it as something little different from that of the Renaissance. This attitude has misrepresented its nature and thereby clouded that which can still lay claim to our interest – a society that had its roots in the classical and Christian traditions (the same intertwined legacy as was inherited by the Renaissance) but which grew to be something other.

For a generation and more one or another form of "Orientalism" has been held to be the besetting sin of western intellectuals, a notion that has at last permeated to those who consider Byzantine art professionally.[2] Yet the nature of Greek Orthodox culture is as ill served by treating it in terms devised for European societies as it is by seeing it as a schismatic variant on medieval civilization or, in the Renaissance view, as a portion of "prehistory" – a fetal, if not abortive, state, beyond which the West has progressed. Following expositions of both these stages, I shall argue that Byzantine art is better regarded as the expression of an "Oriental," that is to say, quite alien culture. Stupendous spectacle that it may have been, it will not best be recovered by chasing after its Greco–Roman vestiges. Some archeologists believe that Boadicea is buried under platform 10 at King's Cross Station. But digging her up will not in itself tell us much about the nature of early Britain. *Tam Britannia quam Byzantium.* An understanding of these (or any other) cultures requires the recognition of our own theoretical attitude towards such accounts; and this depends upon an awareness of the historiographical matrix on which our present stance is grounded. Without these Boadicea can be only a skeleton or, at best, a corpse.

Byzantium in, and after, the Renaissance

We may as well begin with Cennino Cennini, pupil of Agnolo, the son of Taddeo Gaddi who was Giotto's pupil. It was Giotto who, in Cennini's construction, "changed the profession of painting from Greek back into Latin, and brought it up to date."[3] This famous formulation, along with Vasari's notion of the *maniera greca moderna*,[4] is a *locus classicus* for the invention of Renaissance painting. But it has been inadequately scrutinized. According to Cennini, Giotto did two seemingly contradictory things: first, he restored painting to the way in which the *Romans* had practiced it; secondly, he modernized this manner. To understand this declaration requires us to recognize what was obvious to all c. 1400: the Byzantine manner was the way in which all Italians had painted. Everywhere Cennini and his contemporaries looked they saw the art that we call medieval – in the layout of cities, in the buildings that lined their streets, in the frescoes in those buildings. There is no contempt for this manner (as there is in Vasari), no triumphalism in Cennini's conception. The *maniera greca* was simply the past, a past whose superannuation was proved by the fact that the building and painting of his own day were different. To be aware of difference here means to have a sense of history, to be able to see the past as passed.

To be passed over is to go unnoticed and it is precisely this absence of attention to things of the Trecento in records of the Renaissance that is a source of controversy among historians of the period. A prime example is the panel of the archangel Michael today in the Museo di S. Matteo in Pisa (Figure 1.1). Frustrated by the fact that this object went unrecorded until 1923,[5] the art historical debate over its place of origin continues. The means of ascertaining this origin can proceed from neither a general theory of Byzantine "influence" on Tuscan art nor one of Byzantine painters working for foreign clients. More revealing than any plausible account of the picture's source is the amount of scholarly effort that has gone into the attempt to determine this. For our present purposes, the significance of the controversy lies in its participants' disinclination to accept the one undebatable, if minimal, conclusion that it allows – the Italian refusal to distinguish local productions from those of the east Christian world. (Whether this refusal represents a surrender to the Byzantine manner is another, and secondary, issue.) A panel that employs an iconography shared by both regions, one that "looks" Greek but is inscribed in Latin, affirms that very commonality that would fall victim to the self-consciousness made explicit in Cennini's assertion.

His position is an ideological one; it is also one that explains why Quattrocento artists were fundamentally uninterested in Byzantium. For a larger audience, in 1400 the Greeks were a nation of beggars: their emperor was then (and not for the first time) in western Europe pleading for funds, for assistance against the Turks then besieging the inhabitants of Constantinople. Their mental horizon, according to Gibbon, could never accommodate the Renaissance achievement:

> "Your scandalous figures stand quite out from the canvas: they are as bad as a group of statues." It was thus that the ignorance and bigotry of a Greek priest applauded the pictures of Titian, which he had ordered, and refused to accept.[6]

Whether the story is true or not, it speaks volumes about the Enlightenment's attitude towards Byzantium. It is worth investigating this cognitive posture not only because its roots lay in the Quattrocento but also because we, for all our protestations to the contrary, are likewise its heirs. In essence, I shall argue that precisely because Byzantine civilization was irrelevant to the humanists, except insofar as it appeared as a way-station on the road back to antiquity, in the seventeenth and eighteenth centuries it had to be rediscovered. By the nineteenth and twentieth such was Europe's remoteness from this culture that a variety of Byzantiums could exist – one, in the prism of colonialism, an east whose *splendeurs et misères* tantalized artists, architects, and their publics; the other, no less fictive but attainable and made safe for scholarship when viewed through the classicizing lens of the Enlightenment. Rays from an object, even one infinitely distant, prove that the object once existed. When they fail to meet at a single focal point, they also demonstrate the presence of astigmatism.

As a first step towards correction, we need to recognize the difference between the functional and the symbolic roles of Byzantium in the Renaissance; the uses made of this culture were by no means congruent with the West's sympathy (or lack thereof) for the regime that supported it. The distinction is apparent in a number of areas. For example, at the same time as the Latin church was unwillingly discussing papal primacy and the proper nature of the eucharistic host with John VIII and his Patriarch at the Council of Ferrara–Florence (1438–39), Pisanello borrowed the emperor's profile for a famous medal.[7] This likeness lived on in Italian art not as the portrait of a specific individual but as a model for images of Pontius Pilate and the Ottoman sultan. In the hands of a Carpaccio, a Gentile Bellini, the Byzantine, deprived of his race and faith, offered a convenient type for exotic costumes and headdresses, one among many that included Tatars and Mamluks.[8] While the classical and Patristic learning exhibited by Bessarion, Pletho, and George Amiroutzes at the conclave led one scholar to describe the Council as "the greatest historical seminar of the Italian Renaissance,"[9] the impact of their presence was perhaps better assessed by Ihor Ševčenko: "when looked at, these turbaned, bearded and long-robed Platonists appeared more like the denizens of Susa than Athens."[10] At least at the level of appearance, then, in Latin eyes there was little to separate Greek from Turk. The Byzantines got part of what they wanted – the ill-fated Crusade of Varna preached by Eugenius IV – but the Italians got more. In April 1438 Ambrogio Traversari wrote excitedly from Ferrara to his friend Filippo dei Pieruzzi of the books brought by the supplicants from the Bosporos – a beautiful Plato, a Plutarch, Aristotle, Diodoros, Dionysios of Halikarnassos, and "Cyril's big book against Julian the Apostate which we shall take care to copy if we can find the parchment."[11] In short the Latins were aroused by what the Byzantines had conserved; the preservation of the *conservators* was far from their minds, even though the predictable flurry of protests went up when Constantinople finally fell fifteen years later.[12]

Ten months before this event a humanist had already proclaimed one aspect of the West's superiority in the area of its greatest desire, and the mechanism that brought it about:

> I, Lorenzo Valla, corrected this codex of Thucydides, of whom I believe even the Greeks have no more splendidly written or illuminated text, at the command of our blessed lord by divine grace, Pope Nicholas V, working with the very Ioannes who wrote it so well."[13]

No matter that this was a translation – the text had been saved, the desire satisfied.

Like the knights of medieval romances, the humanists justified their lust by exaggerating the threat to their beloved objects. Immediately after the Turkish conquest of the capital, the Venetian Lauro Quirini, writing to the same pope, claimed that 120,000 books had been destroyed.[14] But the great tenth-century Paris Psalter (B.N. gr. 139) was available in the capital when brought out by the French ambassador, between 1557 and 1559, for King Henry III;[15] and the huge copy of the works of Hippokrates (B.N. gr. 2144), commissioned by Alexios Apokaukos about 1338, was among the books selected for Louis XIV from the Seraglio library in Istanbul and sent to Paris 350 years later.[16] The number of unillustrated books preserved, both Christian and "pagan," was vastly greater. If ever "Orientalism" was virulent it is in these tales of Turkish destruction, rumors whose spread we can actually watch in hindsight. Quirini claimed that he had the figure of 120,000 books from Isidore of Kiev, the Greek-born cardinal of Kiev, later appointed Latin patriarch of Constantinople by Pius II Piccolomini.[17] Piccolomini himself, before becoming pope, described the Turks as "the enemy of letters, both Greek and Latin" and saw a "second death for Homer, Pindar, Menander, and all the other famous poets."[18]

Yet, while scholarly contempt for the Byzantines metamorphosed into fear and loathing of the Ottomans, it is clear that such prejudice was not shared by Italians in other circles. Venetians who for centuries had traded along the Golden Horn soon resumed their activities and, in Florence and elsewhere, pragmatists saw in successive sultans not Asiatic terminators but opportunities no less appealing than those that commercial treaties with the Greek emperors had afforded. Condivi tells the story of Michelangelo's and Julius II's mutual pique: sensing in Bayezid II a patron less tyrannical than the pope, the artist threatened to accept the sultan's offer to build a bridge across the Golden Horn and other structures in Istanbul.[19] Whether Michelangelo (or Condivi) was telling the truth is less important than that, early in the Cinquecento, the offer would have been credible.

A century after the Turkish conquest of the city the major part of Byzantine history had slipped from European awareness. Left were the Muslim present and a remote early Christian past, willed into consciousness by the twin forces of confessional appropriation and scholarly antiquarianism. We shall see in a moment how these engines operated upon

1.2   After P. Coecke van Aelst. *Procession of Sultan Süleyman through the Atmeydan* (detail). Woodcut, after 1553. New York, Metropolitan Museum of Art. (Photo: museum.)

the scant fuel provided by Renaissance philology. Visually, the void is suggested by a woodcut after Pieter Coecke van Aelst's *Procession through the Atmeydan* (the "Square of Horses"), i.e., the Hippodrome that had been Constantinople's civic core for more than a millennium (Figure 1.2). One or two of the smaller domes in the background may evoke Middle Byzantine churches, but the scene is dominated by Bayezid II's Firuz Aga mosque on the Divan Yolu in the center and, to the right of this main avenue (the old Byzantine Mesê, or Middle Street), the remains of Theodosius' obelisk, the serpent column from Delphi, and the semi-circular *sphendone*, the hemicycle at the southern end of the Hippodrome. Not one of these monuments is Byzantine: in Coecke's gaze it is as if the period between the fifth and fifteenth centuries had vanished. Caryatids line the square; its arches and trabeated structures, like so many Hollywood props, make a classical backdrop for the oriental spectacle undisrupted by the hieroglyphics on the obelisk. The history of even this monument was rewritten: for the reliefs of Theodosius, his family and his subjects on its base were substituted scenes from Greco–Roman mythology. The scene, one of a series, drawn on the spot in Istanbul in 1533, has been described as "reportage."[20] But the act of reporting, and the content of a report, depend upon a decision as to what is worth reporting, and this decision, of course, upon the audience that the reporter has in mind. If Coecke's drawing echoes the ceremonial entry into cities of the kings and Holy Roman Emperors of his day, and the classical precedents upon which such entries were based, its immediate context was Süleyman I's stunning victory at Mohács seven years earlier, a triumph which brought the Turks to the doorstep of western Europe. Constantinople, which had fallen to the Ottomans in the previous century, was the least of Europe's worries.

Were cultural attitudes toward Byzantium from south of the Alps any less affected by current events? It has been claimed that Lorenzo de' Medici, when he instructed Janus Laskaris to find him not only classical manuscripts but also the "histories of the more recent Greeks,"[21] consciously acknowledged a distinction between Greco–Roman and Byzantine texts. But the difference between, say, Thucydides and Niketas Choniates is a matter of vastly more than chronology. I know of no self-evident declaration that Renaissance Europeans conceived of Byzantium as an objectively alien society, possessed of a mentality that, other than in its religious faith, differentiated it from the world of the Caesars. And it was the use that could be made of this faith that was the wellspring of a renewed interest in the literature of eastern Christianity. Though its main expression did not come until the Fuggers, the merchant princes of sixteenth-century Germany, financed the *Corpus byzantinae historiae* of Hieronymus Wolf and Wilhelm Holtzmann ("Xylander"), the beginnings of this revival can be detected on the eve of the Reformation. At a public disputation at Leipzig in 1519, Luther presented the thesis that the Orthodox Greeks were the repository of a religious tradition and a theology older and purer than that of the Roman church.[22] As so often, revolutionary rupture was supported by appeals to the illusion of conservation.

No such artifice was needed to drum up interest in Venice, where the Byzantine past was a matter of current political concern. The Empire's enduring struggles with enemies from the east were seen as precedents for the history of the Serenissima which, in 1204, had been party to the division of the Byzantine state and had profited mightily from these economic and material spoils but which, in the sixteenth century, lost to the Turks ever more territory and the commercial benefits that this entailed. Popular anger was enflamed, though not kindled, by the production in 1564 of a *Volo a Turco* performed in the Piazza San Marco beneath the bronze horses looted from the Hippodrome of Constantinople and the most public witness to Venice's quondam greatness.[23] At least parallel to, if not contingent upon, this hostility was a resurgent fascination with the events of 1204. Villehardouin's Old French chronicle of the Latin conquest was translated by Giovanbattista Rannusio and in 1556 the Council of Ten commissioned from the translator's son the huge (and neglected) study of the context of that conquest and the benefits that had accrued to Venice.[24] Published first in Latin in 1573 and again in that language and in Venetian dialect in 1604, Paolo Rannusio's book depended heavily on editions of Byzantine historians made from manuscripts assembled in and after the Quattrocento. Italians got their first impressions of the erstwhile rulers of Constantinople from the engravings in this book where their regalia and even poses were applied to the figures of the Latin emperor Baldwin and his family.[25]

If in sixteenth-century Venice Byzantine history was turned to contemporary and local purposes, in Rome it was exploited for doctrinal reasons. Where the Protestants had appealed to an evangelical tradition fantasized as surviving among the Greeks, the Counter-Reformation effectively invited Catholic scholars to prove through their researches the continuity and uniqueness of the apostolic legacy. Pertusi acutely detected the relationship between Tridentine emphasis on the authority of the Fathers and Jesuit preoccupation with Patristic and later texts.[26] But to conclude that this interest resulted in an investigation of medieval Greek history for its own sake would be as far from the truth as to suppose that, when he painted the True Cross cycle in Arezzo,[27] Piero della Francesca had been primarily concerned with the Eastern Empire. While of course Constantine, Helena, and Heraklios bulk large in the frescoes, they are no more important than Adam, the Queen of Sheba, Chosroe, and other protagonists in the story. A purely circumstantial Byzantium is likewise evident in such *epigoni* as Guido Reni's cycle in the funeral chapel for Paul V (1605–21) in S. Maria Maggiore. A concern with early Christian rather than later church history is predictable in the age of Baronius and Bellarmine but nowhere is Byzantium quite so effaced, while remaining the ostensible subject, as in the frescoes in the arch directly inside the Cappella Paolina. Painted by Baglione after 1611,[28] these purport to show the deaths of two imperial adversaries of images[29] – Constantine Kopronymos ("called dung," an epithet due to his alleged defecation during baptism; Figure 1.3) and Leo V, who was assassinated by supporters of his rival and successor while at prayer on Christmas Day, 820 (Figure 1.4). Constantine is shown as a Michelangelesque giant, moribund (if appropriately diapered) in his tent at

1.3 Giovanni Baglione. *Death of Constantine V Kopronymos.* Fresco, after 1631. Rome, S. Maria Maggiore, Cappella Paolina. (Photo: author.)

1.4 Giovanni Baglione. *Death of Leo V the Armenian.* Fresco, after 1631. Rome, S. Maria Maggiore, Cappella Paolina. (Photo: author.)

Strongylon, while Leo, bare-chested and wearing a Roman fighting skirt, falls like Caravaggio's blinded apostle. An angelic figure points to his successor, Michael the Amorian, anachronistically equipped with a radiate crown, as heavenly radiation pierces the vault of "the temple of the Mother of God," the architecture of which would not have struck the early Seicento spectator as in any way remarkable.

These Baroque figures writhing in allegory may seem odd in a Rome newly endowed with the Greek College of St. Athanasius, a papal institution founded in part to demonstrate to its pupils what their most famous member argued was "the perpetual consensus between the western and eastern churches."[30] Earlier in his career, one of its students, the Greek-born Leone Allacci, had advised Catholic scholars on the mysteries of Orthodox architecture and liturgy.[31] But his philological procedure was innocent of archeological concern, being addressed solely to the burning issue of the day, the reunification of the churches. Although Allacci's work was drawn on heavily by DuCange, the most important French Byzantinist of the seventeenth century, it, like the "Louvre Corpus" of medieval Greek texts begun in 1645,[32] is only partially understood if viewed as a product of disinterested antiquarianism.

Where in the sixteenth century French monarchs had been content to patronize scholarly missions to the Levant,[33] by the early seventeenth Louis XIII personally participated in a climate that has been described as "a certain ferment of anti-Ottoman ideas and philobyzantine ideology."[34] In 1612 he translated the *Ekthesis* of the deacon Agapetos, 72 chapters addressed to Justinian I[35] that constituted a proleptic version of the genre later known as the Mirror of Princes. Royally sponsored Byzantine studies provided, first, raw material for Jesuit scholarship and then, in the second half of the century, a set of targets for the empiricist criticism of the *illuminés*. More broadly considered, they played their part in that orientalism which was so abiding an aspect of European taste, one that neither started with Marlowe's *Tamburlaine* (1587) nor ended with Mozart's *Magic Flute* (1791). But it was for its didactic potential that the Byzantine vein was most thoroughly mined. Surpassing the visual preachments of the Cappella Paolina, Jesuit dramaturges found in the legends of its celebrated men and women (Theodora became as well known on eighteenth-century stages as she had been, according to the story, on those of Justinian's time) a seemingly inexhaustible lode. By far the most popular, and enduring, of these was the tale of Belisarius, Justinian's great general, disgraced and blinded in his old age, begging in the streets of Constantinople.

In 1607 there appeared (in Munich?) a piece with the splendid title, "the Tragi-Comedy of Belisarius, the Christian Leader, Fallen from the Happy Heights of Glory to Become an Object of Derision."[36] We are not told how this Latin version fared, but some index to the success of this historico-morality play in early modern Europe is suggested by the fact that the same theme was exploited by Calderón (1659) and Goldoni (1734), not to mention versions by a dozen nonentities.[37] Instead of waning during the Revolution, the subject seems to have become even more popular. A laconically named *Bélisaire* was written by Jean-François Marmontel, secretary of the Académie Française and "Historiographer of France." But, if it still existed, the most telling document might well be the huge canvas on the same theme by François Gérard, unsuccessfully submitted for the grand prize at the French Academy in Rome in 1795.[38] In the absence of visual evidence, we have only his audience's response by which to judge this work: Gérard was ennobled by Louis XVIII and went on to become Napoleon's portraitist. As late as 1847 the picture was saluted in the following terms: "the misfortunes of Belisarius were destined to draw tears from those who had known the rigors of exile."[39] Its disappearance may thus be one of the great losses of European painting. Or perhaps not: its full title was "Belisarius carrying a child bitten by a serpent."

Given the continuing attention to such figures as Heraklios,[40] it would be an exaggeration to say that by the early nineteenth century Byzantium had been trimmed to a myth concerning the era of Justinian. But, even in its invisibility, Gérard's picture leaves little doubt that, drowned in sentimentalism, this iconography disappeared into the maw of European history painting. No doubt the digestion of the eastern Roman empire was aided by the view that it *was* Roman, but this understanding is itself the product of nineteenth-century historiography. The themes of David's and Gérard's time joined seamlessly with the Romanticism of Delacroix, who returned time and again to the

1.5 Eugène Delacroix. *Entry of the Crusaders into Constantinople.* Oil on canvas, 1840–41. Paris, Musée du Louvre. (Photo: Art Resource.)

subject of the Latin conquest of 1204. An early version (1823; Aachen, Suermondt Museum) was effaced in 1840 by his immense canvas, *The Entry of the Crusaders into Constantinople*, now in the Louvre (Figure 1.5). Both the size and the content of this work – almost five meters across – are explained by its commission by Louis-Philippe for the Galeries historiques at Versailles. There, like a fresco in some Venetian hall of state, it dominated the Salle des Croisades, a monument to what, by the time of the July Monarchy, had long been the myth of a monarch who leads his armies into battle. At the center of the picture, Baldwin of Flanders enters the Byzantine capital, the very model of a francophone major-general but proleptically equipped with a turban which, for Delacroix, lent a properly oriental air to the man who would become the first Latin emperor of Constantinople. Other elements have gone misunderstood or ignored. The bearded figure to the left, assaulted by a soldier in the porch of a church outfitted in the Corinthian order, has been read either as the blinded Byzantine emperor, Isaac II Comnenus, but he is not blind; or as a "priest." If he is that, given his papal tiara, he is a very important priest indeed; most likely he is the Patriarch, John X Kamateros, protesting the outrage in the coffered loggia of a classicized Hagia Sophia. But the identification of details is less revealing than the nature of the canvas's reception. In 1855, for instance, Maxime du Camp declared it "un motif à colorations savantes" and its subject as "absolument indifférent" to Delacroix.[41] The latter's interest, in truth, would seem to have been confined to the victims, and their setting a variant on the painter's *Scenes from the Chios Massacres*. Broken jewel-boxes lie among the dead and dying who would not be out of place on the raft of Medusa. The domed precinct to the right could be the Boukoleon ("bull lion") palace, if its naively signifying animal statuary is to be taken seriously. The pathos of the city's inhabitants may have appealed to European sympathies with the Greek rebellion against the Turks, but this distress is played out against the backdrop of Renaissance facades. Byzantium has become a culture conceived in terms of its Greco–Roman inessentials.

Byzantine Art in Modern Scholarship

The mélange of the classical, the Oriental, and the Christian that was manifested in Delacroix's Constantinople became the standard constitution of Byzantine culture for many nineteenth-century French historians.[42] Yet before the century was out, trained archeologists were advocating a much narrower formula for this complex body of production. Thus, for example, in 1893, Alois Riegl maintained that "Byzantine art is nothing more than the late antique art of the eastern Roman empire."[43] We may quickly pass over the acrimonious debate, epitomized in the label *Orient oder Rom*, that racked scholarship in the first two decades of the present century without more ado than to point to the source of the argument's aridity: any attempt to define a culture in binary terms, in the Aristotelian mode that governs modern computer science – a proposition is either so or not so, a machine is either "off" or "on" – is bound to fail. Cultures are not machines, their logic is not binary but "fuzzy" as logicians now use the term. They are multivalent, not bivalent, and exist not as "bits" but as patterns which computers and their absolutist human equivalents can discern but not understand.

1.6 *Washing of the Feet.* Panel, tenth century. Sinai, Monastery of St. Catherine. (Photo: courtesy of the Princeton-Michigan-Alexandria expedition to Mt. Sinai, and Kurt Weitzmann.)

Were the definition of Byzantium's essence as Greco–Roman, the description of its culture as European, merely passing mistakes in logic, these too could be passed over. But, as encapsulated in the title of the largest ever international exhibition of Byzantine art – *Byzantine Art an* [sic] *European Art* – staged in Athens in 1964, this manner of thinking has become endemic in our field. Indeed the Athens exhibition, perpetuated in its catalogue of 740 items,[44] merely canonized the interpretation of Byzantium that had been the common denominator of western European and American scholarship for at least a generation. And even today the "young Turks" (if, in this context, the phrase may be forgiven) who reject much of their predecessors' intellectual framework, still rail against those who judge Byzantine art to be not "European."[45] That this is not the case can be demonstrated with any number of quotations from recent commentary in a dozen different areas of cultural activity. While documents of Byzantine epistolography, history, and philosophy self-consciously bristle with classical allusions and quotations, the field in which the Greco–Roman achievement is most often used as a reference point by modern scholars is without doubt that of art. "The classical" – as a system involving such elements as human proportion, the illusionistic handling of light and shadow, drapery forms, and notional overall "elegance," still used as touchstones in the analysis of Italian Renaissance art – is applied both as a principle of measurement and as a set of particulars to East Christian objects, as the following citations make clear. (The identity of their authors is less important than the attitude that they display in common towards the objects of their study.) Of a tenth-century panel of the *Washing of the Feet* (Figure 1.6), for instance, it has been observed that:

Stylistically, the icon painter stresses comparatively slender body proportions and he works with a strong emphasis on the highlights, revealing the impact of the revival of classical painterly forms after the iconoclastic period."[46]

And of a steatite showing the Hetoimasia (the throne prepared for Christ's second coming) with two angels and four martyrs:

The majestic rhythm of the presentation, the elegance of attitudes and the classical canon of the figures evoke those of the most beautiful ivories of the "Romanos Group" . . . [and] restore the antique spirit sought for during the Macedonian Renaissance.[47]

In these examples, the unsurpassable nature of classical Greece, the mantle of Winckelmann with its folds beautifully draping the human figure, weigh heavily on the historian of Byzantine art. The fault here is *not* the fact that works are treated in terms of their formal qualities. Stylistic analysis remains one of the most powerful weapons in the armory of the historian of culture and one which art historians are especially well equipped to deploy. Rather, these quotations exemplify the analytical tangle that arises when the criteria applied are largely irrelevant to the objects under scrutiny.

It may be objected that such criteria were those that the Byzantines themselves employed. If the literature of the same period rejoices in classical references, are such standards not equally appropriate to contemporaneous works of visual art? To this plea two responses may be made. First, the citation of pagan authors by Byzantine writers was a convention, a socially sanctioned *modus operandi* that was normally pursued in the service of Christian argument – an argument ignored in the commentaries just cited. Secondly, to treat Byzantine art "on its own terms" is, as Paul Lemerle once observed, to fall into a trap that the Byzantines themselves set.[48] We can think only in our own terms, even when what we are thinking about is not something of our own devising.[49] The Byzantines called themselves "Romans" (*Rhomaioi*) and, from the thirteenth century onwards, Hellenes. For us to use such language today, except insofar as we refer to the Byzantines' own awareness of the political, ethnic, and religious overtones that these terms carried, would be not only confusing, but to walk open-eyed into the trap. Yet to insist on "the classical" as a prime standard by which to judge their civilization is to accept complicity in the confusion. The use of "classicism," "naturalism" (or "realism"), and similar norms constitutes what philosophers call a category mistake. It has also led to the sort of circular argument by which works that are said to be of high quality, i.e., those which are perceived as possessing an elevated quantum of "Greco–Romanness," are regarded as metropolitan productions, while those of lesser magnitude in this respect are deemed to be provincial. Almost needless to say, so theoretically feeble an axiom is both easily and frequently extrapolated. The massive ivory box object known as the "David Casket," now in the Palazzo Venezia in Rome, was long judged to be Armenian (or, in a later interpretation, Sicilian) because of its ungainly figure carving; in fact, it is a work of Constantinopolitan manufacture and an early product of the era when "Renaissance" values and style are said to have been the horses on which the best people in town were putting their money.[50]

Such delusions have done more than induce factual mistakes. They have led to the exaltation of questions of minor significance over those that could direct our attention to matters of central importance. The best example is perhaps the already mentioned Paris Psalter, the "classicizing" features of which led to fifty years of dispute: were these features survivals or revivals of antique prototypes? Such far more interesting problems as the nature of a culture that, within the pages of one book, could accept both the thoroughly "Pompeian" composition of David and his muse-like companion *and* a "shield raising" (one means by which early Byzantine emperors were chosen) in which legs unattached to any figure dangle beneath the shield,[51] were left unconsidered.

Involved here is an issue that transcends aesthetics. The paradigmatic role of major commissions is a matter that goes to the heart of this society. Byzantine buildings and images are moments in sequences that can be traced both backwards and forwards in time. A fair number can be seen to be what Roland Barthes called "prophecies in reverse." Setting both the tone and topic for future generations, they rehearsed an established, sometimes millennial past, recapitulating not only what the Byzantines knew but evidently determining what they wanted. This does not mean that no change, no development, occurred:[52] new subjects and modifications of meaning are the stuff of all but the dreariest histories of Byzantine art. But this art's normative tenor results in a generalization that art historians attempt to deconstruct: an overall consistency in the appearance of its expressions. The resemblance between an icon of, say, the tenth century and one of the late twelfth (Figures 1.6 and 1.14) is more marked, and therefore surely of greater import to us, than the differences between them. To dismiss this simply as the manifestation of a "conventional" or "traditional" society is not only a thoroughly conventional and traditional observation but a misrepresentation of the dynamics of its culture. The similarities between icons of quite different dates are better seen as the embodiment of a sort of intertextuality: the later image draws on and proclaims its reference to an exemplary ideal. In this sense Byzantine art may be considered derivative by definition, that definition being supplied by Orthodox theology. The role of the exemplary (*ektupôma*) and its relation to the derivative (*paragôgon*) are set out *in extenso* in the writings of Iconophile polemicists.[53] These works − canonical reading till the end of the Byzantine empire − promoted the idea that, in depicting the holy, an icon, instead of merely representing it, *participated* in all but its essence. They thus formed the core of a theory of images and a doctrine of mimesis utterly at odds with the principles of Greco−Roman and European art in and after the Renaissance.

If enough has been said at least to suggest that the standards of both the ancient and modern worlds are inapposite to Byzantium, there remains to be considered its Christian contemporary, the medieval West. In this case, the grounds for differentiation are more subtle, for our awareness of this society is similarly founded on written records prepared for an elite which, notwithstanding its diversity of origin, used a single, official language and which was responsible for the material circumstances of a state-sponsored, and generally state-serving, church. Byzantium has often been treated as the *alter ego*, with little altered, of western Europe. Yet the latter, which consisted first of the fragments of one portion of the Roman empire and then, from the tenth century, of mutually competing kingdoms, presents a clear contrast to Byzantium which saw itself as a unit, as *the* Roman empire, and thus as an entity that should assimilate its neighbors, incorporating peoples born into different faiths and customs and, where this was not possible, dominate them.

The capacity to realize this end, progressively more asserted than demonstrated, translated into a society which, like medieval China, was exclusive. The *barbaroi* who could not be compelled or, like the Slavs in the ninth and tenth centuries, persuaded to come into the Empire were considered implacable enemies against whom its forces (themselves increasingly comprised of non-Greeks) were properly arrayed. Following the Persians, Arabs, Pechenegs, and Turks, the Latins occupied this frame in the Byzantine gaze. But no later than the late twelfth century – and the period essentially coincides with the reduced impact of Byzantium on their native art and architecture – the Latins saw the Eastern Empire as later western nations regarded Turkey: as the Sick Man of Europe, a legendarily rich, autocratic state living on its past glories and growing ever feebler. This debility was proved by the capture of Constantinople in 1204 and the loss of most of the territory that it still possessed. The Byzantine empire, like love, was eternal as long as it lasted. Momentarily mourned, as we have seen, when it finally fell to the Ottomans in 1453, in the eyes of Europe it became the bedraggled tail of the ancient world. Its culture, because Christian, was considered a curiosity, an attitude that still survives in the awkward agglomeration of "Early Christian" and Byzantine art of our handbooks. Unable to see in the beliefs of this civilization anything more than a source of "symbolism," these same texts yet prefer extinct classicism to generative credence as a justification for our interest in Byzantium.

As a consequence of this choice, much that is characteristic of Byzantine society has been supplanted by notional concerns that were never concerns of its members. To limit ourselves only to aspects that pertain to art, where in any book not intended for specialists can one find useful accounts of such diverse phenomena as the theology of the icon, the stylite saint (Figure 1.7), the eunuch (Figure 1.8), or the aulic ceremonies of Constantinople, all long-lived phenomena in search of even a brief explanation? The first two of these institutions are regarded as infinitely mysterious and virtually abandoned to Russian scholarship (or further mystification); the last two I shall touch on briefly below, if only because they exemplify the "oriental" and thus alien nature of much that went on in Byzantium. It may be that such negligence is unavoidable. Aron Gurevich has observed that when the student of a later culture looks at the activities of an earlier society

> he will notice above all that which is close and understandable . . . anything that responds in some way to his own culture's intentions or that strikes him, on the other hand, by force of contrast and is understood precisely because of the sharp contrast with his own culture.[54]

I have argued that many differential aspects of Byzantium have yet to find adequate representation in our own scholarship. Yet the first part of the Russian historian's observation conforms to what has been suggested above. When we look at Byzantium we recognize the little that we know – the allegedly "classical" aspects of that culture.

This may yet change, as Greek and Latin disappear from the field of modern awareness. Yet where the means of communication are not verbal but visual – i.e., in carving and painting where the raw material upon which stylistic analysis operates is not directly dependent on language – recognition of the inappropriateness of criteria derived from antiquity is likely to come more slowly. More is involved here than a matter of literacy. When the history of twentieth-century pedagogy and scholarship comes to be written, some social psychologist might well observe the extent to which we have been aided by the illusion of closeness to cultures very different from our own, a strategy that eases our discomfiture in the face of palpable evidence for "otherness." This reduces what Gurevich calls "the pathos of distance"[55] between "us" and "them." The shedding of illusions is always a difficult task and one that is made no easier by the fact that our Eurocentric stance towards Byzantium is a *learned* position, inherited from the Renaissance and canonized by the concerns of the Enlightenment. The sincerity of these societies was the sincerity of self-interest. But today we have little to gain and much to lose by appropriating cultures that were (and are) manifestly distinct. To do so is to repeat the Byzantine mistake, to persist in the autistic belief that our civilization is the climax and end product of history. The difficulty of unlearning a learned posture may, however, be softened by the recognition of analogies. (In our own day, the rate of change in social attitudes towards both women and our society's "minorities" has doubtless been accelerated by attention to the model of relations between whites and blacks.) For the art historian such precedents are available in Asian cultures, the study of which, I submit, can be of heuristic value for a better understanding of Byzantium.

Byzantine Art an "Oriental" Art?

Anyone who undertakes to show that much that is essential in the nature of Byzantine art is closer to that of eastern societies than it is to western Europe will be arraigned for moving to the center of this achievement aspects that are "in fact" marginal. If this accusation is levied, I accept the charge, and do so not only because "facts" are hard to come by in the study of medieval art but because what is deemed to be central is as much an artifact as the concept of the peripheral. In the foregoing pages I have suggested the reasons why, in our historiography, that which resembles the dominant characteristics of Greco–Roman art has been the focus of attention. It is time now to scrutinize the particulars of this center and their consequence – the liminal position attributed to those qualities of Byzantine art and thought that do not appear to fit the classical mold.

The most notorious example of this topology is the preponderance in architectural history of church design and construction, as against the relatively minor place accorded to secular building. While it is true of Byzantine palaces that "we have so little left," this argument will not hold for more ordinary structures. If we know little of domestic buildings, it is because we have scarcely looked for them. It may be no accident that, of the lost Imperial Palace in Constantinople (now largely under the foundations of the Sultan Ahmet mosque), the parts best recorded in Byzantine literature are those of the early ninth-century emperor Theophilos who, at least at Bryas (modern Bostanci, an Asian suburb of Istanbul), built "in imitation of Arab [palaces] and in no way differing from the latter either in form or decoration."[56] Another area of the main palace due to him was the Karianos which, in the tenth century, was "used as a *vestiarium* for storing away silken garments." It is in this field that Arab (and earlier, Persian) elements in Byzantine art are most in evidence. Indeed, except where a textile bears names and offices in Greek, it is often difficult to distinguish Byzantine products from textiles made

1.7 *St. Symeon Stylites.* Illuminated manuscript, early eleventh century. Vatican, Biblioteca Apostolica Vaticana gr. 1613, page 2. (Photo: author.)

elsewhere in the Near East. These cultures shared a common repertoire of motifs and techniques and borrowed from each other the names of both particular types of stuffs and the garments into which they were made up; Byzantine texts witness to the employment of Muslim and Jewish workers.[57] The evidence, in sum, is sufficient to call in doubt the enterprise of assigning "national" origins to silks in and after the ninth century. More important for our present purposes, the stylistic and iconographical norms of antiquity are all but silent in this artisanal *lingua franca.*

To this irrelevance we have a sizable body of testimony, produced under optimal conditions, for a test of the uses of textiles in middle and late Byzantium (ninth to fifteenth century) and in the West. In the former, dedicatory and portrait miniatures in books, as well as the likenesses in fresco of scores of donors, show their patrons in the garb in which they chose to present themselves to eternity: these are never the garments historiated with biblical scenes that we find in the early Christian and early Byzantine worlds. In an early eleventh-century picture the group of men to the left, revering St. Symeon the Stylite (Figure 1.7), are Arabs, as their turbans and the *tiraz* band on the arm of one of them make clear. Yet the ornament of their costumes would have been unexceptionable to the manuscript's first audience; rather, such clothing would have helped persuade the Byzantine spectator that in Syria, the land of this long-dead saint, he was still venerated by Christians. Medieval Latins, for their part, declined to distinguish Greek from other eastern Mediterranean silks: both were sufficiently exotic to serve as shrouds for the earthly remains of kings and saints and precious enough to line the *châsses* that contained such relics.

By concentrating on function rather than form, it should be clear that the similarities (and differences) between Byzantium and its Muslim neighbors were not primarily matters of *style*, as the term is normally used. The formal means by which Byzantine culture separated itself were reserved for its overtly Christian expressions: in this domain it is as distinct from Islam as it is from Greco–Roman art, and there can be as little doubt about the self-consciousness of these stylistic choices as there is about the painstaking arguments that the Orthodox used to separate their theological positions from the often strikingly similar tenets of monotheistic Islam.[59]

But beyond the realm of ideological protestation, Byzantines and Muslims look remarkably akin. Whether we look at the pragmatic or the decorative in these cultures, the resemblances are obvious. Consider the case of Leo the Mathematician, an ornament at the court of Theophilos, a renowned student of Ptolemy and Archimedes, and the inventor of an early warning system against Arab raids. The Abbasid caliph Ma'mu-n is said to have offered Theophilos eternal peace and 2000 pounds of gold if he would allow Leo to reside for a while in Baghdad.[60] Leo, apparently like Michelangelo, declined the offer from the East. But the invitation is more significant than the refusal: it reminds us that societies compete only when they share the same interests. Of course the Arabs wanted Leo, as the Americans wanted German rocket scientists in the 1940s or, as today, many nations practice industrial espionage. It would be vain to distinguish between technology, art, and statecraft when considering the automata, the mechanical lions that roared in the Byzantine court of the ninth and tenth centuries, as they did beside the princes of Baghdad and Cairo. Here, too, were thrones that rose and fell, elephant clocks and metal(?) trees alive with (pneumatic?) singing birds. We know next to nothing of how such machines worked in Constantinople. The Arabs produced several versions of the elegantly illustrated *Book of Mechanical Devices*[61] which leave us little wiser. The point is not our ignorance but the shared mechanics and common purposes of the cultures under consideration.

Other eastern societies likewise display greater affinities with Byzantium than the ancient world or the medieval west. One of the signs of Constantinople's transformation from an "open" late antique city to a "closed" medieval enclave was the progressive confinement of imperial rituals to the palace. The audience to whom these played was increasingly an elite, appointed by the emperor rather than constituted by inheritance as in western Europe. More like the Forbidden City of Peking than the itinerant Carolingian court, the palace was a *sanctum* inaccessible to "the people" who had been the nominal seat of authority in the Rome of the Republic and Principate. Within this holy of holies both bureaucracy and ceremony fed upon themselves, multiplying in complexity and number. An intrinsic role in both was played by the class of "beardless ones" who reached high positions and, as suggested by images like that of Leo the *praipositos* and *sakellarios* in the Bible that he commissioned (Figure 1.8), played a perhaps disproportionately large role in the sponsorship of art. Originally associated with a notion of purity, and then, because they could found no dynasty, as especially loyal to the throne, eunuchs became leading generals (Narses) and top financial administrators (John the Orphanotrophos). These high governmental positions were analogous to those that they occupied in both China and Islam but alien to their functions in the West where, in Venice for example, the chief use of *castrati* was in the choir of the state church.

The image of Leo *sakellarios*, shown in his "Sunday best" presenting his book to the Virgin, and through her to Christ, epitomizes the tenth-century court whose protocol required changes of costume within the course of even a single ceremony.[62] But it also demonstrates the cognitive parallels in Byzantine systems of morality, ritual, and patronage. Leo is a sort of ambassador presenting his credentials; on bended knee he assumes the position of the submissive barbarians on the base of the Obelisk of Theodosius. But his

offering cannot be accepted directly by the Lord, remote in an arc of heaven and
distinguished by the attribute of his *nimbus cruciger* and his gesture of blessing. Dwarfing
these male poles, the Mother of God is the mistress of ceremonies, the mediatrix
necessary to the transmission of human pleas and oblations. This message is conveyed by
her eyes which, unlike those of Christ or the donor, are upon the miniature's beholder.

In contrast to European art where, no later than the Trecento, the spectator is just
that, a voyeur vouchsafed a glimpse of a scene from which he or she is excluded, in
Byzantium the beholder is a privileged participant, at once active witness to the transac-
tion and potential recipient of the saint's intercession. Renaissance art in both north and
south knows numerous instances where the protagonist in the picture and the observer
exchange gazes, but in such cases almost never is the depicted figure a sacred personage;
in the art of Greece and Rome direct visual engagement between the human and the

divine is so rare as to be negligible. Supremely in Byzantium, however, Christ or his saints fix the beholder with their stare – a gaze no less terrifying for the inertia and impassiveness that are the hallmarks of this art in the modern, popular view. The medieval west presented the divine in similar ways (for example in the tympana of Romanesque churches) but did not pursue the logic of the image to the conclusion reached in the East – the image of the earthly lord in the same numinous manner. This central, "aweful," larger-than-life attitude is assumed by John VI Kantakouzenos presiding over a church council in a copy of his *Works* in Paris (Figure 1.9). Painted during the emperor's lifetime but some twenty years after he had retired into a monastery, it shows the mid-fourteenth-century emperor with the insignia of his office as the linchpin of a system represented by the bishops and monks about him. This is no "illustration," for there is no direct relationship between the picture and the texts that it precedes. And precisely this absence of dependence characterizes the frontispiece of a *Book of Songs* (Kitâb al-Aghârî) finished in Mosul in 1219 (Figure 1.10). Formal resemblances (and dissimilarities) aside, it is clear that what Ettinghausen calls "the princely style"[63] in medieval Iraq served many of the same purposes as book production in Palaeologan Constantinople.

Treated as if they were Greco–Roman papyri or luxurious books prepared for Italian humanist clients, Byzantine "illustrated manuscripts" have been studied as if extensive narrative cycles, particularly those representing the Scriptures, were their prime form of embellishment. Considered at least quantitatively – surely a valid mode of analysis if we

1.11 (above) Koran frontispiece, 1368–88.
Cairo, National Library (from Ettinghausen,
La Peinture arabe, page 174).

1.12 (above right) *Headpiece to Matthew.*
Illuminated manuscript, early twelfth cen-
tury. Oxford, Bodleian Library, Cod. Auct.
T. inf. 1.10, fol. 24r. (Photo: courtesy of I.
Hutter.)

1.13 (right) *Abu Zayd Addressing an Audience.* Illuminated manuscript, 1222. Paris,
Bibliothèque Nationale, MS arabe 6094,
fol. 147r. (Photo: library.)

wish to understand the norms of a society's production – nothing could be further from the truth. As everywhere else the majority of books was undecorated. Statistically, the next largest category included books with only bands or headpieces of geometric or stylized floral ornament. Such decoration has remained a stepchild neglected by scholars, including the present writer,[64] as they rush to celebrate the anthropomorphic achievements of medieval painters. Yet in the manner of the splendid frontispieces in medieval Korans (Figure 1.11), where the "image of the word"[65] is inlaid in fields of ornament, even so rich a liturgical book as the Codex Ebnerianus in Oxford[66] has as many headbands calligraphically announcing the readings from the Gospels and similar decorations as it does figural scenes. Even where the greater portion of the page is given over to adornment and the titles removed to a position directly above the text (Figure 1.12), the polychrome vegetation is subordinated to the dictates of a symmetry that defies nature. Such carpets "represent" nothing save a splendor worthy of their divine *destinataire*, embellishments that speak at the same time of the mortal patron who has seen fit, as Byzantine dedications put it, to create this glory.

I seek neither to ignore nor to minimize the conceptual gulf that yawns between Byzantine and Islamic art. The latter delights in, even while it formalizes, events in the natural world: the old scoundrel, al-Hariri, stupefies the men of Najrân with tall tales (Figure 1.13) where the archetypal Christian teacher demonstrates his humility to an audience that is the spectator gazing at the mosaic (Figure 1.14, compare Figure 1.6). Yet

1.14   *Washing of the Feet*. Mosaic, late twelfth century. Monreale. (Photo: Alinari.)

both scenes, the profane and the holy, are conventions, repeated across centuries with the same minimal attention to spatial setting and the same emphasis on the mesmerizing power of the protagonists' gestures. Scores of versions of both incidents exist and few differ from the essentials depicted here. Repetition over time assured the Byzantine beholder that he was in the presence of an Orthodox image; rehearsal of al-Hariri's stories, always with the same figure types, in manuscripts from a variety of regions lent to the *Maqâmât*, for all its roguery, the air of an Arab national epic. The narratives of

1.15 (above) *St. Eustratios*. Ivory, tenth century. Luton Hoo, Wernher Collection. (Photo: author.)

1.16 (right) *Priest Seshin*. Wood, 1163–1223. Nara, Hokuen-do of Kofuku-ji (from Lee, *History of Far Eastern Art*, fig. 422).

Greco–Roman mythology, like depictions of the Passion of Christ in and after the Quattrocento, show far more diversity in their telling.

The variation among such western works is a measure of the distance that separates us from medieval Byzantium and Islam. No one today would try to naturalize Muslim culture, to constrain its otherness in the Procrustean bed of European standards and achievements. Yet the attempt to squeeze Byzantium until it fits our ethological and aesthetic presuppositions has been scholarly practice since the Renaissance. The reasons, and misguided justification, for these efforts lie first, I have tried to suggest, in the illusion of classicism that the Byzantines themselves promoted and, secondly, in the extent to which, because they were Christians, we demand that they should be accessible to us in a way that the civilizations of the East are not. But, I have also argued, the study of human aggregations is not susceptible to binary methods; each is a special case of "gray," not a black or white phenomenon. In this light it is silly to argue that Byzantine art was an "oriental" art. But to do so is no sillier than to insist that it was "European."[67] The absurdity of the first proposition is evident if we compare a holy image from Byzantium (Figure 1.15) with one from Japan (Figure 1.16). The wood figure from Nara represents a living being, the priest Seshin, possessed of all the inward intensity that we expect of a Zen Buddhist. The ivory icon, on the other hand, is a fantasy, the conjured likeness of a legendary martyr. Yet, if we go beyond the traditional procedures of philology and archeology, approaches that turn everything to facts, and acknowledge that we explore these figures in the only way we can – that is, through our responses to them – it is both possible and profitable to recognize what they have in common. I leave this exercise to the reader in the hope that, even as he or she perceives the differences between these examples, the distance between them and, more importantly, their distance from us becomes a little less than it seems at first.

2.1   Michelangelo, *Bruges Madonna*. Marble, 1503–1504. Bruges, Church of Onze Lieve Vrouwe.

CHAPTER 2

Italian Sculptors and Sculpture Outside of Italy (Chiefly in Central Europe): Problems of Approach, Possibilities of Reception[1]

THOMAS DACOSTA KAUFMANN

By the late sixteenth century Latinate culture as first introduced in the form of Italian humanism provided a model for grammatical instruction and rhetorical practice from Manila to Minsk.[2] By the same time works of the visual arts possessing a definite Italianate character had also expanded throughout the globe. The iconography of humanism, as evinced by author portraits and frontispieces, was spread in books by authors as widely disparate as the Mexican-born Diego Valadés and the Belorussian Francisk Skarina.[3] In the sixteenth and early seventeenth centuries works comparable in form to those in the peninsula could be found in churches scattered from Macao or Goa (which contain paintings of the sixteenth century) to the highlands of the Andean region in South America, where Bernardo Bitti, a native of Camerino, was active in an area extending from Quito to Sucre during the later sixteenth century, and where the Fleming known as Pedro de Gante designed the Franciscan Church in Quito, which possesses a facade that recalls a triumphal arch.[4]

This essay deals with some of the best known and most striking instances of the spread of Renaissance (and later) visual forms, Italian sculptors and sculpture outside of Italy.[5] From antiquity Italy supplied a source of fine marble. The skill and training of Italians as stonecarvers and bronzecasters were also appreciated elsewhere. Thus Italian sculptors and their products were long in broad demand, especially from the fifteenth century. Yet familiar as the topic may be, this seemingly straightforward case of the expansion of the Italianate still remains to be integrated into a comprehensive picture of what the Renaissance and its consequences might mean outside Italy, as indeed do so many other examples of related phenomena.

For the possible historical significance of many such works, especially those found outside of Europe, is hardly acknowledged in Anglo–American art history. Studies of the history of European art in the early modern period also continue largely to ignore two thirds of the continent, where many major monuments are contained, namely the area east of the Rhine, particularly after about 1530, as they also ignore the area east of the Oder, in almost any period. Very few American art historians study the Iberian peninsula, especially before the so-called Golden Age of seventeenth-century Spain, for that matter. Despite the existence of objects located or made outside Italy that can be considered within the terms of standard definitions of the Renaissance, there is little attention given to what they might reveal about the broader applicability of the idea of the Renaissance, what they might perhaps even imply for a reconsideration of the meaning of the conception, and finally what they might indicate more generally about cultural exchange and interchange.

With all the concerns that are voiced for a more comprehensive art history, and the extensive debate they have provoked, newer trends in Anglo-Saxon art history hardly appear to have affected the discussion of these issues. Instead, many of the older paradigms and canons that had also determined the geographical boundaries and national concerns of the discipline of art history as it was "traditionally" practiced still stay in force.[6] If the term "Renaissance" is used to indicate something more than merely the time period of the fifteenth to the seventeenth centuries, then little has changed in scholarship on the early modern period.

Whatever the ideal of the "Renaissance" may mean in regard to Italy, when applied to the visual arts elsewhere, the term is still usually taken to signify, even celebrate, something described as quite distinct from that in Italy. Both scholarship and teaching on the so-called Northern Renaissance, which effectively still stands in the United States for the Renaissance outside Italy, concentrate almost exclusively on Netherlandish painting in manuscript and on panel from Van Eyck to Brueghel, with attention also being given to German paintings and prints, and some sculpture too, of the era of the Old German masters around Dürer. This point of view is found both in standard textbooks, and in supposedly newer approaches.[7]

There is, however, nothing new in the emphasis on Netherlandish painting up to Brueghel and German artists of the *Dürerzeit*. The consideration of "Renaissance" art outside of Italy has demonstrably often involved a different set of assumptions than that which has governed the study of Italian "Renaissance" art. From at least the early nineteenth century, when art history became an academic discipline in Germany, art of the fifteenth and sixteenth centuries in the north has been understood as something different and distinctive from that in Italy. The "Renaissance" has been used largely either to define a chronological period, as it often still is, or else to designate art of a quality comparable to that of the Italian masters, but distinct from them.

This idea is found in literature c. 1800, as Wackenroder and Tieck's *Herzensgiessungen eines kunstliebeneden Klosterbrüders* suggests. It was developed by art historians in the formative years of the *Gründerzeit* of the mid-nineteenth century, and passed on by important figures in the field such as Heinrich Wölfflin and Georg Dehio. The idea of a national German Renaissance was even used for purposes of political propaganda, both during the 1914–18 war and the years of National Socialism. The notion of a distinctive Northern Renaissance, largely unrelated to and even contrasting with that in Italy, continues to recur in much recent writing, especially in English, where the local or native element is privileged, and the cosmopolitan, Italianate is downplayed or ignored.[8]

The result has been that like many related topics, the subject of Italian sculptors and sculpture outside of Italy not only remains to be integrated into the history of the Renaissance, but also even to be adequately conceptualized. In response, this paper will endeavor to strive towards this process of integration and conceptualization. It will offer a critical review of prior treatments of the topic, and suggest some alternatives to them.

Earlier essays have a further interest in that they imply a view of the general course of the history of European art during the early modern period. The literature to date thus reflects the general development of historiography of the Renaissance. A critique therefore has further relevance to a collection of essays that is devoted to a reconceptualization of the Renaissance.

Broadly speaking, it would seem that the tendencies that have dominated the interpretation of Italian sculpture and sculptors outside of Italy may be described as monographic, nationalistic, stylistic, and anthropological. First, a traditional monographic approach could easily ignore the problem of synthesis. One way of treating the presence of Italian sculpture or the work of Italian sculptors outside Italy was simply to regard such phenomena as examples of an artist's oeuvre. In this kind of account, as it has been evinced in historiography since Giorgio Vasari, a work of sculpture is seen as the product of an individual master. From the late eighteenth or early nineteenth century, writers on art also considered sculpture a product of genius. Sculpture might accordingly be regarded as the mark of biographical incident. In the approach that results, the historical scheme may thus consist of the linkage of a chain of works by individual masters, that are conjoined by bonds of personal association, or perhaps, as also described by Vasari, by progress towards the achievement of some artistic goal. Other, later, treatments of Italian sculptors, for instance a history of sculptors in Poland, often take over this model even when they do not follow Vasari in other regards.[9]

A related perspective, namely that from the peninsula, may however open up a different view. From this perspective, works by major Italian sculptors found outside Italy appear as scattered pieces of evidence of Italian genius. This view is anticipated by the way sculpture is handled in Vasari's account of the pieces by Verrocchio that Lorenzo de' Medici sent Matthias Corvinus in the fifteenth century.[10] Yet many subsequent accounts – of such works as the marble Virgin and Child by Michelangelo (Figure 2.1) that, as Vasari also mentions, was acquired by a Bruges merchant in the early sixteenth century, or the bust of the king and the other projects that Bernini carried out for Louis XIV of France in the seventeenth century, or the works made by Roman sculptors for Mafra in Portugal in the eighteenth century – often do not differ substantially. In many studies of Italian art, such objects may be regarded as important documents of their artists' oeuvres. Nevertheless, they remain distinctive examples of individual genius, further isolated in that they are often unconnected to the milieus in which they were subsequently, or are now, found.

One merit of the most comprehensive series of studies directed to the work of Italians outside Italy was that it overcame this sense of individual isolation. This series treated the *opera* of Italian artists, including sculptors, as examples not of individual genius, but of the genius of the nation or, it may be said, the race. The series thus appeared under the title *l'opera del genio italiano all'estero*. The products of this genius were to be found throughout the ages and throughout Europe, as presented in books devoted to *il genio italiano* in Spain, Austria, Germany, Hungary, Russia, and other countries. In their emphasis upon the comprehensive, collective picture of the national genius of the Italians, these books do not, however, display much concern for local context elsewhere.

The collective approach taken in the series *L'opera del genio italiano all'estero* derives ultimately rather from the Romantic view of cultural products as expressions of the *Geist* or genius of peoples or *Völker*, that is to be traced to authors such as Herder. In nineteenth-century histories of what is now most often called culture (*Kulturgeschichte*), the view of history as an expression of a *Volk* was also spread by Hegelian thinking about art as a form of *Volksgeist*.[11] These ideas were also familiar in Italy (through Benedetto Croce, among others), and it is significant that the series dedicated to *il genio italiano* was published under the imprimatur of ministries of the Italian government, at first of the Mussolini epoch. Some of the earlier volumes in the series bear dates measured in the reckoning of the Fascist era, when some of these ideas were given a fateful twist.[12] Under Mussolini, the idea of Italian genius bringing art and civilization to Europe was one theme of fascist propaganda, that, remarkably enough, was in a way still being promoted as this series was continued into the 1960s.[13]

A spirit not so dissimilar in its chauvinism has often led to widespread neglect of Italianate phenomena outside Italy, and nationalistic presuppositions have also been woven into other approaches. This tone of cultural nationalism has, however, fortunately been alien to much Italian historiography related to the topic, even when the clamor of *campanilismo* still seems to resound in volumes devoted to the impact of individual regions, such as those on the art and artists of the Lombard lakes,[14] and when nationalistic presuppositions have also been woven into other approaches to these questions. It is precisely the international or transnational aspect of artistic contacts that such chauvinistic or culturally nationalistic approaches ignore. Yet as significant as Italian sculpture and sculptors may be outside of Italy, it is also true that what could similarly be called *il genio estero* had a significant presence *in* Italy. To mention just sculpture in one site, in addition to a host of other rather minor talents from beyond the Alps, such major figures as Giovanni Dalmata in the fifteenth century, Giambologna in the sixteenth, François Duquesnoy in the seventeenth or, at the end of that century and the beginning of next, Pierre Legros, along with a flock of other French academicians, were all active in Rome. All these artists, along with whom we should remember the presence in Rome of other important northern painters such as Claude Lorrain, Nicolas Poussin and Peter Paul Rubens, give evidence that the process of artistic exchange was not one-sided, that there was not merely one source of artistic genius in European art.

Moreover, an alternative model has long existed, that developed alongside the attention given to the formulation and evolution of concepts of stylistic periodization in art history. This approach treats Italian artists and art outside of Italy in relation to the general course of development of artistic styles. In this perspective, the activity of Italian sculpture and sculptors, and also of painters and architects, belongs to a continuing history of styles, which Italians convey to the north. In this way Italian artists are regarded not merely as translating works of individual or national genius, but as contributing to the evolution of style epochs outside of Italy. As in Italy, these are seen to progress from the Renaissance, to Mannerism, to the Baroque, to neo-Classicism.

It may even be said that this account has directed so many previous discussions that it has almost become a standard line, at least for older generations of scholars. Jan Białostocki articulated a position that has been adopted by many other art historians, whose opinion he may thus be said to represent. In numerous papers Białostocki regarded the Renaissance as "a system of forms, qualities, artistic functions and themes which dominated art and architecture, decoration and design, and which we call the Renaissance style."[15] Białostocki treated this (and other styles) as, on the one hand, the product of individual Italian artists and, on the other, an indigenous response to them. And so when Białostocki says that the Renaissance came first to the north in eastern Europe, he means quite literally that Italian sculptors and masons of the Quattrocento came first to places like Hungary.[16] In this view Italian forms, including sculpture, were then taken up by local courts, used for particular purposes and functions, and then spread more widely by the local artists and craftsmen who responded to them.

Although it has many virtues, this approach has also created numerous problems, not the least of which is implicated in the very terms employed: the use of stylistic terms to describe unrelated phenomena in regions other than that for which they were created has produced several difficulties. Thus many of the problems that the Florentine–Roman model has entailed for studies of art and culture of the quattrocento and cinquecento elsewhere in Italy itself seem to have been compounded when these conceptions have been applied to art outside Italy.[17] In the first instance, forms related to style epochs such as the Renaissance and Mannerism that are not regarded as contemporaneous in Italy may appear simultaneously in the north. Even where terms might seem to be suitable, a comparison of Italian with northern examples may also indicate the apparently belated or supposedly incorrect nature of stylistic manifestations in the north, thus slanting the interpretation. Moreover, when analyzed further, a term such as Mannerism in any event seems to have limited applicability to phenomena outside of Italy.[18]

Even when Italians made works *in situ* outside Italy, it was only exceptionally, at least in Central Europe, that the Italian artists who came north worked in modes similar to the forms of the Renaissance, or Mannerism, as they have been defined according to the Florentine or Roman paradigm. Many artists came from other regions in Italy, such as the Lombard lakes. The works they produced are different from those of Tuscan classicism, and its successors, and may accordingly seem mannered in contrast, although the legitimacy of this description in this context is questionable.[19]

In answer to some of these conceptual difficulties Białostocki reformulated another heuristic notion: the local stylistic variant. He opposed his understanding of the conception of Mannerism and other international models to the national styles he otherwise also tried to define. Echoing earlier Polish and Czech art historians, Białostocki identified a supposedly more local style, which he distinguished from Mannerism, with which it might be confused. He called this the vernacular. In this he followed the manner of the *Motivenkunde* of historians such as Władisław Husarski in Poland and Antonín Balšánek in Bohemia, in identifying various motifs as pertaining to the vernacular.[20]

Although the examples of the vernacular that have hitherto been adduced are drawn largely from the realm of architecture, it might nevertheless seem that the more general characteristics used to describe the vernacular pertain particularly well to sculpture. In Białostocki's words these are a lack of interest in space composition, an enthusiasm for ornament, and lack of functional thinking – disruption of links between form and content that take on a picturesque or fantastic character of their own.[21] But these features are also not to be identified with any characteristic *genius loci* of eastern Europe, as Białostocki would have it. Similiarities have also been declared to be distinctly German or Italian. In any event, atticas resembling so-called Polish parapets are found independently of the presence of Polish artisans in Hungary (i.e., Slovakia), Austria, and Germany;

2.2 (above)   Boim Family Chapel. Lwów (L'viv).   1609–1615. (Photo: The Institute of Art, Polish Academy of Sciences.)

2.3 (opposite page)   Main facade on the Calle de Liberos, Salamanca University. *C.*1520 (Photo: Bildarchiv Foto Marburg, courtesy of Art Resource.)

graffiti and gables that are said to mark an indigenous Bohemian Renaissance are likewise found frequently in Germany and Austria. Furthermore, in the same time period that Białostocki finds them in eastern Europe, a similar decorative inventiveness, and a tendency towards the planiform, are found for example in Spanish and Spanish American sculpture.[22] The comparison of the Boim Chapel in Lwów (L'viv, Lemberg; Figure 2.2) with the portal to Salamanca University (Figure 2.3) may be telling in this regard, but many works in Latin America, such as the facade of the church at Tepoztlán (Figure 2.4), also suggest similar deviations from the classic norm.

The treatment of a particular material for sculptural details, namely stucco, has also been seen as the sign of vernacular style. But there is nothing particularly localized about the use of this medium, either. Thus one needs to treat with caution, if not skepticism,

2.4 (right)   Dominican Church,
Tepotzlán, Mexico. Completed 1588.
(Photo: Instituto de Investigaciones
Esteticas)

2.5 (below)   Houses of Mikiołaj and
Krzysztof Przybyła Family. Kazimierz
Dolny 1615. (Photo: The Institute of
Art, Polish Academy of Sciences.)

arguments advanced by Białostocki to the effect that the use of stucco, which is said to characterize the sculptors and masons of the Lublin school (Figure 2.7), or the flattened forms in plasterwork seen at Kazimierz Dolny (Figures 2.5 and 2.6), are vernacular.[23] Similar flattened plasterwork forms are found in interiors in other northern realms, including Bohemia and England, where, as in Poland, they are ultimately to be traced to Italian origins. The plasterwork figural decoration on the exterior of Nonsuch castle would probably not have been so dissimilar to Polish examples.[24]

This search for a vernacular therefore seems to have produced exceedingly elusive results. Motifs that have been identified as vernacular in eastern Europe have also been declared at various times to be distinctly German, or Italian. Certainly none of these motifs is unique to the specific regions in which they are supposedly originally located. There is also no way of situating their origins in any one place in Central Europe.

It is quite telling that Italians may in fact have been responsible for the origins of many of the forms that are regarded as vernacular. Architectural motifs that have been associated with the eastern European vernaculars such as stepped gables, parapet-like atticas, along with their constituent forms, come from northern Italy. One can point to the Venetian or northern Italian source of merlon cresting, the Paduan origins of the Kraków Cloth Hall, long attributed of course to Italians, and the north Italian origins of sgraffito decoration. In sculpture, the use of stucco also derives from Italy (the Lublin masters actually came from the Lombard lakes), and it was spread to France by Italians at

2.6   Facade detail, house of Kryzstof Przybyla Kazimierz Dolny, 1615. (Photo: The Institute of Art, Polish Academy of Sciences.)

2.7   Vault of the side aisle, Bernardine Church. Lublin. 1603–1607. (Photo: The Institute of Art, Polish Academy of Sciences.)

Fontainebleau (Figure 2.8) and thereafter by emulation to England: stucco was indeed in many countries an Italian speciality.[25] In another paper, Białostocki raised the possibility that what he elsewhere called the vernacular might be a local redaction of a more general stylistic form.[26] Rather than considering the phenomena adduced by evidence for a distinctive kind of vernacular, it might indeed be better to call them examples of the dialects of an international language, comparable to variants such as types of American English.

It is worth dwelling on the problem of the conceptualization of the vernacular in distinction to the international Italianate, because this way of treating supposedly local artistic forms illuminates the difficulties that art history has in extracting itself from a discussion which is still ultimately grounded – better, troubled – by nationalist premises. This problem is presented by the conception of *il genio italiano*, and it also has many other manifestations in the historiography of Central European art. This sort of approach has indeed so dominated the discussion to date that it has impeded the formulation of many coherent alternatives, as well as developing other insights, such as Białostocki's own idea of artistic dialect.

Nevertheless, another model of diffusion, that is anchored more firmly in anthropology, already exists (although it does not seem to have been inspired by other, more recent, trends in Anglo–Saxon art history). This diffusionist model has been frequently

2.8   Galerie of François I, view from the Vestibule of Honor, Fontainebleau. 1528. (Photo: Bildarchiv Foto Marburg, courtesy of Art Resource.)

2.9   Giovanni Dalmata.
Fragment of an altarpiece from
Diósgyőr. Stone, *c*.1490.
Budapest, Hungarian National
Gallery. (Photo: museum.)

employed in discussions of the Renaissance outside of Italy by scholars other than art historians, and it has begun to be utilized in art history as well.[27] A model of cultural diffusion helps to bolster the insights gained from an approach related to style history, without introducing problems stemming from a possible over-emphasis on novelty or uniqueness, such as is often implied by style history.

In this diffusionist approach questions of influence and interaction – not those of original genius or invention, or those posed by a national problematic – are at stake. The model of cultural diffusion, derived from the anthropological conception of acculturation, makes it possible to deal with issues of cultural influence and intersection, without regarding Italian culture as superior, and hence in reaction needing to lay stress on local identities or national characteristics.

There remains, however, a further problem in utilizing the idea of influence, namely that of underestimating the other side of the question, reception. A model of influence that is related to acculturation still largely suggests an image of a passive recipient, to which influence flows. If, however, a model of diffusion is really meant to suggest a coherent cultural process, without at least an equal emphasis upon the recipient, it may nevertheless be misleading. As Peter Burke has remarked specifically in relation to the question of the "reception" or "diffusion" of the Renaissance abroad, it may seem that "while the Italians were active, creative, and innovatory . . . the rest of Europe was passive . . . a borrower eternally in debt to Italy."[28] Yet both the activity of northern artists in Italy, and the continuation of indigenous traditions, show that this was obviously not the case.

The picture of circulation is certainly more complicated than a simple image would allow of traffic in one direction, from Italy north. Careers of artists who came from abroad to work in Rome, and elsewhere in Italy, and then passed on (or back) to Central Europe, either to remain there or else to stay for only a limited time, evoke a more complex picture than that suggested by the notion of Italy as a source, even if it be desired to retain this notion for limited cases. Giovanni Dalmata provides a good example. As his name implies, Dalmata, properly Duknovich, came from Trogir (Trau) in the present area of Dalmatia, Croatia. After working for the pope and other patrons in Rome, he moved on to the court of Matthias Corvinus in Hungary, where he executed the Madonna of Diósgyőr (Figure 2.9).[29] There are many other examples of the same phenomenon, of which the work of Pietro Francavilla or Adriaen de Vries towards 1600 are familiar.

It is time to consider other approaches. We might try to examine the other side of the coin, to see what the active aspects of reception were that led to the way in which Italian sculptors and sculpture were treated outside Italy. In this connection Burke has proposed that a model like that of literary reception (as used by some scholars of literature) is much more helpful.[30] Not only should we look, as Burke says, at the presence of individual Italians abroad, and find out where they went, at what time, and even, as in Białostocki's account, for what purposes, but how they were received. Ultimately there thus may be involved a more subtle process, as Burke suggests, of creative misinterpretation (one might also say reinterpretation). In the example considered here, Italian sculpture may thus be seen to have been assimilated, absorbed, reworked, domesticated, and transformed.[31]

Furthermore, other anthropological models than that of acculturation are available for adaptation in art history. These include that proposed by Marshall Sahlins.[32] Sahlins presents examples illustrating how cultures interact, mutually misinterpret each other, and selectively adapt elements from each other in a historical manner. The use of such a model might lead to a more comprehensive conceptualization of the relation of the history of European art to broader considerations of European culture.

To stay with the particular subject of Italian sculpture and sculptors outside Italy: one might thus rather wish to investigate what conditions or factors (to use this rather inadequate, but perhaps still necessary, term) there were that either facilitated, and thus created possibilities for, Italian sculpture and sculptors, or made problems (to use the word in another context) for them. In this sort of investigation a foundation is offered by the information and insights gained from other scholarly or interpretive approaches. Stylistic developments and individual accomplishments may consequently also be set in relation to issues of taste and fashion, theoretical motivations, education, and other bases for familiarity with Italian culture. Conversely other issues, including conditions of employment, of generic and technical limitation, of religious inhibition, and even of competition not only from alternatives in the kind of forms and practitioners of sculpture, but also from other mediators of Italianate forms, might be considered as "factors" that might impede reception of Italian sculpture and sculptors.

Białostocki himself suggested that the Renaissance came to eastern Europe as a royal fancy, and the role of taste or fashion can be emphasized, even more than in his account, in the adaptation of newer forms of art, and their spread.[33] Following Jerzy Łoziński and

Helena and Stefan Kozakiewicz, among other scholars, Białostocki suggested for instance how such a taste for the Italianate, in sculpture as in other media, began at the Polish court and spread throughout the country.[34] But Poland is not unique in this pattern. Jolán Balogh and Gyöngy Török have suggested that a similar pattern can be established for sculpture in Hungary.[35] It may also be argued (to contradict Białostocki, who regards the Habsburgs with their multinational empire as alien to the local tradition, while he deals with the Jagellonians whose dynasty was ultimately Lithuanian) that the Habsburgs as well as the Jagellonians set similar patterns, for architecture and sculpture, not only for the Austrian lands, but also for Bohemia. In Germany, too, the courts set the tone for patronage of Italians and the Italianate, as Frederick the Wise of Saxony's commissions for sculpture to Adriano Fiorentino, as well as his patronage of Jacopo de' Barbari, suggest. In all these instances a court center created a fashion that raised expectations for other rulers to follow if they wished to be *au courant*.

In fact, one of the best examples indicating how the adaptation of Italianate forms in architecture and sculpture followed the demands of fashion is suggested by a self-promoting letter that the Lübeck Town Council (*Rat*) received from the *steenhower* Paul van Hofe in 1548. In it van Hofe announces his presence in the city "in order to make some buildings in the antique manner, which antiques one now considers as the highest art, but of which art one finds nothing in the city."[36] In Lübeck, as in much of the Baltic region, a Netherlander might stand for an Italian, but the letter also demonstrates the appeal of fashion in the adaptation of the antique style, of which Italian artists and artisans were the purveyors *par excellence*.

Indeed the *stile all'Italiana* might often serve as a stand-in for those who desired something done in the "antique" style, the *stile all'antica* or *alla Romana*.[37] Here especially Italians or Italian-made sculpture often assuaged a desire for the ancient. This is evinced in the area of collecting as well as that of patronage for, as we have known since Erwin Panofsky's essay on Dürer and the antique, often the classical was seen through the veil of the Italian.[38]

A treatise on how a *Kunstkammer* should be formed that Gabriel Kaltemarkt drew up in 1587 is noteworthy here. Kaltemarkt gives first place to works of sculpture, and esteems antique statuary as the most desirable of all collectors' items. Among contemporary sculptors, however, he places Italians first. Significantly, Kaltemarkt also mentions how copies can be made of ancient works, or casts taken from them.[39] In this realm Italian sculpture again assumes a preeminent position. Kaltemarkt almost seems to suggest that in this regard Florence equals if not surpasses Rome, since it is from Florentine workshops that good copies can be obtained. In any event, this may be why from the time of Filarete's copy of the equestrian statue of Marcus Aurelius (Figure 2.10), which also belonged to the *Kunstkammer* in Dresden where it is still to be found, copies of ancient works of art by Italians found their way into northern collections.[40] This practice continued in later centuries, as is evinced by the copies made by Giovanni Susini, Massimiliano Soldani Benzi, and other sculptors who made bronzes after ancient works for the Prince of Liechtenstein.[41]

A taste for the antique can of course be related to several aspects of Renaissance culture, a huge and complicated subject to be sure. Even the revisionist critique of humanist education provided by Anthony Grafton and Lisa Jardine would allow for the

2.10 Antonio Averlino, called Filarete. Marcus Aurelius on horseback. Bronze, 1465. Dresden, Staatliche Kunstsamm-lungen. (Photo: museum.)

impact of humanist education, founded on ancient sources, on the formation of ethical notions, at least from the late ·fifteenth century,[42] and it is striking how many future patrons of Italian sculptors were actually educated by humanists. To mention but a few, in Poland these include notably kings Jan Olbracht and Sigismund Stary, who were tutored by Filippo Buonacorsi, and Piotr Tomicki, bishop of Kraków, who studied in Bologna with Filippo Beroaldo, among many other figures. In Hungary, outside of prelates who were actually Italian, the most noteworthy figure in this regard is Tomas Bákocz, the patron of the Bákocz Chapel, to whom Filippo Beroaldo dedicated his commentary on Apuleius.[43] In Germany Elector Augustus of Saxony was educated by the Vitruvian translator Rivius; later Habsburgs such as Rudolf II received a thorough humanist education, but the examples could be multiplied. Hence a newer motivation was articulated for the patronage of sculpture from the fifteenth century on. Among other notions revived or encouraged by humanist thought was the ideal of magnificence, which affected many endeavors. In his *Ten Books on Architecture* (7:16), L. B. Alberti indicates how this conception might apply to statuary:

> But, unless I am mistaken, the greatest ornament of all is the statue. It may serve as ornament in sacred and profane buildings, public and private, and makes a wonderful memorial to man or deed.[44]

Certainly contemporary humanist critics related patronage in Central Europe to *themes* including the ethic of magnificence. Politian's remarks on Matthias Corvinus are noteworthy here: "You also build the most magnificent palace by far, and adorn your court [*forum*] with statues of every kind, either bronze or marble."[45] This text indicates that one leading humanist's assessment of a ruler's realization of the ideal of magnificence could thus not be merely a theoretical *desideratum*, but a critical tool used to refer to a patron's actual use of sculpture.

Patrons did not need to learn from humanists how conspicuous consumption might be a sign of status or, as is now said, might help to constitute charisma. Nevertheless, humanist doctrine may have helped direct expenditure towards sculpture and thus may have affected patronage both in an ecclesiastical and in a secular setting. This suggests a more precise connection, and thus provides a better way of understanding the relevance of humanism to the reception of Italianate style than more general statements by scholars like Białostocki to the effect that the history of fourteenth- and fifteenth-century humanism in Central Europe provides a background to the arrival of Italianate forms there. It may even be that the inculcation of doctrines led to a predilection for Italianate works. In other words, as humanist ideas percolated north, so did a need, or taste, for Italian sculpture.

On the other hand, the adoption of stylistic notions that we associate with the humanist ideal of eloquence would also have played an important role in the assimilation of classicizing art. According to principles of rhetorical (and also poetic) decorum, forms were matched appropriately with the content they were meant to express, and with the audience to which they were directed. In this instance noble, magnificent forms that were endowed with the charisma of antiquity would have been appropriate for important monuments of sculpture.[46]

Education and humanist theory were of course not the only conduits for the spread of Italianate cultural ideals. Travel was another stimulus. This is such a familiar topic that it can be passed over briefly; one need but recall Frederick the Wise's journeys through Italy, or Maximilian I Habsburg's Italian campaigns. One of the clearest examples of the impact of travel, though not necessarily on sculpture, involves the Bavarian Duke Ludwig X who, after visiting Mantua, had a place resembling it (to his mind) built in Landshut.

Other elements than taste and fashion, or humanist ideals and education, contributed to the change in taste and fashion. The role of Italians in bronzecasting and in carving marble is obviously pertinent. Italian manufacture of terracotta sculpture is also worth mentioning.[47] But despite Italian pre-eminence in these fields, none of these was exclusively an Italian preserve. On the other hand, stucco was for a large part of the early modern period definitely an Italian specialty. The predominance of Italian sculptors in this medium throughout the region and throughout the era is well known if, as remarked above, sometimes forgotten in historical accounts that over-emphasize indigenous work in other media. In the eyes of one sixteenth-century artist, stucco was, however, distinctly an Italian gift to Central Europe. Aberlin Tretsch, the designer of the Stuttgart *Schloss*, wrote in 1561 that "handwork in stucco is among us a new craft, that Italians brought into the land around 1540."[48] Certainly Italian stucco in the Star Villa near Prague, or in Güstrow in Mecklenburg (Figure 2.11), or in the so-called *Italienisches Bau* in the Landshut residence built for Ludwig X would bear this observation out.[49]

In contrast, it is useful to consider what conditions or elements might have impeded

2.11   Doorway (detail), entry of church, Sabinov (Kisszeben), Slovakia. Stone. (Photo: Institute for Art History, Slovak Acadey of Sciences, Bratislava, Slovak Republic.)

the adaptation of Italian sculpture or the employment of Italian sculptors. Białostocki has remarked on how the adoption of Italian Renaissance solutions was very selective, limited primarily to tomb sculpture of the variety set in niches.[50] By selectivity, Białostocki means that, in comparison, other Italian Renaissance forms, such as *intarsie* or free-standing tombs, did not find their way to Poland. But the question is a broader one.

The broader issue of taste may work in a way which suggests why, conversely, Italian forms and sculpture could also have lost some of their popularity. When, for instance, in the late seventeenth and especially in the eighteenth century a taste for things French replaced that for the Italianate, French sculptors began to assume the places that Italians had once occupied. But this does not entirely explain why from the beginning patrons or clients were more sensitive to Italians' endeavors in some areas, such as tomb sculpture or architectural ornament, than in others.

While in general Italians may have worked in the north in a variety of sculptural media including marble, stucco, or occasionally bronze, even though Donatello also worked in wood there was no continuing major tradition in limewood or oak in Italy to rival the thriving use of these media in the north in the late fifteenth century. In the north the local tradition of working in wood also remained a lively alternative well through the eighteenth century for altarpieces, pulpits, baptismal fonts, and even epitaphs. In certain areas of central Europe, including Silesia, Poland, and Upper Hungary (Slovakia), there may even have existed division of media, of sorts, in which some works were executed by Italians in stone, whereas retables remained tied to the local tradition of working in wood. This is seen in places like Sabinov in Slovakia, where Italians did the doorway in stone (Figure 2.12) while presumably Germanic sculptors worked on the altarpieces

2.12 (opposite page) Master of the Altars of St. Anne (follower of Parol z Levoča). Annunciation Altarpiece from Sabinov (Kisszeben). Polychromed wood, c.1515–1520. Budapest, Hungarian National Gallery. (Photo: museum.)

2.13 (left) Master of the Altars of St. Anne (follower of Parol z Levoča). St. Anne Altarpiece from Sabinov (Kisszeben). Polychromed wood, c.1510–1515. Budapest, Hungarian National Gallery. (Photo: museum).

(Figures 2.13 and 2.14). The same phenomenon may be encountered through the eighteenth century elsewhere.[51]

There is also a social dimension to the question of artistic reception. Opportunities to obtain permanent positions as court sculptors were infrequent. Thus Italians, who might be called to work on individual projects, often in effect had to take on employment *ad hoc*. Furthermore, workshop and guild restrictions would have otherwise inhibited foreigners from settling in many cities or towns. In many places the qualifications needed to become a master would have included the demand that one be a citizen, and the qualifications for citizenship may have depended on property ownership or local birth, or even religion in Protestant regions, thus excluding Catholic Italians. As is well known, itineracy was therefore a feature of the career of many Italian sculptors. It is relatively rare that a continuing presence might be established in one place for long. The result was that there often existed extreme limitations to the lasting local impact of Italians.[52]

Religious beliefs also could have presented impediments. Religious differences *per se* seem in general to have been less of an issue. Thus in Protestant northern Germany and Scandinavia, Italian stuccoists were employed, as they were in orthodox Russia. Yet in Russia other sorts of controls could have been placed on the activity of sculptors. The prohibition against making graven images was interpreted in such a manner that opportunities for making statues were seriously reduced.[53] Thus in Russia until the late seventeenth century Italians served more often as masons or architects than as sculptors.

In the end, it may even be their very success that also restricted chances for Italians. Masons and sculptors who were drawn to Italy to be trained by Italian masters may in many instances have created competition for them. As van Hofe's letter suggests, many Netherlanders often took up in places where Italians did not reach. This is suggested by the pupils of Giambologna, Netherlanders or Germans who had been trained by him in Italy. Moreover, indigenous traditions were often created to challenge Italian hegemony in some fields. And so by the early seventeenth century south German and Tyrolean stucco decoration was thriving in or not far from areas where Italians had earlier been involved in similar projects.

As these last remarks indicate, this essay can at best be considered merely a sketch suggesting where further investigations may be pursued. Nevertheless, a good place to start reframing a more comprehensive view of the Renaissance is with the examination of Italian art and artists outside of Italy.

CHAPTER 3

"Vision Itself Has Its History": "Race," Nation, and Renaissance Art History

CLAIRE FARAGO

In the last two decades, the nineteenth-century epistemological foundations of art history have been the subject of great debate. Despite some fundamental disagreements over the nature of visual images, there is a general consensus on two major issues.[1] First, most art historians now regard as problematic the assumption that all images are at base natural-istic: in fact, almost everyone recommends severing the link between images and nature that has historically been postulated by resemblance theories of representation. Secondly, it has been widely claimed that an adequate theory of representation must take into account the culturally specific circumstances in which visual images function. Yet current theoretical discussions stop short of specifying how we are to define these circumstances. What would be involved in drawing out the implications of our theorizing? How might we establish a relativistic epistemological foundation for art history that adequately defines what "culturally specific circumstances" actually means?

With these issues in mind, the following essay explores the possibility of reconstruing our disciplinary paradigm based on national culture so that it focuses on cultural exchange instead. The history of our discipline has been written as a modernist enterprise. Most narrative accounts have been concerned with the formal features of theory at the expense of the cultural circumstances out of which accounts of artistic change emerged. An examination of *these* cultural circumstances reveals that some of our predecessors were challenged by problems similar to the ones we face today – to revise resemblance theories of representation, to incorporate a multicultural framework, to overcome the Eurocentrisms of our inherited academic practices.

Moreover, the normative status of Italian art established within the discipline by Burckhardt, Michelet, Ruskin, and others played a catalytical role over several gener-ations of art historical revisionist writing. If we treat the writings of our founding fathers as documents of cultural history, rather than purely theoretical contributions, we discover that nineteenth-century theories about the nature of artistic development on the collec-tive or "cultural" level emerged in connection with widespread debates about the evolution of civilization. First, Social Darwinist theories of cultural evolutionism pro-vided the leading paradigm. When Social Darwinism *per se* was no longer the issue, German National Socialism made new demands on art historians and other European intellectuals, who responded to the racism of Hitler's Germany by reinstating an earlier, internationalist view of culture. The revival of the Enlightenment concept of *Bildung* initiated during the Weimar Republic, as Carl Landauer has recently argued, fed American cultural aspirations in the post-World War II period when a growing appreciation for humanist culture was fueled by the presence of recent German emigrés like Erwin Panofsky.[2]

We are still debating the paradigmatic status of Renaissance art and culture – the Renaissance no longer has the same cachet in disciplinary discussions of methodology as it did for Burckhardt or Panofsky, but many of us lament its decline along with other historical subjects in university curricula. I think we can reinvigorate Renaissance studies and other traditional historical fields without becoming mired in old polemics, by reconsidering our inherited assumptions about national culture based on a nineteenth-century assimilationist paradigm. Art historians have, moreover, weighed the methodological problems of using visual evidence in writing cultural history more exhaustively than scholars in any other discipline. We have important contributions to make in constructing a working model of transnational cultural process.[3]

Burckhardt's Notion of Italian Culture

A good place to begin reassessing categories of national culture that interfere with our perception of the complexity of cultural interactions is with Burckhardt's *Civilization of the Renaissance in Italy* (1860). Burckhardt and other nineteenth-century historians helped to construct the historical memories of modern nation-states – not that I wish to suggest that a directly proportional relationship exists between historians and the formation of nation-states. Burckhardt, for instance, refused to take any active political role and became deeply disillusioned with contemporary political trends. An increasingly reclusive member of the Swiss intellectual elite, he opposed the impending formation of the German nation-state. His political views are indirectly expressed in his characterization of "Italian national spirit" as a natural bond that transcends any centralized bureaucratic structure. The terms for his understanding of national community as something bound by common interests rather than any specific form of government had been defined in the late seventeenth century, before modern European national boundaries were established. Accordingly, Burckhardt wrote about Italy as a country organized into political units by regional governments. He saw himself as a modern Dante or a Petrarch, the conscience of the spiritual nation, not as an advocate of large industrial interests.[4]

In light of Burckhardt's explicitly contemporary investment in the history of Italy, and his dread of German unification – even more apparent in his personal letters and historical reflections – it is somewhat perplexing that the concept of Italian Renaissance art and culture that is still associated with his writings has become so detached from the political circumstances in which Burckhardt and his contemporaries wrote history.[5] Why is there no body of critical literature – as there is for other aspects of his thought – that has considered the effects of Burckhardt's views about modern nation-states on our characterization of the Italian Renaissance? According to one of Burckhardt's most famous statements, in the opening discussion of *Civilization of the Renaissance*, in the Italian republics and despots of the fifteenth and sixteenth century

> for the first time we detect the modern spirit of the state [*Staatsgeist*] of Europe, surrendered freely to its own impulses, often displaying the worst features of an unbridled selfishness, outraging every right, and killing every germ of a healthier culture [*Bildung*]. But, wherever this tendency is overcome or in any way compensated, a new fact appears in history – the state as the creation of reflection and deliberation, the state as a work of art [*Kunstwerk*].[6]

Michael Ann Holly, one of the few art historians who has expressed a methodological interest in Burckhardt's writings for its effect on disciplinary practices, argues that Burckhardt's historical narrative was influenced by the actual paintings that he admired, constructed on the principles of centralized geometric perspective (with its single focal point).[7] The key to Burckhardt's frequent verbal portraits and other rhetorical strategies, however, appears to be even more profound – and more interdisciplinary. No historians have traced Burckhardt's use of the word *Kunstwerk* to describe the "State." If we did, we would find its precedents in philosophy and political theory. In political theory, the Thomistic/Aristotelian notion of a "work of art" appeared as a paradigm for productive legislation in discussions by seventeenth-century political philosophers such as Thomas Hobbes, who referred to the state as a "work of art," just as the metaphor appears in Burckhardt's *Civilization*.[8]

Burckhardt also drew on longstanding associations between philosophical "reflection" as the quintessential activity of human judgment and the order that actual works of art manifest. This connection underlies Holly's insightful observation that Burckhardt's narrative structure resembles Renaissance painting constructed on the principles of centralized perspective. But the shared structural traits have a more complex relationship than the stylistic analogy between painting and prose can suggest. John Locke's 1690 *Essay Concerning Human Understanding* is an important philosophical precedent for Burckhardt's abstract idea of the work of art as the product of "reflection and deliberation' – and the original audience of Burckhardt's cultural history, at least its educated members, would surely have recognized this connection from Burckhardt's choice of language.[9] Knowledge is acquired in successive stages, according to Locke. As described by Abbé de Condillac in his supplement to Locke's treatise, when knowledge is finally gained, the order of things within the mind will be displayed simultaneously.[10] Which is to say, the activity of reflection disposes knowledge, arranges it in a manner that is comparable to visual order. This analogy should not surprise us, given the longevity of the theory that cognition proceeds on the model of vision. Descartes and many other philosophers combined the language of rhetoric and optics to distinguish the "clarity" or "distinctness" of ideas represented in the mind from "dark" impressions at the "lowest" levels of conscious attention.[11]

Among the many routes that optical metaphors of cognition traveled from seventeenth-century philosophy to Burckhardt's characterization of the state as the product of reflection and deliberation, one of the most important to single out is the path through Herder, for whom Condillac's essay on human understanding was a fundamental source.[12] Herder shifted history into the center of philosophical thinking in his effort to establish aesthetic theory as a philosophical science that dealt with the reception of beauty. In his day, Herder was unique in approaching works of art created by other cultures and epochs with the analytical model of cognition developed by philosophers. Herder came to understand that it would be impossible for a philosophical theory of the beautiful to exist without history, arguing that time and environment give works of art their particular appearance. Burckhardt, who frequently cited Herder in positive terms, drew on this association: he saw the enduring "Italian national spirit" manifested in its individual works of art, be they despots and republics or paintings, sculptures, works of architecture, rituals, and ceremonies. Not that all these categories were equally accessible as historical evidence – Francis Haskell is quite right to emphasize that Burckhardt never invoked the fine arts individually when he wrote his famous cultural history of the Renaissance or established a theoretical rationale for their use as historical evidence, probably because the relationships between art and history are not straightforward, illustrative ones.[13]

My line of argument would be hopelessly derailed if we were to consider the status of *Zeitgeist* theories in general; the only point I wish to make about the implicit analogies in Burckhardt's writings between actual works of art (as we define them still) and his notion that states are also works of art is that Burckhardt's verbal picture of the Renaissance in Italy testifies to the role that scholars have played in constructing images of national culture. In a sense, Burckhardt's cultural history of Italy is also a self-conscious "work of art" – an artistic imitation of the Italian national spirit insofar as his narrative exemplifies the coherence of the "Italian national spirit" he defines. This is Holly's argument, also Haskell's. Burckhardt gave the Thomistic/Aristotelian definition of a work of art as any composition created by human art a new concrete dimension: a future investigation might inquire to what extent his fundamental contribution to *Kulturgeschichte* was responsible for fusing separate discussions of the notion "work of art" drawn from the literature of art, analytical philosophy, and political theory.

Burckhardt's praise for the Italian national spirit, manifested in local forms of government as well as civic ceremonies and other visible symbols of collective identity, is not only a monumental work of historical writing, it is a nineteenth-century humanist's critique of current politics. In this regard, it is important to bear in mind that there were no nation-states in the sixteenth century. We look in vain for national boundaries on sixteenth-century maps: "Germania" was a geographical location bounded by topographical features, like "Italy," which referred to the Italian peninsula, even as it did at the moment that Burckhardt wrote *Civilization*.[14]

Distinctions between sixteenth- and nineteenth-century forms of national identity are important to our present investigation of disciplinary paradigms. Unfortunately, however, as important as nationalism is as a historical phenomenon, there are no satisfactory criteria for defining what constitutes a nation. In the sixteenth century, England probably came closest to qualifying as a modern nation-state. As Richard Helgerson has recently argued, the emerging English sense of national identity was produced by disenfranchised writers who defended themselves against Italian humanist claims that all foreigners were "barbarians."[15] Cultural boundaries defined in opposition to, or in competition with, Italian humanist values were an important ingredient in the emerging concept of national identity for several hundred years. The rise of centralized, unified, bureaucratic states is, however, a modern phenomenon following changes due to the French and Industrial Revolutions.[16] In the last quarter century, a new generation of scholars has significantly altered the concept of nationalism on which the disciplinary paradigm of art history was fashioned. Ernst Gellner, Eric Hobsbawm, Benedict Anderson, and others of the new generation restrict the modern concept of a nation to the large-scale political units that emerged in the nineteenth century.[17] Anderson, in a study of nationalism outside Europe that has gone far to shift the older definitions, defines a "nation" as an "imagined political community" – "an image of communion, as opposed to an actual meeting" that seeks to align itself with large cultural systems that preceded it, such as the religious community or the dynastic realm.[18]

Part of the current challenge of understanding the history of nationalism is due to the manner in which newly emerging nations in the nineteenth century imagined themselves as antique. Why, asks Anderson, should the nineteenth century need to construct a "nationalist memory" reaching back in time?[19] By producing histories of "national culture," scholars helped to manufacture the modern idea of a nation as an enduring collective. A significant aspect of the *problematic* of "nationalism" is, therefore, to take into account the role of the scholars who produced it. National traditions of historical writing arose in the same period that historians began to make use of specific visual sources to evoke the economic and constitutional realities of societies.[20] Nineteenth-century nationalism has, without doubt, distorted the earlier material. In a classic study on the interrelationship between humanism and Scholasticism in the Italian Renaissance published over four decades ago, Paul Oskar Kristeller warned us against taking up the prejudices of nineteenth-century historians.[21] Yet nineteenth-century ideas of a "nation" or "national spirit" continue to impose on our thinking unstable categories that conflate sixteenth-century notions about time, geography, and culture with the nineteenth-century politics of colonialism, race, and the nation-state. The international character of the humanist movement, as Thomas DaCosta Kaufmann argues in Chapter 2, has been neglected in studies of the Renaissance primarily because scholars in northern and central Europe imposed on the historical material nineteenth-century concerns with their own national culture.

The sixteenth-century sense of national identity was expressed differently, in terms of family or regional ancestry, or by association with the Roman Empire. The dominant forms of collective identity in the sixteenth century were multiple, clustered in overlapping groups defined by family, profession, religion, and region.[22] Europe was organized into monarchies, local republics and despotic city-states, the Holy Roman Empire, and the papacy, but *not* into centralized nation-states in the modern sense. Felix Gilbert observes that, while those living on the Apennine Peninsula were "bound together in a special relationship," there was "astounding" neglect of the national element in the political literature of Italy in the late sixteenth and seventeenth centuries.[23] Richard Goldthwaite recently wanted to argue that the internal economy of the Italian peninsula constituted a form of national unity in the sixteenth century.[24] But the relationship between the relative economic autonomy of loosely associated city-states and a federal national consciousness that did not emerge until the Risorgimento is far from clear.

Nineteenth-century studies of Italian culture deserve to be contextualized in the setting of nationalist politics, not just for the specialist in their writings or in Italian history, but for everyone interested in the status of modern disciplinary practices. Jacob Burckhardt identified "Italy" with "national spirit" on a local level, without a centralized governing structure, in sharp contrast to contemporaneous efforts to unify Germany as an institutionalized nation-state. Burckhardt's formulation of Italian Renaissance culture was transformed by later histories of art written on the Burckhardtian model that construed enduring national identity in conformity with the borders of modern nation-states. Nineteenth-century historians understandably saw nationhood as being in the process of formation since early humanism, but the assumption – according to a new generation of historians of nationalism – is flawed. Many would argue that such a definition of a nation applies nineteenth-century categories to sixteenth-century material without justification. At the same time, the idea of a nation as an enduring, authentic collectivity elides all critical discussion of the ways in which cultural domination has operated.

Burckhardt's discussion of the state as a work of art – his central notion of the Italian Renaissance as a unified cultural entity organized into regional republics and despotic states – is indebted to Herder's innovative cultural pluralism.[25] However, the Herderian assumption that each culture (and each language) remains discrete and incommensurable with any other is untenable today. Edward Said and other critics of the nineteenth-century phenomenon of Eurocentrism argue that cultural domination is the result of consensual assimilation (which leads to precisely the kind of national state Burckhardt advocated).[26] The new generation of historians defines the development of nationalism in terms of distinct stages. Drawing upon the groundbreaking work of Miroslav Hroch, Eric Hobsbawm identifies three criteria for the formation of a nation: both a long and a recent historical association, a long-established cultural elite with a written national literary and administrative vernacular, and a proven capacity for conquest. An important aspect of Hobsbawm's analysis of nationalism has been his rather unexpected finding (surprising because it denies Herder's central assumption) that a common spoken language is rarely present, but a powerful combination of representations – visible symbols of collective practices – "give palpable reality to an otherwise imaginary community."[27] All of these categories are implicated in the category "Italian Renaissance art," but the role of visible symbols in constructing national identity has been barely examined by historians.[28] Why, then, have art historians not jumped into the breach?

Coining of the "Visual Arts"

The impetus for expanding the boundaries of what is culturally intelligible is of course much greater when we take into account our position as authors in a historical continuum. Let us now return to the idea, implicit in Burckhardt's text and rapidly developed by his contemporaries Michelet and Taine, that works of art embody the collective psychology of entire nations and epochs in perceptible form. We no longer take the most sweeping of these claims seriously yet, as David Summers and Francis Haskell have both recently observed, this kind of essentialism still pervades art historical writing and teaching.[29] In 1876, Conrad Fiedler was perhaps the first to use the phrase *bildenden Kunst* (visual art) when he defined the perceptual powers of the entire human race in terms of the assumed visualness of art. "The origin and existence of art," Fiedler wrote, "is based upon an immediate mastering of the visible world by a peculiar power of the human mind. Its significance consists solely in a particular form of activity by which man not only tried to bring the visible world into his consciousness, but even is forced to the attempt by his very nature."[30] Works of art, regardless of how these objects functioned in their societies of origin, were first systematically defined as products of perception and objects of vision by a small group of late nineteenth-century art historians. I am not trying to suggest that these theorists represent all art historians – rather, I want to acknowledge that Fiedler and his German-speaking colleagues are the art historian/theorists who stand accused by a current generation of art historian/theorists of naturalizing the Renaissance metaphor that art imitates nature. Austrian, Swiss, and German writers who assumed that "vision" has its own history, preserved in works of art, did not necessarily see eye to eye with one another; mapping the internal tensions in this field of discourse must wait, however. In the discussion that follows, I will try to suggest, contrary to the current view, that these founders of the discipline of art history made successive attempts to *counter* the humanist, Renaissance model of art.[31]

Paradoxically, in resisting the normative role played by Renaissance art, Fiedler and others who expressed similar views endowed the Renaissance metaphor that art imitates nature with a new level of universality. The notion that all art, regardless of its origins or stylistic conventions, could embody the world view of an entire nation or people, as Panofsky understood in 1915, indicated that "vision" had come to signify metaphorically the entire process from physical sensation to philosophical reflection and deliberation.[32] And this conflation of sight with higher mental processes, as the young Panofsky wrote of Wölfflin's distinction between form and content, is too simplistic.

There is no question that internal dissent existed along generational lines among the founders of the discipline over the definition of the culturally specific circumstances of art – an issue that is now, once again, the focus of critical discussion among a wide range of cultural historians. Why has this dissent escaped the attention of art historians, even in the most recent historiographical critical studies? In the discussion that follows, I suggest that art historians of the nineteenth century worked in an interdisciplinary discursive field dominated by anthropological questions. This intellectual arena, which actually extended into popular culture (as numerous historians of material culture are well aware), was disrupted by the external events of two world wars. During the interval between them, an older view of Renaissance humanist culture, grounded in the Enlightenment concept of *Bildung*, was reinstated at the center of the discipline. *Bildung*, meaning culture or self-cultivation, as it is often translated, was grounded in the view that art is a defining human characteristic of the highest spiritual order, with both universal and historical, culturally specific, characteristics. What the continental concept of *Bildung* did *not* do, because it intentionally sidestepped the issue altogether, was to engage in the longstanding debate over the definition of national, or "racial," character.

Enlightenment Definitions of Art and Culture

Unavoidably, the disease and the cure emanate from the same history.[33] To get a sense of the central intellectual problems that occupied the first truly modern art historians, we must broaden our historiographical understanding of the foundations of art history to include contemporaneous developments in the social and even physical sciences, especially anthropology and the science of race. The main reason this broader context is necessary, as George Stocking aptly puts it, is that we no longer remember the alternatives which the answers were meant to exclude.[34] What the discipline of art history inherited from Enlightenment thought would legitimately be the subject of a set of encyclopedias but, for the sake of identifying a field of discursive practices, the debt of the modern discipline to the Enlightenment might be quickly sketched as a double imperative. On the one hand, art history is still deeply invested in the Enlightenment project of accounting for the particular qualities of "national cultures." On the other hand, art historians are still committed to the Enlightenment project of defining "art" as that which is universally human at the "highest" spiritual level.[35]

The idea that the production of "art" is a distinguishing (and unifying) feature of humanity has a long and complex history in Aristotelian thought. The identification of a distinct "people" or "nation" in terms of their shared practices, habits, and traditions is also very old − originating with the ancient histories of Herodotus and Pliny the Elder − and very complex.[36] Both textual traditions underwent significant modification in the sixteenth century, during the initial period of extensive global contact. Any work of art which is defined as a model of human perception, as literature and the visual arts have been in the western tradition since antiquity, is also the manifestation of a larger complex of cognition. Aristotle's ancient and medieval commentators developed his discussions of the origin of art from individual experience and memory into further distinctions between men and brutes. A new genre of theoretical literature on artistic inspiration and artistic production emerging in the sixteenth century drew substantially on these neo-Aristotelian theories which distinguished art as a peculiarly human capability. According to Aristotle, the difference between human and animal intelligence, and also between human and animal art, required the distinction between human rational fantasy, which is associated with reason and reminiscence, and the fixed imagination of animals, associated with a retentive memory.[37] These theories were applied in some detail to Amerindians, Africans, and other non-European peoples as early as the sixteenth century. We are still in the process of recognizing the repercussions of these acts initiated in the "Age of Discovery."[38]

Print technology encouraged a new, illustrated genre of cultural geography, grounded in the textual tradition of Pliny and Herodotus that distinguished nations in terms of their shared practices, habits, and traditions. As Margaret Hodgen has written of sixteenth- and seventeenth-century precursors to modern anthropological texts, cultural geographies and travel literature organized by nations, cities, and continents according to ancient categories such as customs, religious rites, forms of government, costumes, language, and artistic products, provide an important and frequently visual record of emerging "europocentric" attitudes.[39]

What makes art history especially indebted to Enlightenment thought is the historical conjunction of these two traditionally different ways of defining art. Johann Gottfried Herder's career may exemplify this uneasy marriage at its inception: after completing his fourth and most important treatise on aesthetics, in 1769, Herder put the unpublished manuscript aside and spent the next thirty years writing about art as culture, taking up aesthetics again only at the very end of his life.[40] Despite difficulties, it has not proven feasible to divorce one way of defining art from the other – like the two ends of a seesaw, when one goes down, the other comes up, but they are cut from the same plank. "Art" (the essentialist argument) and "culture" (the materialist argument) express two extremes of the central anthropological problem of defining humanness through "art." Nearly every contemporary discussion of "art" as a manifestation of "culture" suppresses this element of tautology by taking one seat on the seesaw or the other without acknowledging the fulcrum that historically keeps the game in place.[41]

The problem that the double-seated issue of "art" presents for Renaissance art historians is even more complicated. Raymond Williams, the Marxist literary historian who was, not unlike Jacob Burckhardt, concerned to define the field of general change that introduced elements "we can point to as distinctly modern," describes culture as "one of the two or three most complicated" words in the English language.[42] In *Culture and Society, 1780–1950*, Williams argued that, when culture came to mean a mode of interpreting common experience that refers to an area of personal experience, it affected the meaning and practice of art, which became the "center of defense against the disintegrating tendencies of industrialism."[43] Williams pinpointed a decisive change to Herder's concept of culture as a *variable* form of collective identity. Herder defined a nation as a cultural (rather than a sovereign) entity unified by language, custom, costume, gesture, habit, and its artistic productions.[44] For Williams, the historical transformation in the function of art that corresponds in time with theories of cultural relativism was the Romantic rejection of "all dogmas of method," especially those associated with representational art in the academic tradition of naturalism.

But the nesting of art/culture/modern society in this manner cannot adequately conceptualize the contribution of cultural interactions to modern notions of art. We cannot ground *our* attempt to offer alternatives to existing schemes for the study of art organized by national culture on the basis of the modern meaning of culture for the same reason that Williams used to justify his – because "art" and "culture" are the product of the *same* eighteenth- and nineteenth-century effort to define "national identity." The language and theorizing about culture emerged at the same moment in time as the conception that "art" is an object meant for individual, secular aesthetic contemplation. Herder's notions of cultural relativism and his antipathy to systematic "scientific" theories of history are clearly discernible in Burckhardt's writings.[45] Historians of nationalism and of the institutional history of modern academic disciplines, as well as critics of Eurocentrism and postcolonialism, all point out, however, that Herder's idealized notions about cultural integrity and interaction, and the language in which he expressed his ideas, offered an inadequate account of the devastating effects of European colonialism three centuries into the global expansion of European interests.

Whether we are considering exchanges within Europe or on a global scale, our dominant framework has usually been the history of a single civilization presented from its origins to its apogee or decline, without taking into consideration the relationship between politics and the writing of culture. Such a framework is poorly suited to investigating the complex historical record of cultural interaction. Benedict Anderson connects Herder's "blithe disregard of some obvious extra-European facts" to the "private property language" that had such a wide influence on subsequent theorizing about the nature of nationalism.[46] Moreover, Herder's ideas about national identity were, inevitably, informed by the period that is *our* primary subject of study. There is, in this reflexivity, a certain self-fulfilling prophecy, to say the least. *How* Herder's idea of national culture is indebted to the new sixteenth-century literature of cultural geography, the changing status of the visual arts, and other cultural phenomena awaits further investigation. Some problematic aspects of the twinned Enlightenment conception of art emerged, however, only at the end of the nineteenth century. Let us now return to these historiographical issues.

The Emergence of Modern Anthropology and the Redefinition of Culture

The co-construction of the categories "art" and "culture" witnessed in the latter part of the eighteenth century was replayed at the end of the nineteenth century. This continuing synchronicity can hardly be simple coincidence. Stocking observes that, before 1900, among German and Anglo–American writers, the word culture meant degree of culture – that is, culture was understood to be a singular phenomenon which every society possessed to a greater or lesser degree.[47] Stocking makes the case that culture redefined as a progressive development in the mid-nineteenth century revitalized older, discredited theories of cultural evolutionism that (like Herder's) had posited the essential unity of mankind.[48] Cultural difference was theorized, beginning in the late 1860s, by fitting the contemporary humanist model of national culture into a framework of progressive social evolutionism. The modern anthropological idea of cultural plurality, Stocking writes, involved a further rejection of contemporary values. Franz Boas was among the first to use the word culture in the modern plural sense, when he shifted the grounds of inquiry from a search for signs of inherited difference to an investigation of how foreign material was taken up by a people and modified by preexisting ideas and customs.[49]

The western notion that all cultures produce art (not merely artifacts or useful products) emerged gradually over several generations of nineteenth-century art historical writing, and made its earliest mature appearance among the German-speaking art historians and theorists that we have been discussing. This occurred around the same time, or slightly before, Boas began his revolutionary work (in the mid-1890s). In several respects, trends in art historical writing were analogous to concurrent trends in anthropology. The new definition of art as a universal human phenomenon also represented a partial rejection of humanist values. The source of the idea that all art is "visual," intended to function primarily as the object of the special sense of sight – as numerous critics of the foundationalist assumptions of the discipline have rightly pointed out – can be found in Renaissance arguments, such as those advanced by Leonardo da Vinci, whose elaborate defense of painting was built on a tradition of Aristotelian commentary on the function of the senses.[50] Like the anthropological concept of cultural pluralism, however, the late nineteenth-century concept of art as a universal cultural phenomenon displaced Greco–Roman culture from the normative position it had held without exception since the early humanist revival of ancient letters in the fourteenth century.

The term "visual art," which seems too neutral even to have a history, actually made its earliest appearance (first in its German form, as *bildenden Kunst*) in the first formalist theories of art by Fiedler (1876), Wölfflin (1888), Hildebrand (1893), and Riegl (1893).[51] The extent to which disciplinary discourses in art history and anthropology were aware of each other's existence awaits further study. Even now it is clear, however, that a loosely connected group of German-speaking art historians, like the German-educated Boas, tried to stamp out the widespread (and we would say, ethnocentric) notion that the only transcendental works of art are those which emulate the cultural zenith of Greco–Roman antiquity by imitating nature ideally. To a greater degree than Boas's statistically grounded concept of cultural pluralism, however, the new assumption that every culture produces works of "visual art" retained the formalist orientation of earlier racial theories of cultural evolution.[52] Identifying the tensions between this enduring theoretical framework and its changing contents is an enormous task. The following discussion tries to suggest what a productive line of inquiry for this undertaking might be.

Art and Cultural Evolutionism

Our nineteenth-century predecessors frequently expressed their ideas about collective identity in racial categories.[53] Heinrich Wölfflin, the German Swiss art historian who lived in Basel when Jacob Burckhardt was still alive and succeeded him in the Chair of Art History there in 1893, is generally acknowledged as the founder of formalist analysis. Wölfflin, regarding himself as continuing Burckhardt's work, defined the "essential" content of specific works of art within the narrowly circumscribed frame of reference of visual characteristics as manifesting the collective psychology of the "Germanic" or "Mediterranean," "classical" or "Late antique" or "Romantic" spirit. As Wölfflin's muddled distinctions can begin to suggest, "race," epoch, and national identity were often interchanged and conflated in the practice of cultural history.

Since the 1790s, the word "race," signifying permanent hereditary differences between family groups, was considered an important factor in determining peculiar cultural characteristics. The anatomist Georges Cuvier, who claimed that negroes were stupid because they lacked civilization, was an early and influential proponent of the idea that permanent differences in mental capability were inherited "racial" characteristics.[54] Racial qualities, like national characteristics, were considered in some sense innate, inherited, and distinguishing features of family groups. But the scientific concept of race was never clearly distinguished from the older notion of a nation or race of people. What Wölfflin called *Rassencharakter* was something held to be the source of all structures of feeling and thought, *naturally* determined by blood and intellect, a shared assumption over and above the individual.[55] The formal vocabulary of art history, like modernist concerns with the language of the text that developed around the same time, rendered these assumptions implicit:

> it remains no mean problem to discover the conditions which, as material element – call it temperament, *zeitgeist*, or racial character [*Rassencharakter*] – determine the style of individuals, periods, and peoples.
>
> Yet an analysis with quality and expression as its objects by no means exhausts the facts. There is a third factor – and here we arrive at the crux of this enquiry – the

mode of representation as such. Every artist finds certain visual possibilities before him, to which he is bound. Not everything is possible at all times. *Vision itself has its history, and the revelation of these visual strata must be regarded as the primary task of art history.*[56]

Quality, expression, and "mode of representation" were the main components in Wölfflin's history of art as the history of collective vision, based on the assumption – shared with most of his contemporaries – that the outward forms of art manifest the inward feelings of artists.[57] The grounding of formalist analysis in German idealist thought has received a great deal of critical attention from art historians in recent years.[58] In light of all the attention to the history of our formal categories of art, is it not curious that no one has ever pursued the obvious connections between racial character and "mode of representation" in these texts?

What Gombrich calls the dangerous "physiognomic fallacy" is nothing other than the racial theory that mental capabilities of entire peoples can be read out of their physical features and, by extension, out of their collective cultural achievements.[59] Alois Riegl's theoretical contribution, more than the writings of any other individual art historian, is the logical place to begin a serious investigation of how the discipline of art history has struggled to redefine its inherited models of national culture defined in nineteenth-century terms of racial identity. Riegl's open-mindedness to the aesthetic values of other cultures is still considered extraordinary. And, significantly for the present discussion, his career effort to establish art history on a new, more theoretical foundation (still widely recognized as a major contribution to methodology) stemmed from his attempts to reground a discipline formed for the study of Italian Renaissance art.

Yet art historians have isolated Riegl's ideas from the pressing contemporary social and political concerns that Riegl explicitly addressed. The most recent studies still consider primarily the philosophical precedents of his arguments – in Hegel, neo-Kantian philosophy, Herbartian psychology, and positivist history in the tradition of Leopold von Ranke.[60] As Henri Zerner acknowledged two decades ago, however, there is a curious disjunction between the intellectual context in which we discuss Riegl's theories and the evidence of the texts themselves: Riegl's writings, Zerner found, are a "philosophical bricolage" – and the only philosopher Riegl mentions by name is not a philosopher at all, but the neo-Classical sculptor Adolf Hildebrand, one of the first to use the category "visual art."[61] Margaret Iverson suggests that Riegl's strongly worded condemnations of contemporary historical practice were directed against the prominent Viennese architect Otto Wagner.[62] While this interpretation may be valid in the narrowest sense – and Iverson's contribution is certainly to be commended for being the first to acknowledge that the issue of race was a factor at all – it atomizes Riegl's social concerns, neglecting his explicit and far-reaching objective to eliminate Social Darwinism from the writing of art history.

More has been written about Riegl's revolutionary concept of *Kunstwollen* (most literally, "will to artistic expression" or "will to [make] art": there is no consensus on the best translation) than about any other aspect of his thought, yet no one has seriously considered that Riegl's coinage is addressed to theories of cultural evolutionism. Riegl devoted some fifty pages at the beginning of his first major theoretical publication, *Stilfragen/Problems of Style* (1893) to refuting the idea of evolutionary cultural progress proposed by some of his contemporaries. That is, Riegl explicitly criticized the application of Social Darwinism to art history. In the introduction and opening chapter, where Riegl set out his theory of geometric style to refute the materialist theories of his contemporaries, his position is absolutely clear. He rejected theories of cultural history that post a parallel between the physical evolution of the human race and the progress of "civilization." He blames this trend on theories of racial difference that have steadily crept into the writing of art history:

> By this [the predominant intellectual tendency of the last thirty years], I mean the materialist, scientific world view, first promulgated by Lamarck and Goethe and subsequently brought to maturity by Darwin, which has left such grave consequences in its wake even in the field of art history. As parallel to the effort to explain the evolution of the species by means of the purely physical drive for survival, there was also an effort to discover primary and intrinsically physical mechanisms for the intellectual evolution of the human race. Art obviously represented – *or so one thought* – a higher stage of intellectual evolution and therefore could not have been present from the very beginning. First came technology, which concentrated on purely practical matters; then, out of this experience, and only after the culture had somewhat advanced, did art appear on the scene.[63]

Art historians have been content to refer Riegl's objections to Social Darwinism to materialist theories of artistic development. I think we have not sufficiently considered that Riegl's opposition was explicitly addressed to controversies over cultural development extending beyond disciplinary concerns with methodology. Chevalier de Lamarck, a well-known early nineteenth-century biologist cited by Riegl in the above passage, assumed that genetic characteristics are culturally acquired.[64] The fundamental issue at stake was whether racial differences in mental ability existed – and if so, how were they inherited: could cultural acquisitions be passed on from one generation to the next? To investigate these questions, Lamarck searched for perceptible characteristics that could measure human intelligence in a vertical scale classified by "race." Lamarckians are, for this reason, racial formalists who believe that genetic improvements in "races" would result from providing individuals with a better social environment.[65]

In *Stilfragen*, in the same discussion we have begun to examine, Riegl condemned recent methods that trace motifs to their origins on the basis of technique, unaided by conscious artistic invention, citing the German Darwinist archeologist Häckel by name.[66] Riegl's objections to materialist histories of artistic development make far more sense when considered in the context of the wide debate over human evolution between the developmentalists (Darwinians) and the degenerationists (Lamarckians) that extended to the end of the century and beyond. These discussions, beginning in the 1860s, revived eighteenth-century issues of racial difference. In the 1860s, in German, French, and Anglo–American discussions, anthropology provided a new means for reformulating the Enlightenment theory of the essential unity of mankind by acknowledging cultural difference according to racial categories. The proposed theories are important to consider in connection with Riegl's theories because, like his arguments, they revolve around the mental difference between the industrial arts and moral culture.[67] Often, as Riegl objects, only the latter was considered to involve "spiritual progress" in the acquisition of civilization.

The anthropological discussions, extending beyond scientific debates to the popular press, emphasized that aesthetic capability manifested in artistic productions helped to define the degree of cultural progress, and hence the degree of humanness. Darwin's *Descent of Man* (1871) suggests how evolutionary theory was applied *in its crudest form* to cultural history by Riegl's contemporaries. Darwin placed savages at a point intermediary between man and animals — and even lower than some animals: "Judging from the hideous ornaments and the equally hideous music admired by most savages, it might be argued that their aesthetic faculty was not so highly developed as in certain animals, for instance in birds."[68]

E. B. Tylor's *Primitive Culture* (1871), according to George Stocking, set the stage for later definitions of culture as a universal phenomenon by suggesting that all areas of culture can be comprehended as one natural process rooted in primitive savagery. With this move, cultural differences came to be explained in terms of degrees of cultural progress through which every society passes.[69] For our purposes, however, the most significant innovation of Tylor's argument is that for him "spiritual progress" encompassed technology and the crafts as well as the fine arts. The concept of art as a universal and simultaneously "spiritual" phenomenon encompassing crafts was widely disseminated by Tylor's publications and by writings associated with the British arts and crafts movement. Basically the same argument that all forms of human artistic production are "spiritual" rather than "mechanical" by nature is at the core of Riegl's concept of *Kunstwollen* and constitutes his fundamental objection to materialist theories of artistic development.

A similar theory had been articulated even a few years before Tylor's publication by the architect and historian Gottfried Semper. It is well known that the materialist–technical theories of stylistic change developed by Semper's followers were the primary object of Riegl's criticism.[70] Riegl and Semper, however, agreed in two fundamentally important respects: neither ancient Greek culture nor the hierarchy of the "fine arts" should be the source of absolute aesthetic norms. Semper's ideas on "primitive art" — a term he is credited with coining — were soon popularized by his associate in the British arts and crafts movement Owen Jones.[71]

Semper insisted that all the arts, including the utilitarian crafts, are concerned with beauty. His view that weaving is the fundamental source of aesthetic development argued, like Tylor's theory of "primitive culture," for the fundamentally spiritual nature of all human artistic production.[72] Like Riegl, Semper explicitly criticized the exaggerated claims that can be made for technology at the expense of the spiritual nature of all artistic endeavor.[73] And Riegl, in keeping with the theories of both Tylor and Semper (but not the crude simplifications of their Social Darwinist followers), avoided associating inherited aesthetic capabilities graded in a vertical scale with national differences. Instead, he granted every culture its own, incommensurable *Kunstwollen*. *Kunstwollen* — a concept introduced in *Stilfragen* and developed more fully in *Spätrömische Kunstindustrie/Late Roman Art Industry* (1901) — overcomes Riegl's two central objections to the Social Darwinist accounts proposed by his contemporaries and immediate predecessors: hierarchical distinctions in mental capacity among different cultures or peoples, and the reduction of human agency to technical or materialistic causes.

Yet Riegl explicitly did *not* reject Darwin's theory of evolution.[74] Indeed, who would have taken Riegl's scientific theory of art seriously if he *had* objected to the dominant scientific paradigm of his day? Nor did Riegl completely reject the humanist model that granted pre-eminence to ancient Greek civilization. Again, who would have taken Riegl's theory of art seriously if, instead of explaining cultural development, he had rejected the cultural values of his day? Rather, Riegl restricted the use of evolutionary theory and he qualified Winckelmann's aesthetic preferences by placing Greek culture (*and* its Egyptian sources, which Winckelmann had rejected as "monstrous") at the historical (rather than metaphysical) foundation of a continuous artistic progression (rather than a continuous drive towards "perfection"). Riegl's scheme consciously avoids both the comparative method of racial science that had steadily crept into theories of cultural evolutionism and the teleological assumptions of the humanist model of cultural perfection and degeneration. Riegl's contribution, widely recognized today, countered the widely held Enlightenment view that as the Roman Empire degenerated its Greek artistic heritage also declined, by creating a new, positive identity for late antique art.

Modern contemporary critical historians, impatient with essentialism in any form, want to dismiss the Idealist underpinnings of art history altogether. But can we really succeed in this endeavor without considering carefully the fabric of concerns with cultural development into which Idealist philosophy was woven in the foundational era of art history? My own reassessment of nineteenth-century theories of artistic change began with the abrupt (and, I recall, embarrassing) realization that Wölfflin's formalist categories of analysis were inextricably tied to a racial theory of cultural identity. I tried to separate, for an undergraduate audience in a survey of "western art" I taught in 1989, the analytic technique which I respected from the racial theory I could only despise. I found I could not. How much more impossible this intellectual task would be to perform for a discriminating audience of professional peers!

Semper, Kugler, and Burckhardt

It is easy to demonstrate that Riegl addresses key issues in the nineteenth-century debates over racial inequality because he tells us that he did. What Zerner and others call Riegl's attempt to overthrow the supremacy of the individual creator is also, in reference to cultural evolutionism, an attempt to explain continuing cultural identity without resorting to the notion of a cultural hierarchy grounded in innate mental and aesthetic differences among "races." Riegl's theory accounts for the development of various dominant cultures as exactly parallel events, the products of formal laws and historical accident rather than inherited mental capabilities. By his own admission, Riegl's objections to Social Darwinism, central to his program of theoretical reform, were not an isolated reaction: he participated in a project that spans several generations of art historical writing. In the context of fitting the idealized naturalism of Greek art into a relative scale of values, Semper and Riegl proposed the first histories of world art defined in non-representational terms.[75] By turning to the writings of Gottfried Semper, we can suggest, at least in a preliminary manner, how Riegl's immediate predecessors also revised existing notions of national cultural identity.

Semper was among the first writers who systematically tried to dismantle the category of the "fine arts" by advocating the study of other objects of human manufacture. I have already suggested that the arguments of both Semper and Riegl participated in debates over the development of civilization. The terms of this debate become more apparent, however, when we consider how Semper directed his theory of relative aesthetic sensibility against the Swiss historian Franz Kugler, Burckhardt's teacher and mentor.[76] Kugler's *Handbuch der Kunstgeschichte* (1841–42) – organized by national culture and issued in many editions through the end of the century – was the first (and very successful) autonomous history of world art based on visual evidence. According to Haskell, Kugler was the most widely read and influential scholar in the field anywhere in Europe.[77] Kugler has also been portrayed recently as a watershed figure for the recognition of Amerindian cultural achievements. According to George Kubler, Kugler's *Handbuch* marks the moment when anthropologists and art historians went their separate ways. The result of this separate evolution is the aesthetic recognition of Amerindian art and Kugler is to be commended on two counts: he rejected diffusionist fantasies that had long provided Old World roots for all other cultures and, in Kubler's own words, he rejected "the history of tools, which differs from the history of art as does the artisanate from the liberal arts."[78]

Yet, where Kubler sees only the aesthetic recognition of ancient Amerindian art, we can also observe the construction of hierarchical cultural boundaries in a new institutional setting – namely the systematic, academic survey of "world art." For if Kugler's treatment of ancient Amerindian art is a form of aesthetic recognition, it is of a very patronizing sort. Kubler traces Kugler's ideas to Winckelmann's concept of periodization, Alexander Baumgarten's admission of the ugly and monstrous into the realm of sensory awareness, Alexander von Humboldt's illustrations treating world civilization, and G. B. Vico's notions about the primacy of imagination in "humanity's childhood."[79] Kubler acknowledges the need to employ a historiographical framework in conjunction with a theoretical model, but one wishes that he had drawn more attention to the assimilative mechanisms of European writers – for example, when he notes in passing that the question of distinguishing between art and artifact first arose in the sixteenth century, when Amerindian objects entered the collections of European courts.[80]

The perniciousness of distinctions between "art" and "artifact" and of equations between "primitive" and "child" become obvious when we consider their appearance in nineteenth-century racial theory, where the adult primitive was widely believed to be as evolved as the white European child on the basis of his artistic productions and assumed aesthetic capabilities. Moreover, Kugler's treatment of ancient Amerindian monuments as an intermediate stage between the "childhood" of humanity and "true art" has direct historical links with Burckhardt's treatment of the Italian Renaissance. Kugler's *Handbuch* evolved in collaboration with Burckhardt, who provided additional text and the illustrations for the second edition (1848).[81] The extensive collaboration between Kugler and Burckhardt, which extended over many years, provides an unusual opportunity to eavesdrop on the construction of modern subdisciplinary boundaries drawn along cultural lines that, in the final analysis, grants European culture the upper hand.

A running debate between Kugler and Semper also extended for many years. Their generational disagreements provide an unusual opportunity to observe the paradigmatic role played by Renaissance art in the construction of theories of national culture.[82]

Semper, far from agreeing with his predecessor Kugler (*or* with George Kubler) that the crafts and the "fine arts" should be maintained in separate categories, defined "art" as a universal phenomenon. Semper disagreed with Kugler by granting non-figurative "crafts" of non-European cultures the status of "art," and he attacked Kugler's theory that all ancient Greek art and architecture were constructed of "noble white marble," citing extensive archeological evidence in a scathing rebuttal to Kugler's reading of the ancient literary testimony (which conformed closely with Winckelmann's aesthetic preferences).[83] Semper's alternative thesis (which still *followed* Winckelmann and Humboldt) is a climatic theory of human development combined with an Aristotelian analogy between nature and art: populations imitate nature in various ways, but always derive their aesthetic preferences from their natural environment.[84]

Kugler, Semper, and Riegl were all committed to revising the exemplary role of Renaissance art, but they instituted some culturally exclusionary categories of their own. Kugler recognized the artistic merits of civilizations other than those associated with the classical world, but he maintained and even helped to institutionalize long-standing cultural hierarchies. Semper disagreed with Kugler by granting "crafts" of non-European cultures the status of "art," arguing that the aesthetic preferences of each nation or culture are inextricable from the functional value of their manufactures and depend on their natural environment.[85] Semper's idea of cultural relativism was influenced by his knowledge of art forms in non-European cultures, notably the Assyrian discoveries of the 1840s, the London Great Exhibition of 1851, and whatever he found in the ethnographic journals he is known to have read. On the other hand, Semper's newly coined category "primitive art" is still grounded in a European system of values that has nothing to do with the values of the society it is meant to describe.[86] His comparative study of art is, moreover, directly indebted to the scientific principles of his contemporaries such as the anatomist Cuvier, who ranked the "*human* races" according to the beauty of their design, even devising a scale of intelligence on this visual basis, that gave 30 percent to apes, 70 percent to Negroes, 80 percent to Europeans, *90 percent to ancient Greek sculptures of men, and 100 percent to sculptures of divinities.*[87]

Riegl rejected evolutionary theories of cultural development more completely than either Semper or Kugler. Yet Riegl, like Wölfflin and in keeping with most writers of their day, thought it was possible to discern psychological characteristics over and above the individual in cultural "forms of art."[88] And, although he restricted the use of evolutionary theory in cultural history (by rejecting the comparative methods of racial science adopted by Social Darwinists) and although he abandoned the humanist model of cultural growth and decline, Riegl still placed Winckelmann's ideal of Greek cultural achievement at the foundation of his history of artistic progression.

Panofsky

When Panofsky grounded the individual work of art in a richer historical and cultural context than any of his predecessors, he had in mind the difficulty of using visual evidence to write history. Panofsky was certainly aware that cultural bias creeps into historical writing. His most famous discussion of method is probably the essay that introduces *Studies in Iconology*, first published in 1939.[89] The following brief analysis of this essay does not pretend to address the complexity of Panofsky's proposal for eliminating bias by means of an internal set of "correctives and controls." The following analysis aims to uncover Panofsky's *own* cultural biases, grounded in a model of nationalism that we can no longer accept.

Panofsky revised Riegl's formalist notion of *Kunstwollen* and he rejected Wölfflin's distinction between form and content as an over-simplification that confuses vision with higher mental processes of apperception and cognition.[90] At the first stage of "pre-iconographic" interpretation, Panofsky proposes, the condition of being human is sufficient to interpret the meaning of certain gestures and expressions – "everyone can tell an angry face from a jovial one," he writes, though we might have to widen the range of our practical experience by "consulting a book or an expert."[91] Panofsky qualified these remarks by noting that first impressions are no guarantee of a correct interpretation. But even in this qualified form, is Panofsky's claim for the *universality* of gesture and expression justified? Recent studies of colonial art and drama leave no room for doubt that gesture and expression are far more culturally specific than Panofsky gave them credit for being.[92]

Panofsky evidently sensed that his definition of the universality of painting did not completely resolve the problem of how we "naturally" understand visual images, because he added a qualification, which he called "a peculiar problem" – that a work of art may be unrecognizable because of the "incompetence" or "malice aforethought" of the artist.[93] He thus eliminated many hybrid works of art from prolonged consideration and reinforced the normative status of representational practices associated with European styles of optical naturalism. Furthermore, Panofsky's argument makes *undocumented* assumptions about human agency. Products of intercultural contact like colonial maps and pictorial calendar books would not qualify for consideration according to Panofsky's criteria. This is not because maps and calendars fall outside the range of the "fine arts" – Panofsky might have applauded the ingenuity of the art historian who chose this subject matter – but because they conflate European optical naturalism with other, incompatible systems of visual signification. The results often compromise the European pictorial conventions they imitate, but the reasons for these compromises – as Pauline Watts, Thomas Cummins, Eloise Quiñones Keber, Cecelia Klein, and Dana Leibsohn discuss in this volume – are more complex than Panofsky allowed. An indigenous, partially assimilated artist of the colonial period, with knowledge of different pictorial conventions, would have understood European images with a different conception of what and how they communicate from a native European artist. The artist *might* be malicious and he might *not* be professionally trained – but these are separate issues with their own social circumstances.

For a European viewing audience, as the case of the Sapi–Portuguese saltcellar I discussed in the Introduction suggests, the hybrid work of art would reflect on the mentality and intelligence of the artist. We are far from being compelled, however, to evaluate such hybrid objects as the inferior artistic products of cultural miscegenation – as "incompetent" versions of "orthodox" representational practices. We can conceptualize the interaction of different pictorial conventions across cultural boundaries in other terms than aesthetic considerations ("incompetence") or fear ("malice aforethought"). We can think of them rather as evidence of emerging colonial identities.

Panofsky did consider some hybrid images when he turned to the art historian's problem of dealing with regional differences in representational conventions. Such puzzling aspects of images belong to the second stage of interpretation, during which the art historian examines "forms under varying historical conditions."[94] At this stage, the art historian learns what the artist "knew" – for example, that a certain portrayal of Judith combines German and north Italian motifs. Panofsky argues that "a correct iconographical analysis" is always possible, presupposing a "correct identification of the motifs." Yet certain hybrid objects, such as the collectors' items that combine natural and human artistry which Martin Kemp discusses elsewhere in this volume (Chapter 9), intentionally defy stable classification as well as determinate readings. How should we treat these objects?

In the *most* complicated cases of iconographical exchange, between completely unrelated cultures, visual motifs can act as permeable membranes, providing access across cultural boundaries. Yet because similar visual representations usually hold *different* meaning for previously unrelated cultures, visual symbols can be a fundamental source of miscommunication and reinterpretation. The mediating functions of visual symbols in these situations deserve to be carefully studied and articulated. What if every viewer has only partial access to the visual codes? And what if this has always been the case for most images? Such fundamental questions about the nature of signification and visual communication raised by hybrid images encourage theoretical concern with the unstable and shifting signification of signs. Panofsky's modes of interpretation, on the other hand, constitute the third in a series of strategic moves that prevent him from adequately conceptualizing the process of cultural interaction in situations where deterministic readings are impossible. How could *one* interpretation be "correct" if the same image signifies differently for different audiences?

Panofsky's formulation of correctives and controls at the final stage of analysis is the most problematic aspect of his discussion. He proposes that art historians compare their interpretations of the "intrinsic meaning" of individual works of art with the intrinsic meaning of other documents from their milieu, to compensate for the individual historian's "personal psychology and world view." The various humanistic disciplines meet at this ultimate stage of iconological analysis "on a common plane instead of serving as handmaidens to each other."[95] We are fundamentally indebted to Panofsky's interdisciplinary vision, but the history of the humanist values that Panofsky praised should *also* be part of our subject of study. As George Mosse has emphasized in his study of Jewish emigration immediately before and during World War II, scholars, professionals, artists, and other producers of European culture overcame the racism they experienced in their European setting with a global vision of humanity.[96] Panofsky and other assimilated German Jewish intellectuals sidestepped the embattled issues of "racism" and "nationalism" when they revalidated the Enlightenment concept of self-cultivation, or *Bildung*, and conceived of themselves as members of an international community.

In the interval between two world wars, cultural values associated with Italian Renaissance humanism were reinstituted by a European community which saw the sixteenth century through the filter of eighteenth-century Weimar classicism. Carl Landauer argues that the views Panofsky developed in Germany were entirely in keeping with the Romanticist sensibility of Weimar culture. Later, in the post-war period, the presence of German scholars in the United States fed American aspirations for a new cultural identity associated with humanism.[97]

The theoretical and cultural refocusing of disciplinary practices associated, above all, with Panofsky's iconological approach created a major epistemological break in the formation of art historical discourse. Panofsky, like other refugees from Nazism, eliminated all direct consideration of racial theory from his writings. This distinguished generation of scholars rarely hinted directly at the contemporary societal pressures that encouraged them to embrace an internationalist view of culture at the expense of their own German loyalties.[98] Given the political circumstances in Germany in the 1930s, it is not surprising that Panofsky and other liberal intellectuals of his generation dealt with racism by denying the historical role of racial theory altogether.[99] When Panofsky developed a method of art historical interpretation that relocated Italian Renaissance humanist values at the center of the discipline, however, he not only glossed over Riegl's objections to a humanist model of culture that grants priority to Greek antiquity and its modern revival, he gave Renaissance humanism an unprecedented status to govern the interpretation of all forms of art.[100] What should *we* make now of such ideas about the authority of Renaissance culture?

Theorizing Cultural Transition: a Retrospective View

The narrative history of art history would sound quite different if it were to emphasize the investigation of cultural exchange rather than the taxonomy of national culture. Pride of place after Semper and Riegl would go, I think, to intentional transgressions of national and cultural boundaries – confrontations with the border *polizei*, as Aby Warburg called them. Such a history would construct a different genealogy of foundational texts than those with which we are currently most familiar. Arthur Kingsley Porter's 1923 study *Romanesque Sculpture of the Pilgrimage Roads*, for example, would gain in stature because, as Linda Seidel has recently argued, his findings were initially considered problematic because they implied that there were no real regional or national boundaries for art during the Romanesque period of French history.[101]

A revised narrative history of the discipline would also prominently feature Otto Kurz for his lifelong interest in cultural transition, the similar interests of his close friend at the Warburg Bibliothek, Fritz Saxl, and the Institute's visionary founder Aby Warburg.[102] Warburg's transcultural interests in magic and science, which substantially determined the holdings of his famous library and the research interests of its users, would surely be the centerpiece of any revised narrative that stresses the discipline's interest in cultural transformation.

Warburg, like Riegl and Semper, broadened his theoretical understanding of art through the study of non-European culture. In the final analysis, however, we are compelled to dwell upon the limitations of the Warburgian approach to the study of cultural development. An incident from the beginning of Warburg's own career can serve as an illustration. In 1896, Warburg traveled around the southwestern United

States, where he witnessed a Pueblo ceremony – what Warburg called a "serpent ritual"
– that reportedly changed his attitude even towards Florentine art.[103] The published essay
that eventually resulted from this trip is evidence of Warburg's sincere theoretical interest
in the *universal* problem of how art communicates with its audience.[104] His stated
intention, however, was to decipher the workings of contemporary "primitive minds."[105]
Warburg assumed that Pueblo culture evolved according to its own internal dynamic of
cultural progress, despite the fact that Native Americans in the Southwest had lived in
close contact with Europeans since the arrival of the Spanish in 1580.[106] Warburg showed
no interest in the historical process of cultural assimilation among the forcibly accultur-
ated Pueblo people. His assumptions about "primitive" mentality were grounded in
discredited nineteenth-century theories of cultural evolution and racial identity.

On the other hand, even though Idealist assumptions about "primitive culture" are no
longer tenable, Warburg's empiricism, manifested in such observations as "what appears
to be purely decorative ornament must in fact be interpreted symbolically," and his
original interest in the inherent tension that visual symbols embody, contain the seeds of
an approach to cultural interaction that *is* still considered viable today. At present, the
concrete nature of knowledge production through visual images in colonial situations
offers a real test of the semiotic and phenomenological models that have developed in
response to resemblance theories of representation. Despite the organization of the
discipline in terms of outmoded assumptions about collective identity that take for
granted the homogeneity of "national culture" and the hierarchy of the "fine arts,"
awareness of cultural difference *has* contributed significantly to the ways in which
disciplinary methodologies developed. It is understandable that the discipline focused on
national culture, modeled itself on the dominant scientific paradigm (evolution), and
adapted current scientific procedures, such as typological analysis, to its own forms of
evidence when it was professionalized during the emerging period of modern nation-
states.[107] Different questions are potentially most interesting to contemporary scholars,
however, and these questions demand different methodologies and different claims to
knowledge.

So how should we define "culturally specific circumstances" now? Certainly not
according to nineteenth-century notions of national culture or racial identity. To develop
a theory of representation on a relativistic epistemological foundation that treats the social
circumstances in which visual images circulate, it is essential that we take into account
the history of the discipline as it developed out of a broad discursive field about the
nature of human civilization. And the longer history of these discussions, as I have tried
to suggest, revolved around the respective roles played in western thought by mental
operations, such as reasoning, memory, and the imagination, in defining humanness.
Only by understanding our lingering epistemological assumptions can we go beyond
them. Writing parallel accounts of the history of art from mutually exclusive points of
view will not free us from the chains of the past. Not a wholesale rejection of the
western philosophical tradition, nor refusal to see beyond the historical boundaries of our
dominant cultural tradition, nor any other dominating framework, will allow us to
reconceptualize the Renaissance and other historical periods as the international,
multicultural phenomena that they were.

Another major difference between the static notions of cultural identity held by

Panofsky, Warburg, and their colleagues, and any model we might wish to develop today, should be our greater awareness that the discourse of the historian is not univocal: it shifts just as the significance of the work changes according to the historian's interest.[108] One of the greatest challenges facing the discipline of art history today is the challenge of remodeling our inherited notions of national culture, which have been widely discredited outside the field, and replacing them with a dynamic model of collective identity defined in terms of diverse elements that are always in flux and, therefore – like visual images – capable of producing more than one responsible interpretation.

PART 2

Renaissance Theories of the Image

4.1   Raphael. *Sistine Madonna*. Dresden, Gemäldegalerie, Staatliche Kunstsammlungen. (Photo: Foto Marburg/Art Resource, New York.)

CHAPTER 4

Re-visioning Raphael as a "Scientific Painter"

JANIS BELL

RAPHAEL. The name immediately brings to mind such descriptions as "idealized," "classicizing," "balanced," and "restrained." To Winckelmann, Raphael was one step removed from the quiet grandeur and noble simplicity of antiquity, as close as any modern had come.[1] The *Sistine Madonna* (Figure 4.1) was described as an ideal beauty produced by the same ethos that animated the ancient Greeks. To Wölfflin, he was the embodiment of "classic art," a concept constructed upon formal analyses of composition and design.[2] The character of his art was defined in opposition to the painterly, recessional style of the "baroque" which, by contrast, made him look linear and planar. Defined in opposition to his fifteenth-century predecessors, his images had repose and spaciousness in contrast to fussy details and crowding; he was always lucid and not confusing, complex and synthetic in contrast to the simplistic and additive.

And in our survey texts, Raphael remains the epitome of High Renaissance classicism. Gardner's *Art Through the Ages* calls him "the artist most typical of the High Renaissance" who "rendered into form the Classical instinct of his age" and whose "art is almost the resurrection of Greek art at its height."[3] Hartt writes: "in his art . . . the High Renaissance ideal of harmony comes to its most complete expression," and Janson points out that "he is the central painter of the High Renaissance; our conception of the entire style rests more on his work than on any other masters."[4] The qualities identified in his works are grace and dignity, sweetness and lofty idealism, calm reason, balance, and measure.[5] Raphael may *be* all of this, yet his classicism has become a straitjacket, limiting not only our verbalization of his qualities but even our conceptualization of who he was and what he accomplished. Granted, the effluence of new monographs, exhibition catalogues, and comparative studies on Raphael has considerably widened the scope of analysis in many ways. The focus of my essay, however, is not the historiography of Raphael studies, but merely to examine how formalist constructions of Raphael's classicism limit our understanding of his art and its impact. I also make a case for a broader view of the artist. I will argue that the paradigm of Raphael as the epitome of classicism, derived from eighteenth-century aesthetics, has been retrospectively applied to our understanding of his reception in the seventeenth century, leading us to overlook aspects of his impact that do not fit the narrowly defined paradigm of classicism. By presenting new texts and reexamining some previously known, I hope to show through specific examples that the critical reception of Raphael's art was not limited by the parameters of classicism. Furthermore, I suggest that the concept of classicism itself needs to be reconfigured, to the extent that it has been defined as the imposition of order and regularity on a disordered world. The diametric constructions, of which early historians were so fond, set up false polarities that limit not only our concept of Raphael but of the scope and value of the Renaissance. By continuing to participate in these dichotomies (for example, contrasting Renaissance with Baroque or with Mannerism), and by conglomerating dichotomies, we create lopsided structures that misrepresent the complexity and diversity of history.

One way in which classicism has skewed our view of Raphael has been through its conception as an ideal, barely realizable in matter. The notion of a perfect mental idea was voiced by Raphael himself, in his famous letter to Castiglione, as imitation grounded in the experience of nature.[6] But following upon Winckelmann's conception of the classical ideal as a state of perfection realized only in a limited number of Greek statues, the ideal became more etherealized and abstracted. The process reached a culmination in Sydney Freedberg's comprehensive *Painting of the High Renaissance in Rome and Florence*, where classicism was conceptualized as a fragile balance. In this framework, as soon as the classical style matures in the Stanza della Segnatura, Raphael pushes it to its limits in the Stanza di Eliodoro and Tapestry cartoons, and then dissolves it in the Stanza dell' Incendio and other post-1514 works.[7] Michelangelo went through the same pattern of evolution even faster in the Sistine Chapel ceiling due to his "unclassical restlessness," ending with images on the pendentives that "breach classical discipline" and assume the "character of postclassical phenomena of style."[8] Freedberg writes of the Tapestry Cartoons (Figure 4.2):

4.2   Raphael. *Feed My Sheep*. Tapestry cartoon. London, Victoria & Albert Museum. (Photo: Victoria & Albert Museum, London/Art Resource, New York.)

The plateau this stage of style represents is not long inhabitable, and Raphael's tenancy of it is relatively brief. Since this high classicism is an apparent ultimate, it is not susceptible of further development in this same sense. Any measurable progressive sequel could be only toward a region of ideality so high as to verge upon abstractness, and thus upon another, and no longer substantially classical, style."[9]

The pattern of thought is a familiar one in the human psyche, aptly summarized by John Donne in a verse from *Lecture upon the Shadow* (1635):

> Love is a growing, or full constant light;
> And his first minute, after noone, is night.

Like love, classicism has been constructed as an ideal for which the striving is paramount and the consummation is elusive, fragile, and brief. Reaching the zenith is the start of a decline; every thought towards a new goal becomes a negation of the original one.

The generation of connoisseurs weaned on Wölfflin's formalist definition of classicism (of which Freedberg was a part) restricted Raphael's output according to this unattainable ideal of classicism, attributing much of Raphael's post-1514 output to young, unrestrained assistants.[10] Everything not "pure" was not classicism and therefore not Raphael. The practice of connoisseurship may be similar to the parallels that Joseph Grigely has recently identified between eugenic theory and textual criticism in our century.[11] Grigely pointed out that textual criticism, like eugenics, was marked by a methodology defined as rigorous and scientific, and by an ideology focused around purity and the elimination of "corruptions." Connoisseurship similarly sought to eliminate corruptions of the master's intentions by assistants or imitators, and this process was particularly obtrusive and restrictive in the case of artists like Raphael for whom "classicism" was already restricting the parameters of the artist's style.

In addition to reducing the number of authentic works, "classicism" has also skewed our access to the artist's work in several ways. *Colore* is one aspect that has been given relatively little attention, largely as the result of prejudices about its sensuous, irrational, and subjective nature (as well as its links to feminine values); by *colore* I mean not only the choice and arrangement of colors but also all aspects of coloring, including chiaroscuro, finish, and the handling of paint. Lichtenstein and Reilly have shown that the negative assessment of *colore* in Renaissance and seventeenth-century thought represents a continuous tradition of criticism dating back to classical antiquity.[12] It is not a prejudice that we have entirely escaped. As a graduate student, I was discouraged from studying Raphael's color because it was deemed "too subjective." John Shearman pointed out in 1962 in his fundamental study of Leonardo's color and chiaroscuro that the study of color has lagged behind other aspects of art history;[13] and the situation has hardly been redressed in the last thirty years. The number of studies devoted to coloring is minuscule; those which treat it with more than a passing reference are more numerous, but still remain only a small fraction of the hundreds of specialized studies devoted to Raphael, his workshop, and his impact on nearly five centuries of artists and art-lookers.[14]

Other aspects of Raphael's practice have received relatively little attention as well. We are still tied to traditional valuations of the relative merits of the rational and intellectual versus the irrational/emotional, and of the spiritual versus the practical. Renaissance writers stressed the intellectual component of *disegno* and minimized the importance of practice (which they called a "mechanical" art) in order to validate the status of painting, sculpture, and architecture among the liberal arts. Later constructions of artistic genius widened the gap by reducing practice to a set of rules which could be learned by any pupil in the Academy while the innate genius of a few talented men would bubble forth in nourishing conditions of opportunity and education. Today, practice is still frequently seen as tedious, technical, and devoid of theoretical concerns. In the practice of art history, however, we are coming to realize that even unspoken assumptions constitute a theory of sorts, regardless of whatever philosophical inconsistencies lurk beneath the surface. And as Raphael's practice engages the attention of scholars and conservators, we are learning to appreciate these other facets of his genius.[15]

Theory itself has not been immune to restrictive views. Even while the classical ideal is a construct of theory, it limits or, more accurately, excludes theory from its parameters. Alberti's 1436 treatise on painting is admitted as an early expression of the classical ideal (and there are some writers who compare Raphael's art to Alberti's idea of it),[16] but Raphael himself is not envisioned as a painter steeped in theory. The true artist, according to this conception, is "too busy making art" to theorize – as if theorizing had to be equated with writing, and writing with abstraction removed from every day reality. Yet Raphael had a "working" theory of painting that was not equivalent to Alberti's theory of painting although it was certainly indebted to it.[17]

In recent years, Raphael specialists have come to recognize how much our conception of Raphael was confined by this adherence to the ideal of classicism. Interestingly enough, revision was fueled by Italian restorers who cleaned the *Transfiguration* and the Stanza dell' Incendio frescoes, finding signs of Raphael's hand where earlier connoisseurs had seen the work of Giulio and Penni.[18] Now the list of Raphael's authentic works is expanded and the picture of his varied achievements is substantially broadened. Recent monographs by Oberhuber (1982) and by Jones and Penny (1984) present Raphael as a dynamic and experimental painter, ever seeking new problems and new solutions. Younger scholars are examining Vasari's biography and other sixteenth-century texts to understand how Raphael was received and how the critical concepts of his contemporaries can help us to break apart the straitjacket of formalist classicism.[19] It would be misleading, however, to imply that a revisionist view of Raphael has thoroughly transformed Anglo–American studies. James Beck's recent monograph on the Stanza della Segnatura still describes and delimits Raphael with the lofty language of the classical ideal.[20] Indeed, it is language which drives the continuation of that ideal, and which constructs and delimits how we see.

In seventeenth-century studies, this revisionist view of Raphael has taken hold even less. A powerful restraint has been created by formative studies of Raphael's critical fortunes (now "critical reception" in Anglo–American studies) which have identified the early seventeenth century as the germination of the view of Raphael as an ideal "academic" painter.[21] It is not surprising that studies searching for the seeds of the classical ideal in seventeenth- and early eighteenth-century thought have validated retrospectively the line of criticism developed by Winckelmann, Wölfflin, and Freedberg.

According to these authors, the works of Raphael represented the epitome of the selective imitation of nature and ideal beauty distilled from a study of classical antiquity. Bellori (1672) canonized Raphael as the perfect embodiment of the *idea*, the model for avoiding the excesses of *maniera*, which was too far removed from nature, and the excesses of Caravaggio's example, which was too unselective in imitating nature.[22] Monsignor Agucchi, in his unpublished treatise fragment (*c.*1607–15), expressed the seed of this concept through his presentation of Annibale Carracci as a paradigm of idealized imitation whose style was formed by combining the *colore* of northern examples (Lombards and Venetians) with the *disegno* of the Roman works of Raphael.[23] The assessment of Raphael was described as similar in France, where Fréart de Chambray (1662), Félibien (1666–85), and Roger de Piles (1699, 1708) presented Raphael as a model to be imitated for *disegno*, expression, decorum, proportion, but rarely as a complete model for filial imitation.[24] Raphael's *colore* was found wanting, especially by Roger de Piles, who ranked him in his "Balances des peintres" (a score card of 57 painters in four categories) lower than some 22 Italian and northern painters from the sixteenth and seventeenth centuries, including Michelangelo.[25] Félibien also saw him as inferior to Poussin on the argument that Poussin also had theory.[26]

De Piles' explicit criticism has been seen as implicit in the discussions of earlier writers such as Agucchi: if the recipe for Annibale's success had included the coloring of Lombardy, particularly the soft *pastoso* effects of Correggio, then Raphael could not be considered a complete model. He was a model for *disegno*, but his coloring was the opposite of what was desired: hard, or *statuino* as Malvasia would later characterize it.[27] The political intentions of these authors need to be considered, for they were reacting to Vasari's arrogant promotion of central Italian art and trying to establish an alternative that gave equal credence to the products of their own local cultures.[28] But, for the most part, modern writers have been more interested in the roots of classicism, perhaps unconsciously or inadvertently, as we mostly work within existing paradigms. And since the founders who canonized Raphael as an exemplar of "classic art" – Winckelmann and Wölfflin—barely mention color and chiaroscuro, as if these elements were an insignificant feature of his personal style and his historical accomplishment, we have managed to exclude them without discomfort. Thus we have barely escaped de Piles' valuation in our own studies of Raphael's contribution. Indeed, our reevaluation of sixteenth-century *maniera*, Caravaggio, and the Bamboccianti has only pushed Raphael further away from the charm and glamor of a colorist. Furthermore, this analysis has helped to create the picture of a great historical debate in which Raphael has been pitted against Titian as a proponent of *disegno* over *colore*, preparing the way for later formulations of contrasts between linear and painterly, classical and Baroque.

Certainly the validity of the old dichotomies – *disegno/colore*, classic/baroque, linear/painterly – has been challenged in recent decades.[29] Scholars today recognize that these dichotomies are not appropriate guidelines for understanding and categorizing the history of seventeenth-century art. But no new structure has supplanted this construction. Raphael's influence in seventeenth-century Italy is still seen as a filial line proceeding from Annibale Carracci to Domenichino to Poussin to the French Academy and ultimately to eighteenth-century neo-Classicism, in which it is associated with reason rather than emotion, and with a rather dry, linear, planar style. Donald Posner regarded Raphael as the inspiration for Annibale Carracci's departure from the expressive chiaroscuro of his Bolognese style to the "harsh classicism" of his Roman works.[30] Richard Spear saw the imitation of Raphael at the root of what he called Domenichino's "neo-classic abstraction" in the pendentive frescoes at S. Carlo ai Catinari following the greater Baroque exuberance of the S. Andrea della Valle frescoes.[31] Domenichino's subsequent phase is characterized as "hyperclassicism" which has "anti-naturalistic tendencies" such as stiffness, impassivity, and light colors. Anthony Blunt similarly connected Poussin's "severe style" of the 1640s to his renewed study of Raphael's compositions.[32] In these and numerous other examples, the pattern can be identified: Raphael is always associated with stylistic changes that are interpreted as emphasizing drawing and composition over color and chiaroscuro, and with changes that lead painters away from naturalism and towards abstraction.[33]

There is something very wrong with a construct that presents Raphael as a model in the direction leading away from naturalism when his sixteenth-century contemporaries and successors celebrated him for his unprecedented naturalism.[34] Had standards of naturalism changed so dramatically in less than the century between the death of Raphael and the maturity of Poussin, or have we been seeing the evidence through distorted lenses?

Several seventeenth-century texts suggest that we need to revise this picture to recognize Raphael's importance in the early seventeenth century as a model of perspective, of *colore*, and as a *pittore scientifico* (scientific painter) – that is, as a painter steeped in theory. These texts at first seem so totally outside what we have retrospectively come to understand as the canon of the "classical ideal" that my first reaction was to dismiss them as blind adulation. But I soon came to realize that these texts do not negate the validity of other texts which celebrate Raphael for his ideal of beauty, for his decorum, and for his *invenzione*. Rather, they broaden the picture. Each text is a reconstruction of one individual's visual experience in literary terms. We have, in recent years, been much more sensitive to the literary genres which have affected those constructions, and no longer naively "read" the text as a record of pure individual or collective experience, just as we no longer look at a painting as a record of pure, visual truth. Indeed, the antique tradition of art criticism is replete with *topoi* in which perspective and color are celebrated as marvels of naturalism and illusionism. Yet this most ancient, venerable theme has been degraded by modern taste; it has been seen as philistine, simplistic, and appealing to the uneducated. From Winckelmann's *History of Ancient Art*, the imitation of nature in representational art was relegated to the back of the bus, discussed in hushed voices and silently admired, while those in the front pursued a white marble "ideal" that could be verbalized in the new, lofty language of philosophical aesthetics.

This prejudice has affected our reading of Bellori as the writer who first canonized Raphael as the perfect embodiment of the classical ideal. We point to his narrative of Domenichino's obsession with the *School of Athens* (Figure 4.3) in the *Lives*:

> [Domenichino] . . . having remained in the *Stanze* many hours, would return home in the evening and recount his day to Francesco Albano, with whom he lived. He would discourse about the *School of Athens*, explaining its beauty; when asked about the other histories, he would respond that he hadn't seen them. Perplexed by this response, Albano would ask him again, at which point Domenichino would admit that he had just not had the time to think about them.[35]

At the same time, Bellori recognized that others preferred the Stanza di Eliodoro frescoes.

4.3   Raphael. *School of Athens*. Fresco. Vatican, Stanza della Segnatura. (Photo: Vatican Museums.)

He related that Andrea Sacchi, after returning from a trip to Venice and Lombardy to study the works of Titian and Correggio, returned to the Vatican with trepidation, afraid that he would no longer be pleased with Raphael. One look at the *Repulse of Attila* and he "found himself transported by its harmony, finding in it a beautiful mix of Titian and Correggio."[36] His own preference was also for the Stanza di Eliodoro frescoes; in his collection of essays on the Vatican *Stanze*, he described the *Expulsion of Heliodorus* (Figure 4.4) and the *Mass at Bolsena* as Raphael's "greatest manner of painting," which, he insisted, was developed without inspiration from Michelangelo.[37] In the same volume, he used the Sacchi anecdote to demonstrate Raphael's excellence in coloring in an essay comparing Raphael to Apelles. In sum, Bellori recognized the artist's varying appeal to different sensibilities, modifying the view of Raphael's universality inherited from Vasari and Dolce to show a multi-faceted Raphael who appealed to nearly everyone in one respect or another. André Félibien also discussed Raphael's coloring in positive terms. He saw him as Poussin's guide in the painting of color and clair-obscur, setting a precedent for the imitation of nature that allowed Poussin to escape from the "unnatural" conventions of Venetian examples.[38] In his analysis of Poussin's *Rebecca and Eliezer at the Well* (Figure 4.5), Félibien observed how Poussin used light and shadow to define the roundings of individual figures and to describe the placement of figures and objects in space. He noticed that the colors of the draperies as well as the flesh tones of the women

4.4   Raphael. *Expulsion of Heliodorus*. Fresco. Vatican, Stanza di Eliodoro. (Photo: Vatican Museums.)

standing behind the well were slightly diminished with respect to those in front, and singled out the woman in white drawing water from the well as "diminished in the force of drawing and color."[39] Her sunlit shoulder is substantially grayer than the white scarves of Rebecca and the green and red draperies of another in the foreground; she is less finished, with fewer details and less crisp edges. Félibien is here talking about Poussin's use of color and acuity perspective, an aspect of coloring to which the seventeenth century was particularly attuned.[40] Félibien was joined by his contemporaries in praising Poussin for his mastery of "la perspective aërienne,"[41] which involves gradations in color, acuity, and the contrast of light and shadow. Some claimed that in this one area Poussin had surpassed all his predecessors.[42] Félibien's statement that Poussin took Raphael as his guide is part of a larger discourse in which the naturalistic approach of Raphael was seen as an alternative to the color and chiaroscuro of Venetian artists, said to be based upon artifice. His concluding remarks make this clear:

> This style and course of action made his [Raphael's] paintings seem to conform to what one sees in nature: for without the artifice of great shadows and great lights, objects are seen just as they normally appear outside and in open spaces, where one never sees these large masses of light and darkness.[43]

The practice of massing light and shadow was at the core of seventeenth-century French

4.5 Poussin. *Rebecca and Eliezer at the Well*. Oil on canvas. Paris, Musée du Louvre. (Photo: © R.M.N.)

debates on clair-obscur.[44] Dufresnoy and de Piles attributed its inception to Titian, using the metaphor of a bunch of grapes which could be forcefully illuminated as a single entity, or broken apart and illuminated individually, additively, and ineffectively.[45] De Piles would later judge Raphael harshly for coloring without this compositional device, admitting, however, that he began to adopt it in the last eight years of his life. His views had already been made public in his 1668 commentary to Dufresnoy's *De Arte Graphica*.[46] Félibien responded to the challenge to defend Raphael's hegemony, and it is significant that he took the side of scientific optics, exposing the practice of the massing of clair-obscur as a mere artistic convention to be adopted at will and *not* as a scientific principle of nature.

Matteo Zaccolini also took the side of scientific optics. In *Prospettiva del Colore*, he praised Raphael as a model of naturalistic light and shadow. His reference point was totally different from Félibien's, so it is all the more interesting that he reached similar conclusions about Raphael's naturalism: he was writing in the late 1610s in Rome in an artistic climate in which tenebrism was coming increasingly under fire. His writings, together with those of the physician Giulio Mancini, represent the first wave of criticism against the dark grounds and strong contrasts of tenebrist painting.[47] Both thought Caravaggesque lighting was unnatural. Mancini wrote that the system of lighting employed by Caravaggio's followers was "unnatural" because it did not indicate the reflections that normally make forms partially visible in the shadows, whereas the pictures of the Carracci and their school were said to be characterized by a natural light like that of Raphael and the painters of Lombardy.[48] The frequently quoted opinion of Annibale Carracci that Caravaggio's *Judith* was "too natural" (*troppo naturale*) cannot be taken as a comment about coloring; yet it has dominated historical accounts because it fits so well with the dichotomies in which color and chiaroscuro are associated with "Baroque" trends and opposed to "classicism."[49]

Zaccolini compared Raphael's "natural" light and shadow to the "unnatural darkness" of tenebrism. In his treatise on cast shadows (part of a four-volume set on pictorial optics),[50] he harshly criticized painting without reflected light in the shadows, arguing that "the shadows will appear to be total darkness as in night-time, which is not a good imitation of nature, but makes a crude, cutting manner."[51] He even advised against the portrayal of "unnaturally dark shadows" in night scenes, recommending that the painter create a naturalistic setting with carefully placed artificial lights at a distance from the figures.[52] His ideal was a soft, natural light with transparent shadow, which he promoted as "natural" by appealing to the scientific principles of optics. Raphael was his model.

If we examine Raphael's painting of a night scene in the *Liberation of St. Peter* in the Vatican (Figure 4.6), we can understand what he might have celebrated in Raphael's painting of light. Even in the darkest parts, as on the left side of the picture where there is no divine light, moonlight illuminates the sky behind the guards so that their contours are visible. The torch held by a guard standing in the foreground illuminates the steps as well as the limbs of the two seated guards; lusters glisten on their armor, helping to define even the backlit figure in the front. Nowhere is pose, contour, or relief destroyed by night-time obscurity, yet the dramatic pattern of illumination and reflections leaves no doubt that we are witnessing a nocturnal event.[53]

4.6 Raphael. *Liberation of St. Peter.* Fresco. Vatican, Stanza di Eliodoro. (Photo: Vatican Museums.)

4.7   Raphael. *Expulsion of Heliodorus* (detail of leaping page). Fresco. Vatican, Stanza di Eliodoro. (Photo: Vatican Museums.)

Zaccolini mentioned Raphael in three chapters in his *Prospettiva del Colore*, all within the context of discussions of light and shadow. In one instance, he praised the artist's intelligence in the painting of cast shadows, citing the divided shadow in the *Expulsion of Heliodorus* as a cue that a *staffiero* (page) has been caught leaping in mid-air (Figure 4.7).[54] In another passage, he praised Raphael for creating marvelous relief by limiting the use of white to a few highlights.[55] And in a third passage, he praised Raphael's use of light and shadow to create a clear illusion of space with the qualities of sweetness and *unione*.[56]

Zaccolini's discussion of light and shadow in space is closely related to Félibien's description of Poussin's diminution in the distance of "the force of drawing and color." Zaccolini described a practice that I have termed "chiaroscuro perspective" or "*contrast* perspective" to distinguish it from color perspective and acuity perspective, all three components of atmospheric perspective ("la perspective aërienne").[57] Chiaroscuro perspective results from placing the strongest lights and darkest shadows on the foreground figures, with a subsequent graded diminution of the obscurity of the shadows and brightness of the lights as the distance increases. This is demonstrated in Raphael's *The Expulsion of Heliodorus*, a fresco in the Sala di Eliodoro in the Vatican which Zaccolini surely knew (Figure 4.4). The figures of Heliodorus and the angel of the Lord are painted with the greatest contrast between light and dark. Lusters on the armor rise to a pure white, while the shadow of Heliodorus's hip and the opening of the vessel are among the darkest in the entire fresco (Figure 4.8). Even the flesh shows a great contrast range,

4.8 Raphael. *Expulsion of Heliodorus* (detail of Heli-odorus). Fresco. Vatican, Stanza di Eliodoro. (Photo: Vatican Museums.)

4.9 Raphael. *Expulsion of Heliodorus* (detail of high priest). Fresco. Vatican, Stanza di Eliodoro. (Photo: Vatican Museums.)

especially where the light on his elbow is juxtaposed to the cast shadow on his upper arm. By contrast, the distant figure of the high priest at prayer is rendered in a lesser contrast (Figure 4.9). While there are still lusters on the gold drapery, the bronze lamps, and candelabra, the range of modeling tones is reduced in the draperies and the flesh. Figures placed at an intermediate distance show an intermediate contrast range, greater than the distant priest, yet less than the foreground Heliodorus. The foreground figures thus create a scale to which the diminution of light and shadow tones are compared, enabling the viewer to judge the proximity of the object in conjunction with other distance cues, such as diminishing size.

Interestingly enough, there is a direct link between Zaccolini's and Félibien's aware-ness of the role of light and shadow in creating pictorial space. Zaccolini's treatise was copied by Cassiano dal Pozzo in the 1630s, and shown to artists and other intellectuals.[58] Poussin was the most prominent artist who studied it, and perhaps the most enthusiastic. According to Félibien, Poussin brought his own copy of it to France with him in 1640, which he showed to Chantelou and others, and which was mistakenly remembered by some as a treatise by the French painter himself. Félibien nowhere reveals that he himself had seen or read the treatise, but he knew it indirectly through Poussin, albeit trans-formed and improved, for he asserted emphatically that Poussin "demonstrated what he had learned from Padre Zaccolini in his paintings."[59] Indeed, Poussin had modified

Zaccolini's precepts on color perspective to make it more natural, substituting the deep *turchino* blue recommended for remote distances with a desaturated grayish blue-green. Yet Zaccolini's basic principles about the systematic diminution of color and chiaroscuro with regard to the distance from the foreground plane as well as the distance from the light source became a commonplace of French theory in the latter half of the century.[60] Raphael had been the model for both. Ironically, in the eighteenth century, Raphael's images would be "modernized" in some reproductive engravings to conform better to this perspective ideal by exaggerating his systematic use of chiaroscuro perspective.[61]

Zaccolini's opinions are also important for a revisionist view of Raphael in the seventeenth century because he presents Raphael as a learned and scientific painter (*il dotto e scientifico pittore*). We are used to thinking of Leonardo in these terms, because he did research on issues that today are categorized as "scientific." Not Raphael, however, for whom the epithet seems incongruous to those who think of science as a diametric opposite to the humanities. The forging of this dichotomy in the nineteenth century has already been challenged by contemporary opponents of dichotomous thought, and it would take us on a tangential course to explore this charged issue. More pertinent is the meaning of *scientifico* which I translate as "scientific" although the meanings are not completely congruent, for *scientifico* did not mean "engaged in science" in the modern sense of that term; "science" is used in the Aristotelian sense to refer to theoretical knowledge grounded in nature rather than speculation.[62]

Zaccolini's praise of Raphael for painting divided shadows is an example that clarifies why Raphael merited the epithet *pittore scientifico*. Although cast shadows had appeared in early Italian painting (fourteenth and fifteenth centuries), it was not until the sixteenth and seventeenth centuries that cast shadows became an essential feature of pictorial naturalism.[63] Their rendition as two-dimensional surface patterns required little more than the observation of nature; and this was the level at which most painters worked, indicating shadows attached to the base of figures. But the truly accurate rendition of cast shadows required an understanding of optical theory. Most crucial was the concept of shadow as a column or pyramid of darkness extending in the air behind an opaque body until it intersected with any illuminated surface. Thus even if an object were raised above a surface, or detached in some other way, the pyramid of shadow that it projected would still intersect the given surface. Raphael's use of divided shadows to indicate airborne figures in the *Expulsion of Heliodorus* depended upon a basic understanding of this principle.

To art historians working within the paradigms of early modern (eighteenth- and nineteenth-century) aesthetics, Zaccolini's observations would be considered peripheral. Technical matters were denigrated and even at times seen as antithetical to classicism. It became commonplace, for example, to regard the zeal of the fifteenth-century *bottega* for perspective, anatomy, and other details of scientific accuracy as evidence of an attitude precluding classicism. But, as Martin Kemp has recently argued, neither our own distaste for mathematical demonstrations nor our devaluation of the daily humdrum concerns of the practicing artist reflects the values and concerns of the past.[64] Classicism forces upon us a focus on the individual work of art as a pure text. It isolates the work of art from its production, its historical situation and from the accretion of its critical reception and physical change throughout the centuries.

4.10   Matteo Zaccolini. *Shadow from a
Suspended Cube*. Pen and ink with
wash. Florence, Biblioteca Medicea-
Laurenziana, MS. Laur. Ash. 1212[4],
fol. 10v. (Photo: Pneider.)

Zaccolini, however, was a working artist as much interested in process as in product.
Largely unaware of the complexities of diachronic accretions, both literary and historical,
his interest in Raphael was motivated by his own timely recognition of the optics of light
and shadow as an essential feature of perspective practice. Dürer had devised a "method"
for projecting cast shadows which involved determining the shape of the pyramid of
darkness.[65] This had paved the way for early seventeenth-century perspective experts to
discover how the shape of that shadow would change when projected on to any surface
at any distance, by combining the principles of perspective projection with the geometry
of conic sections.[66] In the early seventeenth century, cast shadows were a hot topic,
engaging the attention of Guidobaldo del Monte (*Perspectivae libri sex*, 1600), Franciscus
Aguilonius (*Opticorum libri sex*, 1613), Pietro Accolti (*Inganno degli Occhi*, 1625), Jean
Dubreuil (*Perspective practique* . . . 1642), and Abraham Bosse (*Manière universelle*, 1648).
Zaccolini devoted an entire volume to the projection of cast shadows (*Descrittione dell'
ombre prodotte da corpi opachi rettilinei*) which is by far the most extensive account. He
included the first demonstration of a divided shadow, showing geometric shapes
suspended from a gibbet (Figure 4.10). Similar illustrations would soon appear in the
perspective treatises of Dubreuil and Bosse.

But by the early seventeenth century, the complexity of modern perspective had
pushed many artists to reject mathematical perspective as the foundation of painting and

to question the relevance of sophisticated geometrical demonstrations to artistic prac-tice.[67] Zaccolini insisted upon their relevance, and tried to make the projection of shadows as simple and accessible as possible for the artist who cared about results and had neither the patience nor the inclination to immerse himself in the mathematical determi-nation of the *lineamenti*. Zaccolini argued that mastery need not be achieved only by expertise in mathematics; repeated practice coupled with an understanding of the basic principles of shadows could suffice. Ichnographic (two-dimensional) and isometric per-spective diagrams as well as perspective drawings rendered with wash and white-heightening accompanied his text to facilitate the reader's understanding and copying. Diligence was essential to either approach. What better exemplar than the diligent Raphael, who had produced a convincing rendition of an airborne figure through careful study of the basic principles, without the benefit of mathematical perspective treatises? Looking at Raphael with the eyes of a practicing artist and perspective expert, Zaccolini saw his painting as a singular manifestation of the artist's profound knowledge of theory.

I think it is in this vein too that we have to understand Filippo Gagliardi's admiration for Raphael's use of perspective. Gagliardi was an architectural perspective painter who worked in the Barberini ambient and later became *Principe* of the Accademia di San Luca.[68] He referred to Zaccolini as his teacher (*precettore*) in the preface to his unpublished perspective treatise (probably written in the early 1630s), but the relationship of his ideas to those of Zaccolini have not yet been explored.[69] At the very least, we can state that he inherited Zaccolini's admiration for Leonardo and Raphael.

Gagliardi mentioned Raphael in three places. In the preface, he praised Raphael in the same breath as Dürer. Dürer was deemed "an exceptional draughtsman in everything because he was well educated in mathematics [*aggiustatissimo disegnatore in tutte le sue operationi per essere instrutto nella Mathematica*]" while Raphael was praised as "singular in positioning figures and objects in *istorie* [*unico disponitor d'istorie*]." Gagliardi went on to mention Veronese, the three Carracci, and Domenichino. He then praised the entire group of "great men" (*grandi huomini*) because they "had put the practice of lines into effect, understanding that mathematics is truly the mother of the arts [*hano esercitato la pratica delle linee, conoscendeno che veramente la mathematica e madre delle arti*]." Later in the treatise he commended the fish-scale pattern of bricks that Raphael had designed for the pavement of the *Fire in the Borgo* (Figure 4.11), and the pavement pattern of hexagons in the *Expulsion of Heliodorus* (Figure 4.4).[70] Apparently, these patterns were difficult and tedious to project in perspective diminution. By mastering them, Raphael had demon-strated his facility with perspective as well as his ability to conquer the difficulties of art.

We often forget that Giovanni Paolo Lomazzo had also praised Raphael as an exemplar of perspective. In his *Trattato dell' arte della pittura* (1584), he categorized six types of perspective according to the viewpoint of the observer.[71] Raphael's Roman frescoes were cited as superlative examples of the fourth category, the frontal view at eye-level to the figures, which he explained "had the least amount of foreshortening but was considered just as difficult as the others."[72]

Raphael's mastery of perspective is rather obvious when we compare his first two Roman *istorie*, the *School of Athens* (Figure 4.3) and the *Disputà* (both Vatican Museum, Stanza della Segnatura) with fifteenth-century paintings of crowds. Indeed, it is common-place to observe Raphael's innovation in disposing figures by means of a deep semi-circle that fully uses the fictive architectural space and to compare this with his earlier *Marriage of the Virgin* (Figure 4.12) where the figures are splayed across a narrow shelf in the foreground and the deep space of the piazza recedes like a backdrop.[73] Recent studies have confirmed Raphael's great facility in perspective in the Stanza della Segnatura frescoes: the background architecture of the *School of Athens* was constructed directly on the wall without a cartoon, using a nail and strings to incise lines in the wet *intonaco* as a guide to the perspective construction.[74] Nesselrath reported similar results from technical studies in the Stanza dell' Incendio: the architecture of the *Coronation of Charlemagne* was projected right on the wall, but the *Fire in the Borgo* seems to have been constructed from a full cartoon which was pounced.[75] Nesselrath and Oberhuber have also pointed out Raphael's remarkable experiments with new viewpoints and dispositions of figures in space in his later Vatican frescoes.[76]

Yet we tend to forget this or dismiss it when looking at Raphael's influence in the seventeenth century. Our tendency is to assume that Raphael mastered perspective and then went on to master more interesting things. This pattern is then applied to the history of art on a larger scale: we argue that fifteenth-century artists struggled to master perspective while artists in later centuries mastered it quickly in their early training and then concerned themselves with less technical problems.

This schema does not fit with the details of early biographical sources – for example, that Bellori and Passeri tell us that Domenichino turned to Zaccolini to learn perspective and optics, or that Poussin immersed himself in the 1630s in a study of "classic" optical

4.11   Raphael. *Fire in the Borgo*. Fresco. Vatican, Stanza di Incendio. (Photo: Vatican Museums.)

4.12 Raphael. *Marriage of the Virgin*. Milan, Pinacoteca di Brera. (Photo: Alinari/Art Resource, New York.)

treatises by Alhazen and Witelo as well as Zaccolini's more recent one.[77] Nor does it jive with the prevalence of artistic collaboration in the seventeenth century, when a whole group of artists suddenly emerged as perspective specialists who prepared the architectural perspectives for Domenichino, Guercino, Lanfranco, and a host of others. Here we are not talking about poorly trained figure painters from provincial backwaters, but about those artists who had the benefits of the most advanced artistic education in the academy run by the Carracci. The obscure names of many of these perspective specialists testifies to another aspect of the problem. Perspective mastery has become devalued as a mere technical skill, believed to be lacking originality and invention.

Yet, if we seriously consider the impact of Raphael's perspective as a model for imitation by some seventeenth-century artists, the picture changes. Domenichino will serve as a typical but especially telling example for, as noted earlier, Bellori argued that he studied the Vatican *stanze* with a devotion bordering on obsession. The impact of this study on his own production is revealed in the Bolognese artist's mastery of those features of Raphael's perspective cited as noteworthy by Lomazzo and Gagliardi: of the "frontal view at eye-level," the disposition of figures within a recessional space, and the mastery of herringbone and other geometric pavement designs. The first fruits of this study are revealed in the *Flagellation of St Andrew* (1609) at S. Gregorio Magno, Rome (Figure 4.13)

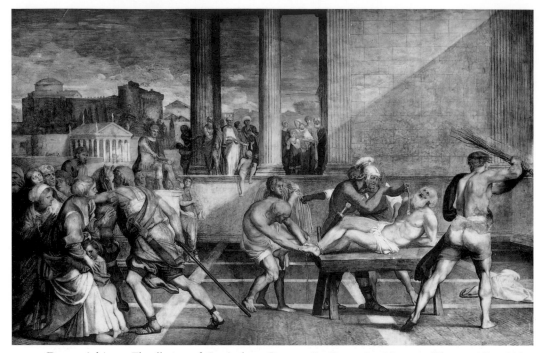

4.13   Domenichino. *Flagellation of St Andrew*. Rome, S. Gregorio Magno. (Photo: Alinari/Art Resource, New York.)

but the Bolognese artist's full mastery is revealed several years later in the frescoes of the Polet chapel in S. Luigi dei Francesi, Rome (1612–15). Spear rightly presents the Polet chapel as Domenichino's most "neo-Raphaelesque" phase.[78] In particular, one notes the rhythmic semi-circular disposition of figures in the *Martyrdom of St. Cecilia* (Figure 4.14) and *St. Cecilia Giving Alms* as well as the construction of complex architectural spaces with assertive pavement patterns.

Why then do "classicism" and Raphael also get associated with Domenichino's late works, such as the pendentives at S. Carlo ai Catinari, Rome (Figure 4.15), and S. Gennaro, Naples, where, in contrast to the Polet chapel images, Domenichino has constructed the figures like a sculptural relief, densely packed into the foreground, projecting outwards towards and overlapping the frame? Spear cites the dense, relief-like compositions of Raphael's *Lo Spasimo di Sicilia* (Prado) and Annibale's paintings in the Herrera chapel as "spiritual" precedents, and connects the changes in Domenichino's style with similar changes in the art of contemporaries like Guido Reni. He argues that the "formal, rigid designs and cooler, lighter colors" of Reni and Domenichino testify to a movement away from "Baroque" naturalism, as manifested in Domenichino's S. Andrea della Valle frescoes in the 1620s.[79] But is "classicism" the appropriate way to refer to these changes? What does this style labeled "hyper-classicism" really have to do with "classicism" in models such as Raphael?

The legitimacy of the Baroque/classic dichotomy as a conscious schism in the Roman art world has been rightly questioned by several writers, among them Spear and especially Harris.[80] As Harris points out, one of the consequences of focusing on the baroque/

4.14 Domenichino. *Martyrdom of St. Cecilia.* Rome, S. Luigi dei Francesi. (Photo: Alinari/ Art Resource, New York.)

classical dichotomy in Roman seventeenth-century painting is that "scholars and critics, blinded by the stereotypes suggested by the two terms, overlook or minimize those qualities in a particular work that do not fit the stereotype while over-emphasizing those that do."[81] Such questioning can be taken even further when we recognize that this dichotomy is essentially based upon a notion of classicism as "unnatural," as the imposition of order and symmetry on an unnatural, irregular world.[82] This paradigm now seems inaccurate in light of the fact that perceptual scientists have ceased to talk about perception as the imposition of order on raw visual data and now talk about a visual system developed to perceive variants and invariants.[83] In the old model, we "perceived" blobs of light and color which we then "ordered" into shapes through cognitive processes that we could recognize as a table edge or as our grandmother. In the new model, we directly perceive shapes, edges, movement, light, and color; even our grandmother is recognized by direct perception because, after learning who she is, we instantaneously connect to the proper neuronal pathway. Visual art involves a mixture of both, and realism has been reconstrued as a relativistic concept related to the balance between a given culture's emphasis on the variant and invariants perceived.[84] Recent scholars have pointed out how much later constructions of classicism as formal order have distorted our view of Greek art, causing us to diminish and devalue the remarkable naturalism of fifth-century art.[85] We can say much the same for the art of Raphael and his contemporaries, art which was exalted by sixteenth- and seventeenth-century viewers for its remarkable naturalism; our modern construction of classicism has led us to minimize these very aspects in our writing of history. We have been so intent upon

4.15   Domenichino. *Justice*. Rome, S. Carlo ai Catinari. (Photo: Alinari/Art Resource, New York.)

distinguishing Renaissance concepts of realism and imitation from photographic realism and the pictorial ideals of nineteenth-century plein-air painting that we often fail to give sufficient emphasis to this aspect of Raphael's art that was greatly admired, and to this aspect of art through the Renaissance: the ability to make things *look* real. Much of this ability depended upon Raphael's "scientific" knowledge of *colore*, of perspective, and of anatomy.

In conjunction with this polarizing of Baroque naturalism to Renaissance classicism, color and chiaroscuro have been shunted into a polarized position. Naturalism is coupled with a dynamic, "Baroque" style; chiaroscuro is equated with tenebrism and strong contrasts; and both are allied with *colore* as opposed to *disegno*. Classicism is what Baroque is not – static, light-colored, linear: the heritage of Wölfflin. Typical of this approach is an analysis of Poussin's *The Death of Germanicus* as having "hot colour and dramatic lighting" which are said to "exemplify the painterly movement away from classicism" and to give it an imprecise and emotional "Baroque" flavor in contrast to the "cool unemphasized colouring" and "emotional detachment" of *Extreme Unction* with its "geometrically placed shadows."[86] The false construction of classicism has pushed "Baroque" into the untenable position of being unclassical, a muddle which seventeenth-century scholars are still working to straighten out.

The writings of Zaccolini and Félibien on chiaroscuro, Gagliardi's pairing of Raphael and Veronese, and the extensive discussions of chiaroscuro in contemporary writings of Pietro Testa and Pietro Accolti, which have been discussed elsewhere,[87] testify to how much we have overlooked by coupling "chiaroscuro" with the "baroque" side of seventeenth-century stylistic alternatives. Chiaroscuro was of great importance and interest to all painters; it is just that we have failed to pay sufficient attention to it in the works of painters categorized as "classicists." Elizabeth Cropper, however, has shown that Poussin and Testa undertook serious study of chiaroscuro, Poussin even consulting copies of Zaccolini's manuscripts.[88] Dufresnoy and Félibien also wrote about chiaroscuro in great detail, as did other "classicizing" Frenchmen (although Dufresnoy is often categorized as "baroque" because of de Piles' later publication of his text).

In conclusion, this discussion of Raphael's *colore* and perspective by seventeenth-century writers alerts us to misguided conclusions that often arise from the application of anachronistic concepts to cultures that did not embrace the same values. However, I am not suggesting that we discard the baby with the bathwater. The terms "classicism," "baroque," and "naturalism" still have a certain usefulness as distinctions, and concepts developed by modern artists and scientists can bear fruitful results when applied, even anachronistically, to the art of the past.[89] We cannot circumvent the conditioning of our vision by our verbal constructs. But we must become aware of the values and historical conditions encoded in these verbal constructs so that we can use them judiciously. "Baroque," "classicism," and "naturalism" should not be exclusive, polarized categories. If "naturalism" is an ideal embracing artists as diverse as Bamboccio, Bernini, Annibale Carracci, Caravaggio, Raphael, and Rubens, our use of the term ought to account for this range of meanings. Perhaps we can devise new historical categories by developing a greater sensitivity to the issues that engaged the artists, critics, collectors, and historians from the cultures we are studying. We must be careful, however, not to follow them blindly for, as Cutler has shown in Chapter 1 of this anthology, contemporaries can often be misguided by their own ideals; and furthermore, we can be misled by giving greater value to a few of the better-preserved texts while overlooking those that are less articulate, unpublished, or difficult to access. Even so, we will still be culturally relative, for the process of sifting and sorting past ideas is structured by our own contemporary categories and perceptions. But we can supplant the black-and-white illustrations and linear texts from which many of us learned art history by working to construct a rich, varied palette in a multilayered hypertext environment. This model gives equal primacy to images and text, thereby bringing us closer to the cognitive experience of perceiving images.

5.1   Gaudenzio Ferrari. *Christ on his Way to the Praetorium* (detail). Polychromed sculpture with other media. Varallo, Sacro Monte. (Photo: Riserva del Sacro Monte di Varallo.)

CHAPTER 5

"Popular" Art in Renaissance Italy:
Early Response to the Holy Mountain at Varallo

ALESSANDRO NOVA

The first Sacro Monte, or Holy Mountain, was founded in the late fifteenth century by the Franciscan Observant Bernardino Caimi. It was established at Varallo (Piedmont), which at that time formed part of the Milanese duchy, and the principal function of the Sacro Monte was to offer an accurate reconstruction of Jerusalem with its environs for those pilgrims who could not travel to the Holy Land. Indeed, an inscription painted over the entrance to Varallo's reproduction of the Holy Sepulchre, recording its completion in 1491, could not have been more explicit: "The Milanese friar Bernardino Caimi designed the sacred places of this mountain, so that those who cannot make the pilgrimage see Jerusalem here."[1] The original scheme was fairly modest, but the number of structures built to display the sculptural groups and frescoes representing Christ's life and Passion, as well as the life of the Virgin, increased considerably during the sixteenth century.

The Sacro Monte reached its apogee under the guidance of Charles Borromeo and his collaborators, who created a network of Sacri Monti in the region between the Lombard lakes and the Swiss border. The reasons for Varallo's later decline, however, were inherently connected to its particular, distinctive characteristics. Indeed, the strong realistic effects of some of the sculptures – such as the use of actual hair, beards, and clothes (Figure 5.1) – which became a hallmark of the Sacro Monte and which had been employed by both artists and patrons to elicit emotional responses from the original viewers, were subsequently regarded as over-dramatic and too "popular"; although what is meant by popular is never further described in the literature on the Sacro Monte.[2] The study of this unique creation, therefore, became the domain of local historians, who were often more interested in the Sacro Monte's devotional significance than in its artistic features.

In recent years, however, a number of erudite and scholarly publications have been devoted to the art of the Sacri Monti.[3] We are much better informed about the origins, histories, and functions of these unusual architectural complexes; and Varallo, the oldest as well as the most impressive Sacro Monte, has been extensively investigated. Yet some of the most compelling issues posed by this extraordinary monument of devotion have attracted little or no attention: first, the close rapport between the Milanese aristocracy and the founders of the Sacro Monte, that is the Franciscan Observants of the Milanese Province; second, the relationship between the friars' sermons and the works of art they commissioned to decorate the "chapels" built at Varallo; third, the way in which these sculptural groups were used by the friars to elicit specific responses from the original audience; finally, the social mix of that audience. All these themes are inextricably interlinked, and here they must be dealt with simultaneously even if, regrettably, in a summary way.

As André Vauchez has pointed out, we know little about the mendicant friars' social background.[4] If we analyze the role they played in fifteenth-century Italy, however, it becomes easier to determine their social origins and education; or at least this is the case with the Franciscan Observants of the Milanese Province. The power, influence, and prestige of these friars expanded dramatically during this period, in part as a result of the special interest in the region shown by the Order's leaders. After all, it was in Milan that St. Bernardino of Siena, the most important figure of the Osservanza movement, first attained popularity: there he delivered a highly successful cycle of Lenten sermons in 1418, and he returned to Lombardy many times.[5] Moreover, the region was frequently visited by other distinguished members of the Osservanza, such as John of Capistrano who preached in Milan in 1440–42.[6] The extent of their sermons' impact can be gauged by the number of Milanese aristocrats who joined the Observants. Among them was the blessed Michele Carcano, who was the successful advocate of public hospitals and of the Monti di Pietà.[7] Others included Bartolomeo Caimi, who specialized in the writing of confessions of faith (formal statements of doctrinal beliefs),[8] Bernardino Caimi, Francesco Trivulzio, and Bernardino de' Bustis, who devoted most of his life to the controversy over the Immaculate Conception.[9] Hence they formed a socially homogeneous group in which each member promoted a specific feature of the Observant program.

The Franciscan Observants are often depicted in the hagiographic literature as the good friars who championed a return to the Order's original ideals in opposition to the decadent and lax behavior of the Conventuals, but by the end of the fifteenth century these friars had acquired a very high social profile: the Observant leaders belonged to the local aristocracy, and they were so well connected with the court that they were also the confessors and spiritual advisors of the Milanese duchesses. The relationship between the Observants and the Milanese aristocracy is a point to which I shall return when I examine the heterogeneous nature of the public that visited the Varallo Sacro Monte. Before addressing this problem, however, it is necessary to discuss the friars' approach to preaching in connection with some of the best known Franciscan devotional tracts.

Preaching was always one of the central activities of the mendicant orders, but for the Franciscan Observants it became their fundamental mission. St. Bernardino himself stated that the sermon was more important than the Mass,[10] and his Lombard disciples also adopted this view. For instance, the church of Santa Maria delle Grazie at Varallo, which was founded at the foot of the Holy Mountain, as well as the other Observant churches of the Milanese Province, were especially designed for preaching.[11] They were usually divided into two clearly separated parts by a gigantic rood-screen wall, or *tramezzo*, which extended to the ceiling of the church. The main altar was placed in the choir reserved for the friars;[12] and even if the Mass could also be celebrated on one of the altars in the nave, where the lay congregation stood, the principal function of this public space

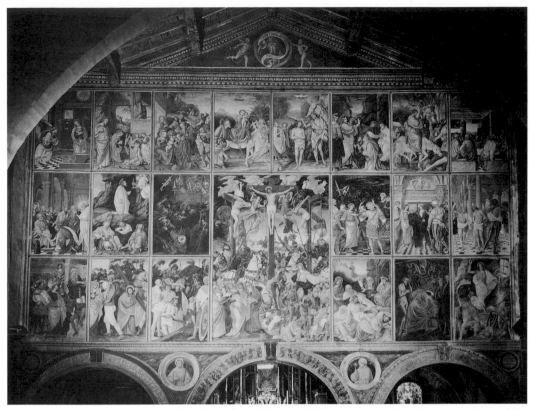

5.2   Gaudenzio Ferrari. *Scenes from the Life and Passion of Christ*. Fresco. Varallo, Santa Maria delle Grazie. (Photo: Riserva del Sacro Monte di Varallo.)

was signalled by the pulpit. From here the friars could deliver their sermons, and in this part of the church they could use the complex cycles frescoed on the rood-screen wall (Figure 5.2) to instruct listeners concerning Christ's life and Passion, from the Annunciation to the Resurrection. That such frescoes were used as didactic tools is confirmed by an extremely rare devotional tract which was published in Milan in 1514, only one year after the completion of the frescoes on Varallo's *tramezzo*.[13] The tract is entitled *These Are the Mysteries that Are on the Holy Mountain at Varallo*, and it was certainly written by an Observant friar, possibly Francesco da Marignano who took Caimi's place after his death. It is a description in forty-seven rhymed octaves of the original Sacro Monte; and this text is further evidence of the ongoing success enjoyed by the empathetic approaches employed in Franciscan devotional literature. The familiar exhortations to the pilgrim to participate in the suffering of Christ by weeping, beating himself or herself, and touching the simulacra are indeed numerous. But for the present argument it is more pertinent to observe that in this tract the pilgrim is instructed to stop at the Observant church before beginning his or her ascent of the Holy Mountain. This is because it was in the church that the pilgrim was "purged of all errors." It was in the church, where the friars preached, that the pilgrim was taught how to approach the journey to the new Jerusalem at Varallo in the correct frame of mind. And, last but not least, it was here that the pilgrim learned that what he or she was going to visit was only a reproduction of the Holy Land.

This public experience was then internalized during the ascent of the Holy Mountain, but when the pilgrims reached the summit they were not free to move around as they wished because they were restricted to guided tours of the holy places given by the friars. Guided tours were traditionally offered by the Franciscans who took care of the Sepulchre in Jerusalem, and the program at Varallo was so true to its model that even this aspect was accurately recreated: inevitably, therefore, the pilgrims' responses to the sacred mysteries of Christ's life and death were directed by the friars. Of course, any work of art is to a certain extent manipulative, but at Varallo the patrons were highly conscious of this aspect. Indeed, the guided tour to the "chapels" of the Sacro Monte was the culmination of the friars' sermons, and the holy places of the original Holy Mountain as created by Bernardino Caimi operated as a kind of visual translation of the sermons transcribed in his *Quadragesimale de articulis fidei* and *Quadragesimale de penitentia*.[14] These collections of sermons were begun around 1488, precisely when Caimi was planning his Sacro Monte, and they differ from otherwise similar productions in that they often quote verbatim long passages from two bestsellers of Franciscan devotional literature: the *Meditations on the Life of Christ* by the Pseudo-Bonaventure and the *Garden of Prayer* attributed to Nicolò da Osimo, who was also an Observant friar.[15]

The choice of such sources seems to imply that Caimi geared his sermons to what we would probably call an unsophisticated or vernacular audience – that is, a mixture of semi-literate lay people, untutored clergy, and the unlettered. And this is particularly interesting in view of the fact that the art of the Sacri Monti has also been classified by other scholars as "popular" because of its intimate as well as intensely emotional realism. Yet the social background of the people who visited Varallo was very heterogeneous: there is little doubt that most pilgrims belonged to the lower social strata, if for no other reason than because the Holy Mountain was explicitly designed for those who could not afford the journey to Jerusalem;[16] but it should not be forgotten that cardinals, members of the Milanese aristocracy, dukes, heads of state, and celebrated humanists did not disparage the simplicity of the Observants' Sacro Monte scheme. Of course, this social melting pot is a common feature of all pilgrimage sites. Here, however, I am concerned neither with the visitors' shared religious practices nor with their spiritual behavior *vis à vis* this peculiar recreation of the Holy Land. What I am trying to analyze, instead, is how the *different* strata of the original audience responded to the *same* veristic and allegedly "popular" or vernacular images. A crucial question therefore arises: how did the connection between verism and popular taste develop in the context of Franciscan patronage and devotion?

It seems to be generally agreed that the Franciscan preachers catered primarily to the masses and, since the classic book by Thode, scholars have often connected the Franciscans with the emergence of realistic tendencies in the art of the Italian Renaissance (i.e., a greater verisimilitude in the representation of the narrative).[17] But the single most important reason why the questions of Franciscan patronage, the vernacular audience, and realism have become part of the same interrelated issue is the emphasis placed by the Order's devotional tracts on the minutest details of everyday life in an attempt to elicit an empathetic response from their readers.

5.3 Gaudenzio Ferrari. *Nativity*. Polychromed sculpture with other media, 1520s. Varallo, Sacro Monte. (Photo: Riserva del Sacro Monte di Varallo.)

From the Franciscan Order's foundation, St. Francis himself had exploited the realistic dramatization of Christ's life, as is clearly shown by the episode of the Christmas crib at Greccio. And some of the earliest Franciscan writings, such as the *The Tree of Life* by St Bonaventure, the *Goad of Love* by James of Milan, and the *Meditations on the Life of Christ*, invited the reader to share in the sufferings of Christ's Passion. These texts are too well known to be discussed here. Yet it is important to remember that the reader was asked to participate in the events of Christ's life not as a spectator but as an actor. When Bonaventure discussed the Nativity (compare Figure 5.3), he encouraged the believer to press his lips upon the Infant's feet; and in the passages dedicated to the Adoration of the Magi and the Purification, the reader was asked to become a companion of the holy kings and to receive the baby Christ in his arms.[18] The Pseudo-Bonaventure expands upon this strategy. He writes: "Kiss the beautiful little feet of the infant Jesus who lies in the manger and beg His mother to offer to let you hold Him a while. Pick Him up and hold Him in your arms. Gaze on His face with devotion and reverently kiss Him and delight in Him."[19] Similar passages are quoted verbatim in Caimi's sermons, and it is therefore likely that what was suggested in the *Tree of Life* and the *Meditations* was realistically performed at Varallo: the Infant's feet were probably kissed by the pilgrims, and it is also possible that the visitors were allowed, not to say encouraged, to hold the statue in their arms.

In this tentative reconstruction of the response experienced by the original audience of the Sacro Monte, it is no less important to remember that a tacit contract between the friars and the pilgrims existed. The latter agreed to submit, as it were, to an empathetic treatment, while the friars guaranteed that what the pilgrims saw was a precise imitation of the Holy Land. Indeed, Caimi's sermons were replete with his own recollections of Jerusalem. He liked to remind his public that he had been the chief guardian of the Sepulchre and that he had shown the real thing to many pilgrims. Moreover, he claimed to be an entirely trustworthy source because he was an eyewitness: he could describe the holy places in the exact order in which he had visited them and, what was more important, he had recorded the exact distances between them.[20] Now, the accuracy in reproducing the topography of Jerusalem and its environs was the greatest innovation introduced at Varallo. More or less faithful copies of the Sepulchre had been built all over Europe well before the foundation of the Sacro Monte,[21] but the Holy Mountain at Varallo was the first attempt to reproduce the Holy Land topographically. And this leads us back to the *Meditations*, one of Caimi's main sources, and to the Franciscan obsession with numbers, dimensions, and distances.

According to the Pseudo-Bonaventure, "Mount Calvary . . . was as far from the gate of the city as our [monastery] is from the gate of Saint Germanus",[22] and he often states the exact distances between holy places. Relics are also precisely measured: as far as the height of the holy cross is concerned, the Pseudo-Bonaventure must rely on information provided by those who had visited Jerusalem, but he can personally guarantee that the table of the Last Supper is square and consists of several boards because he has seen it in Rome, in the Lateran church, where he has measured it.[23] Measurements are of course used as a certificate of authenticity: the Nativity, the Last Supper, the Crucifixion are true events which took place in real locations also because we can measure the manger, the table, and the cross. And to make his readers even more well disposed towards his message, the Pseudo-Bonaventure narrows the gap between them and the distant lands evoked in his narrative by referring to sites familiar to his audience. For example, when he describes how Mary and Joseph were accidentally separated from their Child, he writes: "Very early the next morning they left the house to look for Him in the neighborhood, for one could return by several roads; as he who returns from Siena to Pisa might travel by way of Poggibonsi or Colle or other places."[24]

Similar approaches were adopted in several Franciscan texts and by many Franciscan preachers. It is therefore not difficult to understand why these ingenuous references to the daily life of their audiences, combined with their taste for minute and familiar details, gave rise to the notion that the Franciscans catered to the masses rather than to members of the upper social strata. Likewise, it is easy to see why the strong veristic effects of the art of the Sacro Monte have been inevitably associated with the "realism" of Franciscan sermons and devotional tracts. In all these forms – art, literature, and preaching – we find the same ingredients: empathy and a penchant for the minutest details.

At Varallo these features go to extremes. Hair, beards, and moustaches are often made of horse-hair; some of the statues are dressed in real clothes; and the passion for verisimilitude is so profound that the food on the table of the Last Supper becomes a matter of concern – indeed, during one of the periodic inspections organized by the local bishops, it was strongly recommended that the traditional Easter dish of lamb "be made

5.4 *Christ and St. John the Evangelist* (detail of *The Last Supper*). Polychromed sculpture with other media. Varallo, Sacro Monte. (Photo: Riserva del Sacro Monte di Varallo.)

as if it were roasted" and that fruits which are not in season at Lent should be removed from the table.[25] So great a desire for accuracy seems to us misplaced when we look at the crude statues of Christ and the apostles (Figure 5.4). These are not statues in the traditional sense, but rather dummies covered with real linen draperies which were dipped in plaster to stiffen their folds; yet, to increase the realistic potential of the scene, the statues were made with moveable limbs so that they could be rearranged around the table according to changing circumstances. (However, I want to make clear that this is the only surviving example. The other wood and terracotta statues of the Sacro Monte did not move.)

The final touch of such a *tableau vivant* was probably provided by artificial illumination. Bernardino Caimi's sermons inform us that the Holy Sepulchre and the place where the body of Christ was anointed were perpetually illuminated by oil lamps.[26] It is therefore not implausible that Caimi planned a similar solution for his Lombard imitation, and we do know from two sources that the pilgrims who visited the Sacro Monte could also start their climb up the Holy Mountain at night.[27] The impact provoked by the wounds and scars of Christ's body on those members of the original audience who looked at this statue or at the other narratives of the Passion by candle- and torchlight must have been tremendous; and in this flickering light the statues might have given the impression of moving, of being almost alive (Figure 5.5).

Having said that, however, it is unlikely that this *mise-en-scène* was actually designed to deceive the eyes of the pilgrims. This view is supported by the fact that at Varallo the friars were very diligent in reminding their audience that the places that had been

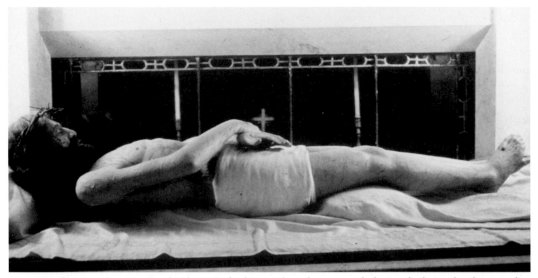

5.5   Gaudenzio Ferrari. *Dead Christ*. Polychromed sculpture with hair, cloth, and other media. Varallo, Sacro Monte. (Photo: Riserva del Sacro Monte di Varallo.)

recreated on the Holy Mountain were only replicas of the real thing. Perhaps this was due to a fear of idolatry but, whatever the reason, the Observants were extremely careful in their handling of this issue. For example, the large stone placed in a niche of the porch outside the Sepulchre is flanked by the following inscription: "This stone is *similar in every detail* to the stone slab which covers the tomb of Our Lord Jesus Christ in Jerusalem."[28] An analogous but now lost inscription was placed inside the chapel reproducing the tomb of the Virgin: "This holy sepulchre is *similar in every detail* to that built at the feet of the Mount of Olives where the body of the most Holy Virgin was buried."[29] The same preoccupation pervades the tract that I have already quoted which functioned as a sort of devotional guide to the pilgrims who visited Varallo in 1514. According to this source the Annunciation takes place in a "place similar to the real one"; the Nativity is staged in a "similar place"; the Adoration of the Magi is "similar"; the Circumcision is in a "similar place"; the Sepulchre is a "holy place similar to the real one"; in the portico outside the Sepulchre is the aforementioned tomb slab which is "similar" to the real one in Jerusalem; and the chapel dedicated to the Ascension of Christ contains a footprint similar to the marble relic preserved on the Mount of Olives.[30] It is therefore obvious that Varallo was purely a reproduction of the real thing, even if a very accurate one. One could argue that the friars were overstating their claims because in Jerusalem there were neither statues nor frescoes, but the 1514 guide to the Sacro Monte makes it clear that the illustrated mysteries were meant to stimulate the viewers' imaginations. This was not a new trend in Franciscan devotional texts. In his *Tree of Life* Bonaventure had already stated that "imagination aids understanding."[31] And the author of the *Meditations on the Life of Christ* had also stressed the role played by imagination in the learning of the Holy Scriptures: "For the sake of greater impressiveness I shall tell [the events of Christ's life] to you as they occurred or as they *might have occurred* according to the devout belief of the imagination and the varying interpretation of the mind."[32] The realistic descriptions which greatly contributed to the enormous popularity of the *Meditations* must be read in the context of these words in the introduction to the book. The reality effect is not the result of a minute description of the events as they *actually* occurred,[33] because this is neither possible nor desirable, but is the product of an interaction between this didactic approach and the efforts of the imagination in the service of faith and contemplation.

The same applies to Varallo: the emphasis placed by current scholarship upon the apparently extreme, sometimes grotesque realism of its images as evidence of its catering primarily to "popular", in the sense of unsophisticated, audiences, misses the main point. The secret of the Sacro Monte's success among widely differing strata of Lombard Renaissance society is not merely in the verisimilitude of its representations, but in the *tension* created between the patrons' desire to reproduce the events narrated in the Gospels and the viewers' imaginative participation in these events. The allegedly exact imitation of Jerusalem's topography, of the distances between the holy places, of precise measurements, as well as the realism of familiar anecdotes, hair, beards, and clothes, entail an inherent tension, based on an acute awareness that this is only a replica concocted to stimulate a contemplative frame of mind in the pilgrims. And this tension helps explain how the *same* vernacular images could affect a very *diversified* public.

Works of art can be inspired by but are eminently different from sermons. Language is flexible and a good preacher can adjust the register of his discourse to different as well as to mixed audiences; but the narratives reproduced at Varallo could not change to meet the different tastes of their viewers. What could change, however, was the response of the public, and this was perfectly understood by the friars who guided the tour of the Sacro Monte and encouraged the pilgrims to supplement the veristic narratives with their own imagination; in other words, the impact of these images varied according to the viewers' culture and education, because it was the involvement of the spectator that completed the reality effect.

We should remember that the art of the Sacro Monte is still all too frequently discussed in its post-sixteenth-century morphology after drastic alterations had been introduced. For example, in one of the projects designed by Galeazzo Alessi (Figure 5.6) to transform one of the original structures into a centralized building with a classical portico – a project which was later implemented – the purpose of the elaborate grilles was to keep the pilgrims outside the chapels and increase the effect of distance.[34]

This was a deliberate rejection of the purpose of the original structures, which pilgrims had been encouraged to enter and experience more directly. In the "chapel" of the Magi, for instance, the spectator had been intentionally caught between two spaces and hence could not help becoming part of the action. In exactly the same way, of course, was the reader of Bonaventure's *Tree of Life* encouraged "to become a companion of the holy kings."[35]

It was in the *tableau vivant* of *Crucifixion*, executed by Gaudenzio Ferrari in the 1520s, that the empathetic strategies were most consistently and successfully exploited (Figure 5.7).[36] On the wall opposite the Golgotha are frescoed groups of onlookers who were not originally visible from the exterior of the chapel, and this suggests that the pilgrims originally entered from the door on the right, stopped in front of the cross, where they were surrounded on all sides by carved as well as painted figures, and finally went out through the door on the left. Like the reader of the *Meditations on the Life of Christ*,

5.6 (right) Galeazzo Alessi. *Design for the Chapel of Adam and Eve*. Pen and ink with wash. Varallo, Biblioteca Civica. (Photo: Riserva del Sacro Monte di Varallo.)

5.7 (below) Gaudenzio Ferrari. *Crucifixion* (detail). Polychromed sculpture with other media, 1520s. Varallo, Sacro Monte. (Photo: Riserva del Sacro Monte di Varallo.)

therefore, the viewer of Varallo was not a spectator but an actor–participant.[37] Similar comprehensive experiences are also described in the 1514 tract: for example, the "chapel" dedicated to the Apparition to the apostles displayed a statue of Christ, with open arms, surrounded by the figures of His disciples frescoed on the wall of this circular structure; and the pilgrim was encouraged to place himself or herself between the simulacrum and the paintings, thus becoming physically as well as emotionally part of the action.[38] This performance engaged most of the viewers' senses: not only sight, but also hearing and touch. Understandably enough, art historians tend to concentrate their analysis on the visual evidence. Yet the narratives of the Sacro Monte elicited a response from the members of many different social strata because they also affected the spectators' other sense organs.

For example, as the pilgrims looked at the narratives, they were encouraged by the friars to recite the most familiar prayers, such as the Our Father and the Creed. And it is possible that the Observants did not reject such practices as those recommended to the Benedictine monks of the Congregation of Santa Giustina by Ludovico Barbo in his *Forma orationis et meditationis* of 1441. For the meditation of Good Friday, Barbo advised the monks to become completely absorbed in the events immediately preceding the erection of the cross in this way: "imagine that you hear the sound of the hammers used to crucify your Lord."[39] In other words, not only the mental image of Christ being nailed to the cross, but also the imaginary sound of the nails piercing His flesh must be used to stimulate the Christian's appropriate emotional response. And it was not only an appeal to the auditory sense: references to weeping and crying in Franciscan devotional texts are innumerable. Space permits me to mention only the many vernacular translations of the *Meditations on the Life of Christ* published in Milan during the 1480s and 1490s, as well as the 1514 devotional tract, all of which repeatedly insist that the reader lament the sufferings of the Lord. Finally, the sense of touch should not be forgotten. At Varallo the pilgrims were encouraged to touch the facsimile tomb of Christ or other relics. For instance, those who touched the replica of Christ's footprint in the chapel of the Ascension were granted a plenary indulgence. It is not difficult to see how such a complex ritual, in which the verism of the narratives, combined with total viewer participation, could appeal to many different types of audience. The works of art that the friars commissioned were not as flexible as their sermons, but the level of the spectator–actor's involvement could be adjusted according to his or her religious feelings and education.

In the foregoing, I have attempted to reconstruct the way in which the pilgrims' responses to the Sacro Monte narratives were directed, although, as we have seen, not entirely preordained by the friars. Naturally, however, it would be useful to possess some written evidence as to the response elicited by Varallo. Fortunately, one such document exists, and it is an invaluable source which records the impressions of an unusually sophisticated visitor.

In September 1507 the humanist Girolamo Morone traveled to this region as the ambassador of the king of France; and, notwithstanding his busy diplomatic agenda, he did not overlook the opportunity of visiting the Sacro Monte. Like many Franciscan Observants, Morone also belonged to one of the oldest and most aristocratic Milanese families. Well known to Machiavelli and Guicciardini, he was one of the most interesting political figures of his time. He was in contact with numerous humanists, and his Latin orations are often praised by modern scholars for their stylish elegance. Morone also wrote extremely polished letters in Latin, and in one of these, written in 1507 and addressed to the poet Lancino Curzio, he informed his friend about his profoundly moving experience of the Sacro Monte at Varallo.[40] Before examining this document, however, it is necessary to say something about the artistic tastes of these two remarkable personalities, because – as we shall see – Morone was concerned with the formal aspects of the Holy Mountain.

Curzio, who is often mentioned in Matteo Bandello's short stories, was a bizarre figure. He roamed the streets of Milan dressed in a Roman toga and kept his hair long as a sign of his opposition to the French invaders, who had imposed a different fashion. His poems were profoundly influenced by Virgil, and his tomb, which was designed by Bambaia, reveals all the qualities of Lombard classicism. He was well acquainted with the most important artists of the time, such as Leonardo, Boltraffio, and Cristoforo Solari, all of whom are mentioned in his works. Moreover, we know that Curzio was also in contact with Andrea Solario since he provided the elegant Latin inscription which is at the bottom of the portrait of Cristoforo Longoni.[41] Solario, who was one of the most important followers of Leonardo, also painted the portrait of Morone (Figure 5.8).[42] And what we know about Morone's artistic patronage is sufficient to reassure us that he had impeccable taste: when he was appointed Great Chancellor by the last Sforza duke, he wasted no time in hiring Bramantino as court painter and architect.[43]

From these sparse notes about their milieu, education, careers, and patronage, it is obvious that Morone and Curzio were perfectly well aware of the best artistic achievement in Renaissance Milan. Yet Morone's letter reveals how deeply he was affected by his visit to the Sacro Monte. He writes: "because of the difficulties and dangers endured by the pilgrims who visit Mount Calvary in Jerusalem, the Franciscans have built in Varallo a copy of the Holy Sepulchre. The events of the Gospels are represented in many chapels into which I was introduced by a pious friar who has seen the place where the real body of Christ is buried. And my guide told me that the distances between these chapels and the structures in which the events are reproduced correspond exactly to the originals. Oh Lancino, I never saw anything more pious or devout; anything that can move the heart in the same way. On this Holy Mountain one is compelled to follow only Christ and to forget about everything else. Everything you see here is superior to all antiquity."[44]

These are strong words in the mouth of a person who was educated in the worship of classical culture; but they illustrate in a very clear way how Varallo's simple images could affect the perception of a sophisticated viewer. It is at this point that I would like to return to the first issue I raised in this paper – that is, the close relationship between the Milanese aristocracy and the Franciscan Observants who founded the Sacro Monte. Varallo is often described as a product of the people's devotional feelings, but this means neither that it was created by them nor that it was exclusively "consumed" by them. On the contrary, as all pilgrimage sites attract a mixed audience, and since a trip from Milan to Varallo took only one or two days,[45] the Holy Mountain was visited by many distinguished personalities during the sixteenth century: by writers such as Morone, Matteo Bandello, and Agostino Gallo; by painters like Lomazzo and Federico Zuccaro;

5.8 Andrea Solario. *Portrait of Girolamo Morone*. Milan, Gallarati-Scotti Collection. (Photo: Alinari.)

by saints and cardinals such as Charles Borromeo, Angela Merici, and Alessandro Crivelli; and by many members of the nobility, for example, Francesco Sforza II and Charles Emanuel of Savoy. Yet it is even more important that the chapels themselves were often financed by local as well as Milanese aristocratic families.

On the basis of what I have said so far, it is obvious that one of my main objectives is to demonstrate that the sculptures of the Sacro Monte were commissioned by discriminating patrons for a mixed audience which included the best educated members of the Milanese society of the time. But this does not mean that some members of the original audience were unaware of the fact that the Sacro Monte's earliest statues, such as the Christ and the apostles of the Last Supper or the figures of the Lamentation which have been recently attributed to the De Donati brothers,[46] belonged to a material culture. This may sound a modern and rather abstract art historical evaluation, but in fact it was the opinion of Girolamo Morone. At the end of his 1507 letter to Lancino Curzio, and after having recounted his moving experience of the Sacro Monte, he adds: "the very simplicity of this enterprise, this structure with no art, and the noble site are superior to all antiquity."[47] The Milanese humanist was moved to tears as a Christian by Caimi's project, so much so that he repeated his pilgrimage three or four times, but he was perfectly aware of the fact that the narratives seen at Varallo did not meet the standards of similar works of art produced by north Italian sculptors. Yet the images of the Sacro Monte could still affect the response of different viewers because the reality effect was completed by the spectator's imagination in the comprehensive theatrical performance set up by the friars.

To conclude, the early history of Varallo's Sacro Monte confirms that when it came to sharing the religious practices of their community, literate and illiterate people were indistinguishable; and that, in the socially mixed environment of a pilgrimage site, the image representing Christ's Passion could arouse intense emotional reactions in any viewer independent of those images' formal merits. Morone's letter, however, makes it clear that a sophisticated visitor would have found these works unsatisfactory from a purely artistic point of view. It is always dangerous to draw broad conclusions from the evidence given by one source, but Morone's letter seems to indicate an awareness of the emerging category of "art" or of "artistic quality" in the modern sense of the term. The same work, therefore, can have a different historical significance if examined from the point of view of the history of style or if analyzed from the point of view of response. Varallo's *sermo humilis*[48] may not have pleased the taste of every viewer but it documents an important aspect of late medieval–early modern religious practices.

CHAPTER 6

Art Theory as Ideology: Gabriele Paleotti's Hierarchical Notion of Painting's Universality and Reception

PAMELA M. JONES

Gabriele Paleotti (1522–97), the Roman Catholic zealot and bishop of Bologna, wrote his *Discorso intorno alle imagini sacre e profane/Discourse on Sacred and Profane Images* of 1582 in response to the Council of Trent's decree that bishops oversee the production of Christian art in their dioceses. In 1584 Paleotti's instructional guide was published in a Latin edition to address a pan-European readership.[1] A discussion of Paleotti's *Discorso* is therefore a fitting place to introduce major issues of post-Tridentine art theory.[2] In this paper, we will uncover the hierarchical world view that Paleotti's discussion of universality and reception presupposes. It will emerge that Paleotti's world view has philosophical and sociological implications of fundamental importance for the subject of this book: the encounter between the "Old and New Worlds."

Paleotti's Claim for the Universality of Sacred Art

Because Paleotti's conception of reception was formulated in terms of painting's role as a universal language, it is necessary to summarize his position on universality. Roman Catholic apologists for art had insisted from early Christian times onward that painting was a universal language, and Paleotti's defense in the *Discorso* drew on this tradition. The notion of painting's universality was, of course, deeply embedded in theology, for Christ, the new Adam, was the "image" of God.[3] To Paleotti, the universality of man-made images was also inextricably tied to the way man perceived art and expressed himself through it. Indeed, according to Paleotti, God gave man the ability to create images to aid his natural desire to know and to represent the similitude of things both material and spiritual. Paleotti further remarked that imitation is the soul of painting, and among God's creatures only man is able to imitate.[4] For these reasons sacred art was essential to man's wellbeing, as Paleotti indicated in the *Discorso*:

> Heretics have denied the efficacy of images. To prohibit their use would be to commit a serious injustice against infinite numbers of people, and perhaps against the majority of the Christian populace, not only because it would constitute depriving them of their sensual ability to gain knowledge [*cognizione*] of necessary things, but also because the

knowledge necessary for the health of the soul would be inaccessible to countless unfortunate illiterates.[5]

Discussions of man's cognitive abilities found in Aristotle's *De Anima* and *Poetics* and Thomas Aquinas's *Summa Theologiae* were the general basis for Paleotti's understanding of human knowledge, including his remark that knowledge begins with the senses.[6] In effect, Paleotti turned Aristotle's statement that "the soul never thinks without an image" inside out and asked whether or not an image (here physical rather than mental) can be counted on to elicit the desired efficacious thought or emotions.[7] Also standard fare was Paleotti's conception of a hierarchy of senses through which knowledge was acquired. Roman Catholics, in contradistinction to Protestants, believed that the eye – not the ear – was the primary cognitive organ because God had given man eyes so that he could look at created things of the world, which were easily seen, as well as at celestial things, which were more difficult to see, and thereby penetrate the significance of God's universe.[8] By contrast, as Paleotti noted in the *Discorso*, the ear was an inferior cognitive organ because the voice was personal, serving merely in a few places at a few times.[9] It was not always possible to obtain words of explanation, and even when it was, auditory sensation had less longevity than visual; images, rather than words, imprinted information on one's memory for a longer time.[10]

Words, of course, were often written and thus visible to the eye. Yet to understand a book, Paleotti maintained, one must understand the language and the author and have the ability and opportunity to learn.[11] Following the lead of numerous iconophiles before him, Paleotti stated that whereas words have limited efficacy, paintings speak a universal language comprehensible to all kinds of persons everywhere: men and women, young and old, learned and ignorant.[12]

Paleotti's orthodox Roman Catholic position – that painting was a universal language – confirmed the power of art. In 1563 the Council of Trent had entrusted bishops with supervising the creation and use of sacred art in their dioceses in hopes that bishops could channel art's power in a positive direction.[13] In response, Paleotti treated in the second book of the *Discorso* every imaginable abuse of both sacred and profane art. These abuses included, for example, the use of heretical and apocryphal subject matter, the depiction of false gods and lascivious figures, and the lack of decorum in general.[14] In a nutshell, Paleotti's purpose in writing the *Discorso* was to ensure that sacred and profane art would move viewers away from vice and towards virtue and the knowledge of God.[15]

Star-gazing, the Viewing Process

Paleotti's explicit description of the viewing process – which has direct bearing on reception – is a remarkable feature of his *Discorso*. He dealt with the viewing process in the context of a discussion of the ends and means of sacred painting. The ultimate end of painting, he declared, is to imitate something in order to persuade persons to practice piety and to direct them to God. Like sacred oratory, sacred painting also has more specific ends, such as moving Christians to penitence, voluntary suffering, charity, disdain for the world, and the obedience and awe they owe God.[16] His detailed description of the viewing process occurs in Book 1, Chapter 22, which is devoted to delight. Remarkably, Paleotti's delight is not aesthetic in character, for he was not interested in artistic style; instead, he regarded delight as part of a hierarchical cognitive process:

> Mankind's knowledge [*cognizione*] is of three sorts: the first is sensual [*animale*], which is had by means of the senses – tasting, smelling, touching, etc.; the other is rational [*razionale*], which, if it also originates in the senses, passes by means of reason and discourse to a higher level and distinguishes universal abstract things from every material thing; the third is supernatural [*sopranaturale*], being born from a divine light infused in us by means of faith, through which we believe and know things that exceed not only the capacity of the senses, but also every human discourse and rational intelligence. We call this spiritual cognition [*cognizione spirituale*], which was given to earthly and innocent souls by the singular grace of God.[17]

Paleotti explained the ascent to knowledge that this visual learning process entailed by describing how a man could look at a starry sky at night. Each level of cognition, Paleotti stated, had its accompanying level of delight, so that if someone looked up at the sky and appreciated in it the beauty of its colors and of its sparkling stars, he experienced sensual knowledge with its concomitant sensual delight. If the same man then began to converse and reason about the relative size of each star, the changeability of the heavens, and the course of the planets and their effects on earthly things, he reached the higher level of rational knowledge with its accompanying delight. The star-gazer would reach the highest level, that of supernatural knowledge with its corresponding spiritual delight, only if – under divine inspiration – he considered how God, in his great providence and wisdom, wanted by means of created things to provide human beings with a staircase by which to ascend to the celestial realm of eternal bliss. Finally, Paleotti noted, because Christian joy could be derived equally from each of the three kinds of delight, Christian law approved of all three.[18] In essence, the three levels of Paleotti's hierarchical cognitive process can be associated with the three rhetorical means: delight, instruction, and moving.[19]

Paleotti went on to apply the relevance of this cognitive process to the act of viewing art. Human beings received sensual delight, that is, "marvelous pleasure and recreation," from "the variety of [paintings'] colors, shadows, figures, and ornaments, and the diverse things represented in them – such as mountains, rivers, gardens, cities, landscapes, and other things."[20] He associated rational delight with imitation in painting:

> Aristotle wrote in the *Poetics* that since man alone among all the other animals was born to imitate, by instinct he derives very great delight and pleasure from imitation. Imitation seems to have been born of the virtue of reason, which is peculiar to man . . . And this imitation, which is so obvious in painting, causes delight. It immediately renders present to man things that are far away. And in the manner of the omnipotent hand of God and of nature, his minister, paintings bring to life in a moment men, animals, plants, rivers, palaces, churches, and all the same works that are seen in this great machine of the world . . . Thus, the more closely paintings imitate life and truth . . . , the more . . . rational delight they carry.[21]

6.1 Agnolo Bronzino.
Martyrdom of St. Lawrence.
Fresco, 1569. Florence, San
Lorenzo. (Photo: Alinari/Art
Resource, New York.)

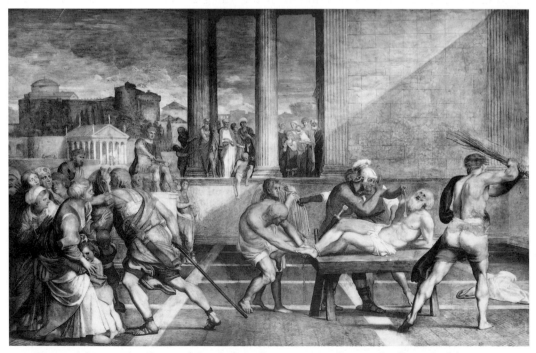

6.2 Domenichino. *Flagellation of St. Andrew.* Fresco, 1609. Rome, S. Gregorio Magno.

Paleotti was not explicit about how one might achieve the most difficult level of spiritual cognition and delight by looking at a painting. He simply stated that pious images helped beholders to achieve this level of cognition, concluding that "we do not doubt that a person who will look at Christian paintings *with purged eyes* [*con occhio purgato*] will be able to participate in all of these delights."[22]

We can illustrate these points with works of art.[23] Paleotti's own discussion made no use of specific artworks because – as surviving indices of the *Discorso* indicate – he planned to discuss individual artists and themes in Books 3–5, which he apparently never wrote.[24] In order to understand Paleotti's attitude towards the viewing process, we will first discuss a painting of the *maniera* style, which was prevalent throughout Europe in the late sixteenth century. A reaction against this style no doubt prompted the objections found in both Paleotti's *Discorso* and the Council of Trent's decree on images to confusing, indecorous art.[25] As an example of *maniera* art we use Agnolo Bronzino's famous *Martyrdom of St. Lawrence* of 1569 (Figure 6.1), a fresco in San Lorenzo at Florence.[26]

Bronzino's *Martyrdom* depicts St Lawrence's gruesome death on a gridiron at the hands of the pagan Romans. If Paleotti had seen Bronzino's painting he would have considered it confusing, for the saint is difficult to find and, once found, to keep one's eyes on, due to the over-abundance of distracting ornament: complicated poses of nude (read "lascivious") figures, an elaborate perspectival schema, and wild gesticulations that do not lucidly convey emotions inherent to the narrative. In short, Paleotti would have found Bronzino's image indecorous because its pictorial embellishment is inessential or, in Augustinian terms, its ornament is merely superficial.[27]

Further light can be shed on Paleotti's theory of art by considering Bronzino's painting in connection with Paleotti's description of the star-gazer in the *Discorso*. It is implicit that Bronzino's *Martyrdom of St. Lawrence* would not lead the viewer to sensual cognition. This is because sensual cognition was dependent on appreciation of a painting's beauty, variety of colors, effects of light, and the variety of its figures and ornaments. Accordingly, the hard, dry style and lack of tonal range (typical of *maniera* style) of Bronzino's painting do not qualify as effective sensory stimulants. And, although Bronzino's painting is full of varied figures and ornaments, surely they contribute to its lack of verisimilitude; that is, the painting's contorted poses, exaggerated gestures, lack of convincing emotional reactions, and so forth, would also prevent the viewer from achieving rational cognition, which Paleotti associated with the close imitation of "life and truth."[28] Thus, to Paleotti, works similar to Bronzino's painting would not be considered efficacious because, lacking the ingredients that promoted sensual and rational cognition, the viewer could not use them to reach spiritual cognition either.

Let us now turn to another well-known depiction of martyrdom, this one painted more than a decade after Paleotti's death: Domenichino's *Flagellation of St. Andrew* of 1609 (Figure 6.2), a fresco in the Oratorio of S. Andrea, San Gregorio Magno at Rome.[29] According to Paleotti's description of the viewing process, Domenichino's painting would indeed lead the beholder to sensual cognition on account of its variety of figures, colors, and shadows; moreover, its imitation of life and truth – seen, for example, in its uncontorted poses, decorous emotions, and convincing spatial relationships – would lead the viewer to rational cognition as well. At that point, the viewer might use it to go on to achieve spiritual cognition.

Although Paleotti was not explicit about how spiritual cognition could be achieved, he remarked that to rise to that level a viewer would need to look at Christian paintings "with purged eyes." Paleotti's use of this phrase surely indicates that he was assuming his viewers to be Roman Catholics. It is likely that these hypothetical viewers were not only the same persons for whom Paleotti wrote the *Discorso* itself – that is, artists and clerical and lay patrons who practiced Roman Catholicism according to the norms established in his diocese – but also the unlettered masses who could benefit from looking at decorous Christian art.[30] More specifically, the *spirituali*, whom Paleotti identified in the *Discorso* as viewers more devoted to spiritual than to material things, certainly qualify as viewers endowed with purged eyes.[31]

The Reception of Sacred and Profane Painting

As we have seen, Paleotti promoted the Church's position that painting is a uniquely powerful universal language. It is hardly surprising, therefore, that Book 2 of the *Discorso*, dedicated to abuses in art, constitutes an attempt to control the messages that sacred and profane art impress on the viewer's memory. Because Paleotti treated the reception of various pictorial subjects chiefly in Book 2 of the *Discorso*, some introductory remarks about this portion of the tract are needed. First, Book 2 does not address such matters as detailed iconographical points, abuses seen in specific individual paintings, and the appropriate ways to decorate various kinds of buildings with works of art; as previously noted, Paleotti intended to discuss these and other topics in subsequent books. Thus, although Book 2 treats abuses in excruciating detail, it cannot be said to introduce all of Paleotti's ideas about reception. This helps explain why some of his points are not fully developed therein. Second, Paleotti's *Discorso* is ambiguous, repetitive, and prolix. If Book 2 of the *Discorso* offers much food for thought, it is by no means easily digestible.

Finally, Paleotti's lack of sensitivity towards artistic style – a distinctive feature of the *Discorso* as a whole – deserves mention because it is incongruous in a tract devoted to art. We have seen that Paleotti's interest in painting lay principally in its power to move viewers. Thus it is surprising that, although he conceived of different kinds of viewers, Paleotti did not conceive of different styles geared to their needs; he did not, for example, adapt the plain, middle, and high styles of ancient rhetoric to his art theory. Not only did Paleotti lack interest in the ways in which individual stylistic features might be exploited to achieve desired rhetorical effects in given pictorial subjects and genres, but he also regarded painters as mere craftsmen who tended to deviate from the architect's definitive plan rather than as men whose creative intellects could be tapped for the benefit of the faithful.[32]

For our purposes, one of the most important aspects of Book 2 of the *Discorso* is that in it Paleotti classified and discussed paintings not according to genre, as one might expect, but rather according to their ends.[33] For example, in individual chapters Paleotti denounced sacred images that he deemed "reckless, scandalous, erroneous, suspect, heretical, superstitious, and apocryphal."[34] These unacceptable sacred paintings could result, for instance, from unwitting errors or deliberate heresy on the part of the patron and/or painter or from the painter's lack of understanding of the subject at hand. To avoid the latter problem Paleotti advised the painter to seek the knowledge of wise men (*uomini savii*).[35] In any case, sacred paintings containing abuses had uniformly negative effects on all beholders, whereas those that were appropriately rendered benefited all beholders.

Paleotti designated as examples of profane art subjects including those that depict evil, thereby inciting beholders to evil; those that treat acts of virtue, thereby inciting them to good; and "indifferent" images which, depending on the nature of the given beholder, could be either beneficial or useless. In other words, some profane subjects were efficacious and others were not. Many further individual abuses were defined and described under the rubric of their ends – including those shared by both sacred and profane paintings, such as the contradiction of truth and of probability.[36] In short, Paleotti's treatment of reception in Book 2 shows that he conceived of the usefulness of a given painting – sacred or profane – as depending on a dynamic, tripartite interchange among the painting, painter, and beholder based on the inherent utility of the image's subject, the degree of accuracy and decorum with which the artist rendered it, and the predisposition of its beholder.[37]

When it was the subject *per se* that undermined the success of this dynamic interchange, Paleotti's mission of purifying art was quite straightforward. In the case of an image of an evil deed, which necessarily incites evil, it is the bishop's duty to make it clear to patrons and artists that the evil subject must not be represented. This was Paleotti's reason for explaining the unacceptability of so many pictorial subjects.

In other cases it was not the subject itself but rather the artist's inappropriate treatment of it that rendered an image inefficacious. Paleotti regarded such abuses – including but not limited to theological and historical mistakes and depiction of saints as lascivious – as breaches of truth and decorum.[38] We have already discussed an example of indecorum in connection with *maniera* art as represented by Bronzino's *Martyrdom of St Lawrence* (Figure 6.1). Here the subject of martyrdom is inherently useful but, as previously noted, Paleotti presumably would have regarded Bronzino's pictorial embellishment of the subject as superficial rather than substantive. Furthermore, in discussing other subjects Paleotti suggested that in order to learn, "ordinary" viewers needed visual stimulants more than did the educated few, yet "ordinary" viewers were paradoxically quite likely to be beguiled by superficial pictorial ornament. This is why superficial ornament and confusing compositions were so detrimental. It is worth noting that although his discussion involved artistic style, Paleotti avoided detailed analysis of it; his notion of the artist's role in the dynamic interchange was rather one-dimensional.

The Viewer

Having discussed subject matter and also the painter, let us now focus on the viewer. In the star-gazer passage Paleotti described three levels of delight and knowledge – sensual, rational, and spiritual – and pointed out that all three were acceptable. But he provided no clue as to the social or intellectual identity of the star-gazer. And when Paleotti went on to describe the hierarchical cognitive process in connection with viewing paintings, his most specific remark about the beholder's identity was that a beholder with "purged eyes" could attain spiritual cognition. To investigate further how Paleotti defined the audience for sacred and profane art we must study other chapters in Book 2 of the *Discorso*.

Paleotti's most detailed discussion of the audience for art in his diocese appears in the final or fifty-second chapter of Book 2. In this chapter he stated that a Christian image is universal if it satisfies four grades or professions (*gradi o professioni*) of persons: painters, educated persons, uneducated persons, and baptized Christians who are more devoted to the spirit than the flesh (*pittori, letterati, idioti,* and *spirituali*).[39] Paleotti added that it was morally useful to apply to the conceit of universal painting the psalm that David used to teach the people (*il popolo*) how to observe the cult of God. Accordingly, *confessio, pulchritudo, sanctimonia,* and *magnificentia* (confession, beauty, holiness, and magnificence), the words David used in Psalm 96:6, should be regarded as the four principal characteristics of sacred painting. Paleotti explained these characteristics in order to distinguish more thoroughly between the four kinds of viewers he listed.

To Paleotti, *confessio* (or confession) corresponded to *disegno*, which painters called the soul of painting or its principal part.[40] Because the artist must master *disegno* (design, in the sense of both intellectual and manual creation) in order to produce acceptable works, *confessio* was the domain of painters and appealed to them. *Pulchritudo* concerned the loveliness of the painting's colors, its grace and beauty; Paleotti declared that such features, perceived through the senses, for the most part satisfy uneducated beholders. These uneducated beholders, the *idioti*, comprise the largest part of the people, and sacred painting was mainly introduced to serve them. In several chapters Paleotti suggested that, to be successful, a painting must correspond to the relatively low intellectual capacity of the uneducated majority. It must either be so clear and well composed that an uneducated person can recognize its subject immediately or be expressed in such a way that persons of greater intelligence can easily instruct the uneducated about it. In the context of artistic style it is important that Paleotti wanted paintings to be clearly composed and highly finished, but let us not overlook the reason for this, which is based on reception: Paleotti deemed clear presentation necessary because the vast majority of viewers were uneducated, sensually inclined, and less intelligent than the educated few.[41] This notion, which runs like a leitmotif throughout the *Discorso*, cannot be over-emphasized. Indeed, it begs revision of Anton Boschloo's implicit characterization of Paleotti as a benevolent populist eager to promote art for the masses.[42]

To return to Paleotti's discussion of Psalm 96:6, he explained that *magnificentia* in painting appeals to educated beholders and persons of high intellect (*letterati* and *persone d'alto intelletto*), who are knowledgeable in the subjects represented in the images, such as ecclesiastical material, secular history, or natural and/or artificial things. It is not enough to create beautiful works on the basis of good *disegno*; artists' works must correspond to the experts' knowledge of the subjects being represented.

According to Paleotti, all baptized Christians embraced *sanctimonia*, or holiness. Man is made of spirit and flesh and, since flesh is heaviest, most Christians, the *sensuali*, are mired in earthly things. Far fewer in number are the *spirituali*, those primarily concerned with spiritual matters. Sacred painting, continued Paleotti, is devoted mainly to the spirit. When viewing sacred paintings, the *spirituali* consequently recognize compositions proportioned to themselves and take pleasure, whereas the *sensuali* recognize compositions dissimilar to themselves and atone.

This discussion of viewers in Book 2, Chapter 52 leads us to expect a similarly detailed treatment of reception throughout the *Discorso*. But this is not, in fact, what Paleotti gives us. Often, as in the passage on the star-gazer, Paleotti failed to distinguish what kind of viewer he was discussing. Nevertheless, Paleotti's discussion of the four kinds of beholders, if summarized according to these salient points, sheds light on less explicit portions of his tract: all viewers with whom Paleotti is concerned are Christians; most of these viewers are uneducated but a few are learned; the uneducated viewers are more sensually inclined and less intelligent than the learned; most viewers are weighted down by cares of the flesh but a few are *spirituali*. Notwithstanding this fourfold classification of beholders in the concluding chapter of Book 2, throughout the rest of the *Discorso* Paleotti consistently emphasized *two*, not four, classes of beholder: the educated and the uneducated.[43]

With these points in mind, we can consider parts of the *Discorso* in which Paleotti discussed the reception of paintings of nature themes. In Chapter 24 of Book 2 entitled "On Profane Paintings Representing Various Things, Such as Wars, Landscapes, Buildings, Animals, Trees, Plants, and the Like," Paleotti distinguished nature themes as subjects that had no inherent virtue but could nevertheless lead to the exercise of virtue. Then, in Chapter 30, entitled "On Vain and Lazy Paintings" – that is to say, those that are indifferent – Paleotti pointed out that nature themes did not necessarily belong in that category. He then explained the appropriateness of such works to different kinds of viewers:

> We know well that although many things may appear to be indifferent, some persons will be able to derive use from them, while others will derive from them nothing but damage. This is due to both the disposition of him who uses the things and the diversity of the ends that the things put forward . . . Thus, one cannot say absolutely that all of these paintings [of nature themes] are useless to all kinds of persons . . . because *he who is endowed with spirit and judgment* can derive great philosophy [even] from birds and fish and flowers and rocks . . . In fact, to this end all created things of this world are visible to our eyes, so that, by means of them, we may enter into knowledge [*cognizione*] and desire of eternal things, which are invisible.
>
> Still, because few are they who can ascend to this [metaphysical] speculation, we, *speaking for the ordinary man* [*l'ordinario*], call paintings good and suitable those that by their nature and propriety represent to us praiseworthy and beneficial things to know for use in human life.[44]

Paleotti made it quite clear that paintings of nature themes could elicit dramatically different responses from beholders. The difference in these beholders was that those "endowed with spirit and judgment" were acquainted with metaphysics whereas "ordinary" persons were not. In short, Paleotti asserted in this passage that the ability to achieve the full benefits from a profane image depended partly on the viewer's predisposition and partly on the subject's efficacy and the artist's use of decorum, for it would be possible for a viewer unfamiliar with metaphysics to look at a landscape painting and benefit not at all.

Before exploring further the character of the viewer unable to ascend to metaphysical speculation when looking at paintings of nature themes, we should briefly consider the type of image Paleotti discussed in his chapter "On Vain and Lazy Paintings." In the

6.3 Annibale Carracci. *Landscape*. Oil on canvas, *c.*1590. Washington, D.C., National Gallery of Art. (Photo: museum.)

passage quoted above, Paleotti seems to be treating landscape and other nature themes devoid of religious narratives. Annibale Carracci's *Landscape* (Figure 6.3), presumably painted in Bologna for a now-unknown patron about 1590, is the sort of subject Paleotti apparently had in mind; there are a few inconspicuous figures in a boat in the middle ground, but it emphasizes untouched nature itself.[45]

The subtlety of Annibale's earthy palette and the delicacy of his effects of light, which evoke the feeling of a gentle breeze moving through the trees, certainly fit Paleotti's specifications for sensory stimulation leading to sensual cognition. And the cropped composition in which trees appear at irregular intervals across and behind the picture plane, rather than being placed as obtrusive coulisses, heightens the verisimilitude of the painting, rendering it conducive to the attainment of rational cognition.

In addition to his treatment of the star-gazer, Paleotti's discussion of nature themes themselves suggests how he believed various different sorts of beholders would react to Annibale's painting. Presumably, "ordinary" viewers – those occupying a low place in God's hierarchical universe – would understand a painting such as Annibale's merely as the depiction of persons enjoying a lovely day outside, whereas the few able to ascend to metaphysical speculation would use such an image of created things just as they used created things themselves: as a staircase leading to the contemplation of celestial things, which could result in the attainment of spiritual cognition.

Paleotti's comment that the staircase of visible created things could lead human beings to knowledge of the invisible spiritual realm is quite revealing. It closely resembles later remarks on the sacred significance of nature articulated in devotional tracts by his younger ecclesiastical colleagues Roberto Bellarmino (1542–1621), the Jesuit theologian, and Federico Borromeo (1564–1631), the reforming Archbishop of Milan. All three men shared an optimistic attitude towards the mundane world and human nature. Unlike St. Augustine, who saw man as living in a state of fallen grace, all three post-Tridentine clerics were more optimistic.[46] Paleotti, however, indicated in the *Discorso* that the knowledge offered by nature paintings was inaccessible to the "ordinary" majority.[47] It is now necessary to investigate further Paleotti's conception of the audience for works of art.

Since Paleotti wrote the *Discorso* to purify art for the benefit of uneducated and educated members of his diocese – the two groups of viewers most often specified in his tract – it is important to note that he implemented in the diocese of Bologna one of the most all-inclusive educational programs in post-Tridentine Europe. This educational program made knowledge – particularly Christian doctrine – accessible to persons of all social classes.[48] Obviously, however, Paleotti's schools were not founded to provide the lower-class person with an education equivalent in scope or depth to that of the aristocrat; it was not in schools of Christian doctrine that the leading theologians, historians, natural philosophers, and so forth were educated. Indeed, even lower-class persons who entered religious orders or the secular clergy failed to gain expertise in most of these fields, which Paleotti identified in the *Discorso* as the wellsprings for pictorial subject matter. This is why Paleotti referred to the majority of his parishioner–viewers as *idioti* – that is, uneducated persons.

Yet it is somewhat surprising that in discussing nature themes in the passage of the *Discorso* cited above, Paleotti designated nature themes as beyond the ken of "ordinary" persons due to their inability to enter into metaphysical speculation. After all, metaphysics was not only typically treated in various genres of ecclesiastical writing – particularly in devotional literature – but also in religious music and sermons, which reached the general public.[49] If "ordinary" viewers had multiple points of access to metaphysics, what was the obstacle they faced in using it to understand paintings of nature themes and thereby grow closer to God? Paleotti provided no straightforward answer to this question, but by attempting to identify more precisely what he meant by "ordinary" persons, we can see more clearly his attitude towards this reception problem.

In the chapter "On Vain and Lazy Paintings," Paleotti made two points about the "ordinary" viewer who could not ascend to metaphysical speculation: first, he is in the majority, and second, he is not among those "endowed with spirit and judgment," to wit the *spirituali*, who are few in number. The "ordinary" majority, therefore, are *sensuali*, persons weighted down by earthly things. We recall that Paleotti tended to conceive of viewers as either educated or uneducated. Although the educated are few and the uneducated are many, this alone seems insufficient reason to identify Paleotti's "ordinary" majority as uneducated persons. But there are other reasons for doing so.

Paleotti's attitude towards the majority as opposed to the educated few emerges pellucidly when rereading his 1582 *Discorso* in light of his 1578 *Instruzzione . . . Per Tutti quelli, che havranno licenza di Predicare nelle Ville, & altri luoghi della Diocese [di Bologna] / Instructions for All Those who will have License to Preach in the Villages & Other Places of the

Diocese [of Bologna].[50] Paleotti's *Instruzzione* belongs to a genre of ecclesiastical writing known as the *instructiones praedicatoribus verbi dei* ("instructions for preaching the word of God"). Unlike rhetorical treatises, the *instructiones* served as practical guides to help preachers eliminate abuses. In fact, this kind of preaching manual provided bishops such as Paleotti with a model for art tracts likewise aimed at curbing abuses. Paleotti's *Instruzzione*, like his *Discorso*, was among the best-known tracts of its kind in post-Tridentine Christendom.[51]

In addition to treating such topics as the preacher's preparation, the themes of sermons, and the observance of feast days, Paleotti's *Instruzzione* considered what the preacher must know in order to interact with his parishioners, whom he called peasants (*contadini*). To this end, Paleotti told clerics that most of their parishioners would be illiterate persons (*persone imperite di lettere*) whose lives were spent in arduous labor and, as a result, had little time for anything but the necessities of life. Just as in the *Discorso* Paleotti instructed painters to avoid treating heretical, apocryphal, useless, or difficult subject matter, so in the *Instruzzione* he instructed preachers along the same lines. Paleotti also entreated preachers to feed to their audiences' "simple intelligences" only what they were capable of digesting.[52]

Paleotti went on to discuss complaints of the poor (*poveri*) and the arguments that preachers should make to help them come to terms with their role in the world order. For example, in the chapter of the *Instruzzione* entitled "Complaints of the Poor," Paleotti stated that the ignorant poor were open to temptation by the devil, for they were apt to think that their miserable conditions precluded any access to paradise. This, Paleotti declared, was not true. Indeed, in his chapter "Reasons that can be Given to Quiet the Laments of the Poor," Paleotti counseled preachers to instruct the poor that God came to earth to save souls, not to distribute goods, and that because excess wealth could make the road to heaven difficult, the road was very accessible to the poor. Most revealingly, in the same chapter Paleotti declared:

> Just as a body has many parts to serve it, the world must have various classes, ranks, and offices of person. They all serve the same body – that is to say, the Holy Church – whose head is Christ, our Savior.[53]

In the chapter entitled "Each Person's Obligations According to His Rank," Paleotti elaborated on the necessity of everyone's fulfilling his duty to God and the Church by living in accordance with the hierarchical structure of the universe.[54] All members of society should be thankful for whatever rank God gave them, and live within these natural confines.

Paleotti's *Instruzzione* and *Discorso* bespeak a similar attitude towards the uneducated majority. In the earlier tract, the *Instruzzione*, we are told that by their very nature – as occupants of a lower rung on the ladder of created things – the majority are inferior to the minority, whose natural superiority accounts for their social superiority. In the later tract, the *Discorso*, we are told that uneducated viewers are more sensually inclined and less intelligent than the educated. These remarks accord well with Paleotti's further statement in the *Discorso* that the uneducated majority cannot benefit from books because to do so requires the "ability and opportunity to learn."

To put this together is easy enough: uneducated persons are by nature lowly, relatively unintelligent sensualists. On the basis of a joint reading of the *Instruzzione* and the

Discorso, therefore, we cannot avoid identifying Paleotti's "ordinary" majority, who are unable to rise to metaphysical speculation when viewing paintings of nature themes, as uneducated *sensuali*. Since everyone must live according to the rank God gave him, the unlettered majority – who lacked the time and opportunity to learn – did not have the knowledge necessary to understand the full range of subjects of sacred and profane art. And, in any case, a leisured majority was unthinkable; leisure and learning might promote social mobility, thereby upsetting God's preordained hierarchy. Yet it is implicit that time and opportunity would not help the majority because they lacked the ability for book learning. Thus Paleotti's notion of reception, which centered on a tension between uneducated versus educated beholders, was conceived in accordance with his world view and, although to twentieth-century readers it is a reprehensible ideology, given Paleotti's time, place, and station in life, it could hardly have been otherwise.

Nevertheless, a ray of hope, a glimmer of Christian optimism, can be seen in Paleotti's attitude towards the ability of uneducated persons to use art to raise themselves to spiritual cognition. The previously mentioned passages of the *Discorso* concerning viewers with a spiritual proclivity do not categorically exclude uneducated persons from the *spirituali*. It is true that Paleotti considered the uneducated majority to be earthbound by nature but he never insisted that exceptions could not occur, or that it was impossible for any member of the majority to see with "purged eyes" and ascend to the spiritual realm. Paleotti never explained how one became a purged-eyed *spirituale* in the first place, and there is no reason to believe that book learning had anything to do with it. Although he failed to address the matter in the *Discorso*, Paleotti himself undertook spiritual exercises to raise his spiritual state, and he certainly believed others could do likewise.[55] In Paleotti's day, it was assumed as a matter of course that very few persons undergoing spiritual exercises would attain the highest spiritual level, but lack of education was apparently not considered a stumbling block in the endeavor.[56]

By way of concluding our discussion of Paleotti's notion of viewer response, let me emphasize that the *Discorso* itself and Paleotti's thought in general warrant much further analysis. Yet even this brief study of his *Discorso* and *Instruzzione* demonstrates that he upheld a conservative, post-Tridentine world view in which the prevailing social and ecclesiastical hierarchies were regarded as microcosmic approximations of the structure of God's perfect macrocosm. Thus Paleotti's world view inevitably informed his notion of the reception of sacred and profane art.

Paleotti's art theory was well known in Europe, but he never traveled to the New World of the Americas and, as far as I know, no one has sought to establish whether or not his *Discorso* and *Instruzzione* were used by priests in the Americas during the sixteenth and seventeenth centuries. Yet when Europeans arrived in the New World, they obviously brought with them preconceptions about sacred art based on post-Tridentine theory in general. It is reasonable to speculate that, in accordance with the hierarchical world order which post-Tridentine art theory espoused, Native Americans, of whatever social class or level of education, were forced into the viewing role that Paleotti's "ordinary" Europeans had been made to play in the Old World of the *Discorso*. The complexity of Old World art theory, analyzed briefly here in light of Paleotti's *Discorso* – only one of many tracts that could be brought to bear on the topic – suggests that an exciting new avenue of inquiry would be the investigation of how Old World art theory was interpreted and put to work in a New World context.

CHAPTER 7

Languages of Gesture in Sixteenth-Century Mexico: Some Antecedents and Transmutations

PAULINE MOFFITT WATTS

> The historical moment can be viewed with a double pair of lenses: one
> focused on the face it actually presents, the other trained on the routes by
> which knowledge of the past has been acquired. The story that every age
> tells, deliberately or by implication, of its own remoter antiquity, sheds a
> reflected light in both directions.
>
> Gertrude Bing[1]

Introduction

In several influential essays, the historian J. H. Elliott has pointed to what he calls the
"blunted" or "uncertain" impact of the New World of the Americas upon the Old
World of Europe in the century following Columbus's voyages. Elliott observes that
European descriptions of the peoples, the flora, and fauna of the Americas were of
necessity filtered, mitigated from the start by a range of criteria. After the initial
encounters of 1492, there could be no such thing as an "innocent eye" for either
Europeans or indigenous peoples.[2]

Why were such filters, such mitigations, necessary? The emergent awareness of a
previously unknown world was potentially deeply disturbing, if not overpowering. This
world called into question the centuries-old, traditional constructs of providential history,
and the geographies and anthropologies subsumed within it. It had to be calibrated into
the workings of European polities, economies, and cultures in ways that would avoid
what Elliott aptly terms "seismic shocks."[3] Put somewhat differently, European writers,
explorers, and cartographers created a variety of grisailles in which the Americas were
distanced in ways that preserved or safely nuanced dominant cultural integrities. Mono-
chromatic and marginated, the peoples of the New World did not come to life in
verisimilar variety and complexity.

Widely read writers such as the humanist Peter Martyr d'Anghiera and the essayist
Michel de Montaigne never saw the Americas. Nor, presumably, did most of their
readers. Even the famous debate between Juan Ginés de Sepúlveda and Bartolomé de Las

Casas regarding the nature of the Amerindians, cast as it was in the *topoi* and formulae of the scholastic *disputatio*, represented the permutations of sixteenth-century Iberian Thomism rather more than the workings of indigenous cultures.

The conquistadors and missionaries who were active in the early decades of the conquest of the Americas also "screened" the peoples whom they encountered, invoking a range of criteria reflective of their varied social, political, and religious backgrounds. Elliott has noted that, broadly speaking, the criteria they employed and their preconceptions "derived from a fusion of classical and Christian values and beliefs, and were now in many instances being filtered through the lens of Renaissance humanism."[4] But such fusions were not without fissures, the lenses were not always pristine.

The decalced Observant Franciscans who inaugurated the so-called "spiritual conquest of Mexico" conceived of themselves as "strangers and pilgrims," in some fundamental way alienated from and transient within their society and history. The work of Johan Huizinga, Gerhard Ladner, and others has shown that this sense of displacement is a feature underlying various modes of medieval and Renaissance thought and behavior. This consciousness of spiritual displacement or "otherness" informed the development of the Franciscan concept of mission operative in sixteenth-century Mexico in a variety of ways.[5]

Franciscan missionary work amongst "spiritual others" – Mongols, Muslims, Jews, the various non-Christian peoples of inner Asia, northern Africa, the western Mediterranean, and Iberia – dates from the lifetime of Francis himself. It may be argued that the ongoing history of such contacts with non-Christian spiritual others generated a "missionary Christianity," even perhaps a characteristic Franciscan "missionary Christianity."[6]

The structures and messages of this "missionary Christianity" are marked by the missionaries' more immediate physical displacement from their native cultural settings and customs as well. It is shaped by the struggle to devise efficacious modes of dialogue and exchange, by the syncretic and adaptive strategies necessitated by the presence of powerful, often deeply disturbing alternatives. In this, Franciscan "missionary Christianity," for example that of Ramon Llull, may be distinguished from those forms of Christianity anchored in more formal settings, though it is surely also related to these forms, as the writings of the mendicant participants in the spiritual conquest of Mexico were related to the debates between Sepúlveda and Las Casas held in Spain.[7]

The identification and study of the criteria, the strategies, and screens of Franciscan "missionary Christianity" in sixteenth-century Mexico present particular methodological challenges. For, initially at least, the monks and indigenous peoples shared no written or spoken language, no history of contacts such as marked the interactions of Christian, Jew, and Muslim in the Old World. One of the important early Franciscan missionaries, Jacopo da Testera, called the language barrier a "wall"; until the monks mastered native languages, their tongues would remain locked in their mouths, he said.[8] How then did the first Franciscans evangelize?

To a considerable degree, it appears that the Franciscans relied upon languages of images and gestures, unfolded in ritual theatres which served at once to initiate the Indians into the Christian cosmos and to mute the phobic reactions of the missionaries themselves to the indigenous religions they confronted. Such languages of gesture, insofar as they are retrievable, can be revealing indicators of social structure and order. Their mnemotic and mimetic techniques encode and transmit collective histories and mores. More particular passages of which these languages are composed may provide a means of delineating and recollecting relationships within a given social order. They might also, in the absence of a common spoken language, initially serve to establish relationships between peoples with different languages, histories, and cultures.[9]

Hence the languages of gestures employed by the Franciscans were complex, sometimes conflicted, repositories of significations traceable back to Greco–Roman antiquity. In order to look at the curious sixteenth-century afterlife of these ancient techniques, we may begin by considering them as antecedents to the historical moment of contact between monks and Nahuas.

Antecedents

The second-century Attic satirist, Lucian of Samosata, tells the story of a singular gift requested of the Emperor Nero by a visiting dignitary named Pontus:

> "Give me," said the Pontian, "your great pantomime, no gift could delight me more." "And of what use can he be to you in Pontus?" asked the Emperor. "I have foreign neighbors, who do not speak our language; and it is not easy to procure interpreters. Your pantomime could discharge that office perfectly, by means of his gesticulations."[10]

Pontus's expectation that Nero's mime could serve him as an interpreter was based upon the assumption that there is a natural, shared language of gestures – an assumption that would be shared by many psychologists, physicians, and art historians today.[11]

But Lucian also recognized a second category of gesture – the conventional gesture. Such gestures are derived from and comprehensible only within specific cultural contexts. This is evident in Lucian's description of the training and function of the pantomime. He must serve the goddess Mnemosyne (Memory); he must acquire and appropriately invoke an extensive knowledge of myth and history, the stock upon which his repertoire is grafted. And, in order to serve as Mnemosyne's medium, the pantomime must be a master or mistress of the mimetic languages of natural and conventional gesture:

> Since it is his profession to imitate, and to show forth his subject by means of gesticulation, he, like the orators, must acquire lucidity; every scene must be intelligible without the aid of an interpreter; to borrow the expression of the Pythian oracle, "Dumb though he be, and speechless, he is heard."[12]

As Lucian suggests here (and indeed elsewhere), the pantomime shares these languages of gesture with the rhetorician. While the environment of the pantomime is the theatre and that of the rhetorician is the legal or political forum, and while the rhetorician speaks and the pantomime does not, for both the entire body is engaged in the process of communication.

The gestures, the postures used by the rhetorician, the establishment of space, and the development of his movements within it are as crucial to his effectiveness as are the content and syntax of his speech. This interweaving of word and speech is treated at length in one of the most influential ancient treatises on rhetoric, Quintilian's *Institutio oratoria*, probably completed by the late first century AD. The section culminates with a nuanced evocation of the special expressive power of the hands:

> As for the hands, without which all action would be crippled and enfeebled, it is scarcely possible to describe the variety of their motions, since they are almost as expressive as words. For other portions of the body merely help the speaker, whereas the hands may almost be said to speak. . . . In fact, though the peoples and nations of the earth speak a multitude of tongues, they share in common the universal language of the hands.[13]

In addition to its dramatic, political, and forensic functions, the language of gestures also played a significant role as an indicator of rank and status in the imperial court circles of the late antique world. Ceremonies such as that of the *adlocutio*, a formal address by the emperor to his army, and the *adventus*, the triumphal arrival of a conqueror or ruler into a city, unfolded themselves in a carefully choreographed sequence of actions and gestures.[14]

But there is a disturbing counterpart to, an inversion of, these pantomimic, rhetorical, and imperial languages of gesture. These are excessive, uncontrolled, or inappropriate gestures. For both Lucian and Quintilian these were embarrassing, distasteful and, above all, ineffective. In his treatise on pantomime, Lucian observed:

> But in Pantomime, as in rhetoric, there can be (to use a popular phrase) too much of a good thing; a man may exceed the proper bounds of imitation; what should be great may become monstrous, softness may be exaggerated into effeminacy, and the courage of man into the ferocity of a beast.[15]

Such excesses had powerful but dangerous effects on the audience. Lucian described a performance he had seen in which the pantomime's "histrionic frenzy" caused the whole house to run berserk, "leaping, yelling, tearing their clothes."[16] Presumably, any departure from the codified gestures of the ceremonies of *adlocutio* or *adventus* would render them absurd and incomprehensible as well. In fact, aberrations such as that described by Lucian are so unconventional that they pass over into the marginated, unorthodox realm of *gesticulation*. They are madness – morally, socially, and politically subversive.

As with many elements of Greco–Roman public culture, these languages of gesture and gesticulation were variously received and adapted by their medieval heirs. Though their ancient frameworks can still be discerned, the medieval codifications of gesture were suffused with other significations derived from the emergent, then dominant, symbols and rituals of Christianity. They can be traced through liturgies and commentaries on the Mass such as those of Honorius of Autun, Sicardus, and Durandus, through manuals of prayer and preaching, and through sacred drama. Gesture and gesticulation are represented in certain lineages of manuscript illuminations as well, particularly those accompanying texts of the plays of Terence, Prudentius's *Psychomachia*, and the *Sachenspiegel* – a thirteenth-century German work describing and illustrating regional legal practices and court procedures.[17]

The mutant languages of gesticulation persist throughout the medieval period as well. These were the languages of jesters, actors, prostitutes, and heretics. Vagrant creatures they were – lascivious, grotesque, yet seductive and somehow necessary. Peripheral to society, but inseparable from it, they adorn the margins of maps and manuscripts, entwined in the patterns and tendrils of border motifs, engraved in stone on the columns that support ecclesiastical edifices and the facades that introduce them.[18]

The complexes of sacred and secular meanings generated by the entertainments of these *gyrovagi*, these *goliardi*, were traced anxiously by theologians, church synods, and councils. Some theologians appreciated the pious adaptation of certain techniques of actors and jesters to the *ars praedicandi*, believing that they might make the messages of Christianity more accessible to unlettered audiences. But these appreciations were always muted by the fear that such syncretisms might be too inflected by residual pagan customs and practices, that they might slide too easily into the shadowy realms of the heretical, the diabolical.[19]

The mendicant orders, particularly the Franciscans, became skilled in the manipulation of the hybrid images and dramas of surviving indigenous folklores and overlays of Christianity. There is no better example of what Carlo Ginzburg has called the "carnivalesque" aspect of primitive Franciscanism than its founder. Through incongruent acts such as stripping himself naked before the Bishop of Assisi, covering his head with ashes and leaving his audience without delivering a sermon or conversing with the Crucified, Francis established himself as a holy man inhabiting a sacred space apart from society. And through his empathetic transmogrified attachments to animals – his sermons to the birds, his taming of the wolf of Gubbio, the incantatory metamorphosis of his body into that of a donkey – he occupied a liminal space between the human and natural worlds.[20]

It is not coincidental that Francis and his followers roamed the frontiers, the border-lands of the world inhabited by their fellow Europeans, and adapted the curious languages sketched above to communications with spiritual "others" within and without the territories of Christendom. In subsequent centuries members of the order that bore his name traveled to other parts of Africa, to inner Asia, and, after 1492, to the New World, where they played a pioneering role in the evangelization of the indigenous peoples of the Americas.

Transmutations

The Franciscan mission to the New World commenced in the decade of the 1520s and was initially the work of decalced Observants. In Iberia, the heart of the Observant movement was located in Estremadura, the home of Hernán Cortés. Cortés appears to have had ongoing connections with the Order, so it was not coincidental that the vanguard of these extremely ascetic and zealous Franciscans, known as the "Twelve," arrived in Tenochtitlán soon after Cortés's conquest of Montezuma's Aztec empire.[21]

On June 17 or 18 of 1524, Cortés met the Twelve, led by Martin of Valencia, at the outskirts of the city. Their journey to Tenochtitlán and their arrival there may be read as a transmutation of the ancient Roman ceremony of *adventus*, but it also involved a characteristically Franciscan inversion of that ritual, an inversion in which Cortés himself participated. The event is described by Bernal Díaz in his *Historia verdadera de la conquista de la Nueva España/The True History of the Things of New Spain*. According to Díaz, when

Cortés received word that the twelve Observants had arrived at the port of Veracruz, he ordered that:

> whichever way they came, the roads should be swept, and wherever they halted, even in the open country, ranchos should be built for them, and that when they reached the pueblos of the Indians they should go out to meet them and should ring the bells . . . and that the natives should carry lighted wax candles and the crosses they possessed – and he ordered the Spaniards with all humility, to fall on their knees and kiss their hands and garments (so that the Indians might observe it and follow their example) and moreover Cortés sent off plentiful supplies along the road and wrote to the Friars very affectionately.[22]

These initial preparations appear to have been modeled after those customarily made for the arrival of important secular and religious leaders, and for the translation of relics during the late antique and medieval periods. The sweeping of roads, the lighting of candles, the display of crosses, and the provision of food and lodging wherever the honoree might stop, are mentioned in a variety of sources. Such actions appear to comprise a distinct initial phase of the ceremony of *adventus* usually known in ancient sources as *synantesis* – the welcome provided by the general populace during the triumphal approach to the host city.[23]

Díaz then relates that as the Twelve drew near the city, Cortés rode out to greet them. The monks approached, not on horseback as would the conqueror in the traditional *adventus* ceremony, but on foot. Díaz says that "the friars were barefoot and thin and their garments ragged" and that "they had no horses but came on foot and were very jaundiced looking." Their poor appearance and the fact that they did not ride horses apparently struck the assembled Aztec leaders, who only recently had regarded the mounted conquistadors as supernatural agents of conquest.[24]

Díaz's account indicates that the inversion of images continued as Cortés dismounted from his horse, divesting himself of the venerable status of equestrian conqueror and assuming the submissive role of the vanquished:

> When Cortés knew that the Friars were approaching he dismounted from his horse, as did all of us, and when we met the reverend friars the first to fall on his knees before Fray Martin de Valencia and to kiss his hands was Cortés himself, and the Friar would not permit it, so he kissed his garments and those of all the other ecclesiastics and so did nearly all the captains and soldiers who were present and Guatomec and the Mexican chieftains.[25]

This variation of the *adventus* ceremony described by Díaz – the language of gestures manipulated by Cortés and Martin of Valencia – inaugurated the "spiritual conquest" of Mexico. Without the use of words the conquerors were able to communicate important relationships among themselves to the assembled Aztec leaders. The participation of the *caciques* in the ritual kissing of Martin of Valencia's robes initiated them into the world of their conquerors and assigned them a rank or status much as the carefully orchestrated gatherings of victors and vanquished in the ancient ceremony of *adventus* had done.[26]

At this point Díaz's account requires supplementation by three important Franciscan chronicles of that order's activities in Mexico. These are Gerónimo de Mendieta's

Historia eclesiástica indiana, Juan de Torquemada's *Monarquía indiana*, and Augustín de Vetancurt's *Teatro Mexicano*. They all report that a series of presentations of doctrine then took place between the monks and the Aztec wise men. A text purportedly recording these exchanges or *colloquios* was discovered in about 1564 by the famous Franciscan missionary and ethnographer, Bernardino de Sahagún. He had found it in the library of the Colegio de la Santa Cruz, which was a school founded by the Twelve and their followers in order to educate the sons of the indigenous elite with the goal of creating an Indian priesthood. Aided by indigenous collaborators, Sahagún transcribed the manuscript and so preserved it.[27]

These *colloquios* were also part of the longer history of ceremonial encounters of the Christian and the non-Christian. As such, they can be placed within the larger context of Franciscan missionary activity in both the Old World and the New. In his edition of the *colloquios* of 1524, Miguel Léon-Portilla has remarked that missionaries in other parts of the world apparently engaged in ritual exchanges of doctrine upon inital contact with the non-Christian, non-European peoples whom they encountered. He cites as examples the disputations which took place between Jesuits and Japanese sages in 1551 and dialogues between Capuchin monks and the wise men of the Pacamao, Tapuytapera, and Iacupen peoples of Brazil in 1613.[28]

The more distant antecedents for such exchanges may be traced in the patterns of religious dialogues between Christian, Muslim, and Jew. Works such as Ramon Llull's *Liber de gentili et tribus sapientibus*, Thomas Aquinas's *Summa contra gentiles*, and polemical and apologetic works by other figures such as Ramon de Peñyafort and Ramon Marti provided enduring models for formal presentation of Christian doctrine to potential converts. Another possible model might have been the *Requerimiento*, a document produced in 1510 at royal command. Designed to be read (in Castilian) to indigenous peoples resistant to Spanish presence in their lands, it offered the option of peaceable submission and guaranteed certain protections. If its terms were rejected, it provided the Spanish *conquistadors* with legal and moral justification for armed combat.[29]

However, the efficacy of such translations of rank and status, such symbolic exchanges of doctrine, appears somewhat ephemeral when compared with other early contacts between the Franciscans and indigenous peoples. Such contacts were consistently marked by the monks' anamorphic relationship to their own bodies and to the "body politic" of their culture. Martin of Valencia's mortification of his body was so extreme that he was no longer aware of it. In his *History of the Indians of New Spain* (written between 1536 and 1541) another of the Twelve, Toribio de Benavente (Motolinía), called Martin diabolically possessed, saying that "As a result of these temptations he became so emaciated that he was little more than skin and bones, imagining at the same time that he was strong and healthy."[30]

This possession was projected on to the natural world, especially the trees and birds so loved by Francis himself: "Prayer left him cold and indifferent. He hated seclusion. Trees seemed to be demons," Motolinía wrote. Suddenly rendered cognizant of his shackles of self-destruction by the simple query of a woman who asked him, "Do you want to kill yourself?", Martin was freed. He "experienced great serenity and peace of mind, relished seclusion, while the trees, which he had previously abhorred, and the birds that sang in them, seemed a paradise to him."[31]

Martin of Valencia's struggles with the devil were not private nightmares or his biographer's hagiographic allegories. They were but *exempla* of the many physical, palpable battles which, according to the plan of providential history encoded in Scripture and prophetic traditions, would mark the approaching end of post-lapsarian time and space.[32] That the decalced Observant Franciscans were ordained to play a special role in these penultimate wars is manifest in the *Obediencia* and *Instrucción* delivered to the Twelve by the Minister General of the Order, Francisco de los Angeles, upon their departure for Mexico. Observing that the world was now in its "eleventh hour," he summoned them to combat with "the ancient serpent" and assigned them the task of "snatching away from the maw of the dragon the souls . . . deceived by satanic wiles, dwelling in the shadow of death, held in the vain cult of idols."[33]

When viewed through such neo-Manichean lenses, the customs and rituals of indigenous peoples sorely tested the Europeans' capacities to absorb and understand. A kind of "culture shock" was triggered by the onrush of impressions resulting from exposure to native customs and rituals; the dances of the Aztecs were apparently particularly disturbing to conquistador and missionary alike. The movements of the participants appeared grotesque to European observers; they were gesticulations, excessive and bestial indicators of diabolical possession. Both Díaz's history and indigenous sources describe an occasion in which a ritual dance led to shocking results.

It occurred in Tenochtitlán, after the initial Spanish occupation but prior to the Noche Triste and the final conquest of the city. Cortés himself was absent and his soldiers were under the command of Pedro De Alvarado. According to the indigenous sources, the time for the annual festival of Toxcatl, held in honor of the god Huitzilopochtli, was at hand. It was the most sacred of Aztec religious celebrations and permission was granted by the occupying Spaniards for it to be held at the main temple of Tenochtitlán.

An account recorded by Sahagún and his collaborators relates that at the very moment that the Dance of the Serpent "was loveliest and song linked to song, the Spaniards were seized with an urge to kill the celebrants. . . . They ran in among the dancers, forcing their way to the place where the drums were played. They attacked the man who was drumming and cut off his arms. Then they cut off his head and it rolled across the floor." A massacre of the dancers then ensued, for which Díaz could offer no adequate explanation.[34]

In his *History of the Indians of New Spain*, Motolinía offered a number of ophidiophobic descriptions of religious ceremonies and dances that he observed. After ingesting certain fungi – the " 'flesh of god,' that is, flesh of the demon whom they worship" – Motolinía reported that

> the Indians soon have a thousand visions, especially of snakes. Being entirely bereft of their senses, they imagine that their legs and body are covered with worms which are eating them alive . . .[35]

The resulting *ekstasis* was, for Motolinía, a "transplanted hell":

> This land was a transplanted hell, seeing how its people would yell at night, some invoking the devil, others in a drunken stupor, and still others singing and dancing. They had kettledrums, trumpets, horns, and large conches, especially at the feasts of

their demons. . . . It was very pitiful to see men created after the image of God, becoming worse than brute animals.[36]

To filter, if not to sublimate and transmutate what seemed to be the diabolically inspired dances and ceremonies of the Nahuas, the Franciscans initially made use of a variety of techniques based on vocabularies of the "natural language" of gestures. The rudiments of Christian doctrine were communicated through pantomime according to the account of Fray Juan de Torquemada in his *Monarquía Indiana*:

> These things were taught by the holy religious men in pantomime, and only in signs; in signalling to the sky and saying that they ought to believe that the only God was there; and turning their eyes to the earth, they signified that there was hell, wherein walked [were] the likenesses of toads and serpents. These were the demons tormenting the condemned souls.[37]

And basic rituals of repentance and penance, in particular the confession, were also conducted without words. Both Motolinía and another early Franciscan, Diego Valadés (who was likely a *mestizo*), describe the methods used in this regard. In his *Rhetorica Christiana* (1579), Valadés explained:

> In confession, by using very ingenious pictures, they show in what ways they have offended God, and they put small stones on the sign on which the vices or virtues are represented in order to indicate how many times they have relapsed back into the same sin.[38]

Through such raw debuts the initial phobic responses of the mendicants gradually gave way to more considered observations and descriptions of the forms, functions, and traditional histories of indigenous ritual dances and ceremonies.

The work of missionary–ethnographers such as the Dominican Diego Durán, the Franciscan Bernardino de Sahagún, and others, revealed that the Nahua singers and dancers were carefully trained in schools called *cuicacalli* or "Houses of Songs." There was then considerable range, precision, and sophistication in the indigenous deployment of song, dance, and drama in the service of religious ritual.[39] The Nahua songs, some of which survive in manuscripts such as the *Cantares Mexicanos*, were dramatic poems built on mixes of voices – they could be monologues, dialogues, colloquies, choruses, or combinations thereof. They served as vehicles for preserving and transmitting theogony and cosmology, or commemorating important historical figues and events. They could be presented in relatively private settings, in presumably aristocratic symposia known as *cohuayotl icniuhyotl* or in more public arenas contiguous to the great temples as part of the public calendar of religious festivals.[40]

These festivals involved elaborate costuming and staging, sometimes using animals and puppets as well as human participants. They unfolded themselves through processions, farces, satires, sacrifices, and other narrative skeins. They (re)enacted myths and histories in a carefully calculated calendrical sequence tied to the larger scans of Nahua astrology and concomitant cycles of cosmic history:

> In this fashion, each ritual became a dramatic enactment of the relationship of the Aztecs to their gods, and through them to the universe itself. In order that the people

might share in and empathize with the realization of this relationship and be taught the religious content of their culture in a dramatic fashion, the role of the particular god whose ritual was being celebrated was literally enacted by a chosen member of the celebrants themselves; the ritual was commemorated in the manner of a passion play.[41]

The parallels between indigenous plays and their own ritual dramas, which depicted important persons and events in post-lapsarian Christian providential history, were not lost on the missionaries. Early on, they began to experiment with fusions of their own *auto sacramentale* with indigenous theatre. In so doing they were forced to confront and negotiate the power and beauty, and the fascination of Nahua dances, and their fear that such dances preserved the ancient religion and so subverted or resisted the processes of conversion. Durán understood this crucial tension well, writing in his chapter on "The God of Dance" that

> All the native lays are interwoven with such obscure metaphors that there is hardly a man who can understand them unless they are studied in a very special way and explained so as to penetrate their meaning. For this reason I have intentionally set myself to listen with much attention to what is sung; and while the words and terms of the metaphors seem nonsense to me, afterward, having discussed and conferred [with the natives, I can see that] they seem to be admirable sentences, both in the divine things composed today and in worldly songs. I believe that there is nothing in general to reprehend in this case. I say "I believe" because there might be a slip here, and they might amuse themselves by remembering their ancient gods and singing the evil and idolatrous chants and perhaps more. These songs were so sad that just the rhythm and dance saddens one. I have seen these danced occasionally with religious chants, and they are so sad that I was filled with melancholy and woe.[42]

The plays, composed first by the Franciscans, then the other mendicant orders and later the Jesuits, were patterned in such a way that they safely encased indigenous processions and dances within orthodox Christian parables and narratives. In his *Historia*, Motolinía described several ceremonies and plays of this sort. These include the procession of the Holy Sacrament on the feast day of Corpus Christi in 1538 and a dramatization of the expulsion of Adam and Eve from the Garden of Eden performed the following year in celebration of Easter. Both the procession and the play took place in elaborate settings which consisted of live animals, an abundance of plants, trees, and topiaries made of flowers, as well as Indians costumed as animals. In this, the missionaries' *autos* can scarcely be distinguished from some of the Nahua rituals described by Durán, particularly those which honored the deity Huitzilopochtli, which had so horrified Cortés's conquistadors.[43]

So the danger that the plays might be overly inflected by residual "pagan" forms and content was always at hand. The sense of danger may well have increased when some missionaries, aided by indigenous collaborators, began to compose plays in Nahuatl. As the anthropologist Louise Burckhart has argued, such collaborations represent negotiated Christianities in which the Nahuas are active agents, in which the missionaries themselves are sometimes missionized. In this process of negotiation, the Nahuas contribute to the conflations and refashionings of the gods of the missionaries – the Trinity, the Virgin

Mary, and the host of saints – in relation to the spectrum of their own deities and modes of worship.[44]

The emergent institution of the Roman Church in Mexico tracked the missionaries' uses of drama, fearful that the *autos* might be unknowing hosts to languages redolent of diabolical possession. The synod of 1555, which marked the beginning of canon legislation in the Americas, cautioned that

> The indigenous peoples of these parts are greatly given to ritual dancing and to other rejoicings which they have held as their custom since their gentility. They now wish to mix with these dances elements which are reminiscent of their pre-Christian history. With the permission of the Holy Council, let us instate and order that when the Indians dance they shall wear no ancient masks, nor use any insignia which might arouse suspicion. Nor shall they sing hymns pertaining to their ancient rituals or history, without their first having been examined by either priest or persons who well understand their language; and such songs which do not directly treat of the Gospel or the Mysteries of our Faith they shall not be permitted to dance before dawn, *nor after the High Mass*, but *only after these hours* and until Vespers.[45]

Such abstract demarcations of the languages of gesture and gesticulation, anchored by the dictates of law and theology, occupy a world apart from the precariously balanced frontiers of histories, actions, and meanings spliced together by monks and Nahuas through their shared ritual dramas.

And, in spite of institutional surveillance, these splicings continued to short-circuit in startling, if not grotesque, incidents. In his recent book *When Jesus Came, The Corn Mothers Went Away*, Ramón Gutiérrez traces tensions that arose because of the Franciscans' efforts to eradicate the *katsina* dances of the pueblo peoples, tensions which ultimately fed into the Pueblo Revolt of 1680. During a performance of the prohibited dance at Isleta, the participants beat a child to death. A Franciscan observer, Fray Salvador de Guerra (who may have been its father), was overcome by his incapacity to screen, to distance the event. According to Gutiérrez,

> Bathed in tears, Fray Salvador stripped himself naked, placed a crown of thorns on his head and a rope around his neck, flagellated himself, and then criss-crossed the pueblo carrying a large cross on his shoulders. The Indians immediately stopped the dance and dispersed, said the friar, because the sight of "the Holy Cross caused them horror."[46]

Fray Salvador's gestures and actions in his moment of acute distress may seem difficult to decipher. But their historical antecedents are easily recognizable. They may be traced back to the penitential asceticism of Martin of Valencia, ultimately to Francis himself. As such they are not simply spasmodic or reflexive. Rather they incant and embody the historical memory and identity of his order and its mission. Fray Salvador's mimetic pantomime provided him with "a precious moment of precarious equilibrium" in the face of the excessive, deadly frenzy of the *katsina* dance.[47]

The historical drama in which Fray Salvador, Martin of Valencia, Motolinía and the other mendicants played such active roles – the "spiritual conquest of Mexico" – unfolds itself, then, not so much in a linear narrative as in a kind of fugue. That is, the voices of the so-called conqueror culture, polyphonic and only partially remembered, reflect conflicted states of religious and political consciousness. These missionaries played out their historical destinies through their contrapuntal relationships to the "body politic" to which they nominally belonged, through estrangement from their own bodies induced by radical forms of self-denial, and finally through their interactions with the otherness of indigenous religions and cultures. The afterlife of the liminal worlds created by the monks and Nahuas, traceable back in part to their respective pre-contact pasts, survives today in the rituals and celebrations of many people living in Mexico and the American Southwest. In this sense, the mimetic and mnemonic power of the ancient language of gestures invoked by Lucian lives on.

From Lies to Truth: Colonial Ekphrasis and the Act of Crosscultural Translation

THOMAS CUMMINS

> Somos Informado que en las Indias hay muchos testigos falsos, que por muy poco interés se perjuran en los pleytos, y negocios . . . Mandamos . . . que con muy particular atencion procuren averiguar los que cometen este delito, castigando con todo rigor . . . .
>
> Charles V at Toledo, August 24, 1579
> (from *Recopilación de Leyes de las Indias*,
> Vol. II, Book 7, Chapter 8, law 3.
> Madrid: Ivian de Paredes, 1681, 296)

An anxious subtext cuts through all genres of early writings and rewritings produced in or about the New World: that the author in producing his text is producing the truth for his reader, that what the author says he knows can be verified and/or that what has been claimed by others is false.[1] Certainly for the European reader of the early travel and conquest histories, the experiential presence of the narrator as witness puts the teller in possession of the truth.[2]

But the establishment of truth in the sixteenth-century New World is something altogether different when it involves the act of communication between Europeans and natives and the retelling of that communication. Here, truth is something that must be negotiated through difference in language, difference in society, difference in culture. All this brings into question the possibility of any communication between Europeans and natives as it unfolds within a contestation of power in which deceit, distrust, and lying constitute some of the principal characteristics that define this contestation. Where, then, could the differences of language and ethnicity find an accepted mutual place of representation through which the truth of ideas, religion, and history could be believed to pass securely from one "other" to the "other"? For the telling of narratives across cultures, there needs to be invented/found a mutually recognized cultural space that forms a permeable and transparent referent through which the words of the other can pass through translation into one's own culture in order to be used as the bearers of truth as evidence, as historical fact, or as religious dogma to be adjudicated, marveled upon, discussed, debated, or ridiculed.[3]

I will argue that pictorial images formed just such a site for crosscultural translation in the New World. Of course, Spaniards learned native languages, transcribing and/or translating them into written form, and elite natives quickly learned to use alphabetic writing to produce documents in their own language or in Spanish. Pictorial images, however, had a different role than the recording and disseminating of information and ideas; they established and authenticated them. After all, the invention of writing was one of the key cultural differentiations that Europeans made between themselves and the peoples of the New World, whereas pictorial images were something they held in common.[4] And this, I would say, is one of the crucial implications of the term "colonial" as it is used to qualify art produced in the New World during the sixteenth and early seventeenth centuries. Its often hybrid appearance appeals to a new set of cultural expectations.[5] The images that were produced in both New Spain and Peru are not mirrors of passive assimilation and acculturation, registers of change. They constitute the location to which the act of looking by Europeans and natives could be mutually and simultaneously directed in order to establish agreement. One cannot talk, then, about a simple evolution from the pictorial to the alphabetic in this century as if it were a natural and logical process.[6] Rather, even as images were increasingly brought forward in texts only through their written descriptions, their existence was presumed to be nonetheless real in terms of their capacity for authentication and truth because they preexisted the text and continued to exist in a myriad of other contexts. This always-presumed existence suggested that, when and if needed, they could be called forth, at least by name, as the originating source for the written words.[7]

The production of images in relation to oral and/or glyphic texts already had many forms in prehispanic America, but the necessity of the production of images in relation to alphabetic texts in the New World is perforce a colonial strategy initiated by Spaniards. It permits, in the midst of charges of lies, distrust, and reticence, a "neutral" site for the correlation of the two cultural texts in order to establish a semblance of truth by which decisions could be made, metaphysics discussed, and histories recorded. This strategy moves throughout various crosscultural narratives as they occur in law, Christian doctrine, history, and ultimately fiction. This strategy, however, is not based upon any articulated or consistent theory about images, rather it is based upon the contingency of the context of and the participants in the narrative. And what I would like to show within the structure of this paper in terms of the order of the evidence presented is that as one moves through the colonial production of truth content in law, in religion, in history, and even in the novel, this strategy of establishing truth through images unravels so as to be seen as absurd within the fiction of crosscultural translation. I begin with the narrative of law in New Spain because it is literally within that narrative that the performance of translation through image as referent is judged absolutely to be acceptable or not as a legitimate presentation to establish truth.

Law

In 1531, a lawsuit was brought by Hernando Cortés in Mexico City against the members of the first Audiencia of Mexico, Nuño de Guzmán, Juan Ortiz de Matienzo, and Diego

Delgadillo who had taken advantage of Cortés's return to Spain in 1528 to take control of lands and resources, particularly in the native town of Huejotzingo, that had been granted to Cortés. In the course of preparing the brief, Cortés's lawyer asked for an extension of time to prepare his case because, as he states:

> it has come to my notice that in this city [Huejotzingo] there are certain leading men [natives] of the said town who have paintings of what the said town gave to the said licentiates. I beseech Your Majesty that you command and compel them to give them [the paintings] to the secretary because from them I make [my] presentation; and I ask that their statements be taken by means of the paintings and by the questionnaire which I have presented in the case and for this I ask an extension of time if necessary . . .[8]

The extension was granted and the paintings, eight in all, were brought to Mexico City along with three witnesses from Huejotzingo. It is thus the existence of the indigenous paintings that draws native participation into the drama of a litigation between Spaniards. The native witnesses are sworn to tell the truth,[9] and then the words of the men from Huejotzingo are translated by an interpreter and transcribed by a notary into the written case. Yet the paintings stand prior to their oath and testimony, and therefore the content of the testimony is not substantiated just by the written transcription of the verbal translation. It is the presence of the paintings placed literally before the view of the witness as he speaks, the interpreter as he translates, and the notary as he writes that forms/creates a common cultural space through which native speech moves (crossculturally) to arrive in a Spanish context as an acceptable form of evidence that will then be evaluated by the court. For example, the response of Esteban, the third witness from Huejotzingo, to a question concerning the forced tribute of corn was recorded as follows:

> And as to the [amount] of maize they have given to the said factor [in 1529], *they have it painted in a painting which he asked to be shown* [Figure 8.1]. *And when he saw it, he said through the said translator, regarding the black images, painted like the combs of the Indians,* that each picture represents four hundred loads of maize and the other seventeen black bands, in the manner of outstretched banners of the Indians, each one of them is twenty loads . . . And concerning the tribute of the year 1530, they sent them all maize which amounts to nine red bands, after the fashion of Indian red combs, and each one of the said bands is four hundred, and of the other red band, painted after the fashion of an outstretched banner, he says that they are twenty loads. All of this said maize he says that they had taken from a granary, which they have depicted there in the said painting . . . And this is what he knows about this question. The said painted paper is signed by me, the said notary and secretary.[10]

In this passage, as emphasized above, the notary takes the reader through a remarkable transformational narrative that charts the crosscultural movement of the witness's testimony from oral Nahuatl words through the painting into a Spanish frame of reference. The transformation can be said to occur in seven acts: 1) the priority of the painting as separate from the individual testimony, "they have it painted in a painting"; 2) the placing of the collective image in the context of the individual witness before he speaks,

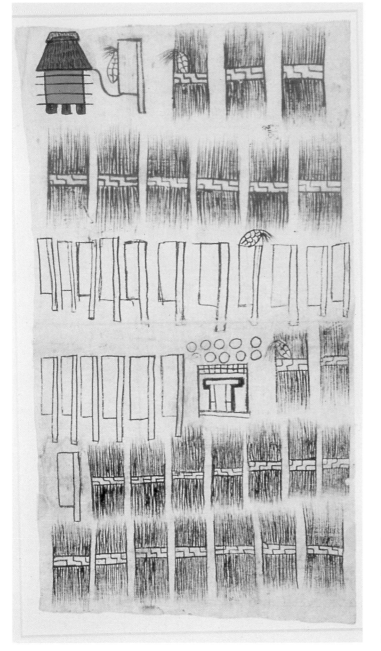

8.1 Anonymous, Mexican. Painting Number 7. Paint on amatl paper, Huejotzingo Codex, c.1530. Washington D.C., Library of Congress. (Photo: library.)

"he asked to be shown"; 3) the viewing of the painting by Esteban, identifying the image to which he will refer his words, "and when he saw it"; 4) the speech of what he sees, "he said"; 5) the oral translation of that speech, "through the said translator"; 6) the transcription of the image into word/text, "regarding the black images"; and 7) the notary's own description of what the image looks like for a Spanish audience, "painted like the combs of the Indians." Only then does Esteban's evidence become apparent in

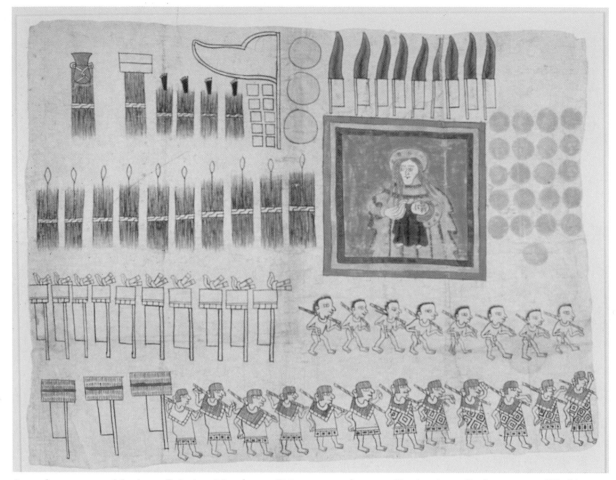

8.2   Anonymous, Mexican. Painting Number 5. Paint on amatl paper, Huejotzingo Codex, *c.*1530. Washington D.C., Library of Congress. (Photo: library.)

terms of what the paintings represent in relation to the interests of the case: "four hundred loads of maize." By naming the referent of the words as they occur in the painting (the black images) and by describing their form by analogy so as to be recognizable to any viewer (like Indian combs) the presentation of the paintings becomes intelligible through translation, both visual and verbal; their validity as evidence, however, is predicated upon their existence prior to the immediacy of the oral testimony itself.

Like Spanish witnesses, all three native witnesses do offer their own experiential presence at the events as validation of their testimony. But it is through the paintings, not their experience, that their words are taken, as García de Llerena's original request to have the paintings presented makes clear: "I beseech Your Majesty that you command and compel them to give them [the paintings] to the secretary because. . . I ask that their statements be taken by means of the paintings." The validity of the narrative of what they had personally seen and heard is predicated upon the existence of the paintings and the agreement of what can be said/written to be seen in them. Thus the transcript of the court case not only contains a description of the image, but a description of the act of seeing the image.

The locus of that agreement within the document is through the notary himself, Alonso Valverde, that supposedly passive agent of transcription, who interjects his own presence in terms of what he sees and hears. So, for example, in transcribing an earlier part of Esteban's testimony, he writes: "All that has been stated is painted on the said paper on which is depicted the said image of Our Lady and which is signed with my rubric."[11] Yet what he actually saw and signed was a painting on bark cloth consisting only of a series of glyphs that stand for objects and numbers and an oddly placed image of the Virgin and Child (Figure 8.2). The image of the Madonna and Child, however, is crucial to the notary's viewing because it is the only figure that allows a completely unmediated recognition that cannot be questioned by a Spanish viewer. To the notary, it is his own pre-possessed sacred cultural icon: "ymagen de *Nuestra* Señora."[12] This unproblematic viewing anchors the notary's viewing of all the other figures as depicting what is said by the Indian witness.[13] Thus the written words of the Spanish notary stand to (re)confirm the truth of the witnesses' oral testimony, not through hearing but through seeing a "truth" to which all the participants in the production of the testimony – witness, court scribe, and official translator – had already sworn to give before the sign of the cross.

However, before truth is finally established in a court of law, the evidence by which truth is decided can be contested, and the defense was given the chance to rebut the evidence presented by Cortés's lawyer. In regard to the witnesses from Huejotzingo and the paintings, the defense charged that:

> The Indians presented by the contrary party lack credibility, and they should not be given credence because they are Indian vassals of the said Marqués and *all Indians in general* are bad Christians, drunks, *liars*, idolaters, eaters of human flesh, vile persons who for anything whatsoever will perjure themselves, and in regard to the paintings that the contrary party presents, even less faith should be paid to them because they are made by the same infidel and barbarous Indians and for it my parties were not consulted and thus they could have painted whatever they wished.[14]

As in any good defense, the character of the witnesses is attacked. But the attack on the credibility of the witnesses from Huejotzingo is not based on individual character, as it is in the case of a Spanish witness, rather it is based on their identity as Indians who by their nature are many evil things but, most important of all, within a court of law, they are liars and perjurers. The paintings, while not to be believed, are not discredited because they are in and of themselves paintings, but because they are made by the Indians. Yet it is the paintings that were called to court as evidence and not the Indians of Huejotzingo as witnesses. The defense thus reverses the order of priority, hoping that by discrediting first the Indians, the paintings and the evidence presented through them will also be discredited. After all, how could any Spaniard in 1531 deny that Indians did eat human flesh, practiced idolatry, were liars? It would appear to be a shrewd defense, playing upon commonly held opinions about the nature of Indians, essential to the very justification of the Spanish presence in New Spain.

Yet the defense failed, and the four judges declared in open court before the two opposing lawyers that: "We find . . . that the party of the said Marqués proved his intention and demand . . . We grant and pronounce it as well proven; and the said licentiates *did not prove their defense pleas nor anything that would be of any use to them.*"[15]

Now, of course, other evidence was presented in the case by both sides, but the court accepted all that was presented by Cortés's lawyer as true. What is crucial here within a colonial context of law is that a forum for the presentation of non-European evidence could be constructed so as for it to be judged as "true" despite the character of the native. The establishment of truth is found to exist in the suspension of distance between words and images: "All that has been stated is painted." Thus the spoken testimony in Nahuatl that is absent in the record appears within the Spanish text through the written reference to the presence of the images at the time of the testimony and the continued presence of the images which are kept with the court case. It is not just that the paintings are authentic, it is that they authenticate what is said and written, not by analogy but by correspondence. And the recognition of a correspondence or correlation between what is seen and said/written establishes sufficiently the conveyance of a "truth" originating in one culture so as for it to be accepted within the parameters of "truth" in the other.

Christian Doctrine

To convey truth across cultures was not just a contingency of the practice of law within a colonial situation. It was fundamental to the rationale for the European presence in the New World, but in this case truth had to be believed to move from European to native. The teaching of Christian truth to the native population was paramount in order to replace the idolatry of a false religion which the natives had been led to practice by Satanic deceit.[16] Here, in contrast to what obtains in a court case, truth preexists man and does not need to be established; however, in the New World it had yet to be perceived by the natives.

Many interrelated strategies were developed by the early missionaries to convey this universal, divine truth.[17] Yet only one means of conveyance, the use of images in sermons and instructional practices to illustrate various aspects of Church doctrine, was claimed to be newly invented in the New World. This claim was based upon divine inspiration – that is, that there is an unparalleled ontological proximity between sacred Biblical truth and the means of its conveyance by pictures because they are equally produced through the agency of a pre-existing God.

Although the use of paintings to teach Christian doctrine has a long history in Christian practice, the Franciscan, Diego Valadés, insists on its Franciscan invention in one of the most detailed descriptions of the practice in both the text and engravings of his *Rhetorica Christiana*, 1579 (Figure 8.3).[18] What then does Valadés mean by this claim? In part, as Pauline Watts discusses gesture elsewhere in this volume (Chapter 7), it refers to the technical use of images as mnemonic aids (within the classical tradition of artificial memory) as a means to instruct the newly converted Indians.[19] But the claim to Franciscan invention is not merely to be seen within the rhetorical production of memory through images. It is the discovery (realization/divine inspiration) that, through images, natives had the capacity to apprehend the truth of the content of what they were being taught to memorize despite their barbarous character. The Franciscan "discovery" resides in the awareness that images produce a site of correlation for a crosscultural transmission of Christian truth. Because the words of one pass to the other through images, Valadés can write: ". . . this art for spreading the Divine Word was so fruitful and so compelling that as soon as the sermon was finished, the Indians themselves began to discuss among themselves the figures that had been explained to them."[20] The authority to speak of the Word of God moves here from the Franciscan voice through the painting to the native voice.

For Valadés, a *mestizo* and fluent in three Indian languages, his own experience validates what he believes to occur; still, he writes in Latin to his European audience. And in order to establish that natives, in viewing these divinely inspired images, were "attracted and led to the knowledge of the true God creator of heaven and earth,"[21] Valadés needs to establish for his reader that the natives, even though they might be as stupid as he says, were capable of producing and therefore perceiving truth. Here stands his dilemma: how can it be demonstrated that the natives not only memorized but perceived the truth through the images shown to them by the Franciscans when before they had only perceived the lies of their many picture books and idols? It is here that Valadés must demonstrate the existence of a mutual cultural space in which comparable truths can be shown to be held by both cultures and for which an image of correspondence can be produced.

Thus Valadés prefaces his discussion concerning the Franciscan use of paintings by leading his Latin readers through a series of examples of the native use of images. He writes in detail about how Mexican merchants kept accurate track of accounts using their paintings, and he compares the pictographic images of Mexican royalty with the hieroglyphs of Egypt. All of this discussion is kept within the secular use of native images so as to present them as being non-idolatrous and hence not false. But Valadés does not rely only on his own written description as proof. Immediately before commencing his discussion of the Franciscan use of images, he invites the reader to contemplate an engraving that illustrates the Mexican calendrical system (Figure 8.4).[22]

The invitation is not innocent. The reader is asked to stop reading and to look at the engraving provided by Valadés before moving on to his description of Franciscan invention. The engraving thus occupies a visual transitional place between Valadés's textual descriptions of native images and European images and it becomes for the reader, now viewer, the site for his or her own act of recognition of a mutual space of cultural agreement that then permits Valadés to imply, but not openly state, a homologous relationship between native and European uses of imagery to convey truth.

But what exactly is the reader asked to see? It is a diagrammatic chart of concentric circles divided so as to show the division of the Mexican year into 18 months of 20 days each. Yet, although the diagram is a European construct, it is not a "pure" European image in the sense that Valadés uses Mexican pictographic images for the 20 day names and 52 year names. This is the only place in all of Valadés's engravings that prehispanic images refer to their prehispanic referent, so it is his only "*mestizo*" image in which European and Mexican forms of representation have equal valiance. The placement of Mexican forms here is not arbitrary. Neither does it serve simply to demonstrate the Mexican way of recording time. It provides the reader with an image in which European and native forms of knowledge have equal and corresponding truth value; Valadés's

8.3 (right)   Diego Valadés. *Franciscan Teaching in Mexico*. Engraving, page 211 [sic], *Rhetorica Christiana*, Perugia, 1579. Providence, The John Carter Brown Library at Brown University. (Photo: library.)

8.4 (opposite page, left)   Diego Valadés. *Mexican Calendar*. Engraving, page 100, *Rhetorica Christiana*, Perugia, 1579. Providence, The John Carter Brown Library at Brown University. (Photo: library.)

8.5 (opposite page, right)   *Mexican Calendar*. Paint on European paper, dated 1549. Inserted into Fray Motolinía, *Memoriales*, MS., 1541. Austin, Library of the University of Texas, Benson Collection. (Photo: library.)

engraving provides an image of the Mexican calendar correlated with the European calendar. And although it is correlated with the Julian calendar, Diego Valadés understood very well that the Christian calendar and its correct calibration was a monumental issue in the 1570s in Rome where he wrote and published the first part of his book. Whether or not he discussed the Mexican calendar with Pope Gregory, to whom he dedicates the *Rhetorica Christiana*, is unclear, but calling attention to it in a publication appearing only three years before the institution of the Gregorian calendar is no minor act. Such a correlation demonstrates the independent and thus pre-existing ability of Mexicans to produce images through which truth could at once be perceived by them and be recognized by a European.[23]

It is no accident that Valadés asks his reader to contemplate this engraving before reading about the miraculous invention of the Franciscans. His tactic of first visually presenting the calendar and its correlation with the European calendar establishes that a place of truth exists within the corpus of native images. This tactic demonstrates to the reader that Mexicans can receive/perceive the Christian truth through the images that the Franciscans present to them. But why does he choose the calendar as the site of his correlation rather than his illustration of the very act of Christian dialogue through image between Franciscan and native (Figure 8.3)? This decision seems especially odd because Valadés tells the reader that he will not offer an explanation of the native calendar

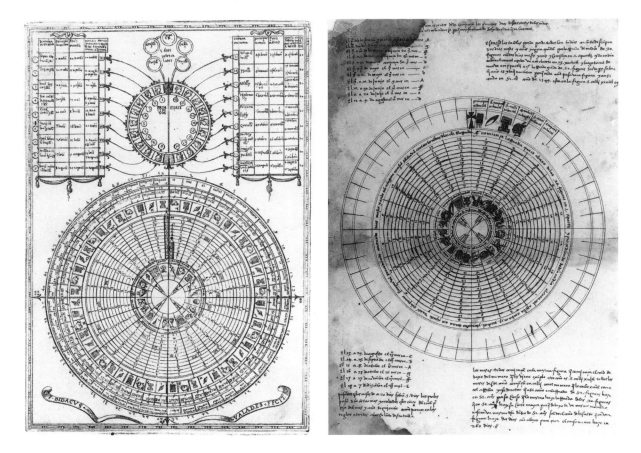

because it ought to be done in the Mexican language.[24] By stating the impossibility of translation and hence explanation for this image while providing an elaborate textual explanation for his illustration of the Franciscan sermon,[25] the calendar image seems to be a place of non-communication.[26] Yet the choice of the calendar image is as tactical as its placement because the calendar had already been privileged by an earlier Franciscan, Motolinía, as the site for recognizing the capacity of certain Mexican images to represent truth through which knowledge of Mexicans could be perceived by the European.[27]

Valadés's source for his engraving is found in Motolinía's 1541 *Memoriales*,[28] into which had been inserted both a description and a drawing, made perhaps by Francisco de las Navas, of the Mexican calendar dated 1549 (Figure 8.5); this drawing also includes a correlation of sorts with the Christian calendar. Its insertion into Motolinía's *Memoriales* as the only visual information in that manuscript for the European reader provides the precedent for Valadés's own placement of his calendar engraving in the *Rhetorica Christiana*.

The drawing of the calendar in Motolinía's manuscript is inserted into Chapter 16 in which Motolinía describes the Mexican calendar, but this, in itself, is not critical to Valadés's choice of the calendar as a sign of the capacity of truth.[29] It is, rather, Motolinía's reference to Chapter 16 in the "Epístola Proemial del Autor . . . ," a dedi-catory letter that begins the manuscript, that suggests why Valadés places such crucial

8.6   Diego Valadés. *Crucifixion.*
Engraving, between pages 220 and
221, *Rhetorica Christiana*, Perugia, 1579.
Providence, The John Carter Brown
Library at Brown University. (Photo:
library.)

truth value in his own engraving. Motolinía writes in his preamble that he will give the
reader the most truthful account of what he has been able to learn.[30] He then lists, as
possible sources for this knowledge, five types of Mexican painted books. He writes,
however, that four of the books are not to be believed in the way in which one believes
the Gospels because they were neither written by John, Mark, Matthew, nor Luke but
were invented by the devil. Motolinía thus creates a kind of medieval typology in which
the four books of the Gospel stand for God's truth in distinction to the four books of the
Mexicans which stand for the devil's deceit. But then Motolinía mentions the fifth book
which stands outside this numerical typology, and it alone is categorized as capable of
conveying truth through its images. This book is the Mexican pictorial account of days
and years or *xihuatonalamatl* as Motolinía calls it. And it is precisely at this place in his
prologue that Motolinía refers the reader to Chapter 16 ("something of this appears
in . . . chapter sixteen") into which has been inserted the drawing of the calendar, the
very source of Valadés's engraving.[31]

   Valadés's invitation to his readers to view his engraving clearly plays upon Motolinía's
own reference to the reader to see his Chapter 16. However, Valadés's appeal reverses
the cultural direction of information through image. Motolinía, as narrator, refers to this
single Mexican source as validating the truthfulness of what he is about to tell his readers
about Mexicans. Valadés seizes upon this image, now already established as standing
outside the typological dichotomy of Christian truth and pagan lies, to demonstrate that

natives were not only capable of producing historical truth through their own pictorial images but, because of that, were capable of perceiving divine truth through Christian images. That is, for Valadés, the image is not a site for the explanation of the native to the European – in fact he rejects that completely. The image is the site that authenticates his claim to his readers, and perhaps himself, of the truthfulness of what the natives say among themselves as they stand speaking in Nahuatl or some other Indian language before the Franciscan paintings.[32]

Here, with Valadés, one moves from the matter-of-fact necessity of a specific crosscultural communication to establish truth in a court of law to the desire to communicate the true faith across culture. Judgment here does not rest in the final opinion of a judge, but in the Final Judgment. Yet just as the *escribano* can believe that he could see in the Huejotzingo paintings all that has been said, so too Valadés can believe that natives could see in the Franciscan images all that has been said to them and that they could now speak among themselves as if they too had experienced and understood the teachings of the Gospels.[33]

Thus, in one remarkable engraving, Valadés presents to the viewer/reader an allegorical image that asserts this claim by creating a pictorial space that collapses differences of time and space (Figure 8.6). Beginning with a print of the Crucifixion, perhaps by Dürer,[34] Valadés moves with his community of native Christians out of the contemporary place of preaching into the space of sacred history. First he displaces the narrative action of the biblical event to the middle ground but without reducing the scale of the figures or altering the style in which they were originally created. In the foreground, he now places a group of figures handled in a different style and scale than those in the middle ground. Here a group of seated natives look into the picture plane and at various parts of the Christian narrative, while a standing Franciscan, perhaps Valadés himself, points to the principal event. This is the same didactic gesture taken by the figure preaching in the pulpit to a congregation of natives seated within the architecture of a colonial church (Figure 8.3). In that engraving, however, no one enters into the illustrations of the Gospel. The paintings of Christ's life do not define the space of action but are merely depicted hanging on the wall of a contemporary church in New Spain. They illustrate the mundane didactic function of images as the pictorial screen for the discourse of a sermon by the gesturing priest. That is, as paintings they still function merely as aids for the illiterate or as what the Jesuit missionary, José de Acosta, calls "libro(s) para los idiotas que no saben leer."[35]

In the engraving of the Crucifixion, however, Franciscan and native have been joined together with the subject of the Gospel image.[36] Valadés thus invents a singular image, marked by two sets of figures and styles such that they all occupy the same space and time. The Latin text in the legend below the image refers to the salvation of mankind through Christ's blood and presumably this is the lesson being articulated by the standing and gesturing Franciscan. But by being in the same space as the crucifixion, Valadés proposes to his European viewer/reader that the Franciscan and the audience in New Spain share the same messianic truth of the Gospel through their common experience such that its sacred meaning can be embraced as re-enacted in the ritual of the Mass. This, then, is not the Baroque theatre of imagery as later produced by someone like Bernini in his sculpture of Santa Teresa. This is a distinctly colonial Renaissance image in which is posited by a *mestizo* the utopian belief in the shared pictorial space of truth.

History: Tovar, Acosta, and Durán

Images proliferated in the New World in order to establish many kinds of truth to varying audiences and contexts. One area that continued to hold fascination for Europeans was knowledge about the native past, both its history and religion. But knowledge of history had to cross through the mediation of the author, and how could the author prove to his reader that what he wrote was true? The textual form of the experiential authority of the author was not always enough and doubts persisted as to *how* the author knew that the histories he recorded were true. Even the Jesuit scholar, José de Acosta, who had spent so many years in Peru studying the history of the Inca, once outside the domain of his own experience had doubts about the truth of historical accounts in Mexico. He expressed these doubts in 1586 in a letter to his Jesuit colleague, Juan de Tovar: "I have enjoyed seeing and studying the Mexican history that you have written and I think that people in Europe will enjoy it also . . . But I wish you would satisfy certain doubts that have occurred to me. In the first place what certainty or authority does this relation or history possess?" He then goes on to ask how such quantities and varieties of information could be remembered over such a long period of time by a people who lacked writing. He ends by asking Tovar: "If you could relieve me of these doubts, the pleasure afforded by this history would not be liable to the suspicion *that it may not be true and certain as a history should be*?"[37]

Tovar understood the doubts and responded, writing that he could have answered immediately but, as he wanted to ensure that his history would find favor with Acosta, he had gone back to check his sources. He describes how he consulted with the old Indian leaders and how he discussed their history with them through their paintings. Like Motolinía and Valadés, he privileges the calendar as the site for establishing the truth of what he knows and writes. Tovar first describes the image of a calendar wheel that was depicted in the history he had already sent Acosta (Figure 8.7), but he also sends a new calendar composed of text and illustrations of the months and days and native feasts, and which is equated with the ecclesiastical calendar as well as the zodiac (Figure 8.8).[38] Both forms of the calendar are asked visually to confirm the temporal structure upon which Mexican history is authenticated ("In these wheels all the events and memorable occurrences that they had in their histories were indicated, *as you will see* in the wheel at the end of the calendar that goes with this [letter].") Tovar notes, however, that the Mexican figures and characters only convey concepts as opposed to "our writing [which] refers to what is written by each word itself without referring to anything else."[39] But the Mexican images became precise through memory so that "many orations were preserved without varying a word from generation to generation until the Spaniards came," when they began to write it down.

That is, historical knowledge is possible in both cultures so that what Tovar has written is true even though the cultural relationship between symbols and their meaning may be different. In the new calendar that Tovar sends to Acosta, this equation is made pictorial so as not to miss the point. An indexical figure literally connects the Mexican system to the European system (Figure 8.9). The figure of a Spaniard is drawn on the page dedicated to a depiction and description of the 17th Mexican month. His placement, however, is outside Tovar's construction of Mexican temporal space, and the

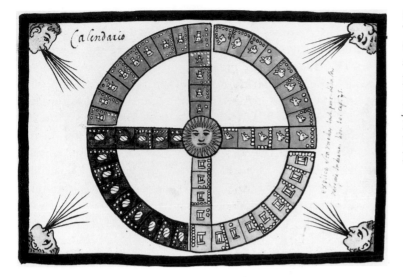

8.7 (left)   Juan de Tovar. Mexican Calendar Wheel. Ink and color on European paper, *Historia*, MS., 1585. Providence, The John Carter Brown Library at Brown University. (Photo: library.)

8.8 (right)   Juan de Tovar. Third and Fourth Months. Ink and color on European paper, *Tovar Calendar*, MS., 1586. Providence, The John Carter Brown Library at Brown University. (Photo: library.)

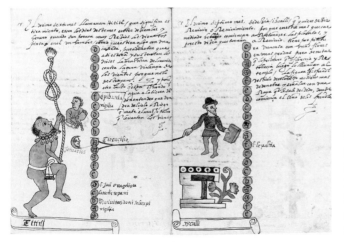

8.9 (left)   Juan de Tovar. Sixteenth and Seventeenth Months. Ink and color on European paper, *Tovar Calendar*, MS., 1586. Providence, The John Carter Brown Library at Brown University. (Photo: library.)

figure gestures across the page and time. His index finger points and is connected by a line that emanates from that finger to the row of 20 day signs on the opposite page which belongs to the sixteenth Mexican month. The line bifurcates to indicate the days in the Mexican month that also mark the end and beginning of the Christian year. The gloss clearly explains that the figure is denotative not illustrative: "the figure of the Spaniard dressed in red serves no more than to denote and signal with a line that comes from the finger where begins the year of the Spaniards."

Yet this figure does more than signal the Christian year. It is the only figure that engages through pictorial gesture with the alphabetic text. His gaze is not turned towards the act described in the gloss, rather the head is turned backward with the eyes looking upward in the direction of the gloss itself, as if in the act of reading it. That is, the figure seemingly becomes the image of its text through its decoding of it. The multidirectional body of the Spaniard, as agent, becomes the contorted transformational gesture of text into image that leads to the intersection of western and Mexican sign systems and their mutual ability to produce comparable meaning. Moreover, what the gloss does not mention is that the figure holds a book in his other hand, the sign of European written knowledge. The denotative image of the Spaniard thus does more than point forward while it looks backward; it collapses the gulf between European written words and Mexican images by holding on to and connecting these two forms of knowledge, just as Tovar himself has done for Acosta.

For Tovar, Mexican images are capable of revealing the truth "as every history should be" and he sends this calendar as part of his reply to Acosta's doubts. But what is problematic in Tovar's defense through an appeal to Mexican images as authenticating the history that Acosta had read and doubted is that Tovar's images (which illustrate his history) are not copies of "true" Mexican images. Rather, they are copies made after copies found in a manuscript made by the Dominican friar, Diego Durán. In fact, Tovar refers to Durán in his letter to Acosta: "In addition [to consulting with native lords to explain their images that came from their libraries], I saw a book made by a Dominican friar, a relative of mine, which was very similar to the ancient library that I had seen and which helped me refresh my memory in making the history that you [Acosta] have now read." Tovar's reference to Durán and his copying of Durán's images and text therefore attribute an authority to Durán's work that is equal to that of native oral and pictorial sources. Yet they are not the same thing because Durán's work already mediates the native sources, so that Tovar is placing as much faith on the mediated illustrations of native sources as on the native sources themselves. How is it then that Durán's version of Mexican history and religion is so authentic for Tovar?[40] Clearly, Tovar is aware that Durán's text and illustrations are based on images taken from Aztec sources, but Tovar also can see clearly that Durán's copyist has transformed the mnemonic Mexican pictographs into Renaissance-style illustrations by placing them in landscapes, within frames, and at the heading of chapters (Figures 8.10 and 8.11).

Yet Tovar accepts their presence in this quasi-emblematic form as the proof of the accuracy of Durán's methods of inquiry because Durán asserts that his illustrations can stand for his original dialogue with natives in which his translation of the mnemonic act of discourse across culture is authenticated by the aura of the antiquity of the native image to which his illustration, as a copy, refers. In his *Libro de los Ritos y Ceremonias*

composed in c. 1579, he begins with a description of Topiltzin, "a great man who once came to this land," saying that "the information that exists about him is great, I saw him painted in the way that he appears above (Figure 8.10), on very old and ancient paper in Mexico City, with a venerable representation. It showed [Topiltzin] to be an old man with a long red beard turning white."[41] Further on in the same first chapter Durán introduces another of his copyist's images:

> I found the painting as you will see it painted on this page next to the painting of Topiltzin no less old and ancient as the other [Figure 8.11], which in order to lend it to me, the Indian from Chiauhtla who had it, made me first swear that I would return it to him. When I had given him my word that when I had copied it I would return it, he loaned it to me . . . He did not leave the side of the painter until he had finished it . . .

Durán then returns to the first image, writing:

Wanting to confirm if this were true I asked an old Indian from Coatepec . . . to tell me whether what was written and painted there was true and as the Indians find it difficult to give explanations unless they can consult the book of their village, he went home and brought back a painting . . . This native narrated the life of Topiltzin to me like the other or better such that I was more than a little contented. He showed me the picture of Topiltzin celebrating feasts, wearing a feathered crown we saw in the painting. It looked very much like the miter that bishops wear on their heads when they say Mass. The painting is this.[42]

Durán compresses, in these passages, the two acts of seeing into a single sentence so that the reader participates, through the illustration, in Durán's own viewing of the original painting ("el cual vi pintado a la manera que arriba aparece"). Durán then describes textually what is seen in the painting, but one is not sure if the description pertains to the original one that Durán saw or to the illustration he provides.[43] That is, he vacillates in his reading of the picture into words in which temporal phenomena, in this case the history of Topiltzin, is presented through the verbal description of the static object. Durán's description pertains both to the absent ancient original and to the present illustration.

Durán's stratagem is important because he has already told the reader in the prologue that ". . . they [Mexicans] distrust us, do not believe us. They will not tell us things they know about the lives of their ancestors."[44] Yet despite this assertion, he must convince his readers that what he is telling them is the truth because the truth was told to him, and this is done by including reproductions of the images through which the natives narrated their history. That the images are said to agree in detail with the oral narratives of the Indians means that what Durán has written, as translated text, is true. The image appears both physically and textually as the sign of Durán's task and method of transferring information crossculturally. But here, unlike the court case of Huejotzingo, the images are the simulacra of a prior oral dialogue between Durán and the native informants, and they function now solely within a written dialogue between the author and the reader. Their presence does not authenticate the text by their own authenticity. They do not stand prior to the text, rather they illustrate the text that describes them. The correspondence between text and image is not now a movement across culture, but is circular within European discourse in which the image reifies the textual authenticity of Durán's own visual and auratic experience. Durán now boldly writes that his copy is the image of what he had seen as it is described in the text.

The presence of images is not, however, necessary to establish the authority of Durán's text and, when Acosta incorporates the texts of both Durán and Tovar into his own work, he simply refers to the images and does not reproduce them.[45] Yet Acosta, by accepting the veracity of these authors, accepts unquestioningly their images as truthful. Tovar's and Durán's images may be copies but as copies they have as their object of imitation the native images through which the originary dialogue across culture took place. Hence they function as natural signs that confirm the texts that Acosta reproduces. They appease by their presence, either as copies or textual reference, the doubts concerning historical knowledge which in Europe was possible because "writing refers to what is written by each word itself without referring to anything else," while in the

Americas that knowledge was possible because of native images and memory which through description and translation could then be conveyed in European alphabetic text.

History and Fiction

As one moves from Durán through Tovar to Acosta there is an ever-increasing distance from the original site of crosscultural discourse through image as it is imagined to occur in the Huejotzingo trial and Franciscan teaching. Yet in all cases, the image and its description stand to displace doubts about the credulity of the speaker/author. The image becomes as much the production of the author, either by finding or copying of the original, as is his text. Its presence plays upon the ambiguity of the image's referent as image. That is, by its nature the image refers by imitation to the thing it reproduces and hence its unmediated immediacy seemingly corroborates independently the textual reproduction of that phenomenon which has been extracted through linguistic and cultural differences.

The fiction of independence is maintained by the presence of authenticity, either as an original or as a copy of the original. The fiction, however, becomes more difficult to sustain in the absence of an original image, as in Peru where there was no comparable prior native pictorial tradition as there was in Mexico. Thus, in one of the few Peruvian pictorial manuscripts, Martín de Murúa's *Historia del Origen y Genealogía Real de los Reyes Incas del Perú*, the reference of most images is not to an independent original source but to the text itself. Here, there is no claim to their status as anything other than as illustrations. For example, Murúa recounts the dream of one of the *akllakuna* (cloistered young women dedicated to the service of the Inca sun god) who sits in the middle of the cloister and listens to the four springs repeat her prayer back to her. He provides two images of this account, the first of which is like many of his other illustrations and pictorially depicts the sleeping *aklla* placed between four fountains (Figure 8.12). But the second image is altogether different and indicates a sensitivity towards the difference between the image as illustration of text and image as conveyance of truth. That is, the second image is presented as an unmediated visualization of proof of what he has written about the wondrous nature of the dream (Figure 8.13). It is a diagram of the cloister filled with the four Quechua words of the *aklla*'s prayer, arranged in a grid pattern of 25 letters such that the first word of the prayer forms the four borders and reads in all four different directions. The letters of the diagonal, central horizontal and central vertical columns also form a pattern in which the words can be read the same way in either direction. Murúa's motive in this case is not illustrative but demonstrative and he writes that "in order *to see if it were true* about which these Indians tell, I wanted to place here on the other side of the page the four fountains and the names and the sad song of Chiquillanto [the *aklla*], in order *to see* by the figure if [the words] were communicated the same in either direction, and *I saw* it to be something marvelous, as the figure *shows*."[46] Here Murúa invites the Spanish reader to discover with him, through his own image, the truth of what has been told to him and that which he is now telling. Together, Murúa and the reader visually enter into the mytho-history of Inca dreams in which the fantasy of the unconscious becomes configured and confirmed by a fantastic image. The image that

8.12 Martín de Murúa. Drawing of Aklla's Dream. *Historia del Perú*, 1590. Formerly Loyola, Jesuit Archive; location now unknown (illustration taken from *Historia del Perú*, ed. Constantino Bayle).

8.14 (above) Miguel de Cervantes Saavedra. *El Ingenioso Hidalgo Don Quijote de la Mancha*, Madrid: Juan de la Cuesta, 1605, pages 32–33. (Photo: author.)

8.13 (left) Martín de Murúa. Diagram of Aklla's Dream. *Historia del Perú*, 1590.

Murúa provides here is completely fabricated, as he acknowledges, based upon his transcription of the oral prayer into the European alphabet, but unlike his other illustrations, it is presented as direct proof. Thus what becomes the authenticating source is not a prior native image (there is none); instead it is the oral text itself which becomes fixed not in a textual narrative transcription with illustration, but in a patterned form of a magical text/image.[47] It is neither one nor the other. What must be suspended here for belief, and in fact is not acknowledged by Murúa, is that the crosscultural act of conveying the miraculous orality of the other's dream becomes visible only by assigning to Quechua words which existed previously in a spoken state, western alphabetic values within a spatial matrix. Their representation as an anagram and a palindrome is thus not a literal translation of Quechua into Spanish, nor words into image in the sense of illustration, rather it is the transfiguration of spoken Quechua into a form of knowledge in which written Quechua words can be shown to reproduce (and therefore show/ prove) the almost indescribable movement of sound in a dream.

Martín de Murúa's image begins as proof to himself and then is offered to the reader as the truth of what Murúa has been told as history, but the fantasy of dreams moves his history perilously close to fiction. Thus the visual gymnastics through which an image is given to the translation of a Quechua word/dream seems, today perhaps, ludicrous and false. Yet Murúa, at one level of crosscultural communication, performs no different an act than Cortés's lawyer, Valadés, Motolinía, Tovar, or Durán. They are all similar attempts to find an acceptable, neutral site upon which the doubts to truth can be put to rest by means of visual confirmation. That all but Murúa's image have been used almost exclusively by modern scholars as the site of iconographic exegesis on Precolumbian symbolic systems demonstrates how powerful this tactic remains.

Yet the credulity that an image engenders for the viewer as the site of crosscultural truth was long ago given the lie, but not in a court of law, nor history (how many history books are still illustrated?), nor philosophy, but in fiction. In Chapter IX, Part I of *Don Quijote*, Cervantes recounts the discovery of the Arabic manuscript that allowed him to continue the narrative "de nuestro famoso Español D. Quijote de la Mancha." However, the imagined discovered manuscript, Cide Hamete Benengeli's *Historia de Don Quijote de la Mancha*, is written in Arabic and Cervantes tells how, in a frenzy of desire, he had it immediately translated for him by a *ladino*, a bilingual Arab.[48] At the same time, Cervantes describes very carefully what is "pintada muy al natural" on the first page of the manuscript. Cervantes performs this act of ekphrasis because he notes that the translator is an Arab and therefore by his very nature cannot be trusted; however, the painting confirms the identification of the manuscript and its translation as true because the image agrees in almost every detail with the verbal description from the manuscript of the Arab.[49] That is, the Arab, although by nature a liar, has his translation confirmed as being true by an image that pre-exists the translation and thus it must first refer to the original Arabic text but then, because it also faithfully illustrates the translation as well, it forms the neutral site/sight of confirmation. But, of course, Cervantes provides no image for his reader (Figure 8.14). There is no site of confirmation of the truthfulness of the translation other than the author who is at once other (Arab) and self (Spaniard), but the reader is beguiled by the promise of the truth said to exist in a painting that is somewhere else.

"Todo aca es mentira"

I have argued here that in the sixteenth century a part of the cultural space that allowed for a place of agreement between the words of different languages and the shared concepts that they signified came to be located in the pictorial image. In part, this neutral territory, composed, like writing, of graphic lines and colors but appealing to sight not sound, is based on the belief in the mutual recognition of what is represented regardless of how it is expressed in the transcription of language into alphabetic text. The words, if written, would not look alike if seen and not pronounced alike if spoken, but the image to which they mutually appeal reveals their truthful relationship. This relationship assumed not only an unproblematic relation between image and its object of imitation but an unproblematic relation between cultural readings as if the pictorial image were a natural sign equally available to all.[50]

Therefore, to describe an image, to discourse on an image, to allow an image to stand prior to the text as that which authenticates it were acts that could be believed to convey truth because of the acceptance of the pictorial image itself, both European and native, as an unmediated access to knowledge across cultural boundaries. These acts are what could be called the ekphrasis of crosscultural translation. That is, the translation, the telling of another's words, has a referent that appears by its nature to be unproblematic and hence that translation too becomes unproblematic if the translation is brought through the screen of the "objective" pictorial image into text.

But if ekphrasis, as a European poetic concept, is the "illusionary representation of the unrepresentable,"[51] then this inherent paradox, when it becomes apparent in the relation of text and image in the New World, reveals the absurd nature of the unproblematic acceptance of the truth content of the image and thereby the translation which is attached to it, because it masks the act of translation itself as being both cultural and verbal. The paradox, however, is double because whereas the European images are mimetic, the native images, as in Mexico, are primarily mnemonic. Yet difference here, too, is repressed for the Spaniard, at least in the early negotiations, so that the pictographic, mnemonic images could be seen to be mimetic through their transformation into alphabetic text; that the narrative of the written text of an oral translation could be believed to be seen in the image which exists prior to both. Ultimately, this repression of difference was effaced by the transformation of mnemonic images into mimetic images so that, for example, although the Franciscan, Bernardino de Sahagún, set about in 1536 studying Nahua culture and society by using pre-contact mnemonic paintings and their oral exegesis, the images found in his 1569 Florentine Codex are mimetic illustrations of his written text.[52] Now completely unproblematic, to a western viewer at least, Sahagún's images stand in that "neutral" ground between the text written in Spanish or Latin and the text written in Nahuatl and pertaining "naturally" to both by their imitation of the mutual object described (Figure 8.15).

If then there is a common thread to what I have called the ekphrasis of crosscultural translation, it is the act of invention/discovery that carries in it the desire for completeness and closure: the existence of something prior that allows for the telling, often in spite of the lying nature of the teller. Certainly the Indies pre-existed the discovery of the Indians but, once their discovery became named, the search for a kind of northwest

Del primero libro

que iamas se puede ver por donde
paso: o como vna saeta, que sale
dela vallesta, con gran impetu,
y llega adonde la endereça el
vallestero sin dexar rastro algu
no, de su passada: Desta manera,
nos acontecio, a nosotros: nacidos en
breue tiempo, se nos acabo la vi
da: y ningun rastro dexamos,
de buena vida: fenecieron se nros
dias, en nra malignidad, y en
nuestro mal viuir: B. Tales co
sas dixeron los peccadores enel in
fierno, con grandissimo dolor de
su coraçon, y con llanto de gran
tristeza, y con lagrimas no reme
diables: porque no quisieron cono
cer, ni seruir al verdadero dios,
criador, y regidor, de todas las co
sas: quando començo su tormento,
entonce començo su llanto, dolor
y lagrimas, y agora estan enel,
y para siempre iamas perseuerará
enel: los que conocen, y siruen
y obedecen, al solo y verdadero
dios, gozaron de sus riquezas. Y go
zos eternos, porque es infinitame
te bueno, y suaue: ansi queda di
cho enel testo de la sagrada escrip

e vntlan, vmpoliuh. intonemiliz.

B. Ocauhquihi, ynintlaçol intlaten
tocanime, iuhqui in, yminchequiz, y
rymixaio, ynintlaocullatel, yninho
quiztlatl, vanyman aic vel motolla
lizque. Auh inquimiximachilia. inqui
metlacumchilia, yntotecuyo dios, qui
nopilhuizque. yniytlatocaiotzin, yni
neaiytonoliztzin: iehua caçanguiz
camocuiltono.xny, yntoteccuyo dios, iuh
ca intcuidatolli intlacpac omito.

8.15   Bernardino de
Sahagún. *Florentine
Codex*, pictorial
manuscript, 1570.
Florence, Biblioteca
Medicea-Laurenziana,
Palat. Col. Cod. 218–

passage across culture continued by means of which truth could pass through the opacity
of linguistic and cultural difference. But in *Don Quijote* the image as a fetish of any such
truth is revealed by its absence. It is not there, it is only said to be there; the reader can
no longer see it. The reader's credulity is twice cajoled by the text. The fictitious
discovery of the Arabic text is translated by the Arab who by his nature is a liar, yet it
is all true because his translation is confirmed by an image which, because it reproduces
what is read in the Spanish text, must then also reproduce what is written in the
unreadable Arabic text. It is the illusory site of correlation of translation.

One has not moved so very far from the *escribano* in the Huejotzingo case in the sense that he could see in a Mexican painting all that had been said. But for the reader of *Don Quijote* there is no image to see, there never was one, but one readily plays the game of fiction. But in the New World, a place to which Cervantes wanted to travel and to which Don Quixote did,[53] truth and reality were not just a clever word game. It was a place where truth was a lie, captured most eloquently in the famous phrase, "I obey but I do not comply," and used in earnest by Spaniards with brutal consequences for the native population. So then, one also can believe Guaman Poma, the native Andean author and illustrator, who, although he produced some 400 drawings in his 1000-page manuscript addressed to the king of Spain, writes about colonial Peru and by extension all of the Americas that "todo aca es mentira (everything here is a lie)."[54] That longed-for place of mutual recognition across cultures is thus held up to us by both Cervantes and Guaman Poma to be a fiction and a lie even as Guaman Poma compulsively drew pictures of it in order to denounce it. Here, in the New World, there is no justice and for this absence to become real, it too must become an image occupied by Spaniard and native.[55]

PART 3

Early Collecting Practices

9.1   Pieter Gerritsz. van Rosestraten (?). *Still Life of the Paston (Yarmouth) Collection*. Norwich, Castle Museum. (Photo: museum.)

CHAPTER 9

"Wrought by No Artist's Hand": The Natural, the Artificial, the Exotic, and the Scientific in Some Artifacts from the Renaissance

MARTIN KEMP

A large seventeenth-century painting in the Castle Museum, Norwich (Figure 9.1), displays a glorious ensemble of natural and artificial objects, scattered across a wide but shallow space in an abundant profusion which is notable even by the cluttered standards of Dutch still life paintings.[1] Of the thirteen items of virtuoso goldsmithery, which comprise the largest group of objects in the painting, at least nine appear to incorporate natural objects, most typically ornamental shells set within elaborate mounts. The intentionally exotic nature of the ensemble is underlined by the parrot, monkey, African youth, giant lobster, and, most literally, by the terrestrial globe which is oriented to display "America," "Mexica," the "Mare Pacifico," "Nuova Guinea," and adjoining geographical features of the Postcolumbian world. The patronage of the picture is reasonably clear. It originated from the Yarmouth (or Paston) Collection and incorporates a selection of the treasures owned by the Pastons of Oxnead Hall in Norfolk, England. Some of the items can be identified with surviving pieces and recognized in an inventory of Sir Robert Paston's holdings.[2] The obvious fascination with objects which owe their origins to the sea is consistent with the overseas travels of Sir William Paston (1610–63), who visited Cairo and Jerusalem and was credited with the assembly of an unrivalled "*Musaeum* abounding with an infinite variety of the most choice and admired rarities." His son, Robert (1631–83), extended his father's collection of "rarities" and was a fashionable builder on a scale that extended the family's wobbly finances beyond their limits.

The interpretive frameworks for the painting are clearly a good deal more complicated than a simple record of the act of possession – and I use the plural, "frameworks," deliberately. The key to the re-assembly of potentially relevant meanings lies generally within the field of the history of collecting, providing this history is taken in its most expansive sense to embrace intricately interconnected motives from religious and secular thought, from art and science, and from the private and public realms. The items in the Paston painting are generically representative of the kind of objects that were to be found in collectors' "cabinets," those pan-European proto-museums which contained what to our eyes are multifarious and heterogeneous assemblages of curious things – of *mirabilia* (items at which to marvel), *exotica* (items from strange realms), *naturalia* (products of nature), *artificialia* (artifacts of human contriving), and *scientifica* (instruments for the pursuit of science and technology), in varying permutations.[3]

A tool for the reconstruction of two of the most conspicuously evident frameworks within which the Paston picture would have made articulate sense to a sophisticated viewer in the periods of late Mannerism and early Baroque is provided by the *Archetypa* of Georg Hoefnagel, the printed assemblage of *naturalia* which was published in 1592.[4] Hoefnagel was closely associated with Prague, the epicenter of *wunderkammer* culture around 1600. His professed concern was to locate human activities in relation to nature, or rather in regard to God's eternal presence as manifested though his work as the supreme artisan of all natural forms. The frontispiece for Book IV (Figure 9.2) articulates this relationship through a series of *vanitas* motifs, most notably the *homo bulla*, by which the pretensions of the human race are equated with the transitory glories of an inflated bubble. At the top of the print Hoefnagel quotes a tag – "genius lives; all else will perish" – which was also used by Andreas Vesalius in the illustration of the skeleton in his great volume of anatomy, and by Tycho Brahe on one of his famed astronomical instruments;[5] while the tablet below the skull reminds the reader of Psalm 102: "As for man, his days are as grass: as a flower of the field, so he flourisheth."[6] The thinly veiled genital allusions in the rotund and penile fruits on the left and right underscore the fleshy impulses to which man is subject. In the subsequent illustrations (Figure 9.3), a particular remedy for the human condition is advocated. This remedy consists of the recognition of the divine artisan and in his worship through our prostration in the face of the transcendent artistry of his handiwork. Thus the "gloria summi Artificis" is displayed through collections of natural artifacts which populate the earth, water, and air. The extraordinary shaping abilities of God are described in terms of the aesthetic of Mannerist design, with a contrived relish for sinuous combinations of curvaceous, sharp, and entangled profiles, and diverse patterns of surface markings. The very self-consciousness of Hoefnagel as a designer – as in the characteristic *trompe l'œil* motifs of the stems clamped to the borderline of the print – reflects his implicit aspiration to be an imitator of the supreme *Artifex* within the scope of what is possible for the human "ape" of nature's wonders.

Comparable *vanitas* motifs are insistently apparent in the Paston painting, with a particular emphasis upon the inexorable march of time and the transitory delights of music. Perhaps there is a direct allusion to the five senses, all of which are expressly stimulated by items within the picture. The girl, who is squeezed rather spacelessly into the foreground, displays full-blown flowers and sombre music for the viewer's attention.[7] She has been feasibly identified as Robert's daughter, Mary, who was less than 13 years old when she died in 1676, and the whole painting may be a *memento mori* in her honor. Yet, as so often with *vanitas* compositions, the ostensible decrying of the worth of worldly glories is visually undermined by an unabashed delight in their rich beauties. A hymn in praise the ability of the human designer to participate in the divine creativity of nature competes manfully with a mournful lament of the kind expressed by Sir Robert himself: "all is so uncertain in this world that no man knows which way to turn himself."[8]

The subject of this paper is to be a group of objects of the kind that play such a conspicuous role in the Paston painting, that is to say artifacts which incorporate natural

9.2 (left) Georg Hoefnagel. *Allegorical Frontispiece*. Engraved by Jacob Hoefnagel, from *Archetypa*, Frankfurt, 1592, book IV. Glasgow, University Library. (Photo: author.)

9.3 (right) Georg Hoefnagel. *Plants, Insects, Snail, and Sea Horse*. Engraved by Jacob Hoefnagel, from *Archetypa*, Frankfurt, 1592, book IV, plate 4. Glasgow, University Library. (Photo: author.)

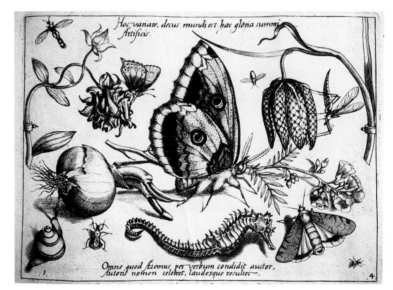

objects in such a way that their original configuration remains apparent, and indeed provides the generating motif for the overall design. It is my contention that objects in this category of the "applied arts" are "cultural migrators" of the most peripatetic kind, and that an examination of their making and use undermines any rigid systems of classification which claim to provide categories or classes through which the spectator's reaction (then or now) might be controlled within clearly delimited parameters. I will be arguing that a complex fluidity, ambiguity, and diversity of meaning characterizes the viewing of such items even in a number of apparently similar contexts in Renaissance societies, and that such viewing undermines any propensity to characterize them neatly in terms of the kind of historical "meta-realities" – such as power, colonialism, pos-

9.4 (right) *Tree-Column*. From the portal of the Chapel of St. Hubert, stone. Amboise. (Photo: author.)

9.5 (below) Giulio Romano. *Design for a Vine Dish*. Pen and ink with wash. Chatsworth, Collection of the Duke of Devonshire. (Photo: Courtauld Institute of Art, courtesy of the Trustees of the Chatsworth Settlement.)

session, oppression, patriarchy, Eurocentrism, and otherness – which now tend to be taken as having a privileged explanatory power.

Although it will not be possible in this paper to tease out all the possible fluidities and potential subversions of categorization, I will endeavor to keep a representative selection of them in play and to signal their presence in relation to some of the individual items I have chosen to exemplify my own artificially defined category. Let us, as a preliminary move, signal some of the "poles" between which the objects potentially migrate. They journey between religious and secular, Catholic and Protestant, godliness and vanity. They cross boundaries between public and private, the secret and the accessible, artisan and noble, high and vulgar taste, functional and decorative, self-aggrandisement and disinterest, financial value and perceived worth in other value systems, center and periphery, domestic and exotic. They effect transformations between artist, artisan, technologist, engineer, scientist, philosopher, and magician in varied compounds. They cross neat divisions between Gothic and Renaissance, classical and non-classical, western and non-western, single style and plural styles, mechanical and intellectual, applied arts and fine arts. The motive power behind these plural migrations is the conscious and continual redrawing of the boundary between the artifice of nature and the artifice of the human agent. As my listing of "poles" indicates, I am setting up an absurdly prolix agenda, but I believe that we can gain a provisional sense of the kind of migrations that are involved through the classic strategy of looking at a selection of illustrated examples which collectively serve to pose the most telling questions.

The motif of the essential contiguity of the natural and the artificial in the conception of human artifacts was very much present in Gothic design, particularly in those later phases of courtly Gothic which display a highly self-conscious wit which is little less developed than that of the Mannerists. A modest but apposite example is provided by the nice tree-column in the portal of the fifteenth-century Chapel of St. Hubert in the Castle at Amboise (Figure 9.4), the chapel that now contains what are taken to be the mortal remains of Leonardo da Vinci – who had himself used this visual pun in the *Sala delle Asse* in Milan, some twenty years before his death at Amboise. In Renaissance terms, the motif drew support from Alberti, perhaps on the basis of Vitruvius's account of the earliest dwellings, but the late Gothic example shows that the Roman sanction was not strictly required.[9] This conscious parading of natural sources for human designs was to become a motif which ran strongly throughout Mannerist production. As a self-consciously "rustic motif" it features in one of Guilio Romano's designs (Figure 9.5), with overtly bacchic resonances, and, as we shall see, it gains special power in the hands of those designers who incorporated direct casts of natural objects into their works, such as Jamnitzer and Palissy.[10] The continuities here seem to erode any system of period labeling, especially any attempt to describe this aspect of the work of Giulio and their successors as "neo-Gothic."

More strictly germane to our present inquiry are those medieval objects that directly incorporate recognizable natural items. Indeed, the fact that the natural objects remained recognizable was essential for the meaning and function of the items. There is both written and visual testimony to the use of exotic treasures from nature as sacred containers in ecclesiastical contexts – chalices, reliquaries, and monstrances composed from ostrich eggs and coconut shells – and as objects of wonder which testify to the

9.6   *Coral Tree Table Ornament with "Serpents' Tongues."* Coral, metal, and fossilized teeth. Vienna, Schatz des Deutschen Ordens. (Photo: Schatz des Deutschen Ordens.)

9.7   *Table Ornament with "Serpents' Tongues" and Topaz.* Coral, metal, topaz, and fossilized teeth. Vienna, Kunsthistorisches Museum, Sammlung für Plastik und Kunstgewerbe. (Photo: museum.)

marvels of God's creation, attracting a public into the church and inducing reverent awe, as well as performing more overtly magical functions.[11] Coral was particularly prized for its talismanic powers, variously protecting against illness and the evil eye, and promoting the growth of teeth in children. One particularly spectacular piece in Vienna (Figure 9.6) doubles up on its magic attributes. From coral branches hang a series of detachable "serpents' tongues" (*natterzungen*) which acted as antidotes to poison when dipped into drink or food.[12] The magic "tongues" (in fact the fossilised teeth of chondricthytes, such as sharks) were prized items in the highest circles of church and state. In 1295 Pope Boniface had acquired no fewer than fifteen "branches of trees with serpents' tongues."[13] The two most spectacular surviving examples, both dating from the fifteenth century, demonstrate that the designers responsible for their mounting have consciously harmonized the natural and the artificial. The designer of the second of them (Figure 9.7) has devised metal branches and calyxes to support the bloom-like tongues, while at the top is a fructiform growth, at the heart of which is a grand topaz.[14] The compound

9.8 Willibald Stoss, after Albrecht Dürer. *Dragon Chandelier.* Reindeer antler and metal, 1522. Nuremberg, Germanisches Nationalmuseum. (Photo: museum.)

ensemble exploits a conscious blurring of the demarcation between the products of nature and man through the use of the late Gothic vocabulary of organically styled shapes, in a manner which is no less knowing than the Mannerist puns of the later sixteenth century.

In case, however, we should feel that we are settling too comfortably into a category of "late medieval magic," it is worth noting that coral could serve as exotic decoration without any apparently direct exploitation of its magic potential. Around 1519, the Elector August of Saxony bought a set of coral-handled cutlery, whose primary function clearly was to impress guests on special occasions.[15] The trouble and expense that was entailed in obtaining such objects from specialist suppliers in distant places was part of the point of the exercise. Later in the century, Battista de Negrone Viale in the port city of Genoa became known as a specialist supplier to European princes of items based on coral obtained via Sicily.[16] Some idea of the response of designers to the importation of exotic materials and the designs can be gained from Cellini's *Autobiography*, where he describes in typically declamatory fashion his conquest of the exotic art of damascening which had been introduced to Spain by the Moors.[17]

A comparably secular context, but a civic rather than a courtly one, provided the setting for one of the most spectacular of all items of interior decoration which incorporated an exceptional *naturalium*. In 1522 Anton Tacher II presented a remarkable and prized set of 34-point reindeer antlers to the city of Nuremberg for their "newly built upstairs chamber" (Figure 9.8).[18] The antlers had been transformed into a seven-light candelabrum in the guise of a three-headed dragon by Willibald Stoss on the basis of a design by Albrecht Dürer. The conjoined qualities of an extraordinary product contrived by nature and by the artists of Nuremberg was designed to lend special distinction to the city's new room, which was built specifically to house the meetings of the seven Electors. There is little doubt that Dürer's contriving of seven lights was intended to allude to the seven luminaries who were to deliberate under its glow. The appropriation of a wonder

9.9   *Ostrich Egg Cup with
Coral*. Vienna,
Kunsthistorisches
Museum, Sammlung für
Plastik und Kunstgewerbe.
(Photo: museum.)

of nature here serves a governmental function, but it is not difficult to envisage the same splendid antlers hanging with mammoth bones and ostrich eggs in a church, or alternatively being pointed out as a hunting trophy in a Saxon prince's *wunderkammer*.

No exotic item had a longer or more varied history of use than the ostrich egg. Through the extensive literature on Piero della Francesca's *Montefeltro Altarpiece*, the egg has become something of a set-piece of the iconographer's art in a way that has worked against its wider consideration in religious and secular frameworks.[19] Durandus had already drawn attention to the ability of ostrich eggs as "marvelous rarities" to draw people into church, as if God has provided a particularly effective visual magnet for his own ends.[20] We know that in 1435 two eggs were located on either side of Duccio's *Maestà* in Siena Cathedral, and the Medici inventory of 1492 records one in the rather different setting of the private devotional space of the chapel in the Palazzo Medici.[21] Although the bestiary legends of the strange and rather negligent habits of the ostrich in incubating its eggs might, as Durandus acknowledged, support their interpretation as symbolizing the way human beings forget the true observance of God, it seems more likely that their presence was generally justified in the same way as was used to sanction the display of griffins' claws and serpents' tongues in churches. The huge eggs were also items that an opportunistic trader might add to the goods he shipped for sale to well-off clients, as happened in the case of Francesco Datini, the much-traveled merchant of Prato, who imported ostrich feathers and eggs, as well as ivory tusks.[22] Once purchased, it would be open to the owner of an egg to endow it with whichever of the potential significances might be most appropriate in whatever context it was placed.

It is not surprising that ostrich eggs became star items in the *wunderkammer*, occasioning some of the most elaborate settings of any natural items. The spectacular example in Vienna (Figure 9.9), made for the Augsburg cabinet of Archduke Ferdinand II of Tyrol, uses liberal quantities of coral to provide a dense tangle of organic shapes around the smooth geometry of the shell.[23] The egg itself is directly supported by an ostrich, which is held captive on collar and chain by a "native" hunter and holds in its mouth a horsehoe – alluding to its legendary appetite. The function of such an extraordinary ensemble in a cabinet was in a sense obvious: it served as a marvel which gave pleasure and pride to its owner and induced pleasure and awe in the privileged visitor. But the very compound nature of the ostrich cup gave it a multivalent quality, in which it could play with equal efficacy on the spectator's potential interest in aspects of magic, in Plinian natural science, in the meaning of animals as outlined in the medieval bestiary, in the surpassing skill of the divine *Artifex*, in the virtuoso achievements of the human hand and eye, and so on. The way that different cabinets were laid out supplied different kinds of primary order within which the same object could potentially converse in a number of rather different languages. The magnificent cabinet assembled by Archduke Ferdinard of Tyrol at Ambras was arranged by materials in Plinian fashion, whereas the Elector August of Saxony concentrated on tools and instruments in his collection at Dresden.[24] Samuel Quiccheberg, who may justly be regarded as the theorist of the *wunderkammer*, advocated an elaborate scheme of micro- and macrocosmic analogies through which the cabinet would become a *teatrum sapientiae*, much like Giulio Camillo's "memory theatre."[25] However, I believe that much of the life and sustained fascination of the collections for highly sophisticated viewers lay in the refusal of many of the individual objects to submit docilely to precise categorization. Rather, they manifest the interconnectedness of things in the manifold of nature, what Francis Bacon was to call the "shuffle of things" in his prescription for a "goodly huge cabinet,"

> wherein whatsoever of the hand of man by exquisite art or engine has made rare in stuff, form or motion, whatsoever singularity, chance, and the shuffle of things, hath produced; whatsoever nature has wrought in things that want life and may be kept; shall be sorted and included.[26]

There is indeed a certain subversion involved in the making of an object like the Vienna ostrich cup, which may be generically categorized as a drinking chalice but which has become elaborated to the point where function becomes more a matter of visual type than genuine utility. A nice recognition of this issue occurs in a letter of 1550 to Duke Cosimo in Florence from Jacopo da Trezzo, a specialist modeler and carver of rock crystal, who inquired whether the Duke wanted "a cup for drinking or just to look good."[27] Looking at the vessels, it is not always easy to tell whether they were "utilitarian" and we know that some of the notably exotic vessels were actually used for drinking. The Fuggers possessed a "mounted ostrich egg with a silver cover in a black case, together with the book used for welcoming."[28] But the utility would have been at most strictly limited to particular occasions or functions, like the Fuggers' ceremony of welcome for prestigious visitors. Today such "cups" are removed both from their utilitarian and intellectual contexts. We are now likely to see them displayed as works of "applied art," but an object like the Vienna ostrich cup, which we are now most likely to see in the context of a modern display devoted to German goldsmiths' work, would coexist at least as comfortably with an astrolabe, a landscape in *pietre dure* (the variegated stones for which the Florentines were famed), a painting by Arcimboldo, or an ingenious mechanical model.[29]

The kinds of conscious and artful fluidities involved in the conceiving of such objects are perhaps best exemplified in the highly regarded nautilus and strombus shell cups, of which some superb examples are displayed in the Paston picture. Such *indianische Schneggen* were the subject of high-level international exchange and trade. From Philipp Hainhofer in 1610 we learn that the Duke of Württemberg had bought a collection of shells for some 1,200 florins, and that 6,000 florins-worth had been presented by the Dutch states to the king of France.[30] The beautiful material of the shells, when polished, and their miraculous design by God in his "Mannerist" mode, made them particularly treasured items which occasioned elaborate mounting. When devising the setting for a shell, the most knowing designers exploited a deliberate conflation of human and natural design. A British *Nautilus Cup* of 1585 in the Fitzwilliam Museum, Cambridge (Figure 9.10), stands as a typical representative of the European fashion.[31] Indeed, it has been suggested that it was made by a Dutch goldsmith who fled from the Spanish in 1576. The stem of triton and dolphin serves to emphasize the watery theme which runs throughout the design, and the artist has taken the opportunity to echo the design of the natural shell, both in the accompanying "creepy-crawlies" and in the more abstract ornamental motifs. The natural objects were themselves often worked by the human hand in some way – this particular example had been cut by a Chinese artist, enhancing its exotic status – to disclose the inherent beauty of nature's contrivances. The designer's conspiracy with nature is equally well expressed in those "shell" cups in which the shells are carved by the human hand from a prized substance like rock crystal. In many of the engraved designs (Figure 9.11), which played such an important role in broadcasting the latest styles across Europe, it is often unclear whether the body of the object is a decorated shell or an entirely man-made confection. From the point of view of what was being implied about the human and natural design, the ambiguity was a large part of the point.

A general air of exoticness was clearly a major factor in many of the pieces' impact. The more exotic the better. Coconuts had long been known and highly regarded, in secular and ecclesiastical settings alike, and the Seychelles nut – the *coco de mer* – came to assume an even higher level of rarity and geographical novelty. In spite of the somewhat unprepossessing surface qualities of the nuts, the very wonder of them as surprising

9.10 *Cup with Engraved Nautilus Shell.* Cambridge, Fitzwilliam Museum. (Photo: museum.)

9.11 Cornelius Floris, after Enea Vico. *Shell Cup.* Engraving. Private collection. (Photo: author.)

artifacts of nature justified their working and setting in the most stylish manner. A notable example of a coconut cup, made in Nuremberg around 1540 by Melchior Baier and Peter Flötner and owned by the Holzschuher family, has been adorned with what is literally an orgy of decorative motifs, including a base with a pair of rutting sheep, and a woman reaching out to rouse a man's penis, and a cover decorated with a satyr ministering large quantities of wine to a semi-recumbent figure.[32] The shell itself is decorated with various erotic activities carved in low relief in a strikingly "antique" manner. The cup illustrated here (Figure 9.12) is more sober in design and content, but it shares the secularism of the Holzschuher cup, in this case by reference to hunting in the scenes carved on the neck and the statue of the armed Pallas-Athene on the cover. The vocabulary of the design associated with such Seychelles nuts is generally different from that called forth by the maritime shells. Like the Holzschuher cup, the stem is here composed from the knottily organic motif of a creeper spiraling around a gnarled trunk, as favoured by Dürer. The character of the artifact of nature suggests, as it were, the mode that the human designer should adopt.

A particularly inventive response by a designer, probably Nikolaus Pfaff, to a rhinoceros horn – one of the most prized and magically potent of all the rarities – shows

9.12 *Coconut Cup with Cover*. Seychelles nut and metal. Cambridge, Fitzwilliam Museum. (Photo: museum.)

9.13 Nikolaus Pfaff (?). *Rhinoceros Horn Cup with Warthog Tusks*. Vienna, Kunsthistorisches Museum, Sammlung für Plastik und Kunstgewerbe. (Photo: museum.)

how an exotic object can evoke an appropriately exotic mode from a virtuoso master (Figure 9.13).[33] The horn itself is carved with scary and mysterious organic motifs. Strange heads, human and animal, emerge from coralline branches, while on the cover two African warthog tusks are set on either side of a demonic, dragon-like head that openly recalls oriental designs. Such an object not only makes articulate sense in the context of the *naturalia*, *exotica*, and *artificialia* of the cabinet of marvels, but it can also be

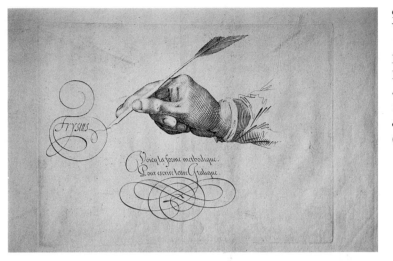

9.14 (left) Jan van den Velde. *Instruction in the Writing of the Italic Hand.* Engraved by Simon Frysius, from *Spieghel der Schrijfkonste*, Rotterdam, 1605. London, Victoria & Albert Museum. (Photo: author.)

9.15 (right) Jan van den Velde. *Instruction in the Writing of the Netherlandish Hand.* Engraved by Simon Frysius, from *Spieghel der Schrijfkonste*, Rotterdam, 1605. London, Victoria & Albert Museum. (Photo: author.)

located in a complex dialogue between European collectors and products of other cultures.[34] An adequate discussion of this dialogue clearly lies outside the feasible scope of the present essay, but I should like for the moment to say that the types of viewing and interpretation accorded to objects from, say, China, Africa, India, Precolumbian America, and Persia, should be seen as resistant to simple generalization as the contents of the *wunderkammer* were resistant to a single type of categorization. There was a plurality of reaction to objects in what we would call different styles, and the Mannerist designers themselves could operate in a plurality of geographical and chronological styles both between and within particular items. Something rather comparable to the virtuoso changes of manner which a designer like Pfaff could accomplish in goldsmithery is provided by Jan van den Velde in his writing-book of 1605, in which Frysius's stylish engravings show the virtuoso hand of the writing master literally coming to grips with a variety of old and new "hands," including Italic and Dutch styles (Figures 9.14, 9.15).[35]

9.16 Wenzel Jamnitzer. *The Merckel Table-Centre*. Amsterdam, Rijksmuseum. (Photo: museum.)

Van den Velde's book also serves to introduce us to another subversion – or at least an intended subversion – of stock frames of reference, that is to say the intellectualizing of the "crafts," in such a way that what had previously been taken as rudely mechanical pursuits acquired a theoretical base. Whether we are dealing with a social art like dancing, a military craft like gunnery, the skill of writing, or the trade of the potter, we find written tracts being produced to promote the intellectual and social status of their practitioners. The goldsmith who embodied the increasingly insistent insertion of the most select of craftsmen into a philosophical orbit was Wenzel Jamnitzer in Nuremberg. As the devisor and illustrator of a most spectacular treatise on the perspective of the five Platonic solids, in which the cosmological connotations of his highly decorative variations are underlined, Jamnitzer left no one in any doubt about his claims.[36] Indeed, his whole practice as a "craftsman" undertaking work on commission from noble patrons cast him in the guise of a universal *artifex* who would fear no aspect of the intellectual, visual, or technical challenges posed by God's creation.

Jamnitzer's most spectacularly "decorative" complexes in the "decorative arts," the great table fountains and ornaments, are in fact his most intellectualizing creations, involving philosophical programs, high aesthetic ambition, and extreme technical virtuosity in a way which rivals in condensed form the building and decoration of a complete suite of rooms – including the plumbing. The two greatest schemes, both commenced in 1556, no longer survive. One was planned for Archduke Ferdinand of Tyrol and was to involve the antiquarian, engineer, and courtly entrepreneur, Jacopo Strada.[37] The theme was to center on Adam and Eve in Paradise. In 1557 and 1559 there are records of the casting of small animals and insects directly from nature, involving a specialist in such items, Matthias Zündt. Although the grandiose project was abandoned in 1561, Ferdinand's taste for the nature casts had been fired, and in 1565 he ordered two dozen small animals and grasses. The other major project was a table fountain for Maximilian II, and, though no longer extant, it was described in a way that allows a partial reconstruction.[38] About ten foot high, its overall configuration assumed the form of the Imperial Crown, and its subject-matter was based on a comprehensive program of micro-macrocosmic analogies, involving the elements, seasons, rivers, human pursuits, and so on, with moving parts driven by marvelous displays of water power and clockwork. The description records, in tones of awe, that everything was included in its compass – "Physica, Metaphysica, Politica, and many fine Philosophical and Poetic ideas."

Some idea of the visual richness of such ensembles can be gained from a more "modest" piece commissioned in 1549 by Nuremberg City Council (Figure 9.16). In this case, the dominating image is of the earth and its abundance, with a figure of Mother Earth supporting the elaborate "fruit bowl."[39] Densely abundant life casts are combined with decorative motifs in classical and mauresque styles, while the voluptuousness and exotic costume of Earth suggests a merging of antique and Indian sources. The virtuoso stylistic plurality and the blurring of the demarcations between the natural and the artificial were designed to inculcate wonder precisely because the transformative skill of the *artifex* has transcended the normal boundaries of things. Life casts from animals and plants became specially prized objects in their own right, and relatively few artists mastered the secrets of making them. Philipp Hainhofer reported to Duke Philipp that Christoph Lencker, the goldsmith, "has a large snake cast entirely of silver and a number of little lizards that were cast by old Lorenz [Dhem, the Augsburg goldsmith]. . . He paid eight florins for a lizard and refuses to sell any of them, looking on them as treasures: there is no chased work on them, but they are entirely cast from life."[40]

The most famous of all the artists who managed to annex the skills of nature herself was the great potter, Bernard Palissy. His name today is almost wholly identified with a special kind of *rustique figeurine* (Figure 9.17) in which life casts of notable fidelity and detail are scintillatingly combined with the vitreous glazes which cost Palissy many years of hard experiment.[41] The aim was, in his own words, to create works which "do not appear to involve any appearance or form of the art of sculpture, nor any labor of the hand of man."[42] Like the grotto described by Ovid, the boundaries of art and nature appeared to have become permeable: the "architecture" around Diana's bathing pool was apparently "wrought by no artist's hand, but nature by cunning hand had imitated art, for she had shaped a native arch of the living rock and soft tufa."[43] Palissy's own grottoes, for which he became especially famed, may legitimately be regarded as the supreme realizations of the metamorphic motif in the late Renaissance.[44]

Palissy was, however, more than a supremely ingenious craftsman-designer. His writings, too little read by historians of art and science alike, set his creations in a strongly argued framework of natural philosophy, in which he becomes the cunning accomplice

9.17 Bernard Palissy. *Dish with Animals Cast from Life*. Glazed ceramic. London, Wallace Collection. (Photo: Wallace Collection.)

of nature through the understanding of her secrets. He was, not surprisingly, full of awe for the divine creator. Looking at the lustrous shell in the cabinet of M. Rasce, he challenges the human artificer to make a cup from the same materials. The result would be "more precious than gold":

> Why do they [the craftsmen] not observe from what the fish has formed such a beautiful house, and take similar materials to make a beautiful vase? The fish that made the said shell is not as glorious as man – it is an animal which has little form – and yet it is able to do what man is unable to achieve.[45]

When he came to devise a radically new form of secure fortress to protect those who, like himself, suffered attack and persecution on religious grounds, he founded his design on the spiral of a shell.[46] The debate about the houses of animals and man was an old one, with Aristotelian antecedents.[47] Palissy's own position – that a direct inquiry of nature provides the basis on which true knowledge of design can be acquired – is the central theme of his two treatises, published in 1563 and 1580. Cast in the form of vigorous arguments between "theory" and "practice," his writings sustain a tough polemic against metaphysically inclined philosophers and above all against alchemists, who would claim presumptuously to assume God's creative mantle. Casting himself as an "unlettered" man of practice – though in reality he espouses quite a sophisticated version of the micro-macrocosmic analogies – he proclaimedly stands as the true investigator of "the beautiful order which God has placed in the earth," literally excavating his understanding of the earth's generative powers with his hands when making his pottery, grottoes, and fountains.[48]

It is not difficult to imagine Palissy's magical creations thriving in the context of the alchemical culture of the Medician Court in later sixteenth-century Florence, and he was himself the recipient of noble and royal patronage on a large scale in France. But his empiricist attitudes were consciously opposed to the alchemists' speculations, and were accompanied by unshakeable Huguenot convictions which placed his courtly career in jeopardy. As in other incidents that we have examined, the intellectual motivations and social associations of apparently similar cultural artifacts might not be similar at all.

The kind of items of nature admired and recreated by Palissy were very much those of the collector's cabinet, and he had established one of his own – "in which I have placed many admirable and monstrous things, which I have drawn out of the matrix [*matrice*] of the earth."[49] His cabinet certainly contained objects which would have graced any princely *wunderkammer*, but his collection was not princely and its primary thrust was idiosyncratically Palissian. Such differences serve to remind us that simple generalizations about power and possession need to be carefully scrutinized when we look at the European vogue for cabinets in the later sixteenth and early seventeenth centuries. The founders of the great cabinets were not all princes aiming to conquer territory and promote political power through ownership. The famous cabinet established in Bologna by Ulisse Aldrovandi, Professor of *fossilibus, plantis, et animalibus*, was a pedagogic tool for the philosophical understanding and ordering of nature, while the character of Ferrante Imperato's collection in Naples was given a particular shape by his professional interest in medicines.[50] However, even in such "scientific" cases we would probably be wrong to impute just one driving motivation to the assemblers of the cabinets. The sheer acquisitive momentum needed to assemble a grand cabinet over a period of time appears to have consumed energy from a set of interlocked motivations. Even if we may regard the princely cabinets of Rudolf II and Ferdinand as expressions of their personas as rulers, we should not doubt that other motives, such as curiosity, delight, scientific wonder, and magic, were necessary accompaniments and corollaries to the more political impulses. Although we now tend to think of power as a secular means and end in itself, it could be conjoined in the Renaissance with genuine piety in a way that we now find difficult to grasp. I am prepared to believe that there is a measure of truth in Anselm de Boodt's claim in his 1609 book on gems and stones that "the Emperor was not attracted to them in order with the help of their luster to increase his own importance and majesty, but to understand through the medium of precious stones the grandeur and infinite power of God, who was able to combine in such minute particles the beauty and the force of all other things on earth, and in this way to have before his eyes a permant reflection of the brilliance of the Deity."[51]

Confirmation of the multivalent personality of the cabinets is found in the activities of Philipp Hainhofer, whose correspondence has already proved to be a rich source in this study. Hainhofer created what might almost be called "off-the-peg" cabinets of natural

9.18 Philipp Hainhofer. *Kunstchrank*. Mixed media, 1632. Uppsala, University of Uppsala. (Photo: University.)

and artificial wonders. In 1632 he supplied an elaborate *kunstchrank* for presentation to King Gustavus Adolphus of Sweden by the Councillors of Augsburg (Figure 9.18). The structure had originally been assembled for another patron, but Hainhofer rapidly stocked it to meet the Councillors' urgent request. This incident suggests that Hainhofer's cabinets were not necessarily patron-specific to a high degree, and that they resulted from a mixture of planning and opportunism. They were set up in such a way that they could be interpreted philosophically by a learned recipient like the Swedish king without necessarily having been compiled at each stage according to a rigidly preconceived

9.19 (opposite page)   Philipp Hainhofer. *Kunstchrank*. Detail of decoration with coral and Seychelles nut cup, 1632. Uppsala, University of Uppsala. (Photo: University.)

program. Each *kunstchrank* would have been contrived to exercise plural appeals, so that it had the ability to respond to the individual demands of its purchaser (and by implication of subsequent owners). The survival, virtually intact, of the *kunstchrank* presented to Gustavus Adolphus testifies to a notable staying power.[52] Like a walk-in *wunderkammer*, the Uppsala cabinet can be approached at various levels, from high philosophical seriousness to amused curiosity. It contains in microcosm a range of natural, magical, scientific, and artificial curiosities from the four continents, similar to that in a full-scale cabinet, including small silver casts from nature, dried animal skins, scientific and domestic tools, musical instruments on a diminutive scale, and devices driven by clockwork. Inset into the cabinet is a diverse assemblage of cameos, reliefs, engraved plaquettes, *pietre dure*, etc., in which the ancient and the modern, and the secular and the religious jostle for attention. On the top is a mountain of rock crystal and variously colored corals, at the summit of which is a ewer composed from a decorated Seychelles nut with a Venus cover (Figure 9.19). The way that the ewer can unexpectedly be detached for use exploits function as a form of surprise. We should remember that the nut was an antidote to poison, as were the coral branches, two of which have been carved to display literally repellent gestures (*fighe*) at their tips. The whole ensemble has been designed with such complexity of function and meaning as to unhinge any gross generalization about its intended and actual appeal – beyond the commonplaces that possession of such a cabinet signified status and inferred intellectual sophistication.

Looking back over the necessarily limited selection of objects illustrated here, I think we can see how they lent themselves to ordering and classification in various ways – often with explicit or implicit resonances to microcosms and macrocosms – and yet at the same time achieved much of their power and fascination because they seemed to transcend the most obvious divisions, most notably that between art and nature. The sixteenth-century viewer, like the present-day visitor to a museum, approached the extraction of meaning from artifacts through a series of classificatory categories of a more or less definite kind, but the nature of the objects themselves played a delightful game with the viewer's expectations. Above all, they were objects of wonder, whether that wonder arose from human ingenuity, local and distant, or from nature's prodigious powers of generation, familiar and exotic. The institutionalized rigidities of our present-day classifications have often resulted in the kind of items we have studied being housed in different buildings from objects that were originally their companions. The nexus of associations and the fluid transgression of boundaries which was so important for their functioning has been largely obscured. Considered more fully within their original contexts they can be seen again as objects of incredible visual and conceptual richness – as potentially restless migrants in a richly cosmopolitan world which can be comfortably simplified only at the historian's peril.

CHAPTER 10

Animals as Cultural Signs:
A Medici Menagerie in the Grotto at Castello

CLAUDIA LAZZARO

In the Renaissance animals were understood in a variety of ways, but above all in terms of contemporary conceptualizations of nature, which ranged from a domesticated nature, altered or tamed by humans, to wild nature, an uncontrollable force in opposition to civilization. In this sense, animals are cultural signs, embodying a complex of ideas about nature which also define and sustain contemporary notions of civilization and culture. In this society, the paradigms of nature and culture, wild and civilized, were both in opposition and interlocked. The wildness of animals contrasted with human culture, but appropriating that wildness was also a demonstration of human power and magnificence. Such assumptions about animals and their relationship to humans inform visual representations, collections of both living animals and images of them, spectacles, and rituals – from public animal fights to diplomatic gift-giving. Classical antiquity played a profound role in this, providing models for the paradigms of nature and culture as well as the specific representations of them, from works of sculpture to the spectacles of animal slaughter.

Animals were generally conceived of not independently of humans, but in complex relationships with them. Animals provided food, clothing, and medicine, but equally, they reflected human values, virtues, and conduct in heraldry, symbols, emblems, and many other ways.[1] The enthusiasm for animals in the Renaissance was not disinterested. Animals were understood within a system of associations: they were significant to contemporaries because they embodied multiple associations (from literature, history, mythology, and so on) and symbolic meanings on many different levels. This way of thinking derived from classical antiquity, but it was vastly extended by the end of the sixteenth century. The study of animals increased dramatically as well, following the precedents of classical texts and accompanied by a new empirical observation. In the sixteenth century, the different ways of knowing animals, from ancient authority, direct experience, symbolic meanings, and multiple associations, coexisted, even if in direct conflict.

A great impetus to the study of animals was the variety of unfamiliar ones that entered Europe through the encounters with other continents from the late fifteenth century. Since the ancients had already known Asia and Africa, the exploration of these two continents was framed as one of rediscovery of classical antiquity. As antiquity provided the framework for understanding animals in general, so it also gave a means for comprehending the new animals to appear in Europe. This was one of the strategies of assimilation and domestication through which the strange was made familiar.[2] The newly known animals were also assimilated into existing ideas of wild, savage, and barbarian, as were the continents that they signified.[3] In the ensuing hierarchical conceptualization of the world, by the end of the sixteenth century the spectrum from civilized to wild came to characterize the relationship of Europe with the other known continents and cultures.

I

The point of departure for my investigation of these issues and the principal vehicle for presenting them is an artificial grotto in a sixteenth-century Medici garden filled with sculpted animals, both native species and those from Asia and Africa. My aim is at the same time to provide an interpretive framework for this grotto and to address the larger issues in sixteenth-century culture that have been suggested here, along with the role in them of visual representations. I begin with and repeatedly return to the example of the grotto, but intermittently the text digresses to focus on various aspects of animals and the crosscultural encounters that they illustrate.

The garden at Castello (Figure 10.1), on the outskirts of Florence, is the first of the

10.1   View of the garden, Villa Medici. Castello, begun 1537. (Photo: Art Resource.)

10.2   Grand Ducal Crown in the Grotto Vault, Villa Medici. Castello. Mosaic, 1565–1572. (Photo: author.)

grand gardens created by the Medici rulers in the sixteenth century. It was begun about 1537 for Cosimo de' Medici immediately after his election as head of the government of Florence. From the start a grotto was planned for the retaining wall at the back of the geometric garden, but the existing interior decoration – the surface of rough calcified concretions or stalactites and the carved animals – belongs to a second project, from 1565 to 1572. The date and something of the significance of the grotto decoration can be deduced from the mosaic in the vault representing the grand ducal crown (Figure 10.2), which was granted to Cosimo in 1569. At that time Giorgio Vasari was in charge of completion of the garden, and presumably he also designed the grotto. The sculptor of the animals may have been the little-known Antonio di Gino Lorenzi. The present neo-Classical exterior of the grotto dates from the eighteenth century.[4]

Inside the spacious grotto there are three niches, at the back and sides, each with a great tub above which stand over 36 large-scale sculptures of animals (Figures 10.3, 10.4, and 10.5). Distributed among the three groups are native species, both domestic and wild – a goat, lamb, and wolf, a horse, three different European deer, a bear, bull, the auroch or wild ox of Europe, and various others. There are also one or two prominent non-European animals from Asia and Africa in each niche – in the center niche (Figure 10.3) an Indian elephant in addition to the familiar lion; a North African camel in the right (Figure 10.4); and in the left a giraffe and an Indian rhinoceros (Figure 10.5). These are joined by smaller non-native species, a gazelle in the center, a leopard, Indian goat, and monkey in the right, and another monkey in the left niche. The animals in this remarkable collection are carved of colored hard stones – some corresponding with the animal's natural coloration, as in the gray granite of the rhinoceros; some known by their association with the ancients, as in the *giallo antico*, the yellow marble from Siena called

10.3   Central niche of the Grotto, Villa Medici. Castello, 1565–1572. (Photo: author.)

ancient yellow, of the lion; and others only recently discovered, such as the veined marbles of the horse, the monkey in the left niche, and the central tub.[5] The tubs in the side niches are carved with friezes: one of fish, the other of shellfish. Bronze birds, sculpted by Giambologna, were also originally attached to the walls. Most are housed in the Bargello Museum in Florence – a pigeon, New World turkey, thrush, falcon, eagle, and owl.[6] In the vault of the grotto playful masks are fashioned of shells and pebbles. Although the grotto displays a great variety of fauna and a wide range of natural materials, the animals do not represent an encyclopedic collection of known species in the late sixteenth century, but rather one that presents specific messages about the power and magnificence of the Medici, conveyed through general concepts of nature and culture, wild nature and civilization.

II

Modern studies of the grotto have examined it in the context of Medici imagery and the themes in the rest of the garden. Most posit an allegorical meaning for the whole, with reference to a literary text or mythological figure.[7] Implicit in these interpretations are various assumptions of the discipline of art history and about the Italian Renaissance. The traditional art historical approach is to ask the meaning of the specific animals in this particular context and to seek a literary text which the collection in some way illustrates. My approach includes the iconographic, but also goes considerably beyond it. Some of the animals do have specific symbolism and they may correspond with a text, but they do so because the symbols and stories, like the animals generally, draw on contemporary constructs of nature and culture and conventional ways of representing them in images, texts, and social practices. To understand how contemporaries could have apprehended the messages in the grotto, it is necessary to look at both the specific meaning of individual animals for the Medici and the larger meanings for this culture of animals in general as well as particular configurations of them. Since the concern here is with visual representations, it is also necessary to examine the pictorial conventions, cultural assumptions, and intellectual expectations that mediate between the animals and their representation. In the grotto the most familiar animals, the domestic and native ones, are generally the most naturalistic. The strange could no more be "truthfully" reproduced in images than into words. Visual representations can domesticate and assimilate the wild and strange as well as convey associations, symbolic meanings, and cultural constructs. These approaches to the animals in the grotto are essential to its interpretation since there are no human figures or narrative references, only the animals themselves and their rustic setting.

In the sixteenth century, sculpted animals were an appropriate decoration for such a grotto, since it was a commonplace that animals lived in caves, mountainous areas, and forests. In the playful reiteration of nature in Renaissance gardens, representations of

10.4 Right niche of the Grotto, Villa Medici. Castello, 1565–1572. (Photo: author.)

10.5 Left niche of the Grotto, Villa Medici. Castello, 1565–1572. (Photo: author.)

10.6   Water tricks in the
Grotto, Villa Medici.
Castello, 1565–1572. (Photo:
Ralph Lieberman.)

animals, whether made of topiary, paint, or stone, were accordingly located in grottoes,
the *bosco* or wood, and parks. There are numerous recorded examples in central Italian
gardens, beginning with the topiary animals in the fifteenth-century gardens of the
Medici in Florence and of the Rucellai outside of town. In the sixteenth century
fountains were ornamented with animals of every kind, and sculpted animals inhabited
the woods and parks of Latium – the Sacred Wood at Bomarzo, the park at Bagnaia, and
the Boschetto of the Villa Mattei in Rome. They were also featured in several grottoes,
all of them in Medici gardens in Tuscany: in addition to Castello's, the ram's head, goats,
and she-goat in the Boboli Grotticina, the animals carved on the exterior of the Grotto
of Cupid at Pratolino, and the sculpted and painted animals in the Grotta Grande at the
Boboli.[8] Although common to Renaissance gardens, the representation of animals seems
to have had a specific significance to the Medici.

    The grotto at Castello was the admitted inspiration for an imaginary grotto in a text
from the end of the sixteenth century by Agostino del Riccio, which described an ideal
garden of a king. The fantastic grotto in Riccio's ideal *bosco* contained 29 different
animals. In his account, reasoning visitors puzzle out the identity of each species.[9] In
contrast to them, the animals (there as well as in other garden sites) signify nature in at
least two of the ways it was construed in the Renaissance. The domesticated sheep, goats,

and ram suggest the pastoral view of nature, in harmony with humans, which was celebrated in the popular literary genre. The wild animals, including the non-European examples, and the rocky cliffs, caves, and forests where they roam, refer to a nature that is *not* domesticated, that is wild or savage, *selvaggio* in Italian. (Dragons and unicorns, both of which have specific garden associations, are among the few mythological animals in Renaissance gardens.) In Riccio's evocation of his imaginary grotto, the gate suddenly slams shut, and, as at Castello, the visitors are soaked by unsuspected torrents of water from the hidden water jets in the floor (Figure 10.6). These *scherzi d'acqua*, water tricks or jokes of water, recall the jokes and tricks of nature, which could be uncontrollable and destructive. The recreation of them through play, in water tricks, is a way of domesticating the force of nature.[10] Garden grottoes functioned similarly: they imitate woodland caves and thus domesticate wild nature. Although the grotto at Castello with its regular interior form does not look very wild to our eyes, contemporaries would have read it as such for the signifier of wild in the rough coating of stalactites lining the walls and vaults. Exemplifying the playful, shifting relationships of art and nature in Renaissance gardens, these stalactites *were* in fact natural materials, which came from the hills beyond the garden, or so Vasari claimed.[11] The grotto at Castello domesticates wild nature through imitation and also through the reuse of natural materials in a patently artificial setting. The representations of animals (with real horns and tusks) similarly domesticate the force of nature.

III

In the city, actual living animals, not only sculpted ones – indeed wild animals – were kept in captivity. Here, the force of nature was not domesticated, only restrained, dominated by the captor who thereby appropriated its power.[12] In Florence wild animals were a conspicuous presence from at least the thirteenth century. Wild animals, particularly lions, the official animal of Florence, were kept by the Signoria from the early fourteenth century in stables near Palazzo Vecchio (there were 24 in 1410). They were moved to a site near the botanic garden at San Marco, where they remained for over two hundred years, from 1550 until 1777.[13] The Marzocco, the emblematic representation of the Florentine lion, and the living examples that it signified were conflated in the caged lions and in the public rituals in which they participated. Other animals were also kept, some of them acquired through gifts, in a long and widespread tradition of collecting wild animals, and over time increasingly exotic ones, as signifiers of power and magnificence. In Florence the custom dated from at least 1291, when a leopard and other wild animals were given to the Commune, and led ultimately to the much more extensive collections of the Medici in the sixteenth century.[14] These animals conferred prestige on the government or ruler who possessed them by their rarity, grandeur, and fierceness, but also by their captivity.

The animals in the Florentine menagerie acquired their various meanings for contemporaries through the social practices in which they were involved. Not merely kept, but explicitly displayed, they impressed, entertained, and epitomized the wild and strange against which culture and the familiar could be defined. The lions – together with the buildings, relics, and nunneries that the king of Norway toured in 1474 – constituted the renown of Florence.[15] Later, in their location at San Marco, the animals could be observed by passers-by on the street and from a viewing area in the adjacent amphitheater.[16] The Frenchman Montaigne's journal of his visit to Florence in 1580, like so many others, considered the animals worthy of enumeration. In addition to the stable of horses, he saw a camel, some lions and bears, and two animals that were unfamiliar to him: "a sheep of a very strange shape" and a tiger ("an animal the size of a very big mastiff and the shape of a cat, all marked in black and white")[17] – typically, the strange was described in terms of the familiar. The Scotsman Fynes Moryson, at the end of the century, noted yet more of the "fierce wilde beasts" kept by the duke: five lions, five wolves, three eagles, three tigers, a wild cat, bears, leopards, and wild boars. The large and ferocious animal that he identified as an Indian Mouse ("with a head like our Mise, but a long hairie taile") may have been a monkey. Some visitors were privileged to view the animals in the company of their ultimate masters: the keeper told Montaigne that Grand Duke Ferdinando and Duchess Christina came with "gentlemen" to watch the animals.[18]

These caged animals also appeared in public spectacles, which were controlled displays of wildness, staged for Florentines and foreign visitors alike. These included horse races and jousts, animal fights on a small scale in the viewing amphitheater, and, above all, the spectacular fights or *caccie*, literally "hunts," as they were called, in the great piazzas. In these *caccie* mostly wild animals, but also some domestic ones, were pitted against each other and incited to violence. In the fifteenth century two such animal fights were held in Florence in honor of visiting foreign dignitaries and there were many more in the sixteenth century. The earliest *caccie* were in 1439 and again twenty years later, for the visit of Count Galeazzo Maria Sforza, son of the Milanese duke, together with Pope Pius II.[19] In the great spectacle in 1459, as in later ones, the Piazza della Signoria was blocked off and bleachers set up within it. Wild boars, wolves, bulls, wild horses, dogs, and other animals were let into the square. Then lions were introduced in anticipation of a bloody battle.[20] Lions – kings of the beasts, symbols of pride, and emblems of Florence – were pitted against other wild animals with a hoped-for show of force in entertainment meant to be read on multiple levels, all of which together would impress foreign visitors with the prowess of their hosts. A contemporary poem characteristically interweaves different readings of the events, effortlessly comprehending the lions as multivalent signs, signs with several, simultaneously perceived meanings. The poem explains how the lions walked around the piazza with a proud spirit, while the other animals trembled. The lion attacking a horse is referred to as a Marzocco (the emblem of Florence), showing itself to be the ruler of the beasts.[21] On the other hand, when the lions did not fight after this show of force, their pacific behavior was interpreted as an indication of the friendship between the Sforza count and the Commune of Florence.[22]

Both symbolism and violence increased in the much more prevalent *caccie* of the sixteenth century within the altered political climate of the Medici dukes and grand dukes. In 1514 (the year of the election of Pope Leo X, the first Medici pope, and two years after the return of the Medici to Florence, ousted in 1492) a memorable animal fight numbered among the entertainments for the feast of San Giovanni, the city's patron saint. According to a contemporary, two lions, bears, leopards, bulls, buffaloes, stags, and many other beasts of various kinds participated, as well as horses and dogs. Since the lions were unwilling to fight, apparently intimidated by the tumult of the crowd, they were provoked by men thrusting lances from the shelter of mobile contraptions in the form of a tortoise and a porcupine.[23] In this spectacle the lions assumed an additional association with the newly elected Medici pope, who, in choosing the name Leo, identified himself and the papacy with Florence. The lions, however, remained reluctant to act out either the political messages encoded in the fight or the contemporary concept of wild animals, which is that they demonstrate their wildness by fighting.

Despite the passive animals, that day's events brought home the relationship of the animals in captivity and on public display to the forces of nature that they epitomized. The city square was transformed into a natural setting, with a large fountain in the center for the animals to drink and around a mock wood with dens for them to hide. The crowd in the piazza was composed of Florentines, including women and children, as well as Romans and other foreigners. As they all watched, stallions and a mare in heat were introduced, who this time did the expected, to the dismay of contemporary observers.[24] If the topiary and sculpted animals in gardens domesticated and tamed wild nature, this recreation of a natural setting in the circumscribed area of the piazza represented the opposite: thoroughly undomesticated wild nature urged to manifest its wildness in the civilized city. The forces of nature were at the same time unleashed and controlled by the force of the local authority, in a spectacle that was perhaps also intended to unleash and, through a reversal of the social order, to harness, the populace.[25]

Under the Medici dukes the *caccie* became more frequent, staged for a wider range of festivals including carnival and weddings, and more violent, featuring not only incitements to fight but also wholesale slaughter of animals. In February 1541 in Piazza della Signoria, two lions fought with a bull and many large dogs.[26] During the carnival of 1545 in Piazza Santa Croce on three successive days bulls were slaughtered, alongside a battle of lions, bears, a wild boar, stag, and other animals.[27] Similarly, in the sixteenth-century papal hunts in the countryside, violence, particularly the slaughter of wild animals, served as both entertainment and demonstration of human power. A new set of hunting practices had changed the character of the hunt from active sport to passive spectacle.[28]

For the lavish festivities celebrating the wedding of Grand Duke Francesco I and Joanna of Austria in 1565 a slaughter of bulls took place in all the piazzas. Another spectacle was the slaying of a stream of animals (rabbits, hares, roebucks, foxes, porcupines, and badgers, then stags, boars, and bears, and finally some wild horses). The obvious parallel with the imperial Romans was not lost on contemporaries. In the account of the wedding it was noted explicitly: the chase was seen as "again renewing the ancient pomp of the Roman hunts."[29] Once again, however, the animals in captivity would not respond as their counterparts in the wild, or rather, in accordance with contemporary notions of the behavior of wild animals, which the fights and hunts attempted to recreate artificially in both the city and the countryside. As was common practice, the animals were not left to their instincts: a great tortoise filled with men was introduced into the arena to excite a "most fierce" lion so that it would fight with a "valiant" bull.[30] As a demonstration of Medici power and magnificence following ancient precedent, humans appropriated the wildness of animals and did violence to them, first by provoking, then by killing them.

IV

There was a reciprocal relationship between the representations of the animal kingdom in the city square and those in art, both of which did not represent natural animal behavior so much as the cultural construction of wild nature, with which human civilization could be contrasted. The lion fights in the piazza actualized images known through art from antiquity to contemporary times, at the same time that the fights must have inspired their visual representation. In the art of classical antiquity many lion combats are depicted, some of them on sarcophagi which have at each end a lion slaughtering another animal – boar, antelope, ram, goat, horse, stag, and so on.[31] Such imagery continued through the Middle Ages, as in the original Florentine Marzocco, which took the form of a lion victorious over a wolf.[32] The renewal of animal fights in the piazzas was accompanied by a similar interest in art. Images of animals became a distinct genre from the fifteenth century and fighting animals comprised a significant number of them in both paintings and prints. A Florentine engraving of about 1460 (Figure 10.7) depicts wild animals, lions and leopards, attacking horses and oxen, in this instance perhaps directly inspired by events of the previous year in the piazza. In another fifteenth-century engraving, dogs attack a bear. An engraving by Lucantonio degli Uberti represents a contest between a dragon and a lion and lioness, presumably after a drawing by Leonardo and perhaps the inspiration for the sculpted group at Bomarzo.[33] One of several sketchbooks with animals is that of the Venetian Jacopo Bellini, which includes a number of drawings of lions, at rest as well as attacking one or more horses.[34] Piero di Cosimo's *Hunting Scene* in the Metropolitan Museum in New York belongs to a series illustrating the development of humankind from the initial state of the world, following classical thought: that is, the age of stone before Vulcan, the discovery of fire, and the consequent civilization of humans.[35] The *Hunting Scene* represents a time when humans were like wild beasts, which is demonstrated in the painting by both animals and humans fighting.

In Vasari's tales of animal pictures, the Medici references are conspicuous from the fifteenth century to his own time in the later sixteenth. He relates that for the Medici palace Paolo Uccello painted some stories of animals. One represented lions fighting, another juxtaposed wild and pastoral nature (a serpent fighting a lion in the presence of a country girl and her ox).[36] Also for the Medici palace, Pesellino painted a *spalliera* (a wooden panel) of animals, some *cassoni* (chests) with scenes of jousts on horseback, and canvases with lions and animal fights, which were still there in Vasari's time.[37] This interest continued in the sixteenth century, when Cosimo I owned Piero di Cosimo's animal sketchbook and had a study painted like a garden bower with every sort of bird by Bacchiacca, also known for his animal specialization.[38] Modern scholarship adds to Vasari's list many other examples of Cosimo's collection of animal subjects, including Bacchiacca's sketchbooks of animals, a painting of lions, bronzes of serpents fighting, and so on.[39] Animals and animal fights may have been popular subjects for interior decoration, but in the Medici residences they also reinforced the association of wild nature with the power of the ruler, while the preponderance of lions made unmistakeable the identification of Florence with its Medici rulers.

As the number and violence of the animal fights in the piazzas increased in the sixteenth century, evoking ancient Roman precedents more explicitly, contemporary

10.7 (left) Anonymous, Florentine. *Wild Animals Attacking Horses and Oxen*. Engraving, *c*.1460. (Photo: Louvre, Collection Rothschild © Réunion des Musées nationaux.)

10.8 (right) Giambologna. *Lion Attacking a Horse*. Bronze statuette. (Photo: Walters Art Gallery, Baltimore.)

artistic representations of lively animal encounters also received greater inspiration from ancient models. A colossal Greco–Roman group of a lion attacking a horse, which stood on the Capitoline Hill in Rome since the fourteenth century, was reproduced many times, in drawings and two engravings.[40] Late in the sixteenth century the same group inspired a bronze statuette by Giambologna (Figure 10.8); a companion piece of a lion attacking a bull also followed ancient precedents from coins and other objects.[41] Although not as inexpensive and readily disseminated as prints, the statuettes were similarly portable and reproduceable. Different versions and variations on a type attest to their wide currency.[42] As we have seen, the literal animal combats in the piazzas of Florence act out a concept about animals, which is that they demonstrate their wildness by fighting, and also another concept, that the harnessing of this wildness in a staged fight is a demonstration of power. Encapsulating and enshrining the fights in dramatic visual representations is a parallel expression of power – witness the giving of Giambologna's statuettes as diplomatic gifts.[43] Antiquity profoundly influenced all this, and much else, as we shall see, of the way of construing the world and representing it in rituals in the fifteenth and sixteenth centuries.

V

Animals do fight, but not always; "fighting animals" is instead a cultural construct, which can be seen again in another of its manifestations, the paradigm of paired enemies. Animals were understood as having innate antipathies, some observed in nature, others known from the lore of classical antiquity and its later evolution in medieval bestiaries.[44] Common pairs include the cat and mouse and wolf and lamb, but equally legendary was the innate hatred of camels for horses, noted in antiquity by Pliny the Elder in his *Natural History* and passed on until the late sixteenth century when Giovanvettorio Soderini related it again in a treatise on domestic animals.[45] Also from antiquity, the rhinoceros was known as the adversary of the bear, since an epigram by Martial contained the trope of a rhinoceros tossing a bear. This image came to characterize their enmity and was repeated and given fixed pictorial form in the hierogylphic and emblematic literature of the second half of the sixteenth century, as in the emblem from Joachim Camerarius, *Symbolorum et emblematum* of 1595 (Figure 10.9).[46] Another famous enmity was that between rhinoceros and elephant, which was described by Pliny and widely disseminated in the Middle Ages. The paradigm of paired enemies, and this particular example, also determined how contemporaries dealt with Asian and African animals, known to antiquity but later only through lore, when the actual animals appeared in Europe. One of the gateways into Europe for animals, as for much else, was Portugal, as a result of its extensive voyages down the coast of Africa and to India. In 1515 in Lisbon, where both a rhinoceros and an elephant had just arrived from India as diplomatic gifts, a fight was staged between them.[47] Again, however, the animals defied the expectations of them: the young elephant took flight at the first sight of his opponent.

Several of these legendary enemies inhabit the grotto at Castello, but the consequent displays of wildness are strikingly absent. The camel and horse both occupy the right niche, oblivious to each other (Figure 10.4). The left niche (Figure 10.5) contains a bear and a rhinoceros, equally unconcerned with each other's presence. There is some conflict, but only among a few much smaller animals. In the left niche the dog appears to glare at the jumping cat on the other side of the greyhound and a lamb lies beneath the wolf. In the right niche a dog is overturned at the feet of a boar; beneath the prancing horse another similarly sized, but unidentifiable, animal lies supine. These illustrate the fighting behavior of animals, but they are far outweighed by the general remarkable lack of violence. The animals for the most part stand in static poses, or in

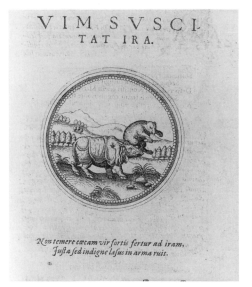

10.9 (above) Joachim Camerarius. *Rhinoceros Tossing a Bear*. Engraving, *Symbolorum et emblematum*, 1595. (Photo: author.)

10.10 (right) Francesco Ubertini, called il Bacchiacca. *Gathering of Manna*. Oil on canvas, *c.*1540–1555. Washington, D.C., National Gallery of Art, Samuel H. Kress Collection. (Photo: museum.)

active ones, but without any interaction. Even the overturned animals seem calculated in their placement. The aim of these groupings of animals is something other than a demonstration of their wildness.

As fighting animals are a cultural construct, so too are animals who are *not* fighting, particularly the coexistence of wild and domestic animals. Again the *topos* derives from classical antiquity, in texts such as Virgil's *Eclogues*, in which this peaceful coexistence is a metaphor for the harmony of the golden age.[48] It has a long history and may be more familiar from later paradise and peaceable kingdom paintings. One contemporary representation of wild and domestic animals coexisting in a harmony not found in nature is Bacchiacca's *Gathering of Manna* in the National Gallery in Washington of about 1545 (Figure 10.10). In this painting sixteen kinds of animals ranging from Asian giraffe to northern European brown bear form an implausible collection for the most part inappropriate to the setting of the biblical story (Exodus 16).[49] They suggest not the precise geographical setting, but the generic one – the wilderness. The harmony among the animals reflects the narrative: the discontent of the Israelites was quelled by the miraculous nourishment. It also reinforces the significance of the manna as a type of the Eucharist with its ultimate promise of salvation and, with it, paradise. The animals, therefore, serve several functions in the translation from narrative text to visual image: the non-European, "strange" animals identify the setting not in particular terms, but as wild or other; the harmony among such a variety of animals presents metaphorically and visually the human harmony of the narrative text. It may also allude to the moral lesson of the story by suggesting an earthly paradise analogous to the heavenly one. The animals in this painting, as in the grotto and elsewhere, have a significance of their own, independent of the narrative, which reinforces but does not illustrate it.

In the grotto at Castello, likewise, the overall absence of fighting between wild and domestic animals and among the large, wild ones signifies harmony. In this case, as in the Bacchiacca painting, harmony in nature is associated with the idea of nourishment, keyed by the presence of the unicorn in the central niche (Figure 10.3), the only mythical animal in the grotto. Unicorns were a common image in the sixteenth century. Their existence was much debated; nevertheless, in 1569 Cosimo de' Medici spent a considerable sum for the horn of one, whose powers were well known.[50] Unicorns were believed to purify water with their horns, while other animals wait patiently and harmoniously by the water source.[51] Because of this legendary ability, in garden fountains unicorns denote spring water.[52] In the grotto it was appropriately spring water that formerly spurted from mouths, horns, and ears of the animals, and seeped from the stalactites on the walls. Since building aqueducts to bring spring water to Florence was one of the accomplishments of Cosimo, the animals in the grotto suggest a further political reading: the spring water brought by Cosimo tames the wild beasts and creates harmony, as his good rule does to his state. Since the central niche carries the most overt Medici symbolism, as we shall see, it is not surprising that all the examples of conflict are relegated to the side niches.

VI

Classical antiquity provided precedents for animal hunts, artistic models for fighting animals, accounts of animal antipathies, and much more — the conceptual framework for the understanding and study of animals. Renaissance natural history was based on the writings of Aristotle, Pliny the Elder, and other ancient authors, made possible through the translation and, with the invention of the printing press in the fifteenth century, the publication of ancient texts. Pliny's *Natural History* was first published in 1469, followed by at least 46 editions in various European languages by 1550.[53] In the fifteenth and sixteenth centuries Asian and African animals were similarly known via the ancients, since many had been familiar to them. Elephants, camels, giraffes, and many others were described in Pliny's *Natural History*, Ptolemy's *Geography*, and Strabo's *Geography*. The Latin translation of Ptolemy's *Geography*, made early in the fifteenth century, was a bestseller by mid-century, even before it was printed in 1475. Ptolemy's Latin text was the source for most of the parts on Asia in Sebastian Münster's *Cosmographia* of 1544.[54] Classical antiquity profoundly influenced Renaissance thinking. Anthony Grafton has noted as well that Latin humanist culture was incorporated into vernacular culture: Münster's text was written first in German and only six years later translated into Latin.[55]

In the extensive literature commemorating the first encounters of Europeans with America, one of the persistent themes is the way in which the New World was understood through the framework of the old, particularly Christianity and classical culture.[56] This is especially the case for the exploration of the new worlds of Asia and

10.11 Giovanni da Udine. Loggetta of Cardinal Bibbiena. Fresco, c.1516. Vatican. (Photo: Vatican Museums.)

Africa. Columbus read Ptolemy's *Geography*,[57] but in a more limited framework the influence of antique texts was far more precise, particularly on the voyages of exploration to the Levant. One of the first in the early fifteenth century was Cyriacus of Ancona's journey to Egypt, following an itinerary that corresponded precisely with the places mentioned by Strabo, one of Cyriacus's favorite authors, who wrote (in Greek) six geo-historical books on Asia.[58] In the mid-sixteenth century Melchior Lorck, one of the itinerant artists who went to the Levant, sought the true sources of classical antiquity.[59] The process of exploration of Asia and Africa was framed as one of rediscovery of classical antiquity. As a result, through the sixteenth century, the animals discussed in ancient texts were privileged. That the animals in the grotto at Castello are only from worlds known to the ancients and do not include any American examples, except the turkey, reflects a broader situation,[60] although we shall see that more particular reasons influenced the choice of species.

The relationship between the discovery of non-European worlds and the rediscovery of classical antiquity is apparent in the decoration of the Vatican Loggetta of Cardinal Bibbiena, which was painted about 1516 by Giovanni da Udine. The decorative scheme was directly inspired by the recently discovered frescoes in the Domus Aurea, the Golden House of Emperor Nero, as well as other sites that have not survived. Vasari relates that Raphael and Giovanni da Udine were among the first to see some of these ancient painted rooms and that they were stupefied by them. Giovanni da Udine's Loggetta in the Vatican (Figure 10.11) is uncannily similar to its Roman model. In the vault, climbing plants delineate compartments, as in its ancient prototypes, and painted inside each is one of the exotic animals of Pope Leo's menagerie (visible on close inspection at the top of the photograph). Among them are several of the animals in the Castello grotto – a camel, boar, giraffe, and elephant. Vasari also noted among Giovanni da Udine's frescoes in the Vatican a chameleon, civet cats, apes, parrots, lions, baboons, and mandrills.[61]

The rediscoveries of ancient decorative schemes and of the animals of Asia and Africa were nearly contemporaneous and in the minds of contemporaries they were associated, as the Loggetta decoration illustrates. Antiquity provided the paradigm for understanding the animals just as the gridwork *all' antica* provided their painted setting in the Vatican. These exotic, or rather "strange," as they were termed, animals were made familiar by their assimilation into the classical tradition, as Michael Ryan has argued in a broader context.[62] It should be remembered that in Renaissance Italy these animals were conceptualized as "strange," different from the known, rather than "exotic," a term not in currency until the eighteenth century and one that suggests a fuller sense of both what constitutes the identity of the familiar and what must be its opposite in the other.[63]

VII

In the sixteenth century the flourishing activity of naturalists was characterized by a reliance on ancient authority as well as by empirical observation. The geographical range and number of species studied expanded greatly and the 1550s saw several important publications. The Frenchman Guillaume Rondelet studied marine life on the French coast; Pierre Belon wrote a treatise on birds and published his observations on fauna and flora on his travels to Egypt and the Levant. The first of two encyclopedic works was published from 1550 to 1558, Konrad Gesner's four-volume *Historiae animalium*, named after Aristotle's treatise, whose general classification it followed. Almost fifty years later the Bolognese naturalist Ulisse Aldrovandi began publication of a twelve-volume *Natural History*, published from 1599 to 1648.[64]

The texts of Gesner and Aldrovandi followed the model of Pliny's *Natural History* in not only describing the animals, but also cataloging their history, habitat, legends, and symbolism. Gesner added to this basic information all known associations, etymology, practical and medicinal uses to mankind, and symbolism derived from the animal's actions, character, and appearance. These last were formulated in proverbs, hieroglyphs, and emblems. The concern of Gesner's and Aldrovandi's texts was not only the animals themselves, but their significance to humans. Much of it was derived from sources in classical antiquity, often through the intermediary of contemporary literature. Gesner presented the animals as they were understood by contemporaries – in a complex system of similitudes, which Foucault has called the *episteme* of the sixteenth century. In the particular context of natural history, William Ashworth has termed this an emblematic world view, for both the system of associations and the myriad hidden meanings of everything in the cosmos.[65] The ways in which animals had meaning to contemporaries also increased enormously over the second half of the sixteenth century. The manifestations of this are in works on hieroglyphics and emblematics. These included Piero

Valeriano's *Hieroglyphica* (Basel, 1556), which concerns the allegorical significance of animals, and Joachim Camerarius's monumental *Symbolorum et emblematum* (1593–1604), an emblem book of natural history in four volumes with 400 emblems, each of which involves an animal or plant. The emblem of the rhinoceros tossing a bear (Figure 10.9) is from this text; there are also a giraffe, camel, elephant, and other Asian and African animals.

Again, exotic animals were easily assimilated into this emblematic world view since many of those newly known in the sixteenth century had an established cultural history from antiquity. For animals from America and others unknown to the ancients, meanings and emblems might be invented anew,[66] but others received only brief accounts without the traditional list of associations. The understanding of animals began to change only in the seventeenth century, and then only through texts devoted exclusively to the animals of the New World, for which there were no known similitudes or hidden meanings.[67]

The numerous publications in natural history in the sixteenth century were guided, in varying measures, by ancient authority, the growing system of similitudes, and also a new empirical observation, aided by the representational skills developed by artists from the fifteenth century.[68] If observation conflicted with the first two, it did not cancel them out. The same is true in representations of animals. Empirical observation was a significant aspect of fifteenth- and especially sixteenth-century representations, but it did not displace other ways of knowing the world. The function of images, even in many of the natural history texts, was not exclusively the production of scientific knowledge, understood in modern terms, but rather the illustration of the subject in its cultural matrix: not the actual animal, but the contemporary understanding of it, which required instead a normative image.

Some of the normative images represent the animal sitting, standing, and acting out characteristic gestures and actions. For example, at Castello the mountain goat in the left niche (Figure 10.5) is represented in a typical pose of grazing among the rocks. A number of these images were derived from the great repertoire of animals in ancient sculpture, such as the colossal group of the lion fighting a horse. As in the natural history texts, many sixteenth-century images follow models from antiquity, which were modified by observation. The bull at Castello (Figure 10.3) repeats a common ancient type with its turned head, folds of skin on the neck, prancing pose, and tail swung back over its torso. The static quality of the grouping in the grotto derives in part from the use of such models and types, some in profile; even when active or looking out, they are not interactive with the surrounding space or a posited viewer. Repetition of a model was also a means of making associations or hidden meanings evident. The wild boar, or *cinghiale*, in the right niche (Figure 10.4) is a very close copy of a specific ancient sculpture, one highly esteemed in the sixteenth century, which was given by Pope Pius IV to Cosimo de' Medici in 1560.[69] The sculpture thus sets up a series of associations between the wild animal, ancient sculpture, the papacy, and the ruler of Florence. Other models came from pattern books, such as the fourteenth-century book from the studio of the Lombard painter, Giovannino de' Grassi. The seated leopard in the right niche of the grotto in its characteristic and aristocratic pose (Figure 10.4) follows a familiar, normative image which ultimately derives from Egyptian sculpture, mediated by a profile leopard in another Lombard sketchbook of about 1400. A version of this type appeared later in the fifteenth century in Benozzo Gozzoli's fresco of the Procession of the Magi in the Medici palace,[70] which may have been inspired by the actual procession to the Medici palace that followed the *caccia* in 1459 during the festivities in honor of the Sforza count and the pope.[71]

Representations of animals had a long history, despite inaccuracies and unchecked by further observation from nature. Just as the sources of knowledge about animals were interlocked, so too were those for their illustration, again because animals were not so much important in their own right as in a grid of associations. Illustrations to natural history texts were no different in reusing earlier images, particularly, but by no means exclusively, when the actual animal was not available for observation.[72] In this one large sixteenth-century collection, the grotto at Castello, the images derive from ancient sculpture, pattern books, long medieval tradition, and treatises on natural history (such as the greyhound from Gesner in the left niche), as well as travel literature, emblem books, and other sources, as we shall see. In some component, empirical observation was also incorporated into the representations, just as the horns and tusks are real, not sculpted.

VIII

The strange animals from Asia and Africa were likewise assimilated into existing visual traditions, which reinforced associations in an increasingly complex web of meaning. The Indian single-horned rhinoceros, for example, was very rare in Europe. There were only eight from the sixteenth through the eighteenth centuries, but the image of the animal was in fact very common. The rhinoceros that was supposed to fight the elephant in Lisbon in 1515 was the first seen in Europe since the third century. A sketch of it was sent to Nuremberg and found its way into the hands of Albrecht Dürer. The German artist's famous woodcut of a rhinoceros (Figure 10.12), made in 1515 after the sketch, provided the almost universally accepted image of the animal for almost three centuries, in spite of its glaring inaccuracies and the existence of a more correct representation. The plated animal in the grotto at Castello (Figure 10.13) is also based on Dürer's with the fictitious, and here exaggerated, dorsal spiral horn. The inscription on most editions of the woodcut is from Pliny, who told of its fight to the death with the elephant. The same image was used to illustrate the device that Paolo Giovio made for Alessandro de' Medici featuring the rhinoceros, which was first published in 1556.[73] The animal was chosen because its character exemplified Alessandro's own: the duke ruled with an iron hand against much opposition and said of himself that he entered every difficult enterprise determined to win or die.[74] After the murder of Alessandro in 1537, the device was ironically appropriate. It has been suggested that Dürer's woodcut, with its double horn and plates reminiscent of contemporary armor, illustrates the *idea* of the animal better than a more accurate image might.[75]

The giraffe, like the rhinoceros, was practically unknown in Europe before the fifteenth century and was not commonly known there until the nineteenth. The normative image in the Renaissance was also based ultimately on the first encounter with the actual animal in the fifteenth century and it persisted because of a particular cultural resonance. On his voyage to Egypt in about 1443, Cyriacus of Ancona saw a giraffe and

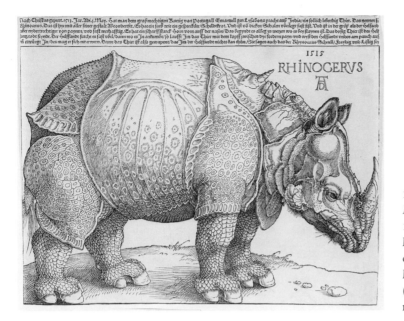

10.12 Albrecht Dürer. *Rhinoceros.* Woodcut, 1515. New York, The Metropolitan Museum of Art, Gift of Junius Morgan, 1919 (19.73.159). (Photo: museum.)

made a drawing of it in a letter, which is known in several copies.[76] The bridled animal in the manuscript in Florence provided the model for later versions in that city. A Florentine engraving (Figure 10.14), apparently based on this drawing but reinforced by the living animal, was used to illustrate a description of the giraffe's arrival in Florence in 1487 as a diplomatic gift.[77] The steeply sloping rear body with short hind legs, long thin neck and large head, may be influenced by the imperfect knowledge that the ancients had of the animal. Called a *camelopardalis*, it was understood as a hybrid of more familiar creatures: a camel for its great size, a leopard for the spots, and a lion in the hind quarters and flanks.[78]

Although the Florentine giraffe died soon after, it had a long afterlife in representations. In Piero di Cosimo's late fifteenth-century painting of Vulcan and Aeolus in the National Gallery of Canada in Ottawa (Figure 10.15) there is a giraffe in the right distance. It follows the same type derived from Cyriacus's letter, although livelier, with a prancing leg and an unnaturalistically curving neck. The sculpted giraffe in the grotto at Castello (Figure 10.13) retains this majestic, slim neck, but returns to the earlier, more static versions with firmly parallel forelegs. The giraffe in Bacchiacca's painting of the *Gathering of Manna* in Washington (Figure 10.10), with a neck like that in Piero di Cosimo's Vulcan, also belongs to this distinctly Florentine tradition.[79] There is a different tradition of giraffe representations in Germany; and in his treatise on animals, Gesner illustrated both types.[80]

But what is the giraffe doing in Piero di Cosimo's painting of the mythological story of Vulcan, god of fire, and Aeolus, god of winds, teaching humans the uses of fire, which is generally associated with a series of the early history of man, including the *Hunting Scene* in New York?[81] The giraffe and also a camel (very small, in the middle distance, to the left of the horse) are as inappropriate to the setting of the story in Sicily as the animals in Bacchiacca's *Gathering of Manna* are to the locale of that story. The giraffe

10.13 Rhinoceros, giraffe, and monkey, left niche of the Grotto, Villa Medici. Castello, 1565–1572. (Photo: author.)

reminded contemporaries of the important diplomatic gift, but the two exotic animals also reflect the theme of the painting, which is about progress towards civilization from the barbarian state depicted in the Hunting Scene with the fighting animals. The ancient Greek author Strabo, who wrote the first account of the giraffe, believed it to be a domestic animal; the camel was well understood as a domestic animal in the Renaissance. These non-European, "strange," but also domestic, animals are present as signifiers of the theme of the painting, the early stages of civilization. That they should have such an association is an equally significant issue, to which we will return.

The fixed representation of the camel was crystalized in one of the travel journals of the explorers to the Middle East, André Thevet. A Frenchman whose journey to the Levant between 1549 and 1553 resulted in his *Cosmographie de Levant* (Lyons, 1554 and

10.14 (left)   *Giraffe*.
Engraving, late fifteenth
century, Vatican MS.
Chigi G II 36.148v.
(Photo: Vatican library.)

10.15 (above left)   Piero di Cosimo. *Vulcan and Aeolus*. Oil and
tempera on canvas, *c*.1485–1490. Ottowa, National Gallery of
Canada. (Photo: museum.)

10.16 (right)   André Thevet. *Camel*. Woodcut, *Cosmographie de
Levant*, 1554. (Photo: British Library.)

est Gamal. Voila les choses principales , & dignes de memoire,que ïay veu du tems que ieſtois par dela,non pas que
ie demouraſſe en ladite ville de Conſtâtinoble,ains de l'autre
coté de la Mer , à Pere, appellee au tems paſſé Galate, ou de
preſent trafficquét les Chreſtiens viuás ſouz l'Egliſe Római
ne,ayás Femmes, Enfans,Maiſons,& Temples propres pour
prier le Souuerain,& ouir ſa parole, eſtans ſeulement tribu-
taire au grand Turq, ſelon le taux des tributs ordinaires.Là
demourent les Embaſſadeurs de France,& pour le iourdhui
monſieur d'Aramon bien aymé du grand Turq,& des gens
de vertu,faiſant grâd accueil aux Chreſtiens allans par dela.
Et en ſon abſence y eſtoit le Signeur de Cambray , tenant
ſon lieu & penſant des affaires du Roy, pres la perſonne du
grand Signeur : homme tres ſongneux & amateur des ver-
tus , & de gens de bonnes lettres , & qui ha prins vne peine
k   2   ſingul

10.17   Camel, right niche of the Grotto, Villa Medici. Castello, 1565–1572. (Photo: author.)

1556), Thevet described several exotic animals including a giraffe, hippopotamus, croco-dile, elephant, camel, lion, and wild ass, which were illustrated with woodcuts.[82] The figure of the camel (Figure 10.16) includes features observed from life, but the combi-nation of a camel with a monkey riding its back is a pictorial construct, a recurring image repeated in the grotto at Castello (Figure 10.17). (This monkey, of a type commonly known in Europe, is called a Barbary ape.) The association of camel and monkey derives from an old medieval type of a monkey riding a bear,[83] and dates from at least the late fifteenth century, the date of a *cassone* panel in the Metropolitan Museum in New York. This panel faithfully follows the biblical text in depicting camels in the procession of the Queen of Sheba, although the monkeys on the camel's backs are the artist's addition. The monkey illustrates the domesticity of the camel, standing in for its human counter-part and at the same time relegating the animal to the earlier stages of civilization implied in Piero di Cosimo's painting. The fruit-eating monkey in Thevet's woodcut and also in the Metropolitan painting ultimately derives from late antiquity and was a frequent image from the late thirteenth century. In the Castello grotto this monkey type is also present, but in another niche (Figure 10.13). In contrast to its exotic companions at Castello, a rhinoceros and the giraffe inspired by Cyriacus's early voyage, the apple-eating monkey as well as the leg-scratching one riding the camel were familiar in western art from manuscript borders and other sources.[84] The living specimens of the exotic animals were known, although they remained thoroughly foreign, probably through the eighteenth century. The representations of them, however, made the strange animals familiar, domesticating them through their assimilation into a long visual tradition.

IX

Collections of non-European animals, as well as their representations, were very popular among rulers and aristocrats. They indicated a literal contact with the enlarged world and implied a metaphorical possession of it. In the second half of the fifteenth century, Lodovico Gonzaga's garden at Mantua contained exotic birds.[85] Parakeets were prized by popes since the fourteenth century, but particularly by Pope Leo X.[86] Civet cats, which Pope Leo also kept in his menagerie, were brought in by European merchants from North Africa and their perfume fetched a high price.[87] The aristocratic greyhound was imported from England and in Italy the oriental greyhound, the *saluki*, was especially popular. Their presence at the Medici court is recorded in a number of images.[88] In the early sixteenth century Giovanni Cornaro in Venice owned a gazelle, newly arrived in Italy, probably from North Africa. When Duke Alfonso d'Este I of Ferrara learned this in 1520, he immediately commissioned a painting of it from Titian.[89] The array of animals in the Castello grotto reflects these other contemporary collections with its gazelle in the central niche (Figure 10.3), the greyhound in the left (Figure 10.5), and Giambologna's bronze birds (now removed).

Keeping menageries of large and wild animals as a sign of power was an old custom, as we have seen with those of the Florentine Republic, the Medici Duchy, and Pope Leo X in Rome. Cosimo de' Medici's second son, Cardinal Ferdinando, likewise spent a large sum on animals. He kept bears, lions, ostriches, and other wild animals in his villa in Rome and moved them with him to Florence in 1588 when he returned to assume the position of grand duke.[90] Giving such animals as gifts was also a common practice among the most distinguished rulers of Europe, including members of the Medici family. Like the animal fights in the piazzas, this was another ritual of power inspired by ancient Roman tributes and those of Byzantine, Near Eastern, and North African rulers.[91] In 1542 the Viceroy of Naples sent two tigers to Duke Cosimo in Florence.[92] His successor, Francesco, in 1572 sent to Albrecht V of Bavaria a miscellany of exotica, including parrots, Indian sheep, and crocodiles.[93] Francesco received in turn three elks in 1587, sent from Sweden by a merchant from Lucca, which were the first of this northern European animal to be seen in Florence.[94] These gifts are witness to international relations in the sixteenth century, as well as to the continuation of a long tradition of viewing rare animals, preferably also both very large and wild, as diplomatic currency.

Among such gifts were major ones to members of the Medici family, which were recorded in artistic representations, poems, and other contemporary accounts and became part of the family lore. The gifts were also an early and significant means of contact between Florence and the worlds beyond Europe. In 1487 the Sultan of Egypt, seeking diplomatic aid, sent an embassy to Lorenzo the Magnificent bearing precious objects and exotic animals. Among the former were a Chinese dish and other pieces of porcelain, which later inspired Grand Duke Francesco to attempt to reproduce the blue and white ware.[95] The animals included a giraffe, camels, monkeys, lion, and Indian goats, all of which are represented in the grotto at Castello. The giraffe, which caused a great stir, was the first ever seen in Florence and only the second in Italy – the first was in Rome in 46 BC when Julius Caesar returned in triumph from Africa.[96] This extraordinary animal, little known even in antiquity, signified to contemporaries Lorenzo's foreign standing.[97]

The distinct tradition of Florentine representations served to identify the animal with the place that was so honored by its presence.

In the system of exchange and language of diplomacy of the Renaissance, gifts were a two-sided commodity.[98] On the election of a new pope, foreign sovereigns were expected to send a gift of obedience. King Manuel I of Portugal wanted favors and concessions from Pope Leo X and thus in 1514 gave him a spectacular gift which both highlighted his own magnificence and bestowed it upon the recipient. Along with spices, gold, gems, rare plants, parakeets, Indian fowl and dogs, a cheetah, and a Persian horse, and amidst much pomp, his ambassador presented to Leo an Indian elephant. The animal delighted all of Rome, not least the pope.[99] The gifts acknowledged Portugal's mastery over lands in Asia, Africa, and America, while also implying that the newly conquered realms submitted to papal authority.

The elephant, above all, made an enormous impression, as no living elephant had been seen in Rome since antiquity. Before its death in 1516, it was paraded in Roman festivals, affectionately named "Annone," and drawn by Raphael.[100] A drawing from the circle of Giulio Romano (Figure 10.18) preserves a livelier, if more fantastic, elephant type than Raphael's, in active poses more reminiscent of the beloved pet described in contemporary accounts.[101] This elephant type, with a furled trunk and the small ears of the Indian elephant, which were given an almost decorative scalloped outline, provided the model for the Elephant Fountain made by Giovanni da Udine in 1526 for the Villa Madama in Rome of Cardinal Giulio de' Medici (later Pope Clement VII). Best seen in Francisco d'Hollanda's drawing (Figure 10.19), the elephant head, whose trunk served as a water spout, was placed in an *all' antica* setting. Vasari claimed that it imitated a fountain

10.18   Circle of Giulio Romano. *Elephant Studies.* Oxford, Ashmolean Museum. (Photo: museum.)

10.19   Francisco d'Hollanda. *Elephant Fountain at the Villa Madama in Rome*. Madrid, Biblioteca Escorial 28.I.20. (Photo: Fotografia Cedida y Autorizada por el Patrimonio Nacional.)

10.20   Elephant, central niche of the Grotto, Villa Medici. Castello, 1565–1572. (Photo: author.)

in the so-called Temple of Neptune on the Palatine, which was discovered in the same year.[102] The culture of classical antiquity provided the framework for understanding this animal, and, as with Giovanni da Udine's frescoes in the Vatican of a decade earlier, the sculpted image was framed within the classical decorative vocabulary of an ancient monument, one similarly only just discovered. (The classical vocabulary here consists of the grotesque decoration, garlands, rustic pebbles, and also the mosaic that is missing from Francisco d'Hollanda's drawing, as well as the sarcophagus that served as a basin.)

The representation of the elephant in the central niche at Castello (Figure 10.20) alludes to both the recipient of the extraordinary gift, Pope Leo X, and to Pope Clement VII, whose fountain immortalized it. Any elephant could have made the association with Leo, but this elephant, an unmistakable descendant of the type in both drawing and fountain, with its projecting, furled trunk and scalloped ears, made reference to Clement's sculpted animal as well. In the sixteenth-century *episteme* of similitudes, analogies were inferred from visual resemblance. With its appearance in the grotto of Cosimo I, this particular representation of the elephant, through its accumulated associations, could signify the power of the Medici dynasty, epitomized in the elephant gift. The same was true of the rhinoceros. Since the elephant gift was such a success, in the following year King Manuel shipped off to the pope a yet more rare specimen, the rhinoceros that he had just received from India. Although the animal perished during its journey from Lisbon to Rome, its carcass was preserved. The sculpted rhinoceros in the grotto (Figure 10.13) recalls the great gift to Pope Leo. Its form follows Dürer's woodcut, which was also the model for Alessandro de' Medici's emblem emphasizing the indomitable will of both animal and duke. The rhinoceros, like the elephant and giraffe, was incorporated into a Medici myth; the representations of these animals, through the repetition of visual signs which carried multiple associations, was similarly ideological.

Gifts of animals were mediated by other representations as well, which reflected current practice and interpreted it for contemporaries. These lavish gifts recall scenes of the Adoration of the Magi, which from the fifteenth century at least included exotic animals such as the camel and the leopard. In the sixteenth century animals in Adoration scenes increased in number and variety, corresponding with the social reality of diplomatic gift-giving. Vasari's painting of the Adoration of the Magi in Rimini, for example, presents an extravagant entourage of horses, elephants, and giraffes.[103]

10.21   Andrea del Sarto. *Tribute to Caesar in Egypt*. Poggio a Caiano, Villa Medici, 1521. (Photo: Art Resource.)

X

More pertinent in political terms, the animals and other precious objects presented among contemporaries as diplomatic gifts evoked ancient tributes, and this association was made explicit through images. In the early sixteenth-century decoration of the grand *salone* of the Medici villa of Poggio a Caiano, diplomatic gifts to Lorenzo are conflated with an ancient tribute to Caesar. The villa was built in the fifteenth century by Lorenzo the Magnificent, with whom it was closely associated, and the later decoration was commissioned by Pope Leo X. The scene of the *Tribute to Caesar in Egypt* (Figure 10.21) was painted by Andrea del Sarto in 1521 (and later extended by Alessandro Allori in 1582).[104] While the subject purports to be from ancient history, the giraffe in the distance and the Indian goats, lion, and parrots in the left foreground were gifts to Lorenzo the Magnificent in Florence from the Sultan of Egypt, not to the Roman emperor.[105] The association would have been clear since the only giraffe known to contemporaries was the one given to Lorenzo and thus identified with him. The Sultan of Egypt's embassy arrived 34 years before the *Tribute to Caesar* was painted, still within memory. Later the reference was made explicit by Raffaello Borghini in his discussion of the *salone* in *Il Riposo*, dialogues on art which were published in 1584.[106] It may have seemed necessary by then to jog the memory of an event that had taken place almost a century earlier, or perhaps the new and more complex program for the room, which had just been completed, required such explication.

The way in which the *Tribute to Caesar* was represented underlines the allusion to the Medici event and its conflation with an ancient Roman tribute. The giraffe with its long, graceful neck and curiously proportioned body belongs to the type familiar from other Florentine images – the engraving accompanying a description of the gifts in 1487 (Figure 10.14), Piero di Cosimo's painting of Vulcan and Aeolus (Figure 10.15), and, over twenty years later, Bacchiacca's *Gathering of Manna* (Figure 10.10). In addition to the telling giraffe, the other animals painted in the scene, including the monkeys, civet cat, chameleon, and the New World turkey and horses added by Allori, reinforce the idea of homage from all parts of the known world.[107] The setting of this tribute is presumably Egypt (recalling the Sultan of Egypt), which is interpreted as a classical city with a circular temple, round arch, and statuary.[108] The silhouette of the giraffe, framed by the distant mountain, is juxtaposed with the statue on a pedestal, the visual relationship between classical artifact and exotic natural creature suggesting again the parallel between redis-covery and discovery.

The larger context of the *Tribute to Caesar* at Poggio a Caiano is the grand *salone* with its classicizing barrel vault decorated with four scenes of ancient Romans in a villa striking for its temple front. The fresco in its setting also establishes, even more strongly than the Vatican *loggie* and the Elephant Fountain, the relationship of the new worlds to both contemporary situation and classical tradition. The ancient past was used typically to give authority to the present and also to represent the non-European worlds in a role of subservience. The tributes that signified these worlds implied that they were submissive to the dominant authority of the classical ruler, be he Caesar or Lorenzo.

In later tributes the identification of contemporary ruler and ancient emperor was complete and the classical gloss no longer necessary. In 1546, twenty-five years after the

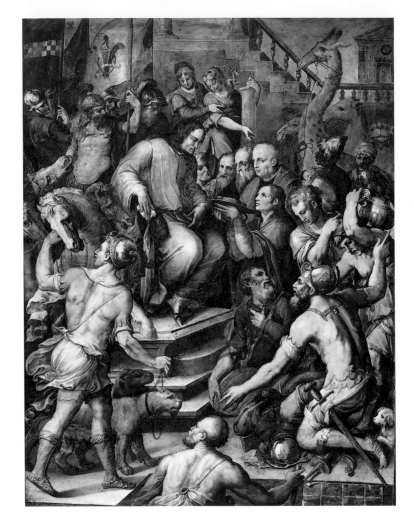

10.22   Giorgio Vasari.
*Tribute to Lorenzo the
Magnificent.* Florence,
Palazzo Vecchio, 1556.

Poggio a Caiano scene, Vasari and his shop painted in the Palazzo della Cancelleria in
Rome a scene of tribute to Pope Paul III. The enthroned Farnese pontiff himself accepts
the gifts of various nations, among them a giraffe, two camels, and an elephant. The
legend suggests that a golden age will ensue from the dispensation of an upright and
equitable order.[109] The tribute signified the power of the recipient, which extended to
foreign lands – in this case the spread of Christianity. The harmony of the animals gives
visual form to the idea of a golden age resulting from his good rule. A decade later Vasari
painted for Cosimo I the *Tribute to Lorenzo the Magnificent* in the Palazzo Vecchio in
Florence, following the Cancelleria model (Figure 10.22). The scene of the seated
Lorenzo accepting various gifts represents not a single historical event, but a conflation
of different episodes. Together they present the idea of tribute with all its implications.
Among the gifts is the Sultan's giraffe, with its characteristic long, curving neck. (Behind
it are the shadowy figures of two camels, which Vasari indicated were also presented to
Lorenzo.) Vasari explains how the giraffe underlines Florence's uniqueness. Nothing

similar, he noted, had ever come into Italy, and neither the Portuguese nor the Spaniards in India and in the New World had ever found a giraffe.[110]

A significant aspect of the political propaganda of the later Medici beginning with Cosimo I was the emphasis on continuity in the Medici family, merging the two branches to create a family dynasty and blurring the distinction between republic and principate.[111] The two paintings of the tribute to Lorenzo work to this end, since both Lorenzo and Pope Leo received such animals and both Leo and Cosimo had Lorenzo's tribute represented (the second in the apartments of Leo in the Palazzo Vecchio). The grotto at Castello, begun in the 1560s, about a decade after the Palazzo Vecchio rooms, continues this program of propaganda. We have seen how individual animals were associated with more than one member of the Medici family. The predominant non-European animals represented there were received in one or another of the tributes. It was not necessary to include a recipient of the gifts as well, since the central animals (Figure 10.3) stand in for both Florence and her succession of Medici rulers. The lion, proud king of the beasts, alludes simultaneously to the Florentine Marzocco, Pope Leo X, and Grand Duke Cosimo. The goat at its side resembles Cosimo's astrological sign, the capricorn. The four-horned ram nestled beneath the lion is the device of Cosimo's son, Francesco, who was made regent in 1564.[112] Without ambassadors or recipients, the grotto carries associations of tribute, dynasty, and the power of the Medici, along with the civilizing of wild nature and the harmony of good rule.

XI

In the grotto Medici power is defined in terms of the greatly increased knowledge of the world and the concomitant interest in defining differences, both within Europe, which was emerging as a concept, and between Europe and the other continents. This is evident in a number of publications, some that we have seen: Ptolemy's and Strabo's geographies and the *Descriptio Asiae et Europae* of Aeneas Sylvius Piccolomini in the fifteenth century; and in the sixteenth, Leandro Alberti's *Descrittione di tutta Italia* (1550); the cosmographies of Sebastian Münster, André Thevet, and others; the accounts of voyages, several collected in G. B. Ramusio's *Delle navigationi et viaggi* (1554), and the travel journals that led to the guidebooks of the next century.[113] Many new maps were produced from the late fifteenth century. Some, begun in the years between 1550 and 1575, formed part of princely decorative schemes – in the Vatican, the Palazzo Vecchio in Florence (commissioned by Cosimo in 1563), and the Farnese palace at Caprarola.[114] Following a long tradition, these maps contained images of the distinctive fauna of different regions, particularly those newly known.[115]

By the end of the sixteenth century the four continents were represented in personifications, in which animals play an important role. An early example of them appeared in Cesare Ripa's *Iconologia* of 1603, similar to others that ultimately derive from the frontispiece of Abraham Ortelius's *Theatrum Orbis Terrarum*, published in Antwerp in 1570.[116] In the personifications, the continents are characterized by the relationship of nature and culture, on a spectrum from civilized, the standard for which was set by Europe, to barbarian, embodying qualities of wild nature. This hierarchy of civilization

di frutti, perciòche come dimoſtra Strabone nel luoco citato di ſopra, e
queſta parte ſopra tutte l'altre feconda , & abondante di tutti quei beni ,
che la natura ha ſaputo produrre, come ſi potrà vedere da alcune ſue parti da noi deſcritte .

Si rappreſenta che tenghi con la deſtra mano il tempio , per dinotare,
ch'in lei al preſente ci è la perfetta , & veriſſima Religione , & ſuperiore
à tutte l'altre .

Moſtra con il dito indice della ſiniſtra mano Regni , Corone, Scet-
tri, Ghirlande , & altre ſimili coſe , eſſendo che nell' Europa vi ſonno i
maggiori, e più potenti Principi del Mondo; come la Maeſtà Ceſarea,
& il Sommo Pontefice Romano , la cui auttorità ſi ſtende per tutto ,
doue hà luocho la Santiſſima , & Cattholica Fede Chriſtiana . Il
quale

AFRICA.

VNA donna mora , quaſi nuda, hauerà li capelli creſpi, & ſparſi, te-
nendo in capo come per cimiero vna teſta di elefante , al collo vn
filo di coralli , & di eſſi à l'orecchie due pendenti , con la deſtra mano ter-
rà vn ſcorpione , & con la ſiniſtra vn cornucopia pien di ſpighe di grano;
da vn lato appreſſo di lei vi ſarà vn ferociſſimo leone , & da l'altro vi ſaranno alcune vipere , & ſerpenti venenoſi .

Africa vna delle quattro parti del Mondo è detta Africa, quaſi apriea,
cioè vaga del Sole , perche è priua del freddo, ouero è detta da Afro vno
de diſcendenti d'Abraham, come dice Gioſeffo .

Si rappreſenta mora , eſſendo l'Africa ſottopoſta al mezo dì , & parte
di eſſa

10.23 *Europe* (above left); 10.24 *Asia* (above right); 10.25 *Africa* (bottom left); 10.26 *America*
(bottom right). Cesare Ripa. Engravings, *Iconologia*, 1603. (Photos: author.)

Namque feras alijs tellus maurusia donum Præbuit, huic ſoli debet ceu victa tributum.
Il cornucopia pieno di ſpighe di grano denota l'abondanza , & fertilità
frumentaria dell'Africa, della quale ci fa fede Horatio .

Quicquid de Libycis verritur areis .
Et Gio: Boemo anch' egli nella deſcrittione, che fà de'coſtumi , leggi ,
& vſanze di tutte le genti , dice che due volte l'anno gl' Africani mietono
le biade, hauendo medeſimamente due volte nell'anno l'eſtate. Et Ouidio
nel quarto libro delle Metamorfoſi anch'egli .

Cumque ſuper Libycas victor pendebat arenas
Gorgonei capitis guttæ cecidere cruentæ,
Quas humus excerptas varios animauit in angues ;
Vnde frequens illa eſt, infeſtaque terra colubris .

A M E-

DONNA ignuda, di carnagione foſca, di giallo color miſta, di vol-
to terribile , & che vn velo rigato di più colori calandogli da vna
ſpalla à trauerſo al corpo , le copri le parti vergognoſe .

Le chiome ſaranno ſparſe , & à torno al capo ſia vn vago , & artifitioſo
ornamento di penne di varij colori .

Tenga con la ſiniſtra mano vn'arco , con la deſtra mano vna frezza , &
al fianco la faretra parimente piena di frezze, ſotto vn piede vna teſta hu-
mana paſſata da vna frezza , & per terra da vna parte ſarà vna lucertola,
ouero vn liguro di ſmiſurata grandezza.

Per eſſer nouellamente ſcoperta queſta parte del mondo gli Antichi
Scrittori non poſſono hauerne ſcritto coſa alcuna, però mi è ſtato meſtie-
ri ve-

is conveyed through dress, attributes, and animals. Ripa, important for the tremendous influence on painters of his handbook, repeats the essential elements of his models, but reduces, heightens contrasts, and emphasizes the animals. The illustration of Europe (Figure 10.23) closely follows the text, which describes "the first and principal part of the world," as crowned, dressed in regal garments, and seated on two crossed cornucopias, indicating the fertility of the continent. Behind her in the illustration is a horse, the quintessential embodiment of European aristocratic and classically based culture, as witnessed by equestrian monuments and portraits of rulers and generals and by the horse's role in jousts, hunts, and warfare (here alluded to by the lances). At the feet of Europe are emblems of the Christian religion and an owl, book, musical instruments, and other attributes of the liberal arts – denoting, Ripa explains, Europe's superiority in all these endeavors.

None of the other continents is accompanied by indications of cultural accomplishments: they are defined only by flora, fauna, and geography in a descending scale of civilization. Asia (Figure 10.24), in rich garments, is represented with fruit, flowers, an incense burner denoting its spices and aromatic substances, and a camel. We will recall that in Piero di Cosimo's Vulcan and Aeolus (Figure 10.15) a camel was a signifier of the early stages of civilization. Africa (Figure 10.25), nearly nude in the text, but in the illustration only suggestively displaying a bare leg, wears an elephant headdress and holds a scorpion and cornucopia. She is accompanied by a "most ferocious" lion (rather domesticated in the illustration), poisonous snakes, and vipers. All this suggests a wild and uncivilized continent. Finally, America (Figure 10.26), with only her shameful parts covered, Ripa explains, wears a feathered headdress and holds a bow and arrow. One foot rests on a head pierced with an arrow, demonstrating the barbarity of her people. Beside her is a reptile, called a lizard in the text and although seemingly innocuous in the woodcut, explained as a ferocious animal which devours not only other animals but also humans.[117] The animals were selected not only because they are native to the respective regions, but equally importantly, as signifiers of the cultural paradigms that informed the personifications.

Animals were part of a construct of nature; wild animals spoke to assumptions about the force of nature. The public animal hunts and visual representations of fighting animals were demonstrations of this wildness, but also of the power of the individual or state that harnesses the wildness. Exotic animals indicated the magnificence of their owners, because of their rarity and expense, but also because they signified less civilized, more wild, or barbarian parts of the world. In the animal tributes the appropriation of the force of nature that the exotic animals signified is also a demonstration of the domination of a superior civilization, be it Florence, the Catholic Church, or Europe. Classical antiquity is a key element in the assumptions and paradigms behind this set of associations. It provided the foundation for natural science and the familiarity with Asia and Africa that made their fauna and flora accessible to study. The tenacious imitation of the ancients was also an obstacle to their study.[118] Models from classical antiquity served as well to legitimate Europe's claims of superiority and authority. For much of the next two centuries classical forms and paradigms continued to dominate and define western, and especially Italian, culture. The cultural biases embedded in Ripa's personifications of the continents were also a long-enduring legacy of the Renaissance.

II.I *Codex Vaticanus B* screenfold. Pictorial manuscript, sixteenth century. Vatican, Biblioteca Apostolica Vaticana, Codex Vaticanus 3773. (Photo: author, courtesy of the Akademische Druck–u. Verlag sanstalt.)

CHAPTER 11

Collecting Cultures: A Mexican Manuscript in the Vatican Library

ELOISE QUIÑONES KEBER

Even as Renaissance Italy was recovering the letters, scholarship, and arts of classical antiquity, European expansionism was giving impetus to the passion for another kind of collecting. Vessels returning from newly encountered lands to the west were laden not only with goods destined for European markets but with other kinds of unexpected wonders – hitherto unknown plants, animals, and even peoples, *made* objects as well as raw substances, trinkets as well as treasure. Resulting from the expansion of geographic rather than historical horizons, these exotica made a different kind of impact on Renaissance intellects and appetites.[1]

The relationship of "collecting" to the darker side of European exploration, with its expropriation of native lands and possessions, cannot easily be ignored.[2] Ironically, however, the collecting, like the explorations, began a process that would eventually result in the relativization of European culture – that is, the shifting of European culture from its central position, or at least the viewing of it in relationship to other cultures.[3] One outcome of this process is the creation of terms like "Europocentric" and "Eurocentric" to express new perceptions about old relationships.

Today the results of this European passion for possession have helped to provide both the means and the materials for re-encountering the cultures of the non-European peoples who were once dispossessed. In the case of ancient Mexico, there is no doubt that those items that were amassed in Europe by sixteenth-century collectors are indispensable for reconstructing the art history – and history – of the late prehispanic period that preceded the first European contact.

Even before 1519, when Hernando Cortés dispatched his famous first shipment of gifts and booty to his sovereign Charles I of Spain (Emperor Charles V), Mexican treasure resulting from Juan de Grijalva's exploratory voyage along the eastern coast of Mexico in 1518 had already been relayed to Spain. Extant inventories of these items describe hundreds of finely worked articles that today we would call Precolumbian art. Several of these objects are particularly crucial survivals since the few examples of them that exist today are found for the most part in archives and museums in Europe rather than in their native land. These include pictorial screenfold books that consisted of figural and symbolic images, like the Codex Vaticanus 3773 (Codex Vaticanus B) now in the

Biblioteca Apostolica Vaticana in the Vatican (Figure 11.1);[4] finely wrought crystal or gold adornments, like the gold eagle-head lip ornament now in the Museo Civico in Turin;[5] meticulously crafted precious stone mosaics, like the mosaic mask now in the Museo Nazionale Preistorico e Ethnografico Luigi Pigorini in Rome;[6] and brilliantly colored, painstakingly assembled featherwork items, like the famous quetzal-feather headdress now in the Museum für Völkerkunde in Vienna.[7]

The Mexican objects found in sixteenth-century collections are thus undoubtedly important for what they can tell us about prehispanic art history. But can they also disclose anything about Renaissance art history? Can these objects shed any light on prevailing attitudes toward other cultures during the Italian Renaissance? Did the collecting of these works have any direct or indirect influence on the development of the history of western art, at that time or thereafter?

With their history of 400 years in European repositories, these Mexican objects can certainly be said to have a European as well as a Precolumbian art history. This fact has, of course, long been recognized by curators of collections that include early examples of Mexican (and other non-western) objects (and "art"), as well as by historians of collecting and of museums.[8] With some exceptions, art historians, especially those specializing in European art, have generally seemed less cognizant of, or perhaps less interested in exploring, the ramifications of the "strange" and "wonderful" images that increasingly began to appear in European collections and archives from the time of the Renaissance on.

Indeed, the responses of Renaissance Europe to indigenous American artifacts began to be recorded as early as Columbus's voyage.[9] In terms of documentation related to Mexico, they are revealed in a number of ways, including written descriptions and reactions of Europeans to objects produced there;[10] inventory lists of Mexican treasure destined for European beneficiaries;[11] related inventories of Mexican items in European collections;[12] actual surviving examples of the types of objects that were most prized and collected;[13] works produced in Mexico for a European market; European drawings, engravings, and adaptations of prehispanic items, actual or fanciful; and Mexican pieces incorporated into European art works.[14] Although each type of object or documentation reveals a different aspect of Europe's response to the foreign artifacts, it can be argued that collectively they disclose much not only about European curiosity about the "New World" but about the aesthetic and intellectual predilections of the period.

Aside from goldwork, which seems to have been esteemed mainly because of the value of its constituent material, and featherwork, which seems to have elicited admiration because of its exotic appearance, perhaps no other Mexican objects attracted as much attention as pictorial manuscripts. Made of long strips of stucco-coated bark-paper or animal skin that the Indian artists covered with brightly painted images then folded back and forth to create screenfold books, they appear to have been especially valued works. It is no accident that of the fifteen indisputably preconquest manuscripts that survive, thirteen are in Europe. These screenfolds undoubtedly ranked high in the hierarchy of "New World" curios since Europeans regarded books and written records as hallmarks of civilization. The provenance of the Codex Vindobonensis, one of the preconquest Mexican screenfolds that arrived in Europe in the sixteenth century and is now in the Nationalbibliothek in Vienna, illustrates the value these manuscripts had for the

European collector. Within a period of about twenty years this Mixtec screenfold passed from emperor to king to pope to cardinal.[15]

Surprisingly, none of the surviving prehispanic screenfolds is Aztec (Nahua), the dominant culture in ancient Mexico at the time of European contact. The production of painted manuscripts was an ancient and flourishing craft when the Spaniards first arrived in Mexico, and manuscripts were among the first items Cortés selected to ship back to Spain.[16] The virtual disappearance of preconquest manuscripts in Mexico thus attests to the thoroughness with which the task of eradicating "pagan" books was carried out by conquistadors, missionaries, and bureaucrats. In light of this, we might ask whether removing the painted screenfolds from their original setting permitted them to be viewed in Europe with less suspicion. Was the geographic decontextualization of these manuscripts part of a sanitizing process that rendered them into harmless curiosities in European repositories?

Because all preconquest Aztec manuscripts have been lost or destroyed, this category of Aztec art is known today only through later, usually modified, colonial copies. And here again, many of the finest examples are to be found in European repositories, where they seem to have been collected almost as avidly as the preconquest originals. Interestingly, these copies began to be made very soon after European contact, even while preconquest examples were still available. Many of these copies are composite works that were produced by grouping together replicas of disparate types of indigenous manuscripts. We can thus surmise that they were created precisely to render pictorial compendia of the beliefs, practices, and history of the "New World" for a curious European audience.[17] We might also ask whether recopying the prehispanic screenfolds, often on European paper and in the form of a European book or codex, was another attempt at disengaging the indigenous manuscript from its suspect origins and authors and of exorcising the contents of those sections that were devoted to what were regarded as pagan gods, idolatrous religious beliefs, and superstitious rituals (Figure 11.2).

Among these colonial compilations is a Mexican manuscript called the Codex Vaticanus Latinus 3738 (Codex Vaticanus A), which is now in the Biblioteca Apostolica Vaticana. Made up of both images and texts, this large, bound volume of 101 folios offers a specific and revealing early example of the encounter of Renaissance Italy with a non-western cultural artifact.[18] In fact, cooption rather than encounter seems more to the point in this case. Even the formal Latin name of this Mexican manuscript shows how thoroughly it was subsumed into a European setting. Its other unofficial names divulge a bit more about its Mexican identity and history. The manuscript is also called the Codex Ríos, after Pedro de los Ríos, who is identified in the manuscript itself as a Dominican friar who lived in Mexico and compiled it. Given these historical circumstances, it is likely that Ríos, actually a lay brother, probably served as a Spanish missionary. Sixteenth-century chapter reports of the Dominican Order reveal few facts about him. He is, for example, first documented in Mexico City, the capital of New Spain, as early as 1541, and he died before 1565 in Puebla, another city in which Dominican missionaries were especially active.[19] The manuscript's other unofficial designation as Codex Vaticanus A distinguishes it from another Mexican manuscript later acquired by the Vatican library, the preconquest Codex Vaticanus B mentioned above.

Like other exotic curiosities that found their way into aristocratic collections through-

11.2   *The Aztec goddess Chalchiuhtlicue.* Codex Vaticanus B, pictorial manuscript, sixteenth century. Vatican, Biblioteca Apostolica Vaticana, Codex Vaticanus 3773, page 53. (Photo: author, courtesy of the Akademische Druck-u. Verlag sanstalt.)

out Europe, the inclusion of the Codex Vaticanus A in an Italian repository demonstrates the range of interests of sixteenth-century Italian collectors. Not only do these collections demonstrate an awareness of the newly encountered lands, but amassing objects produced by their inhabitants seems to have been one way for Europeans to incorporate these alien cultures into a rapidly expanding world view.

Mexican manuscripts, whether prehispanic originals or colonial copies, must have been something of a revelation for European collectors. Illustrations of Indians produced and circulated throughout Europe in the sixteenth century almost invariably depicted them holding simple weapons like bows and arrows and clubs, occasionally a rudimentary tool, and even human limbs, but never a book. The inhabitants of the Americas were variously shown as hunters, fighters, farmers, and acrobats, but never as thinking beings. One of the few works that revealed the spectrum of Aztec existence was Bernardino de Sahagún's voluminous and lavishly illustrated manuscript called the *General History of the Things of New Spain*.[20] Never published, one version of it disappeared after being sent from Mexico to King Philip II of Spain in the late 1570s and re-emerged only in the 1790s in the Biblioteca Medicea-Laurenziana in Florence.[21]

The painted manuscript copies that surfaced in European collections likewise displayed evidence – indeed, they were graphic evidence – of the cultural and intellectual activities of the inhabitants of the "New World." Furthermore, the commentaries in these manuscripts show the first responses of Europeans to the socio-cultural systems devised by these peoples, their religious and ritual structures, political institutions, and economic arrangements.

Because it has been altered for European consumption, the Codex Vaticanus A is even more revealing of European collecting proclivities than the simpler acquisition of "original" preconquest manuscripts. Since the colonial copies were consciously constructed, they reveal those aspects of indigenous culture that were incorporated to intrigue a

11.3 *The Aztec goddess Chalchiuhtlicue. Codex Vaticanus A*, pictorial manuscript, sixteenth century. Vatican, Biblioteca Apostolica Vaticana, Codex Vaticanus 3738, fol. 17v. (Photo: author, courtesy of the Akademische Druck-u. Verlag sanstalt.)

European reader and elicit his admiration or stir his acquisitiveness. Interestingly, although the Codex Vaticanus A is a colonial document produced during the second half of the sixteenth century, it focuses chiefly on Aztec life as it existed at the time of European contact about half a century earlier (with the exception of the pictorial history that extends into the early viceregal period and terminates in 1562). Possibly it was the "antique" character of this distant culture that was thought to be of most interest to a European reader. Because the Codex Vaticanus A is not unique but part of a group of manuscript copies, we can also surmise that there must have been a viable European market for these types of documents to justify the amount of time, talent, money, and materials expended to produce them.

11.4 *Events in Mexico, 1507–1509. Codex Vaticanus A,* pictorial manuscript, sixteenth century. Vatican, Biblioteca Apostolica Vaticana, Codex Vaticanus 3738, fol. 85r. (Photo: author, courtesy of the Akademische Druck-u. Verlag sanstalt.)

11.5 *Mexican women in costume. Codex Vaticanus A,* pictorial manuscript, sixteenth century. Vatican, Biblioteca Apostolica Vaticana, Codex Vaticanus 3738 fol. 61r. (Photo: author, courtesy of the Akademische Druck-u. Verlag sanstalt.)

Some sections of the Codex Vaticanus A have counterparts in surviving preconquest manuscripts, demonstrating that colonial copies, or sections of them, were ultimately derived from indigenous prototypes. One of these parts is a divinatory almanac (*tonalamatl*, or book of days), which features images of elaborately attired deities and other supernatural forces that influenced the fates of the days depicted (Figure 11.3). A second part represents another well-established indigenous category, the historical annals whose images portray rulers, conquests, astronomical occurrences, and other major events (Figure 11.4). In these two areas the Vatican codex is pictorially cognate with another sixteenth-century colonial manuscript called the Codex Telleriano-Remensis, which is now in the Bibliothèque Nationale of Paris.[22]

Other parts of the Codex Vaticanus A do not appear either in the Codex Telleriano-Remensis or as a standard feature of other ancient Mexican manuscripts. Apparently these sections were painted specifically for the Codex Vaticanus A. One of these is referred to today as an ethnographic section because it portrays indigenous people and their activities. One folio, for example, shows two women in typical costumes (Figure 11.5), and another depicts a warrior in battle array (Figure 11.6). Other images portray sanguinary ritual practices – ever-compelling for the European viewer – like the sacerdotal acts of penitential bloodletting (Figure 11.7) and human sacrifice (Figure 11.8, top). Another section represents Aztec cosmology. The first two facing folios of the Codex Vaticanus A, for example, depict the Aztec cosmos with its thirteen celestial layers and nine levels of the underworld (Figure 11.9). This is the only extant depiction of this concept, which is otherwise known only from textual descriptions set down in the sixteenth century. Other sections show similarly rare representations of the destruction of the four worlds (or Suns) that preceded what the Aztecs believed to be their present cosmic era of the Fifth Sun. The addition of these ethnographic and mythological sections, unique features of the manuscript, were undoubtedly made by the compiler to provide for the intended European reader a fuller picture of ancient Mexican customs and, significantly, of their beliefs.

11.6 *Mexican warrior. Codex Vaticanus A*, pictorial manuscript, sixteenth century. Vatican, Biblioteca Apostolica Vaticana, Codex Vaticanus 3738, fol. 58v. (Photo: author, courtesy of the Akademische Druck-u. Verlag sanstalt.)

11.7 *Bloodletting ritual. Codex Vaticanus A*, pictorial manuscript, sixteenth century. Vatican, Biblioteca Apostolica Vaticana, Codex Vaticanus 3738, fol. 55r. (Photo: author, courtesy of the Akademische Druck-u. Verlag sanstalt.)

11.8) *Sacrificial ritual. Codex Vaticanus A*, pictorial manuscript, sixteenth century. Vatican, Biblioteca Apostolica Vaticana, Codex Vaticanus 3738, fol. 54v. (Photo: author, courtesy of the Akademische Druck-u. Verlag sanstalt.)

Above all, what distinguishes the Codex Vaticanus A from other colonial Mexican manuscript copies is the extensive commentary, written in Italian, that accompanies the voluminous images. Other manuscripts may preserve native language texts, albeit transcribed into European script, or include annotations written in Spanish, but the Codex Vaticanus A is the only colonial Mexican manuscript to feature a lengthy, systematically composed Italian text to explicate its images.

While the images of the Codex Vaticanus A have been fairly faithfully copied from traditional models, the text, written by two scribes, represents a European intrusion, and a highly mediated one. Although based to a great extent on the scattered glosses of the Codex Telleriano–Remensis, the commentary has been expanded far beyond the scope of the earlier manuscript. The Codex Vaticanus A not only describes what is drawn on the page, as does the Codex Telleriano–Remensis, but it goes to great lengths to attempt to explicate it for a European audience and through a European lens. The commentator was interested in translating for his Italian readership not just words or images but a whole culture. The written text thus presents a curious blend of indigenous lore, analogies made between Indian and European/Christian traditions, and oftentimes fanciful speculations on their meanings. In passages where the commentator finds resemblances between indigenous and Christian personages and practices – a discovery that both fascinates and dismays him – his responses likewise take different, somewhat contradictory forms. He may allude to scripture to support the similarities he sees or deplore what he believes to be the tricks of the devil in ensnaring a gullible Indian population.

On folio 55r (Figure 11.7), for example, after first describing the way in which the Mexican priests drew blood from their tongue and ears, the commentator of this section goes on to say:

> From all of this we see a resemblance [that is, to known history], and we see that this race descends from the Jews, since all the ceremonies [described in] this chapter follow the text of Leviticus, such as the law that says that the common people shall not touch sacred things; or as it says in Exodus, that in the temple there must always be light and incense and trumpets and stoles. [The commentator here voices a belief, which persisted until the nineteenth century, that the indigenous inhabitants of the New World were descendants of the lost tribes of Israel.] The great difference lies in the nature of one of their priests and one of ours, and theirs conforms to the kind of gods they worshiped; their priests were black and dirty, and stinking and abominable, because that is the way their god is. But the priests of the true God had to be holy,

11.9 *The Aztec cosmos. Codex Vaticanus A*, pictorial manuscript, sixteenth century. Vatican, Biblioteca Apostolica Vaticana, Codex Vaticanus 3738, fols. 1v–2r. (Photo: author, courtesy of the Akademische Druck-u. Verlag sanstalt.)

clean, without stain and filth . . . those who . . . scripture says were whiter than milk, the color of ancient coral, more beautiful than sapphire. . . .[23]

The Eurocentrism evident in these comments may stir our amusement or dismay, and it would be simple to dismiss these words as being of little value from either a Mexican or European perspective. Yet, given the extensiveness of the text, it seems clear that the commentator wanted to understand, and to make understood, this perplexing culture and its expressions. Thus he tells us: their history is really our history; their ceremonies are like ours; their gods are like ours; their priests are like ours. But discrepancies between their world and ours are the work of the devil, for as the text goes on to say:

> . . . [it can be seen that] from our own cleanliness we can know how great is the cleanliness of the lord to whom we offer sacrifice. So, it is not out of keeping that these high priests of the devil were dirty and black and abominable like the devil himself.

The commentator(s) of the Codex Vaticanus A thus tried to carry out the task of explication principally in two ways. The first was by identifying items or acts and describing their function by analogy with European examples. The second was by supplying a plausible causal explanation for exotic beliefs and practices. In the religious and ritual sections of the manuscript, this usually takes the form that these gods and their cults originated through diabolical interference.[24]

The first part of this methodology is even more clearly exemplified by another folio that features the wind god Quetzalcoatl (Figure 11.10). Glosses that accompany the individual images tell the reader: this is a god, his name (Quetzalcoatl), his items (thorn, incense burner), his temples (house of fasting, house of communal fasting, house of fear, prison of sadness), and so on. In the text below the figures, it is the resemblances to Christian practices that capture the commentator's attention:

> This Quetzalcoatl . . . seeing that the sins and sufferings of the world were not ceasing, they say was the first to begin to invoke the gods and to make sacrifices to them. Thus also he was the first to do penance in order to appease the gods in order that his people might be pardoned. They say that he sacrificed himself, drawing his own blood with thorns and other forms of penance.[25]

What may appear to us today as the naivete and prejudice of the commentator's remarks should not distract us from the serious intent or lead us to a total rejection of his efforts. Given the intensive and systematic character of the commentary, it seems apparent that the commentator wanted to describe the paintings accurately, to get them right. The effort to get things right must be noted, even if the analogies used to identify or clarify foreign personages and objects eventually came to be seen as deficient and distorting, or as expressive of the deleterious side of Christian and European attitudes toward the inhabitants of the Americas. Notwithstanding the negative aspect of the endeavor, we might in fact see in the commentary of the Codex Vaticanus A, as well as in those of other annotated Mexican manuscripts, the first seeds of a critical history – and critical art history. But critics of today must not stop at critiquing the prejudices (that is, prejudgments) of the sixteenth century, they must also critique their own. Contemporary

11.10 *The Aztec god Quetzalcoatl. Codex Vaticanus A*, pictorial manuscript, sixteenth century. Vatican, Biblioteca Apostolica Vaticana, Codex Vaticanus 3738, fol. 7v. (Photo: author, courtesy of the Akademische Druck-u. Verlag sanstalt.)

awareness of Eurocentric attitudes posits the need to critique them, but without forgetting the intellectual development that generated the initial awareness.

From reading the commentary it seems evident that, unlike some other colonial manuscripts, the Codex Vaticanus A was not created primarily to preserve indigenous traditions or to inform the Spanish monarchy or its administrators about the new realms under its command. Rather, the manuscript was made for the enlightenment of an Italian patron. Indeed, the opulent physical features of the manuscript – its painted pages, grand folio size, elegant handwriting, and encyclopedic scope – suggest that it was created as a presentation copy for an Italian recipient, whose name has unfortunately been lost to us.[26]

So striking is the Italian connection that some scholars have speculated that the Codex

Vaticanus A may have been copied from Mexican sources in Italy and by a non-Indian artist; others, however, opt for a Mexican origin.[27] If the former is the case, this would indicate that the manuscript might even have been an Italian commission specifically produced for an Italian collector. In any event, it is not known how the manuscript first came to rest in the Vatican library. Its listing as item 3738 in the Rainaldi inventory of the Vatican collection, compiled between 1596 and 1600, securely places it there by the late sixteenth century.[28] But certain circumstantial evidence suggests that it (or perhaps the model from which it may have been copied) may have arrived in the Vatican library even earlier, possibly about 1570.[29]

The hybrid form of this unusual Aztec–Italian document represents the transformation of a Mexican manuscript into a western-style codex. For its Italian collector, it became – even if it was not called such at the time – an ethnographic document recast in an accessible Europeanized format. But the Europeanization of the manuscript went beyond the use of materials such as paper and ink and the reorientation of the images to read from left to right. More importantly, the whole notion of the native book was being rethought as its components were reshaped.

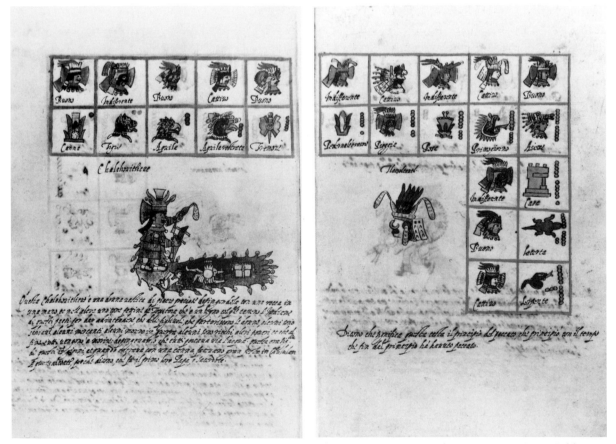

11.11   *Fifth divinatory period. Codex Vaticanus A*, pictorial manuscript, sixteenth century. Vatican, Biblioteca Apostolica Vaticana, Codex Vaticanus 3738 fols. 17v–18r. (Photo: author, courtesy of the Akademische Druck-u. Verlag sanstalt.)

For example, in the divinatory section (*tonalamatl*) of preconquest screenfolds like the Codex Vaticanus B, the continually repeating divinatory and ritual cycle was visually expressed by the horizontally extended painted panel with the 260 days of the cycle divided into 20 contiguous 13-day segments (Figure 11.1). This is visually communicated even more emphatically in the *tonalamatl* section of the preconquest Codex Borgia, another Mexican screenfold in the Vatican library. There the first ten segments of the ritual-divinatory cycle read from right to left on the bottom half of each panel, and the second ten read from left to right above them in the top half of the panels. In the corresponding section of the postconquest Codex Vaticanus A, however, the *tonalamatl* has been fractured into discrete, sequential units or pages, a rearrangement that not only fails to communicate the cyclical aspect of the ritual-divinatory cycle but also hampers a proper understanding of this repeating ritual round in indigenous ideology. Placed on two facing folios, each 13-day divinatory period is visually disconnected from those before or after it (Figure 11.11).

In addition, in this new format, the images, the main constituents of the indigenous manuscript, have been reduced and moved to the upper section of the folio to make room below for the addition of a written (that is, alphabetic) text. Divested now of the interlocking frames that surrounded the figural images, as well as of some of the accompanying items that related to divinatory rituals or the divinatory sphere of the deity, as shown in the Codex Vaticanus B (Figure 11.2), the deity patrons of the Codex Vaticanus A now float in an indeterminate space (Figure 11.11). Visual attention now focuses on the grandly costumed individual figures rather than on the interrelated augural system of days, deities, and divinatory forces. In a parallel way, the commentary below the figure concentrates on describing general features about the patron rather the system of which it was a part. On folio 17v of the Codex Vaticanus A, for example (Figure 11.3), the commentator describes the water goddess represented (Chalchiuhtlicue or Jade Skirt), her costume, and the insignia she bears. But her role in the divinatory rituals of the 13 days under her sway is ignored.

Furthermore, the Italian text now bears the weight of communicating information to the reader, in contrast to the reliance on the images and accompanying oral recitation that had been prevalent during the prehispanic period. The final form of the Codex Vaticanus A thus represents not just a different mode of recording and "reading" information, but a new way of thinking about the content of a culture. The codex form of the Europeanized manuscript visually expresses the estrangement of the manuscript from the contributory role it once played in the participatory augural activity carried out between individual and priest. The new format thus correlates to the solitary act of reading that characterizes what has been described as an isolating literacy. The effort to understand orality as constituent of cultures, differentiating them from "literate" (alphabetic) ones in important ways, especially in their modes of knowing and social consequences, has engaged some recent scholars.[30] Orality is said to unite speaker with hearer in a dialogical immediacy and allow the past to become present in performance (ritual), whereas writing is said to isolate audience from speaker and to reify the past. The transmutation from screenfold to codex illustrates this transcultural shift.

What seems to emerge from these considerations is that attempts to arrive at understanding by establishing context through such means as exhaustive description, appropriating or transmuting indigenous taxonomies and categories, or imposing extrinsic ones, turn out to be essentially unrealizable projects. No complete specification or description of a culture, especially of an outside one, seems possible. The intellectual artifact of critical (art) history arrives, if not at self-consumption, then at exhaustion. It consumes itself by depleting all the available resources (analogies/categories) western culture has to explain the other. It exhausts itself by an ever more detailed description of the "native context" that it finds still capable of further description. These shortcomings would seem to necessitate the abandonment of all centrisms, even when ironically the only way of understanding the other – and the art of the other – is by way of analogies born of the centrism one seeks to escape.

Over time the European discipline of history, with its interest in indigenous languages and categories, has led to an inevitable recognition of the problem of "the native point of view" and of the impossibility of experiencing it in western terms. Interest in an ever more detailed description of context has similarly led to an understanding of foreign images as unlike European ones, indeed as "other," to be appreciated precisely as signs and symbols of a different world view and to be understood by way of analogy with the familiar. An immediate or intuitive understanding of these images has proved to be illusory. However approached by the various methodologies of art history, they remain truly "other." As such, they announce the limits of the western point of view and liberate the art of non-western others to be really "other."

PART 4

Mediating Images:
Developing an Intercultural Perspective

Von der neüwen welt

darūß võ den völckern andere kaufftē/vñ sind võ vns gangen/mit dem geding/dz sy zū vns nach fünff tagen vff das höchst sorgten wider zekummen/wann wir ir so lang warteten/vnd also haßen sy den weg angriffen vnnd wir die widerfart zū vnsern schiffen genen.

12.1 Grüninger. *Women Clubbing Member of Vespucci's crew.* Woodcut, *Dis büchlin saget,* 1509.
(Photo: British Library.)

CHAPTER 12

Wild Woman in Colonial Mexico: An Encounter of European and Aztec Concepts of the Other

CECELIA F. KLEIN

In his introduction to *Marvelous Possessions*, one of numerous texts focused on Renaissance Europe's reactions to the peoples of the so-called New World, Stephen Greenblatt forewarns his reader that he has tried "less to distinguish between true and false representations than to look attentively at the nature of the representational practices that the Europeans carried with them to America and deployed when they tried to describe to their fellow countrymen what they saw and did [there]." I gather that Greenblatt found this task fairly difficult, because he writes at times like a repentant sinner still attracted to the devil: "I *catch myself constantly straining* to read into the European traces an account of what the American natives were 'really' like – but *I have resisted as much as I can* the *temptation* to speak for or about the native cultures as if the mediation of European representations were an incidental consideration, easily corrected for" (emphases mine). Greenblatt's reason for resisting any claim to knowing the "other" is by now familiar: "We can be certain only that European representations of the New World tell us something about the *European* practice of representation".[1] There can be, in other words, no real epistemological interaction across cultural boundaries. One cannot ever know his "others."

The poststructuralist critique of representation, which grew out of the writings of twentieth-century French intellectuals such as Roland Barthes, Michel Foucault, and Jacques Derrida, has been embraced by a number of students of the conquest and colonization of the New World.[2] Its popularity derives in large part from general belief that such critiques provide a solution to the thorny problem of Eurocentrism in the literature on indigenous America. Stung by criticism launched by sub-alterns[3] and multiculturalists, as well as dissident historians and "ethno-anthropologists," and sensitized to the increasingly well-documented Renaissance European tendency to perceive the New World in familiar and ultimately reductive forms, Americanists have recently become aware of the naivete inherent in using European texts and pictures as literal, essentially transparent reflections of the Amerindian past. In rejecting the idea that the Renaissance's documentary sources – whether visual or textual – constitute a glass window looking out on Europe's "others," more and more authors on both sides of the

Atlantic instead have moved to treat those sources more like a modern mirror, as an opaque surface capable only of reflecting back to us an image of ourselves.

I doubt that Greenblatt meant to be read as casting blanket disapproval over all attempts to reconstruct the reality of the New World "other," and I am relieved that he himself, trained as he is in Shakespearian Renaissance culture, refrained here from personally undertaking to make one. There can be nothing so grim as the assumptions about, and consequent misrepresentations of, indigenous American thoughts and practices that have been offered up by Europeanists in the course of providing poststructuralist "insights" into the conquest and colonization periods.[4] Whether or not Greenblatt's personal intent was to discourage future attempts to understand the American indigene, however, the fact is that poststructuralism in general has tended to do so. If, as Peter Mason has argued, the European vision of America is necessarily a distorted view of native reality because representions "refer only to other representations, and not to the truth of the represented," then it follows that there is no gain in pursuing that truth, that reality.[5] This message has not been lost on younger Americanists in particular, many of whom have deduced from these axioms that it is simply impossible to reconstruct and understand the early culture history of the New World native. Since that is the case, these scholars have concluded, they can better spend their energies studying their own reflections in the mirrors of history. Never mind the history, the "truth," of their "others."

What follows is an effort to demonstrate that, however cloudy the image may be destined to remain for us, it *is* possible to see something in the glass beside ourselves. Representations, in other words, do not just refer to other representations; they can refer in part to other "realities" as well. This exercise also will attempt to show that we can only identify and fully understand the nature and range of colonial-period representational processes if we can locate those points at which Renaissance representations both resembled and differed from indigenous modes of conceptualization. We need, in other words, to be certain that it is indeed only ourselves – and not some "other" as well – whose image we are seeing in the glass.

I will develop these points through investigation of the impact of the medieval and Renaissance motif of "Wild Woman" on Central Mexican representations of the Aztec goddess Cihuacoatl. Previous scholars have already demonstrated a tendency for early sixteenth-century European explorers and their illustrators to represent native women of Brazil in terms of the female counterpart of the violent, cannibalistic "Wild Man" of European lore.[6] Susi Colin, for example, points to a woodcut illustrating the 1509 Strassburg edition of Amerigo Vespucci's account of his voyages to America, which depicts a crew member cunningly distracted by several Guarani women while another woman prepares to club him from behind. In accordance with Vespucci's text, and as seen in the background, the senseless sailor was subsequently dragged into a cave to be roasted and eaten (Figure 12.1).[7] Like Wild Woman, these Guarani women are naked and have long, unkempt hair. This is important because, to the north, Spanish mendicants in Central Mexico were describing an Aztec goddess whose disheveled appearance and destructive behavior likewise recall Wild Woman. Most commonly called by the Nahuatl name of Cihuacoatl, "Woman Snake," this deity's statue had, according to the Dominican friar Diego Durán, "a huge open mouth and ferocious teeth," while her hair

12.2   Lucas Cranach the Elder. *Cannibal Eating Baby*. Woodcut. 1510–15. New York, The Metropolitan Museum of Art, Harris Brisbane Dick Fund, 1942 (42.45.2). (Photo: museum.)

was long and "bulky." Because she was "always famished," Durán claims, she was fed a roasted captive every day; when sated, she flung a thigh from her dark temple, crying out, "Take this for it has been gnawed on!"[8] The Franciscan Bernardino de Sahagún described Cihuacoatl as a "savage beast" and claimed that she recently had "eaten" a infant boy in his cradle, a report bearing eerie resemblance to European tales in which Wild Man and, especially, Wild Woman, who were always hungry, kidnapped and ate other women's babies (Figure 12.2).[9]

Fray Gerónimo Mendieta's 1596 report that Cihuacoatl could change herself into a serpent or a lovely young woman who enticed men into intercourse so that she could kill them reinforces the suspicion that the goddess was perceived in terms of Wild Woman.[10] In European lore, Wild Woman was often an anti-social slave to nature who lived alone, usually in remote caves or forests. Normally grotesque in appearance, with long matted hair and naked sagging breasts, she nonetheless was able to turn into a lovely young woman who seduced men into her remote wooded or mountainous lair in order to drive them mad if not devour them. Such creatures are still widely feared in Mexico and Maya-speaking areas today. Among the Chorti Maya in Guatemala, for example, there is still talk of a wild and ugly, long-haired and fanged creature – half-snake, half-woman – whose name is Siguanaba, an hispanicization of the Aztec name Cihuacoatl. Like Wild Woman, Siguanaba appears on trails at night, usually disguised as a man's lover, in order to trick him into illicit intercourse. If her victim, upon seeing her true identity, refuses her advances, the seductress scratches him with her long claws and drives him mad with terror.[11]

To my knowledge no colonial Mexican text states specifically that either Wild Man or Wild Woman influenced European perceptions of the Aztecs. Tales of Wild Man and Wild Woman certainly had been popular back home in medieval Spain, however, appearing there in both literature and folklore. In the fourteenth century many Spanish stories focused on a *serrana*, or mountain girl, who, although lovely in appearance, waylaid and brutalized travelers who strayed into her wild domain. One *serrana* reportedly lived in a cave surrounded by the bones of the men she had enticed there.[12] In the *Libro de buen amor*, moreover, a *serrana* appears as a grotesque creature with long breasts and a hairy neck. Stanley Robe suggests that stories of such threatening women were carried to New Spain by colonists of the lower classes, giving rise in time to the widespread Middle American belief in "*la llorana*" (the weeping woman), who wanders at night along streams and watercourses with long, matted hair and "a face that inspires horror."[13]

It is entirely possible, if not probable, therefore, that Wild Woman's image shaped Sahagún's contention that Cihuacoatl had "devoured" an infant. It would be a mistake, however, to conclude from this that her cannibalistic proclivities were entirely foreign to Aztec tradition. On the basis of reported Aztec beliefs that do not find ready counterparts in European countries, it can be argued instead that colonial assertations that Cihuacoatl consumed babies owe something to prehispanic beliefs, as well. As the acknowledged patroness of Aztec midwives and parturient women, we are told, Cihuacoatl was responsible for determining her clients' success or failure in producing healthy babies, and midwives and parturients accordingly prayed to her for easy delivery.[14] Although there is no evidence that dead children were thought to have been literally devoured by the goddess in prehispanic times, it is clear from the foregoing that she was already held responsible for infant deaths by the time of contact. Cihuacoatl's reputed cannibalism in the colonial period therefore cannot be understood solely in terms of European stereotypes of Wild Woman.

The differences here between Wild Woman's relation to children and that of Cihuacoatl points up further misunderstandings that can arise from focusing exclusively on European modes of representing the New World "other." For unlike Wild Woman's, Cihuacoatl's prehispanic role was actually ambivalent; she was as capable of benevolence as of hostility, and as likely to manifest it. Her decision to grant or take an infant's life depended not so much on her own innate disposition, which was neither kindly nor unkindly, as on whether or not her clients acted appropriately both before and during labor.[15] That she was understood to have tremendous creative potential as well as destructive powers is reflected in the fact that she was addressed as "Our Mother" and by her frequent role in Nahua myth as mother or guardian of the gods.[16] In emphasizing the goddess's destructive powers to the exclusion of her creative potential, then, colonial representations of her role and nature reduced the complexity and ambivalence of beliefs about her to a simpler, univalent form that better fitted the European template cut for Wild Woman.

The tensions and slippage created by the collison of traditional Aztec and Renaissance European concepts of mythic women are equally evident in the graphic realm, where

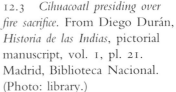

12.3 *Cihuacoatl presiding over fire sacrifice*. From Diego Durán, *Historia de las Indias*, pictorial manuscript, vol. 1, pl. 21. Madrid, Biblioteca Nacional. (Photo: library.)

native artists were employed by Spaniards to illustrate mendicant texts detailing native histories, beliefs, and customs. Whereas the European authors were free to recast native testimony into more familiar European forms and languages, the illustrations to their writings were produced directly by the Aztec "other." This is not to say that these native artists of the colonial period were not themselves influenced by European values and artistic modes of expression. It is increasingly clear that, as descendents of the Aztec aristocracy, most had been systematically exposed to European artistic techniques and imagery – as well as to Roman Catholic values, European languages, and alphabetic writing – at one of the several schools early established by the church expressly for this purpose.[17] However, although these artists were certainly in a position to assess their own past by European standards, and although they surely must have done so, at least some of them possessed some culturally transmitted knowledge of the nature of, and rationales for, earlier indigenous practices and beliefs.[18] This native perspective, however altered by the events of subordination, exploitation, and the needs of Spanish patrons, often included not just memories, however blurred, of how things once were, but also some idea of how things once might have looked.

It is significant, then, that Durán's native illustrator twice depicted the ravenous Cihuacoatl, once in anticipation of her grisly dinner (Figure 12.3), the second time

12.4   *Cihuacoatl*. From
Diego Durán, *Historia de
las Indias*, pictorial
manuscript. vol. 1, pl.
20. Madrid, Biblioteca
Nacional. (Photo:
library.)

simply standing alone, her long hair hanging loose and her large, snarling mouth wide
open, with her teeth exposed and her tongue protruding (Figure 12.4). The figure closely
resembles an illustration produced for Sahagún of an Aztec *auiani*, or harlot, whose loose,
windblown hair contrasts so markedly with the bound-up hair characteristic of married
Aztec women.[19] Margaret Arvey has suggested that this hairdo was derived, not from
native custom or artistic convention, but from European print and book illustrations of
"women of easy virtue"; these included Eve, Venus, and personified vices such as
Licenza and Heresia.[20] Books and single-sheet prints were certainly early imported into
the Americas from the Old World and thus would have been accessible to native students
trained in the European way of making pictures.[21] Long, disheveled hair, however, as we
have seen, was also characteristic of the European Wild Woman, for whom a snarling
visage was also appropriate (Figure 12.5). It may well thus have been Wild Woman
herself who served as a model for Cihuacoatl's coiffure.

But, again, do these paintings of Cihuacoatl reflect *only* European artistic and moral

12.5 (left)   Anonymous, French. Wild Woman. Detail of scene of Alexander in combat, *Le livre et la raye histoire du bon roy Alizandre*. Illuminated manuscript, early fifteenth century, fol. 51. London, the British Library. (Photo: library.)

12.6 (bottom left)   *Cihuacoatl*. Mexican, stone. Mexico City, Museo National de Antropología e Historica. (Photo: Instituto National de Antropologia e Historia, México, D.F.)

12.7 (bottom right)   *Cihuacoatl's face*. Drawing after image reproduced in 12.6. (From Caso, *Calendarios prehispanicos*, 204, fig. 3).

codes? Pre-Hispanic Aztec stone reliefs depicting Cihuacoatl suggest otherwise. These preconquest images should never be ignored in our analyses of the colonial encounter, for they represent the "texts" of the Aztecs themselves. To refuse to heed them is tantamount to denying the "other" a voice in the discussion of ways in which their world was represented. It cannot be discounted, then, that Cihuacoatl appears in these pre-contact images with a head of long, unruly hair (Figures 12.6 and 12.7). Jeanette Peterson has argued that such twisted locks referred to the goddess's close association with the zoomorphic earth, whose vegetation was understood to be its hair.[22] As vegetation, Cihuacoatl's wild tresses would have been seen as a source of nourishment for people and animals and thus as beneficial and positive; as such they would not have borne the same connotations as Wild Woman's.

Peterson, however, shows quite clearly that in preconquest Nahua imagery this sacred "hair" takes the form of a particular wild grass known as *malinalli*, a name that means "twisted." The name may derive from the plant's form, growing as it does in clusters of long, unruly leaves, but twistedness itself was a pan-Mesoamerican metaphor for wrong-doing, danger, hostility.[23] In Aztec ideology, moreover, the plant was associated with suffering, sickness, and death, further suggesting that it had negative as well as positive connotations.[24] The implication seems clear: not only did Cihuacoatl have long, unbound tresses well before the Spanish conquest, but her tangled locks already connoted super-natural power, wildness, and physical danger, as well. The native artist who illustrated Sahagún's text on the Nahua harlot therefore may well have used new, European stylistic conventions to depict her loose, unkempt hair, but in doing so he drew upon a curious convergence of indigenous and European ideas specifically associating such hair with female sexuality and its dangerous powers.[25]

In the years immediately following the Spanish conquest, Cihuacoatl was assigned even more negative attributes as her powers came to be represented less and less as ambivalent, and more and more as unilaterally terrifying and harmful. In Europe a similar fate had befallen Wild Woman, whose physical attributes and nasty habits increasingly overlapped with those of the witch.[26] This association was at one level a logical one, because European witchcraft had come to be primarily identified with women. Often depicted in European prints and book illustrations as naked, old, and toothless, with sagging breasts and wild, unbound and matted hair, the witches in these images usually either brew noxious ointments, reportedly made by mixing together body parts, herbs, and/or poisonous toads, or fly through the air at night on a broom or animal (Figure 12.8).[27] Like Wild Woman, they were believed to be shape-shifters, capable of turning into animals or beautiful young women who seduced and destroyed foolish men, and to steal and devour other women's children.

Witches therefore shared with Wild Woman a proclivity to meddle in sexual, in particular reproductive, matters, and were held responsible for every form of sexual deviance and wrongdoing. A list of such evils would include many of the same items ascribed to Wild Woman: homosexuality, carnal lust, adultery, impotence, sterility, abortion, and infant death.[28] Of these the most serious was apparently sexual immoder-ation, as the *Malleus Maleficarum*, a report prepared for the church in 1484 following several outbreaks of alleged witchcraft in Germany, states categorically that "all witchcraft comes from carnal lust."[29]

Because Cihuacoatl was associated with human reproduction and sexuality in prehispanic times, the Spaniards readily identified her with the European witch. Her prehispanic role as patroness of midwives may have facilitated this identification, as European witches in the fifteenth century were particularly apt to be equated with midwives, whom the church and the wealthy merchant class viewed as a threat to professional doctors. In Italy, at least, members of the medical profession who served the more affluent members of society were drawn from that same social class, educated in urban universities, and, perhaps most important, invariably male. They and their patrons

12.8 Hans Baldung Grien. *Witches' Sabbath*. Engraving, 1510. (Photo: Amsterdam, Rijksmuseum.)

protected their interests by denouncing unschooled curers, especially women, as witches.[30] Such official distrust of midwives and healers would have been equally appropriate in Mexico, where midwives and female curers in general already played important roles, sometimes assuming positions of considerable prestige and power.[31] Their power over reproduction, moreover, would have been particularly threatening to a Spanish clergy preoccupied with sexual morality and legitimacy. This is implied by a sixteenth-century Nahuatl play in which St. Francis banished to hell some witches, played by Indians, because they were "of the kind who with their native drugs very easily produce abortions."[32] Such witches must have seemed fairly numerous to the Spaniards, to judge by José Acosta's claim that most Mexican sorcerers were old women.[33] Fray Toríbio de Benevente, known in Mexico as Motolinía, complained that virtually all Indian women were midwives.[34]

Although, as Noemi Quezada points out, native *curanderas* (female curers) and midwives at first were largely tolerated in colonial Mexico due to a shortage of European doctors, there is no doubt that they were persecuted by the Inquisition. Although relatively few Indians, and even fewer curers, were publicly punished in Central Mexico, a number were convicted, and in 1526 at least one was hanged just outside Mexico City.[35] In Spain a major sphere of Inquisitorial activities had been directed toward

12.9 *Tzitzimitl. Codex Magliabechiano*, pictorial manuscript, fol. 76r. (Photo: Florence, Biblioteca Nazionale Centrale.)

punishment of sexual sins, a concern that was early carried across the Atlantic to New Spain.[36] It is logical that the focus of such concerns would have been transferred there to the prehispanic goddess of fertility and reproduction, Cihuacoatl, and to the women she patronized: Indian midwives and healers.

There is little doubt that in New Spain the church's attitude toward healers, magicians, and Indian women in general was shaped by European ideas about witchcraft and sorcery. Mexico's first bishop, Juan de Zumárraga, who later took over the Inquisitorial powers of the mendicants, had just returned from investigating a resurgence of witchcraft in the Basque country prior to relocating in New Spain in 1528. His chief assistant in the extirpation process had been Fray Andrés de Olmos, who also moved to New Spain, and who there authored, in addition to an entire treatise on Nahua witchcraft, some of the earliest prose sources we have on native religion and history in general. At the time that he wrote, Olmos was well versed in the ideas of Fray Martín de Castañega, whose book on witches was published in Spain in 1529. In that book Castañega identifies all magicians as ministers of the devil, the majority of them women, whom he characterizes as "sinks of iniquity."[37]

Spanish fears of curers, and in particular female curers, also derived in part from the knowledge that some women back home in Spain used incantations and charms to lure a recalcitrant man into marriage, bring a straying husband back home, or, failing either, emasculate him. The hated practice had either spread to Mexico from Spain or was already in place there, for both Indian and non-Indian women engaged in love magic in colonial New Spain.[38] The Spaniards equated such erotic sorcery with the worst forms of witchcraft, perhaps because European witches were believed to work harm through spells and amulets. More than one author has linked the colonial Mexican representation of female immorality with the character of a prostitute called Celestina, who, in a popular late fifteenth-century Spanish play by Fernando de Rojas, indulges in erotic sorcery. Since Aztec women who behaved like Celestina accordingly were associated with witchcraft in colonial Mexico, it again follows that Cihuacoatl was perceived by the Spaniards as a witch.[39]

Still, if Cihuacoatl's association with the occult in the colonial period allowed her to be identified with the European witch, it nonetheless again had roots in preconquest times. This can be demonstrated through examination of the same prehispanic stone reliefs that depict the goddess with twisted malinalli hair. For at the bent knees and elbows of these early Aztec figures appear grotesque profile faces with round eyes and large teeth suggesting that her joints have an identity, if not a life, of their own. The motif reappears in colonial depictions of the Tzitzimime, a largely female group of "demons" whom the Spaniards identified with witches (Figure 12.9), and figures prominently in Durán's report that an Aztec official who, prior to the conquest, had impersonated the "Lord of Hell" at a royal funeral, wore masks with mirrors on his shoulders, elbows, knees, and stomach.[40] It is true that Durán's description closely matches medieval miniature depictions of the devil with faces representing his sins on his knees and shoulders – and sometimes on his chest, stomach, or buttocks – and that it is thus likely that the description recalled such images to Spaniards (Figure 12.10).[41] Because joint masks appear in prehispanic images of Cihuacoatl, however, we are prevented from drawing the false conclusion that joint marks in colonial imagery derived exclusively from these visual European conventions for evil powers.

That Cihuacoatl's joint marks signified her own extraordinary powers is supported by prehispanic images and beliefs found elsewhere in Indian America. Durán himself wrote that the shining masks worn by the impersonator of the Aztec "Lord of the Underworld" "represented eyes on all these parts" that made it look "as if he could see in every direction."[42] The reference suggests the powers of a seer, one whose profession included clairvoyance and divination. Elsewhere in the Americas it was indeed shamans, clairvoyant religious practitioners, and healers who engaged the spirits of the dead and other supernaturals both as helpers and as enemies, who are described in comparable terms. Alaskan Inuit shamans, for example, sing of the deity from whom they derive their

12.10 (right)   Anonymous, French.
Satan with joint masks. Pen and ink,
fifteenth century. (From Didron,
Christian Iconography, vol. 1, fig. 135).

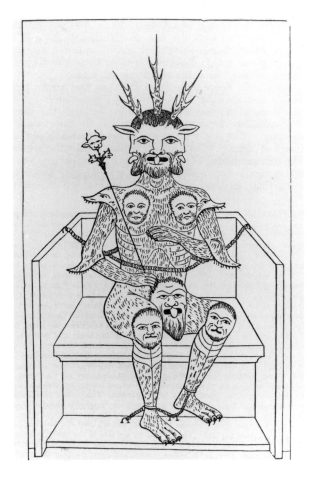

12.11 (opposite page)   *Coyolxauhqui,
defeated sister of Huitzilopochtli.*
Mexican, stone. Mexico City, Museo
National de Antropología e Historia.
(From Solís, *Gloria y fama*, pl. 87).

power: "My whole body is covered with eyes: Behold it! Be without fear! I see all around."[43]

In Greenland, however, it is specifically "black magic," or "sorcery," as opposed to "white magic," that is suggested by small masks carved at the joints of wood figures of *tupilaks*, monstrous beings sent out by shamans secretly to pursue and kill people.[44] Similarly, well to the south, in Ecuador, the tribal Jívaro shaman, under the influence of a narcotic called *natema*, hallucinates that his demon helpers have emerged on his arms and shoulders as "a thousand eyes" ready to search the night for his enemies. The appearance of these spiritual assistants alerts him, as well, that he now possesses the special powers of Tsungi, the first shaman.[45]

Throughout Indian America, finally, the sorcerers' spirit helpers tend to take the form of reptiles and amphibians. Mexican shamans today inflict harm by sending frogs, toads, snakes, and lizards into the victim's body through its orifices and points of articulation.[46] The practice sounds suspiciously European, since reptiles and amphibians were widely used by European witches for the same purpose.[47] However, an anonymous early colonial Mexican text preserved in French states that the Aztecs "took the earth for a goddess, and painted her as a fierce toad with mouths in all the joints, full of blood,

saying that she swallows and eats all [of it]."[48] Images thought to represent this deity reveal profile faces with large eyes and mouths at the knees and elbows, and bear such a startling resemblance to prehispanic depictions of Cihuacoatl that a relationship between the two supernaturals has long been posited.[49]

I know of no European belief in a powerful, supernatural amphibian of this nature, whereas supernatural frogs and toads play important roles in Amerindian mythology. The Mohave of the southwestern United States, for example, told ethnographers that their female "witches" derived their powers from the first witch, named Frog, who was the daughter of the oldest deities and extremely dangerous.[50] Cihuacoatl's monstrous joints, then, most likely connoted her extraordinary magical powers and conceivably identified her with the very first, and thus the most powerful, of all Nahua sorceresses, from whom all subsequent workers of magic — both good and bad — derived their powers. In this they both resemble the devil's joint masks in their role of signs of supernatural power and potential danger, and diverge from them in their capacity to signify the power to work good as well. Once again an ambivalent Aztec symbol was reduced in the colonial period to a closely related yet unilaterally negative symbol.

Perhaps the best evidence that joint marks signified occult powers well before the conquest resides in the iconography of the large, circular, late fifteenth-century stone relief that was discovered in 1978 at the foot of the right stairway of the Aztec main twin temple-pyramid in Mexico City (Figure 12.11). The right side of that pyramid was dedicated to the national patron god Huitzilopochtli (Hummingbird Left), whose statue was housed in the temple at the top. The relief depicts a bleeding, nearly naked, decapitated and dismembered woman identifiable as Huitzilopochtli's sister whom, according to colonial accounts of the Aztec migration into the Valley of Mexico, he had slain when she challenged his authority.[51] The dangerous woman appears in this relief, significantly, with monstrous masks at her knees, elbows, and heels.

In colonial texts such insubordination is expressed in terms of witchcraft, sorcery, and black magic. For example, in a related version of the Aztec migration myth, Huitzilopochtli abandons another asocial kinswoman, this one named Malinalxochitl (Malinalli Flower), specifically because she was a "great sorceress." It would be easy to dismiss this association of insurgency with sorcery as a result of the Spanish tendency to view all magical practicioners – especially females – as potential fomenters of political resistance.[52] In colonial Mexico it was often local shamans – especially the women – who led uprisings against Spanish control, incurring thereby almost blanket suspicion and persecution by the authorities. The author of our narrative, however, describes the woman's occult actions in terms that betray the indigenous roots of the link, noting that Malinalxochitl's offense lay specifically in eating people's hearts and calves (i.e., legs). I am aware of no European parallel to this notion, whereas certain magicians in Aztec Mexico were indeed referred to as *tecotzcuani*, "muscle-eater," and *teyollocuani*, "heart-eater."[53]

It is worth noting, too, that Malinalxochitl worked her evil magic by calling for the aid of "all the centipedes and spiders,"[54] for, in at least one prehispanic Aztec stone relief, spiders, centipedes, a worm, and a scorpion all appear in Cihuacoatl's tangled malinalli hair (Figure 12.12). Cihuacoatl, like Malinalxochitl, it follows, must have been a powerful magician. Nahua magical practitioners, including healers, reportedly ground up spiders, centipedes, scorpions, worms, and other poisonous creatures, together with tobacco leaves and the hallucinogenic seeds of the indigenous *olioliuhqui*, or Morning Glory plant, to create a powerful, hallucinogenic ointment. This ointment in turn was used to communicate with the gods and to cure the sick; when spread on the skin, it was believed to protect the wearer against danger.[55] Such brews clearly predated the conquest but the Spaniards quickly associated them with the dangerous ointments concocted by European witches for the purpose of inflicting great damage. Father Augustine de Vetancourt complained in the seventeenth century that Aztec ointments allowed their "priests" to converse with "the devil," and that in his day they were still being used for sorcery.[56] The insects in Cihuacoatl's hair, then, for the prehispanic Aztecs would have represented the sources of her power, which had the potential to cure and aid people as well as harm them. To the colonial viewer steeped in European lore about witches, in contrast, they would have connoted only the latter.

As a New World extension of the Old World Wild Woman-*cum*-witch, Cihuacoatl soon came to be personally identified with the devil. In mid-sixteenth century painted manuscripts, her features were grafted on to those of the mythical destructive, nocturnal creatures collectively known as Tzitzimime, who, the mendicants preached, were demons and devils. The best example appears in Codex Magliabechiano, where a frightening female with tousled hair and monstrous joints, as well as clawed hands and feet, wears a skirt decorated with the same shell border seen earlier in the same manuscript on Cihuacoatl (Figures 12.9 and 12.12). Like Cihuacoatl's, too, this woman's face is skeletal. Despite the similarities, however, the codex commentator identified the figure not as Cihuacoatl, but as "Tzitzimitl," the singular form of Tzitzimime. That only the negative, horrific aspect of Cihuacoatl was relevant here is further evident in the

12.12 *Cihuacoatl. Codex Magliabechiano*, pictorial manuscript, fol. 45r. (Photo: Florence, Biblioteca Nazionale Centrale.)

creature's other attributes. Her hair and chest, for example, are covered with a necklace of bloody, disembodied human hearts and hands, while a human liver forms her pectoral. Sacrificial banners adorn the head while the protruding tongue takes the form of a sacrificial knife. The former further link the being to occult practices since similar banners are said to have been worn in the hair of some Aztec sorceresses.[57] Olmos identified the Tzitzimime with the *tlatlatectolo*, Nahua sorcerers who, the Spaniards contended, inflicted harm on other people.[58]

The need to press Aztec supernaturals into the Roman Catholic mold was so over-riding that some friars preached that female sorcerers, under the influence of *ololiuhqui* or some other hallucinogen, actually copulated with Satan.[59] The idea that female witches had sexual intercourse with the devil was a fundamental tenet of Old World Catholicism and a major reason that the Church had denounced witchcraft as heresy in the fourteenth century.[60] It is not surprising, in view of this, that Cihuacoatl early in the post-Conquest period seems to have assumed the role of bride of Satan. In Codex Ríos her shell-tipped skirt appears, along with a row of sacrificial banners in her hair, on the goddess named Micticacihuatl, or Mictlan Woman, whose name identifies her as co-ruler of the under-world land of the dead, called Mictlan (Figure 12.13). Micticacihuatl also wears a skull at her back like that worn by prehispanic stone-carved figures of Cihuacoatl. In the Codex Ríos scene she faces her husband Mictlantecuhtli, "Mictlan Lord," who is identified in the accompanying glosses as both the "lord of the infernal region," meaning hell, and "Tzitzimitl, the same as Lucifer." Mictlantecuhtli, moreover, sits in the gaping mouth of a monstrous head clearly based on the zoomorphic medieval European manscript con-vention for hell (Figure 12.14). In the Codex Ríos image, then, Cihuacoatl, prehispanic patroness of human reproduction and female sexuality, fuses with the goddess of the Aztec underworld who has herself become reconfigured as the bride of Satan. Elsewhere in mendicant writing of the period, it is Cihuacoatl herself who is identified as "the wife of the god of the infernal regions."[61]

Cihuacoatl's importance in New Spain was shortlived, however, because the European devil himself was, after all, male. Cihuacoatl, accordingly, was eventually deprived of her femininity, and her identity subsumed by that of the death god-turned-devil himself. This transformative process can be seen in Codex Magliabechiano, where the skeletal Mictlantecuhtli (Figure 12.15), clearly identified by name on the facing pages and wearing a male loincloth while seated in the pose reserved for men, twice appears with the sacrificial banner headdress and monstrous joints typically characteristic of female supernaturals like Cihuacoatl. Throughout the manuscript, the commentator refers directly to Mictlantecuhtli as a demon or devil and, on folio 73, deplores as "abominable" the cannibalistic rites taking place before him.[62] The ultimate effect was to conflate Cihuacoatl's form and role with the devil's, in the process eclipsing her original significance altogether.

Cihuacoatl's transformation into the death god proceeded apace on a title page to

12.13 (right) *Mictlantecuhtli and his wife Micticacihuatl as the rulers of Hell*. Detail, *Codex Ríos*, fol. 2v, from Corona Nuñez, vol. 3, lam. III. (Photo: courtesy Secretaria de Hacienda y Crédito Público.)

12.14 (left) *The Jaws of Hell*. Detail from the Winchester Psalter, illuminated manuscript. London, British Library, MS Cotton Nero c IV, fol. 24. (Photo: library.)

12.15 (right)
Mictlantecuhtli with joint masks and banners. Codex Magliabechiano, pictorial manuscript, fol. 79r. (Photo: Florence, Biblioteca Nazionale Centrale.)

12.16 (left)   Title page engraving from Antonio de Herrera, *Descriptio Indiae Occidentalis*, 1622. (Photo: The John Carter Brown Library at Brown University.)

12.17   *Huitzilopochtli.*
Engraving from Allain
Manesson Mallet, *Description
de l'Univers*, Paris, 1683, 5,
fig. 135. (Photo: The John
Carter Brown Library at
Brown University.)

Antonio de Herrera's *Historia general*, which was first published in Spain in 1601 (Figure
12.16). There we see a skirted figure, kneeling in the pose appropriate to Aztec women,
that was directly drawn from the Codex Magliabechiano depiction of the goddess
Cihuacoatl. Below, the figure is clearly labeled as "the god of the dead."[63] The same
figure, now without a label, appeared one last time, in 1683, in an engraving in Allain
Manesson Mallet's *Description de l'Univers*, published in Paris (Figure 12.17). Reduced
now to a tiny, unidentified occupant of a niche placed to the right of the top of the page,
the goddess yields the stage to a gigantic figure of the Aztec national patron god
Huitzilopochtli. It is Huitzilopochtli who here assumes the role of the devil, this time
taking his popular Spanish form of a giant he-goat.[64] In this engraving, then, Cihuacoatl
loses not only her name, gender, and importance, but all reference to her prehispanic role
as an ambivalent goddess of fertility and childbirth, as well. The colonial need for Wild
Woman appears, by this time, to have completely dissipated.

It seems clear, then, that Wild Woman was indeed present in colonial Central Mexico,
and that she influenced early colonial representations of the Aztec goddess Cihuacoatl.
Colonial-period representations of Cihuacoatl often recalled, if they did not directly

derive from, European representations of both Wild Woman, particularly in her aspect of witch, and the Christian devil. As a metaphor for the evils and vices that threatened Catholic and crown interests, she helped to abet the colonizing process by shaping representations of Aztec belief in terms that were meaningful and familiar to Europeans. Through verbal and visual images of Cihuacoatl, accordingly, threatening subversive and immoral behavior was condemned via association with witchcraft, satanism, and heresy. In this sense, then, the postmodernist axiom holds true that we see a reflection of the European mind-set in the glass of colonial Mexican history. When we look into that glass for Cihuacoatl, in other words, it is Wild Woman who stares back at us.

But is this, and need it be, all we can see there? The manuscript paintings we have been looking at were, after all, all painted by native artists whose descendents in places still speak the native language and who still hold beliefs that clearly had no place in Europe. These images and voices of the Mexican "other," as we have seen, can sometimes be related to the thousands of surviving Mexican artworks that predate the conquest. What these prehispanic images and ethnographic reports have shown us is that the European Wild Woman could make herself at home in colonial Central Mexico precisely because the Aztecs, however different from the Spaniards, had expressed their values and concepts in metaphorical terms that were often remarkably congruent with those of Europe. In places the Aztecs even used some of the same visual signs, such as joint marks, to convey what was often a related, yet always slightly different, social and moral message. It was this very parallelism in the semiotic codes of these two very different cultures that allowed the Spaniards to reshape and reduce prehispanic beliefs and concepts so as to conform to their own European templates. The glass we look at, therefore, is transparent as well as reflective; it can provide a glimpse of native reality that qualifies our understanding of the European imprint. Without an analysis of these insights into the "other," a scholar following Greenblatt might well have attributed exclusively to Europeans what were often similar, and therefore more easily altered, indigenous modes of representing alterity, thereby missing entirely an important insight into the way that representation operates in a colonizing context.

To refrain from trying to understand pre-contact Latin American cultural history so as to avoid Eurocentric misrepresentation of the "other" is therefore to foreclose all hope of ever perceiving the full range and nature of human representational practices. It precludes all hope of simultaneous perception of similarity and difference, condemning us to see instead only one or the other of these at any given time. The complexity and subversive manipulations of representational practices are obscured by such myopia. Unless western scholars continue to try to identify the tropes and structures that their own cultural templates have tended to deform or mask, they can never really *know* whether − or to what degree − the west's representations speak to its own semiotic practices as opposed to someone else's. Without Cihuacoatl, in other words, we cannot claim to have accurately identified the presence of Wild Woman in colonial Mexico.

Our partiality, our unwillingness even to try to hear the "other," at the same time can only imply to Mexicans today that *their* native ancestors' modes of telling had no effect on colonial representations − that they were and are, in fact, simply unimportant. Surely this is a form of Eurocentrism potentially more arrogant and misleading than the projected fears and fantasies postmodern critics have exposed.

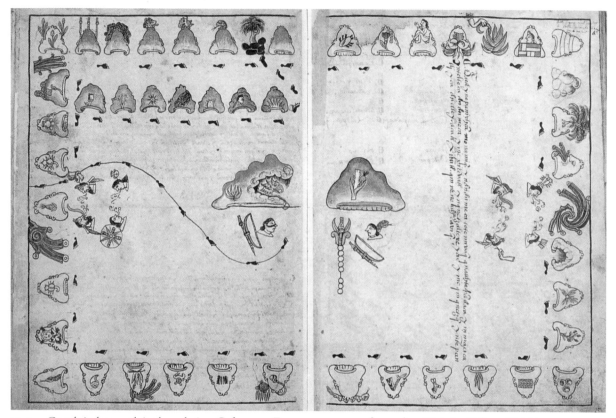

13.1 *Cuauhtinchan and its boundaries.* Color on European paper, from the *Historia Tolteca-Chichimeca, c.*1545–1565. Paris, Bibliothèque Nationale, Ms. 46–50, fols. 35v–36r. (Photo: author.)

CHAPTER 13

Colony and Cartography:
Shifting Signs on Indigenous Maps of New Spain

DANA LEIBSOHN

> If it is true that the imperialists study their colonial charges, it is equally
> true that the charges study their masters – with great care and cunning.
> Who shall say which understands the other more?
>
> Woodrow Borah, *Justice by Insurance*

In New Spain, between 1530 and 1630, indigenous painters created hundreds of maps.
These cartographic representations – usually depictions of towns and nearby lands –
played an integral role in the colonial process. In the first century after the Spanish
conquest maps often served as legally binding documents and were among the most
frequently commissioned of all indigenous paintings. Moreover, both Europeans and
indigenous people accepted maps as credible representations of their territory. Indigenous
maps, however, never supplied their viewers with an unambiguous image of the actual
world. No map does. Rather, cartographs engender landscapes: in assembling the signs of
disparate sites and objects, they fuse imaginary and physical traits. As persuasive images,
maps constitute and mediate relationships in the world. For the indigenous maps of New
Spain, this implies that visual representations carried forth and extended the colonial
enterprise; they did not simply mirror it. Thus the images recorded on maps inaugurate
as well as document colonial practice.

A comparison of two maps – each created by an indigenous painter around 1550, each
showing the community of Cuauhtinchan – highlights this point (Figures 13.1 and 13.2).
Set side by side, these paintings indicate how ephemeral the bond was between what
actually existed in the world and the presence or absence of signs on maps. For example,
near the center of one map stands a hill glyph with one side cut away to expose an eagle
within (Figure 13.1). With this, the first map-maker has signed the town of
Cuauhtinchan, a Nahuatl word meaning "Home of the Eagles." Surrounding this glyph
are other hill forms, suggesting that the places represented by these signs encircle the
community of Cuauhtinchan just as they frame the cut-away hill glyph. In contrast,
the second map depicts Cuauhtinchan as a church and plaza centered within an
orthogonal grid (Figure 13.2). Neighboring communities are also shown as gridded areas
rather than as a series of hill glyphs. Cuauhtinchan again appears towards the center of

13.2 *Mapa de Cuauhtinchan #4* (detail). Color on indigenous paper, *c.*1560–1563. Mexico City, Museo Nacional de Antropología e Historia.

the painting although the other towns no longer circle the community; instead, they are linked via a network of roads which binds the sites to one another as it anchors them to a specific geography. Because of their common focus and temporal origin, the differences in these images cannot be attributed to any actual metamorphosis of the landscape itself. The differences reveal that, in their assimilation of churches and grids, indigenous maps convey many things: only some of them inscribed on the ground. Indeed, the paintings suggest that the "ground" of indigenous maps is no less metaphysical than physical.

In the following pages, I maintain that indigenous maps reveal as much about the actual transformation of geographical territory under Spanish rule as they do of the interaction between European and prehispanic systems of representation, and ultimately, the interaction between Europeans and indigenous people. By examining the fate of three signs – the hill glyph, the church, and the grid – this paper argues two points. First, I demonstrate that neither capitulation to foreign impositions nor explicit resistance dominated native responses to European introductions. Rather, on maps, indigenous representational practices shaped and organized the incorporation of signs of European origin. Second, and more importantly, I contend that the negotiations transacted across the surfaces of maps are paradigmatic of the colonial enterprise in New Spain. Because the church and the grid are implicated in colonial policies of domination, their debut and persistence on maps was neither an inevitable nor innocent matter of cultural exchange. This means that the way we interpret maps impinges directly upon our construal of colonization.

After 1550 various combinations of churches and grids became the prime signifiers for indigenous communities; yet as signs, churches and grids behaved quite differently. Churches proliferated on maps, insinuating themselves into the landscape in multifarious ways. The grid, on the other hand, was less conspicuous and its use was always circumscribed. In spite of this divergence the two signs intertwined, and, taken together, they illuminate a process wherein European record-keeping practices were brought together with prehispanic-style representations. In the semiosis of maps, signs of European and indigenous origin were each reframed by the other.

Moreover, the cultural exchanges that have left their trace on indigenous maps suggest that although Spaniards occupied key political and economic positions, their hegemony did not mold all colonial interaction. Indigenous people, even though marginalized and subordinated, played an active role in their emergence as colonial subjects. Here I resort to an analysis of what Michel de Certeau calls the tactics of everyday life, "the ingenious ways in which the weak make use of the strong, thus lend[ing] a political dimension to everyday practices."[1] It is my conviction that only by entering the map at this level – noting the ways people live out their lives, day by day, under a colonial regime – that we can begin to make sense of the transactions that occurred across cultural borders. It is in this sense, rather than that of a coherent ideological or propagandistic program, that this paper considers the politics of colonization and cartography.

A la Carte: Maps and their Makers

It is well known that indigenous people suffered immensely in the wake of the Spanish conquest. Not only did they experience military defeat, but extraordinarily harsh physical and cultural depredations followed upon the heels of their domination. Before the turn of the seventeenth century, thousands perished from diseases introduced by Europeans. Those who survived were required to adopt the morals and precepts of a foreign religion and scores of people were subjected to the policy of *congregación* which forcibly grouped scattered settlements into European-style towns under the aegis of the Christian church.[2]

Even so, the presence of Europeans did not affect all regions of New Spain, nor all her inhabitants, in the same way. Coercion and threat of punishment notwithstanding, many features of prehispanic culture persisted well into the colonial period.[3] A reading of indigenous written and painted documents suggests that among Nahuas, Tarascans, Mixtecs and Zapotecs interactions with foreigners in the narrow spaces and distant corners of New Spain – rather than the officious *Audiencias* staged in the halls of Mexico City – formed the warp and woof of colonial experience. Of central importance in indigenous communities is not "the Spanish conquest," but local struggles for control of resources and positions of power: access to plots of land, access to local tribute revenues, and access to symbolic and economic privileges that separated commoners from nobles.

Because land and its control were seminal to all residents of New Spain, maps were never neutral images. The settings in which indigenous cartographic records circulated underscore this point. By far the greatest number of maps were legal documents proffered during contests for natural resources and territory. Most commonly, maps were commissioned by administrators and submitted with binding oral and written testimonies before authorities in land grant applications, official inquiries, and *congregaciones*.[4] Yet native map-makers did not work only for "colonists." Although legal channels were dominated by Europeans, map patrons included other indigenous people – community leaders or groups seeking a favorable judgment in claims brought against Spaniards, their slaves, or other native communities.[5]

It is critical to note that Spaniards as well as Nahuas, Mixtecs and others wielded maps in these endeavors, for the multiple ethnicity of the patronage system indicates that by the late sixteenth and early seventeenth centuries many audiences acknowledged and cultivated the power of maps. Spaniards and indigenous people alike expected – in fact relied upon – maps as persuasive and compelling representational instruments.

Yet legal contention did not spawn all native mapping. Some documents, like the maps (or *pinturas*) of the *Relaciones Geográficas*, were made explicitly for presentation before the royal government in Spain.[6] Other cartographic images fell outside the purview of Spaniards; produced for use within native communities, these maps fulfilled indigenous requirements.[7] The historical situation, then, is complex: native map-makers worked for a variety of patrons and they crafted images for use in heterogeneous social contexts. A survey of these documents confirms that map-makers followed no single model or set of guidelines. Much of a map's "look" depended upon the occasions and audiences for which it was created.

The vast majority of native map-makers, as was the case with the maps themselves, circulated in settings dominated by Spanish and indigenous authorities. Only a few names have come down to us – from signatures vouching for the accuracy of particular maps and from written documents accompanying certain images – yet it seems that many painters working between 1530 and 1630 were literate people of significant social standing. Moreover, these painters facilitated the discourse between two worlds; they acted as "go betweens" in several capacities. Some map-painters exhibit intimate knowledge of prehispanic graphic conventions, suggesting that they were trained as *tlacuilo* (scribes) before the Spanish conquest – a role reserved for people of privilege and noble birth.[8] Many of these men must have served as mentors to apprentices at the local level, for the commitment to preconquest traditions did not die out with the first-generation painters.[9]

A number of map-producers also received training in European graphic conventions from mendicant friars. An integral aspect of colonization involved inculcating the sons of indigenous nobles with skills valued by Europeans, and, under the tutelage of Franciscans, Dominicans, and Augustinians, young men across New Spain were indoctrinated with Christian morality and European literacy skills.[10] Taught to read and write Spanish, their own languages, and sometimes Latin, these noblemen emerged equally qualified to fulfill the role of friars' assistants or local administrators. Study of the conventions and iconography of European pictorial imagery also formed part of the mendicant curriculum and among the young nobles' lessons and practice sheets there appear emulations of European Renaissance motifs.[11]

Given that map-makers served diverse patrons and that they were educated by *tlacuilo* and friars, it is not surprising that their images intermingle preconquest features with European introductions. What is of particular interest are the ways in which the two representational systems intertwine. My concerns lie with practices that can be traced across the colony, yet it is impossible to disregard regional differences and individual deviations. Because there was no over-arching policy on map-making nor an official program for training indigenous map-makers, both pattern and idiosyncracy are to be found. This facet of early colonial life is fundamental. In New Spain, most people – not only map-makers – improvized pragmatic responses to colonization according to their understanding of official policy, local cultural standards, and individual abilities.

Cartographic Palimpsests

If maps painted by indigenous people in the first century after the Spanish conquest weave together elements of prehispanic and European origin, it is preconquest traditions of representation that provide a thick layer of ground upon which European introductions were inscribed. Pre-Hispanic conventions for depicting territory, settlement, and space influenced the ways in which new representational practices were assimilated into the map-makers' repertoire. Because no native maps from before the conquest survive, direct attestations to prehispanic mapping practices are lacking.[12] Yet a sense of these traditions can be assembled by examining early colonial maps like the depiction of Cuauhtinchan (Figure 13.1). Sprinkled with hill glyphs but revealing no trace of churches or grids, this map depends heavily upon conventions with prehispanic roots. Fundamental to the painting, for example, are its emphases on itinerary, toponyms, and historical narrative – emphases known from prehispanic paintings.[13]

Although the map of Cuauhtinchan offers the viewer a tableau of the community's boundaries, it also presents an itinerary. The map-maker has drawn a visual list of places. The footprints, which define an uninterrupted path past each location, underscore the peregrine framework of the image. Because the hill glyphs are of similar shapes and sizes, and equal distances separate them, the painting implies that each named site is essentially the same as its neighbors. Moreover, the alternation of place glyphs with blank spaces in a regular pattern collapses the actual distances between sites. Over 30 kilometers separate some adjacent locations while less than 10 kilometers divide others. Yet the map reveals none of this. Indeed, the map-maker has elided references to the mountains and valleys that travelers would encounter in their journey from one place to the next. In so aligning the boundary sites, and in repressing the differences that occupy the spaces between them, the map-maker proffers an itinerary of named landmarks strung together like rosary beads on a looped cord.

Toponymy rather than topography organizes the map of Cuauhtinchan: 52 sites are identified, although few clues about their appearance are provided. We cannot discern from the map alone which hill glyphs stand for features of the landscape and which denote communities. The map-maker has used stylized hills as signs for both natural features and indigenous towns. These place glyphs allow the painter to distinguish one location from another, not so much by shape or profile – as this tends to be standardized – but by an affix which cues a name. Thus a reed identifies one hill-form as Place of the Reeds, a place distinct from all others, just as a straw mat marks another, identical hill as Little Place of the Straw Mat (Figure 13.3).

Indigenous painters could map a variety of places by using such conventionalized signs. We cannot, however, take these images at face value and assume, for instance, that Little

13.3   *Cuauhtinchan and its boundaries* (detail). Color on European paper, from the *Historia Tolteca-Chichimeca*, *c.*1545–1565. Paris, Bibliothèque Nationale, Ms. 46–50, fols. 35v–36r. (Photo: author.)

Place of the Straw Mat was in actuality a diminutive site. Before and after the conquest, the fundamental units of social and territorial organization in Central Mexico were called in Nahuatl *altepetl*, a term reducible to *atl* (water) and *tepetl* (hill).[14] Signs such as that for Little Place of the Straw Mat could therefore cue the name of a natural landmark as well as a native settlement. In the indigenous system, then, ambiguity colored the relationship between the shape of the glyph, the naming affix, and the actual place. Without previous knowledge of a region and its history, it was impossible to know which of the place glyphs represent *altepetl* and which topographic features. Put simply, the indigenous precedent did not set landscape (nature) apart from human communities (culture) – at least not in visual terms.[15]

Following prehispanic convention, the Cuauhtinchan image collates signs for landmarks with those of settled communities (Figure 13.1). Yet in contrast to certain types of European maps, territory is not the primary theme. This map commemorates the founding of Cuauhtinchan in the year 8 Reed and the marking out of primordial community boundaries. The footprints that circumscribe the perimeter of the field, the small figures of ancestral founders, and the date at the center of the painting all sustain this reading of the image. The map implies that this specific geographical arrangement does not *a priori* exist independently of the cultural world. Rather, the terrain unfolds because a suite of significant events calls these particular sites together. In a crucial sense, history is the pre-text for geography. Landscapes are produced by narratives that disclose events which transpire at the feet of certain mountains, along the banks of specific rivers, and within the boundaries of individual communities. The map establishes a nexus where history and landscape conjoin.

When artists portrayed the lands of New Spain as a sequence of toponyms, and when they intertwined images referring to historical narratives with those referring to the physical world, long-held understandings of spatial relationships and symbolic geography motivated them. Like palimpsests in which new entries are made on top of old, these layered compositions provided the foundation for postconquest mapping.

*   *   *

An Edifice of Signs: the Christian Church

One of the features that most sharply separates early colonial maps from preconquest paintings is a new conception of territory. Instead of sequences of hill glyphs drawn together through narrative, indigenous maps produced for legal purposes generally portray the lands of New Spain free from explicit references to historical event.[16] To a large extent, this shift away from narrative and itinerary derives from judicial requirements for maps issued by the Viceregal government of New Spain. In land grants, for example, specifications for an acceptable map were explicitly provided. Such charts were to depict the town and ranches nearest the site of the prospective grant, the distances between locations, and the lands and untilled fields which would remain.[17] These stipulations, based on Spanish protocol, indicate that the distribution of land in the sixteenth-century present, not the past, was the object of concern. The pre-eminent role assigned to cartography thus became the visual description of an extant landscape.

This change in focus, in which views of territorial tableaux rather than narrative and itinerary perspectives dominate cartographic paintings, was not, strictly speaking, forced upon indigenous painters. Native map-makers learned – through a combination of coercion, trial and error, and pragmatic instruction – what colonial authorities would deem appropriate. If the broad guidelines set out for land grant and other legally binding maps established a framework for native painters, there was still considerable flexibility in how a map-maker might reconcile his skills and conceptions with the details required by his patrons. Consequently, the transfiguration of narrative representations of territory into conventions more in keeping with Renaissance Europe proceeded across marshy and ill-defined terrain: by 1630 both forms of map-making were still in existence. And although in official arenas European concerns for visually descriptive scenes ultimately displaced prehispanic interests in peregrination and narrative, this was not the case in local map production where hybridity persisted well into the nineteenth century.[18]

A survey of cartographic documents painted in the century following 1530 reveals that indigenous map-makers used churches more often than stylized hill glyphs as the primary sign for towns. A familiar element on European maps, the church became the favored sign for a settled community only by infringing upon the semiotic domain of the hill glyph. One common practice among map-makers working during this period was to sign native towns with both hill glyphs and churches. The two signs might be set side by side, echoing one another, or churches could stand atop traditional hill glyphs.[19] An image from Veracruz dating to 1572, however, provides a variation on these modes of doubling (Figure 13.4). To identify the towns of Maxtlatlan and Almolonca, the scribe supplemented hill glyphs with portals and crowned the hillock with crosses.[20] By fusing prehispanic and European conventions, the map-maker fashioned signs that bear the stamp of Christian society but that also maintain ties to an older order of representation. Maxtlatlan and Almolonca emerge as towns that are no more – or less – Christian than indigenous.

Although these Christianized hill glyphs may strike us as odd, it would be a mistake to read this map as simple confusion about which sign-system was more appropriate. Instead, I believe we are witnessing a fundamental change in indigenous representations of place. Prior to the conquest it was not necessary to visually differentiate natural features from towns: hill glyphs were sufficient markers for mountains, hills, canyons, and communities. This was not so in the regions mapped by European cartography. Landscape – mountains, rivers, and coast line – were rendered in conventionalized but naturalistic detail (Figure 13.5). Moreover, large cities could be distinguished from natural landmarks as well as from smaller towns through the use of churches, towers, and other buildings.[21] After the Spanish conquest indigenous painters were influenced by these mapping practices and, by the turn of the seventeenth century, native map-makers were replicating European notions of landscape, albeit in their own way.

On a map of Otumba and the surrounding region, dating from 1590, hill glyphs form a mountainous spine running vertically along the center of the painting (Figure 13.6). Because of their size and color, they dwarf the churches. Yet it is the churches that operate as signs for towns. In the case of one town, Ajuluapa (shown at the far right), the church glyph has not only been labeled in Spanish, but – in a practice reminiscent of

13.4 (right)   *Map Showing Communities of Maxtlatlan and Almolonca, Veracruz*. Color on European paper, 1572. Mexico City, Archivo General de la Nación. *Catálogo de Ilustraciones 4*: #1561, Tierras, vol. 2676, exp. 9, f. 11. (Photo: archive.)

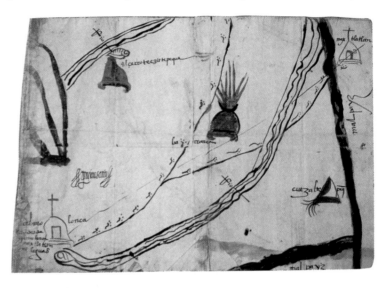

13.5 (left)   Bolognino Zaltieri. *Il Disegno del Discoperto della Nova Franza*. Engraving, 1566. Chicago, The Newberry Library. (Photo: library.)

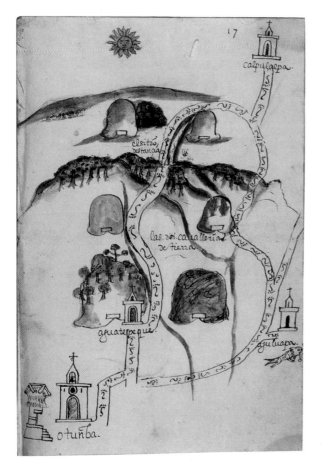

13.6 *Map of Otumba and nearby communities, Mexico.* Color on European paper, 1590. Mexico City, Archivo General de la Nación. *Catálogo de Ilustraciones* 5: #2160, Tierras, vol. 2782, exp. 15, f. 17. (Photo: archive.)

prehispanic traditions – it is also signed with an affix. In contrast, the hill glyphs have become anonymous. Neither written text nor glyphic affix distinguishes one from the other. The promontories are visually striking, but only as part of a backdrop of landscape. As hill glyphs are converted from toponyms to topographic cues, a seam in the fabric of the map opens. Places where people live are separated from regions where they do not.

I am arguing, then, that church signs advanced their privileged place on the maps of New Spain at the expense of indigenous hill glyphs. At first, this process was one of decentering rather than outright substitution. In graphic terms, the image from Otumba makes this point: hill glyphs loom large in the background, but they no longer designate sites where residents conduct daily life (Figure 13.6). Those activities, the map suggests, are managed exclusively under the aegis of Christianity. As hill glyphs are marginalized, their ability to mark a place with moral or sacral conviction is usurped by signs of the church. Thus the church, as a sign, performs an ideological function. Visually, the painted edifice indexes the Christianization of conquered lands. As on the map of Otumba, the distribution of churches indicates that all communities are Christian communities. The map identifies no settlement in this region that has escaped conversion. In implying that only those places stamped by the moral authority of the Church are proper

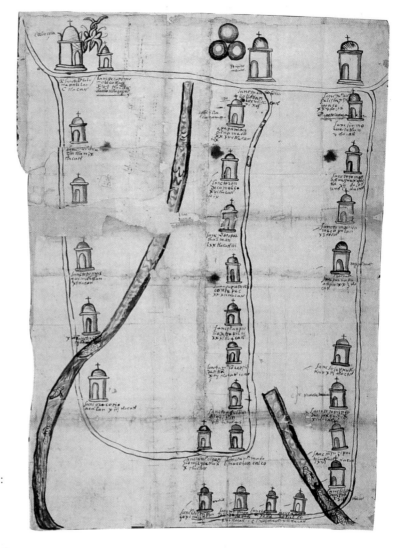

13.7 *Map of San
Bartolomé Malila and
nearby communities,
Hidalgo.* Color on
European paper, *c.*1599.
Mexico City, Archivo
General de la Nación.
Catálogo de Ilustraciones 2:
#593, Tierras, vol. 64,
exp. 7, f. 201. (Photo:
archive.)

sites of occupation, the Otumba map projects the destiny of this foreign institution on to
the territory of New Spain.

In contrast to the map of Cuauhtinchan which alternated hill glyphs and empty spaces
(Figure 13.1), maps with churches and hills provide considerably more information about
the ways that people occupied specific geographies. Even so, maps were conservative
documents. And even after church signs established a firm place for themselves on the
ground of indigenous maps, cartographic representations were overwhelmingly
toponymic in conception. Indeed, the church became the paradigmatic toponym.

Conventionalization of form and architectural features makes it impossible to read the
churches on a 1599 map from Hidalgo as specific buildings (Figure 13.7). An hieratic
scale distinguishes the main town of San Bartolomé Malila, in the upper left-hand corner,
from smaller settlements under its sovereignty. But, by and large, the map does not
record the actual appearance of any single church. This is emphasized by the disjunction

between the imagery of the map and its written glosses.[22] According to the Nahuatl text, the largest town in the region had over 100 tribute-paying residents, the smallest only three. Yet the map imagery glides over these differences, distinguishing the administrative center of the district but none of the other communities. All of the outlying towns, regardless of their size, are signed with churches uniformly drawn. In this way, the church sign behaves much like the hill glyphs on the Cuauhtinchan map (Figure 13.1): it functions toponymically to locate where in the graphic field a community stands.

As was the case with the hill glyphs, the difference between buildings rests upon their names – now, spelled out alphabetically. The Christianized towns of Santa Maria Montasco and San Augustín Chiquitlan are evoked by standardized representations of a church and a short label. While the relationship between picture and text is not identical to that of hill glyph and affix, a parallel result is achieved through their coupling. Churches with written words label and differentiate individual communities just as hill glyphs with pictorial affixes identify places like Place of the Reeds and Little Place of the Straw Mat on the map in figure 13.1.

This is not to suggest that the substitution of church and writing for glyph and affix was an uncomplicated process. The point I want to stress here is that churches absorbed the toponymic function of hill glyphs. To a degree, the toponymic role assigned the painted buildings parallels European practice; churches also served as toponyms on European maps. Because native painters were exposed to such documents, we cannot be surprised to find church signs performing analogously. Nevertheless, it would be misguided to see the practice of indigenous map-makers as simply appropriation, for there is much to suggest that the prehispanic representational system was too deeply rooted and too conservative to yield easily to foreign conventions.

Of Grids and Maps

Centuries before the Spanish conquest, the vast city of Teotihuacan spread in a grid-like pattern across the heart of Central Mexico. And in the fifteenth century, certain parts of Tenochtitlan, the capital of the Aztec state, were also laid out according to a rectilinear web of pathways. Even so, few prehispanic communities adopted this arrangement, and representations of gridded spaces are quite rare. It would seem that prior to the arrival of Europeans, grids lacked the cultural imperative they gained after the conquest.

Among Spaniards, the colonial enterprise was steeped in a discourse of utopic ideals. One facet of this involved arranging newly settled lands into identical, geometrically defined and rectilinear parcels. In this system, life could be organized into regular units that reflected the measured order befitting a Christian kingdom on earth; and, at the same time, the ground was prepared for authoritative control and supervision. The gridding of New Spain was therefore a process doubly motivated. Its mission was inspired by both utopic ideals and a will to dominate.[23]

Exemplary in this regard was the policy of *congregación* which gathered natives together and resettled them in towns that, often as not, followed orthogonal ground plans.[24] These newly arranged settlements were by definition Christian settlements. Imposed and laid out by friars, the gridded towns were segregated according to a hierarchy of spaces. The central plaza, with its church and administrative buildings, took pride of place; it dominated and supplied a matrix of evenly sized blocks that extended to the community's periphery.

Although the desire to found gridded towns was a familiar topos in Spanish statements of policy,[25] it nonetheless met with varied degrees of realization. Not all *congregaciones* led to the inscription of orthogonal grid-plans, nor did a church grace the main plaza of every new settlement. Indeed, the actual transformation of the native landscape into rectilinear communities with central squares proceeded unevenly across New Spain.[26]

Thus we should tease apart two independent factors that contribute to the appearance of grids on indigenous maps. First, the implementation of Spanish projects for native communities met with both success and failure. The will of colonial policy-makers to establish grid-plan towns was powerful, but so, too, was native resistance. Resettlement in gridded towns was rarely accepted passively. Rather, its achievement was possible only with the assistance of coercion, if not force. Second, what actually occurred on the ground substantiates only some of the roles assigned to grids by indigenous map-makers. Just as the transformation of native *altepetl* into Spanish-style *pueblos* was complex so, too, was the plotting of orthogonal patterns on maps and their symbolic relationship to landscape.[27] Across New Spain, myriad indigenous towns were redesigned between 1530 and 1630, yet this experience was not the only – or even the primary model – for native depictions of grids. Of equal consequence was an intertextual dialogue of images:

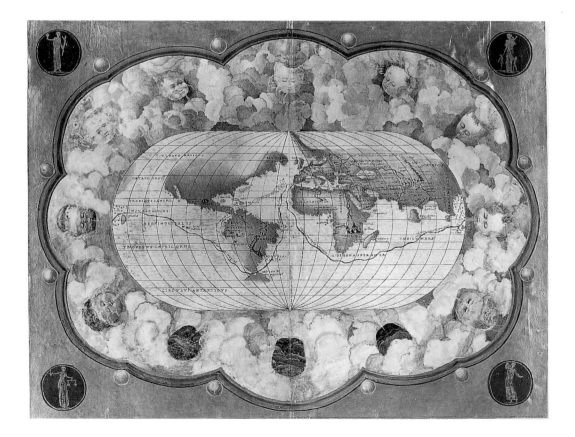

European maps and diagrams functioned as models for indigenous map-makers who harbored their own concepts of how to adumbrate territory.

The legacy of the grid in European cartography owed much to ancient Ptolemaic geography, and Renaissance map-makers certainly inherited this tradition. Yet Hubert Damisch connects the Renaissance with fundamental changes in the cartographic use and connotative moorings of the orthogonal diagram.[28] Analyzing the grid as an ideological projection as well as a form of representation, he implicates it not only in a renewed will to command territory, but also in an emergent moral regime. Throughout the Middle Ages, the uniform interstices designated by a lattice of lines marked *terra cognita*, beyond which laid an ill-defined frontier. In the wake of the European Renaissance, however, grids assumed another function. Rather than differentiating settled communities from lands untamed, evenly laid lines segmented the entire map into a net of uniform spaces (Figure 13.8). In providing an armature for distributing objects in space, orthogonals defined the boundaries of the cartographic document itself. As the ground for maps, the grid furnished a matrix for experiencing the world.[29]

Working far outside European intellectual circles, but with a familiarity of Renaissance cartographic developments, indigenous map-makers cast the grid in a very different role. In a map of Minas de Zumpango from 1580, for example, the grid functions not as a proper cartographic "ground," but as yet another figure (Figure 13.9).[30] Tethered to the edges, the grid emerges as one more element set upon the map.

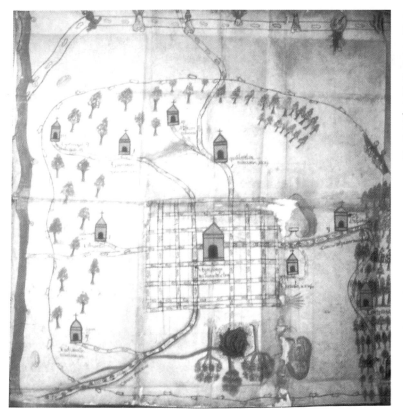

13.8 (opposite page) Battista Agnese. *World Map.* Painting on paper, *c.*1536–1564. Providence, The John Carter Brown Library at Brown University. (Photo: library.)

13.9 (left) *Map of Minas de Zumpango.* Color on European paper, from *Relación Geográfica,* *c.*1580. Madrid, Réal Academia de la Historia. (Photo: library.)

In effect, the Minas de Zumpango map-maker treats the grid according to a well-established tradition: for him, it is a toponymic sign. Yet, unlike the church and hill glyph, the mesh of lines never stands alone on indigenous maps – at least one ecclesiastical building always accompanies the web. The significance of the grid is therefore bound to that of the church. Often a gridded "shadow" radiates across the landscape from the edifice, and the net of bisecting roads amplifies the privilege of the church and its claim to cartographic authority. In this context, the grid serves primarily to describe what could not necessarily be seen; it visually demonstrates that under the aegis of the Christian Church communal spaces were surveyed, ordered, and contained.

We anticipate that grids will describe the shape and arrangement of civic space; and we expect them to reveal more about the appearance of towns than either hill glyphs or church signs. And at times they do – but not in every instance. On the map of Minas de Zumpango (Figure 13.9), a mesh of intersecting roads arranged around a centralized church stands for the town. Yet the uniformly shaped, empty blocks disclose very little about Minas de Zumpango. Moreover, footprints – arranged in a pattern of one per block on either side of the street – signal movement, but no actual path of travel is betrayed. This gridded image, then, is not simply a descriptive exercise. Rather, it imparts a geometric ideal that existed with greater reality in the imaginary, utopic space of the cartographer's mind than it ever did on the ground.[31]

As components of idealized spatial projections, grids splay towns before the panoptic, exploratory gaze of map viewers. Convolutions of topography and human occupation are ironed out into a lattice-work of anonymous districts.[32] As it cancels the possibility of random deviation, the uniform geometry of the grid demarcates the ideal order of a Christian community. Consequently a preordained civility materializes within its blocks. Moreover, the grid permits only two courses of communal transfiguration: it allows greater density and efficiency of occupation; or it unfurls itself, pushing the limits of *terra cognita* towards the fringes of the map. Both of these possibilities undermine the narrative potential of maps and direct attention away from sequential travel across the painted page.

As utopian prescriptions and as actual descriptions, grid-worked spaces leave few openings for preconquest narrative and itinerary traditions whose remnants remain in footprints that plod along the roads of many an early colonial map. In the Minas de Zumpango painting, a trail of prints skirts the edges of the chart, circumscribing not only the main town but also the smaller communities under its jurisdiction and the forests adjacent to them (Figure 13.9). Other elements retained from preconquest paintings include the two hill glyphs and the large expanses of blank space. Although these features are not completely banished, they are marginalized and the map implies that the church and grid are ascendant. The intersecting web of lines that forms Minas de Zumpango dwarfs the hill glyph which it abuts and, by skewing the relative scale of the two signs, the grid emphasizes ecclesiastical triumph. Presumably, the community stood in the shadow of a mountain that was far more vast than the town at its feet. Yet the painting inverts the scale and, in so doing, reverses the symbolic status of landmark and Christianized town.

The Minas de Zumpango map is prescient of the turn that would eventually sweep across indigenous cartography. Yet the relationships among grids, churches, and hill glyphs were never definitively settled in the sixteenth century. Dominating the 1579 map

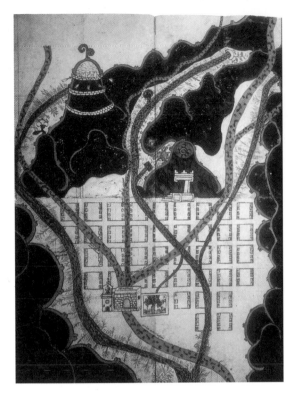

13.10 *Map of Texúpa, Oaxaca.* Color on European paper, from *Relación Geográfica,* 1579. Madrid, Réal Academia de la Historia. (Photo: library.)

(Figure 13.10) is the gridded town of Texúpa. The 39 blocks, each marked with eight house symbols, suggest that the gridding of Texúpa had been carried out with great rigor.[33] Yet this image also subverts the integrity of the grid in a number of ways. As three large roads cut across unnamed streets and blocks they pass through city lots and over conventionalized houses as if slicing through phantoms or mirages. Further compromising the material status of the grid are the motifs of prehispanic origin. Stylized hill glyphs, some marked with affixes, are posted beside the apparition-like grill; their dark masses form a menacing landscape. And towards the center of the map, at the lattice's upper edge, a temple stands before a hill glyph. Together, the two form a toponym for Texúpa. Pressed to the margins of the town, however, the prehispanic signs no longer suffice as visual invocations of the community. Now they stand guard like sentries, insuring that the grid is cancelled before it encroaches upon the regions where hill glyphs, and perhaps other indigenous traditions, still prevail.

Figures of Place: Between the Church and the Grid

There can be no doubt that indigenous map-makers in New Spain accommodated signs of the church and the grid quite differently. Testifying to this are the nearly 400 maps painted between 1570 and 1630: over 300 have churches, but fewer than 40 have grids. Moreover, of those paintings that feature an orthogonal mesh, nearly all were created for the Spanish crown. It is tempting to read this disparity as evidence that native map-makers anticipated some of their viewers' conceits. Perhaps painters sensed that royal officials longed, if not demanded, to see signs of the order they unfurled across the lands they now ruled. While this may have been the case in a few instances, I believe that there were more profound motives behind the uneven appropriation of churches and grids from European sources.

Its ability to evoke meaning on many levels buttressed the success of the church sign. Churches could replace hill glyphs without undermining the vigor of the toponym. The intrusion of painted buildings into native maps grafted additional meanings on to the hill glyph. Yet, ultimately, the church sign did not counter toponymic forms of representation, forms that had their roots in the prehispanic past. Moreover, by the end of the sixteenth century, nearly every indigenous community of any size had at least one church. Usually built by local residents, these structures became the focus of community identity and pride. Consequently it is not surprising that in the landscapes they charted, map-makers found ample room for churches.

Responses to the grid took a more ambivalent – if not halting – path. This is not coincidental. At one level, the grid of Renaissance Europe ran against the grain of prehispanic mapping conventions. Orthogonal diagrams can define the shape and limits of individual towns, but they cannot – by themselves – signal where a community is located. Unlike the church or the hill glyph, indigenous map-makers found no toponymic advantage to the grid. Throughout the colonial period, however, native conceptions of mapping privileged toponomy. It would seem, then, that the paucity of grids stems from an indigenous unwillingness to abandon a coveted representational device.

The resistance is not, however, strictly cartographic. As blueprints for colonial towns, grids arrived laden with spiritual and political connotations. Entangled as they are in the most violent metamorphoses initiated by the Spanish – conversion to Christianity and *congregación* – grids were hardly innocent signs. Hence we might construe the languishing of the orthogonal mesh on maps as a silent circumvention of European designs on native lands, and, additionally, as a rejection of the achievements Europeans claimed in New Spain.

It is certainly true that indigenous map-making proceeded hand in glove with colonization. And the signs on native maps conspired with the moral and material transfigurations of that world. But even as the Church tried people for idolatry and forced them to live in newly congregated towns, indigenous documents only rarely describe territory or mirror responses to colonization in an obvious way. Indeed no map, neither Spanish nor indigenous, set out to verify what was "really" happening in the sixteenth century.

If we obsessively follow maps and trust them as guides, then we must also recognize their semiotic and ethical equivocation. The cartograph constructs its own visual discourse – a discourse that folds within itself the symbolic and the unconscious as well as the political, moral and economic order of affairs. Thus in the web of interlocking social contingencies that we call history, the map is simultaneously implicated and constitutive. Some of these processes uncoiled on the ground: prehispanic temples were razed and churches rose in their stead, communities were resettled and grids were organized under Spanish auspices. Other interactions transpired in the domain of representational convention and record-keeping. Indigenous painters reflected upon their craft via a mixture of prehispanic traditions and European introductions; the shimmer of memory and change therefore structured the association of signs on the map.

Finally, that which was molded by desire and imagination must be taken into account. This includes those things indigenous painters willingly acknowledged – both on the ground and on their maps – and those things that map-makers and their patrons helped each other to envision. These are concerns no less real than the furrowing of orthogonal lines in the earth.[34] If there exists any common fabric within the heterogeneity of indigenous maps, then it is spun when desire, painting conventions, and historical circumstances intermingle. It is this tenuous thread that binds hillocks to churches and churches to grids on the maps of New Spain. And it is the texturing of these filaments that lends grain and tooth to matters of colonization.

14.1 Luca Signorelli. Fresco (general view), 1499–1504, Cappella Nuova, Orvieto Cathedral. (Photo: Scala/Art Resource.)

CHAPTER 14

Luca Signorelli's Rule of Antichrist *and the Christian Encounter with the Infidel*

JONATHAN B. RIESS

The characterization of the decade of the 1490s in western Europe as one of eschatological anxiety, and the belief that Luca Signorelli's murals in the Cappella Nuova of Orvieto Cathedral (1499–1504; Figure 14.1) be ranked among the foremost expressions of this ferment, are ideas that have assumed the aura of historical truisms.[1] It can, indeed, be reaffirmed that Signorelli's scenes of universal cataclysm and Last Judgment, so rare in the history of Italian art, do distil an epoch of millennial expectation. (We must not overlook the fact, however, that Fra Angelico had begun decoration of the chapel about half a century earlier.[2]) Less well appreciated is the possibility that the massive representation of the *Rule of Antichrist* (Figure 14.2), one of Signorelli's contributions to the decorative scheme, alludes to the censure of Jews and Muslims and to the enduring conviction that their resistance to Christianity be understood within an apocalyptic framework.[3] Signorelli's fresco, in this sense, condemns the forces perceived as the greatest enemies of the Church and so illustrates the continuing way in which Renaissance Christian Europe cast the encounter with the infidel in terms of its own world view.

John Calvin wrote, some years after Signorelli's murals were completed, that "Among Catholics nothing is more discussed or well known than the anticipated coming of Antichrist."[4] There is truth to this for the period of concern to us. Antichrist is, in any case, one of the most important figures in medieval and Renaissance apocalypticism. The medieval view of history includes prophetic pronouncements treating the future, known and based chiefly on the Revelation of St. John the Evangelist, or the Apocalypse, and sees as its leading protagonist the powerful and ominous figure of Antichrist. The advent of this great dread adversary of God – the Final Enemy – will be heralded by certain signs. An agent of the devil and Satan's chief weapon in the struggle ahead, Antichrist is in every sense the antithesis of Christ. His followers will be seduced through fear, bribes, false miracles, and the sheer potency of the Evil One's preaching into believing that he is the true Christ returned. The hegemony of Antichrist will come to an end, so the account of the future concludes, by the coming of Christ in Majesty. Antichrist will be destroyed, the universe will come to an end, and Christ will call the living and dead to judgment.[5]

14.2   Luca Signorelli, *Rule of Antichrist*. Fresco, 1499–1504, Cappella Nuova, Orvieto Cathedral. (Photo: Alinari/Art Resource.)

The Antichrist legend grants a preeminent role to Jews. Antichrist is himself said to be born a Jew, his agents are of the faith, and his many Jewish supporters identify their messiah with him. We must recognize as well that Islam was also implicated in popular versions of the myth, often being very directly associated, if not identified, with Antichrist, commonly conceived as the embodiment of the forces arrayed against the Church.[6] Thus the crusading enthusiasm and fervid anti-Judaism of the epoch, leading features of the world of ideas and events that shaped the *Rule of Antichrist*, were imbued with an apocalyptic aura through association with the Final Enemy.[7]

The *Rule of Antichrist* is the pivotal scene in an encyclopedic program illustrating the last things. The decorations in the Cappella Nuova of Orvieto Cathedral, as noted, span a half-century of activity. In the vaults, that region started by Fra Angelico in 1447 and completed by Signorelli at the outset of his labor in 1499, is Christ in Majesty presiding over a vast representation of the heavenly council. Below, on the chapel walls (the area conceived and painted by Signorelli alone), are pictured the *Antichrist*, the *End of the World*, the *Resurrection*, the *Damned Led into Hell*, *The Damned*, the *Coronation of the Elect*, and the *Entry of the Elect into Heaven*. Finally, in the basement section of the walls, is portrayed a grouping of portraits of pagan and contemporary authors accompanied by scenes drawn from their writings. These are individuals who anticipate and sustain,

14.3   Luca Signorelli, *End of the World.* Fresco, 1499–1504, Cappella Nuova, Orvieto Cathedral. (Photo: Alinari/Art Resource.)

through various signs and devices, the truth of the apocalyptic vision laid out above them.[8]

Although the mural program is of unprecedented sweep, its prevailing theme is clear enough: the triumph of the Church over evil, as personified by Antichrist, and the triumph, through everlasting life in heaven, of those who withstand the temptations of the Evil One. The sequence of events in the *Rule of Antichrist*, as we move from the middle foreground into the left background, leads us first through the various means the Evil One employs to attain power, to, finally, his destruction, this last episode propelling us into the adjoining mural of the *End of the World* (Figure 14.3). The order of Antichrist tableaux and the sequence of murals thus correspond to the rise and fall of the Evil One and to the larger unfolding of events he sets in motion.[9]

The legend of Antichrist is, historically, a malleable political and religious instrument, and Signorelli, consistent with tradition, grants aspects of the story an explicit contemporaneity.[10] Only one of the mural's reflections of the events of the time is, however, of interest to us here: the special manner in which Jews and Muslims are condemned, or, more accurately, demonized. To the left of the preaching Antichrist at the center of the mural is a wealthy ally reaching into a purse with one hand and giving money to an indigent woman with the other, a unique realization of Antichrist's use of bribes in his

14.4   Luca Signorelli,
Rule of Antichrist (detail).
Fresco. 1499–1504,
Cappella Nuova,
Orvieto Cathedral.
(Photo: Alinari/Art
Resource.)

ascent to power (Figure 14.4).[11] The purse of this ally is decorated with a six-pointed device suggestive of the star known as the Mogen David or Shield of David. The device, while perhaps not the Shield of David itself, seems in any case to be a variant on the so-called Jew-badge required by many medieval and Renaissance municipalities to identify members of the faith. The yellow color of the emblem, and of the dress of the figure, as well as the green head covering and the conspicuously opulent clothing, are attributes that mark him more specifically as a usurious Jew,[12] although, in a large sense, the ostentatious dress simply bespeaks the sinful inclinations that lead to damnation.[13]

The dark complexion of the figure, a readily evident physical parallel with both the preaching Antichrist and the whispering devil at his side, suggests that the gift-giving Jew is himself a species of devil incarnate. Dark-skinned denotations of evil abound in European art; the common portrayal of Judas comes first to mind. Ripa's image of Sin is dark, it is relevant to note, because he is said to be "impure."[14]

The Jew's sharp and pointed beard, like his dark skin, was another well-established aspect of the medieval Jewish caricature and serves to draw further attention to his kinship with evil: the beard suggests the goat's beard, or goatee, and so refers to the presumed favorite animal of the Jews and Satan, and is symbolic, more specifically, of lechery. Thus the presence of women near the Jew denotes a demonic association, the presumed lecherous instincts of Satan and, through him, of his Jewish servants.[15] Finally, the usurious aura about Signorelli's Jew is itself a satanic impulse, for usury was of course said to be a crime against Christ, a crime in which, predictably, the devil was assumed to play a part. This is reflected in art, to cite but one example, in scenes of financial transactions where the devil assists Jews.[16]

The analogues between Signorelli's Antichrist and Jew reflect deeply ingrained traditions of medieval and Renaissance anti-Judaism. The Jew, as Trachtenberg has described him, was conceived as a creature of Satan, "not a human being but a demonic, a diabolic beast fighting the forces of truth and salvation with Satan's weapons." The Jew joins with the devil and his minion, Antichrist, as the great and inexorable enemy of Christ, vilified most savagely, and allied most closely with the devil, in the Jew's putative routine desecration of the host.[17] Christendom was engaged in a holy war of extermination against the Jews, "lest Satan," again in Trachtenberg's words, "inherit the earth and truth and salvation be lost." The true and ultimate enemy in the struggle against evil was not the Jew himself, but rather Satan who supposedly works through the Jew, as he does through Antichrist.[18]

Signorelli is not alone in portraying the Jew in deadly alliance with Satan; this demonization is widespread in the arts throughout the later Middle Ages and Renaissance – one of the first dated images of a Jew carries the superscription *"Aaron fil diaboli"* – assuming many different modes of expression, some relatively mild in nature (the popular print series of the sixteenth century showing the devil assisting Jews in the bathhouse), others utterly repugnant (those showing a sow, as mother, feeding her Jewish offspring, the so-called *Judensau*).[19]

A relevant matter of broad import, one that helps introduce other aspects of Signorelli's usurious Jew, concerns the remarkable fact that the Jew in European culture had come to be regarded, well before 1500, not so much as infidel but as arch-heretic. This followed from the notion that Judaism was not an independent faith but a demonic perversion of the one true body of belief.[20] Thus the religion of the Jews could be persecuted as relentlessly as were other forms of "heretical" belief. The Jews were, inevitably, thought to have been the dark force behind various schismatic sects. And so among the first charges brought against these sects was that they were products of "judaizing." The issue of Jewish plots was in the air around 1500 as the Spanish Inquisition was in full swing and, although technically beyond its jurisdiction (like Muslims and pagans), the Inquisitorial bodies were nevertheless able to sate their hatred by pursuing Jews and, still more assiduously, Jewish converts to Christianity.[21] The directing hand of Antichrist was discerned everywhere: records indicate that in at least one case the messianic expectations of Jewish converts to Christianity were linked to the Evil One. The association of Jew with Antichrist, however, is one that goes back, as we have seen, to the very origins of the legend and the association was a defining thrust of Catholic thought beginning in the early Middle Ages.[22]

The Christian net for the capture of Jews and other agents of Satan was spread wide to draw within it Muslims as well, for were they not also obviously in league with and abetted by the Jews? Muslim incursions were, therefore, construed at various times as forms of Jewish sabotage. All of this is but part of a larger phenomenon, or fantasy, in which the Muslims were identified as demons or as Antichrist himself (as we have observed), were believed to be in league with the Jews, and were even thought to have assisted in the Crucifixion. Cohn posits, in the face of this miraculous cooperation of the two faiths in the popular demonology of the Middle Ages and Renaissance, that the only reason Christians were somewhat more obsessed with Jews than with Muslims was that they "lived scattered through Christian Europe."[23]

How do these ties between infidels and heretics apply to Signorelli's Jew and to his relationship with Antichrist and Satan? The figure (Figure 14.4) is, I believe, a hybrid individual, an amalgam of the two chief enemies of the Church. In this way he relates directly to Antichrist's association with opposition to the Church, to his role as heresy incarnate.[24] Given the perception of a secret partnership between Jew and Muslim it is fitting that in other contemporary works of art physiognomic features as well as details of costume often make it difficult to distinguish between representatives of the two religions, an equivocal situation directly related to the Orvieto Jew.[25]

Although the profile of the figure suggests readily the Jewish stereotype in contemporary art, it is also similar to depictions of Muslims; those by Pintoricchio, for example, come to mind. The sunken cheeks, the tight-lipped harsh expression and elongated eyes, and the simple fact that the figure is in extreme profile which allows these features to be seen clearly – all these were characteristics connected to the common representation of both Jew and Muslim.[26] The ostentatious dress of Signorelli's Jew suggests, as observed, the rich garments customarily worn by usurers, but the dress might also designate an oriental potentate, an impression underscored by the fact that his earring and sash were the fashion among Muslim men, particularly Moors.[27] Two other details situate the figure more securely within a Spanish ambience; he becomes, in the end, a composite of Sephardic Jew and Moor. The purse conforms closely to the Spanish style of the time, and the distinctive headgear is still more certainly Spanish: the tight headpiece (known as a caul) with a hat worn over it appears widely in Spanish painting of the period.[28]

The "Jew" poses not only his personal threat but also functions, it would seem, as representative of all the exotic enemies of Christendom. His composite dress and type, which does not appear to correspond with any national or ethnic modes and manners, was possibly adopted by Signorelli from contemporary theatrical costume – an appropriate choice, if this supposition is correct, given the possibility that an Orvietan Antichrist drama might be reflected in the *Rule of Antichrist*.[29]

The figure of the usurer combines within himself some of the larger foundations of the fresco. The beginnings of the medieval epoch of crusades and of the vehement medieval persecution of the Jews are closely allied historical phenomena and are related, among other factors, to the desire to preserve the unity of the Church as it came to be challenged both internally and externally.[30] It may simply be a matter of fortuitous contingencies that the 1490s was a decade of inquisition and, especially through the efforts of the papacy, of the promotion of a crusade, but it is not unreasonable to suggest that in medieval and Renaissance Europe it is the recurring condemnation of Jew and Muslim that appears to provide the energies and direction for such contingencies.

The presumption of a Muslim–Jewish conspiracy was most directly connected with the interpretation of contemporary events in Spain. This should not be unexpected. The proclivity to cast history within an eschatological framework, even so far as to determine policy on the basis of hoped-for millennial outcomes, was a feature of the reign of Ferdinand and Isabella – "the Catholic kings," as their compatriot Pope Alexander VI had titled them in 1494 – in part because of the expulsion of the Jews just two years earlier, an event many believed would hasten the advent of the millennial kingdom, and one, possibly, that helped inspire Alexander's own anti-Jewish policies.[31] The exactly contemporaneous Christian conquest of Granada (1492) dramatically underscored the sense of eschatological association between the anti-Jewish and anti-Muslim campaigns of the day. Ironically, the expulsion of the Jews would bring to pass the Spanish Christian's worst fear: many Jews fled to the Orient, an event which prompted one sultan to thank the Spanish for having sent him some of his best subjects, and so the much-dreaded Jewish–Muslim alliance was indeed forged.[32]

Many have remarked upon the extraordinary number of Spanish millennial prophecies around 1500. These visions, generally Joachimist in character, are best epitomized by Columbus's pronouncements concerning the divinely inspired ambitions of his voyages. The prophecies envisioned Spanish leadership of a crusade to retake the Holy Land from the Antichrist Turk, to convert Gentiles, Greek Christians, and finally Jews, and thus to prepare the way for the Second Coming.[33]

Vincent Ferrer's sermons on Antichrist of the late 1300s and early 1400s, and the interpretation of the Apocalypse by Annio da Viterbo of 1480, are important theological sources for the *Rule of Antichrist*, and these sources further the impression of a distinctly Spanish cast to Signorelli's apocalyptic program, especially to the paired condemnation of Jews and Muslims.[34] Proclaimed the "Angel of the Apocalypse" during his lifetime, the Spaniard, Vincent Ferrer, was cited by many theologians of the fifteenth century as the authoritative voice on Antichrist and the approaching kingdom of God. I have written elsewhere that Vincent's significance to Signorelli was given explicit expression through the inclusion of a portrait of the saint: the prominent Dominican in the middleground, a figure who stands in every way as the antithesis to the preaching Antichrist, is similar to the widespread portrait type that appeared in art following Vincent's canonization in 1455.[35]

"Like an invincible athlete," the ebullient bull of canonization reads in part, "he had as his mission the refutation of the Jews and Saracens, and of other infidels."[36] Vincent's sermons dwell on the Jewish origins of Antichrist. His rabid anti-Judaism, as well as the persecutions that he helped foment, were invoked by the Spanish in the 1490s as precedent and license for their own actions and policies, while Jews at the time of the expulsion thought back to Vincent as emblematic of the terrible trials to which they had been subjected in the past. Thus in a Spanish reprint of the most vicious censure of the Jews in the sphere of Antichrist illustration (1497), there is appended a dedication to Vincent. I should point out that the image of the Jew in this life of Antichrist is marked by a physiognomic distortion more extreme than that found at Orvieto, and that the identifying emblem the figures wear approximates the one displayed by Signorelli's Jew (Figure 14.5).[37]

Also important to Signorelli's formulation is Annio da Viterbo's fervent denunciation of the Muslim as Antichrist, apparently the most popular of Renaissance accounts of the life of the Evil One. Annio's profound hatred of the Jew, and espousal of the crusade,

14.5 (right) *Antichrist Preaching, Entkrist.* Woodcut, *c.*1472, Strasbourg [?]. Frankfurt am Main, Stadt Bibliothek.

14.6 (below) Luca Signorelli, *Rule of Antichrist* (detail). Fresco, 1499–1504, Cappella Nuova, Orvieto Cathedral. (Photo: Scala/Art Resource.)

are the themes of his interpretation of the Apocalypse, first printed in 1480 and in wide circulation by the late 1490s. A high point in the renown of author and text coincides with Signorelli's period of activity in Orvieto: from 1499 to 1502 Annio served as Alexander's Master of the Sacred Palace, chief interpreter and guardian of the faith.[38] Possibly in recognition of the affinities of his apocalyptic thinking with that of Spain, Annio expresses throughout his writings a respectful, even obsequious, attitude towards the Spanish royal house. His history of Spain, printed in 1498 with the assistance of Alexander, glorifies Ferdinand and Isabella as the chief ornaments of modern civilization.[39] The Jewish policies of Spain were doubtless one source of appeal of "the Catholic kings" to Annio. His was among the most strident of anti-Jewish voices of the 1490s in Rome; a diatribe of 1497 contends that Christians who deal in any fashion with Jews should be excommunicated, condemns usury, and extols the virtues of the *monte de paschi*, the approved money-lending houses of the Church.[40]

These last comments bring us back to the mural, and to the usurious, composite figure of Jew and Moor. The dominant image in the *Rule of Antichrist* is of course not this individual, nor is it even the figure of Antichrist. It is, rather, the enormous structure that rises behind them (Figure 14.6). This is, most likely, the third Temple of Solomon, the one built by Herod and known to Christ, who prophesied its destruction.[41] Antichrist, according to biblical interpretation, was to make the Temple the center of his cult and reign.

Signorelli's structure, significantly, is turned away from the altar and is oriented towards the succeeding scene of the *End of the World*. Here, in this latter mural, is pictured what is likely the same building in ruins. We may take this to be symbolic of the vanquishing of the world of paganism and Judaism and to allude to the superseding of the Old Dispensation by the New. Thus Giles of Viterbo, in his opening oration at the Fifth Lateran Council, spoke of how the new Church of Rome would last forever while the Old Law, symbolized by the Temple of Solomon, would not endure.[42]

Christians of the Renaissance persevered in the medieval habit of mind of seeing all forces outside the Church within the framework of their apocalyptic program – Antichrist as Jewish Messiah, Antichrist as Muslim. The fury with which the Spanish armies of conquest swept through the Americas several years after Signorelli had completed his Orvieto murals in 1504 is, in this sense, an expression of the same blindness with which European Christians encountered other peoples and faiths much closer to home. And were not the "Indians" of the New World one of the Lost Tribes? And was not their conversion, and that of the Jews, to be the last great event of End-Time?[43] The legend of Antichrist and the attendant hatred of Jews, as pictured in Orvieto, stands, in short, as a broad expression of the enduring Christian demonization of other faiths and cultures.

Iconology, Ideology, and Cultural Encounter: Panofsky, Althusser, and the Scene of Recognition

W. J. T. MITCHELL

> If we knew by some concatenation of circumstances that a certain Negro sculpture had been executed in 1510, it would be meaningless to say that it was "contemporaneous" with Michelangelo's Sistine ceiling.
>
> We have all seen with our own eyes the transference of spoons and fetishes of African tribes from the museums of ethnology into art exhibitions.
>
> Erwin Panofsky

"Intercultural contact" is among other things an encounter of real persons, flesh-and-blood individuals. Of course they bring with them an enormous amount of baggage: languages, codes of behavior, histories, institutions, technologies – in short, everything that goes to make up a culture. But the cultures never meet except in concrete encounters, doubly imbricated experiences of "self–other" relations.

What gives the history of art something specific to say about these encounters is its special relation to the field of visual culture. The history of visual "art," if we were to follow Panofsky's guidance, would not be concerned with the whole field of visual culture, but only with that part that has aesthetic status, and is *intended* to be taken as art.[1] But Panofsky was also quick to admit that he could only maintain these aesthetic boundaries by circular and self-contradictory arguments: the distinction between artistic "monuments" and secondary "documents" is always shifting and relative, and the idea of the aesthetic as something "we just look at . . . without relating it . . . to anything outside itself" (11) is immediately betrayed by Panofsky's appeal to the intention behind the object. Similarly, Panofsky's attempt to segregate the subdisciplines of art history by spatio-temporal "frames of reference" (7) (most notably the frame called "Europe") is immediately belied by the two quotations I have prefixed to this essay. It would be "meaningless to say" that African sculpture was contemporaneous with European art, but "we have all seen with our own eyes" their juxtaposition in our own immediate frame of reference.[2] Evidently the sayable and the seeable are operating at cross-purposes in

Panofsky's conception of the boundaries of his discipline. But then his notion of iconology always implied a broader ambition than European art (or even visual art in general), one that would address both nonwestern and non-artistic visual images, and explore the whole field of human visuality and visual experience.

Intercultural contact is mediated in crucial ways by vision. The greeting with the other is, in some fundamental sense, necessarily face-to-face. Before words are said, there is a sighting, a meeting of eyes, a gesture of mutual recognition. One may have already "met" the stranger indirectly, through verbal communications, descriptions, pictures, tokens of friendship, but the visual encounter in a specific place and time is crucial.

Many forms of visual contact between cultures are, of course, quite unfriendly, filled with misrecognition, distortion, and a disfiguration of the other. Stereotypes (as the very word suggests) are pre-eminently visual images, mechanically reproduced caricatures that do violence to the people(s) they represent. Racism is not only an attitude, or a thing people say and do to each other, but a way of seeing that imposes an "optical regime" on the racial other, creating an entire *gestalt*, a moving image in space and time, that seems like a transparent (re)presentation to the racist. The meeting of gazes is then far from mutual, but an enactment of power relations, a site of mutual anxiety, resentment, and guilt. The slave is not supposed to raise his or her eyes to meet those of the master; the natives require watching; children should be seen and not heard. Women (who always form a culture within a culture) typically find themselves in intricate rituals of visual power and pleasure in their contacts with the culture of men. Cultures based in gender, sexual orientation, or in any sense of shared minority status (think here of "sensory minorities" like the blind and deaf) are also likely to experience the visual field in radically different ways from those of the dominant culture. The experience of seeing and being seen is not just "socially constructed," but a foundational moment in the construction of the social.

To say all this is, of course, only to remind ourselves of what should be obvious, that the general problem of "intercultural contact" and the specific dimension of visual culture are inseparable. The boundaries between people(s) are both mediated and blocked by visual institutions, by practices of observation, representation, surveillance, and by blindnesses and modes of invisibility. The cultural other is typically (and paradoxically) "seen as" an "invisible man" or woman, simultaneously marked as visually readable and available, and as inscrutable, elusive, and illegible.

Whether or not a revised version of Panofsky's iconology is the best way to study the paradoxical structure of intercultural visual contact is far from clear. One fundamental problem with iconology is suggested by the roots of the very word, promising a discursive science of images, a mastering of the icon by the logos, and then delivering an ensemble of "world-pictures" and "world-views" (most notoriously, the very idea of "perspective") that come back to haunt the master-discourse. The icon in iconology is like a repressed memory that keeps returning as an uncontrollable symptom. Intercultural and interpersonal contact may be mediated by vision, but that is no guarantee that a "science" of the visual image will provide an Archimedean perspective from which to make these contacts intelligible. Or perhaps an Archimedean perspective is exactly what iconology has given us, and unintelligibility has been the result.

In *Iconology* I argued that there are two key moves required for a reconstruction of iconology as a dialectical and critical discipline. The first is the resignation of the hope for a scientific theory of visual images, and a redescription of the basic "object" of iconology as the *encounter* of word and image, the readable and the visible. When this encounter is examined in specific historical circumstances, and in relation to recurrent traditions such as the *paragone* or "contest" of the visual and verbal arts, it invariably reveals itself as a social struggle, a battle between professions, genders, classes, or cultures staged as the dissonance between types of signs (word and image) or modes of communication (the readable and the visible). The "bottom line" of the word–image division is probably species difference, the boundary between the human and the animal, culture and nature, a division that is then reinscribed within accounts of intercultural difference. Thus language and speech and writing are the attributes of "man." The image is the medium of the subhuman, of the "dumb" brute, the savage, the child, the woman, the masses. These stereotypes of the social meaning of the word–image difference are all too familiar, as is the disturbing counter-tradition, that "man" is created "in the image" of his maker. One basic argument of *Iconology* was that the very name of this "science of images" bears the scars of an ancient division and a fundamental paradox that cannot be erased from its workings.

The other key move for a revived iconology follows directly from the first: it is a mutually critical encounter with the discourse of ideology, understood as an analysis of the process by which social and cultural hierarchies are naturalized by (among other things) visual regimes. I attempted to stage such an encounter in the final chapter of *Iconology* by working through the constitutive figures of the *camera obscura* and the fetish in Marx's account of ideology and commodity. I want to extend that discussion here by shifting from the "apparatus" of ideology (especially its figures of optical technologies) to its *theatrical* figures, what might be called its "scenes of recognition."

Panofsky gives us the "primal scene" of his own iconological science in the introductory essay to his *Studies in Iconology*:

> When an acquaintance greets me on the street by removing his hat, what I see from a *formal* point of view is nothing but the change of certain details within a configuration forming part of the general pattern of color, lines and volumes which constitute my world of vision.[3]

Panofsky's subsequent elaboration of this scene as a hierarchy of ever more complex and refined perceptions is familiar to all art historians: the "formal" perception gives way (is "overstepped") to a "sphere of subject matter or meaning," the "factual" identification of the formal pattern as an "*object* (gentleman)" – that is, a thing that has a *name*. This level of "natural" or "practical experience" Panofsky associates anthropologically with savages (the Australian bushman), and it gives way, in turn, to a secondary level of "conventional subject matter," or meaning. The "realization that the lifting of the hat stands for a greeting belongs in an altogether different realm of interpretation." Finally, the greeting reaches the level of global cultural symbol: "besides constituting a natural event in space and time, besides naturally indicating moods or feelings, besides conveying a conventional greeting, the action of my acquaintance can reveal to an experienced observer all that goes to make up his 'personality,'" a reading that takes this gesture as "symptomatic" of a "philosophy," a "national, social, and educational background."

These four terms − form, motif, image, and symbol − are overlapped to construct a three-dimensional model of interpretation that moves from "pre-iconographical description" of "primary or natural subject matter," to "iconographical analysis" of "secondary or conventional subject matter," to "iconographical interpretation" of the "intrinsic meaning or content," the (iconological) world of "symbolical values" (14). The movement is from surface to depth, from sensations to ideas, from immediate particulars to an insight into the way *essential tendencies of the human mind* were expressed by specific *themes* and *concepts*" (15; emphasis Panofsky's).

There are plenty of reasons to accept the naturalness of the scene of greeting as a starting place for the explanation of painting. The silent, visual encounter, the gesture of raising the hat, the motif of "gesturality" as such, may seem simply inevitable as a basic example, since it captures one of the central features of western history painting, the language of the human body as a vehicle for narrative, dramatic, and allegorical signification. We might also look forward to Michael Fried's accounts of gesture in Modernist painting and sculpture to reinforce a sense of Panofsky's scene as inevitable and natural.[4] But suppose we resisted these natural inevitabilities, and questioned the scene itself. What might we notice?

First, the banality and minimal interest of the scene, its empty typicality as an emblem of something like "bougeois civility," the mutually *passing* recognition of subjects who take no interest in one another, *say nothing* to one another, and go on with their business. The example is not important, of course; it *exemplifies*, stages, even flaunts its insignificance, lack of importance. It does not deserve harsh, picky scrutiny or judgment. It is not dignified enough to be the subject of a painting − no great history, epic, or allegory is being enacted. It is just there to exemplify the *minimal* features of visual communication and representation; it provides a baseline from which to measure more complex, more important forms of visual representation.

Second, the transformation of this simple, social encounter (the men passing in the street) into the encounter between a subject and an object (the perception and "reading" of an image, a painting), and finally into the encounter between two "objects" of representation (the two passing figures − "gentlemen" − staged for us in Panofsky's own "theoretical scene"). "Transferring the results of this analysis from everyday life to a work of art" (5) we find the "same three strata" − forms as objects; objects as images; and images as symbols. Panofsky on the street greeting an acquaintance becomes a figure for his encounter with the individual painting; the "scene" of greeting between iconologist and icon becomes the paradigm for a science of iconology.

Third, the construction of a hierarchical structure deployed as a narrative sequence from simple to complex, trivial to important, natural to conventional, "practical" to "literary" or "philosophical" knowledge, analytic to synthetic understanding, primitive, savage confrontation to civilized intersubjective encounter. Early stages are "automatic" (3), later ones are reflective, deliberative. In our inability to recognize the subject of a painting "all of us are Australian bushmen."

Fourth, the opposition between "iconography" and "iconology" deployed as a reverse narrative, in which the higher level precedes the lower in a hierarchy of control. Thus "our practical experience had to be controlled by an insight into the manner in which objects and events were expressed by forms . . ." (15); the fact "that we grasp these qualities in the fraction of a second and almost automatically, must not induce us to believe that we could ever give a correct pre-iconographical description of a work of art without having divined, as it were, its historical 'locus.' " (11)

Fifth, the privileging of literary painting in which "images" of the human body and its gestures are the principal bearers of meaning, and the marginalizing of non-literary forms ("landscape painting, still-life, and genre") as "exceptional phenomena, which mark the later, oversophisticated phases of a long development" (8). No mention of abstract art or other forms "in which the whole sphere of secondary or conventional subject matter" (i.e., literary images) is "eliminated." No mention of pictorial traditions that impose severe constraints (including prohibitions) on the representation of the human form.

Sixth, a homogenizing of these oppositions and hierarchies into an "organic whole" – the "essential tendencies of the human mind" accessible to the "synthetic intuition" of the iconologist.

Simply to list these features is probably sufficient to demarcate the outlines of a critique that would question the homogeneity of the iconological process. The "control" of lower levels of perception by higher levels immediately suggests the possibility of resistance; Modernism becomes intelligible, for instance, precisely as a resistance to Panofsky's iconology and its Romantic hermeneutic, its literary/figural basis, and its familiar array of analytic/synthetic oppositions. Panofsky's is an iconology in which the "icon" is thoroughly absorbed by the "logos," understood as a rhetorical, literary, or even (less convincingly) a scientific discourse.

But there is more to do here than simply to note the way Panofsky's method reproduces nineteenth-century conventions or undermines its own logic in the play of its figurative language. We need to ask (1) what stands between this scene, its extrapolation, and the hoped-for "science" of iconology; why is this scene inconvenient for that goal, and what other scenes might serve it better? This question will take us ultimately back to Panofsky's essay on perspective; (2) what can we learn from Panofsky's canny choice of the primal scene of greeting? How might this scene be revisited by a postmodern iconology, or (as I should prefer to label it) a *critical* iconology?

One thing a critical iconology would surely note is the resistance of the icon to the logos. Indeed, the cliché of postmodernism is that it is an epoch of the absorption of all language into images and "simulacra," a semiotic hall of mirrors. If traditional iconology repressed the image, postmodern represses language. This is not so much a "history" as a kernel narrative embedded in the very grammar of "iconology" as a fractured concept, a suturing of image and text. One must precede the other, dominate, resist, supplement the other. This otherness or alterity of image and text is not just a matter of analogous structure, as if images just happened to be the "other" to texts. It is, as Daniel Tiffany has shown, the very terms in which alterity *as such* is expressed in phenomenological reflection, especially in the relation of speaking Self and seen Other.[5]

Critical iconology, then, is what brings us back to the men greeting one another silently in the street, the constitutive figure or "theoretical scene" of the science of iconology – what I have called the "hypericon."[6] It would be all too easy to subject this scene (as I have partly done) to ideological analysis, to treat it as an allegory of bourgeois civility built, as Panofsky reminds us, upon a "residue of medieval chivalry; armed men used to remove their helmets to make clear their peaceful intentions" (4). Instead, let us subject a different scene – an explicitly ideological one – to an iconological analysis.

The scene is Althusser's description of ideology as a process which "hails or interpellates concrete individuals as concrete subjects."[7] Ideology is a "*(mis)recognition* function" exemplified by several of what Althusser calls "theoretical scenes" (174). The first scene:

> To take a highly "concrete" example, we all have friends who, when they knock on our door and we ask, through the door, the question "Who's there?", answer (since "it's obvious"), "It's me". And we recognize that "it is him", or "her". We open the door, and "it's true, it really was she who was there." (172)

This scene immediately coupled with another – a move into the street:

> To take another example, when we recognize somebody of our (previous) acquaint-ance ([re]-connaissance) in the street, we show him that we have recognized him (and have recognized that he has recognized us) by saying to him, "Hello, my friend," and shaking his hand (a material ritual practice of ideological recognition in everyday life – in France, at least; elsewhere there are other rituals). (172)

How do we "read" these scenes of greeting in comparison with Panofsky's? First, they are slightly more detailed, more "concrete," as Althusser puts it – in quotation marks. The social encounter, similarly, is slightly more intimate and consequential – a mutual greeting of acquaintances, friends, gendered persons, not a one-way token of civility that could as well pass between anonymous strangers. Althusser's scene is a prelude to a narrative or dramatic encounter, a dialogue of which these are the opening words; it brackets the visual and privileges the blind, oral exchange – the greeting through the closed door, the "Hey, you there!" of an unseen caller in the street – "the most commonplace everyday police (or other) hailing."[8] Panofsky's is a purely visual scene; no words are exchanged, only gestures, and we are led to expect nothing further from the passing acquaintances. Panofsky never tips his hat in return; he withdraws into an anatomy of his own perceptual and interpretive activity, the three-dimensional interpret-ation of an object in visual/hermeneutic space.

These are the constitutive "theoretical scenes" of two sciences, Panofsky's science of images (iconology) and Althusser's science of (false) consciousness (ideology). The sym-metry is imperfect, of course. Iconology is the science; ideology is supposed to be the object of a science. Ideology is a theoretical object, not a theory; it is the bad symptom that has to be diagnosed. Iconology is the "diagnostician" (15) according to Panofsky; the (good) "symptoms" are the cultural symbols he interprets with his "synthetic intuition" – those theoretical objects (other men, paintings) encountered in the primal scene of visual recognition and greeting.

Let us now stage a recognition scene (as opposed to a mere comparison) between Panofsky's iconology and Althusser's ideology by asking each to recognize and "greet" itself in the other. Iconology recognizes itself as an ideology, that is, as a system of naturalization, a homogenizing discourse that effaces conflict and difference with figures of "organic unity" and "synthetic intuition." Ideology recognizes itself as an iconology, a putative science, not just the object of a science. It makes this discovery most simply by recognizing and acknowledging its origins (etymological and historical) as a "science of ideas" in which "ideas" are understood as images – the "science" of Destutt de Tracy and the original "ideologues" of the French Revolution.[9]

The point of this greeting, then, is not simply to make iconology "ideologically aware" or self-critical, but to make the ideological critique iconologically aware. This critique cannot simply enter the discussion of the image, or the text–image difference, as a super-method. It intervenes, and is itself subjected to intervention by its object. That is why I have called this notion of iconology critical and dialectical. It does not rest in a master-code, an ultimate horizon of History, Language, Mind, Nature, Being or any other abstract principle, but asks us to return to the scene of the crime, the scene of greeting between Subjects – between the speaking and the seeing Subject, the ideologist and the iconologist. What we learn from this greeting is that the *temptation to science*, understood as the panoptic surveillance and mastery of the object/"other" (individual or image) is the "crime" imbedded in these scenes. It is not staged directly for us; the figures merely engage in more or less conventional social greetings. To "see" the crime, we need to remove the figures and examine the stage, the space of vision and recognition, the very ground which allows the figures to appear.

The presentation of this empty stage, the foundational image of all possible visual–spatial culture, is precisely what Panofsky offers in the perspective essay.[10] This paper, as Michael Podro has argued, makes a double (and contradictory) argument about Renaissance perspective: first, that "it has no unique authority as a way of organizing the depiction of spatial relations, that it is simply part of one particular culture and has the same status as other modes of spatial depiction developed within other cultures"; second, that it "provides an absolute viewpoint for interpreting other constructions."[11] Perspective is a figure for what we would call ideology – a historical, cultural formation that masquerades as a universal, natural code. The continuum of "homogeneous infinite space" (187) and the bipolar reduction to a single viewpoint/vanishing point at the "subjective" and "objective" ends of visual/pictorial space provide the structure or space in which Panofsky's three-dimensional iconology makes sense. Perspective is thus both a mere symptom, and the diagnostic synthesis which allows interpretation to be scientific, and symptoms to be made intelligible.[12] Panofsky comes close to saying this explicitly in the concluding remarks of the perspective essay:

> Just as it was impossible for the Middle Ages to elaborate the modern system of perspective which is based on the realization of a fixed distance between the eye and the object and thus enables the artist to build up comprehensive and consistent images of visible things; just as impossible was it for them to evolve the modern idea of history, which is based on the realization of an intellectual distance between the present and the past, and thus enables the scholar to build up comprehensive and consistent concepts of bygone periods. (28)

Panofsky's iconology takes perspective as one of its historical/theoretical objects at the same time that it regards "the modern idea of history" as itself modeled on the perspective system. The history of pictorial representation turns out to be intelligible only inside a theoretical picture that is itself supposed to be "inside" that history.

The equivalent stage in Althusser's notion of ideology is unveiled when he moves to "the formal structure of ideology" which, he informs us, "is always the same" (177). Althusser's example for the universal structure of ideology (which he says could be replaced by any number of others, "ethical, legal, political, aesthetic ideology, etc.") is "Christian religious ideology." Specifically, he invokes the theological greeting or "interpellation of individuals as subjects" by a "Unique and central Other Subject" (178), i.e. God. The relation established in this greeting is one of mirroring and subjection or dominance: "God is thus the Subject, and Moses and the innumerable subjects of God's people, the Subject's interlocutor–interpellates: his *mirrors*, his *reflections*. Were not men made *in the image* of God?" (179). The stage on which the ideological greeting of individuals occurs, then, is something like a hall of mirrors:

> We observe that the structure of all ideology, interpellating individuals as subjects in the name of a Unique and Absolute Subject is *specular*, i.e., a mirror-structure, and *doubly* specular: this mirror duplication is constitutive of ideology and ensures its functioning. Which means that all ideology is *centered*, that the Absolute Subject occupies the unique place of the Center, and interpellates around it the infinity of individuals into subjects in a double mirror-connexion such that it *subjects* the subjects to the Subject, while giving them in the Subject in which each subject can contemplate its own image . . . the guarantee that this really concerns them and Him. (180)

It should be noted that this is the moment when Althusser's ideological "scenes" give way to the possibility of a "science," a general account of "the formal structure of all ideology." It is hard to ignore the irony, however, in grounding a scientific theory of ideology in a model drawn from theology. Of course Althusser stands outside this model; he views it from afar — puts it, as Panofsky might say, "in perspective" for us. If we can see that ideology is a hall of mirrors, perhaps we can smash the mirrors and rescue the oppressed subjects from the all-powerful Subject. Or can we? Is this "formal structure of all ideology," like Panofsky's perspective, a peculiar historical formation which will pass when relations of production, reproduction, and the social relations deriving from them are transformed? Or is it (also like Panofsky's perspective) a universal, natural structure which absorbs social forms, all historical epochs in its purview? If Althusser takes the first alternative (the model as specific historical formation) he forsakes his claim to science and universality; the structure of Christian religious ideology might *not* be replicated exactly in "ethical, legal political, aesthetic ideology, etc." The "etc." might include formations quite different from the religious, and religious ideology itself would of course vary with history and culture. If Althusser takes the second alternative, and insists on the universal, scientific generality of the specular model, he becomes, like Panofsky, an iconologist who has an ideology and does not know it.

How can we stage a greeting of Panofsky and Althusser that is anything more than an impasse between science and history, a fatal mirroring of ideology and iconology? What can the French Marxist philosopher and the German Kantian art historian do for each other besides tip their hats in the street? Can they "hail" each other, as Althusser dramatizes it, from the opposite sides of a closed door, and expect any recognition, any acknowledgment other than the misrecognition of the "everyday police" suspect?

Perhaps not, except insofar as we map out the common space they occupy, which is simply the placement of the recognition scene at the center of their reflections. The main importance of *recognition* as the link between ideology and iconology is that it shifts both "sciences" from an epistemological "cognitive" ground (the knowledge of objects by subjects) to an ethical, political, and hermeneutic ground (the knowledge of subjects by subjects, perhaps even Subjects by Subjects). The categories of judgment shift from terms of cognition to terms of recognition, from epistemological categories of knowledge to social categories like "acknowledgment." Althusser reminds us that Panofsky's relation to pictures begins with a social encounter with an Other, and that iconology is a science for the absorption of that other into a homogeneous, unified "perspective." Panofsky reminds us that Althusser's local instances of ideology, the greeting of subject with subject (s/s), are all staged within a hall of mirrors constructed by the sovereign Subject (S/s), and that the ideological critique is in danger of being nothing more than another iconology. These reminders do not get us out of the problem, but they may help us to recognize it when we see it.

NOTES

ACKNOWLEDGMENTS

1 Curriculum development was supported by a grant from the Women's Integration Project at the University of Colorado, funded in part by the Ford Foundation. My initial syllabus is published as Farago, "Renaissance Art out of the Canon: Art, Gender, and Cultural Diversity, 1500–1600."

INTRODUCTION

1 Abbé Dubos, *Réflexions critiques sur la poësie et sur la peinture*, Paris, 1719; and Abbé Batteaux, *Les beaux arts réduits à un même principe*, Paris, 1746; both cited in Kristeller, "The Modern System of the Arts," 18–20.

2 On European participation in long distance trade systems before the fifteenth century, see Abu-Lughod, *Before European Hegemony*. Thanks to George Gorse for this reference.

3 Albrecht Dürer recorded in his diary entry of August 27, 1520: ". . . For I have seen therein wonders of art and have marvelled at the subtle *ingenia* of people in far-off lands. And I know not how to express what I have experienced thereby." Translated excerpt of a longer description cited in Panofsky, *Albrecht Dürer*, I, 209.

4 Burckhardt's contributions include a historical guide to the visual arts in Italy and other writings on art and architecture; see Burke, Introduction to Burckhardt, *The Civilization of the Renaissance in Italy*. White, "Burckhardt: Historical Realism as Satire," in *Metahistory*, 230–264, and R. Klein, "Burckhardt's Civilization of the Renaissance Today," in *Form and Meaning*, 25–42, are both excellent essays for art historians to consult. On Burckhardt's characterization of the Middle Ages, see Aers, "A Whisper in the Ear of Early Modernists," with references. On Burckhardt's treatment of gender, see the overviews in Migiel and Schiesari, Introduction to *Refiguring Woman*, 1–18; and M. Ferguson, Quilligan, and Vickers, Introduction to *Rewriting the Renaissance*, xiv–xxxi. The present essay does not present a comprehensive picture of historiography; for parallel developments in France, Germany, and England, see the study by Haskell, *History and Its Image*.

5 Haskell, *History and Its Images*, 368, argues that the aesthetic value attached to painting, sculpture, and architecture precluded their availability as merely historical evidence for nineteenth-century historians including Burckhardt, a circumstance that encouraged him to turn to popular culture. This hypothesis sounds reasonable, but it is difficult to test. The following argument begins from a somewhat different premise, which is that Burckhardt's book is a cultural text in its own right that helps us understand how categories of "high" and "low art" emerged around this time.

6 Burke, *The Italian Renaissance*, 8–9, takes his term from a group of social anthropologists who call themselves "ethnographers of communication."

7 Kristeller, "The Modern System of the Arts," found that the broader meaning of "fine" or "beaux arts" included music and poetry. He credits Abbé Charles Batteaux with popularizing this system of the fine arts in his influential treatise, *Les beaux arts réduits à un même principe* (1740), followed by Diderot and the Encyclopédistes, and culminating in German thought and criticism during the second half of the eighteenth century that established a philosophical theory of beauty and the arts on equal standing with the theory of truth and ethics (Kant, *Kritik der Urteilskraft*, 1790).

8 An extensive literature exists on Burckhardt's description of the state as a work of art/ *Kunstwerk* (*Civilization*, 20; *Die Kultur*, 1–2); see Ossola, "Rinascimento e Risorgimento: Punti di Interferenza," with references to the Italian scholarship; and Aers, Burke, and White (all as in n. 4). I have discussed the history of Burckhardt's metaphor in political thought with implications for emergent notions of "art" elsewhere, in "The Status of the 'State as a Work of Art.'"

9 See further discussion in my contribution to this volume, "'Vision Itself Has its History'" (Chapter 3).

10 Among the earliest contributions see Alpers, "Is Art History?"; other significant contributions include Bryson, *Vision in Painting*; Krauss, "The Story of the Eye"; Summers, "'Form,' Nineteenth-Century Metaphysics and the Problem of Art Historical Description"; Preziosi, *Rethinking Art History*; and Bryson, Holly, and Moxey, Introduction to *Visual Theory*. From an anthropological perspective, see the valuable essay by Fabian, "The Other and the Eye: Time

and the Rhetoric of Vision," in *Time and the Other*.

11 See W. Ferguson, "Humanist Views of the Renaissance." Petrarch had already emphasized the distinction between Roman history and the Christian "barbarian" era that followed it, but Leonardi Bruni, *Historiarum Florentini*, begun in 1415, created a true scheme of periodization in terms of the rise and decline of states. Bruni used Filippo Villani's essay (c. 1382) which had, even earlier, treated the decline and revival of literature and painting.

12 Vasari, *Le vite de' più eccellenti pittori, scultori, e architettori*, I, Preface; see discussion in Panofsky, *Renaissance and Renascences*, 33–35.

13 Said, *Orientalism*, 28 ff.; and see further, "Orientalism Reconsidered," in *Europe and its Others*.

14 Amin, *Eurocentrism*, vii.

15 According to Amin, a transnational European consciousness postdates 1945.

16 Amin, *Eurocentrism*, ix, and see further, 85–117. One of the most contentious arenas of critical debate has been generated in response to the problematic study by Bernal, *Black Athena*, which is most valuable for its critique of nineteenth-century historiography; see "The Challenge of Black Athena," special issue of *Arethusa* 8:1 (Fall 1989). Thanks to Melanie McHugh for this reference.

17 Maxime Rodinson, *Europe and the Mystique of Islam*, points to the difference between the medieval European vision of Islam and the appearance in Europe of a theory of world history accompanied by a global political project.

18 *The Early Years of Art History in the United States* is an important contribution to our knowledge of university curricula and the individual scholars who developed them. Current interdisciplinary interest in the history of "primitivism" is part of the same trend to historicize "modernism" by reconstructing its broader social context; see, for example, Torgovnick, *Gone Primitive*; Hiller, ed., *The Myth of Primitivism*. Scholarship on the institutionalization of the academic disciplines in the nineteenth century during the era of emerging nationalism is extensive, but see the foundational study by Ringer, *The Decline of the German Mandarins*.

19 For example, see Hanke, *Aristotle and the American Indians*; Elliott, *The Old World and the New 1492–1650*; O'Gorman, *The Invention of America*; Pagden, *European Encounters with the New World*; and Richard Trexler, *Church and Community*.

20 See *Knowledges. Historical and Critical Studies in Disciplinarity*, especially Preziosi, "Seeing through Art History," 215–231.

21 See n. 4 and for an art historian's perspective, see Andrée Hayum, "The Renaissance as a Historical Concept."

22 Gates, Introduction to *"Race", Writing, and Difference*. For an excellent critical study of racial theory which documents numerous intersections with aesthetic theory that deserve further investigation, see Stepan, *The Idea of Race in Science*. See also, my contribution to the present volume (Chapter 3).

23 *Women, "Race," and Writing* is the first major study to address problems related to the later notion of "race" and to conceive of research programs.

24 Anderson, *Imagined Communities*, xiv.

25 Kelly, "The Doubled Vision of Feminist Theory."

26 Exhibitions include: Kenseth, ed., *The Age of the Marvelous*; Laurencich-Minelli, et al., *Bologna e Il Mondo Nuovo*; Washington, D.C., National Gallery, *Circa 1492: Art in the Age of Exploration*; Small with Jaffe, *1492: What Is It Like to Be Discovered?*; New York Historical Society, *Imagining the New World: Columbian Iconography* (no catalog); Danforth, *Encountering the New World 1493 to 1800*; New York, Metropolitan Museum, *Mexico: Splendors of Thirty Centuries*; Doggett, et al., ed., *New World of Wonders*.

27 Exhibition planners who wish to dispel entrenched narrratives must actively discourage them and propose alternatives, which is not an easy task. What might be called the museum effect has been discussed by Alpers, "The Museum as a Way of Seeing," and others in *Exhibiting Cultures*. See also, Hooper-Greenhill, *Museums and the Shaping of Knowledge*.

28 Schama is a Europeanist historian of seventeenth-century Dutch culture, the French Revolution, and other areas. Bhabha is a leading theorist of colonial discourse analysis, whose ideas are discussed later in this Introduction.

29 H. Bhabha, "Double Visions."

30 S. Schama, "They All Laughed at Christopher Columbus," 33.

31 *Ibid.*, 40.

32 Kuhn, *The Structure of Scientific Revolutions*, 90. On the historian's ability to discover the determination of shared scientific paradigms and the rules that are associated with them, see 43 ff.

33 See, on the medieval period, Ovitt, *The Restoration of Perfection*; and Cahn, *Masterpieces*. On the Renaissance, see Kristeller, "Modern Systems of the Arts"; Farago, *Leonardo da Vinci's "Paragone."*

34 On the neo-Aristotelian tradition of the internal senses and the literature on art, see Summers, *The Judgment of Sense*, whose argument *in nuce* is that "the development of art based on point of view at the dawn of the modern period was deeply bound up with the Aristotelian notion

that the human soul, from sensation upward, is suited to its world, and with the further notion that the beautiful itself is conformity to human sense before it is evidence of transcendental value" (citing page 2).

35 See Gilbert, *Renaissance Concepts of Method*. "Art" could also refer to a craftsman's guild; see Epstein, *Wage Labor & Guilds in Medieval Europe*.

36 Blier, "Imaging Otherness in Ivory," especially 390–391, with further evidence that the ornament of these ivories derives from textile patterns that carried cosmic significance, often concerning the land of the dead. For the object reproduced here, see Bassani and Fagg, *Africa and the Renaissance: Art in Ivory*, cat. n. 31. I thank Suzanne Blier for consulting with me on the condition of this object. The term "salt-cellar" is of nineteenth-century origin, according to Blier, 390.

37 On the Renaissance concept of decorum as applied to painting, see R. W. Lee, "Ut pictura poesis"; and Baxandall, *Giotto and the Orators*.

38 The principal evidence for attributing these views to Michelangelo (during the 1520s and 1530s, in connection with designs for the Laurentian Library) is Vincenzo Danti's *Il Primo Libro del Trattato delle perfette proporzioni* (Florence, 1567), in which Danti associates *grotteschi* with chimeras, which are "new compounds and things that seem sometimes almost invented by art itself." See Summers, "Michelangelo on Architecture," 150; on Renaissance views in connection with ancient painting, see Dacos, *La Découverte de la Domus Aurea*, 121–135.

39 Danti, in *Trattati d'arte*, ed. Barocchi, I, 235; citing the English translation in Summers, "Michelangelo on Architecture," 150. Danti grafted a new scientific vocabulary on to a longstanding conception of the artistic license that painters share with poets: Cennino Cennini and Leonardo da Vinci inverted Horatian critical ideals in very similar terms when they wrote about artistic invention as a process of the imagination which enables the artist to combine different natural elements into novel, fantastic wholes. Vitruvius, *De architectura*, Bk. 5.5.2, and Horace, *Ars Poetica*, are the two main ancient sources of Renaissance discussions of the decorum of ornament; see further, Pollitt, *The Ancient View of Greek Art*, Introduction and *passim*; and Summers, *Michelangelo and the Language of Art*, 455, 496–497. The ancient sources of "exoticism" have recently been a focus of attention in two major exhibitions: see the review by Frederick Bohrer, of *Europa und der Orient, 800–1900* (1989) and *Exotische Welten, Europäische Phantasien* (1987).

40 December 5, 1563; see *Canons and Decrees of the Council of Trent*, ed. Schroeder, 216.

41 Pagden, *European Encounters with the New World*, 78, calls attention to similar rhetorical strategies in the expository writing of both Columbus and Bartholomé de Las Casas, whose prose style Pagden associates with Augustinian tradition and legal methods for presenting direct experience.

42 Even theorists as different from each other as the Neapolitan artist–archeologist Pirro Ligorio and the Milanese painter-turned-theorist Giovan Paolo Lomazzo agreed that *grotteschi* and other products of the imagination serve a serious didactic function, which was to signify allegorically. In the 1570s, Pirro Ligorio wrote at great length about *grotteschi*, arguing for their allegorical significance while condemning "errors against nature" in terms shaped by the ecclesiastical writer Gilio da Fabriano (see following note). Similar attempts to justify *grotteschi* can be heard in the arguments of Lomazzo, *Trattato dell'arte de la pittura*, 1584, 369, who compared *grotteschi* to emblems or *imprese*—presumably to defend the artist's *concetti* by comparing them to erudite humanistic play. Lomazzo also wrote a book called *I Grotteschi* (Milan, 1587), in keeping with this definition. See Coffin, "Pirro Ligorio on the Nobility of the Arts"; on Lomazzo, see Summers, *Michelangelo and the Language of Art*, 496–497; and Ossola, *Autunno del Rinascimento*, 198–209.

43 On Aldrovandi's collection and scientific illustration, see Laurencich-Minelli, "Museography and Ethnographical Collections in Bologna during the Sixteenth and Seventeenth Centuries," in *The Origins of Museums*, and *Bologna e il Mondo Nuovo*; and Olmi, *Inventario del Mondo*, 21–161. Paleotti's views are often equated with those of his unbending contemporary Gilio da Fabriano, author of a 1564 treatise to correct the abuses of painters and best remembered for his objections to Michelangelo's late paintings. I will argue that Paleotti was much more openminded than Gilio, despite his continuing concern with the same issues of decorum and naturalness as his predecessor.

44 For the texts, see Paleotti, *Discorso intorno alle imagini sacre e profane, diviso in cinque libri*, Bologna, 1582, books 1–2 reprinted in *Trattati d'arte*, ed. Barocchi, II: 117–509. Aldrovandi's correspondence with Paleotti extends over many years. His 1582 letter about *grotteschi* is published in *Trattati d'arte*, II: 512–517. Aldrovandi also wrote a treatise on painting, entitled *Modo di esprimere per la pittura tutte le cose dell'universo mondo, e Narrazione di tutti i generi*

principali delle cose na[tura]li et artificiali che ponno cadere sotto la pittura, dated November 1582, published in *Scritti d'arte*, ed. Barocchi, IV; 923–930 and related to these discussions.

45 Remarkably for an ecclesiastical writer defending the Tridentine Decree on sacred images, Paleotti admitted that painters *should* be allowed to represent novel things that seem to lie outside the order of nature – such as "monsters of the sea and land and other places" – as long as they actually do exist; Paleotti, in *Trattati d'arte*, ed. Barocchi, II: 425; see also 382–389. This position is also much more tolerant of *grotteschi* than that adopted by Cardinal Carlo Borromeo (see *Trattati d'arte* III: 44). The central point in these considerations was the distinction between the delusions of a dissolute person and the true visions of a prophet. Thomas Aquinas addressed the question by differentiating between the eternal substance of an object and its accidental, external appearance: the mutation in appearance (of the host) was external to the visionary's eyes, but caused by the imagination of a dissolute person who mistook the image for the thing itself, thus was captivated by demonic illusions (*Summa theologica* 3.76.8). The same arguments and sources were used in Spanish America; see MacCormack, "Calderás *La Aurora en Copacabang*." Some of the essays in the present volume are concerned with the complex effects of these assumptions in Latin America; see especially the contributions by Watts (Chapter 7), Cummins (Chapter 8), Quiñones Keber (Chapter 11), and Klein (Chapter 12). In the same period, chivalric romances and their successors in travel literature presented the same difficult problem of distinguishing between fantasy worlds and real places; see Pagden, *European Encounters with the New World*, 64; and further, Campbell, *Witness and the Other World*; Pratt, *Imperial Eyes*.

46 Aldrovandi, in *Trattati d'arte*, ed. Barocchi, II: 513, emphasis mine. The principles guiding artistic invention, not the utility of scientific illustration *per se*, was the issue at stake, as Aldrovandi's closing remarks on *grotteschi* make clear.

47 Marian Hobson, *The Object of Art. The Theory of Illusion in Eighteenth-Century France*, vii, makes an apt distinction between the history of European perceptions of art and the history of conceptions of this perception. The latter is concerned primarily with the critical literature of art, but ultimately the two subjects are inseparable. The phrase "*perception* of art" is itself deeply invested in Christian–classical concepts, as this volume of essays suggests at many junctures.

48 Pagden, *European Encounters with the New World*,

21.

49 Citing Bhabha, "Signs Taken for Wonders," 156.

50 Bhabha, "Signs Taken for Wonders," 161.

51 Bhabha, "Of Mimicry and man."

52 For an excellent overview, see Stepan, *The Idea of Race in Science*, 93–110, and *passim*; and Stocking, *Race, Culture, and Evolution*, especially 45–48. For a similar critique of Bhabha's ahistorical use of the concept of fetishism, see Young, *White Mythologies*, especially 143–144. Thanks to Dana Leibsohn for bringing this excellent study to my attention.

53 Hybridity or intermixture, according to Boas's empirical study of American Indian populations in the Northwest (1894), had "a favorable effect upon the race" in terms of its physical characteristics and fertility, as cited by Stocking, *Race, Culture, and Evolution*, 172.

54 For other criticisms of Bhabha's oversimplification of colonial authority, see JanMohamed, "The Economy of Manichean Allegory"; and Parry, "Problems in Current Theories of Colonial Discourse".

55 Clifford, "On Ethnographic Allegory," 98–121, in *Writing Culture*.

56 Greenblatt, *Marvelous Possessions*, 4.

57 Pratt, *Imperial Eyes*, 6, coins the term "contact zone" to refer to "the space of colonial encounters, the space in which peoples geographically and historically separated come into contact with each other and establish ongoing relations, usually involving conditions of coercion, radical inequality, and intractable conflict."

58 Aristotle, *De anima*, is the foundational text, but the commentary tradition is a complex and synthetic one; see Bundy, *The Theory of Imagination in Classical and Medieval Thought*; Summers, *Judgment of Sense*; Pagden, *The Fall of Natural Man*; Zapalac, "*In His Image and Likeness*."

59 See n. 1.

60 Eco, *Limits of Interpretation*, 34–54. Eco makes the suggestive remark that the nature of any communicative system can be found in the "roots of artistic openness" (page 54), but the main point of his discussion, which is framed as a critique of Peircian theory of unlimited semiosis and Derrida's position that nothing exists outside the text, is that the act of indication links signs to the extra-linguistic or extra-semiotic world, so that agreement about semiosis is produced outside semiosis. In Eco's reading, the idea of community is the intersubjective reality that semiosis builds up. Eagleton, *Ideology of the Aesthetic*, 405, offers a critique of Jürgen Habermas's theory of communicative action that could be leveled against other semiotic attempts, such as Eco's, to theorize consensus at the collective level. Eagleton

regards Habermas's ideal speech community as an updated version of Kant's community of aesthetic judgment, noting that the Frankfurt School's attempt to theorize a universal pragmatics has been criticized most forcefully by postcolonial critics (see the summary of controversy over universal pragmatics in Benhabib, *Critique, Norm, and Utopia*), who question how far Habermas's theory goes to acknowledge the individual particularities of the community. A systematic semiotic critique of discursive practices based on the lingering assumption that cultures are discrete would be a welcome addition to current discussions.

61 Derrida, *Truth in Painting*, 7–8.

I   THE PATHOS OF DISTANCE

1 Lévi-Strauss, *Tristes tropiques*, 31. This and all subsequent translations, unless otherwise specified, are my own.

2 I refer to the papers read by R. S. Nelson, A. J. Wharton, A. Taylor, and B. Zeitler at the annual meeting of the College Art Association at Chicago in February 1992, in a session that had as its common theme the modern construction of Byzantium and its chronological and geographical neighbors as "the Orientalist Other." See the *Abstracts and Program Statements* of this meeting, 174–176. While I suggest that exactly the opposite is the case, I do not see my contribution as in conflict with these arguments. The paradox dissolves when we seek, in the words of one of the participants, to understand the contexts in which Byzantine art was received by western audiences. On the larger issue of the various sorts of Orientalism in western responses to Byzantine culture, see Cameron, *Use and Abuse*, 3–31.

3 Cennini, *Handbook*, 2.

4 Cf. Cutler, "*La questione Bizantine.*"

5 Van Marle, *Development* 1, 296, where it is briefly mentioned. The first extended discussion was by Lasareff, "Duccio," 159–160, who declared it to be "Byzantine, painted on Italian soil."

6 *Decline and Fall*, chap. 49, 5, n. 14.

7 Weiss, *Pisanello's Medallion*.

8 Raby, *Oriental Mode*, especially 18 and nn. 4–7.

9 Setton, "Byzantine Background," 70.

10 Šučenko, "Intellectual Repercussions," 291, cited by Setton.

11 Mercati, *Ultimi contributi*, 24–26.

12 Pertusi, *La Caduta* and *Testi inediti*.

13 Cod. Vat. lat. 1801: "hunc Thucydidis codicem, qualis nullis, ut opinor, unquam apud ipsos grecos vel scriptus vel ornatus est

magnificentius, idem ego Laurentius iussu sanctissimi domini nostri Nicolai divina providentia pape Quinti recognovi, cum ipso Ioanne, qui eum tam egregie scripsit." I owe this reference to the kindness of Anthony Grafton.

14 Pertusi, *Testi inediti*, p. 75.

15 M.-D. Germain in *Byzance*, no. 261.

16 B. Mondrain in *Byzance*, no. 351.

17 At least in his best-known report on the Turkish sack (Pertusi, *La Caduta*, 2), Piccolomini gives no estimate of the number of books destroyed.

18 Pertusi, *La Caduta* 2, 54.

19 Condivi, *Life*, 37. For a slightly earlier project of 1502–03, involving a bridge to be built by Leonardo da Vinci for Bayezid II, see Babinger, *Briefschaften*, 120–135 and figs. 21–23.

20 Marlier, *Pierre Coeck*, 72.

21 "Historika neoterôn Hellênôn", Pertusi, *Storiografia*, 12.

22 Pertusi, *Storiografia*, 40.

23 For the literature on this event, see Pertusi, *Storiografia*, 64 n. 162; see now Jacoff, *Horses of San Marco*.

24 Rannusio, *Della guerra*.

25 Rannusio, *Della guerra*, plates V–VII; Pertusi, *Storiografia*, plates IV–VI.

26 Pertusi, *Storiografia*, 72.

27 Still most conveniently represented in Clark, *Piero*, plates 31–97.

28 For the program, see Noack, "Kunstpflege," 196–197.

29 While opposing icons and relics, Constantine V vigorously defended the cult of the True Cross. See Hollingsworth in the *Oxford Dictionary of Byzantium*, 501.

30 Leo Allatios (Leone Allacci), *De ecclesiae occidentalis atque orientalis perpetua consensione*. Cologne, 1648.

31 Allatios, *Newer Temples*.

32 For this state-supported venture, see Pertusi, *Storiografia*, 82–93.

33 Of which the best-known issue is perhaps Gyllius, *Topographia*.

34 Pertusi, *Storiografia*, 80.

35 In *Patrologia graeca*, ed. J.-P. Migne, vol. 86, part 1: cols. 1163–1185.

36 Jakob Bidermann, S. J., *Comico-tragoedia de Belisario duce Christiano, ab summa gloriae felicitate in extreme infortuni ludibrio prolapso*.

37 For these see Pertusi, *Storiografia*, 96–98, who claims that the tale of Belisarius is to be found in the *Patria*, largely a collection of Byzantine legends first translated in 1596. I do not find the story of the blinded Belisarius in this text. It recurs, however, in post-Byzantine popular literature, on which see Knös, "Bélisaire."

38 The picture was preserved in the collection of

the Duke of Leuchtenburg in Berlin until at least 1912. See n. 39.

39 Lenormont, *François Gérard*, 39. Tastes change: in 1912, when the canvas formed part of an exhibition in St Petersburg, F. Monod (in the *Gazette des Beaux-Arts*, 4th ser., 7 [1912], 197) described it as an "énorme et détestable pensum juvenile commis avec une application religieuse."

40 I do not know if there were later performances of the opera *L'Eraclio* which, with the libretto of Nicola Berengani and music by Pietro Andrea Ziani, was a *succès fou* in the late seventeenth century (performed at Venice 1671, Milan 1678, Munich 1690, and Bologna 1692), but some might dearly wish for its revival.

41 Cited by Johnson, *Paintings*, 99.

42 Thus Bayet, *L'Art byzantin*, 317. Similar recipes were formulated by Charles Diehl and Gabriel Millet.

43 Riegl, *Stilfragen*. I cite the recent translation by Evelyn Kain, *Problems of Style*, 240. A broader report on nineteenth-century attitudes is unnecessary here, given the penetrating account by Spieser, "Hellénisme."

44 *Byzantine Art an European Art*.

45 See Barber, "Art and Worship," 7, 12.

46 Weitzmann, *Sinai Icons*, 93.

47 J. Durand in *Byzance*, no. 175: "Le rythme majestueux de la mise en scène, l'élégance des attitudes et le canon classique des personnages évoque ceux des plus beaux ivoires du 'groupe Romanos' [et] relèvent aussi de l'esprit antiquisant de la Renaissance macédonienne."

48 Lemerle, *Cinq études*, 251.

49 Cutler and Oikonomides, "An Imperial Byzantine Casket."

50 Cutler, *Aristocratic Psalters*, figs. 245, 250.

51 The nature and degree of change in Byzantine culture both *vis à vis* antiquity and in its own development have been central issues in recent scholarship. See, e.g., Kazhdan and Cutler, "Continuity," and Speck, "Die Byzantiner."

52 Thus the ideas of John of Damascus, conveniently available in translation in Mango, *Art*, 169–172; the standard edition of John's works is his *Schriften*, ed. B. Kotter, 5 vols., Berlin 1969–1988. The less familiar argumentation of Nikephoros, Patriarch of Constantinople (806–815), is analyzed by Barber, "The Body within the Frame," to which I am indebted for the observation that immediately follows.

53 The characterization of visual works as "realistic," found frequently in Byzantine documents, has recently come to be understood as a description of the beholder's response rather than as that of the work's style of representation. For this important insight, see James and Webb, "Ekphrasis and Art."

54 Gurevich, *Historical Anthropology*, 8. The restricted gender is in the original.

55 *Historical Anthropology*, 55.

56 *Theophanes Continuatus*, trans. Mango, *Art*, 160.

57 See the summary by M. Martiniani-Reber in *Byzance*, 372–373 and, at fig. 2 in her essay, a reproduction of the inscription on a silk in Aachen testifying to its Byzantine origin.

58 For a selection, see *Byzance*, nos. 101–105, 128–130, 132, 133, 280–289.

59 Corrigan, *Visual Polemics*, 78–103.

60 *Theophanes Continuatus*, 185–191.

61 For the various editions of the *Kitâb al-Hiyal*, see al-Jazari, *Book of Knowledge*, and, for Byzantine practice, Brett, "Automata."

62 Cameron, "*Book of Ceremonies*," 129.

63 Ettinghausen, *Peinture arabe*, 61, and, on the problem of such frontispieces, 64–66.

64 Cutler, *Aristocratic Psalters*, passim.

65 Dodd, "The Image of the Word."

66 The only adequate treatment is Hutter, *Corpus* I, no. 39.

67 See n. 44 above.

2 ITALIAN SCULPTORS AND SCULPTURE OUTSIDE OF ITALY

1 This paper combines two lectures, "The Renaissance and Art Outside of Italy: Trends and Possibilities of Interpretation," Annual Meeting, Renaissance Society of America, Duke University, Durham, N.C., 13 April, 1991; "Italian Sculptors and Sculpture in (Central) Europe: Problems and Possiblities of Reception," International Conference on Italian Sculpture and Sculptors North of the Alps, 1500–1800, International Research and Exchanges Board and the Polish Academy of Sciences, 1991. A report on the second conference was published by Jerzy Kowałczyk, "Konferencja polsko-amerykanská Rzeźba i rzeźbiarźe włoscy na pólnoc od Alpi 1500–1800," *Biuletyn Historii Sztuki* 54, n. 1 (1992), 107–110. A Polish translation of the second paper, as delivered, may also appear in *Biuletyn Historii Szluki*.

2 The spread of humanism, and of Renaissance culture in Europe, has been the subject of two recent collections: Goodman and MacKay, ed., *The Impact of Humanism on Western Europe* and Porter and Teich, *The Renaissance in National Context*, which provide a background for the discussion here. The reference to Manila applies of course to the Spanish (particularly Jesuit) presence there; in general the extra-European experience of the Renaissance merits consideration.

3   Valadés, *Rhetorica Christiana* (1579) is now available in reprint with a Spanish translation, *Rétorica cristiana*. Skarina is most accessible in a book by Chamiarytski, *Francisk Skarina*; see also more completely *Frantsysk Skaryna i iaho Chas. Entsyklapedychny Davednik*.

4   Good photographs of Goa and Macao (Macau) are available in Teague, *In The Wake of the Portuguese Navigators*. For Bitti, see in particular de Mesa and Gisbert, *Bernardo Bitti*, with further references; for Quito, Vargas, *Historia del Arte Ecuatoriano*.

5   I am well aware that Italy lacked a coherent identity before its unification in the nineteenth century, that Italians thought of themselves in different terms, according to regional distinctions, and that these distinctions were also thought to pertain to matters of style. It also seems to be the case that some of these differences were perceived outside Italy, in that citizens of various Italian centers received different characterizations. Nevertheless, Italy and Italians also stood for something quite distinctive. Popular stereotypes, as well as contrasting Venetians with Romans, also portrayed Italians in a more general way (for this subject, see Hale, *The Civilization of Europe in the Renaissance*, 51 ff.). More important, the Italianate was perceived, especially in Central Europe, as the *welsch*: *Welschlandt* meant Italy, without any distinction being made between the individual parts of the peninsula. A similar problem exists between various parts of Germany before its unification in the nineteenth century, but this did not stop Germans from the fifteenth century on from distinguishing between the *welsch* and the *deutsch* (for which see Baxandall, *The Limewood Sculptors of Renaissance Germany*). When in the seventeenth century Prince Karl Eusebius of Liechtenstein said that the architecture of *Welschlandt* was to be emulated (see Fleischer, ed.), he meant Italy in general, and other Central European authors spoke similarly. Thus, even if Italian speakers could make distinctions between art in various parts of the land, it seems legitimate to treat attitudes towards art and artists from the peninsula without further qualifications: the operative distinction seems to be the general Italianate quality.

6   For more on this point, see my "What is 'New' about the 'New Art History'?" 515–520.

7   For an example of a textbook, see Snyder, *Northern Renaissance Art*. For a "newer" approach, see Koerner, *The Moment of Self-Portraiture in German Renaissance Art*.

8   These paragraphs restate some of the arguments advanced in my "Introduction," *Art and Architecture in Central Europe 1550–1620*. See also *Drawings from the Holy Roman Empire*, 4–8.

9   See for example Kozakiewiczowa, *Rzezba XVI Wieku w Polsce*.

10 Vasari, *Le Vite*, ed. Milanesi, 3: 361. For this work by Verrocchio, see the references in Balogh, *Művészet Mátyás Király Udvarában*, 1: 513 ff.

11 The critique of E. H. Gombrich, "In Search of Cultural History," reprinted in *Ideals and Idols*, 24–59, is pertinent here. For Herder see also Berlin, "Herder and the Enlightenment," in *Vico and Herder*, 143 ff.

12 For example, Hermanin, *Gli artisti in Germania*, dated "Anno XII E. F."

13 In Morpurgo, *L'opera del aenio Italiano all'estero*.

14 I refer here to the otherwise quite useful volumes *Arte e artisti dei laghi lombardi*. A similar series is sponsored by the neighboring canton of Ticino, Switzerland, e.g. Karpowicz, *Artisti Ticinesi in Polonia nel '600*, and *Artisti Ticinesi in Polonia nel '500*.

15 As far as Italian sculpture and sculptors outside of Italy are concerned, Białostocki's most comprehensive consideration of the theme is found in his important *The Art of the Renaissance in Eastern Europe*, from which the quotation is taken (page 1). The problems engaged him in many papers, however, from at least the time of his classic essay on "Mannerism and the Vernacular in Polish Art." See also "Renaissance Sculpture in Poland and its European Context: Some Selected Problems."

16 Compare *The Art of the Renaissance in Eastern Europe*.

17 These are discussed for example in Brown, "Painting and History in Renaissance Venice" and, more generally, *eadem*, *Venetian Narrative Painting in the Age of Carpaccio*.

18 See my "The Problem of Northern 'Mannerism': A Critical Review."

19 As is indicated most comprehensively by *Arte e Artisti dei Laghi Lombardi*, but there are many other artists from other regions in northern Italy who worked beyond the Alps. In this essay my use of the word "vernacular" picks up on Jan Białostocki's introduction of the term, appearing first in "Mannerism and the Vernacular." Similarly, my use of "international Italianate" is employed in contrast with this notion, to make a distinction with regional styles. The conception of "international" is employed to indicate a broader stylistic movement, such as was implied by "mannerism"; "Italianate" indicates, in general, art and artists originating in the peninsula, in most instances having some connection to a classicizing style, whatever its derivation or deformation.

20 Husarski, *Attyka polska i jej wpływ na kraje sąsiedie*, and Balšánek, *Štíty a motivy attikové v éské renaissance*.

21 Białostocki, "Mannerism and 'Vernacular.'"
22 Białostocki, "Some Values of Artistic Periphery," tacitly made a similar comparison between Latin American and eastern European art, although not on this point.
23 See Białostocki, *The Art of the Renaissance in Eastern Europe*, 86, 88, and "Renaissance Sculpture in Poland," 287; again Husarski, *Kamienice renesansowe w Kaimierzu Dolnym*, provides the lead for this approach.
24 See Summerson, *Architecture in Britain*, 28, 33–37, with notes.
25 Atticas resembling so-called Polish parapets are also found independently of the impact of Polish artisans in Hungary (Slovakia), Austria, and Germany; sgraffito decoration and gables that are said to mark an indigenous Bohemian Renaissance are likewise found elsewhere, as in Germany, or Austria. The issues in regard to central Europe are discussed in my review of Białostocki, *The Art of the Renaissance in Eastern Europe*. See also my *Court, Cloister and City*.
26 Although he did not accept its consequences, in a 1975 lecture "Rinascimento Polacco and Rinascimento Europeo", published in *Polonia–Italia. Relazioni Artistiche*, where he otherwise repeated several of the themes of his other papers on the question, Białostocki did introduce this idea.
27 See for example Glick and Pi-Sunyer, "Acculturation as an Explanatory Concept in Spanish History." This particular diffusionist model has been consciously adapted to a discussion of Spanish painting of the sixteenth and seventeenth centuries in a recent synthesis by Brown, *The Golden Age of Painting in Spain*, vii.
28 Burke, *The Renaissance*, 27.
29 For Giovanni Dalmata, see Balogh, *A Művészet Mátyás Király*, 489–493, and *eadem, Die Anfänge der Renaissance in Ungarn*, 184–187, with references to earlier literature, Röll . . . *Giovanni Dalmata*.
30 For the different applications of reception history and theory in literature in relation to art history, see my "Reception Theory."
31 Burke, *The Renaissance*, 28.
32 In *Islands of History*.
33 Białostocki, *The Art of the Renaissance in Eastern Europe*, 11.
34 Łozinski, *Grobowe Kaplice kopułowe w Polsce 1520–1620*. There are numerous articles and studies by Helena and Stefan Kozakiewicz on this subject: most accessible is *Renesans w Polsce* (also available in other languages).
35 Their contributions are most accessible in *Matthias Corvinus und die Renaissance in Ungarn*; Balogh's *summa* is *Die Anfänge der Renaissance in Ungarn*.

36 "um allhier einige Gebaude in antiker Weise zu machen, welche Antiken man jetzt für die höchste Kunst erachte, von welcher Kunst man aber hier in der Stadt nichts finde." Quoted in Zaske and Zaske, *Kunst in Hansestädten*, 88.
37 See E. H. Gombrich, "The Style *all'antica*: Imitation and Assimilation."
38 "Dürers Stellung zur Antike," trans. in *Meaning in the Visual Arts*, 236–294.
39 See Gutfleisch and Menzhausen, "'How a Kunstkammer should be Formed': Gabriel Kaltemarckt's advice to Christian I of Saxony."
40 See *The Splendor of Dresden*, 85, no. 47, ill.
41 See for example *Liechtenstein. The Princely Collections*, nos. 45, 55–62.
42 Grafton and Jardine, *From Humanism to the Humanities*.
43 A convenient overview of the Hungarian situation is available in essays by Leslie S. Domonkos, "Bildung und Wissenschaft," and Peter Kulcsár, "Der Humanismus in Ungarn," in *Matthias Corvinus und die Renaissance in Ungarn*, 55–72.
44 "Ma l'usanza de le statue fu la piu egregia di tutte, conciosia ch'elle sono buone per adornare gli edificii sacri, ed i secolari, ed i pubblici ed i privati; e serbano con loro una rimembranza maravigliosa e degli uomini e de le cose." The translation is taken from Alberti, *On the Art of Building in Ten Books*, 240.
45 "Regiam construis idem longe magnificentissimam forumque tuum simulachris omne genus vel aeneis vel marmoreis exornas"; quoted in Balogh, *Die Anfänge der Renaissance in Ungarn*, 163.
46 For another example of the possible application of this principle in central Europe, see my "The Eloquent Artist: Towards an Understanding of the Stylistics of Painting at the Court of Rudolf II." The argument is extended in *Court, Cloister and City*.
47 This subject is the topic of continuing research by Dorothea Diemer, and was discussed by her in a presentation at the Polish–American conference, cited in n. 1.
48 "Das Gypser Handwerk ist bei uns in Deutschland ein neu Handwerk, das die Italiaener um 1540 ins Land gebracht haben," quoted by Karling, "Les Stucateurs Italiens en Suède," 291.
49 The most convenient place to find all these works discussed is Hitchcock, *German Renaissance Architecture*; see also *Arte e Artisti dei Laghi Lombardi*.
50 Especially in "Renaissance Sculpture in Poland."
51 These subjects are discussed at greater length in *Court, City and Cloister*.
52 I have omitted mentioning the notion of an

economic basis to social life, not because I do not regard it as important, but because I think it does not explain much about why Italians went north, nor where, nor what they were required to do. Of course Italians looking for work might have gone to places where they could find it, if they could not find employment at home. But sculpture can also be situated in a wider context of patron–client relationships. Spending money on the arts, and patronizing religious foundations, has a long history. The thesis of cultural expenditure thus does not in itself explain why the visual arts in particular should have become an outlet for consumption from the fifteenth century, nor why Italian sculpture and sculptors in particular should have been favored. Other elements of cultural mediation were clearly also at play.

53 Some of the rare surviving sculpture from the period in Russia not only indicates the kind of work that was done, but what Italians would have been up against: see *Gates of Mystery. The Art of Holy Russia*, no. 42, 157–159; the essays in this catalogue should also be consulted for background to the subject broached here.

3 "Race," Nation, and Renaissance Art History

The following remarks will be developed in a longer study, "Art as Institution: A History of the Category 'Visual Art'". Thanks to all my contributors and colleagues, mentioned by name in the general Acknowledgments to this volume, to Michael Ann Holly for discussing Burckhardt scholarship with me, and to responsive audiences at the New York Institute of the Fine Arts (March 11, 1994) and the Department of Art History at the University of California at Los Angeles (May 2, 1994). Elizabeth Warren-Turnage and Clarence Sheffield helped me chart unfamiliar terrain with their masters' theses on Semper and Riegl, respectively, cited in the following notes. A Faculty Fellowship from the University of Colorado enabled me to write this essay.

1 A revisionist generation of art historian/theorists is adopting relativistic approaches to the nature of signification that have been developed in structural linguistics, cultural anthropology, and literary studies. Some would transfer to our understanding of images a semiotic view of language as a signifying system based on convention; see Bal and Bryson, "Semiotics and Art History"; Bryson, Holly, and Moxey, Introduction, *Visual Theory*; Moxey, "The Politics of Iconology." Others reject the assumption that the paradigm of

language can adequately account for our understanding of images; see Summers, "Real Metaphor"; Gombrich, "On Physiognomic Perception"; Kubler, *Esthetic Recognition of Ancient Amerindian Art*.

2 Landauer, "Erwin Panofsky and the Renascence of the Renaissance."

3 I borrow the word "transnational" from processual anthropology, where the term was first proposed in the 1940s; see Schiller, Basch, and Blanc-Szanton, "Transnationalism." Thanks to Teresa Wilkins for this reference.

4 "It is evident that the general political uncertainty in Italy during the fourteenth and fifteenth centuries was of a kind to excite in the better spirits of the time a patriotic disgust and opposition. Dante and Petrarch, in their day, proclaimed loudly a common Italy, the object of the highest efforts of all her children. It may be objected that this was only the enthusiasm of a few highly instructed men, in which the mass of people had no share; but it can hardly have been otherwise even in Germany, although in name at least that country was united and recognized in the emperor one supreme head." (Burckhardt, *Civilization of the Renaissance*, 96; *Kultur*, 65). As the rest of the passage makes clear, Burckhardt's comparison is between the expression of national unity manifested through its cultural productions and institutionalized nationhood: "The first patriotic utterances of German literature . . . read like an echo of Italian declamations. And yet, as a matter of fact, Germany had been long a nation in a truer sense than Italy ever was since the Roman days. France owes the consciousness of its national unity mainly to its conflicts with the English, and Spain has never permanently succeeded in absorbing Portugal, closely related as the two countries are. For Italy, the existence of the ecclesiastical state, and the conditions under which alone it could continue, were a permanent obstacle to national unity, an obstacle whose removal seemed hopeless."

5 Italian historical scholarship is a notable exception, although its concerns have been limited to Italian national history; see the excellent essay by Ossola, "Rinascimento e Risorgimento: punti di interferenza."

6 Burckhardt, *Civilization*, 20.

7 Holly, "Past Looking," and "Cultural History as a Work of Art." Writing in the vein of Hayden White's *Metahistory*, Holly argues that works of art of the period compositionally prefigure their own historiographic response – representational practices encoded in works of art continue to be encoded in their commentaries ("Past Looking," 38).

8 Hobbes, *Leviathan*, 1651, 81–82, cited by Caygill, *Art of Judgement*, 19: when Hobbes compared the productive legislation which "makes" a commonwealth with God's creation of the world, the underlying paradigm of the work of art connoted an illusory unity like anamorphic art, a metaphor fueled by Hobbes's interest in optics (Caygill, 19–22). Caygill, 11–18, argues that discussions of the difficulties of judging beauty grounded in Scholastic Aristotelianism have, from Pico della Mirandola to Kant, pointed to the difficulties of judgment in general. Caygill, 37 ff., argues that distinctly British and German traditions of political thought developed out of this Thomistic discourse which was *also* directed to the judgment of beauty. Further study of the range of these discussions of the state as a work of art are needed: was the organization of the "work" identified with the new empirical approach to science?

9 Locke, *An Essay Concerning Human Understanding*, defined the two mainsprings of cognitive activity as sensation and "reflection," which combines and abstracts the contents of the mind to produce its "compositions" or ordered assemblages of knowledge. "Reflection" is the "Fountain, from which experience furnisheth the Understanding with Ideas, [which] is the Perception of the Operations of our own Minds within us" (Locke, *Essay*, II, i, §4; cited by Norton, *Herder's Aesthetics and the European Enlightenment*, 19, a study on which the following summary is substantially based). Descartes, *Discourse on Method*, 1637, provided the terms of this debate and Kant laid the foundation for the modern assumption that art is the model of perception with the argument that fine art (*schöne Kunst*) elicits pleasure considered as a "mode of cognition": "aesthetic art, as art which is beautiful, is one having for its standard the reflective judgement" (*Critique of Judgment*, n. 44 [citing Meredith, 306]). Kant's terms closely resemble sixteenth-century arguments beginning with Leonardo da Vinci's claim that painting is communicable to "all generations of the universe." See my "Leonardo da Vinci's Defense of Painting." For the longer history of the Aristotelian tradition that describes cognition on the model of vision, see Tachau, *Vision and Certitude in the Age of Ockham*; Summers, *The Judgment of Sense*; and the critical essay by Fabian, *Time and the Other*.

10 Condillac, *The Logic*, I, ii; cited by Norton, *Herder's Aesthetics and the European Enlightenment*, 25. Condillac constructed his entire philosophy around the analytic method. Norton rightly emphasizes the polemical component of Condillac's attack on the synthetic method (which begins from first principles). "Analysis" is still based on Aristotle's "double method," for it includes the processes of "decomposition" and "recomposition."

11 I have located examples in rhetorical theory as early as the fifteenth century; see my *Leonardo da Vinci's "Paragone*," 329–330. See also Lindberg, *Theories of Vision*.

12 The recent revival of interest in Herder has produced an extensive bibliography. My brief historiographical sketch is in no way meant to serve as an analysis of Herder's philosophical thought. See the cogent discussions of the scholarship and of Herder, by Barnard, Introduction to *Johann Gottfried Herder on Social and Political Culture*; and Norton, *Herder's Aesthetics and the European Enlightenment*, especially 40–52, with further references. What other philosophers called "reflection," Herder called "*Besonnenheit*" or presence of mind, the innate human characteristic that enables the production of language. It is worth noting that Barnard and Norton reject the older view that Herder was aligned with the extreme Romanticism of Johann George Hamann, and Norton argues that traditionaal accounts of Herder have decontextualized his thought from the philosophical method of analysis that his ideas addressed.

13 Haskell, *History and its Images*, 331–339.

14 The exception is, of course, England, whose geographical boundaries coincide with its political ones: my suggestion, based on a survey of maps in the collection of the John Carter Brown Library, deserves further investigation.

15 Helgerson, *Forms of Nationhood*, writes this about the self-estranged position of a single generation of younger Elizabethans, who were "removed from their artisanal backgrounds, schooled in the alien values of Greco–Roman antiquity, and directed to the service of the newly consolidated monarchic state" (citing page 17). Haskell, *History and its Images*, 173, reveals that the fate of Italian culture at the hands of barbarian invaders was a continuing concern for Italian historians such as Ciampini and Muratori, for whom the art of Ravenna provided a focal point of discussion in the eighteenth century.

16 For a rare discussion of the Renaissance as an international, heterogeneous movement during a time when the "sense of national identity was weak," see Burke, "The Uses of Italy," in Porter and Teich, eds., *The Renaissance in National Context*. European imperial expansionism and nationalist ideology began with sixteenth-century discourses of nation-

hood; see A. Smith, *Theories of Nationalism*, and P. Anderson, *Lineages of the Absolutist State*.

17 Hobsbawm, *Nations and Nationalism*, 9, with an excellent overview of recent scholarship that has completely revolutionized the field in the last three decades.

18 Anderson, *Imagined Communities*, 12.

19 Anderson, *Imagined Communities*, xiv.

20 Haskell, *History and its Images*, 212, who does not, however, draw the same conclusions, cites the work of William Roscoe (1790s), Simonde de Sismondi (1807–18), John Gillies (1786), Winckelmann, and others. These writers drew on the ethnic origins of nations.

21 Kristeller, "Humanism and Scholasticism in the Italian Renaissance." Kristeller urged us to develop more pluralistic forms of vision: part of his statement is cited as an epigram at the beginning of *Reframing the Renaissance*.

22 Italy became a united kingdom in 1861 under Vittorio Emanuele II; see further, D. M. Smith, *Italy and its Monarchy*. This second renaissance known as the Risorgimento succeeded in opposition to the papacy of Pius IX, which probably had some bearing on Burckhardt's view that the papacy stood in the way of the unification of Italy in the sixteenth century (see n. 4). Thanks to Michael O'Connell for this suggestion.

23 F. Gilbert, "Italy," 23–31, in *National Consciousness*. Dante, Petrarch, and others had argued for national unity based on language, but their concerns translate into special interests when we consider that the Tuscan dialect they advocated was spoken only in central Italy, from where the advocates themselves hailed.

24 R. Goldthwaite, *Wealth and the Demand for Art in Italy*.

25 For discussions of the limitations of Herder's cultural pluralism, see Pagden, *European Encounters with the New World*, 179–183; White, *Metahistory*, 69–80. A somewhat different view is expressed by Berlin, *Vico and Herder*, who argues that Herder was a cultural relativist who practiced a "non-aggressive form of nationalism."

26 See Said, "Opponents, Audiences, Constituencies, and Community," 7–32, in *The Politics of Interpretation*; Eagleton, Jameson, and Said, *Nationalism, Colonialism, and Literature*.

27 Hobsbawm, *Nations and Nationalism*, 37–71, citing page 71 here; Hroch, *Social Preconditions of National Survival in Europe*.

28 I have pursued Burckhardt's characterization of the state as a work of art in another essay, "The Status of the 'State as a Work of Art.'"

29 Summers, "'Form,' Nineteenth-Century Metaphysics, and the Problem of Art Historical Description," 382; Haskell, *History and its Images*, 234 and 273. Both Summers and Haskell cite Gombrich's argument that the "physiognomic fallacy" is indebted above all to Hegel's central thesis, which is that "history becomes the determination of a peculiar national spirit" that imparts "a common stamp" to religion, political constitution, ethics, the legal system, customs, science, art, and technical skills. Hegel's list of categories shows that his thinking is, at some remove, indebted to the same cultural geography tradition as Herder.

30 Fiedler, *On Judging Works of Visual Art*, 43–44.

31 An excellent discussion of emerging trends of formal and stylistic analysis that discusses the work of Michelet at length is found in Haskell, *History and its Images*, although the author does not consider the problematic of ethnocentrism considered here; for the textual tradition to which Michelet and his contemporaries are tied, a study that considers the history of ethnocentrism in depth, see Pagden, *European Encounters with the New World*. Both studies have reinforced and expanded my thinking, as citations throughout this essay indicate.

32 Panofsky, "Das Problem des Stils in der bildenden Kunst."

33 Bhabha, "Double Visions."

34 Stocking, *Race, Culture, and Evolution*, 11, in a discussion of historically conditioned disciplinary fragmentation in the behavioral sciences which were in the past much more integrated than they are today. Stocking argues that present anthropologists – and the same is true for present art historians – will be better able to understand historical contributions if they are able to distinguish between questions that have long since been answered, questions which are still open, and questions which we would no longer even recognize as such.

35 Podro, *Critical Historians of Art*, xx, gestures towards the same distinction when he considers the contemporary historian's critical responsibilities: "If a writer diminishes the sense of context in his concern for the irreducibility of autonomy of art, he moves toward formalism. If he diminishes the sense of irreducibility in order to keep a firm hand on extra-artistic facts, he runs the risk of treating art as if it were the trace or symptom of those other facts."

36 Campbell, *Witness and the Other World*, with an excellent discussion of historical concepts of the grotesque in the writings of Eusebius, Egeria, Jerome, John Mandeville, William of Rubrick, and their sixteenth-century successors such as Columbus, Walter Raleigh, and Montaigne.

37 Aristotelian distinctions about various mental operations were also institutionalized in the western classification of the human sciences, based on *Posterior Analytics* 99b–100a; *Metaphysics* 981a4 ff. Aristotle claimed that animals possess a kind of wisdom and even foresight, but they work without inquiry, deliberation or intelligence, working instead according to nature, which corresponds roughly to what we call instinct (*Physics* 199a20–30; *Historia animalium* 588a23–31; *De partibus animalium* 648a5–8; and *Nicomachean Ethics* 1141a28); see Summers, *The Judgment of Sense*. In Christian doctrine, in line with the idea of God's complete freedom of will, all species were created distinct and occupy a specific place in the divine hierarchy. According to Albertus Magnus, pygmies and apes are intermediaries between man and beast in this sense: only man forms universals and distinguishes virtue from vice; but even apes and pygmies learn from past experience, speak, and possess a kind of imitation of art and reason ("Symia," *De animalibus*; cited by Janson, *Apes and Ape Lore*, 83–88).

38 The issues involved extend beyond the scope of the present essay, but see my "The Classification of the Visual Arts in the Renaissance"; and further, on the philosophical context of arguments about Amerindians, see Pagden, *The Fall of Natural Man*; on emerging concepts of racial identity, see *Women, "Race," & Writing*. The following discussion here will touch upon the centrality of neo-Aristotelian, Chirstian views of humanness in nineteenth-century racial theory.

39 Hodgen, *Early Anthropology in the Sixteenth and Seventeenth Centuries*. I use Hodgen's term "europocentric" to distinguish it from the distinctly nineteenth-century practice of Eurocentrism; see discussion in the Introduction.

40 Norton, *Herder's Aesthetics and the European Enlightenment*, 11, citing the fourth *Kritisches Wäldchen*, completed in 1769, and *Kalligone*, 1800.

41 Witness debates between Summers and Moxey, as cited in n. 1.

42 Williams, *Keywords*, 76–82.

43 Williams, *Culture and Society*, xv–48, citing page 42 here.

44 Herder's French contemporary Diderot also defined culture as an aggregate which constitutes national character according to climate and the moral element, as Pagden, *European Encounters with the New World*, 148, has recently discussed.

45 Unlike his teacher Kant and others who detached the concept of beauty in a work of art from actual examples, Herder – like Burckhardt and many art historians who followed him – advocated a theory of the beautiful grounded in specific historical circumstances. Herder's writings on cultural history, which chronologically and philosophically follow his early interest in aesthetics, have been traced to earlier eighteenth-century French sources like the Abbé Dubos, who also attempted to explain historical diversity or cultural variation on universal principles (Dubos, *Réflexions critiques sur la poësie et sur la peinture*, 1748). The present discussion does not trace the dissemination of these ideas in French art history, but see Haskell, *History and its Images*, 226–253, who finds that precedents set by Herder and Hegel enabled Michelet, like Burckhardt, to use visual evidence in an incomparably more imaginative spirit than his predecessors. Haskell credits Michelet with the innovation of formalist analysis that draws connections between national characteristics and visual elements.

46 Anderson, *Imagined Communities*, 67. For an excellent analysis of the outcome in the first modern industrialized nation, see Barrell, *The Political Theory of Painting from Reynolds to Hazlitt*.

47 Stocking, *Race, Culture, and Evolution*, 80–87, 101, and *passim*. See Herder, *The Philosophy of Man*.

48 Stocking, *Race, Culture, and Evolution*, 48.

49 Stocking, *Race, Culture, and Evolution*, 80 ff., discusses the work of Edmond B. Tylor as an important transitional figure between the cultural evolutionism of the 1860s and Boas's anti-evolutionist views, because Tylor proposed a dynamic concept of cultural evolution which proposes that every society passes through the same stages.

50 See my *Leonardo da Vinci's "Paragone."*

51 Fiedler, *Über die Beurteilung con Werken der bildenden Kunst*, 1876; Wölfflin, *Renaissance und Barocke*, 1888; Hildebrand, *Das Problem der Form in der bildenden Kunst*, 1893; Riegl, *Stilfragen*, 1893. I am not sure who deserves credit for coining the term. An even earlier occurence is the periodical *Zeitschrift für bildenden Kunst*, published from 1866 to 1932 (vols 1–65).

52 A critique of Boas's nationalistic concept of culture is beyond the scope of this essay, but see further the historical critique by Cordell, *The Prehistory of the Southwest*.

53 Michelet and Taine's sweeping claims for the manner in which the defining characteristics of different nationalities could be accessed by imaginative contemplation of their artistic productions, however reckless their methods

may have appeared to some, appeared to others to unlock the long-held potential of visual evidence (Haskell, *History and its Images,* 257–273, 358). Haskell argues further, 333–337, that Burckhardt's superior historical understanding put him among those who realized all too well (for Burckhardt did not include his beloved fine arts in his history of Italian culture) that visual evidence does not have an unequivocal relationship to social and political events.

54 Cited by Stepan, *The Idea of Race in Science*, 14. Pagden, *European Encounters with the New World*, 11, cites sixteenth-century precedents of the idea of polygenism, early challenges to the Greco–Christian notion of the integrity of the human race.

55 My wording is based on Gates, Editor's Introduction, *"Race," Writing, and Difference*.

56 Wölfflin, *Kunstgeschichtliche Grundbegriffe*, 12: ". . . es bleibt ein unverärchtliches Problem, die Bedingungen aufzudecken, die als stofflicher Einschlag – man nenne es Temperament oder *Zeitgeist* oder Rassencharackter – den Stil von Individuen, Epochen, und Völkern formen./ Allein mit einer Analyse auf Qualität und auf Ausdruck hin ist der Tatbestand überhaupt noch nich erschöpft. Es kommt ein drittes hinzu – und damit sind wir zu dem springenden Punkt dieser Untersuchung gelangt –: die Darstellungsart als solche. Jeder Künstler findet bestimmte 'optische' Moglichkeiten vor, an die er gebunden ist. Nicht alles ist zu allen Zeiten möglich. Das Sehen an sich hat seine Geschichte, und die Aufdeckung dieser 'optischen Schichten' muß als die elementarste Aufgabe der Kunstgeschichte betrachtet werden." Translation cited from *Principles of Art History*, 11; my emphasis.

57 Long before the modern period, the evolving historical association of outward form and inward feeling can be traced in commentaries on Aristotle's discussion of the faculties of the soul. The internal faculty of the *estimativa*, to use the Aristotelian terminology of St Thomas Aquinas, has the ability to apprehend the inwardness of a thing in its external appearance (as when the sight of the wolf causes the lamb to flee): see Summers, *The Judgment of Sense*, 207 ff. Aristotelian psychological theory and its contribution to western aesthetic theory have been studied, with respect to the ancient world, by Bundy, *The Theory of Imagination*; during the medieval period, by Harvey, *The Inward Wits*; and for the Enlightenment, see Caygill, *The Art of Judgement*.

58 In addition to the citations in the preceding notes, see Krauss, "The Story of the Eye"; Bryson, *Vision in Painting*; and Preziosi, *Rethinking Art History*. See my remarks in the Introduction. Outside the discipline of art history, related critiques of the privileged role of vision in western philosophy have included anthropological questions; two excellent essays to consult are de Certeau, *The Writing of History*, and Fabian, *Time and the Other*.

59 See nn. 1 and 27.

60 My own knowledge of the scholarly literature has benefited from discussions with Clarence Sheffield and his "A Critical Study of Alois Riegl's *Spätrömische Kunstindustrie*." Outside the discipline of art history, there is substantial critical literature on the nineteenth-century foundations of modern humanistic disciplines, which includes the following: Gay, *Weimar Culture*; Ringer, *The Decline of the German Mandarins*; Keylor, *Academy and Community*; and Craig, *Scholarship and Nation Building*. Thanks to Martha Hanna for her bibliographic suggestions. Within the discipline of art history, where a "crisis in the discipline" has been the subject of considerable discussion for the past decade (see the special issue of *Art Journal* dedicated to this topic, ed. Henri Zerner, 42, n. 3 [1982]), discussion has revolved around problems of methodology and the art historian's proper object of study, but I suspect that more attention in the near future will focus on nineteenth-century historiography. Among recent contributions to the disciplinary debates, see Belting, *The End of the History of Art?*; Holly, *Panofsky and the Foundations of Art History*; Preziosi, *Rethinking Art History*, "The Question of Art History," and "Seeing Through Art History."

61 Zerner, "Alois Riegl," 188, n. 17.

62 Iverson, *Alois Riegl*, 25–30.

63 Riegl, *Problems of Style*, 21; my emphasis.

64 See further, Stocking, *Race, Culture, and Evolution*, 234–269; Degler, *In Search of Human Nature*, 85–86. Theories of culturally acquired genetic characteristics were discredited in the late nineteenth century (replaced by race theory based on absolute genetic differences). Riegl's reference to Goethe may refer to Goethe's close association with Lavater, who encouraged theories of genetic inheritance based on *visual* characteristics (*Essai sur la Physiognomie*, 1781). On Goethe's racist image in the nineteenth-century popular press, see Mosse, *Toward the Final Solution*, 26.

65 Most Lamarckians opposed miscegenation for this reason; see Stocking, *Race, Culture, and Evolution*. Stocking shows that many writers at the end of the nineteenth century combined elements of Lamarckian, pre-Darwinian thinking with some of Darwin's ideas. The

following synopsis of anthropological issues is based substantially on Stocking.

66 Riegl, *Problems of Style*, 22.

67 Anthony Pagden argues that distinctions between passive, mechanical imitation and active, synthetic invention were already crucial to eighteenth-century European discussions of the differences between civil and savage behavior. Herder, a key philosopher who contributed to these distinctions (see also my discussion above), considered imaginative grasp a collective trait that varies by nation; see Pagden, *European Encounters with the New World*, 146 and 170–177, tracing the source of Herder's ideas to natural law theorists such as Grotius and Puffendorf. The complex history of racial identity grounded in artistic production deserves further investigation.

68 Darwin, *The Descent of Man and Selection in Relation to Sex*, I, 64, as cited by Stepan, *The Idea of Race in Science*, 54.

69 Stocking, *Race, Culture, and Evolution*, considers Tylor's theory of cultural progress an important step toward modern anthropological notions of cultural relativism culminating in the work of Franz Boas and his students.

70 See Mallgrave, Introduction to Semper, *The Four Elements of Architecture*. Mallgrave does discuss Semper's sources in racial science in depth, but his valuable historical findings are tucked away in the specialized source scholarship.

71 Many scholars have written about the importance of the 1851 Exhibition and the Arts and Crafts movement on Semper's views. Warren-Turnage, "Towards a Theory of Ornament," 29–41, who develops this line of argument further, notes that Semper, like Owen Jones and other members of the British Arts and Crafts circle with whom he associated during his stay in London in the 1850s, praised the "natural instinct" for harmonious design in "primitive" societies like those of the Native Americans. Owen Jones, *The Grammar of Ornament*, 1856, popularized Semper's views.

72 Semper revised Vitruvius's classical theory of architecture, according to which ornament *followed* function, to argue that the human desire to create beauty was *coeval* with practical needs. See Warren-Turnage, "Towards a Theory of Ornament," 25; Ettlinger, "On Science, Industry, and Art: Some Theories of Gottfried Semper"; and Mallgrave, "The Idea of Style," 173.

73 Riegl, *Problems of Style*, 23.

74 Riegl, *Problems of Style*, 23; on Darwin's application of evolutionary theory to differentiate the aesthetic capabilities of different cultures, see Stepan, *The Idea of Race in Science*, 48–56;

and the Introduction to the present volume.

75 Olin, *Forms of Representation*, in another context, stresses the representational element of Riegl's art theory; see Brush, review of Olin, Iverson, and Riegl, *Problems of Style*, especially 356.

76 Podro, *Critical Historians of Art*, 152–53, also cites Anton von Springer's disagreement with racial theories. The present discussion is not intended to be a definitive account of nineteenth-century objections to racial theory: the texts await further study from this perspective.

77 Haskell, *History and its Images*, 305. Kugler's text was reissued in numerous editions, some of which had new introductions and notes, by Charles Eastlake and others. Kugler's study set the standard for many similar publications.

78 Kubler, *The Esthetic Recognition of Ancient Amerindian Art*, 2–3, 130–131. Accounting for the presence of visual similarities in distinct cultures appears to be Kubler's central concern throughout the study. Kubler rejects nineteenth-century diffusionist theories of cultural dissemination and their lingering assumptions about crosscultural exchange: the existence of cultural contact is not in doubt, but the means by which we detect its presence is (citing page 27).

79 A geneology of ideas that Kubler, *The Esthetic Recognition of Ancient Amerindian Art*, 131, offers *without* any critical comment (aside from citing the "recent appreciation" of Kugler by Udo Kultermann [1966]).

80 Kubler, *The Esthetic Recognition of Ancient Amerindian Art*, 18. Most notably, Kubler recognizes the historical sources of inherited categories of analysis when he discusses the work of his own student Donald Robertson, who recognized that Bernardino de Sahagún "rearranged the elements of his archive to fit the cognitive system of medieval encyclopedias" (158–161).

81 The second edition of Kugler's *Handbuch der Kunstgeschichte*, 1848, which divides world art into early art, Classic art, medieval art, and modern art, was illustrated under Burckhardt's supervision. Burckhardt's observations on Italian architecture appeared in 1867, in volume 4 of Kugler's general history of architecture; cited by Haskell, *History and its Images*, 335.

82 There is no opportunity in this short essay to examine the relationships among the views of Kugler, Burckhardt, and Winckelmann. Haskell, *History and its Images*, 338, argues that Burckhardt's notion of the Italian Renaissance was opposed to his predecessors in an important way: it was not prompted by the discovery of the ancient world, but by

the growth of individualism epitomized in the new artistic spirit of optical naturalism, culminating in the late work of Raphael. Winckelmann's aesthetic theories and practices are key to the eighteenth-century view of the Renaissance; see Bell, Chapter 4 in this volume; and on the important homosocial context of Winckelmann's aesthetic views, see Richter, *Laocoon's Body and the Aesthetics of Pain*, with further references.

83   Semper, *The Four Elements of Architecture*, 89, citing Kugler.

84   On the precedent of these theories in Humboldt (who was also one of Kugler's most important sources), see Pagden, *European Encounters with the New World*, 37; on the history of climatic theories of differential cultural development beginning in the early seventeenth century, see Gerbi, *The Dispute of the New World*.

85   Newton, "Primitive Art: A Perspective," credits Semper with being the first writer to use the term "primitive art." I owe this reference to Beth Warren-Turnage.

86   Mallgrave, "The Idea of Style: Gottfried Semper," 153–56, citing Vogt, *Gottfried Semper*, xvi.

87   Cited by Stepan, *The Idea of Race in Science*, 14, citing Lawrence, *Lectures on Physiology*, 335; my emphasis.

88   See Nisbet, *History of the Idea of Progress*.

89   On the philosophical context for Panofsky's "correctives and controls" in relation to the views of Cassirer, Heidegger, and Mannheim, see Hart, "Erwin Panofsky and Karl Mannheim"; Summers, "Meaning in the Visual Arts as a Humanistic Discipline."

90   Panofsky, "The Concept of Artistic Volition" (1920), establishes a direct link between his iconological approach and the project of defining a universal category of the "visual arts" when he notes that his reinterpretation of Riegl's *Kunstwollen* is a continuation of his earlier essay, "Das Problem des Stils in der bildenden Kunst" (1915).

91   Panofsky, *Studies in Iconology*, 9.

92   In this volume, see Watts, Chapter 7, with further references. Panofsky's interest in expression is indebted to Warburg, who was keenly interested in Darwin's theory of expression in men and animals; see Landauer, "The Survival of Antiquity," 82.

93   Panofsky, *Studies in Iconology*, 9.

94   Panofsky, *Studies in Iconology*, 11.

95   Panofsky, *Studies in Iconology*, 16.

96   Mosse, *German Jews Beyond Judaism*. On the mass emigration of Jewish art historians, see the extensive chronicle in Eisler, "*Kunstgeschichte* American Style."

97   Landauer, "The Survival of Antiquity," notes in his discussion that Goethe and Schiller were favorite poets of Panofsky and his associates at the Warburg Bibliothek in Hamburg. Panofsky, like Warburg, also accepted Darwinian ideas about the universality of human expression, thus emphasizing the importance of evolutionist scientific theories to the discipline of art history by focusing on the expressive aspects of figurative art. See Panofsky, "Das Problem des Stils in der bildenden Kunst." This topic deserves more attention than it has yet received. For Landauer's more recent analysis of Panofsky's contribution to American culture, see n. 2.

98   See Moxey, "Panofsky's Melancolia," on Panofsky's conflicting national loyalties, and further, Landauer, "The Survival of Antiquity."

99   The sensitive issues go beyond racial *theory* to personal experience of racism. Compare the attitude expressed by Ernst Gombrich, leading proponent of the effort to expunge all forms of essentialism from art history, reminiscing about his upbringing in Vienna: "Another thing that is often said is that the Viennese contribution to the modern world was in large part Jewish. That is a considerable oversimplification, and one would have to analyse it at much greater length to establish whether it were true. It is a question, anyway, of no particular interest except to racists . . ." (Gombrich and Eribon, *Looking for Answers*, 14).

100 For recent critiques of Panofsky's humanistic bias, see Holly, *Panofsky and the Foundations of Art History*; and Moxey, "Panofsky's Concept of 'Iconology.'" Moxey, 268, argues that Panofsky's discussion of pictorial perspective as a symbolic form in a "diachronic system of interpretation serves only to privilege the Renaissance above all other periods under consideration." Other aspects of Panofsky's "humanist bias," according to Moxey and Holly, include (1) his choice of subject matter that tends to coincide with the values of the academic "hierarchy of genres"; (2) his reliance on a (narrow-minded) tradition of aesthetic judgments; and (3) neglect of the conditions of reception. See further in this volume, Mitchell, Chapter 15, n. 12.

101 Seidel, "Arthur Kingsley Porter," in *The Early Years of Art History*, citing page 103.

102 On Kurz, Saxl, and Warburg, see Gombrich, *Tributes*.

103 See Saxl, "Warburg's Visit to New Mexico."

104 This article was delivered as a lecture in Germany to a so-called "non-professional audience" in 1923. Warburg's concept of "primitive mentality" is ultimately indebted to

the theories of cultural evolutionism associated with E. B. Tylor, but his immediate intellectual debt is to Ernst Cassirer's theory of symbolic forms. Along with Cassirer, Warburg believed that images, defined broadly to include gestures and performances as well as static works of art, grew out of the human need to unify the manifold data of sensation in a lasting, tangible, and visual manner. I am indebted to Karen Lang, "Immediacy to Mediation: Ernst Cassirer, Aby Warburg, and the 'Struggle' of Symbolic Forms," unpublished manuscript, for this succinct formulation. Lang, 7, further argues that Warburg disagreed with Cassirer over the crucial issue of cultural unity: in all of his writings, Warburg demonstrates how symbols embody an inherent tension. Warburg's intuitive understanding of the nature of visual symbols has much in common with contemporary theories of polysemous signification.

105 Warburg, "A Lecture on Serpent Ritual," 277.
106 See further, Gutiérrez, *When Jesus Came, the Corn Mothers Went Away*; Silverberg, *The Pueblo Revolt*.
107 For a brilliant analysis of the racial and medical language that informed nineteenth-century textual criticism and is still in use, see Grigely, *Textualterity*.
108 Moxey, "The Politics of Iconology," 30.

4   RE-VISIONING RAPHAEL

I wish to thank Claire Farago, the editor of this volume, for her helpful comments; Kathleen Brandt for much guidance in the early stages of writing; Pamela Jones for acting willingly as a sounding board; Sheila ffolliott, Nancy Edwards, and Marcia Hall for additional comments; the Kress Foundation and the Mellon Foundation for supporting my research during fellowships at the Villa I Tatti and the American Academy in Rome; and the staff of both those institutions as well as the Biblioteca Laurenziana, Florence; the Biblioteca Herziana, Rome; and the Accademia di S. Luca, Rome, for providing access to research materials.

1 Winckelmann, "Reflections on the Imitation of Greek Works in Painting and Sculpture," 75. See Leppmann, *Winckelmann*, 115. See also Stafford, "Beauty of the Invisible," 65–78.
2 See Wölfflin, *Classic Art*, 73–139 and *Principles of Art History*, passim. On Wölfflin's contribution to the development of formalist art criticism, see Podro, *Critical Historians*, 96–116.
3 Gardner, *Art through the Ages*, 8th edn., 610.
4 Hartt, *Art: A History*, 687–688; Janson, *History*

of Art, 449.
5 See also Honour and Fleming, *The Visual Arts*, 386, who state that Raphael translated "Michelangelo's superhuman, demonic sculptural vision [on the Sistine ceiling] . . . into something much less overpowering . . . ," but they take a more revisionist view and do not use "classicism" as a label.
6 Golzio, "Raphael and his Critics," 611–612.
7 Freedberg, *Painting of the High Renaissance*, 112–132, on the Segnatura frescoes; 151–167, on the Eliodoro frescoes; 264–293, on the Tapestry cartoons; and 293–312, on the Incendio frescoes.
8 Freedberg, 92–110 and 112.
9 Freedberg, 266.
10 See Freedberg, 270–271, 306–307; Hartt, *Giulio Romano*, is a manifestation of this tendency to assign dramatic and "unrestrained" images or parts of images to Raphael's assistants.
11 Grigely, *Textualterity*, Chapter 1.
12 Lichtenstein, "Making up representation," 77–87; and *Couleur eloquente*; and Reilly, "Writing Out Color," 77–99. The unavailability of color photographs has also limited research.
13 Shearman, "Leonardo's Color and Chiaroscuro," 13.
14 Hall's recent *Color and Meaning* devotes considerable attention to Raphael as does Posner [Brandt]'s earlier *Leonardo and Central Italian Art*. See also Caron, *The Use of Color by Painters in Rome* and "Choices Concerning Modes of Modeling;" and Shearman, *The Princeton Raphael Symposium*. Among modern writers who integrate color analyses into monographs, see Oberhuber, *Raffaello*; Jones and Penny, *Raphael*.
15 See the important collection of essays in Shearman and Hall, *The Princeton Raphael Symposium*; Nesselrath, "Art Historical Findings" and "La Progettazione dell' Incoronazione di Carlomagno'," and Mancinelli, "Raffaello e l'Incoronazione di Carlo Magno."
16 Stridbeck, *Raphael Studies*, vol. 2, 7–12; Rosenberg, "Raphael and the Florentine Istoria," 182–184.
17 Here I wish to acknowledge my debt to numerous writings by Elizabeth Cropper and David Summers which build upon the assumption that we can deduce "working" or "workshop" theory from the evidence of the works themselves. Although David Stone, *Theory and Practice*, has criticized such methods as circular reasoning, deduction of underlying principles from external manifestations is a well-accepted method of analysis which lies at the very foundation of art history. The connoisseurship of Guercino upon which he builds the second part of his dissertation and his subsequent publi-

cations such as *Guercino. Master Draftsman*, could not exist without deducing assumptions from the works of art themselves.

18 Mancinelli, *A Masterpiece Close-Up: the Transfiguration* with bibliography (52) to earlier publications dealing with authorship, and Mancinelli, "Raffaello e l'Incoronazione di Carlo Magno"; Nesselrath, "Art Historical Findings" on the *Fire in the Borgo*.

19 See, among others, essays in *Oltre Raffaello* by Rossi and D'Amico; in *Studi su Raffaello* by Pinelli, Arasse, and Maltese; *Raffaello: Elemento di un Mito*; Alice Kramer, "Vasari on Painting"; and Patricia Rubin, *Giorgio Vasari, Art and History*. For bibliography 1972–1982, see *Raphael. A Bibliography* by RILA.

20 Beck, *Raphael: the Stanza della Segnatura*.

21 Some classic studies are Blunt, "Legend of Raphael"; Golzio, *Raffaello nei documenti*, and "Raphael and his Critics"; Muntz, *Les historiens et les critiques de Raphael*; Thuillier, "Polémiques autour de MichelAnge"; and Argan, "Raffaello de la critica" in Hamoud, 7–17.

22 Bellori, *Le Vite*, Borea edn., 90–91, and see also his *Descrizione delle imagini dipinte*.

23 Agucchi's treatise fragment was reprinted in Mahon, *Studies in Seicento Art*, for which see especially 111 ff., 252, 257. For the original publication see Mosini, *Diverse figure*.

24 See Pigman, "Versions of Imitation in the Renaissance" (with previous bibliography). In addition to the bibliography cited in n. 21 above, see Rosenberg, "Raphael and France"; Teyssèdre, *L'histoire de l'art*; R. Demoris, Introduction to Félibien, *Entretiens* (1987), 61–70; *Raffaello: Elementi di un Mito*; and Mason, *Raphael et la Seconde Main*.

25 Included at the end of his *Cours de peinture par principes* (1708), Raphael received 12 out of 20 in coloring, but still had the highest total of all artists, for he received the highest marks in composition, expression, and *dessein* (design). For discussion, see Teyssèdre, *Roger de Piles* and Puttfarken, *Roger de Piles*.

26 Félibien, *Entretiens*; Demoris, Introduction to *Entretiens*, 61–70.

27 Perini, "Lessico tecnico," 227. See also Dempsey, "The Carracci and the Devout style," 85, and Dempsey, "Carracci Reform of Painting," 240 and 246.

28 Many have said this of Dolce's ranking of Raphael below Titian as evidence of Venetian chauvinism, and it is a commonplace in the literature on Scanelli, Malvasia, and other northern Italian writers. See Roskill's Introduction to Dolce, *Dolce's Aretino*.

29 On the inappropriateness of *disegno/colore* and classic/baroque, see Harris, *Andrea Sacchi*, 26–37, and Montagu, *Alessandro Algardi*, vii–viii

and 58–63. For a critique of Wölfflin's approach, see Briganti, "Baroque Art," 255–267, and Martin, *Baroque*. On the drawing/color dichotomy in the sixteenth century and its historical development, see Poirier, "Studies on the concepts of *disegno*, *invenzione* and *colore*," and "The *disegno–colore* controversy reconsidered"; and Freedberg, "*Disegno* versus *colore*."

30 Posner, *Annibale Carracci*, 111–125.

31 Spear, *Domenichino*, 65–66.

32 Blunt, *Art and Architecture in France*, 284–297.

33 There have been some notable exceptions on Caravaggio's imitation of Raphael's *Transfiguration*: Spear, "Leonardo, Raphael and Caravaggio"; and Argan, "Caravaggio e Raffaello" in Hamoud (ed.). Pauline Maguire, *Poussin in France: Chantelou's Collection*, Ph.D. dissertation, Columbia University, 1994, which deals with Poussin's interest in Raphael, is another notable exception.

34 In the sixteenth century, Raphael's coloring was also greatly praised for its sweetness, softness, and *unione* as well as its convincing naturalism (of relief, light) and decorum. See my forthcoming "The Critical Reception of Raphael's Coloring in the Sixteenth and Early Seventeenth Centuries," *TEXT* 8, 1994.

35 Bellori, *Vite*, Borea edn., "Life of Domenichino," 358.

36 Bellori, *Vite*, Borea edn., "Life of Sacchi," 558.

37 Bellori, *Descrizione delle imagini dipinte*, 90.

38 Cropper, *Ideal of Painting*, 135–136. Félibien, *Entretiens*, vol. 4, entr. 8, 116: "Que si le Poussin n'a pas toujours suivi les maximes des Peintres Venitiens dans l'épanchement des ombres et des lumières par de grandes masses, ni suivi entièrement leur conduite dans la manière de coucher ses couleurs, pour aider à donner plus de relief aux corps, il a travaillé sur un autre principe. Il a pris Raphael pour son guide; et fonde sur les observations qu'il faisoit continuellement en voyant la nature, il a fort bien sceu détacher, comme je viens de vous dire, toutes les figures par la diminution des teintes, et par cette merveilleuse entente qu' il avoit de la perspective de l'air."

39 Félibien, *Entretiens* vol. 4, ent. 8, 103–104.

40 See my "Zaccolini's Theory of Color Perspective."

41 Aerial perspective, as commonly known in English, confuses the meaning with the more common meaning of the term to indicate a perspective view from above. The correct term is "atmospheric perspective."

42 Nicaise, "L'Ecole d'Athènes," 18, cited in Giovanni Previtali's introduction to Bellori, *Vite*, Borea edn., p. xiv, n. 1. See also Bosse, *Traite des pratiques géométrales*, 20, cited in

Thuillier, "Corpus Poussinianum," 121.

43 "Cette manière et cette conduite fait dans ses Tableaux un effet conforme à ce que l'on voit dans la nature: Car sans l'artifice des grandes ombres et des grands clairs, on y voit les objets tels qu'on les découvre ordinairement dans le grand air et en pleine campagne, ou l'on ne voit point ces fortes parties de jours et d'obscuritez," Félibien, *Entretiens*, vol. 4, entr. 8, 116; see also the discussion of this passage in Cropper, *Ideal of Painting*, 135–136.

44 Verbraeken, *Clair-obscur*; Teyssèdre, *Roger de Piles*; Puttfarken, *Roger de Piles' Theory*. See also my "Chiaroscuro."

45 Dufresnoy, *De Arte Graphica*, precept 31, lines 279–8, § 283, Dryden trans. 168–172; and precept 33, lines 325–329, g 329, Dryden trans. 173–174.

46 Dufresnoy, *De Arte Graphica*, de Piles' commentary § 204, 145–146. For his later criticism, see *Abrégés*, 172–3.

47 My "Seventeenth-century Appraisals" gives a fuller account with bibliography.

48 Mancini, *Considerazione sulla pittura*, 109–110.

49 Malvasia, *Felsina pittrice*, I, 344.

50 Laurentian Ashburnham MS 1212¹⁻⁴, entitled "De colori," "Prospettiva del colore," "Prospettiva lineale," and "Della descrittione dell'ombre prodotte da corpi opachi rettilinei." The date of the treatise is discussed in Bell, "The Life and Works." The treatises were discovered by Carlo Pedretti; see his "Zaccolini Manuscripts."

51 Laur. Ash. MS 1212⁴, fol. 64b–65: ". . . perche altrimenti senza il temperamento del Lume reflesso il detto spatio ombroso non sarebbe ombra ma si dimostrarebbe di dense tenebre, come di notte tempo, il che non essendo buona imitatione, farebbe maniera cruda, tagliente."

52 Laur. Ash. MS 1212², 9.23, fol. 72r; see my "Seventeenth-century Appraisals." "Prospettiva del colore" is organized into seventeen books, and each book is subdivided into chapters. References to the treatise will include the book number, a period, the chapter number, and the folios. A transcription of the treatise is available in my "Color and theory"; I am working on an annotated edition to be published by Cambridge University Press.

53 Hall, *Color and Meaning*, 95, mentions this work briefly as an example of Raphael's interest in the chiaroscuro mode which involves great contrasts between light and shadow. I am not disputing this analysis. The issue is not whether there is chiaroscuro contrast, but how contrasts are manipulated. Zaccolini saw Raphael in comparison to tenebrist paintings which have even more abrupt contrast and less reflected light.

54 Laur. Ash. MS 1212², "Prospettiva del colore" 9.6, "Dell' Ombra divisa dall' opaco," fols. 58v–59r.

55 Laur. Ash. MS 1212², "Prospettiva del colore" 16.16, "Le figure molto lumeggiate si dimostrono di poco relievo," fols. 141r–142v.

56 Laur. Ash. MS 1212², "Prospettiva del colore" 9.16, "Nelli lontani non si debbono porre ombre troppo gagliarde," fols. 69 r–v.

57 See my "Color and Theory," 220–225; and Kemp and Bell, "Perspective."

58 See my "Cassiano dal Pozzo," 122–125.

59 Félibien, *Entretien* 7, vol. 4, 16. See my "Cassiano dal Pozzo," 124; and on Poussin's debt to Zaccolini, Cropper, "Poussin and Leonardo."

60 For example, Testelin, *Sentimens*, 32.

61 An example is Nicholas Dorigny's engraving of the *Death of Ananias* (dated before 1787), which is constructed in terms of chiaroscuro perspective, whereas the reproductions of Raphael's contemporaries, Agostino Veneziano and Ugo da Carpi, are not. See Pezzini, *Raphael invenit*, 26–28 (cat. nos. 21, 22, 23).

62 The Accademia della Crusca in 1612 defined *scienzia* as "notizia certa di che che sia, dependente da vera cognizione de' suo' principi."

63 Hills, *Light of Early Italian Painting*, 129–132; Meiss, "Some Remarkably Early Shadows."

64 Kemp, page 3 and *passim*.

65 Kaufmann, "Perspective of Shadows," 274–275.

66 Kemp, *Science of Art*, 53–104, especially 90 and 103; see also Kemp's overview in "Geometrical Perspective," especially 103 and 112; and Bauer, "Experimental Shadow Casting" on the relationship between cast shadows and perspective theory.

67 See Kemp, *Science of Art*, 84–85 and on later debates in France, 119–131; and see also Fiorani, "Abraham Bosse" and "Theory of Shadow Projection."

68 Marshall, *Codazzi*, 519–556, contains the most extensive discussion to date of Gagliardi's architectural perspectives and much new biographical information.

69 See my "Filippo Gagliardi," 117, on the date of the treatise; his connection with Zaccolini is briefly discussed in my "Life and Works."

70 Gagliardi, unpublished MS in the Accademia di San Luca, Rome, carta 11 and 18 respectively.

71 Lomazzo, *Scritti sulle arti*, Ciardi edn., 235–238.

72 Lomazzo, *Scritti sulle arti*, Ciardi edn., 237.

73 See the masterful analysis in Freedberg, *Painting of the High Renaissance*, 112–128; but nearly every monograph on Raphael treats this issue to some extent.

74 Winner, "Autoritratto," 88. For more information on Raphael's working methods in the

School of Athens, see Borsook, "Technical Innovation"; and Cappel, "A Substitute Cartoon."

75 Nesselrath "Art Historical Findings," 45. See also his "La progettazione."

76 Nesselrath, "Art Historical Findings," 48, on the "V-Effekt" construction previously used in the Repulse of Attila and Miraculous Draught of the Fishes; Oberhuber, Raffaello, 117.

77 See my "Cassiano dal Pozzo," for further discussion.

78 Spear, Domenichino, 58–59.

79 Spear, Domenichino, 67.

80 Spear, Domenichino, 66; Harris, Sacchi, 27–30.

81 Harris, Sacchi, 29.

82 See Gombrich, Norm and Form, 94: "the more a painting . . . mirrors natural appearances, the fewer principles of order and symmetry will it automatically exhibit. Conversely, the more ordered a configuration, the less will it be likely to reproduce nature."

83 J. J. Gibson seems to have been the main proselytizer of these concepts, which are now widely used. See his Senses Considered as Perceptual Systems and "Ecological Approach." See also Livingstone, "Art, Illusion and the Visual System."

84 Hagan, Varieties of Realism, and Steer, "Art History and Direct Perception."

85 Childs, "The Classic as Realism." See also Hallett, "Origins of the Classical Style in Sculpture," for his assessment and classification of previous views, even though his own position is less radical and depends, to some extent, on the conceptualization of Raphael's "classicism" as a compromise between naturalism and order (82).

86 Brigstocke, "Classical Painting," 209.

87 Cropper, Ideal of Painting.

88 Cropper, "Poussin and Leonarao."

89 I am thinking, for example, of how analyses of warm and cool might be useful in analyzing effects of coloring before the eighteenth century.

5 "Popular" Art in Renaissance Italy

An expanded version of this paper was delivered at the Mellon Colloquium organized by the Institute for Advanced Study in Princeton, March 4–5, 1993, "The Religious Orders and Culture in the Middle Ages and the Renaissance." I would like to thank a few colleagues and friends who offered valuable comments as well as bibliographical references both before and after the conference: Ingrid Baumgärtner, Nicole Bériou, Giles Constable, David Ekserdjian, Claire Farago, Jack M. Greenstein, Jeffrey Hamburger, Claire Hills, Thomas DaCosta Kaufmann, Irving Lavin, Marilyn Lavin, and Philip Sohm.

1 "Frater Bernardinus Caymus de Mediolano . . . Sacra huius Montis excogitavit loca ut hic Hierusalem videat qui peragrare nequit."

2 See, for example, Butler, Alps and Sanctuaries, 249–251, who, however, was genuinely interested in the Sacri Monti.

3 The most recent scholarly book is Vaccaro-Riccardi's Sacri Monti, in which one can find numerous bibliographical references.

4 Vauchez, Ordini mendicanti, 12.

5 Moorman, A History of the Franciscan Order, 458–459.

6 Moorman, A History of the Franciscan Order, 521.

7 On Carcano see Baxandall, Painting and Experience, 41; Rusconi, "Michele Carcano da Milano," 196–218; Rusconi, "Carcano, Michele," 742–743; Rusconi, "Dal pulpito alla confessione," 267; Rusconi, "'Confessio generalis'," 205–206.

8 Rusconi, "Manuali milanesi di confessione," 123–131.

9 Rusconi, "La predicazione francescana sulla penitenza," 68–95; Alecci, "Busti, Bernardino," 593–595; Antoniazzi Villa, "A proposito di ebrei, francescani, Monti di Pietà," 50–51; Rusconi, "Dal pulpito alla confessione," 268–269; Rusconi, "'Confessio generalis'," 208; Meneghin, I Monti di Pietà, 26.

10 Moorman, A History of the Franciscan Order, 459. See sermon number III in Bernardino's celebrated cycle delivered in Siena in 1427: Bernardino da Siena, Prediche volgari, sul campo di Siena, I, 149.

11 For this point and the following arguements, see Nova, "I tramezzi in Lombardia fra XV e XVI secolo," 197–215.

12 My analysis of the history, function and decoration of the Franciscan Observant rood-screens has been confirmed and partly revised by Imesch Oehry, Die Kirchen der Franziskanerobservanten in der Lombardei: she argues (103–106) that an altar was also placed in the nave at the foot of the tramezzo, but there is no evidence to support this view.

13 A facsimile edition of the tract is in Stefani Perrone, Questi sono li Misteri.

14 For these collections of sermons and the suggestion that the Holy Mountain at Varallo was a precise translation of Caimi's sermon on the Passion of Christ, see the excellent article by Longo, "Alle origini del Sacro Monte di Varallo," 44–58 and 66.

15 For the attribution of the Garden of Prayer to Nicolò da Osimo, see Longo, "Alle origini del Sacro Monte di Varallo," 62. According to Picciafuoco, Fr. Nicolò da Osimo 1370?–1453, Vita. Opere. Spiritualità, 146–147, the work was attributed to Nicolò by Sbaraglia in the early nineteenth century, but it is unlikely that

Nicolò was the author of this very popular text. However, the *Garden of Prayer* was printed in 1494 as an appendix to Nicolò's *Quadriga spirituali*, and its frontispiece was reused for another Franciscan text, the *Monte dell' oratione*. It is therefore likely that the *Garden of Prayer* was written by a Franciscan Observant friar.

16 For the considerable costs of a pilgrimage to Jerusalem, see Pinto, "I costi del pellegrinaggio in Terrasanta," 257–284.

17 Thode, *Franz von Assisi und die Anfänge der Kunst der Renaissance in Italien*. The first edition was published in 1885.

18 Bonaventure, *The Soul's Journey into God. The Tree of Life. The Life of St Francis*, 129–131.

19 *Meditations on the Life of Christ*, 38.

20 For the text of Caimi's sermons, see Longo, "Alle origini del Sacro Monte di Varallo," 19–98.

21 Krautheimer, "Introduction to an 'Iconography of Mediaeval Architecture,'" 1–33.

22 *Meditations on the Life of Christ*, 332.

23 *Meditations on the Life of Christ*, 311.

24 *Meditations on the Life of Christ*, 89.

25 "Si finga cotto a rosto": the text of the inspection organized by Monsignor Taverna is transcribed in Testori-Stefani Perrone, *Artisti del legno*, 167.

26 Longo, "Alle origini del Sacro Monte di Varallo," 42.

27 Hood, "The Sacro Monte of Varallo," 301–302.

28 "Questa pietra è *in tutto simile* a quella con la quale fu coperto il sepolcro del nostro Signore Gesù Cristo in Gerusalemme" (Galloni, *Sacro Monte di Varallo*, 45; emphasis mine).

29 "Questo Santo Sepolcro è *affatto simile* a quello ove fu riposto il corpo della Santissima Vergine che trovasi alle falde del Monte Oliveto" (Stefani Perrone, "La 'Gerusalemme' delle origini," 39; emphasis mine).

30 Stefani Perrone, *Questi sono li Misteri*, 24–25, 31, 33, 35: "luogo simile al vero"; "simil luoco"; "somigliato"; "luoco simile"; "luoco sancto asomigliato."

31 Bonaventure, *The Soul's Journey into God. The Tree of Life. The Life of St Francis*, 120.

32 *Meditations on the Life of Christ*, 5; emphasis mine.

33 For the notion of reality effect see Barthes, "The reality effect," 11–17.

34 Alessi, *Libro dei Misteri*, I, fol. 16r.

35 Bonaventure, *The Soul's Journey into God. The Tree of Life. The Life of St Francis*, 130.

36 I discuss Gaudenzio's recreation of the Golgotha because it has replaced the original, and now lost, Crucifixion. It goes without saying that Gaudenzio's works are qualitatively superior to the narratives of the earliest phase of the Sacro Monte (e.g., the Christ and the apos-

tles of the Last Supper), but the way in which these works were experienced by the public was similar.

37 An analogous interpretation is in De Vecchi, "Annotazioni sul Calvario," 109–118.

38 Stefani Perrone, *Questi sono li Misteri*, 34.

39 "Finge te audire sonitum malleorum conficatium dominum tuum" (Gentile, "Testi di devozione," 178–179).

40 On Morone, see Machiavelli, *Lettere*, 440–444; Dandolo, *Ricordi inediti di Girolamo Morone*; Promis-Müller, *Lettere ed orazioni latine di Girolamo Morone*, 148–149 (for the letter to Curzio).

41 On Curzio, see Bandello, *Novelle*, 196–197, 729–731; Melfi, "Curti Lancino," 487–488; Agosti, *Bambaia*, 14, 120–123. For Solario's portrait of Cristoforo Longoni in the National Gallery in London, see Brown, *Andrea Solario*, 143–144.

42 Brown, *Andrea Solario*, 233, 284.

43 Mazzini, "La pittura del primo Cinquecento," 593.

44 ". . . libuit divertere in montem qui Varallo adiacet et ad orientem vergit, in quo intenderam sacellum a Minoribus aedificari ad instar eius quod in Calvariae monte, ubi dominus et servator noster Iesus Christus passus est, magno christianorum concursu, maximis laboribus periculisque visitare solet. Igitur supra radicem montis obviam factus est mihi sacerdos, illius ordinis primas, vir tum religiosus, tum eius situs callentissimus, ubi vere corpus Iesu sepultum fuit qui me per clivos contiguos modo ascensu, modo discensu facili deducens in singula sacella introduxit in quibus imagines repraesentantur, sicuti passionis Domini mysteria ordine successivo in evangelio enarrantur . . . Eaque omnia ad instar locorum veri sepulcri pari distantia, pari structura eisdemque picturis et figuris facta affirmabat. Profecto, mi Lancine, nil vidi unquam magis religiosum, magis devotum, quod corda magis compungeret, quod caetera omnia negligere et solum Christum sequi compelleret. Cessent iam Romanae quas aiunt stationes, cesset ipsa profectio Hierusalem; novum hoc et pientissimum opus omnia refert" (Promis-Müller, *Lettere ed orazioni latine di Girolamo Morone*, 148–149).

45 Morone was still in Varallo on September 30, 1507, but he was back in Milan on October 1 (Promis-Müller, *Lettere ed orazioni latine di Girolamo Morone*, 150–152).

46 Shell-Venturoli, "De Donati," 652.

47 "Ipsa fabricae simplicitas et sine arte structura ingenuusque situs omnem superant antiquitatem" (Promis-Müller, *Lettere ed orazioni latine di Girolamo Morone*, 149).

48 For the notion of *sermo humilis* (humble rhetorical style), see the classic essay by Auerbach in *Literatursprache und Publikum*, 25–63.

6 ART THEORY AS IDEOLOGY

1 The classic biography remains Prodi, *Paleotti*. The standard reprint edition of Paleotti's tract is that of Barocchi in *Trattati*, vol. 2, 117–509. All citations herein of Paleotti's *Discorso* refer to Barocchi's edition. The Latin edition of 1584 was printed in Ingolstadt. In addition to Barocchi's excellent annotated edition of the *Discorso* and Prodi's chapter on it (vol. 2, 527–562) in the book cited above, see the following studies of the tract: Ossola, "'Ut pictora poesis': Paleotti," 63–75; Boschloo, *Annibale Carracci*, vol. 1, 121–141. (Boschloo's main concern was with the possible influence of Paleotti's art theory on art in his diocese, particularly that of the Carracci family of painters; causality of this sort is beyond the scope of my study.) Paleotti's tract is also discussed by Scavizzi in "La teologia cattolica," 171–213. Paleotti indicated on the first page of the Preface to the *Discorso* that he was responding to the Council of Trent's decree. See Paleotti, *Discorso*, 119.

2 I do not mean to imply that post-Tridentine art theory was monolithic; for differences between ecclesiastical points of view of the time, see, for example, n. 47. Nevertheless, all post-Tridentine art theorists were interested in how best to persuade the viewer to Christian truth, and they all had a hierarchical world view. Thus Paleotti's *Discorso* is characteristic of generally held post-Tridentine ideas, even though on certain individual points he disagrees with some of his ecclesiastical colleagues.

3 The bibliography on image theory is vast. On its articulation in a post-Tridentine context, see discussion and full bibliography in my *Federico Borromeo*, esp. 117–126. For its earliest formulations, see Ladner, "The Concept of the Image," 1–34; Kitzinger, "The Cult of Images," 83–150.

4 Paleotti, *Discorso*, Bk. 1, Chapter 4, 139–141. In Paleotti's day, certain concepts were discussed in gender-limited language which, for the sake of historical accuracy, I have also used throughout this study. Here, the metaphysical distinctions were between God and "man" and beast; Paleotti therefore used the word "*l'uomo*". Paleotti nearly always used exclusionary language. Accordingly, where his language is not gender-specific neither is mine and where he uses the word "man" so do I.

5 Paleotti, *Discorso*, Bk. 1, Chapter 24, 224–225. I have translated this passage in such a way as to make Paleotti's points emerge with greatest possible clarity. Here, my translation is not consistently literal but, instead, tends towards paraphrase. Paleotti wrote of "*infiniti poverelli che non sanno leggere.*"

6 In her exemplary edition of the *Discorso*, Barocchi has traced the sources of Paleotti's ideas. In this brief study, which relies on Barocchi's foundation, I have therefore kept analysis of the sources at a minimum, and will refrain from repeating her citations of them.

7 See Aristotle, *De Anima*, Bk. 3, Chapter 7, 141.

8 For further discussion of the relative cognitive merits attributed to the eye versus the ear, see my *Federico Borromeo*, 71 and 118–119.

9 Paleotti, *Discorso*, Bk. 1, Chapter 4, 139–140.

10 Paleotti, *Discorso*, Bk. 1, Chapter 18, 207–208 and Chapter 23, 222.

11 Paleotti, *Discorso*, Bk. 1, Chapter 23, 221. His words are "*l'ingegno e la commodità d'imparare.*"

12 Paleotti, *Discorso*, Bk. 1, Chapter 23, 221. St. Basil and Gregory of Nyssa had stated in patristic times that paintings served as books for the illiterate masses; by Paleotti's day it was a well-worn topos. On early apologetics see Kitzinger "The Cult of Images"; Pelikan, *Imago Dei*.

13 The decree on images was promulgated at the twenty-fifth session of the Council of Trent on December 3–4, 1563. For the text of the brief decree see Waterworth, *Canons and Decrees of the Sacred Oecumenical Council of Trent*, 233–236.

14 The entire second book of the *Discorso* was dedicated to a discussion of abuses.

15 Paleotti, *Discorso*, throughout; for example, Bk. 1, Chapters 20 and 21, 212–216.

16 Paleotti, *Discorso*, Bk. 1, Chapters 18–21, 207–215.

17 It should be noted that not all ecclesiastical theorists were uninterested in style. For example, Archbishop Federico Borromeo of Milan (1564–1631), Paleotti's younger colleague, showed great interest in and sensitivity to artistic style. See my *Federico Borromeo*. For the quotation, see Paleotti, *Discorso*, Bk. 1, Chapter 22, 216–217.

18 Paleotti, *Discorso*, Bk. 1, Chapter 22, 217–218.

19 In order to indicate the ascending importance of the rhetorical means as applied to painting, Paleotti predictably invoked St. Augustine's famous dictum concerning sacred oratory: "To delight is a sweetness, to instruct is a necessity, to move is a victory." See Paleotti, *Discorso*, Bk. 1, Chapter 21, 215–216. For Augustine's remark, see Migne, ed., *Patrologia Latina*, vol. 34, Bk. 4, Chapter 12, line 27 on col. 100. Augustine actually mentioned the means in a different order: instruction, delight, and mov-

20 Paleotti, *Discorso*, Bk. 1, Chapter 22, 218.

21 Paleotti, *Discorso*, Bk. 1, Chapter 22, 218–219.

22 Paleotti, *Discorso*, Bk. 1, Chapter 22, 220.

23 We do not aim to assert a direct influence of the *Discorso* on any individual paintings whatsoever. The establishment of such causality is irrelevant to our study.

24 For the indices to Bks. 3–5, see Paleotti, *Discorso*, 504–509.

25 The Council of Trent's decree on images stated "Let so great care and diligence be used . . . by bishops, as that there is nothing seen [in sacred art] that is disorderly, or that is unbecomingly or confusedly arranged, nothing that is profane, nothing indecorous." Paleotti made many comparable comments in the *Discorso*, throughout. For the decree, see Waterworth, *Canons and Decrees of the Sacred Oecumenical Council of Trent*, 235–236.

26 Bronzino lived from 1503–1572. For Bronzino's fresco, see McCorquodale, *Bronzino*, 149 and 154.

27 Augustine distinguished between substantive and superficial ornament in various tracts. See, for example, his correlation of inner beauty with truth in *De Bono Viduitatis* as reproduced in Migne, ed., *Patrologia Latina*, vol. 40, cols. 445–446.

28 It might also be noted, in connection with Bronzino's *Martyrdom*, that Paleotti objected in general to the use of a great number of figures and actions in a painting primarily with the aim of exhibiting artistic expertise; this, he felt, simply distracted viewers. Paleotti, *Discorso*, Bk. 2, Chapter 33, 412.

29 For Domenichino's fresco, see Spear, *Domenichino*, vol. 1, cat. no. 33, 155–157.

30 Paleotti, *Discorso*, 119–122. Paleotti stated that he had composed the tract in such a way as to maximize comprehensibility. Not only the manner in which information was presented, but also the fact that the *Discorso* was composed in the vernacular rather than in Latin, is noteworthy in this context.

31 See discussion below of the *spirituali*.

32 Paleotti does discuss the fundamentals of painting, its basis in *disegno*, coloring, use of shadows, and so forth. But, as Barocchi pointed out, his discussions are insensitive and he tends to see artistic qualities objectively as ornaments divisible from the work itself. Paleotti, *Discorso*, throughout, esp. 282–285, 379–82, and 496–503. Barocchi, *Trattati*, n. 2 to page 210 on 641.

33 In her edition of Paleotti's *Discorso*, Barocchi made this point; see n. 1 to page 385.

34 Paleotti, *Discorso*, 270–289. Paleotti's words are: "*temerarie, scandalose, erronee, sospette, eretiche, superstiziose, apocrife.*"

35 Paleotti, *Discorso*, Bk. 2, Chapter 6, 270–279.

36 Paleotti, *Discorso*, 289–479.

37 According to Paleotti, images serve to aid the three powers of the soul: the intellect, will, and memory. Looking at images piously, he states, "makes good desires grow and helps abolish sin; it excites in us the pious wish to imitate the lives of the glorious saints who are represented." Images, of course, also help us remember the events depicted. Paleotti, *Discorso*, Bk. 1, Chapter 18, 207–208.

38 Paleotti, *Discorso*, Bk. 2, Chapters 5 and 6, 275–279 and Chapter 11, 294–296.

39 Paleotti, *Discorso*, 496–501.

40 Paleotti, *Discorso*, 498.

41 On paintings' necessary characteristics, see Paleotti, *Discorso*, Bk. 2, Chapter 33, 408 "*chiaro*" and 412 "*compartendo con ordine*"; Chapter 52, 501 "*opere ben finite*." The characteristics of the uneducated majority are addressed throughout the tract. In addition to Bk. 2, Chapter 52, see, for example, Bk. 1, Chapter 23, 221.

42 Boschloo, *Annibale Carracci*, throughout. Boschloo never explicitly terms Paleotti a populist, but he gives the impression that Paleotti's concern with the masses was more enlightened than is tenable.

43 Paleotti, *Discorso*, throughout. Paleotti uses these terms for educated viewers: *letterati, dotti, studiosi, intelligenti*, and *persone di maggior intelligensa*. To indicate uneducated viewers, he uses these terms: *idioti* (most frequently), *indotti, ignoranti, semplici*, and *ordinarii*. He also uses *il popolo* and *il volgo*, often with qualifying modifiers.

44 Paleotti, *Discorso*, 384–385; my emphasis.

45 For Annibale's painting see Posner, *Annibale Carracci*, vol. 2, cat. no. 50 on page 231; also Posner's cat. no. 91, 278–279 in *The Age of Correggio and the Carracci*. As Posner states, the painting's dimensions suggest that it was intended to be an overdoor decoration. Annibale's painting postdates the *Discorso*, but we do not claim that it was influenced by the tract.

46 On the Christian optimism of Bellarmino and especially Borromeo, as well as Augustine's point of view, see my *Federico Borromeo*, 33–6 and 76–89.

47 It is impossible to determine what Bellarmino felt about this point because he did not discuss art in his writings. In his art tracts Borromeo failed to address the relative cognitive merits of various viewers, but his devotional writings do suggest – however obliquely – that he was more optimistic about the ability of unlearned persons to ascend the spiritual ladder. For example, in the tenth *oratione ragionamento* (con-

versational prayer) of his *I Ragionamenti spirituali* (*Spiritual Conversations*), Borromeo discussed five modes of contemplating Christ's Passion. The first mode entailed meditating on the episodes of the Passion as historical events. Significantly, Borromeo pointed out that many persons denigrated this mode, calling it base and unimportant, but that he himself found it particularly efficacious precisely because it was so easy to perform that a person of any level of intelligence or knowledge could accomplish it successfully. See Borromeo, *I Ragionamenti spirituali*, fols. 132r–136r. It is worth noting here that hierarchical methods of devotional prayer practiced in post-Tridentine Italy likewise bespeak the world view characterized in our study of Paleotti. For full discussion, see my *Federico Borromeo, esp.* 64–95.

48 Prodi, *Gabriele Paleotti*, vol. 2, 182–187. At their high point, Paleotti's schools of Christian doctrine served approximately 7,000–10,000 boys and girls aged four to twelve. These numbers were paralleled only by the schools of Christian doctrine in Carlo Borromeo's diocese of Milan.

49 I would like to thank Thomas Worcester, s.j., for discussing with me the uneducated parishioner's access to metaphysics. The bibliography on devotional literature, sermons, and religious music is vast. On devotional literature, see my *Federico Borromeo*, 33–37 and 64–95. On sermons, see O'Malley, *Praise and Blame*; McGinness, "Rhetoric and Counter-Reformation Rome". On sacred music, see Carter, *Music in Italy*.

50 The full title of this tract is: *Instruzzione Di Monsignore Illustrissimo et Reverendissimo Cardinale Paleotti, Arcivescovo di Bologna Per Tutti quelli, che havranno licenza di Predicare nelle Ville, & altri luoghi della Diocese di sua Signore Illustrissimo* (*Instructions of the Illustrious and Very Reverend Monsignor Cardinal Paleotti, Archbishop of Bologna, for All Those who will have License to Preach in the Villages & Other Places of the Diocese of His Very Illustrious Lordship*). My citations are to the manuscript in the Vatican Library listed in the general Bibliography.

51 On the *instructiones* in general, see McGinness, "Rhetoric and Counter-Reformation Rome," 197–232. In addition to that of Paleotti, the most famous manuals of this genre were those of Carlo Borromeo (1538–84) and Roberto Bellarmino.

52 Paleotti, *Instruzzione*, fols. 4r–5v. Paleotti's exact words are *"facile intelligensa."*

53 Paleotti, *Instruzzione*, fol. 9r. His phrase is *"varij stati, gradi, & ufficij di persone."*

54 Paleotti, *Instruzzione*, fols. 10v–11r. The chapter's title is *"Obligo di ciascuno secondo lo stato suo."*

55 Paleotti devoted ten days per year to performing St Ignatius of Loyola's *Spiritual Exercises*, on which see Prodi, *Paleotti*, 36.

56 On this point, see n. 47.

7 LANGUAGES OF GESTURE

1 Bing, "A. M. Warburg", 309.

2 Elliott, *The Old World and The New 1492–1650*, especially "The Uncertain Impact" and "The Process of Assimilation"; "Renaissance Europe and America: A Blunted Impact?" in Chiapelli, ed., *First Images of America*, 11–23.

3 Elliott, "Renaissance Europe and America: A Blunted Impact?", 17.

4 Elliott, " Renaissance Europe and America: A Blunted Impact?", 21.

5 Huizinga, *The Waning of The Middle Ages*; Ladner, "*Homo Viator*: Medieval Ideas On Alienation and Order,"; Sumption, *Pilgrimage: An Image of Medieval Religion*.

6 On Franciscan missionary work in the medieval period see, *inter alia*, Daniel, *The Franciscan Concept of Mission in The High Middle Ages*; Simonut, *Metodo d'evangelizzazione dei francescani*; Richard, *La papauté et les missions d'orient au moyen âge*; Van den Wyngaert and Mensaert, *Sinica Franciscana*, publishes texts pertinent to Franciscan missionary work in the thirteenth and fourteenth centuries.

7 On Llull's life and many writings, see Bonner, *Selected Works of Ramon Llull*; Hillgarth, *Ramon Llull and Llullism in Fourteenth-Century France*. For some discussion of Llull's "missionary Christianity," see Watts, "Talking to Spiritual Others: Ramon Llull, Nicholas of Cusa, Diego Valadés."

8 Testera's letter, signed by seven other prominent mendicants, was addressed to the Emperor Charles V and dated May 6, 1532. It is printed in *Cartas de Indias*, 62–66.

9 A thought-provoking recent study of the roles that rituals and ceremonies, private and public, play in the transmission of culture is Connerton, *How Societies Remember*. See also Bremmer and Roodenburg, ed., *A Cultural History of Gesture*, which has a useful bibliography.

10 Fowler and Fowler, trans., *The Works of Lucian of Samosata*, Vol. 2, *Of Pantomime*, 238–263. The passage quoted is on page 256.

11 There is a large literature on this subject. Publications which I have found particularly useful in shaping this piece include Barasch, *Giotto and the Language of Gestures*; Gombrich, "Ritualized Gesture and Expression in Art,"

and his *Aby Warburg: an Intellectual Biography.*

12 Lucian of Samosata, *Of Pantomime*, 255.

13 Quintilian, *Institutio oratoria*, xi.iii. 85–87.

14 These ceremonies, and others, are the subject of important studies such as Brilliant, *Gesture and Rank in Roman Art*; L'Orange, *Studies in the Iconography of Cosmic Kingship*; MacCormack, *Art and Ceremony in Late Antiquity*; McCormick, *Eternal Victory: Triumphal Rulership in Late Antiquity, Byzantium and the Early Medieval West.*

15 Lucian of Samosata, *Of Pantomime*, 261. See also Quintilian, *Institutio oratoria*, xi.iii, 65–87.

16 Lucian of Samosata, *Of Pantomime*, 261–262.

17 An important recent study of gesture focusing on the medieval period is Schmitt, *La Raison des Gestes dans l'Occident Médiéval*. See also his article "Gestas-Gesticulatio." On illuminations of Terence, see Jones and Morey, *The Miniatures of the Manuscripts of Terence*; on Prudentius, see Stettiner, *Die illustrierten Prudentiushandschriften*. A facsimile of the *Sachenspiegel* now in Heidelberg has been published by Koschorreck, *Der Sachenspiegel.*

18 Witkowski, *L'Art profane à l'église, ses licences symboliques, satiriques et fantaisistes*. More general works include Bernheimer, *Wild Men in the Middle Ages*; Friedman, *The Monstrous Races*; and Camille, *Image on the Edge.*

19 In addition to the article and book by Jean-Claude Schmitt cited above, see Casagrande and Vecchio, "L'Interdizione dei giullare nel vocabulario clericale del XII e del XIII sécolo"; Leclerq, *Ioculator et saltator*. "S. Bernard et l'image du jongleur dans les manuscrits"; Waddell, *The Wandering Scholars*, especially Chapter VIII, "The Ordo Vagorum" and Appendix E, "Councils on the *Clericus vagus* or *Joculator*"; and Chailley, "La danse religieuse au Moyen Âge."

20 For these and other similar incidents, see Thomas of Celano's first and second lives of St Francis, published in *St Francis of Assisi: Writings and Early Biographies*. On the ludic techniques of the early Franciscans, see Ginzburg, "Folklore, magia, religione."

21 Bernal Díaz, a lieutenant in Cortés's army, reports that Cortés had written to Francisco de los Angeles, Minister General of the Observants, requesting that he send friars to instruct the Indians and that the "Twelve Apostles" arrived in response. See Bernal Díaz del Castillo, *The True History of the Things of New Spain*, Vol. 3, 369. On Cortés's associations with the Observant Franciscans, see De Lejarza, "Franciscanismo de Cortés y cortesianismo de los franciscanos"; Elliott, "The Mental World of Hernán Cortés." A recent study of the region which produced significant numbers of

early secular and ecclesiastical emigrants to the New World is Altman, *Emigrants and Society.*

22 Bernal Díaz, *The True History of the Things of New Spain*, 369.

23 Useful discussions of the complex history of the ceremony of *adventus* are to be found in the works by Brilliant, MacCormack, and McCormick cited in n. 14. See also MacCormack's "Change and Continuity in Late Antiquity: The Ceremony of *Adventus*." On the adaptation of the *adventus* ceremony to the translation of relics, see Holum and Vikan, "The Trier Ivory, *Adventus* Ceremonial and the Relics of St Stephen." On subsequent medieval transmutations of the *adventus* ceremony see Kantorowicz, "The 'King's Advent' and the Enigmatic Panels in the Doors of Santa Sabina" and his *Laudes Regiae: a Study in Liturgical Acclamations and Medieval Ruler Worship*. Two of the most important Franciscan chroniclers of the orders' activities in Mexico during the sixteenth century, Gerónimo de Mendieta and Juan de Torquemada, also present the arrival of the Twelve within the context of the *adventus* model. Their treatments are briefly discussed by Phelan, *The Millennial Kingdom of the Franciscans in New Spain*, 33–35.

24 Bernal Díaz, *The True History of the Things of New Spain*, Vol. 3, 369.

25 Bernal Díaz, *The True History of the Things of New Spain*, Vol. 3, 369.

26 MacCormack, *Art and Ceremony in Late Antiquity*, 42–43, points out that "in short, the ceremony of *adventus* in Rome, just as elsewhere, provided a vocabulary for the encounter of different types of persons, and for their convergence into one group." The Franciscans were still employing variations of the *adventus* ceremony in the seventeenth century in their evangelization of New Mexico according to Gutiérrez, *When Jesus Came, The Corn Mothers Went Away*, 99.

27 For a history of the modern rediscovery of this text and its editions, see León-Portilla, ed., *Los Diálogos de 1524 según el texto de Fray Bernardino de Sahagún y sus colaboradores indígenas*, "Estudio Introductario." It has been translated into English by Klor de Alva, "The Aztec–Spanish Dialogues of 1524." See also his interpretive study, "La historicidad de los coloquios de Sahagún."

28 León-Portilla, *Los Diálogos de 1524*, 16–17. Recent studies of some of the techniques employed in the exchange of religious doctrine in medieval and early modern crosscultural encounters include Kedar, *Crusade and Mission: European Approaches toward the Muslims*; Elison, *Deus Destroyed: the Image of Christianity in Early Modern Japan*; Spence, *The Memory Palace of*

Matteo Ricci.

29 Pertinent studies include Chazan, *Daggers of Faith: Thirteenth-Century Christian Missionizing and Jewish Response*; Cohen, *The Friars and the Jews: the Evolution of Medieval Anti-Judaism*; Southern, *Western Views of Islam in the Middle Ages*; Schwoebel, *The Shadow of the Crescent: The Renaissance Image of the Turk.* The approaches of three Christians to dialogue with the non-Christian are treated in Watts, "Talking to Spiritual Others". On the *Requerimiento*, see Hanke, *The Spanish Struggle for Justice in the Conquest of America*, 31–36. Pagden, *Hernán Cortés: Letters From Mexico*, n. 27, 453–455 provides an excellent brief description of the genesis and uses of the document.

30 Toribio de Benavente (Motolinía), *History of the Indians of New Spain*, 229–231.

31 Motolinía, *History of the Indians of New Spain*, 229–31; 370–371.

32 On conceptions of providential history operative among Columbus, the first conquistadors, and missionaries active in the New World, see Watts, "Prophecy and Discovery: On the Spiritual Origins of Christopher Columbus's Enterprise of The Indies' "; Flint, *The Imaginative Landscape of Christopher Columbus*; Kadir, *Columbus and the Ends of the Earth*; Phelan, *The Millennial Kingdom of the Franciscans in the New World*; Watts, "The New World and the End of the World: Evangelizing Sixteenth-Century Mexico." For the larger historical framework, see Reeves, *The Influence of Prophecy in the Later Middle Ages* and *Prophetic Rome in the High Renaissance Period.*

33 Facsimiles of the originals of the *Obedienca* and *Instrucción* are published in Ocaranza, *Capítulos de la Historia Franciscana*, III–VIII. The *Obediencia* is in Latin and the *Instrucción* in Castellan. These texts have been edited with an interpretive study by Meseguer Fernández, "Contenido misionológico de la *Obediencia* e *Instrucción* de Fray Francisco de los Angeles." For the text of the passage translated, see page 492.

34 For translations of several indigenous accounts of the massacre, see Léon-Portilla's *The Broken Spears.* The passage quoted is on pages 74–76. For Díaz's version, see *New Iberian World*, Vol. 3, 306–307.

35 Motolinía, *History of the Indians of New Spain*, 96.

36 Motolinía, *History of the Indians of New Spain*, 96. Motolinía's belief that the Nahuas were diabolically possessed is echoed by other early mendicant chroniclers such as Diego Durán, a Dominican, and Juan de Grijalva, an Augustinian. See, for example, Durán's Introduction to his *Historia de las Indias de Nueva España*; Grijalva's *Crónica de la Orden de N.P.S. Augustin en las provincias de la Nueva España*, Chapters XV, XX, XXII–XXIV.

37 Fray Juan de Torquemada, *Monarquía Indiana*, Book 15, Chapter 13, 31: "Estas cosas, que predicavan à los principios estos benditos Religiosos, era con mudez, y solas señas, señalando al Cielo, y diciendo estat alli el solo Dios, que avian de creer; y bolviendo los ojos à la Tierra, señalavan el Infierno, donde à semejança de los Sapos, y Culebras, que andan por ella, estavan los Demonios atormentando a los Condenados." This is a reprint of the Seville, 1615 edition. The English translation is from Ravicz, *Early Colonial Religious Drama in Mexico*, 31.

38 Valadés, *Rhetorica Christiana*, 95. See also Motolinía, *History*, 198; for the original Castellan, Motolinía, *Historia*, 95–96. Watts, "Hieroglyphs of Conversion: Alien Discourses in Diego Valadés' *Rhetorica Christiana*," provides further information regarding the Franciscans' uses of images and gestures in their efforts to communicate with and convert the indigenous peoples they encountered.

39 See Durán, *Book of the Gods and Rites*, Chapter XXI: "The God of Dance", 287–300; on Sahagún's *Informantes* and other pertinent sources such as the *Codex Ramirez*, see Ravicz, *Early Colonial Religious Drama*, Chapter 1: "Prehispanic Background of Religious Drama." Studies of missionary theatre in sixteenth-century Mexico include Arróniz, *Teatro de evangelización en Nueva España*; Rojas Garciedueñas, "El teatro franciscano en Méjico durante el siglo XVI"; Trexler, "We Think, They Act: Clerical Readings of Missionary Theatre in 16th Century New Spain."

40 See Ravicz, *Colonial Religious Drama*, 12, for some discussion of the *cohuayotl icniuhyotl* which she defines as "collaborations" or "reunions of friends." In addition to her first chapter, see Garibay Kintana's important discussion in *Historia de la literatura nahuatl*, Vol. 1, Chapter 6, "Poesia Dramatica."

41 Ravicz, *Colonial Religious Drama*, 9. On the background for the *auto sacramentale*, see Hardison, *Christian Rite and Christian Drama in the Middle Ages*; Donovan, *The Liturgical Drama in Medieval Spain*; Eisenbichler, *Crossing the Boundaries.*

42 Durán, *The Book of Gods and Rites*, 299–300.

43 For Motolinía's descriptions, see *History*, 152–170. Cf. Durán, *Book of Gods and Rites*, 295–298.

44 Burckhart, "A Nahuatl Religious Drama of c. 1590." See also her important book *The Slippery Earth.*

45 For the text of this decree, see Garibay Kintana,

Historia de la Literatura Náhuatl, Vol. 2, 97. The English translation is from Ravicz, *Colonial Religious Drama*, 40–41.

46 Gutiérrez, *When Jesus Came, The Corn Mothers Went Away*, 123.

47 Gombrich, *Aby Warburg*, 296. It is worth noting that vestiges of sixteenth-century dances and ritual dramas survived into the modern period, embedded in the popular forms of the so-called "dances of conquest." A number of nineteenth-century scripts for such dances and their sources are introduced by Carmen Val Julian in a brief essay titled "Danses de la Conquête: une Mémoire Indienne de l'Histoire?" This piece also includes a very useful bibliography.

8 COLONIAL EKPHRASIS

All translations are by the author.

1 Charges and counter-charges of lying and/or purposeful misrepresentation abound as part of the very formation of the discourse of the Americas. One can think, for example, of Bernal Díaz del Castillo's justification for writing his version of the history of the conquest of Mexico. Yet none is perhaps more direct than Mendieta's 1569 letter to Philip II advocating the position of the Mendicants' evangelical policy towards the native population. In it he cautions the king that he is like a blind man in regard to the Indies and that he needs the reports of eyewitnesses in order to be informed: however, not all are to believed, "for in no part of the world did avarice and lying reign more supreme . . ." (cited in Phelan, *The Millennial Kingdom*, 84–84.)

2 Greenblatt, *Marvelous Possessions*, 117–151.

3 This is what de Certeau implies in his description of the heterological tradition "in which the discourse about the other is a means of constructing a discourse authorized by the other"; de Certeau, *Heterologies*, 68. Like Greenblatt (*Marvelous Possessions*), de Certeau's understanding of this discourse is situated within the parameters of a dialogue between Europeans within Europe and any dialogue that takes place within the Americas is absent in terms of its being meaningful there. Instead, it is always about the taking back to the center (Europe), to reconstruct the periphery (the other) as if the center has not expanded to the periphery in which the need for a multiplicity of discourses between "others" is generated.

4 "casi . . . todo el mundo se ha usado (la pintura) . . . ninguna nación de indios que se ha descubierto en nuestros tiempos usa de letras ni escritura," Acosta, *Historia*, Book VI, Chapter iv.

5 I use the word hybrid purposely to replace the unfortunate term syncretism which, as Henrique Urbano ("Syncretismo y Sentimiento Religioso en los Andes") has discussed, implies an alliance of equals against a common threatening enemy. My use of hybrid derives from Bhabha's use of the term in relation to colonial and postcolonial cultural production; see Bhabha, *Location of Culture*.

6 For the theory of an evolutionary replacement of images by writing based upon a model of competition between writing and images see Lockhart, *The Nahuas after the Conquest*, 326–373, especially 331. For a much less mechanistic and more socially fluid discussion of the relation between writing and image production, see Gruzinski, *The Conquest of Mexico*, 7–97.

7 For example, in New Spain the *Historia de los Mexicanos por sus pinturas* is a written text that is based upon the information recorded in the preexisting pictorial sources. In Peru it is the transcription of the information recorded by *khipus* (colored knotted strings) in *Relación de la descendencia, gobierno y conquista de los Incas*.

8 Kahler, *The Huejotzingo Codex*, 85.

9 "por la dicha lengua fue rescibido su juramento en forma devida de derecho so cargo del qual prometio decir e declarar la verdad," Kahler, *The Huejotzingo Codex*, 114.

10 "quel mayz que al dicho fator an dado lo tienen pintado en una pyntura que pidido le fuese mostrado e vista por el dijo por la dicha lengua que diez e seys pinturas negras de manera de peynas de indios cada pintura es quatrocientos cargas de mayz e ortos diez e seyte Rayas negras a manera de vanderyllas de yndios derechas quecada vna de dellas es viente cargas . . . E que del tributo del año de quinientos e trienta les enbyaron todo el maiz que se montan nueve Rayas coloradas . . . e otra Raya colorada pintada de manera de vandera derecha dize que son veinte cargas todo el qual dicho mayz dixo que abian sacado de una trox que alli en la dicha pintura trayan pintada . . . e questo sabe desta pregunta el qual dicho papel de pyntura va señalado de mi el dicho escribano e Receptor," Kahler, *The Huejotzingo Codex*, 122–123; emphasis mine.

11 "lo qual todo que dicho es esta pintado en el dicho papel En que esta figurada la dicha ymagen de Nuestra Señora e señalada de my señal," Warren, *The Huejotzingo Codex*, 119.

12 For an understanding of this image within the context of a native reading see Cummins, "The Madonna and the Horse." My discussion here of the Huejotzingo images represents the opposite or European side of the possible read-

ing of these paintings in a bicultural context. My two studies should be read as companion pieces that attempt to articulate separately two simultaneous viewings within the context of the production of the court document.

13 This does not mean that all that is said by the witness is all that is represented to the view of the witness. Thus the use of the colors black and red as mnemonics for distinguishing years which is recorded in the written text is also the unacknowledged inscription of the presence of the original Huejotzingo scribe, not unlike the presence of the Spanish notary through his rubric.

14 "los yndios presentados por la parte contraria no hazen fee ni se les deven de dar credito porque son yndios vasallos del dicho Marques y todos los yndios generalmente son malos xptianos borrachos mentirosos ydolatras comen carne vmana personas viles que por qualquier cosa se perjuraran y a las pinturas que presenta la parte contraria mucho menos se les debe de dar fee porque son hechas por los mesmos yndios infieles y barbaros y para ellos no fueron citados por mis partes y asy pudiern pintar todo lo que mas quisieran," Kahler, *The Huejotzingo Codex*, 164; emphasis mine.

15 "Fallamos . . . que la parte del dicho Marques provo su yntención e demanda . . . damos la e pronunciamos la por bien prouada e los dichos licenciados no prouaron sus excebciones ni cosa alguna que les aproveche damos las e pronunciamos por no prouadas," Kahler, *The Huejotzingo Codex*, 174–176.

16 From Mexico to Peru, native religion is claimed to be the result of Satan's deceit practiced on the Indians; see, for example, Sahagún, *Códice Florentina*.

17 Such strategies included learning native languages and teaching reading, writing, Spanish, Greek, and Latin to the children of the native elite; see Gruzinski, *Conquest of Mexico*.

18 See, for example, Baxandall, *Painting and Experience in 15th Century Italy*, 40–46. Baxandall's citation from the *Zardino de Oration*, 1454, elucidates the same mechanisms for memorizing church teachings according to *imagenes* and *locaii*.

19 Palomera, *Fray Diego Valadés*; Taylor, "El Arte de Memoria" and Watts, "Hieroglyphs of Conversion."

20 Valadés, *Rhetorica Christiana*, 96.

21 Valadés, *Rhetorica Christiana*, 95.

22 Valadés, *Rhetorica Christiana*, 94.

23 My discussion of this aspect of Valadés's image has benefited from Pauline Watts's analysis in "Hieroglyphs of Conversion"; see especially 419–424.

24 Valadés, *Rhetorica Christiana*, 100.

25 As in other of his images, Valadés keys his textual explanation of specific pictorial elements in the engraving by using corresponding letters in the image that refer to the section in the text that explains them.

26 For example, Maza ("Fray Diego Valadés," 124) writes: "No trae Valadés ninguna explicación de este grabado, por lo que creo es *puramente ilustrativo*"; emphasis mine.

27 The calendar as a representation of time in relation to human activity seems in general to have been privileged by Europeans as a means of calibration and coordination between European and native American cultures. Even Guaman Poma, the Andean author and artist of the *Nueva Corónica u buen gobierno* (c. 1615), creates only one exact equivalence between prehispanic Andean culture and colonial Andean culture and that is in his series of drawings of the two calendars. Certain aspects of archeo-astronomy and art history in which computer simulations of ancient skies are used to interpret prehispanic iconography still assume an unproblematic relationship between the two forms of representation. For a general discussion of the western representations of nonwestern concepts of time and space, see Fabian, *Time and the Other*, 105–142.

28 Kubler and Gibson, *The Tovar Calendar*, 69; and Maza, "Fray Diego Valadés," 124.

29 I have avoided a discussion of which version of Motolinía's manuscript Valadés actually used, whether it was the lost book of Motolinía or the sixteenth-century copy by another hand of the *Memoriales* now in the Latin American collection of the library of the University of Texas, Austin. If it were the lost manuscript that Valadés used, I would suggest that it too included a drawing of the calendar similar to what is inserted in the *Memoriales*. Valadés's use of both Motolinía's textual description and the calendar wheel image demonstrate that he has collapsed these two discrete parts into his engraving. For a discussion of the versions of Motolinía's manuscripts, see E. O'Gorman, "Estudio," XXI–LII.

30 "diré aquí lo por más verdadero he podido averiguar," Motolinía, *Memoriales*, 3–4.

31 "Habia entre estos naturales cinco libros . . . de figuras y caracteres . . . Los quatro de estos libros no los ha de creer . . . como los Evangelios, porque ni los escribieron Juanes, ni Lucas, ni Marcos, ni Mateos, mas fueron inventados por los demonios. El uno, que es de los años y tiempos, de este se puede tomar crédito, que es el primero, porque en la verdad aunque bárbaros y sin escrituras de letras, mucha órden y manera tenían de contar los mesmos tiempos y años, fiestas y dias, *como algo*

de esto parece en la primera parte del tratado y (décimo) sexto capítulo," Motolinía, *Memoriales,* 5. Motolinía's qualifying phrase "aunque bárbaros y sin escrituras de letras" finds resonance in Valadés's qualifying statement just before he asks his reader to view the engraving of the calendar "cum adeo sint stupidi tamquam in crasso aere nati." That is, truth occurs here despite the *topos* of Indian character just as it does in the court case of Huejotzingo.

32 There is the underlying notion here that the transmission of Christian dogma across culture is something more easily done by seeing than saying. Direct verbal translation leads to misperception; see Burkhart, *The Slippery Earth,* 15–45.

33 Valadés is almost utopian here in that he posits a kind of reciprocity between native representation and European representation so that, just as the Mexican glyphic system can be used in confessional dialogue in which the native act passes through native representation to become a moral transgression in the Christian universe of the Spaniard in order to be absolved, so too the Franciscan images are given over to the Mexicans and now become the center of a native Christian discourse. But as Greenblatt suggests (*Marvelous Possessions,* 121–122 and n. 2, 186), this gift allows for almost no authentic reciprocity in the exchange of representation between Europeans and the peoples of the New World because "Christian universalism – the conviction that its principal symbols and narratives are suitable for the entire population of the world – commits it to the unconstrained circulation of its mimetic capital."

34 Palomera, "Introducción," XVII.

35 "Book(s) for idiots who don't know how to read," Acosta, *Historia,* Book 6, Chapter. vi.

36 This image of the viewer being in the same space as that in which Christ is crucified seems to be in line with Ignatius de Loyola's injunction in his *Spiritual Exercises* to be present as Christ is crucified. What, if any, relation Valadés had with Jesuits while in Rome is unclear. However, there is a temporal overlap with the presence of the Jesuit, Matteo Ricci. Ricci sailed in 1578 to China to begin his evangelical work which included creating a memory system very much like the one described by Valadés; see Spence, *The Memory Palace of Matteo Ricci,* 1–24. In fact, the so-called "memory palace" of Matteo Ricci is similar to the description and engraving by Valadés of the atrium and its four *posas* that serves as his example of a kind of "memory palace" in New Spain. The Jesuits adapted a number of other missionary practices instituted by the Franciscans. For example the *Colloquios,* or

dialogues between Catholic and Aztec priests written by Bernardino de Sahagún, made use of a dialogic form also used by Jesuits in Brazil and China.

37 Emphasis mine. I have based my translation on a study of the letters which are in the John Carter Brown Library, Providence, R.I. A translation – at times loose – of the exchange between Acosta and Tovar appears in Kubler and Gibson, *The Tovar Calendar,* 77–78.

38 The doubt expressed by Acosta to Tovar about the truthfulness of Aztec history is discussed by Mignolo, "On the Colonialization of Amerindian Languages," 309–323. I have greatly benefited from this discussion; however, Mignolo is concerned with the exchange of alphabetic writing between the two Jesuits whereas Tovar's response is prefaced by a letter but is substantiated by images. It is the exchange of images, therefore, that I feel is crucial. In the letter of response by Tovar he asks Acosta to look at the calendar where "vera en la rueda que va alado de ese calendario que va con esta donde *ponen un español con un sombrero y sayo colorado poniendolo por señal del tiempo en que los españoles entraron en esta tierra.*" Acosta surely looked at the figure because in his chapter, "Del Modo de letras y escritura que usaron los mexicanos," he writes, "conforme al año en que sucedían cosas memorables, las iban pintando, con las figuras y caracteres que he dicho, *como poner un hombre pintado con un sombrero y sayo colorado en el signo de Caña, que corría entonces, señalaron el año que entraron los españoles en su tierra . . .*", Acosta, *Historia Natural,* Book 6, Chapter. vii; emphasis mine.

39 "Pero es de advertir que aunque tenian diversas figuras y caracteres con que escribieron las cosas no era tan suficientemente como nuestra escritura que sin discrepar por las mismas palabras refirirse cada una lo que estaba escrito solo concordaban en los conceptos," Kubler and Gibson, *The Tovar Calendar,* 77.

40 The complexity of Durán's position, in which the gathering of knowledge about Indians creates an ambiguity, is explored by Todorov, *The Conquest of America,* 202–218.

41 Durán, *Historia . . . de Nueva España,* vol. 1, 9. My translations are slightly different in places to give a more exact rendition than found in the standard translated edition of Durán, *Book of the Gods and Rites,* translated by F. Horcasitas and D. Heyden.

42 Durán, *Historia de . . . Nueva España,* 13–14.

43 This issue is complicated further by the fact that many of Durán's illustrations are cut from an older manuscript and pasted on to the existing codex. Durán, *Book of the Gods,* xxi–xxii.

44 Durán, *Historia de . . . Nueva España,* 5.

45 Acosta's first chapter (*Historia* 389–390) of Book Six that begins the social and political history of the Inca and Aztec is entitled: "Que es falsa la opinón de los que tienen a los indios por hombres faltos de entendimiento." He begins his demonstration of native abilities in the next chapter (391–392) writing: "comenzando pues, por el repartimiento de los tiempos y computo que los indios usaban, que es una de las más notorias muestras de su ingenio y habildad. . . ." He then describes precisely the calendar wheel sent to him by Tovar and writes: "Y así ví yo en el calendario que he dicho, señalado el año que entraron los españoles en México, con una pintura de un hombre vestido a nuestro talle de colorado que fué el hábito del primer español que envió Hernando Cortés." He again refers to this figure in Chapter vii on writing; see n. 38 above.

46 "para ver si era verdad lo que acerca desto cuentan estos indios, quise poner aquí a las espaldas las cuatro fuentes y los nombres, y canto trizte de Chiquillanto, para ver por la figura si se comunicaban unas a otras, y vi ser cosa maravillosa, como la figura lo muestra," Murúa, *Historia*, 425–426.

47 Where Murúa derived his inspiration from for this kind of image is unclear and, although there is a superficial affinity with Ramon Llull's work, no relationship has been established. Parallel images are found in a later text written in Lima celebrating the dedication of the new church of San Francisco. "Las gracias de Roma, que oy goza esta casa, la Caridad, que en ella se profeffa en la oracion de su perpetua coro fundado, se fignifica en un laberinto de letras: leido al modo de la eternidad, de arriva, abajo, directa ó retrogredemente. Raro, Amor, Roma Ora

> R.A.R.O.
> A.M.O.R.
> R.O.M.A.
> O R. A R"

This is then followed by an anagram within a picture of a sailboat both of which are based on the surname of the Franciscan priest, Luis Cervela ("ser vela"); see Miguel Suárez de Figueroa's *Templo de N. grande patriarca San Francisco*, 1675, folios 17v–18v.

48 Cervantes, *Don Quijote*, 38–41.

49 Bergmann, *Art Inscribed*, 126–127.

50 See Krieger, *Ekphrasis*, 11–12.

51 Krieger, *Ekphrasis*, xiii–xvii. I employ Kreiger's discussion of "ekphrasis" in place of any specific Renaissance definition of the term because I want to move away from the boundaries of meaning set by sixteenth-century academic and artistic discourse. The employment of concepts such as "ekphrasis" were not fixed by such boundaries. They were deployed rather than theorized as the boundaries of Renaissance Europe moved to the Americas and the abyss of Modernity.

52 Bernardino de Sahagún is one of the great European minds of the sixteenth century and the scholarly literature on his various writings is vast. His innovative techniques for investigating culture place the intellectual and spiritual development of the Renaissance within the colonial expansionism of early modern Europe; see, for example, Jorge Klor de Alva, "Sahagún and the Birth of Modern Ethnography," in *The Work of Bernardino de Sahagún*, 31–52.

53 The first copies of *Don Quijote* were shipped to Peru in 1606, less than a year after they were printed, and by 1607, the characters of Don Quijote and Sancho Panza were mimicked in a pageant staged in the backwaters of a mining town in colonial Peru; see Leonard, *Books of the Brave*, 300–312.

54 Guaman Poma de Ayala, *Nueva corónica*, 1114.

55 See Adorno, *Guaman Poma*.

9 The Natural, the Artificial, the Exotic, and the Scientific

The preparation of this essay was greatly facilitated by the work of Lila Yawn-Bonghi, who acted as my research assistant during my semester as Dorothy Ford Wiley Visiting Professor at the University of North Carolina, Chapel Hill.

1 Wenley, "Robert Paston"; and Hayward, *Virtuoso Goldsmiths*, no. 688. Wenley convincingly argues that the painting should be dated to between 1676 and 1679. He suggests that it was painted by Pieter Gerritsz. van Rosestraten, a Dutch artist who worked in Britain.

2 The strombus shell cup beside the youth's left shoulder, lying with its mouth towards the spectator, is in the Castle Museum, Norwich; the silver-gilt flagon which he holds, dated 1597–98, is one of a pair in the Untermeyer Collection, Metropolitan Museum, New York; the silver nautilus cup supported by a seated figure is in the Rijksmuseum, Amsterdam; the nautilus cup of 1592 with a stem of two satyrs is in the Prinsenhof Museum, Delft; and the mother-of-pearl bottle is in a private collection in London (Hayward, *Virtuoso Goldsmiths*, no. 690). The engraved cup mounted on a claw foot is recognizable in the inventory as "a shell engraven with the story of Atalanta standing on an eagle's foot of silver" (Wenley, "Robert Paston", 130).

3 The literature on the cabinets is now very large, but in the present context see especially Kaufmann, "Remarks on the Collections of Rudof II," and *The Mastery of Nature*; Impey and MacGregor, ed., *The Origins of Museums*; Kenseth, ed., *The Age of the Marvelous*; Balsiger, *Kunst- und Wunderkammer*.

4 For Hoefnagel, see Kaufmann, *The School of Prague*, 85 and 207–208, and *The Mastery of Nature*, 11–48, 79–99 and 186; Vignau-Schuurman, *Die emblematischen Elemente*; and L. Hendrix, "An Introduction to Hoefnagel and Bocksay's *Model Book of Calligraphy*," in *Prag um 1600*, ed. Fučiková, 110–117.

5 See Kemp, "Temples of the Body and Temple of the Cosmos."

6 As Psalm 103 in the King James Bible.

7 The part-song book is difficult to read reliably, given the damaged state of this part of the picture, but the most clearly legible words, "death's black," underscore the *vanitas* theme.

8 Wenley, "Robert Paston," 124.

9 L. B. Alberti, *De re aedificatoria*, IX, 1, perhaps inspired by Vitruvius, II, 1. See also Kris, "Der Stil 'rustique.'"

10 Hayward, *Virtuoso Goldsmiths*, 345, no. 67. More generally for life casts, see Kris, "Der Stil 'rustique'"; Leithe-Jasper, *Renaissance Master Bronzes*, nos. 16 and 17 (two casts identified as Paduan, and associated with Severo da Ravenna); and Kenseth, ed., *The Age of the Marvelous*, nos. 51–55.

11 Schlosser, *Die Kunst- und Wunderkammern*; A. Legner, ed., *Die Parler*; and Gilbert, "The Egg Reopened."

12 J. Fritz, *Goldsmiedekunst*, no. 506; Scheicher, "Korallen": Tescione, *Il corallo*. Precisely the same elements of coral and "serpents' tongues" are seen to the right of the saint in Petrus Christus's *St Eligius* in the Metropolitan Museum of Art, Lehman Collection.

13 J. -M. Massing in *Circa 1492*, 130; Kohlhaussen, *Nürnberger Goldsmiedekunst*, no. 252; Zammit-Maempel, "Fossil Sharks' Teeth"; Rudwick, *The Meaning of Fossils*, 30–1; and Oakley, *Uses of Vertebrate Fossils*, 63–5. See Kolhaussen, no. 253 for "serpents' tongues" in assocation with figures of Abraham and the Virgin and Child in a Tree of Jesse.

14 J.-M. Massing in *Circa 1492*, no. 12; Kolhaussen, *Nürnberger Goldsmiedekunst*, 162–3.

15 Hackenbroch, "A Set of Knife, Fork, and Spoon"; *The Splendor of Dresden*, no. 248.

16 Hackenbroch, 184.

17 Cellini, *Vita*, 64–65, for his efforts to surpass the decoration on Turkish daggers.

18 J.-M. Massing in *Circa 1492*, nos. 209 and 210; and Kohlhaussen, "Ein Drachenleuchter."

19 See especially Gilbert, "The Egg Reopened."

20 Durandus, *Rationale divinorum officiorum*, 42–43.

21 Gilbert, "The Egg Reopened," 254–255.

22 Origo, *The Merchant*, 97.

23 Schlosser, *Kunst- und Wunderkammern*, 61 and fig. 50; and Scheicher, "Korallen," 3348.

24 J. Menzhauzen. "Elector Augustus's *Kunstkammer*. An Analysis of the Inventory of 1587" in *The Origins of Museums*, ed. Impey and MacGregor, 62–68.

25 Quiccheberg, *Inscriptiones*; Kaufmann, *The Mastery of Nature*, 181; and Kenseth, *The Age of the Marvelous*, 84.

26 Bacon, *Gesta Grayorum*, in *Works*, 7, 335; Kaufmann, *The Mastery of Nature*, 184–187, where the hermetic flavour of the enterprise is noted.

27 Hayward, *Virtuoso Goldsmiths*, 45.

28 Hayward, *Virtuoso Goldsmiths*, 35.

29 For landscapes and other images in *pietre dure*, see Baltrusaitis, *Aberrations*, 60–75; and Fock, "Pietre Dure work at the Court of Prague and Florence," 445. For Arcimboldo, see Kaufmann, *The School of Prague*, and *The Mastery of Nature*, 100–128. For remarks on how we classify "scientific instruments," see Kemp, "Style and Society in Some Instruments of Art."

30 Doering, "Philipp Hainhofer." For shells in the decorative arts, see Rasmussen, "Mittelalterliche Nautilusgefaesse"; and Woldbye and von Meyenberg, *Konkylien*.

31 Hayward, *Virtuoso Goldsmiths*, 402, no. 661; Glanville, *Silver in Tudor and Early Stuart England*, 322–3; and Tait, *Waddesdon Bequest*, 93.

32 Pechstein, *Deutsche Goldsmiedekunst*, 99, no. 3; and Kohlhaussen, *Nürnberger Goldsmiedekunst*, no. 469; Hayward, *Virtuoso Goldsmiths*, no. 271. For nut cups generally see R. Fritz, *Die Gefasse aus Kokonuss*, and for this cup see no. 46.

33 *Prag um 1600*, no. 339.

34 A convenient review of European collecting of imported artifacts is provided in the essays by E. Bassani and M. McLeod, J. Raby, J. Ayers, O. Impey, and R. Skelton in *The Origins of Museums*, ed. Impey and MacGregor.

35 Van den Velde, *Spieghel der Schrijfkonste*; Whalley and Kaden, *The Universal Penman*, no. 99.

36 W. Jamnitzer, *Perspectiva corporum regularium*, Nuremberg: Gotlicher Hulff, 1565; see Kemp, *The Science of Art*, 62–64.

37 Hayward, *Virtuoso Goldsmiths*, 46; Schönherr, "Wentzel Jamnitzers Arbeiten"; Bott, ed., *Wenzel Jamnitzer un die Nürnberger Goldsmiedekunst*.

38 Hayward, *Virtuoso Goldsmiths*, 129–130; Schürer, "Wentzel Jamnitzers Brunnen"; A. Lhotsky, *Die Geschichte der Sammlungen*, II, 325; for Jamnitzer's life casts, see Pechstein, *Deutsche Goldschmiede-*

kunst, nos. 9 and 10.

39   Hayward, *Virtuoso Goldsmiths*, no. 416.

40   Hayward, *Virtuoso Goldsmiths*, 209.

41   Kris, "Der Stil 'rustique' "; Kemp, "Philosophical Pots,"; Amico, "Les céramiques rustiques"; Ward Jackson, "Some Main Streams."

42   Palissy, *Recepte Veritable*, 133.

43   Ovid, *Metamorphoses*, 3, 157–162.

44   For grottoes, see Miller, "Domain of Illusion"; Châtelet-Lange, "The Grotto of the Unicorn"; and Baltrusaitis, *Anamorphic Art*, 61–70 (discussing Solomon de Caus).

45   Palissy, *Discours admirables*, 1580; 106.

46   Palissy, *Recepte veritable*, 216.

47   Dickerman, "Some Stock Illustrations of Animal Intelligence in Greek Psychology"; and Kemp, "From 'Mimesis' to 'Fantasia,' " 354.

48   Palissy, *Discours admirables*, 105.

49   Palissy, *Discours admirables*, 3v–4r.

50   See Olmi, "Science–Honour–Metaphor" and Laurencich-Minelli, "Museography and Ethnographical Collections in Bologna" in *The Origins of Museums*, ed. Impey and MacGregor, 5–16 and 17–23.

51   De Boodt, *Gemmarum*, Preface.

52   Boström, "Philipp Hainhofer and Gustavus Adolphus's *Kunstchrank* in Uppsala," in *The Origins of Museums*, ed. Impey and MacGregor, 90–101.

10   ANIMALS AS CULTURAL SIGNS

I would like to thank the many individuals who made valuable comments at public presentations of this material. I am particularly grateful to Paul Barolsky, Dana Leibsohn, Randolph Starn, and Andrew Weislogel for reading and commenting on a first draft, and to William Ashworth, Charles Zika, and Vojtech Jirat-Wasintynski for bringing to my attention several important references.

1   Thomas, *Man and the Natural World*, for the understanding of nature in relationship to humans. For other aspects of the interaction of nature and culture, see Lazzaro, *Renaissance Garden*, especially Chapter 1.

2   Much of the recent scholarship on cultural encounters, especially with America, examines the various strategies of assimilation. I have benefitted in particular from Elliott, *Old World and the New*; Grafton, *New Worlds, Ancient Texts*; Mason, *Deconstructing America*; Pagden, *Fall of Natural Man*; and Ryan, "Assimilating New Worlds."

3   For concepts of wildness, see White, "Forms of Wildness," especially 150–157.

4   For the dating and history of the grotto, see Wright, "Castello," 202–207. For a discussion of the grotto and its garden context, see Lazzaro, *Renaissance Garden*, and Acidini Luchinat, *Castello*, 1992, 108–123. Avery, *Giambologna*, 151, attributes the animals to Cosimo Fancelli in the 1550s.

5   Acidini Luchinat, *Castello*, 114, notes some of the particular stones. The new quarry of colored marbles was discovered in 1563, shortly before work resumed in the grotto. The purple variegated marble of the tub in the center niche was one of the most favored of the marbles called *mischio* or mixed, this one commonly called *misto da Seravezza*. On the discovery of the quarry, see Campbell, "Observations," 2:114, and on colored stones, see Morrogh, "Vasari and Coloured Stones," 309–320.

6   Avery, *Giambologna*, 151–154 and 267–268, cats. 122–128; and Micheletti, " 'Ritratti di Uccelli,' " 2: 408–414.

7   Châtelet-Lange, "Grotto of the Unicorn," 51–58, concludes that the grotto illustrates the Greek *Physiologus* and must have allegorical significance; Wright, "Castello," 298–300, determines that the grotto represents Orpheus taming the beasts with his lyre (based on one early seventeenth-century account which noted a statue of Orpheus there, although no earlier visitors mention it), which has an allegorical significance for the contemporary situation of Cosimo de' Medici in Florence; Conforti, "Grotta," 71–80, discusses the grotto in terms of Cosimo de' Medici's identification with Orpheus, replacing an earlier program which played on the identification of Cosimo with Neptune and Pan; Mourlot, " 'Artifice naturel,' " 2:340, discusses the grotto only briefly and generally as a glorification of Cosimo; and my own discussion in *Renaissance Garden*, 178–181, emphasizes the Medici references of individual animals.

8   See my *Renaissance Garden*, 137–140, 200, 202–206, 266–267, and 311, n. 58.

9   Heikamp, "Agostino del Riccio," 80–89.

10   For water tricks in gardens, see my *Renaissance Garden*, 65–68; for a broader treatment of nature's jokes, see Findlen, "Jokes of Nature," 292–331.

11   Vasari, *Le Vite*, 1: 141. In the same passage, Vasari explains that these rustic fountains are "simili alle salvatiche fonti che naturalmente sorgono nei boschi [similar to the wild springs that emerge naturally in the woods.]"

12   Tuan, *Dominance and Affection*, 70–78.

13   Volpi, *Feste di Firenze*, 18–19, n. 2, who notes that the street, Via dei Leoni, still records their presence; Lloyd, *African Animals*, 40; and Simari in *Natura viva*, 27.

14 Volpi, *Feste di Firenze*, 18, n. 2.

15 Trexler, *Public Life*, 326.

16 Simari in *Natura viva*, 27–28.

17 *Montaigne's Travel Journal*, 65.

18 Moryson, *Itinerary*, 1: 325, also noted by Avery, *Giambologna*, 147.

19 Trexler, *Public Life*, 263, n. 158; and Hatfield, "Unknown Descriptions," 232–237.

20 Volpi, *Feste di Firenze*, 16–20, where different accounts of the number of lions are given, from 4 to 26. Landucci, *Diario fiorentino*, 347, remembered only two lions on the occasion of more than sixty years earlier. Lloyd, *African Animals*, 39.

21 Volpi, *Feste di Firenze*, 19. "I gran leoni andavan passeggiando/ Per la gran piazza coll'animo fero:/ Tutti gli altri animali si stan tremando./ Con un gran salto altissimo e leggero/ Sopr'un cavallo un marzocco avventossi,/ Mostrando delle bestie esser l'impero. . . ."

22 Volpi, *Feste di Firenze*, 20. According to two contemporary observers (Volpi, 17), the animals were spurred on by a Trojan horse-like giraffe, filled with brave men (though another identified it as a *palla* or ball).

23 Landucci, *Diario fiorentino*, 345–347; and Lloyd, *African Animals*, 39–40.

24 Landucci, *Diario fiorentino*, 346, and Masi, *Ricordanze*, 143–144, who both note that many foreigners, including Romans and four cardinals in disguise, attended. Trexler, *Public Life*, 508–509, interprets the events in the piazza as a representation of the violence and biological forces, no different from those of animals, that were part of Florentine history.

25 See Bakhtin, *Rabelais*, especially Chapter 3 on popular festive forms and the carnivalesque for symbolic actions, ritual violence, and social reversals, albeit in a different context. Berner, "Florentine Society," 225, suggests that this type of civic ritual "served to release some of the tensions so characterstic of Florentine life. . . . It gave momentary and controlled play to sentiments and feelings which give rise to and were the expression of the more violent aspects of this society." He notes, 226, n. 96, that 40,000 Florentines attended the *caccia* in 1589 and also remarks on the juxtaposition of savagery and elegance.

26 Landucci, *Diario fiorentino*, 376.

27 Plaisance, "Politique culturelle," 3: 136.

28 Kruse, "Spectacle of Slaughter," 45–64, especially 50–51.

29 Vasari, *Vite*, 7: 580.

30 Vasari, *Vite*, 8: 580–581.

31 Toynbee, *Animals in Roman Art*, 65.

32 Fader, "Piazza della Signoria," 24.

33 The engraving of wild animals attacking horses and oxen is catalogued in Hind, *Early Italian Engraving*, 1: 62, no. A.II.3 and *Illustrated Bartsch*, 244–245, where the print is associated with a lost painting by Uccello in the Medici palace, which is noted below. Dogs attacking a bear is in *Illustrated Bartsch*, 211, no. 8(145); Lucantonio's engraving is in Hind, 1: 214, no. D.III.4. Levenson, *Italian Engravings*, 281, notes two additional prints after Leonardo's drawing. Also perhaps based on a lost drawing by Leonardo is the *Combat of Animals* by the Master of the Beheading of St John Baptist, Levenson, 438, no. 159. The connection with the Bomarzo sculpture group was first proposed by Lang, "Bomarzo," 427.

34 Eisler, *Genius of Bellini*, 80–89, plates 4–13.

35 Panofsky, "Early History of Man," 33–67, especially 51–56; and Fermor, *Piero di Cosimo*, 62–74 and 78–81, with additional bibliography. This painting and Piero's *Return from the Hunt*, also in the Metropolitan Museum, are based loosely on the recently rediscovered and newly published text of Lucretius, *De rerum naturae*, Book V. Another painting generally thought to belong to the same series, *Vulcan and Aeolus*, is discussed below.

36 Vasari, *Vite*, 2: 208.

37 Vasari, *Vite*, 3: 37. Milanesi notes that such a panel, not by Pisellino, but by his father Pisello, is listed in Lorenzo the Magnificent's inventory of 1492. This or another was referred to by a contemporary and is identifiable in the inventory of the possessions of Lorenzo di Pierfrancesco in 1499, in Shearman, "Collections," 20 and 25.

38 Vasari, *Vite*, 4: 138, and 6: 455. For Bacchiacca's study, painted some time before 1547, see also Schaefer, "Studiolo of Francesco," 137.

39 Massinelli, *Bronzetti*, 74.

40 Bober and Rubinstein, *Renaissance Artists*, 219 and pl. 185; and Haskell and Penny, *Taste and the Antique*, 250–251. One of the drawings after the classical group is by Jacopo Bellini, among his other sketches of lions.

41 Avery and Radcliffe, *Giambologna 1529–1608*, 186–188, cats. 170, 171, and also cats. 166, 172, 173, and 174; Avery, *Giambologna*, 59–60 and cats. 139–141.

42 Leithe-Jasper, *Master Bronzes*, 226–227.

43 Avery, *Giambologna*, 235, and see n. 41.

44 Bestiaries ultimately derived from a second-century Greek text, called the *Physiologus*. On the history and content of medieval bestiaries, see McCulloch, *Medieval Bestiaries*; and George and Yapp, *Naming of the Beasts*.

45 Pliny, *Natural History*, 8.26.68; Soderini, *Trattato*, 185.

46 Cole, "Dürer's Rhinoceros," 1: 241 and 341.

Martial (*Spect.* 22) wrote that the rhinoceros "tossed a heavy bear with his double horn." The image was repeated in Valeriano's *Hieroglyphica* and Joachim Camerarius' *Symbolorum et emblematum.*

47 Cole, "Dürer's Rhinoceros," 1: 337; Lach, *Asia*, 2, Part 1: 159 and 161–162; and Clarke, *Rhinoceros*, 155–162.

48 Virgil, Eclogue 4.22, "cattle will not fear the lion's might," in *The Eclogues*, 57. The literary *topos* of harmony between wild and domestic animals deriving from Virgil is noted by Toynbee, *Animals*, 21. A similar image is in the prophecy of Isaiah (11:6), in which the wolf dwells with the lamb, the leopard with the kid.

49 Friedmann, "Bacchiacca," 151–158; and Nikolenko, *Bacchiacca*, 59, fig. 71.

50 Tongiorgi Tomasi in *Livorno e Pisa*, 545. The existence of the unicorn is debated in Bacci, *L'alicorno.*

51 Châtelet-Lange, "Grotto of the Unicorn," 52–56, discusses the source of this *topos* from the Greek *Physiologus* and gives relevant examples, both literary and artistic, from Lorenzo de' Medici's *Selve d'amore* of the last quarter of the fifteenth century, to a painting by Filippino Lippi of the end of the century, and an engraving by Jean Duvet of about 1540 with exotic and European animals facing each other on either side of a stream. I disagree with her thesis, however, that the grotto illustrates this account.

52 See my *Renaissance Garden*, 135.

53 *Age of the Marvelous*, 219–220; and Lloyd, *African Animals*, 23.

54 Ruthardt Oehme, introduction to the expanded 1550 edition of Münster, *Cosmographei*; and *Age of the Marvelous*, 302–303.

55 Grafton, *New Worlds, Ancient Texts*, 48–54 on Ptolemy, and 97–111 on Münster.

56 See n. 2.

57 Grafton, *New Worlds, Ancient Texts*, 77.

58 Lehmann, *Cyriacus of Ancona*, 12.

59 Lach, *Asia*, 2 Part 1: 90.

60 Christensen, "Image of Europe," 257–258, makes this point on a larger scale.

61 Vasari, *Vite*, 6: 551–555, and 4: 362. Dacos and Furlan, *Giovanni da Udine*, 23–24 and 44–45, and see 45 for a detail of the camel, giraffe, elephant, and boar in the vault.

62 Ryan, "Assimilating New Worlds."

63 Vasari refers to non-European animals as "animali strani," "bizzarri animali," and "altri animali più strani." The first use of "esotico," denoting flora, fauna, etc., from other continents, is in 1736; the word is more common in the second half of the eighteenth century.

Vocabolario degli Accademici della Crusca, 5: 307.

64 Hoeniger, "Plants and Animals," 130–148; Lcy, *Zoology* 126–134 and 154–155; and Lloyd, *African Animals*, 34–36 and 78–94.

65 Foucault, *Order of Things*, 17–45; and Ashworth, "Emblematic World View," 303–332. My discussion owes much to Ashworth, and also to Harms, "Natural History and Emblematics," 67–83.

66 Harms, "Natural History and Emblematics," 67–69, with the example of new emblems for the bird of paradise.

67 Ashworth, "Emblematic World View," 318–319.

68 Ackerman, "'Naturalism' and Scientific Illustration," 1–17, and "Artists in Renaissance Science," 94–129, deals with some of the issues discussed here in the fifteenth century through the 1540s.

69 Haskell and Penny, *Taste and the Antique*, 161–163, cat. 13. It was reportedly excavated together with other figures in a hunting scene and was displayed in the Uffizi (where it remains) by 1591 with two dogs and a man. For the date of the gift (1560) and of its arrival in Florence (1567–68), see Davis, "Galleria," 33 and 43, n. 56. Acidini Luchinat, *Castello*, 117, states that the existing boar in the grotto was executed in 1791–92 by Innocenzo Spinazzi, although she gives no archival reference or documentation. If this is true, the question remains whether the replacement is a copy of the original, which seems the most likely hypothesis. (The garden at that time was in the possession of the Lorenese ruler of Tuscany, Ferdinand III.)

70 Lloyd, *African Animals*, illustrates the Lombard sketchbook, 60, pl. 39, and Gozzoli's fresco, 58, pl. 37.

71 Volpi, *Feste di Firenze*, 20–21 and n. 22.

72 Ashworth, "Persistent Beast," 46–66, and "Marcus Gheeraerts," 132–138. Ackerman, in "'Naturalism' and Scientific Illustration," and "Artists in Renaissance Science," makes a similar point.

73 The above account is derived from Clarke, *Rhinoceros*, 9, 16–27, 109, and 155–162; Cole, "Dürer's Rhinoceros," 1: 337–356; and Lach, *Asia*, 2, Part 1: 158–171. Clarke, 109 and fig. 79, also notes an engraving after Dürer's woodcut by the Florentine Enea Vico of 1548.

74 Giovio, *Ragionamenti*, 37–39; Langedijk, *Portraits*, 1: 238, n. 1.38r.

75 Knight, *Zoological Illustration*, 15–16. Clarke, *Rhinoceros*, 20–22, notes the similarity of the animal's plates to the armor in one of Dürer's drawings.

76 Lehmann, *Cyriacus of Ancona*, 10, and fig. 33 illustrates the manuscript in the Biblioteca

Medicea-Laurenziana.

77 Donati, "La Giraffa," 147–168; Lloyd, *African Animals*, 51 and fig. 33, for the engraving in Sigismondo Tizio's "Historiae Senenses," Bibl. Vaticana, Ms. Chigi. G.11.36, and for the relationship to Piero di Cosimo's painting. For the engraving, see also Hind, *Early Italian Engraving*, 5: 307 and vol. 7, pl. 911. Masi, *Ricordanze*, 18, tells of its death soon after.

78 Lloyd, *African Animals*, 96; Cuttler, "Exotics," 161–179; and Joost-Gaugier, "Lorenzo and the Giraffe," 91–94.

79 Friedmann, "Bacchiacca," 154, notes the relationship to Piero di Cosimo's.

80 An illustration of a giraffe was published in 1486 in the account of Bernhard von Breydenbach's journey to the Holy Land, *Peregrinatio in Terram Sanctam*, with a stockier and shorter neck, long horns, and a horse-like body. Erhard Reuwich made the original drawings and later woodcuts after them for this publication; Benesch, "Orient as Inspiration," 247. Almost a century later, in 1559, another engraving was produced after a drawing of Melchior Lorck, made in Constantinople. The greatly extended neck in the print is emphasized by the minute scale of the accompanying trainer. It is illustrated in Strauss, *German Single-Leaf Woodcut*, vol. 3, fig. 15. On Lorck, see Lach, *Asia*, 2, Part 1: 89–90. Lloyd, *African Animals*, 89, figs. 61 and 62, illustrates the two images in Gesner.

81 Panofsky, "Early History of Man," 45–47; Bacci, *Piero di Cosimo*, 89, no. 21; and Fermor, *Piero di Cosimo*, 77–81. This painting and the artist's *Finding of Vulcan on Lemnos* are based on Virgil's *Aeneid*.

82 Lach, *Asia*, 2, Part 1: 88, notes that André Thevet collected and made drawings, from which woodcuts were made by Jean Cousin and his shop.

83 Janson, *Apes and Ape Lore*, 264. The same image was repeated again in another travel journal a few years later.

84 Janson, *Apes and Ape Lore*, 15–16 and 43–44; and see the one illustrated in Lloyd, *African Animals*, 15, fig. 9. Janson, 110–111 and Plate XIa, notes an ape in a mid-thirteenth-century English manuscript border eating a fruit with one hand and scratching his leg with another, which must have been a more common motif than his single example suggests.

85 Lightbown, *Mantegna*, 103.

86 Dacos, "Présents américains," 61, n. 19.

87 Lloyd, *African Animals*, 73.

88 Spallanzani, "Saluki," 360–366.

89 Shapley, "Bellini & Cornaro's Gazelle," 27–30; and also Herbert Friedmann, "Cornaro's Gazelle," 15–22.

90 Andres, *Villa Medici*, 1: 176 and 306, and 2: 125, n. 354.

91 Cuttler, "Exotics," 165, gives a number of examples.

92 Landucci, *Diario fiorentino*, 377; and Lapini, *Diario fiorentino*, 103.

93 Schaefer, "Studiolo of Francesco," 101–102.

94 Lappini, *Diario fiorentino*, 258.

95 Loehr, "Medici and China," 68–69.

96 Landucci, *Diario fiorentino*, 52–53; Vasari, *Vite*, 8: 114; Donati, "Giraffa," 247–268; Lloyd, *African Animals*, 49–52; Kliemann, *Poggio a Caiano*, 15–17 and 19–20; and Joost-Gaugier, "Lorenzo and the Giraffe," 94–95.

97 Trexler, *Public Life*, 460.

98 On diplomatic gifts, see Trexler, *Public Life*, 323–326.

99 Lach, *Asia*, 2, Part 1: 136–139; and Bedini, "Papal Pachyderms," 75–90.

100 Lach, *Asia*, 2, Part 1: 135–149; and Winner, "Raffael," 71–109.

101 Winner, "Raffael," 104–105. The drawing is variously attributed to the circle of Raphael or that of Giulio Romano.

102 Vasari, *Vite*, 6: 556; Dacos and Furlan, *Giovanni da Udine*, 149–150; and Coffin, *Villa in Renaissance Rome*, 252–253.

103 Corti, *Vasari*, 70, cat. 50.

104 Shearman, *Andrea del Sarto*, 1: 78–79 and 85, and 2: 246, no. 57; Kliemann, *Poggio a Caiano*, 15–22; and Cox-Rearick, *Dynasty and Destiny*, 107–110, and 87–116 for the *salone*. This is one of four historical allegories decorating the *salone*. Andrea del Sarto's *Tribute to Caesar* and Franciabigio's *Triumph of Cicero* were planned by Paolo Giovio; the second two belong to a later program by Vincenzo Borghini. There are questions about both which Caesar (Caesar Augustus or Julius Caesar) and which tribute, since Vasari, *Vite*, 5: 36, identified it only as a tribute of animals to Caesar, and Raffaele Borghini later specified the tribute to Caesar in Egypt (Kliemann, 22; and Cox-Rearick, 108–110). The fresco is not intended as an accurate representation of an historical scene and does not appear to correspond with a specific event.

105 Landucci, *Diario fiorentino*, 52–53, lists the giraffe, goats, wethers, and a large lion; Vasari, *Vite* 8: 114, notes parrots, monkeys, camels, and the giraffe. Others, in Kliemann, *Poggio a Caiano*, 16 and 173, add the brown race-horse. Cox-Rearick, *Dynasty and Destiny*, 107, argues that the scene alludes to Pope Leo X primarily and Lorenzo only secondarily, while Kliemann, 19, believes the reverse.

106 Borghini, *Il Riposo*, 626, explained that it signified when Lorenzo was presented with foreign animals.

107 Vasari, *Vite*, 5: 36, in the life of Andrea del

Sarto, identifies the animals as "pappagalli . . . che sono cosa rarissima; . . . capre indiane, leoni, giraffi, leonze, lupi cervieri, scimie. . . ." Kliemann, *Poggio a Caiano*, 18, identifies the animal facing the dog as a civet cat, which is likely given the resemblance to the figure in Belon's *Observations*, illustrated in Lloyd, *African Animals*, fig. 71, who notes, 97, that the Florentine consul in Alexandria owned one. For Allori's additions, see Bardazzi and Castellani, *Poggio a Caiano*, 2: 513.

108 On the comparison of ancients and exotics, see Ryan, "Assimilating New Worlds," 527–529 and *passim*.

109 Schiavo, *Cancelleria*, 154–155; and Kliemann, *Poggio a Caiano*, 23, who records the legend: "Aureum saeculum condit qui recto aequabilique ordine cuncta dispensat." The invention was by Paolo Giovio, the same who designed the first program at Poggio a Caiano. On the room, see also Robertson, *Alessandro Farnese*, 57–68.

110 Vasari, *Vite*, 8: 113–115; Kliemann, *Poggio a Caiano*, 22–23; and Allegri and Cecchi, *Palazzo Vecchio*, 137. The invention was probably by Cosimo Bartoli.

111 Berner, "Florentine Political Thought," 179–186. This is one of the themes of Cox-Rearick, *Dynasty and Destiny*.

112 Valeriano's first book of the *Hieroglyphia*, on the lion, was dedicated to Cosimo; Langedijk, *Portraits*, 2: 889, no. 42.89r, for Francesco's device. The ram also referred to Francesco's astrological sign, Aries. Also in the niche is a bull, which may allude to Cosimo as well, since a charging bull is on one of his medals. Langedijk, 1: 491, no. 27.149r.a.

113 Hay, *Europe*, 99–106; and Christensen, "Image of Europe," 257–280. For Leandro Alberti, see Hay, "Italian View," 381–388.

114 Schaefer, "Studiolo of Francesco," 1: 151. Those in the Vatican palace were executed in 1559–60 by Ignazio Danti, who also worked in the Palazzo Vecchio; those at Caprarola were begun in 1575. For the Palazzo Vecchio, see also Allegri and Cecchi, *Palazzo Vecchio*, 303.

115 George, *Animals and Maps*, 24 and *passim*.

116 Ripa, *Iconologia*, 332–339. The personifications are not in Ripa's first unillustrated edition of 1593. For sixteenth-century personifications of the four continents, see *America: Bride of the Sun*, 301–304; Honour, *New Golden Land*, 84–89; Honour, *European Vision of America*, 112–119; and Le Corbeiller, "Miss America and Her Sisters," 207–223. (The frescoed personifications at the Villa Farnese at Caprarola of 1574 do not follow the same tradition from Ortelius.) Hay, *Europe*, 104–

105, discusses the significance of Ripa's images.

117 For the superiority of western culture, in addition to the sources noted above, see also Cole, "Sixteenth-Century Travel Books," 59–67.

118 This has been suggested in a larger context by Elliott, *Old World and the New*, 15–16, and 32; and by Grafton, *New Worlds, Ancient Texts*, 6.

11   COLLECTING CULTURES

1 Vaughan, "People of Wonder," 12, suggests that collection was an essential part of New World exploration and conquest. Specimens were an indispensable part of the mission, not only as proof of arrival but as evidence of the marvels encountered.

2 For expanded discussions of "possession" (appropriation, violation, seizure, etc.) of the "New World," see especially Pagden, *European Encounters*, and, although somewhat less reliable in the reading of sixteenth-century chroniclers of Mexico, Greenblatt, *Marvelous Possessions*.

3 Doggett, Hulvey, and Ainsworth, "New World," 34, for example, link the interest in the new peoples, plants, and animals revealed by sixteenth-century voyagers to an interest in studying diverse cultures and the rise of modern anthropology.

4 In 1972 the Codex Vaticanus B was reproduced in a photographic facsimile that preserved its screenfold form and wooden covers.

5 Saville, *Goldsmith's Art*, is still an indispensable source for this nearly obliterated category of Mexican art.

6 See Nicholson with Quiñones Keber, *Art of Aztec Mexico*, 171–173, for a description and history of this remarkable mask. Heikamp, *Mexico and Medici*, 12, identifies it as a mask mentioned in an inventory of the Guardaroba of Cosimo I de' Medici of Florence.

7 See Feest, "Koloniale Federkunst," 173–178, for a discussion of the collection of featherwork items in this museum.

8 See, for example, the various articles in Impey and MacGregor, *Origins of Museums*. See also works that deal with early European images of the Americas, such as Doggett, Hulvey, and Ainsworth, *New World*; Kenseth, *Age of the Marvelous*; and Honour, *New Golden Land*.

9 Fuson, *The Log*, 75–77. On the morning of the day he landed, Columbus formally "took possession" of the island on which he landed, and by the afternoon had begun trading with its inhabitants for items that he disappointedly

judged to be of little value. See also Greenblatt, *Marvelous Possessions*, 52–54, for his comments on Columbus' claim to have "taken possession" of the first islands that he encountered. He rightly queries why it was that Columbus thought to take possession of them if he believed that he had landed in the Indies, a location already known to Europeans since the time of Marco Polo in the thirteenth century.

10 Certainly the best known of these early reactions to New World objects is that of the artist Albrecht Dürer who, in the journal of his journey to the Netherlands in 1520, recorded his amazement at the "strange" and "wonderful works of art" he saw in Brussels. Despite the glowing terms in which he described these Mexican objects, he failed to include a single drawing of any of them. For an English translation of this much-quoted passage, see Massing, "Early European Images," 515.

11 Saville, *Goldsmith's Art*, contains inventories of the Cortés shipments between 1519 to 1526.

12 For inventories of Mexican objects in the Medici collections, see Heikamp, Mexico and Medici, 34–38. See also Nowotny, *Mexikanische Kostbarkeiten*, for early Americana now in the Museum für Völkerkunde in Vienna, and Feest, *Mexico*.

13 Examples of these early collected pieces are rarely found in "fine art" museums in Europe but rather in ethnographic museums such as those in Berlin (Museum für Völkerkunde), Vienna (Museum für Völkerkunde), and London (Museum of Man, British Museum).

14 For examples of the last three categories, see, e.g., Honour, *New Golden Land*; Chiappelli, *First Images*; and a host of quincentennial-related books and exhibition catalogues, such as Kenseth, *Age of the Marvelous* and Danforth, *Encountering the New World*.

15 Heikamp, *Mexico and Medici*, 9, reports that the screenfold now called the Codex Vindobonensis Mexicanus I was believed to have been sent by Cortés to Charles V, who presumably gave it to King Manuel I of Portugal, who presented it to Pope Clement VII (Giulio de' Medici), from whom it was passed on to Ippolito de' Medici then Nicolaus Capuanus, a German cardinal. After leaving Italy, it passed through the hands of several more owners before it finally coming to rest in the Nationalbibliothek in Vienna.

16 Pagden, *Letters*, 45. Cortés reports that in this shipment he sent "two books which the Indians have," but he does not describe their appearance or contents further.

17 Sturtevant, "Sources for European Imagery," 30–31, notes that another type of compendium, the popular costume books of the sixteenth and seventeenth centuries, also provided Europeans with information about the costumes and customs of diverse peoples around the world. Doggett, Hulvey, and Ainsworth, *New World*, 88, also point out that relatively few American examples were included in these costume books. Those that were tended to be repeated with variations that almost always included feather outfits and accessories, which became stereotypical depictions of native American clothing.

18 The Codex Vaticanus A has been reproduced in a facsimile edition, although in a slightly reduced format.

19 See the *Actas provinciales*, which is still in a Mexican archive, and the *Actas capitulares*, which is now part of the Bancroft Library at the University of California, Berkeley.

20 The most accessible edition of this work is Anderson and Dibble's English translation of the Florentine Codex, as the copy of Sahagún's *Historia* now in the Laurentian Library is commonly called. The numerous illustrations are lithographic copies reproduced in black and white.

21 Heikamp, *Mexico and Medici*, pages 20–21, proposes that the Mexican scenes frescoed on the ceiling of the former Armory of the Uffizi by Lodovico Buti derive from images in Sahagún's *Historia*. Arranged by Ferdinando de' Medici, after a project initiated by his predecessor Francesco de' Medici, the Armory adjoined the Tribuna, which was used to display works of art, including some objects from the Americas.

22 See my *Codex Telleriano-Remensis* for a color reproduction and an analysis of this manuscript.

23 English translation by James Cascaito and the author of the Italian commentary on fol. 55r, Codex Vaticanus A.

24 For a perceptive discussion of Nahua–Christian moral dialogue, the Nahua (Aztec) concept of "deity," and the imposed (albeit transformed) Christian concept of the devil in Nahua thought see Burkhart, *The Slippery Earth*, especially 39–45.

25 English translation by James Cascaito and the author of the Italian commentary on fol. 7v, Codex Vaticanus A.

26 Although the first Italian recipient of the Codex Vaticanus A is not documented, a number of names suggest themselves. Among these are various members of the Medici family, especially Cosimo I and his sons Francesco and Ferdinando (the latter a cardinal in Rome before succeeding as grand duke of Florence), all of whom were greatly interested in "New World" explorations; see n. 20. Given the Dominican connection of the Codex Vaticanus

A, another possibility is Pope Paul VI, a Dominican who was pope from 1566 to 1572, a period when the manuscript (or its prototype) may have been produced.

27 Glass and Robertson, *Guide*, 186.

28 Inventarium, vol. 4, 424.

29 Images reproduced from the Codex Vaticanus A and published in the early seventeenth century apparently derived from Cardinal Amulio, the Vatican librarian who died in 1570. Glass and Robertson, *Guide*, 137, 186, summarize the early history of the manuscript, based largely on the description first given by Franz Ehrle, a prefect of the Vatican library, in his commentary on the Codex Vaticanus A.

30 On participatory oral culture versus isolating literacy, see Walter J. Ong, *Orality and Literacy*, especially "Orality, Community and the Sacred," 74–75, and "The Inward Turn: Consciousness and the Text," 178–179.

12   WILD WOMAN IN COLONIAL MEXICO

Much is owed to many people who have helped me to develop this paper. I would like to thank in particular Cynthia Pinkston for assistance with the medieval data and my research assistant, Annika Rosenberg, for her time and highly honed library skills. Cecile Whiting, Jim Herbert, Tom Cummins, and Claire Farago each gave the first draft a thoughtful reading, and conversations with Jeanette Peterson have helped me to eliminate some errors. I am also grateful to Dumbarton Oaks for a Fellowship in Pre-Columbian Studies that allowed me to research and write the initial version of this study. More recently, the project was supported by the UCLA Academic Senate in the form of a 1993–94 Research Grant.

1 Greenblatt, *Marvelous Possessions*, 1991, 7.

2 See, e.g., Todorov, *Conquest of America*.

3 On the significance of this term, which refers to the members of any dispossessed culture, see Spivak, "Can the Subaltern Speak?"

4 For elaboration of this point, see Coronil's review, "Discovering America Again."

5 Mason, *Deconstructing America*, 7–8.

6 Bucher, *Icon and Conquest*, 46–64.

7 Colin, "Wild Man."

8 Durán, *Historia de las Indias*, vol. 1, 125.

9 Sahagún, *Florentine Codex*, vol. 1, 11; vol. 8, 8. For detailed discussions of European representations of Wild Man and Wild Woman, see Bernheimer, *Wild Men in the Middle Ages*; Husband, *Wild Man*; and White, "Forms of Wildness."

10 Mendieta, *Historia eclesiastica indiana*, 91.

11 Wisdom, *Chorti Indians*, 406–407; Blaffer, *Black Man*, 150.

12 Irizarry, "Echoes of the Amazon Myth," 60–63. For more on reports of Amazons in the New World, see Leonard, *Books of the Brave*, 36–37, 52.

13 Robe, "Wild Man," 40–41. Robe points out that tales of La Llorona extend into Central America as well, thus increasing the likelihood of their Spanish origin. Although Estelle Irizarry links these wild girls of the Spanish sierra to the mythical Amazons of Greco–Roman times, themselves reportedly heard of, if not sighted, by European conquerors and explorers in the Americas, the *serranas*' resemblance to Wild Woman seems far more obvious; see Irizarry, "Echoes of the Amazon Myth," 60–63.

14 For details on Cihuacoatl's identification with motherhood and her role in delivery, see Sahagún, *Florentine Codex*, vol. 6, 161–169; vol. 2, 236.

15 Excessive sexual activity during pregnancy was believed to harm a fetus, for example, while some sex was necessary lest it become sickly and die; see Sahagún, *Florentine Codex*, vol. 6, 142–143, 156.

16 Sahagún, *Florentine Codex*, vol. 2, 236; Velazquez, 1975, *Codice Chimalpopoca*, 124–125.

17 For more on the schooling of Aztec males descended from the former nobility, see Robertson, *Mexican Manuscript Painting*, 42–45, and Peterson, *Paradise Garden Murals*, 50–52. The first school for Aztec boys was set up in Texcoco in 1523 and the best known, the Colegio de Santa Cruz at Santiago Tlatelolco, was founded in 1536. Students were taught Latin, logic and rhetoric, philosophy, music, and writing, as well as what was described as "Indian medicine."

18 On the debate over the likelihood that native artists working for writers such as Sahagún "remembered" much about the meanings of preconquest symbols and traditional ways of rendering them, see Arvey, "Sex, Lies and Colonial Manuscripts," 16–17. Arvey outlines a fundamental disagreement on this issue between Peterson, who sees these artists as well versed in native artistic conventions, and Ellen Baird, who does not. See Peterson, "Florentine Codex Imagery," and Baird, "Artists of Sahagún's Primerios Memoriales." Arvey tends to side with Baird.

19 Sahagún, *Florentine Codex*, vol. 10, fig. 107.

20 Arvey, "Women of Ill Repute," 182–184," and "Sex, Lies and Colonial Manuscripts," 26–32. The penitent Magdalene, of course, also had very long, unkempt hair.

21 For more on European illustrated books and prints imported into sixteenth-century New Spain, see Baird, "Sahagún's *Primeros*

Memoriales," and *Drawings of Sahagún's Primeros Memoriales*; and Peterson, *Paradise Garden Murals*, 65–77.

22   Peterson, "Sacrificial Earth," 3–5.

23   Peterson, "Sacrificial Earth," Figures 1b, 3–5, 23; Klein, "Woven Heaven," 6–12, and "Snares and Entrails." Today in the Nahuatl-speaking community studied by Allan Sandstrom, malevolent wandering souls of people who died bad deaths or had been forgotten by their kinsmen emerge from "filthy, tangled places" in the underworld to spread disease, misfortune, and death. Their names sometimes include the word for "filth" and they are often described as walking on tip-toe or – significantly – as severely pigeon-toed; see Sandstrom, *Corn is Our Blood*, 252, 312. An association of twistedness with wandering, or homelessness, is also implied in the Codex Mendoza commentator's identification of a figure whose hands and feet are twisted as a "*vagamundo*" (wanderer, vagrant); Echeagary, *Códice Mendocino*, pl. 70r.

24   Peterson, "Sacrificial Earth," 116, 122.

25   Arvey, "Women of Ill-Repute," 182, and "Sex, Lies and Colonial Manuscripts," 26 ff.

26   Bernheimer, "Wild Men."

27   On these ointments, see Caro Baroja, *World of the Witches*, 85, 90–91, 164.

28   On the nasty habits of European witches see, in particular, the *Malleus Maleficarum*, especially pages 14, 45–47, and 125, and Caro Baroja, *World of the Witches*, 91–93.

29   *Malleus Maleficarum*, 47. On witches and crossroads, see Caro Baroja, *World of the Witches*, 73, who says that at night witches met the devil and the eternally damned at crossroads.

30   "No one does more harm to the Catholic Faith than midwives," *Malleus Maleficarum*, 66. On the Renaissance tendency for educated, typically male doctors and their upper-class patrons to try to discredit midwives and unschooled curers, who were typically female, by charging them with practicing witchcraft rather than medicine, see Ehrenreich and English, *Witches*, 4–18.

31   Brinton, "Nagualism," 41–46. Elsewhere in Indian America female shamans, although often rarer than male shamans, are considered to be far the more powerful and therefore dangerous; see Stewart, "Witchcraft Among the Mohave," 316, and Harner, "Supernatural World," 17.

32   Foster, *Motolinía's History*, 119.

33   Foster, *Motolinía's History*, 99; Acosta, cited in Brinton, "Nagualism," 18.

34   Foster, *Motolinía's History*, 99.

35   This hanging occurred in Tlaxcala; see Quezada, "Inquisition's Repression," 37–38, 42; Klor de Alva, "Colonizing Souls," 4–5, 12; Moreno de los Arcos, "New Spain's Inqui-

sition," 29; Greenleaf, "Zumárraga," 57–58. The situation was apparently more dire in the Maya-speaking area, as Sherman claims that the bishop of Verapaz hanged five witches, all of them apparently women; see Sherman, *Forced Native Labor*, 448, n. 7.

36   Kamen, *Inquisition and Society*, 205, 211–213.

37   On Zumárraga's and Olmos's extirpation of and ideas about witchcraft, see Olmos, *Tradado de hechicereias*; Caro Baroja, *World of the Witches*, 149–151; Cervantes, *Idea of the Devil*, 19; and Moreno de los Arcos, *New Spain's Inquisition*, 29.

38   Sánchez Ortega, "Sorcery and Eroticism"; Quezada, "The Inquisition's Repression." Vestiges of this early form of female "sorcery" remain in many rural parts of Mexico today; see, e.g., Brinton, "Nagualism."

39   Caro Baroja, *World of the Witches*, 101; Johnson, "Women in Early Historical Writings, 52, n. 27.

40   Durán, *Historia de las Indias*, vol. 2, 311–312.

41   Didron, *Christian Iconography*, vol. 2, 22, 118. The devil's extra faces probably derive from a class of monstrous acephalic beings called Blemmyae that were reported in the first century AD by Pliny the Younger to inhabit the wild fringes of the world; see Boone, "Incarnations of the Supernatural," 77.

42   Durán, *Historia de las Indias*, vol. 2, 180–183.

43   Underhill, *Red Man's Religion*, 89, quoting Weyer.

44   Weyer, *Eskimos*, 313; Holtved, "Eskimo Shamanism," 24.

45   Harner, "Supernatural World," 15.

46   On joints as points of entrance for shamanic spirit helpers, see, e.g., Stewart, "Witchcraft among the Mohave," 319. Jill Furst has developed an interesting argument that the Aztec frequently dismembered the sacrificial victim so as to release its *tonalli*, or soul, into the earth's atmosphere where its "heat" was believed to enhance plant and animal growth; Furst, "Mexica–Aztec Conceptions." See, also, Adams and Rubel, "Sickness and Social Relations," 341.

47   *Malleus Maleficarum*, 172.

48   Mendieta, *Historia eclesiastica*, 81.

49   See, e.g., Klein, "Rethinking Cihuacoatl," figs. 6b, 7a.

50   Stewart, "Witchcraft Among the Mohave," 316.

51   Matos Moctezuma, *Great Temple*, 39–42.

52   Brinton, "Nagualism," 43–44; Johnson, "Women in Early Historical Writings," 17. Sahagún, *Florentine Codex*, vol. 11, 3, calls certain magical practitioners "guardians of tradition, debasers of people." See Silverblatt, *Moon, Sun, and Witches*, 187, 195, for discussion

of comparable concerns in colonial Peru.

53 López Austin, "Cuarenta clases," 87–92.

54 Alvarado Tezozomoc, *Crónica mexicayotl*, 28.

55 Brinton, "Nagualism," 16; Cervantes, *Idea of the Devil*, 23. For discussion of European witches' ointment, see Caro Baroja, *World of the Witches*, 85, 90–91, 164.

56 Peterson, "Sacrificial Earth," 117, 120–121; Vetancourt, cited by Brinton, "Nagualism," 16. Malinalxochitl, it should be noted, upon being abandoned by Huitzilopochtli, went to the place now known as Malinalco, renowned at the time of the conquest as a place of witchcraft.

57 Torquemada, *Monarqui a indiana*, vol. 1, 178.

58 Cited in Burkhart, *Slippery Earth*, 103.

59 Acosta, *Natural and Moral History*, vol. 2, is cited by Cervantes, *Idea of the Devil*, 23, as writing that Mexican priests turned into witches who saw and spoke with the devil under the influence of *ololiuhqui*. See Brinton, "Nagualism," 29, for more ethnohistorical evidence that sorcery was perceived in colonial Mesoamerica in terms of the alliance between witches and the devil. Today the Mixe of southern Mexico believe that witches receive their power from Luzbel, or the devil. Lipp, *Mixe of Oaxaca*, 161, notes that, while this is "not inconsonant with Mixe traditional beliefs," the idea of the devil's patronage of witches is most likely European.

60 On the European belief that witches mate with the devil, see Russell, *Lucifer*, 296–297.

61 Philips, *Historia de los mexicanos*, 630.

62 Boone, *Codex Magliabechiano*, 212–213.

63 Boone, *Codex Magliabechiano*, 47, 49.

64 Boone, *Incarnations of the Aztec Supernatural*, 83. For discussion of the popularity in Spain of representations of the devil as a he-goat, see Caro Baroja, *World of the Witches*, 160.

13 COLONY AND CARTOGRAPHY

Many of the ideas in this paper were first presented at the meeting of the International Congress of Americanists in 1991 and the College Art Association in 1992. I thank Daniel Bridgman, William Hanks, Rachel Hoffman, Rebecca Horn, Arthur Miller, and Barbara Mundy, as well as my fellow Fellows at Dumbarton Oaks in the fall of 1992 for their critiques of and comments on earlier drafts of this work.

1 Certeau, *The Practice of Everyday Life*, xvii.

2 Outside of individual imaginations, there was no single homogeneous institution known as "the Church," nor was there a consistent body of practice and thought called "Christianity." Differences existed between the seculars and regulars in sixteenth-century New Spain, and, in addition, differences separated Franciscans, Dominicans, and Augustinians from each other. Moreover, variations in practice existed at the local and regional level. The "aegis of the Christian Church," then, meant many different things within the colonial context.

3 See, for example, Burkhart, *The Slippery Earth*; Gibson, *Tlaxcala* and *The Aztecs*; and Lockhart, *The Nahuas*.

4 The majority of early colonial maps housed in the Archivo General de la Nación in Mexico City fall into this category. For discussion of these images, see Gruzinski, "Colonial Maps," and Mignolo, "Diatopical Understandings." Photographs of the AGN paintings appear in the *Catálogo de ilustraciones*.

5 While it is clear that indigenous map-makers served a variety of audiences, the details of the patronage system – the ways in which map-makers were commissioned, whether they were paid and how much, the degree to which coercion figured in the agreements between painter and patrons – remain obscure.

6 In response to a questionnaire inquiring about the lands and peoples of New Spain issued by Philip II in 1577, communities across the colony prepared written responses and maps for the crown. Painted between 1579 and 1586, many of the Relaciones Geográficas maps were executed by indigenous artists, others were made by local officials of European or Spanish origin. Transcriptions of the texts of the Relaciones and several of the maps appear in Acuña, *Relaciones Geográficas*. For discussions of the maps, see Robertson, "The Pinturas," 243–278; and Mundy, "Maps of the Relaciones."

7 In indigenous communities, for example, paintings known as cartographic histories served as local historical records, combining sites in the landscape with scenes from important events in the past; see Glass, "Survey of Pictorial Manuscripts," 3–81; my "Primers for Memory"; and Robertson, *Mexican Manuscript Painting*, 179–182. Cadastral paintings were also made to register the distribution of landholdings among residents of native towns and to facilitate the collection of local tribute; see, for example, Williams, "Mexican Pictorial Cadastral Registers," 103–126; and "Rural Tlaxilacalli," 187–208.

8 The Nahuatl word *tlacuilo* means, literally, "one who writes and paints," and in prehispanic Central Mexico the two arts were inextricably linked. Before the Spanish conquest, only people of high status (perhaps only members of the prehispanic priesthood) were trained to execute pictorial images and glyphic signs on

pieces of animal skin, bark paper, or cotton cloth; see Robertson, *Manuscript Painting*, 27.

9   The mechanisms for training people at the local level are not well understood; however, the spread of map-making probably followed a path similar to that of alphabetic writing. Certainly indigenous people were first trained to read and write by mendicant friars, yet alphabetic literacy became largely self-perpetuating within about 50 years. In Central Mexico, for example, by the close of the 1570s, most communities of any size had one or two notaries who could read and write in Nahuatl and fulfill local needs; see Lockhart, *The Nahuas*, 335–345. A similar scenario may pertain to map-makers, some of whom may also have worked as notaries.

10   Robertson, *Mexican Manuscript Painting*, 40–45. On the coercive actions of friars in their pursuit of literate natives, see especially Gruzinski, *La colonisation*, 3–100; Klor de Alva, "Language, Politics and Translation," 345–366; and Mignolo, "Literacy and Colonization," 51–96.

11   Robertson, *Mexican Manuscript Painting*, 38–45.

12   Based on the absence of tangible precedents, Miller has argued that indigenous maps were a postconquest invention; "Transformations of Time and Space," 164. For a contrary opinion, see Boone, "Glorious Imperium," 162.

13   See, for example, the *Codex Nuttall*, a prehispanic Mixtec screenfold.

14   On the importance of *altepetl* in Central Mexico, see Lockhart, *The Nahuas*, 14–58.

15   Glyphic representations of water are the primary exception to this; most often they refer not to communities but to actual bodies of water. Moreover, within the indigenous graphic system, it was possible to distinguish those hill glyphs that stood for communities from those that did not. This was accomplished by pairing an additional sign – such as a temple – with the hill glyph. In the *Codex Mendoza*, for example, burning temples coupled with hill glyphs stand for conquered communities. Yet it is the presence of the temple that makes this clear. Hill glyphs that stand apart from other qualifying signs do not visually differentiate between landscape and settlement.

16   Cartographic histories, paintings that retained a joint interest in geography and historical narrative, continued to be produced for use in indigenous communities. Their appearances in legal contexts, however, were limited. In contrast, within the corpus of maps executed intentionally for presentation to judicial authorities, historical referents are largely absent. As the vast majority of maps painted from 1530–1630 were made for legal settings, this shift away from history and narrative is significant.

17   Mundy, "Maps of the Relaciones." See her chapter, "The *Merced* Map and the *Relación Pintura*," for a helpful summary of the early colonial land grant process and especially the role assigned to maps.

18   The images described in Oettinger, *Lienzos coloniales*, stand as a case in point.

19   This coupling may echo the prehispanic convention of pairing temples with hill glyphs (see n. 15). This is not to suggest that churches simply replaced temples on native maps – the relations between these two signs are complicated both graphically and ideologically. My point here is only that the joining of a hill glyph and building – particularly a building with strong corporate and religious connotations – has prehispanic precedents.

20   Barbara Mundy first called my attention to this image and its fusion of signs, and so I thank her for the reference.

21   On the development of European cartography, particularly in the period leading up to and including the Renaissance, see Campbell, "Portolan Charts," 371–463; Damisch, "La grille," 30–40; Harley, "The Map and the History of Cartography"; Harvey, *Topographical Maps*; Keuning, "History of Geographical Map Projections," 1–24; and Schulz, "View of Venice," 425–474.

22   The map was executed during a preliminary investigation for a *congregación*, Archivo General de la Nación, *Tierras*, volume 64, expediente 7.

23   Kubler, *Mexican Architecture*, 94, suggests that no specific significance can be attached to the grid plan in New Spain. Rather, he sees it as an oft-chosen solution to civic planning with precedents in both Europe and America. While his point is well taken, I believe that the historical circumstances enveloping the spread of gridded towns across the colony justifies a more political reading. For other construals of the ideology of grid-plans in the New World, see Markman, "The Gridiron Town Plan," 471–490; and Mundy, "The Grid Plan," in "Maps of the Relaciones Geográficas."

24   A number of resettlements were imposed on native communities towards the mid-sixteenth century; however, the policy of *congregación* had its greatest impact in the early seventeenth century; see Gerhard, "Congregaciones de indios," 347–395 and Simpson, *Administration of the Indians of New Spain*. On *congregaciones*, see also Cline, "Civil Congregations," 349–369; and Lockhart, *The Nahuas*, 44–46. Kubler does not deal explicitly with *congregaciones*, but discusses the laying out of indigenous towns under the supervision of friars more generally; see *Mexican Architecture*, 85–90.

25   See, for example, the Laws of Burgos of 1512–

13, Simpson, *Administration of the Indians of New Spain*; and the Royal Ordinances of 1573, Nuttall, "Royal Ordinances," 249–254.

26 Although there can be no doubt that colonial policies gave birth to grid-plan towns, efforts to relocate and re-form indigenous communities faced native resistance which often undermined these projects; see Gibson, *The Aztecs*, 282–287. The causal relationship between colonial policy and the spread of grid plans in New Spain therefore remains undeniable but also unresolved.

27 Kubler, "The Colonial Plan of Cholula," 92–101, has made this point with regard to the Relación Geográfica map from Cholula. He maintains that the painting of the gridded town makes visible Cholula's social organization – which derives from prehispanic arrangements – not simply its physical appearance.

28 Damisch, "La grille," 30–40.

29 For an insightful discussion of the relations between this cartographic development and the advent of perspective in Renaissance Europe, see Damisch, "La grille," 30–40; and *The Origin of Perspective*.

30 In this, the grid has been deployed in ways that parallel its use in European maps created from antiquity through the Renaissance; see Harvey, *Topographical Maps,* and Certeau, *The Practice of Everyday Life*, 120.

31 The map of Minas de Zumpango is not alone in this. A number of indigenous maps from the sixteenth century depict idealized projections that relate tangentially to the actual form of the town. In some cases, these maps represent communities planned but not yet constructed. In other instances, the map-maker uses the grid as an ideological construct or as a form for charting social relations; see, for example, Kubler, "The Colonial Plan of Cholula," 92–101, and Mundy, "The Grid Plan," in "Maps of the Relaciones Geográficas."

32 I know of less than a handful of sixteenth-century indigenous maps that identify by name the districts of gridded towns.

33 At the time this Relación Geográfica map was executed, approximately 750 people called Texúpa their home. On the eve of the Spanish conquest, however, 12,000 had resided in this district; see Kubler, *Mexican Architecture*, 92. On the relationship between this map and the actual community of Texúpa and its environs, see Bailey, "The Map of Texúpa," 452–479.

34 On the ways that the imaginary affects and gives rise to actual events and responses, see, for example, Damisch, *The Origin of Perspective* and the analysis of nationalism set forth by Anderson, *Imagined Communities*.

14 LUCA SIGNORELLI S *RULE OF ANTICHRIST*

This essay is a significantly altered version of a section of one chapter in my forthcoming book on Signorelli's mural of the *Antichrist* (*The Renaissance Antichrist: Luca Signorelli's Orvieto Frescoes*, Princeton: Princeton University Press, 1995).

1 See, most notably, Chastel, "L'Apocalypse" (1952), who argues that Savonarola be identified as Signorelli's Antichrist, an interpretation that has been accepted by most historians. For a contrasting point of view, note my "Republicanism."

2 For the history of the chapel and the fresco decorations see, most notably, Fumi, *Il Duomo*, 88 ff. Regarding the rarity of Italian considerations of the Last Judgment, as well as some of the reasons for this phenomenon, see Freyhan, "Joachimism," 214–215.

3 On the apocalyptic dimension to medieval anti-Judaism consult Lewis, "Tractatus advaesus Judaeos," 544–545 and 554 ff., and, for the general setting for the Muslims as apocalyptic adversaries consult, among many sources, Patrides, "The Bloody and Cruell Turke," 126–135; and Southern, *Western Views of Islam*, 22 ff.

4 Cited by Trachtenberg, *The Devil and the Jews*, 39.

5 The best introductions to the medieval and Renaissance Antichrist are Emmerson, *Antichrist in the Middle Ages*, and Chastel, "L'Antéchrist," 177–186.

6 The Jewish role in the legend is well summarized by Emmerson, *Antichrist in the Middle Ages*, especially 89–91, 100, and 134–135. For the Muslim role see Alexander, "The Legend of the Last Roman Emperor," 53.

7 Regarding the associated ideas of crusade and apocalyptic thinking see Setton, *Papacy and the Levant*, vol. 2, 524 ff.

8 On the chapel iconography, note my forthcoming *The Renaissance Antichrist*, and my "Republicanism," 157–185.

9 The standard source for the life of Antichrist was the biography written by Adso Dervensis (*De ortu et tempore Antichristi*) in c. 954. The basic events in Signorelli's representation follow Adso, although almost certainly through intervening texts.

10 The most obvious contemporaneous reference is made through the several portraits of rulers in the mural, on which see my forthcoming *The Renaissance Antichrist*.

11 For Antichrist's use of bribes, see Adso, *Antichristi* (trans. J. Wright, in *Play of the Antichrist*), 104.

12 For conspicuous dress as an attribute of the

usurious Jew see Roth, *Jews in Italy*, 211. I am not the first to suggest that the figure is a Jew. See also Chastel, "L'Apocalypse," 128–129. Regarding the green hat, yellow garments and symbol as emblematic of the usurer, see Kisch, "The Yellow Badge," 26 ff. (The yellow color was symbolic of Judas's betrayal of Christ for pieces of gold.) The purse device seems a free play on the circle and six-pointed star, both of which were used widely, although the latter somewhat later (the sixteenth century), and then not widely (Rubens, *Jewish Costume*, 80 ff.). Perhaps Signorelli's design was meant to conjure up the yellow rings identified with usury (Zafran, "Iconography of Antisemitism," 13). On the dress of poor women during the period, which is close to the dress of Signorelli's figures, note Hartley, *Medieval Costume*, 109 ff.

13 See, for example, Vincent Ferrer's preachment on the subject as collected by Brettle: *San Vincente*, 182.

14 Ripa, *Baroque Imagery*, 164. For the dark-skinned Judas see, for example, Signorelli's own *Institution of the Eucharist* (Cortona, Museo Diocesano, 1512), or, best known of all, Leonardo da Vinci, *The Last Supper* (Milan, Santa Maria delle Grazie, 1497). Regarding the linkage between Judas and Antichrist see Burton, *The Devil*, 231. For the dark color of Satan see Burton, *Lucifer*, 132–133. For the swarthy complexion of the Jew in art, note Blumenkranz, "Le Juif," 35.

15 Trachtenberg, *The Devil and the Jews*, 46. See, for example, the comments of Vincent Ferrer (Brettle, *San Vincente*, 183), who notes that Jews "mix with the Christians, especially women and do much harm."

16 For a summary of the attitude of the medieval Church toward usury refer to Little, *Religious Poverty*, 42 ff., and note Fuchs, *Die Jüden*, 13, for Satan, usury, and the Jew in art.

17 Trachtenberg, *The Devil and the Jews*, 18 and 20, and Bröwe, *Die Eucharistischen Wünder*, 128–138. The exaltation of the Eucharist is the cornerstone of the overall program of murals in the Cappella Nuova, and the condemnation of Jewish (and Muslim) doubts about the efficacy of the Sacrament is one theme of the mid-trecento murals in the neighboring Cappella del Corporale.

18 Trachtenberg, 21.

19 Regarding the first anti-Judaic images see Lewis, "Tractatus," 546 ff. Note, too, Fuchs, *Die Jüden*, 13, 20, 114 ff and 124 ff.

20 Trachtenberg, 170 ff, especially 174; and Lewis, 544.

21 Edwards, *Jews in Christian Europe*, 111 ff.

22 See Trachtenberg, 32, for Jewish converts and, for the more general alliance of Jew and Antichrist, see Cohen, "Esau as Symbol," 39; and Cohn, *The Pursuit of the Millennium*, 78–79.

23 Cohn, 76, and Trachtenberg, 40.

24 Leff, *Heresy in the Later Middle Ages*, 1: 73–78, and 2: 536–541.

25 See the hybrid figure painted by Filippino Lippi that Geiger characterizes in a similar way (*Filippino Lippi*, 81), and certain late fifteenth-century images noted by Blumenkranz, "Le Juif," 74–75, and by de Hevesy, "Une *Histoire Turque*," 286–296.

26 Regarding the portrayal of Muslims by Pintoricchio, see de Hevesy, "Portraits of the Borgias," 70. Among Italian representations of Jews conforming to this physiognomic stereotype see the Judas in Cosimo Rosselli, *Last Supper* (Sistine Chapel, 1482). Among contemporary Spanish works note Juan de Flandes, *Ecce Homo* (Valencia Cathedral, c. 1510). For a general consideration of the Jewish facial type in art see Zafran, "The Iconography of Antisemitism," 20–21.

27 Vecellio, *Habiti antichi e moderni*, 133. For the earring, as worn by Turks, see Bruhn and Tilke, *A Pictorial History of Costume*, pl. 269, nos. 52, 61 and 63.

28 For the purse see Anderson, *Hispanic Costume, 1480–1530*, 86–87, and for the headgear see 35 ff.

29 Newton, *Renaissance Theatre Costume*, 106, who also writes of a comparable theatrical invention for another contemporary Antichrist depiction, the costumes in the Bosch Prado *Epiphany*. Regarding the Antichrist drama and its importance for Signorelli see my "Republicanism," 165–166.

30 Trachtenberg, *The Devil and the Jews*, 11.

31 See O'Callaghan, *A History of Medieval Spain*, 659, concerning Alexander's regard for the Spanish monarchs. Note the following concerning the millennialism of the court ideology: Sweet, "Christopher Columbus and the Millennial Vision of the New World," 374; Phelan, *The Millennial Kingdom of the Franciscans*, 5 ff; and Kagan, "The Spain of Ferdinand and Isabella," 55–61. For a general assessment of Spanish apocalypticism see Reeves, *Prophecy*, 358. Regarding Spanish and papal coordination of the persecution of Jews, see Llorentes, *l'Inquisition d'Espagne*, 290 and 330 ff, and Lea, *History of the Inquisition*, vol. 1, 174 and 178. On Alexander's Jewish policies in general consult Ferares, "La Medaille dites de Fourvières," 227 ff and Vogelstein and Rieger, *Des Jüden in Rom*, 23–28. For a less harsh view of Alexander's share in the persecution see Edwards, *Jews in Christian Europe*, 11–12.

32 On the resettlement of the Jews, see Roth, *History of the Jews*, 260. For the comment of the Sultan, see *Jewish Encyclopedia*, vol. 11, 500.

Note also Gerber, *The Jews of Spain*, 145–175.

33 Regarding the nature of the prophecies, see Watts, "Prophecy and Discovery," 34; Thorndike, *Magic and Experimental Science*, vol. 4, 101–131; and Prosperi, "New Heaven and New Earth," 279–303.

34 My forthcoming *Renaissance Antichrist* provides a detailed discussion of Annio's and Vincent's beliefs concerning Antichrist.

35 Consult my "Republicanism," 162, for identification of the Dominican. Regarding the importance of Vincent's preachment, see Brettle, *San Vincente*, 14–17 and 173–195, and Fages, *Histoire de Saint Vincent*, vol. 2, 413 ff. For Vincent's importance in Orvieto consult Fumi, *San Bernardino*, 18. As to the origins of the designation "Angel of the Apocalypse," see Fages, vol. 1, 322–326.

36 Fages, *Histoire de Saint Vincent*, vol. 2, 337. On the importance of the bull in the appreciation of Vincent's fame note Oakley, *The Western Church*, 261.

37 On Vincent's anti-Judaism see Gorce, "Vincent Ferrier (Saint)," cols. 3033–3045. Wistrich comments that, although he led efforts against the Jews, Vincent did nevertheless resist taking violent measures against them (*Antisemitism*, 35). See Synan, *The Popes and Jews*, 142–143, and Lea, *Inquisition*, vol. 1, 112, on how Vincent's anti-Jewish militancy was a prelude to later persecutions. Note Hockers, "New Chronicles on the Expulsion of the Jews," 201–228, for the enduring Jewish fear of Vincent. See Alba, ed., *Del Anticristo*, 62, for the reference to Vincent, and for the appended note to a Rabbi Isaac titled "*Contra errores Iudaeorum*" in the Spanish reprint of the German *Entkrist*, a life which was first printed in 1472 (Kelchner, ed., *Der Entkrist*). The illustration reproduced here from the *Entkrist* comes from the original German edition. A new set of images was made for the Spanish reprint.

38 On the complex early history of Annio's text (*De futuris christianorum triumphis in Saracenos*), see Thorndike, *Magical and Experimental Science*, vol. 4, 264–265 and 265, n. 24. For Annio's life see my "Republicanism" and Caporali, ed., *Annio da Viterbo*. Regarding the early publishing history of the text see Hain, *Repertorium Bibliographicum*, vol. 1, nos. 1123–1129 (124–125).

39 Weiss, "Annio da Viterbo," 435, Consenza, *Dictionary of Italian Humanists*, vol. 1, 197, and Thorndike, *Magical and Experimental Science*, vol. 4, 267.

40 The text in question is "Questiones super multeo Judaico et civili et divino; Pro monte pietatis, Viterbo, 1497" (*Biblioteca Vaticana*, 1131). Annio's knowledge of the important Hebraic texts was, in spite of his anti-Judaism, impressive (Roth, *Jews in the Renaissance*, 141–142).

41 See Krinsky, "The Temple of Jerusalem," 2, for a brief history of the structure. Note Bousset, *Antichrist Legend*, 160–163, and Emmerson, *Antichrist*, 38 and 42, for the place of the Temple in the myth of Antichrist. Only Cruttwell, *Signorelli*, 71, and Perali, *Orvieto*, 156–157, have suggested that this is the temple constructed by Antichrist rather than the Temple of Solomon, although I myself was at one time in agreement with this latter identification ("Republicanism," 163).

42 As cited by O'Malley, *Giles of Viterbo*, 122.

43 Concerning the New World myth of the Jews and Indians see Phelan, *The Millennial Kingdom of the Franciscans*, 24–25. For a comment on the significance of the conversion of the Jews in the history of End-Time, note Reeves, *Joachim of Fiore*, 11, 50 and 68.

Epilogue

See Section 1 of the Consolidated Bibliography for full citations of the following references.

1 Panofsky's arguments for the proper "aesthetic" boundaries of art history are principally located in his 1940 essay, "The History of Art as a Humanistic Discipline." Panofsky made a basic distinction between the natural sciences and the humanities, but he also saw them as complements: "the succession of steps by which the material is organized into a natural or cultural cosmos is analogous, and the same is true of the methodological problems implied by this process" (citing page 7). For further discussion of this text, see my essay, "What Is Visual Culture?" forthcoming in the proceedings of the Panofsky Centennial Symposium at the Institute for Advanced Study, Princeton.

2 The two remarks on African art appear in "The History of Art as a Humanistic Discipline," 7, 13.

3 *Studies in Iconology*, 3. See Joan Hart's discussion of Panofsky's modeling of this scene on a similar one in the writings of Karl Mannheim, "Panofsky and Mannheim."

4 See Fried, "Art and Objecthood."

5 Tiffany, "Cryptesthesia: Visions of the Other."

6 See *Iconology*, 5–6, 158, and the related concept of the "metapicture" in Chapter 2.

7 Althusser, "Ideology and Ideological State Apparatuses (Notes Toward an Investigation)," in *Lenin and Philosophy*.

8 Althusser, 174.

9   See my discussion of the French ideologues and the history of ideology in *Iconology*, 165–66.

10   First published as "Die Perspective als 'symbolische Form'" (1927).

11   Podro, *The Critical Historians of Art*, 186.

12   Joel Snyder urges caution on this point, arguing that Podro "misunderstands an implicit inner/outer distinction made by Panofsky." "The painters," claims Snyder, "believed that perspective provided an 'absolute standpoint.' But the understanding of perspective from the standpoint of a neo-Kantian, twentieth-century art historian shows that it does not have a special privileged, natural claim upon us. Panofsky takes the latter to be his contribution to the study of perspective and the inner view to be the prevailing, uninformed position" (correspondence with author). I agree that Panofsky believes in some such distinction between the painter's and the iconologist's "perspective," but I think Panofsky's practice, choice of examples, and model of analysis undermines it. It is not that Panofsky believes that pictorial perspective, literally understood, is a universal, ahistorical norm, but that this model, with all its figural and conceptual furniture (surface-depth, three-dimensionality, the "subject/object" paradigm for the relation of beholder and beheld) is imbedded in the rhetoric of Kantian epistemology.

CONSOLIDATED BIBLIOGRAPHY

I HISTORIOGRAPHY AND CRITICISM

Abu-Lughod, Janet L. *Before European Hegemony: The World System A.D. 1250–1350*. New York and Oxford: Oxford University Press, 1989.

Aers, David. "A Whisper in the Ear of Early Modernists; or, Reflections on Literary Critics Writing the 'History of the Subject.'" *Culture and History 1350–1600: Essays on English Communities, Identities and Writing*, ed. D. Aers, 177–202. Detroit: Wayne State University Press, 1992.

The Age of the Marvelous, ed. Joy Kenseth. Hanover: Hood Museum of Art and Dartmouth College: The Stinehour Press, 1991.

Alberti, Leon Battista. *On the Art of Building in Ten Books*, trans. Joseph Rykwert, Neil Leach, and Robert Tavernor. Cambridge, Ma. and London: Harvard University Press, 1988.

Allatios, Leo. *The Newer Temples of the Greeks*, trans. A. Cutler. University Park, Pa.: The Pennsylvania State University Press, 1969.

Alpers, Svetlana. "Is Art History?" *Daedalus* 106 (1977), 1–13.

Alpers, Svetlana. "The Museum as a Way of Seeing." *Exhibiting Cultures*, 25–32.

Althusser, Louis. "Ideology and Ideological State Apparatuses (Notes Toward an Investigation.)" *Lenin and Philosophy*, tr. B. Brewster, 209–219. New York: Monthly Review Press, 1971.

Amin, Samir. *Eurocentrism*, trans. R. Moore. New York: Monthly Review Press, 1989.

Anderson, Benedict. *Imagined Communities: Reflections on the Origin and Spread of Nationalism*. Rev. edn., London and New York: Verso, 1991.

Anderson, Perry. *Lineages of the Absolutist State*. London: NLB, 1974.

Aristotle. *The Works of Aristotle Translated into English*, ed. W. D. Ross. 12 vols. Oxford: Clarendon Press, 1910–52.

Arte e artisti dei laghi lombardi, ed. Edoardo Arslan. 2 vols. Como: Tip. editrice A. Noseda, 1959 and 1964.

Babinger, Franz. *Spätmittelalterliche fränkische Briefschaften aus dem grossherrlichen Seraj zu Stambul*. Munich: R. Oldenbourg, 1963.

Bal, Mieke and Norman Bryson. "Semiotics and Art History." *Art Bulletin* 73 (1991), 174–208.

Balogh, Jolán. *Die Anfänge der Renaissance in Ungarn. Matthias Corvinus und die Kunst*. Graz: Akademische Druck-u. Verlag sanstalt, 1975.

Balogh, Jolán. *Művészet Mátyás Király Udvarában*. Budapest: Akademiai Kiado, 1966.

Balšánek A. *Štíty a motivy attikové y české renaissance*. Prague: Ceská Matice Technika, Ročnik, 1902.

Barber, Charles. "From Transformation to Desire: Art and Worship after Byzantine Iconoclasm," *Art Bulletin* 75 (1993), 7–16.

Barber, Charles. "The Body within the Frame: a Use of Word and Image in Iconoclasm," *Word and Image* 9 (1993), 140–153.

Barnard, F. M. *Introduction to J. G. Herder on Social and Political Culture*, ed., trans., and intro., F. M. Barnard. Cambridge: Cambridge University Press, 1969.

Barocchi, Paola, ed. *Scritti d'arte del cinquecento*. 9 vols. Turin: Giulio Einaidi Editore, 1977.

Barocchi, Paola, ed. *Trattati d'arte del cinquecento*. 3 vols. Bari: Giuseppe Laterza e Figli, 1961.

Barrell, John. *The Political Theory of Painting from Reynolds to Hazlitt: "The Body of the Public."* New Haven and London: Yale University Press, 1986.

Bassani, Ezio and William B. Fagg. *Africa and the Renaissance: Art in Ivory*, ed. S. Vogel with C. Thompson, with an essay by Peter Mark. New York: Center for African Art and Prestel, 1988.

Batteaux, Abbé Charles. *Les beaux arts réduits a la même principe*. Paris, 1746.

Baxandall, Michael. *Giotto and the Orators. Humanist Observers of Painting in Italy and the Discovery of Pictorial Composition*. Oxford: Clarendon Press, 1971.

Baxandall, Michael. *The Limewoood Sculptors of Renaissance Germany*. New Haven: Yale University Press, 1980.

Bayet, Charles. *L'Art byzantin*. Paris: Picard, 1904 (1st edn., Paris: Quantin 1883).

Belting, Hans. *The End of the History of Art?*,

trans. C. S. Wood. Chicago and London: The University of Chicago Press, 1987.

Benhabib, Seyla. *Critique, Norm, and Utopia: A Study of the Foundations of Critical Theory.* New York: Columbia University, 1986.

Berlin, Isaiah. "Herder and the Enlightenment." *Vico and Herder,* 143–216.

Berlin, Isaiah. *Vico and Herder: Two Studies in the History of Ideas.* New York: The Viking Press, 1976.

Bernal, Martin. *Black Athena. The Afroasiatic Roots of Classical Civilization. I. The Fabrication of Ancient Greece 1785–1985.* New Brunswick: Rutgers University Press, 1987.

Bhabha, Homi. "Double Visions." *Artforum International* 30:5 (1992), 85–89.

Bhabha, Homi. "Of Mimicry and Man: the Ambivalence of Colonial Discourse." *October* 28 (Spring 1984), 125–133.

Bhabha, Homi. "Signs Taken for Wonders: Questions of Ambivalence and Authority under a Tree Outside Delhi, May 1817." *Critical Inquiry* 12/1 (Autumn 1985), 144–165.

Białostocki, Jan. "Mannerism and the Vernacular in Polish Art." *Walter Friedländer zum 90. Geburtstag. Eine Festgabe seiner europäischen Schüler, Freunde, und Verehrer,* 47–57. Berlin: De Gruyter, 1965.

Białostocki, Jan. "Renaissance Sculpture in Poland and its European Context: Some Selected Problems." Samuel Fiszman, ed., *The Polish Renaissance in its European Context,* 281–290. Bloomington and Indianapolis: Indiana University Press, 1988.

Białostocki, Jan. "Rinascimento Polacco and Rinascimento Europeo." *Polonia–Italia. Relazioni Artistiche dal Medioevo al XVIII Secolo.*

Białostocki, Jan. "Some Values of Artistic Periphery." *Themes of World Art,* ed. I. Lavin, I, 6–11. 3 vols. University Park, Pa.: Pennsylvania State University Press, 1992.

Białostocki, Jan. *The Art of the Renaissance in Eastern Europe.* Ithaca and Oxford: Cornell University Press, 1976.

Blier, Suzanne. "Imaging Otherness in Ivory: African Portrayals of the Portuguese c. 1492." *Art Bulletin* 75 (1993), 375–397.

Boas, Franz. *The Mind of Primitive Man* (1911), rev. edn., New York: The Macmillan Co., 1938.

Bohrer, Frederick. Review of *Europa und der Orient, 800–1900* and *Exotischen Welten,*

Europäische Phantasien. Art Bulletin 73 (1991), 325–330.

Bologna e il Mondo Nuovo, ed. L. Laurencich-Minelli. Exhibition catalogue. Museo Civico Medievale, Bologna: Grafis Edizioni, 1992.

Brett, Gerard. "The Automata in the Byzantine 'Throne of Solomon.'" *Speculum* 29 (1954), 477–487.

Brown, Jonathan. *The Golden Age of Painting in Spain.* New Haven and London: Yale University Press, 1991.

Brown, Patricia Fortini. "Painting and History in Renaissance Venice." *Art History* 7 (1984), 263–94.

Brown, Patricia Fortini. *Venetian Narrative Painting in the Age of Carpaccio.* New Haven and London: Yale University Press, 1988.

Bruni, Leonardi. *Historia Florentina,* intro. D. Acciaioli. Venice: Jacobus Puteus, 1476.

Brush, Kathryn. Review of Riegl, *Problems of Style;* Olin, *Forms of Representation in Alois Riegl's Theory of Art;* and Iverson, *Alois Riegl. Art Bulletin* 76 (1994), 355–358.

Bryson, Norman. *Vision in Painting. The Logic of the Gaze.* New Haven: Yale University Press, 1983.

Bundy, M. W. *The Theory of the Imagination in Classical and Medieval Thought.* University of Illinois Studies in Language and Literature, XII. Urbana: University of Illinois Press, 1927.

Burckhardt, Jacob. *Die Kultur der Renaissance in Italien* (1860). Cologne: Phaidon, 1956.

Burckhardt, Jacob. *The Civilization of the Renaissance in Italy,* trans. S. G. C. Middlemore (1904), intro. P. Burke, notes by P. Murray. London: Penguin Books, 1990.

Burke, Peter. *The Italian Renaissance: Culture and Society in Italy.* Rev. edn., Princeton: Princeton University Press, 1987.

Burke, Peter. *The Renaissance.* Atlantic Highlands, N.J.: Humanities Press International, 1987.

Byzance. L'art byzantin dans les collections publiques françaises, ed. Jannic Durand. Paris: Réunion des Musées nationaux, 1992.

Byzantine Art an [sic] European Art. Ninth Exhibition held under the Auspices of the Council of Europe. Athens: Department of Antiquities and Archaeological Restoration, 1964.

Cahn, Walter. *Masterpieces: Chapters on the History of an Idea.* Princeton: Princeton

University Press, 1979.

Cameron, Averil. "The Construction of Court Ritual: The *Book of Ceremonies*" in *Rituals of Royalty, Power and Ceremonial in Traditional Societies*, eds. D. Cannadine and S. Price. Cambridge: Cambridge University Press, 1987.

Cameron, Averil. *The Use and Abuse of Byzantium: an Essay on Reception.* Inaugural lecture, Chair of Late Antique and Byzantine Studies. London: King's College, 1972.

Campbell, Mary. *Witness and the Other World: Exotic European Travel Writing, 400–1600.* Ithaca and London: Cornell University Press, 1988.

Canons and Decrees of the Council of Trent: Original Text with English Translation, ed. and trans. Rev. H. J. Schroeder, O.P. St. Louis and London: B. Herder Book Co., 1941.

Caygill, Howard. *Art of Judgement.* Oxford and Cambridge: Basil Blackwell, 1989.

Cennini, Cennino d'Andrea. *The Craftsman's Handbook,* trans. D. V. Thompson, Jr. New Haven: Yale University Press, 1933.

Certeau, Michel de. *The Writing of History* (1975), trans. T. Conley. New York: Columbia University Press, 1988.

Chamiarytski, V. A. *Francisk Skarina.* Paris: UNESCO, 1980.

Circa 1492. Art in the Age of Exploration ed. Jay A. Levenson. Exhibition catalogue. Washington, D.C., National Gallery of Art, 1991.

Clark, Kenneth. *Piero della Francesca.* London: Phaidon, 1951.

Clifford, James. *The Predicament of Culture: Twentieth-Century Ethnography, Literature, and Art.* Cambridge and London: Harvard University Press, 1988.

Clifford, James and George E. Marcus, eds. *Writing Culture: The Poetics and Politics of Ethnography.* Berkeley: University of California Press, 1986.

Coffin, David. "Pirro Ligorio and the Nobility of the Arts." *Journal of the Warburg and Courtauld Institutes* 27 (1964), 191–210.

Condivi, Ascanio. *The Life of Michelangelo,* trans. A. S. Wohl. Baton Rouge: Louisiana State University Press, 1976.

Cordell, Linda. *Prehistory of the Southwest.* San Diego–Toronto: Academic Press, Inc., 1984.

Corrigan, Kathleen. *Visual Polemics in the Ninth-Century Byzantine Psalters.* New York: Cambridge University Press, 1992.

Craig, John. *Scholarship and Nation Building: The Universities of Strasbourg and Alsatian Society 1870–1939.* Chicago and London: University of Chicago Press, 1984.

Cutler, Anthony and Nicolas Oikonomides. "An Imperial Byzantine Casket and Its Fate at a Humanist's Hands." *Art Bulletin* 70 (1988), 77–87.

Cutler, Anthony. "La 'questione bizantina' nella pittura italiana: una visione alternativa della maniera greca." *La Pittura in Italia. L'alto medioevo,* ed. C. Bertelli, 335–354. Milan: Electa, 1994.

Cutler, Anthony. *The Aristocratic Psalters in Byzantium.* Bibliothèque des Cahiers archéologiques, 13. Paris: Picard, 1984.

Dacos, Nicole. *La Découverte de la Domus Aurea et la Formation des Grotesques à la Renaissance.* Studies of the Warburg Institute, vol. 31. London: The Warburg Institute, University of London and Leiden: E. J. Brill, 1969.

Danforth, Susan. *Encountering the New World 1493 to 1800,* intro. W. McNeill. Providence, R.I.: The John Carter Brown Library, 1991.

Danti, Vincenzo. *Il primo libro del trattato delle perfette proporzione di tutte le cose che imitare e ritrarre si possano con l'arte del disegno.* Florence, 1567.

Darwin, Charles. *The Descent of Man and Selection in Relation to Sex.* 2 vols. London: Murray, 1871.

de Mesa, José and Teresa Gisbert, *Bernardo Bitti, un pintor manierista en Sudamerica.* La Paz: Division de Extension Universitaria, Instituto de Estudios Bolivianos, Universidad Mayor de San Sanres, 1974.

Degler, Carl. *In Search of Human Nature. The Decline and Revival of Darwinism in American Social Thought.* New York and Oxford: Oxford University Press, 1991.

Derrida, Jacques. *The Truth in Painting,* trans. G. Bennington and I. MacLeod. Chicago and London: University of Chicago Press, 1987.

Documentary Culture. Florence and Rome from Grand-Duke Ferdinand I to Pope Alexander VII. Papers from a Colloquium Held at the Villa Spelman, Florence, 1990, ed. E. Cropper, G. Perini, and F. Solinas, intro. E. Cropper. Villa Spelman Colloquia, 3. Bologna: Nuova Alfa Editoriale, 1992.

Dodd, Erica. "The Image of the Word. Notes

on the Religious Iconography of Islam." *Berytus* 18 (1969), 35–80.

Dubos, Abbé Jean-Baptiste. *Critical Reflections on Poetry and Painting*, trans. T. Nugent. 3 vols. London: Nourse, 1748.

Dubos, Abbé Jean-Baptiste. *Reflexions critiques sur la poësie et sur la peinture*, 4th edn. 3 vols. Paris: P.-J. Mariette, 1740.

Eagleton, Terry. *The Ideology of the Aesthetic*. Oxford and Cambridge, Ma.: Basil Blackwell, 1990.

Eagleton, Terry, Frederic Jameson, and Edward Said. *Nationalism, Colonialism, and Literature*, intro. S. Deane. Minneapolis: University of Minneapolis Press, 1990.

The Early Years of Art History in the United States: Notes and Essays on Departments, Teaching, and Scholars, ed. C. Smyth and P. Lukehart. Princeton: Princeton University Press, 1993.

Eco, Umberto. *The Limits of Interpretation*. Bloomington–Indianapolis: Indiana University Press, 1990.

Eisler, Colin. "*Kunstgeschichte* American Style: a Study in Migration." *The Intellectual Migration. Europe and America, 1930–1960*, ed. D. Fleming and B. Bailyn, 544–629. Cambridge: Harvard University Press, 1969.

Elliot, J. H. *The Old World and The New 1492–1650*. Cambridge: Cambridge University Press, 1970.

Epstein, Steven. *Wage Labor and Guilds in Medieval Europe*. Chapel Hill and London: University of North Carolina Press, 1991.

Ettinghausen, Richard. *La Peinture arabe*. Geneva: Skira, 1977.

Ettlinger, L. D. "On Science, Industry and Art: Some Theories of Gottfried Semper." *Architectural Review* 136: 809 (July 1964), 57–60.

Europe and its Others: Proceedings of the Essex Conference on the Sociology of Literature, ed. Francis Barker, 2 vols. Colchester: University of Essex, 1983.

Exhibiting Cultures: the Poetics and Politics of Museum Display, ed. I. Karp and S. Lavine. Washington and London: Smithsonian Institution Press, 1990.

Exotische Welten: Europäisches Phantasien. 6 vols. Stuttgart: Württenbergischer Kunstverein et al., 1987.

Fabian, Johannes. "The Other and the Eye: Time and the Rhetoric of Vision." *Time and the Other. How Anthropology Makes its Object*, 105–141. New York: Columbia University Press, 1983.

Farago, Claire. "The Classification of the Visual Arts during the Renaissance." *The Shapes of Knowledge from the Renaissance to the Enlightenment*, eds. R. Popkin and D. Kelley, 23–48. Dordrecht and London: Kluwer Academic Publishers, 1991.

Farago, Claire. *Leonardo da Vinci's "Paragone," a Critical Interpretation with a New Edition of the Text in the Codex Urbinas*. Leiden and Cologne: E. J. Brill, 1992.

Farago, Claire. "Leonardo da Vinci's Defense of Painting as a Universal Language." *Word and Image Interactions: A Selection of Papers*, ed. M. Heusser et al., 125–133. Basel: Niese, 1993.

Farago, Claire. "Renaissance Art Out of the Canon: Art, Gender, and Cultural Diversity, 1500–1600." *Women of Color and the Multicultural Curriculum: Transforming the College Classroom*, ed. L. Fiol-Matta and M. Chamberlain, 152–156. New York: The Feminist Press and The City University of New York, 1994.

Farago, Claire. "The Status of the 'State as a Work of Art': Re-Viewing Burckhardt's Renaissance from the Borderlines." *Cultural Exchange between European Nations during the Renaissance*, ed. G. Sorelius and M. Srigley, 17–32. Acta Universitatis Upsaliensis, Studia Anglistica Upsaliensia, 86. Stockholm: Almqvist & Wiksell, 1994.

Ferguson, Wallace. "Humanist Views of the Renaissance." *American Historical Review* 45 (1939), 1–23.

Ferguson, Wallace. *The Renaissance in Historical Thought: Five Centuries of Interpretation*. Cambridge, Ma.: Harvard University Press, 1948.

ffolliott, Sheila. Review of *Circa 1492: Art in the Age of Exploration*, exhibition and catalogue. *William and Mary Quarterly* (1992), 387–392.

Fiedler, Conrad. *On Judging Works of Visual Art*, trans. H. Schaefer-Simmern and F. Mood, intro. H. Schaefer-Simmern. Reprint with corrections. Berkeley–London: University of California Press, 1978. Originally published as *Über die Beuteilung von Werken der bildenden Kunst*, 1876.

Findlen, Paula. "The Museum: Its Classical Etymology and Renaissance Genealogy." *Journal of the History of Collections* 1/1 (1989), 59–78.

Frantsysk Skaryna i jaho Chas. Entsyklapedychny

Davednik, ed. I. P. Shamiakin. Minsk: Vvdavetstva Belaruskakila Savetskakila gentsykla pcdykila imkila Petruskila Brofuki, 1988.

Fried, Michael. "Art and Objecthood." *Art forum* (Special Issue, Summer 1967), 12–23.

Gates of Mystery. The Art of Holy Russia, ed. Roderick Grierson Exhibition Catalogue. Fort Worth: Inter Cultura, n.d. [1993].

Gates, Henry Louis, Jr., ed. *"Race," Writing, and Difference*. Chicago and London: University of Chicago Press, 1986.

Gay, Peter. *Weimar Culture: the Outside as Insider*. New York: Harper & Row, 1968.

Gerbi, Antonello. *The Dispute of the New World. The History of a Polemic, 1750–1900*, trans. J. Moyle. Pittsburgh: University of Pittsburgh Press, 1973.

Gibbon, Edward. *The Decline and Fall of the Roman Empire*. New York: Modern Library edition, 3 vols., n.d.

Gilbert, Neal. *Renaissance Concepts of Method*. New York: Columbia University Press, 1960.

Glick, Thomas F. and Oriol Pi-Sunyer. "Acculturation as an Explanatory Concept in Spanish History." *Comparative Studies in Society and History* 11 (1969), 136–154.

Goldthwaite, Richard. *Wealth and the Demand for Art in Italy 1300–1600*. Baltimore and London: The Johns Hopkins University Press, 1993.

Gombrich, E. H. "In Search of Cultural History." 1969. Reprinted in *Ideals and Idols. Essays on Values in History and in Art*, 24–59. Oxford: Phaidon, 1979.

Gombrich, E. H. "On Physiognomic Perception." In *Meditations on a Hobby Horse and Other Essays on the Theory of Art*, 45–55. London and New York: Phaidon, 1963.

Gombrich, E. H. "The Style *all'antica*: Imitation and Assimilation." In *Norm and Form. Studies in the Art of the Renaissance*, 129–136. London and New York: Phaidon Press, 1971.

Gombrich, E. H. *Tributes: Interpreters of Our Cultural Tradition*. Ithaca: Cornell University Press, 1984.

Gombrich, Ernst and Didier Eribon. *Looking for Answers: Conversations on Art and Science* (1991). New York: Harry N. Abrams, 1993.

Goodman, Anthony and Angus MacKay, ed. *The Impact of Humanism on Western Europe*. London and New York: Longman, 1990.

Grafton, Anthony and Lisa Jardine. *From Humanism to the Humanities. Education and the Liberal Arts in Fifteeenth- and Sixteenth-Century Europe*. Cambridge, Ma.: Harvard University Press, 1986.

Greenblatt, Stephen. *Marvelous Possessions: the Wonder of the New World*. Chicago: University of Chicago Press, 1991.

Grigely, Joseph. *Textualterity: Art, Theory and Textual Criticism*, Ann Arbor: University of Michigan Press, 1995.

Gurevich, Aron. *Historical Anthropology of the Middle Ages*. Cambridge: Cambridge University Press, 1992.

Gutfleisch, Barbara and Joachim Menzhausen, "'How a Kunstkammer Should Be Formed': Gabriel Kaltemarckt's Advice to Christian I of Saxony on the Formation of an Art Collection, 1587." *Journal of the History of Collections* 1 (1989), 3–32.

Gutiérrez, Ramón. *When Jesus Came the Corn Mothers Went Away: Marriage, Sexuality, and Power in New Mexico, 1500–1846*. Stanford: Stanford University Press, 1991.

Gyllius, Petrus (Pierre Gilles). *De Constantinopoleos topographia lib. IV*. Leiden: Elzevier, 1632 (first edition, 1516).

Hale, John. *The Civilization of Europe in the Renaissance*. London: Harper Collins, 1993 and New York: Atheneum, 1994.

Hanke, Lewis. *Aristotle and the American Indians: A Study in Race Prejudice in the Modern World*. Chicago: H. Regnery Co., 1959.

Hart, Joan. "Reinterpreting Wölfflin: Neo-Kantism and Hermeneutics." *Art Journal* 42 (1982), 292–300.

Harvey, E. Ruth. *The Inward Wits: Psychological Theory in the Middle Ages and Renaissance*. Studies of the Warburg Institute, vol. 6. London: The Warburg Institute, University of London, 1975.

Haskell, Francis. *History and its Images: Art and the Interpretation of the Past*. New Haven and London: Yale University Press, 1993.

Hayum, Andrée. "The Renaissance as a Historical Concept." *Abstracts and Program Statements 1993*, 55–56. 81st Annual Conference, Seattle, February 2–6, 1993. New York: College Art Association, 1993.

Helgerson, Ralph. *Forms of Nationhood: The Elizabethan Writing of England*. Chicago and London: University of Chicago Press, 1992.

Hendricks, Margo. See *Women, "Race," and Writing*.

Herder, Johann Gottfried. *The Outlines of a Philosophy of Man*, tr. T. Churchill. New York: Bergman, 1966.

Herder, Johann Gottfried. *Sämmtliche Werke*, ed. B. Suphan. 33 vols. Berlin: Weidmannsche Buchhandlung, 1877–1913.

Hermanin, Federigo. *L'opera del genio Italiano al' estero. Gli artisti in Germania*. Rome: Libreria dello stato [1934]–43.

Hildebrand, Adolf. *Das Problem der form in der bildenden Kunst* (1893). Strassburg: Heitz, 1901.

Hiller, Susan, ed. *The Myth of Primitivism. Perspectives on Art*. London and New York: Routledge, 1991.

Hitchcock, Henry-Russell. *German Renaiassance Architecture*. Princeton: Princeton University Press, 1981.

Hobsbawm, Eric. *Nations and Nationalism since 1780. Programme, Myth, Reality*. Cambridge: Cambridge University Press, 1990.

Hobson, Marian. *The Object of Art: the Theory of Illusion in Eighteenth-Century France*. Cambridge and Sydney: Cambridge University Press, 1982.

Hodgen, Margaret. *Early Anthropology in the Sixteenth and Seventeenth Centuries*. Philadelphia: University of Pennsylvania Press, 1964.

Hollingsworth, P. A. *Oxford Dictionary of Byzantium*, ed. A. P. Kazhdan et al., 501. New York: Oxford University Press, 1991.

Holly, Michael Ann. *Panofsky and the Foundations of Art History*. Ithaca–London: Cornell University Press, 1984.

Holly, Michael Ann. "Cultural History as a Work of Art; Jacob Burckhardt and Henry Adams." *Style* 22 (1988), 209–218.

Holly, Michael Ann. "Past Looking." *Critical Inquiry* 16 (1990), 371–395.

Holly, Michael Ann. See also *Visual Theory*.

Hooper-Greenhill, Eilean. *Museums and the Shaping of Knowledge*. London and New York: Routledge, 1992.

Horace. *Ars poetica*.

Hroch, Miroslav. *Social Preconditions of National Revival in Europe*. Cambridge: Cambridge University Press, 1985.

Husarski, W. *Attyka polska i jej wpływ na kraje sasiedie*. Warsaw: Towarzystwo wydawnicze, 1936.

Husarski, W. *Kamienice renesansowe w Kazimierzu Dolnym*. Lublin, 1950.

Hutter, Irmgard. *Corpus der byzantinischen Miniaturhandschriften*. 4 vols. Stuttgart: Hiersemann, 1977 to date.

Impey, Oliver. See *The Origins of Museums*.

Iverson, Margaret. *Alois Riegl: Art History and Theory*. Cambridge, Ma.: London: The MIT Press, 1993.

Iverson, Margaret. "The Primacy of Philosophy. Review of Holly, *Panofsky and the Foundations of Art History*." *Art History* 9 (1986), 271–274.

Jacoff, Michael. *The Horses of San Marco and the Quadriga of God*. Princeton: Princeton University Press, 1993.

James, Liz and Ruth Webb. "'To Understand Ultimate Things and Enter Secret Places': Ekphrasis and Art in Byzantium." *Art History* 14 (1991), 1–17.

JanMohammed, Abdul. "The Economy of the Manichean Allegory: The Function of Racial Difference in Colonialist Discourse." *Critical Inquiry* 12 (Autumn 1985), 59–87.

al Jazari, Ibn al-Razzaz. *The Book of Knowledge of Ingenious Mechanical Devices*, trans. and annotated by D. R. Hill. Dordrecht and Boston: Reidel, 1974.

Johnson, Lee. *The Paintings of Eugène Delacroix: A Critical Catalogue*, III. Oxford: Clarendon Press, 1986.

Jones, Owen. *The Grammar of Ornament* (1856). Reprint. New York: Van Nostrand Reinhold, 1982.

Kant, Immanuel. *Critique of Judgement*, trans. J. C. Meredith. Oxford: Clarendon Press, 1964.

Karling, Sten. "Les Stucateurs Italiens en Suède." *Arte e Artisti dei Laghi Lombardi* 2.

Karpowicz, Mariusz. *Artisti Ticinesi in Polonia nel '500*. Lugano: Repubblica e Cantone del Ticino, 1987.

Karpowicz, Mariusz. *Artisti Ticinesi in Polonia nel '600*. Lugano: Repubblica e Cantone del Ticino, 1983.

Kaufmann, Thomas DaCosta. *Court, Cloister and City: The Art and Culture of Central Europe 1450–1800*. London and Chicago: Weidenfeld and Nicholson, and Chicago University Press, 1995.

Kaufmann, Thomas DaCosta. *Drawings from the Holy Roman Empire. A Selection from North American Collections*. Princeton: Art Museum, Princeton University in association with Princeton University Press, 1982.

Kaufmann, Thomas DaCosta. "Introduction,"

Art and Architecture in Central Europe 1550–1620. An Annotated Bibliography. Boston: G. K. Hall, 1988.

Kaufmann, Thomas DaCosta. Review of Białostocki, *The Art of the Renaissance in Eastern Europe. Art Bulletin,* 68 (1978), 164–169.

Kaufmann, Thomas DaCosta. "The Eloquent Artist: Towards an Understanding of the Stylistics of Painting at the Court of Rudolf II." *Leids Kunsthistorisch Jaarboek* 1 (1982), 119–148.

Kaufmann, Thomas DaCosta. *The Mastery of Nature: Aspects of Art, Science, and Humanism in the Renaissance.* Princeton: Princeton University Press, 1993.

Kaufmann, Thomas DaCosta. "The Problem of Northern 'Mannerism': A Critical Review." In *Mannerism: Essays in Music and the Arts,* ed. S. E. Murray and Ruth I. Weidner, 89–115. West Chester, Pa.: West Chester State College, 1980.

Kaufmann, Thomas DaCosta. "What is 'New' about the 'New Art History'?" Philip Alperson, ed., *The Philosophy of the Visual Arts,* 515–520. New York and Oxford: Oxford University Press, 1992.

Kaufmann, Thomas DaCosta. "Reception Theory," in *The Dictionary of Art,* eds. H. Brigstocke and J. Turner. London: Macmillan, forthcoming 1996.

Kazhdan, Alexander and Anthony Cutler. "Continuity and Discontinuity in Byzantine History." *Byzantion* 52 (1982), 429–478.

Kelly, Joan [Gadol]. "The Doubled Vision of Feminist Theory. A Postscript to the 'Women and Power' Conference." *Women, History and Theory. The Essays of Joan Kelly,* 51–64. Chicago and London: University of Chicago Press, 1984.

Keylor, William. *Academy and Community: The Foundation of the French Historical Profession.* Cambridge: Harvard University Press, 1975.

Klein, Robert. *Form and Meaning: Essays on the Renaissance and Modern Art,* trans. M. Jay and L. Wieseltier, foreword H. Zerner. Princeton: Princeton University Press, 1970.

Knös, Börje. "La Légende de Bélisaire dans les pays grecs." *Erasmus* 58 (1960), 237–280.

Knowledges. Historical and Critical Studies. See Preziosi, Donald.

Koerner, Joseph. *The Moment of Self-Portraiture in German Renaissance Art.* Chicago: Chicago University Press, 1993.

Kozakiewicz, Helena and Stefan. *Renesans w Polsce.* Warsaw: Arkady, 1976.

Kozakiewiczowa, Helena. *Rzeźzba XVI Wieku w Polsce.* Warsaw: Panstwowe Wydawnictwo Naukowe, 1984.

Krauss, Rosalind. "The Story of the Eye." *New Literary History* 21 (Winter 1990), 283–297.

Kristeller, Paul O. "Humanism and Scholasticism in the Italian Renaissance." 1945. Reprinted in *Renaissance Thought and Its Sources,* ed. M. Mooney, 85–105. New York: Columbia University Press, 1979.

Kristeller, Paul O. "The Modern System of the Arts: a Study in the History of Aesthetics." *Journal of the History of Ideas* 12 (1951), 496–527, Part One; 13 (1952), 17–46, Part Two.

Kubler, George. *Esthetic Recognition of Ancient Amerindian Art.* New Haven and London: Yale University Press, 1991.

Kugler, Franz. *Handbuch der Kunstgeschichte.* Stuttgart: Ebner & Senbert, 1842.

Kuhn, Thomas. *The Structure of Scientific Revolutions,* 2nd rev. edn. Chicago: Chicago University Press, 1970.

Landauer, Carl. "Erwin Panofsky and the Renascence of the Renaissance." *Renaissance Quarterly* 47 (1994), 255–281.

Landauer, Carl. "The Survival of Antiquity: The German Years of the Warburg Institute." Ph.D. dissertation, Yale University, 1984.

Laurencich-Minelli, Laura, ed. See *Bologna e il Mondo Nuovo.*

Lawrence, William. *Lectures on Physiology, Zoology, and the Natural History of Man. Delivered at the Royal College of Surgeons.* London: James Smith, 1822.

Lee, R. W. "*Ut pictura poesis*: The Humanist Theory of Painting." *Art Bulletin* 22 (1940), 197–269.

Lee, Sherman. *A History of Far Eastern Art.* 4th edn. Englewood Cliffs, N.J.: Prentice-Hall, and New York: Harry N. Abrams, 1982.

Lemerle, Paul. *Cinq études sur le XIᵉ siècle byzantin.* Paris: Centre National de la Recherche Scientifique, 1977.

Lenormant, Charles. *François Gérard, peintre d'histoire. Essai de biographie et de critique.* Paris: A. René, 1847.

Lévi-Strauss, Claude. *Tristes tropiques.* Paris: Union générale d'éditions, 1955.

Liechtenstein. The Princely Collections. Exhibition catalogue. New York: Metropolitan Museum of Art, 1985.

Lightbown, R. W. "Oriental Art and the Orient in Late Renaissance and Baroque Italy." *Journal of the Warburg and Courtauld Institutes* 32 (1969), 228–279.

Lindberg, David C. *Theories of Vision from Al-Kindi to Kepler.* Chicago and London: University of Chicago Press, 1976.

Locke, John. *An Essay Concerning Human Understanding,* ed. P. Nidditch. Oxford: Clarendon Press, 1979.

Lomazzo, Giovanni Paolo. *Rime: nelle quali ad imitazione de i Grotteschi usata da" pittori. . . .* Milan: Paolo Gottardo Ponzio, 1587.

Lomazzo, Giovanni Paolo. *Trattato dell'arte de la pittura, scoltura et architettura.* Milan: P. G. Pontio, 1584.

Łoziński, Jerzy. *Grobowe kaplice kopulowe w Polsce 1520–1620.* Warsaw: Panstwowe Wydawnictwo Naukowe, 1973.

MacCormack, Sabine. "Caldera's *La Aurora en Copacobana*: The Conversion of the Incas in Light of Seventeenth-Century Spanish Theology, Culture, and Political Theory." *Journal of Theological Studies* 33 (1982), 448–480.

Mallgrave, Harry Francis. "The Idea of Style. Gottfried Semper in London." Ph.D. dissertation, University of Pennsylvania, 1983.

Mallgrave, Harry Francis. See also Semper.

Mango, Cyril. *The Art of the Byzantine Empire 312–1453.* Englewood Cliffs, N.J.: Prentice-Hall, 1972.

Marlier, Georges. *Pierre Coeck d'Alost: La renaissance flamande.* Brussels: Robert Finck, 1966.

Matthias Corvinus und die Renaissance in Ungarn. Exhibition catalogue. Schallaburg, Austria: Schloss Schallaburg, 1982.

Mercati, Giovanni. *Ultimi contributi alla storia degli umanisti. 1. Traversariana* (Studi e testi, 90). Vatican City, 1939.

Mexico. Splendors of Thirty Centuries. Exhibition catalogue, intro. O. Paz. New York: Metropolitan Museum of Art, 1990.

Mitchell, W. J. T. *Iconology: Image, Text, Ideology.* Chicago and London: University of Chicago Press, 1986.

Mitchell, W. J. T., ed. *The Politics of Interpretation.* Chicago and London: Chicago University Press, 1983.

Mitchell, W. J. T. "What is Visual Culture?" In *Proceedings of the Panofsky Centennial Symposium, 1993,* Institute for Advanced Study, Princeton, forthcoming.

Morpurgo, Enrico. *L'opera del genio Italiano all'estero. Gli artisti in Austria.* Rome, 1962.

Mosse, George. *German Jews beyond Judaism.* Bloomington: Indiana University Press and Cincinnati: Hebrew Union College Press, 1985.

Mosse, George. *Toward the Final Solution. A History of European Racism.* Madison: University of Wisconsin Press, 1985.

Moxey, Keith. "The Politics of Iconology." *Iconography at the Crossroads,* ed. B. Cassidy, 27–31. Princeton: Princeton University Press, 1993.

Moxey, Keith. "Panofsky's Concept of 'Iconology' and the Problem of Interpretation in the History of Art." *New Literary History* 17 (Winter 1986), 265–275.

Moxey, Keith. "Panofsky's Melancolia." *Künstlerischer Austausch/Artistic Exchange. Akten des XXVIII Internationalen Kongresses für Kunstgeschichte, Berlin 15–20, 1992,* ed. T. Gaehtgens, 681–691. Berlin: Akademie Verlag, 1993.

Moxey, Keith. See also *Visual Theory.*

National Consciousness, History and Political Culture in Early–Modern Europe, ed. Orest Ranum. Baltimore and London: The John Hopkins University Press, 1975.

New World of Wonders: European Images of the Americas 1492–1700, ed. Rachell Doggett, with M. Hulvey and J. Ainsworth. Exhibition catalogue. Washington, D.C., The Folger Shakespeare Library. Seattle and London: University of Washington Press.

Newton, Douglas. "Primitive Art: a Perspective." *The Nelson A. Rockefeller Collection, Masterpieces of Primitive Art.* New York: Alfred A. Knopf, 1978.

Nisbet, Robert. *History of the Idea of Progress.* New York: Basic Books, Inc., 1980.

Norton, Robert. *Herder's Aesthetics and the European Enlightenment.* Ithaca and London: Cornell Univesity Press, 1991.

O'Gorman, Edmundo. *The Invention of America. An Inquiry into the Historical Nature of the New World and the Meaning of its History.* Bloomington: Indiana University Press, 1961.

Olin, Margaret. *Forms of Representation in Alois*

Riegl's Theory of Art. University Park, Pa.: Pennsylvania State University Press, 1992.

Olmi, Giuseppe. *Inventario del Mundo. Catalogazione della natura e luoghi del sapere nella prima età moderna.* Bologna: Società editrice il Mulino, 1992.

Olschki, Leonardo. "Asiatic Exoticism in Italian Art of the Early Renaisance." *Art Bulletin* 26 (1944), 95–106.

The Origins of Museums: the Cabinet of Curiosities in Sixteenth- and Seventeenth-Century Europe, ed. Oliver Impey and Arthur MacGregor. Oxford: Clarendon Press, 1985.

Ossola, Carlo. *Autunno del Rinascimento: "Idea del Tempio" dell' arte nell' ultimo Cinquecento.* Florence: Leo S. Olschki Editore, 1971.

Ossola, Carlo. "Rinascimento e Risorgimento: punti di interferenza." *La Corte nella Cultura e nella Storiografia. Immagini e posizioni tra Otto e Novecento,* ed. C. Mozzarelli and G. Olmi, 205–236. Rome: Bulzoni, 1983.

Ovitt, George, Jr. *The Restoration of Perfection. Labor and Technology in Medieval Culture.* New Brunswick and London: Rutgers University Press, 1987.

Pagden, Anthony. *European Encounters with the New World. From Renaissance to Romanticism.* New Haven and London: Yale University Press, 1993.

Pagden, Anthony. *The Fall of Natural Man. The Amerindian and the Origins of Comparative Ethnology.* 2nd edn. Cambridge: Cambridge University Press, 1986.

Paleotti. Gabriele. *Discorso intorno alle imagini sacre e profane.* Bologna, 1582. Reprint, ed. Paola Barocchi in *Trattato d'arte del Cinquecento,* vol. 2, 117–509. Bari: Giuseppe Laterza e Figli, 1961.

Panofsky, Erwin. *The Art and Life of Albrecht Dürer.* Princeton: Princeton University Press, 1971.

Panofsky, Erwin. "The Concept of Artistic Volition," trans. K. Northcott and J. Snyder. *Critical Inquiry* 8 (Autumn 1981), 17–33. Originally published as "Der Begriff des Kunstwollens" (1920).

Panofsky, Erwin. "Dürers Stellung zur Antike," *Jahrbuch für Kunstqeschichte* 1 (1921–22), 43–92. Translated in *Meaning in the Visual Arts,* 236–294. Garden City, N.Y.: Doubleday, 1955.

Panofsky, Erwin. "The History of Art as a Humanistic Discipline." *Meaning in the Visual Arts,* 1–25. New York: Doubleday and Co., 1955.

Panofsky, Erwin. "Die Perspective als 'Symbolische Form,'" *Aufsatze* (1927), 99–167. English translation published as *Perspective as Symbolic Form,* ed. Sanford Kwinter, tr. Christopher S. Wood. Cambridge, Ma: Zone Books, 1991.

Panofsky, Erwin. "Das Problem des Stils in der bildenden Kunst." *Zeitschrift für Ästhetik und Allgemeine Kunstwissenschaft* 10 (1915), 460–467.

Panofsky, Erwin. "Zum Problem der Beschreibung und Inhaltsdeutung von Werken der Bildenden Kunst." *Logos* 21 (1932), 103–119.

Panofsky, Erwin. *Studies in Iconology. Humanistic Themes in the Art of the Renaissance.* 1939. New York: Harper and Row, 1962.

Panofsky, Erwin. *Renaissance and Renascences in Western Art.* 1960. New York and London: Harper & Row, 1972.

Parry, Benita. "Problems in Current Theories of Colonial Discourse." *Oxford Literary Review* 9 (1987), 27–58.

Pertusi, Agostino. *La Caduta di Costantinopoli.* 2 vols. Milan: Mondadori, 1976.

Pertusi, Agostino. *Storiografia umanistica e mondo bizantino.* Palermo: Istituto Siciliano di studi bizantini e neoellenici, 1967.

Pertusi, Agostino. *Testi inediti e poco noti sulla caduta di Costantinopoli.* Bologna: Patron, 1983.

Podro, Michael. *The Critical Historians of Art.* New Haven and London: Yale University Press, 1982.

The Politics of Interpretation, ed. W. J. T. Mitchell. Chicago and London: University of Chicago Press, 1983.

Pollitt, J. J. *The Ancient View of Greek Art: Criticism, History, and Terminology.* New Haven and London: Yale University Press, 1974.

Porter, Roy and Mikulás Teich, eds. *The Renaissance in National Context.* Cambridge: Cambridge University Press, 1992.

Pratt, Mary. *Imperial Eyes: Travel Writing and Transculturation,* London and New York: Routledge, 1992.

Preziosi, Donald. *Rethinking Art History: Meditations on a Coy Science.* New Haven and London: Yale University Press, 1989.

Preziosi, Donald. "Seeing Through Art

History." In *Knowledges. Historical and Critical Studies in Disciplinarity*, eds. E. Messer-Davidow, D. Shumway, and D. Sylvan, 215–231. Charlottesville: University Press of Virginia, 1993.

Preziosi, Donald. "The Question of Art History." *Critical Inquiry* 18 (Winter 1992), 363–386.

Raby, Julian. *Venice, Dürer and the Oriental Mode*. London: Sotheby, 1982.

Rannusio, Paolo (Paulus Ramnusius). *Della guerra di Costantinopoli per la restituzione de gl' imperatori Comneni fatta da Sig. Venetiani et Francesi, l'anno 1204, libri 6*. Venice 1604.

Refiguring Woman. Perspectives on Gender and the Italian Renaissance, ed. and intro. M. Migiel and J. Schiesari. Ithaca and London: Cornell University Press, 1991.

Rewriting the Renaissance. The Discourses of Sexual Difference in Early Modern Europe, eds. M. Ferguson, M. Quilligan, and N. Vickers. Chicago and London: University of Chicago Press, 1986.

Richter, Simon. *Laocoon's Body and the Aesthetics of Pain: Winckelmann, Lessing, Herder, Moritz, Goethe*. Detroit: Wayne State University Press, 1992.

Riegl, Alois. *Die spätromische Kunstindustrie nach den Funden in Österreich-Ungarn*. Part I. New edition. Vienna: Osterreich Staatsdruckerei. 1927. Reprint. Darmstadt, 1973. (Original edn. 1901.)

Riegl, Alois. *Late Roman Art Industry*, trans. R. Winkes. Rome: Giorgio Bretschneider, 1985.

Riegl, Alois. *Problems of Style. Foundations for a History of Ornament*, trans. E. Kain, notes and intro. D. Castriota, preface H. Zerner. Princeton: Princeton University Press, 1992. (Original edn. Berlin 1893.)

Riegl, Alois. *Stilfragen. Grundlegungen zu einer Geschichte der Ornamentik*. 1893. Facsimile reprint. Hildesheim and New York: Georg Olms, 1975.

Ringer, Fritz. *The Decline of the German Mandarins: the German Academic Community, 1890–1933*. Cambridge: Harvard University Press, 1969.

Rodinson, Maxime. *Europe and the Mystique of Islam*, tr. R. Veinus. Seattle and London: University of Washington Press, 1987.

Röll, Johannes. *Giovanni Dalmata*. Worms: Hernesche Verlagsgesellschaft, 1994.

Sahlins, Marshall. *Islands of History*. Chicago and London: University of Chicago Press, 1985.

Said, Edward. "Opponents, Audiences, Constituencies, and Community." *The Politics of Interpretation*, 7–32.

Said, Edward. *Orientalism*. New York: Pantheon Books, 1978.

Saxl, Fritz. "Warburg's Visit to New Mexico." In *Lectures*, I, 325–330. London: The Warburg Institute, University of London, 1957.

Schama, Simon. "They All Laughed at Christopher Columbus." *The New Republic*, January 6 & 13, 1992, 30–40.

Schiller, Nina Glick, Linda Basch, and Cristina Blanc-Szanton. "Transnationalism: a New Analytic Framework for Understanding Migration." *Towards a Transnational Perspective on Migration: Race, Class, Ethnicity, and Nationalism Reconsidered*, eds. Schiller, Basch, and Blanc-Szanton, 1–24. Annals of the New York Academy of Sciences, 645. New York: The New York Academy of Sciences, 1992.

Scritti d'arte. See Barocchi, Paola, ed.

Semper, Gottfried. *The Four Elements of Architecture and Other Writings*, trans. H. F. Mallgrave and W. Hermann, intro. H. F. Mallgrave. Cambridge: Cambridge University Press, 1989.

Setton, Keith M. "The Byzantine Background to the Italian Renaissance." *Proceedings of the American Philosophical Society* 100 (1956), 1–56.

Ševčenko, Ihor. "Intellectual Repercussions of the Council of Florence." *Church History* 24 (1955), 291–323.

Sheffield, Clarence. "A Critical Study of Alois Riegl's *Spätrömische Kunstindustrie*." M. A. thesis, University of Colorado at Boulder, 1990.

Silverberg, Robert. *The Pueblo Revolt*. Lincoln and London: University of Nebraska Press, 1970.

Small, Deborah with Maggie Jaffe. *1492: What Is It Like to Be Discovered?* New York: Monthly Review Press, 1991.

Smith, Anthony. *Theories of Nationalism*. 2nd edn. New York: Holmes & Meier, 1983.

Smith, Denis Mack. *Italy and Its Monarchy*. New Haven and London: Yale University Press. 1989.

Snyder, James. *Northern Renaissance Art*. New

York: Abrams, 1985.

Speck, Paul. "Waren die Byzantiner mittelalterliche Altgriecher, oder glaubten sie es nur?" *Rechtshistorisches Journal* 2 (1983), 5–11.

Spieser, Jean-Michel. "Hellénisme et connaissance de l'art byzantin au XIXᵉ siècle," in *Hellenismos. Quelques jalons pour une histoire de l'identité grecque*. Actes du Colloque de Strasbourg 25–27 octobre 1989, ed. S. Said. 337–362. Leiden and New York: E. J. Brill, 1989.

Spivak, Gayatri Chakravorti. "Explanation and Culture: Marginalia" (1979). Reprinted in *In Other Words: Essays in Cultural Politics*. New York and London: Methuen, 1987, 103–117.

The Splendor of Dresden. Five Centuries of Art Collecting. Exhibition catalogue. Washington, D.C., National Gallery of Art, 1978.

Stepan, Nancy. *The Idea of Race in Science: Great Britain 1800–1960*. London and Basingstoke: Macmillan Press and Hamden, Ct.: Archon Books, 1982.

Stocking, George, Jr. *Race, Culture, and Evolution. Essays in the History of Anthropology*. New York and London: The Macmillan Company, 1968.

Summers, David. "'Form,' Nineteenth-Century Metaphysics and the Problem of Art Historical Description." *Critical Inquiry* 15 (1989), 372–406.

Summers, David. "Meaning in the Visual Arts as a Humanistic Discipline," paper delivered at the Panofsky Centennial Symposium, "Meaning in the Visual Arts: Views from the Outside," Institute for Advanced Study, Princeton, October 1–3, 1993.

Summers, David. *Michelangelo and the Language of Art*. Princeton: Princeton University Press, 1981.

Summers, David. "Michelangelo on Architecture." *Art Bulletin* 54 (1972), 146–157.

Summers, David. "Real Metaphor: Towards a Redefinition of the 'Conceptual' Image." *Visual Theory*, ed. N. Bryson, M. A. Holly, and K. Moxey, 231–259.

Summers, David. *The Judgment of Sense. Renaissance Naturalism and the Rise of Aesthetics*. Cambridge: Cambridge University Press, 1987.

Summerson, John. *Architecture in Britain 1530–1830*. 6th rev. edn. Harmondsworth: Pelican Books, 1977.

Tachau, Katherine. *Vision and Certitude in the Age of Ockham: Optics, Epistemology, and the Foundation of Semantics, 1250–1345*. Leiden and New York: E.J. Brill, 1988.

Teague, Michael. *In The Wake of the Portuguese Navigators*. Manchester: Carcanet in association with the Calouste Gulbenkian Foundation, 1988.

Theophanes Continuatus, ed. I. Bekker. Bonn: E. Weber, 1838.

Thomas Aquinas. *Summa Theologiae*, ed. Blackfriars. 60 vols. New York and London, 1964–1976.

Tiffany, Daniel. "Cryptesthesia: Visions of the Other." *American Journal of Semiotics* 6:2/3 (1989), 209–219.

Torgovnick, Marianna. *Gone Primitive: Savage Intellects, Modern Lives*. Chicago: University of Chicago Press, 1990.

Trattati d'arte. See Barocchi, Paola, ed.

Trexler, Richard. *Church and Community, 1200–1600: Studies in the History of Florence and New Spain*. Rome: Edizioni di storia e letteratura, 1987.

Tylor, Edward B. *Primitive Culture: Researches into the Development of Mythology, Philosophy, Religion, Language, Art, and Custom*. 1871. 2 vols. 3rd rev. edn. London: John Murray, 1891.

Valadés, Diego. *Rhetorica christiana*. Perugia, 1579. Facsimile, with Spanish translation, *Rétorica cristiana*. Mexico City: Universidad Nacional Autonoma de Mexico, Fondo de Cultura Economica, 1989.

Vargas, José Maria. *Historia del Arte Ecuatoriano*. Quito, 1963.

Vasari, Giorgio. *Le Vite de' più eccellenti pittori, scultori ed architettori*, ed. Gaetano Milanesi. Florence: Sansoni, 1878. New edn., including the text of the 1550 and 1568 editions, ed. R. Bettarini and P. Barocchi. 6 vols. to date. Florence: Sansoni, 1966– .

Visual Theory. Painting and Interpretation, ed. N. Bryson, M. A. Holly, and K. Moxey. London: Harper Collins, 1991.

Vitruvius. *The Ten Books on Architecture*, trans. Morris H. Morgan. Cambridge, Ma.: Harvard University Press, 1914.

Vogt, Carl. *Lectures on Man. His Place in Creation, and in the History of the Earth*. London: Anthropological Society, 1864.

Wagner, Otto. *Moderne Architektur*. Vienna: A. Schnoll & Co., 1896.

Warburg, A. "A Lecture on Serpent Ritual." *Journal of the Warburg and Courtauld Institutes*

2 (1938–39), 277–292.

Warren-Turnage, Elizabeth. "Towards a Theory of Ornament." M. A. thesis, University of Colorado at Boulder, 1993.

Weiss, Roberto. *Pisanello's Medallion of the Emperor John VIII Palaeologus*. London: British Museum, 1966.

Weitzmann, Kurt. *The Monastery of Saint Catherine at Mount Sinai. The Icons. 1. From the Sixth to the Tenth Century*. Princeton: Princeton University Press, 1976.

White, Hayden. *Metahistory. The Historical Imagination in Nineteenth-Century Europe*. Baltimore and London: The John Hopkins University Press, 1973.

Williams, Raymond. *Culture and Society 1780–1950*. New York and London: Harper & Row, 1958.

Williams, Raymond. *Keywords. A Vocabulary of Culture and Society*. New York: Oxford University Press, 1976.

Wölfflin, Heinrich. *Kunstgeschichte Grundebegriffe*. 1915. Munich: F. Bruckmann, 1929.

Wölfflin, Heinrich. *Principles of Art History. The Problem of the Development of Style in Later Art*, trans. M. Hottinger. 1932. New York: Dover Publications, 1950.

Wölfflin, Heinrich. *Renaissance und Barock: Eine Untersuchung uber heren und Enstehung des Barockstils in Italien*. Munich: T. Ackermann, 1888.

Women, "Race," and Writing, ed. Margo Hendricks and Patricia Parker. London and New York: Routledge, 1994.

Young, Robert. *White Mythologies: Writing History and the West*. New York and London: Routledge, 1990.

Zapalac, Kristin. "*In His Image and Likeness.*" *Political Iconography and Religious Change in Regensburg, 1500–1600*. Ithaca and London: Cornell University Press, 1990.

Zaske, Nikolaus und Rosemarie. *Kunst in Hansestädten*. Cologne: Bohlau, 1985.

Zerner, Henri. "Aloïs Riegl: Art, Value, and Historicism." *Daedalus* 105 (Winter 1976), 177–188.

II Theories of Images

Acosta, José de. *Historia natural y moral de la Indias*. Ed. Edmundo O'Gorman. México: UNAM, 1940.

Adorno, Rolena. *Guaman Poma: Writing and Resistance in Colonial Peru*. Austin: The University of Texas Press, 1986.

The Age of Correggio and the Carracci. Exhibition catalogue. Washington, National Gallery of Art; New York, Metropolitan Museum of Art; and Bologna, Pinacoteca Nazionale, 1986.

Agosti, Giovanni. *Bambaia e il classicismo lombardo*. Turin: Einaudi, 1990.

Alberti, L. B. *On Painting*, trans. with an Introduction and notes by John R. Spencer. New Haven: Yale University Press, 1966.

Alberti, L. B. *Opere volgare*, ed. C. Grayson. Vol. 3. Bari: Giuseppe Laterza e Figli, 1973.

Alberti, Leon Battista. *On Painting and On Sculpture: the Latin Texts of De Pictura and De Statua*. Ed. and trans. Cecil Grayson. London: Phaidon, 1972.

Alecci, Antonio. "Busti (de' Busti, de' Bustis, de Busto), Bernardino." *Dizionario biografico degli italiani*. 15. Rome: Istituto della Enciclopedia Italiana, 1972, 593–595.

Alessi, Galeazzo. *Libro dei Misteri. Progetto di pianificazione urbanistica, architettonica e figurativa del Sacro Monte di Varallo in Valsesia (1565–1569)*, ed. Stefania Stefani Perrone. 2 vols. Bologna: Forni, 1974.

Altman, Ida. *Emigrants and Society: Extremadura and Spanish America in The Sixteenth Century*. Berkeley and Los Angeles: University of California Press, 1989.

Antoniazzi Villa, Anna. "A proposito di ebrei, francescani, Monti di Pietà: Bernardino de' Bustis e la polemica antiebraica nella Milano di fine '400." *Il Francescanesimo in Lombardia. Storia e arte*. Milan: Silvana Editoriale, 1983: 49–52.

Argan, Giulio. "Caravaggio e Raffaello." *Caravaggio e i Caravaggeschi*, 19–28. Rome, 1974.

Argan, Giulio. "Raffaello e la Critica." *Studi su Raffaello*, eds. Micaela S. Hamoud and Maria Letizia Strochi, 7–17. Urbino: Quattro Venti, 1987.

Aristotle. *Aristotle. De Anima*, trans. with an Introduction and notes by R. D. Hicks. Cambridge: Cambridge University Press, 1907.

Auerbach, Erich. *Literatursprache und Publikum in der lateinischen Spätantike und im Mittelalter*. Bern: Francke, 1958.

Bandello, Matteo. *Novelle*, ed. Giuseppe Guido Ferrero. Turin: UTET, 1974.

Barasch, Moshe. *Giotto and the Language of Gestures.* Cambridge: Cambridge University Press, 1987.

Barthes, Roland. "The reality effect." *French literary theory today. A reader,* ed. Tzvetan Todorov, 11–17. Cambridge: Cambridge University Press, 1982.

Bauer, George. "Experimental Shadow Casting and the Early History of Perspective." *Art Bulletin* 59 (1987), 210–219.

Baxandall, Michael. *Painting and Experience in Fifteenth Century Italy. A Primer in the Social History of Pictorial Style.* Oxford: Oxford University Press, 1972.

Beck, James. *Raphael: The Stanza Della Segnatura.* New York: Braziller, 1993.

Bell, Janis. "Cassiano dal Pozzo's Copy of the Zaccolini Manuscripts." *Journal of the Warburg and Courtauld Institutes* 51 (1988), 103–25.

Bell, Janis. "Color and Theory in Seicento Art: Zaccolini's *Prospettiva del Colore* and the Heritage of Leonardo." Ph.D. dissertation. Brown University, 1983.

Bell, Janis. "Some Seventeenth Century Appraisals of Caravaggio's Coloring." *Artibus et Historiae* vol. 14, no. 27 (1993), 103–129.

Bell, Janis. "The Life and Works of Matteo Zaccolini (1574–1630)." *Regnum Dei* 16 (1985), 227–258.

Bell, Janis. "Zaccolini's Theory of Color Perspective." *Art Bulletin* 75 (1993), 91–112.

Bell, Janis. "Chiaroscuro." *Dictionary of Art,* eds. Hugh Brigstocke and Jane Turner. London: Macmillan, 1995.

Bell, Janis. "Filippo Gagliardi on Leonardo's Perspective." *Achademia Leonardi Vinci* (1992).

Bellori, Giovan Pietro. *Descrizione delle imagini dipinte da Raffaelle d'Urbino nel Palazzo Vaticano, e nella Farnesina alla Lungara: con alcuni ragionamenti in onore delle sue opere, e della pittura, e scultura.* Rome, 1695.

Bellori, Giovan Pietro. *Le Vite de' pittori, scultori e architetti moderni* (1672). Ed. Evelina Borea, Intro. Giovanni Previtali. Torino: Einaudi, 1976.

Bergmann, Emilie. *Art Inscribed: Essays on Ekphrasis in Spanish Golden Age Poetry.* Cambridge: Harvard University Press, 1979.

Bernardino da Siena. *Prediche volgari sul Campo di Siena 1427,* ed. Carlo Delcorno. 2 vols.

Milan: Rusconi, 1989.

Bernheimer, Richard. *Wild Men in the Middle Ages.* Cambridge, Ma.: Harvard University Press, 1952.

Bhabha, Homi. *The Location of Culture.* London: Routledge, 1994.

Bing, Gertrude. "A. M. Warburg." *Journal of the Warburg and Courtauld Institutes* 28 (1965), 299–313.

Blunt, Anthony. *The Pelican History of Art: Art and Architecture in France.* Harmondsworth: Penguin Books, 1982.

Blunt, Anthony. "The Legend of Raphael in Italy and France." *Italian Studies* 13 (1958), 2–20.

Bonaventure. *The Soul's Journey into God. The Tree of Life. The Life of St Francis,* ed. Ewert Cousins. New York, Ramsey, and Toronto: Paulist Press, 1978.

Bonner, Anthony. *Selected Works of Ramon Llull (1232–1316).* 2 vols. Princeton: Princeton University Press, 1985.

Borromeo, Federico. *I Ragionamenti spirituali.* Milan, Ambrosiana. Ms. Trotti 494, n.d.

Borsook, Eve. "Technical Innovation and the Development of Raphael's Style in Rome." *Revue d'Art Canadienne* 12 (1985), 127–36.

Boschloo, A. W. A. *Annibale Carracci in Bologna. Visible Reality in Art after the Council of Trent.* 2 vols. The Hague: Ministry of Cultural Affairs, Recreation, and Social Welfare, Government Publishing Office, 1974.

Bosse, Abraham. *Traité des pratiques géometrales et perspectives enseignées dans l'academie royale de la peinture et sculpture.* Paris: Abraham Bosse, 1665.

Bremmer, Jan and Herman Roodenburg, eds. *A Cultural History of Gesture.* Ithaca: Cornell University Press, 1991.

Briganti, Giulio. "Baroque Art." In *Encyclopedia of World Art,* II, 255–267.

Brigstocke, Hugh. "Classical Painting in Rome in the Age of the Baroque." *Apollo* 117 (1983), 208–15.

Brilliant, Richard. *Gesture and Rank in Roman Art: the Use of Gesture to Denote Status in Roman Sculpture and Coinage.* Memoirs of the Connecticut Academy of Arts and Sciences, 14. New Haven: Yale University Press, 1963.

Brown, David Alan. *Andrea Solario.* Milan: Electa, 1987.

Burkhart, Louise. "A Nahuatl Religious Drama of *c.*1590." *Latin American Indian Literatures Journal: a Review of American Indian Texts and Studies* 7 (Fall 1991), 153–171.

Burkhart, Louise. *The Slippery Earth: Nahua–Christian Moral Dialogue in Sixteenth-Century Mexico.* Tucson: University of Arizona Press, 1989.

Butler, Samuel. *Alps and Sanctuaries of Piedmont and the Canton Ticino.* London: Fifield, 1881.

Camille, Michael. *Image on the Edge: the Margins of Medieval Art.* Cambridge, Ma.: Harvard University Press, 1992.

Canons and Decrees of the Council of Trent. See Waterworth, J.

Cappel, Carmen B. "A Substitute Cartoon for Raphael's Disputà." *Master Drawings* 30 (1992), 9–30.

Caron, Linda. "Choices Concerning Modes of Modeling during the High Renaissance and after," *Zeitschrift für Kunstgeschichte* 48 (1985), 476–489.

Caron, Linda. *The Use of Color by Painters in Rome from 1524 to 1527.* Ph.D. dissertation. Bryn Mawr College, 1982.

Cartas de Indias. Madrid, 1877.

Carter, Tim. *Music in Late Renaissance and Early Baroque Italy.* Portland, Or.: Amadeus Press, 1992.

Casagrande, Carla and Silvana Vecchio. "L'Interdizione dei giullare nel vocabulario clericale del XII e del XIII sècolo." *Il contributo dei giulleri alla drammaturga italiana delle origini.* Viterbo, 1977, 207–258.

Cassanelli, Luciana, and Sergio Rossi. *Oltre Raffaello: aspetti della cultura figurativa del cinquecento romano.* Exhibition catalogue. Rome: Multigrafica Editrice, 1984.

Cervantes Saavedra, Miguel de *El Ingenioso Hidalgo Don Quijote de la Mancha* (1605). Paris: A. Everat, 1835.

Chailley, Jacques. "La danse religieuse au moyen âge." *Arts Liberaux et Philosophie au Moyen Âge, Actes du Quatrième Congrès Internationale de Philosophie Médiévale, Université de Montreal, 27 August–2 Sept., 1967.* Paris, 1969, 357–380.

Chazan, Robert. *Daggers of Faith: Thirteenth-Century Christian Missionizing and Jewish Response.* Berkeley and Los Angeles: University of California Press, 1989.

Childs, William A. P. "The Classic as Realism in Greek Art." *Art Journal* 47/1 (1988), 10–14.

Cohen, Jeremy. *The Friars and the Jews: the Evolution of Medieval Anti-Judaism.* Ithaca: Cornell University Press, 1982.

Connerton, Paul. *How Societies Remember.* Cambridge: Cambridge University Press, 1989.

Croix, Horst de la, and Richard G. Tansey. *Gardner's Art Through the Ages.* 8th edition. San Diego: Harcourt Brace Jovanovich, 1986.

Cropper, Elizabeth. "Poussin and Leonardo: the Evidence of the Zaccolini Manuscripts." *Art Bulletin* 62 (1980), 570–83.

Cropper, Elizabeth. *The Ideal of Painting: Pietro Testa's Düsseldorf Notebook.* Princeton: Princeton University Press, 1984.

Cropper, Elizabeth. "Tuscan History and Emilian Style." *Emilian Painting of the 16th and 17th Centuries.* Symposium Proceedings, CASVA, National Gallery of Art, Washington, D.C., 49–62. Bologna: Nuova Alfa, 1987.

Cummins, Tom. "The Madonna and the Horse: Alternative Readings of Colonial Images." *Phoebus* 9, forthcoming.

Dandolo, Tullio. *Ricordi inediti di Gerolamo Morone gran cancelliere dell' ultimo duca di Milano.* Milan: Besozzi, 1855.

Daniel, E. Randolph. *The Franciscan Concept of Mission in the High Middle Ages.* Lexington: University Press of Kentucky, 1975.

De Piles, Roger. *Abrégés de la Vie des Peintres* (1699). Paris, 1715.

De Piles, Roger. *Cours de Peinture par Principes* (1708). With an introduction by Jacques Thuillier. Paris: Gallimard, 1989.

De Piles, Roger. *Cours de Peinture par Principes* (1708). With an introduction by Thomas Puttfarken. Nîmes: Jacqueline Chambon, 1990.

De Vecchi, Pierluigi. "Annotazioni sul Calvario del Sacro Monte di Varallo." In *Fra Rinascimento, Manierismo e Realtà. Scritti di storia dell' arte in memoria di Anna Maria Brizio,* ed. Pietro C. Marani, 109–118. Florence: Giunti Barbera, 1984.

De Certeau, Michel *Heterologies: Discourses on the Other,* trans. B. Massumi. Theory and History of Literature, vol. 17. Minneapolis: University of Minnesota Press, 1986.

Dempsey, Charles. "The Carracci and the Devout Style in Emilia." *Emilian Painting of the 16th and 17th Centuries.* Symposium Proceedings, CASVA, National Gallery of Art,

Washington, D.C., 75–87. Bologna: Nuova Alfa, 1987.

Dempsey, Charles. "The Carracci Reform of Painting." *The Age of Correggio and the Carracci*, 237–54. Washington, D.C.: National Gallery of Art, 1986.

Dolce, M. Ludovico. *Dolce's Aretino and Venetian Art Theory of the Cinquecento (Dialogo Della Pittura Intitolato L'Aretino)* (1557). Ed. and trans. Mark Roskill. CAA monograph 15. New York: New York University Press for CAA, 1968.

Donovan, Richard B. *The Liturgical Drama in Medieval Spain*. Toronto: Pontifical Institute of Mediaeval Studies, 1958.

DuFresnoy, Charles Alfonse. *De Arte graphica – l'art de la peinture, traduit en François, Comm. & trans. Roger De Piles*. Paris, 1668.

DuFresnoy, Charles Alfonse. *The Art of Painting . . . with Remarks: Translated into English with an Original Preface, Containing a Parallel Between Painting and Poetry*. Trans. John Dryden, comm. Roger De Piles. 2nd edn. London, 1716.

Durán, Diego. *The Book of the Gods and Rites and the Ancient Calendar*. Ed. Fernando Horcasitas and Doris Heyden. Norman: University of Oklahoma Press, 1971.

Durán, Diego. *Historia de las Indias de Nueva España e Islas de la Tierra Firme* (c.1579). Ed. Angel Garibay. 2 vols. México, D. F.: Editorial Porrúa, 1967.

Eisenbichler, Konrad. *Crossing the Boundaries: Christian Piety and the Arts in Italian Medieval and Renaissance Confraternities*. Kalamazoo: University of Michigan Press, 1991.

Elison, George. *Deus Destroyed: the Image of Christianity in Early Modern Japan*. Cambridge, Ma.: Harvard University Press, 1991.

Elliott, J. H. "Renaissance Europe and America: a Blunted Impact?" F. Chiapelli, ed., *First Images of America: the Impact of the New World on the Old*, 1, 11–23. 2 vols. Berkeley: University of California Press, 1976.

Elliott, J. H. "The Mental World of Hernán Cortés." *Royal Historical Society Transactions* 17, 1967, 41–58; reprinted in J. H. Elliott, *Spain and Its World 1500–1700*. New Haven: Yale University Press, 1989, 27–41.

Elliott, J. H. *The Old World and the New 1492–1650*. Cambridge: Cambridge University Press, 1970.

Fabian, Johannes. *Time and the Other*. New York: Columbia University Press, 1983.

Félibien, André. *Entretiens sur les vies et les ouvrages des plus excellens peintres anciens et modernes (I et II)*. Edited by Réne Démoris. Paris: Société d'Édition "Les Belles Lettres," 1987.

Félibien, André. *Entretiens sur les vies et les ouvrages des plus excellens peintres anciens et modernes* (Trévoux, 1725). 6 vols. Farnborough: Gregg Reprint Co., 1967.

Fiorani, Francesca. "Abraham Bosse e le prime critiche al *Trattato della Pittura* di Leonardo." *Achademia Leonardi Vinci*, V (1992), 78–95.

Fiorani, Francesca. 'The Theory of Shadow Projection and Aerial Perspective. Leonardo, Desargues and Bosse." *Actes du Colloque International Girard Desargues, November 1991*, 267–282. Paris: C.N.R.S., 1991.

Flint, Valerie I. J. *The Imaginative Landscape of Christopher Columbus*. Princeton: Princeton University Press, 1992.

Fowler, H. W. and F. G. Fowler, trans. *The Works of Lucian of Samosata*. 4 vols. Oxford: Clarendon Press, 1905.

Fréart de Chambray. *Idée de la Perfection de la Peinture*. Le Mans, 1662; reprint Gregg International, 1968.

Freedberg, Sidney. "*Disegno* Versus *Colore* in Florentine and Venetian Painting of the Cinquecento." *Florence and Venice: Comparisons and Relations. Conference Proceedings, 1976–77*, ed. Sergio Bertelli, Nicholas Rubinstein, and Craig H. Smyth, II, 309–322. Villa I Tatti, The Harvard University Center for Italian Renaissance Studies, 5. Florence: La NuovaItalia Editrice, 1977.

Freedberg, Sidney. *Painting of the High Renaissance in Rome and Florence*. Cambridge, Ma.: Harvard University Press, 1961.

Friedman, John Block. *The Monstrous Races in Medieval Art and Thought*. Cambridge, Ma.: Cambridge University Press, 1981.

Gagliardi, Filippo. Untitled MS. Treatise on Perspective. Rome: Accademia Di S. Luca, c. 1630.

Galloni, Pietro. *Sacro Monte di Varallo. Origine e svolgimento delle opere d'arte*. Varallo: Camaschella e Zanfa, 1909–14.

Garibay Kintana, Angel María. *Historia de la literatura nahuatl*. 2 vols. México: Editorial Porruá, 1953–54.

Gentile, Guido. "Testi di devozione e iconografia del Compianto." *Niccolò dell'*

Arca. Seminario di Studi, 167–211. Bologna: Nuova Alfa Editoriale, 1989.

Gibson, J. J. "The Ecological Approach to the Visual Perception of Pictures." *Leonardo* 11 (1978), 227–235.

Gibson, J. J. *The Senses Considered as Perceptual Systems*. Prospect Heights, Il.: Waveland Press, 1966.

Ginzburg, Carlo. "Folklore, magia, religione." *Storia d'Italia* 1. Turin, 1972, 603–676.

Golzio, Vincenzo. *Raffaello nei documentia nelle testimonianze dei contemporanei e nella letteratura del suo secolo*. Vatican City, 1936.

Golzio, Vincenzo. "Raphael and His Critics." In *The Complete Work of Raphael*, 607–44. New York, 1969.

Gombrich, E. H. *Norm and Form: Studies in the Art of the Renaissance*. London: Phaidon, 1978.

Gombrich, E. H. *Aby Warburg: an Intellectual Biography*. Chicago: Chicago University Press, 1986.

Gombrich, E. H. "Ritualized Gesture and Expression in Art." *Philosophical Transactions of The Royal Society of London*. 251: 772 (1966), 393–401.

Greenblatt, Stephen. *Marvelous Possessions*. Chicago: The University of Chicago Press, 1991.

Grigely, Joseph. *Textualterity: Art, Theory and Textual Criticism*, Ann Arbor: University of Michigan Press, 1995.

Grijalva, Juan de. *Crónica de la orden de N.P.S. Augustin en las provincias de la Nueva España. En quatro edades desde el año 1533 hasta el de 1592*. Mexico: Ioan Ruyz, 1624.

Gruzinski, Serge. *The Conquest of Mexico*. Cambridge: Polity Press, 1993.

Guaman Poma de Ayala, Filipe. *Nueva corónica y buen gobierno* (1615). Ed. J. Murra and R. Adorno, trans. J. Urioste, 3 vols. Mexico: Siglo Veintiuno, 1980.

Gutiérrez, Ramón. *When Jesus Came, The Corn Mothers Went Away: Marriage, Sexuality, and Power in New Mexico, 1500–1846*. Stanford: Stanford University Press, 1991.

Habig, Marion, ed. *St Francis of Assisi: Writings and Early Biographies*. Chicago: Chicago University Press, 1983.

Hagen, Margaret. *Varieties of Realism*. Cambridge: Cambridge University Press, 1985.

Hall, Marcia. *Color and Meaning: Practice and Theory in Renaissance Painting*. New York: Cambridge University Press, 1992.

Hallett, C. H. "The Origins of the Classical Style in Sculpture." *Journal of Hellenic Studies* 16 (1986), 71–84.

Hamoud, Micaela S., and Maria Letizia Strochi. *Studi Su Raffaello*. Urbino: Quattro Venti, 1987.

Hanke, Lewis. *The Spanish Struggle for Justice in the Conquest of America*. Boston: Little Brown, 1965.

Hardison. O. B. *Christian Rite and Christian Drama in the Middle Ages*. Baltimore: Johns Hopkins Press, 1965.

Harris, Ann Sutherland. *Andrea Sacchi*. Princeton: Princeton University Press, 1977.

Hartt, Frederick. *Art: a History of Paintings, Sculpture, Architecture*. 2nd edn. 2 vols. New York: Harry N. Abrams, 1985.

Hillgarth, J. N. *Ramon Lull and Lullism in Fourteenth-Century France*. Oxford: Clarenden Press, 1971.

Hills, Paul. *The Light of Early Italian Painting*. New Haven: Yale University Press, 1986.

Holum, K. G. and G. Vikan. "The Trier Ivory, *Adventus* Ceremonial and The Relics of St Stephen." *Dumbarton Oaks Papers* 33 (1979), 113–133.

Honour, Hugh, and John Fleming. *The Visual Arts: a History*. 2nd edn. Englewood Cliffs, N.J.: Prentice-Hall, 1986.

Hood, William. "The Sacro Monte of Varallo. Renaissance Art and Popular Religion." *Monasticism and the Arts*, eds. Timothy Verdon with John Dally, 291–311. Syracuse: Syracuse University Press, 1984.

Huizinga, Johan. *The Waning of the Middle Ages*. London: E. Arnold & Co., 1924.

Imesch Oehry, Kornelia. *Die Kirchen der Franziskanerobservanten in der Lombardei, im Piemont und im Tessin und ihre "Lettnerwände."* Architektur und Dekoration. Essen: Die Blau Eule, 1991.

Janson, H. W. *History of Art*. 3rd edn. New York: Harry N. Abrams, 1986.

Jones, Leslie Webber and C. R. Morey. *The Miniatures of the Manuscripts of Terence Prior to The Thirteenth Century*. Princeton: Princeton University Press, 1931.

Jones, Pamela M. *Federico Borromeo and the Ambrosiana. Art Patronage and Reform in Seventeenth-Century Milan*. Cambridge: Cambridge University Press, 1993.

Jones, Roger, and Nicholas Penny. *Raphael.* New Haven: Yale, 1983.

Kadir, Djelal. *Columbus and the Ends of the Earth: Europe's Prophetic Rhetoric as Conquering Ideology.* Berkeley and Los Angeles: University of California Press, 1992.

Kahler, Mary E. ed., J. Warren, trans., "The Harkness 1531 Huejotzingo Codex," In *The Harkness Collection in the Library of Congress,* 49–210. Washington, D.C.: Library of Congress, 1974.

Kantorowicz, E. *Laudes Regiae: a Study in Liturgical Acclamations and Medieval Ruler Worship.* Berkeley and Los Angeles: University of California Press, 1946.

Kantorowicz, E. "The King's Advent' and the Enigmatic Panels in the Doors of Santa Sabina." *Art Bulletin* 26 (1944), 207–231.

Kaufmann, Thomas DaCosta. "The Perspective of Shadows: the History of the Theory of Shadow Projection." *Journal of the Warburg and Courtauld Institutes* 38 (1975), 258–87.

Kedar, Benjamin Z. *Crusade and Mission: European Approaches Towards The Muslims.* Princeton: Princeton University Press, 1984.

Kemp, Martin, and Janis C. Bell. "Perspective." *The Dictionary of Art*, ed. Hugh Brigstocke and Jane Turner. London: Macmillan, 1995.

Kemp, Martin. "Geometrical Perspective from Brunelleschi to Desargues." *Proceedings of the British Academy* 70 (1984), 89–132.

Kemp, Martin. *The Science of Art: Optical Themes in Western Art from Brunelleschi to Seurat.* New Haven and London: Yale University Press, 1990.

Kitzinger, Ernst. "The Cult of Images Before Iconoclasm." *Dumbarton Oaks Papers* 8 (1954), 83–150.

Klor de Alva, J. Jorge. "The Aztec–Spanish Dialogues of 1524." *Alcheringa/Ethnopoetics.* 4: 2 (1980), 52–193.

Klor de Alva, F. Jorge. "La historicidad de los coloquios de Sahagún." *Estudios de cultura nahuatl.* 147–84. Mexico: Instituto de Investigaciones Historica, Universidad Nacional Autónoma de México, 1982.

Klor de Alva, F. Jorge. "Sahagún and the Birth of Modern Ethnography." *The Work of Bernardino de Sahagún*, ed. J. Klor de Alva, H. B. Nicholson, and E. Quiñones Keber, 31–52. Austin: University of Texas Press, 1988.

Koschorreck, Walter. *Der Sachsenspiegel in Bildern aus der Heidelberger Bilderhandschrift.* Frankfurt am Main: Insel Verlag, 1976.

Kramer, Alice. "Vasari on Painting: the Critical Content of the Lives." Ph.D. dissertation. Columbia University. 1991.

Krautheimer, Richard. "Introduction to an 'Iconography of Mediaeval Architecture.'" *Journal of the Warburg and Courtauld Institutes* 5 (1942), 1–33.

Krieger, Murray. *Ekphrasis the Illusion of the Natural Sign.* Baltimore: The Johns Hopkins Press, 1992.

Kubler, George and Charles Gibson. *The Tovar Calendar.* c. 1585. Memoirs of the Connecticut Academy of Arts and Sciences, 11. New Haven: Yale University Press, 1951.

L'Orange, H. P. *Studies in The Iconography of Cosmic Kingship in the Ancient World.* New Rochelle, 1982.

Ladner, Gerhart B. "Homo Viator: Medieval Ideas on Alienation and Order." *Speculum* 42 (1967), 233–259 reprinted in his *Images and Ideas in the Middle Ages: Selected Studies in History and Art,* 2 vols. Rome, 1983; 2: 937–974.

Ladner, Gerhart. "The Concept of the Image in the Greek Fathers, and the Byzantine Iconoclastic Controversy," *Dumbarton Oaks Papers* 7 (1953), 1–34.

Leclerq, Jean. "Ioculator et saltator. S. Bernard et l'image du jongleur dans les manuscrits." *Translatio Studii: Manuscript and Library Studies honoring Oliver L. Kapaner,* ed. Julian G. Plante, 124–148. Collegeville, Mn.: St John's University Press, 1973.

Lejarza, F. de. "Franciscanismo de Cortés y cortesianismo de los franciscanos." *Misionalia Hispànica,* 43–136. Madrid, 1948.

León-Portilla, Miguel. *The Broken Spears: the Aztec Account of the Conquest of Mexico.* Boston, 1962.

León-Portilla, Miguel, ed. *Los diálogos de 1524 según el texto de Fray Bernardino de Sahagún y sus colaboradores indígenas.* Mexico City, 1986.

Leónard, Irving. *Books of the Brave.* Cambridge: Harvard University Press, 1949.

Leppmann, Wolfgang. *Winckelmann.* London: Victor Gollancz, 1971.

Lichtenstein, Jacqueline. *La Couleur éloquente: rhétorique et peinture à l'âge classique. Idées et recherches.* Paris: Flammarion, 1989.

Lichtenstein, Jacqueline. "Making up Representation: the Risks of Femininity." *Representations* 20 (1987), 77–87.

Livingstone, Margaret S. "Art, Illusion and the Visual System." *Scientific American* 258/1 (1988), 78–85.

Lockhart, James. *The Nahus after the Conquest.* Stanford: Stanford University Press, 1992.

Lomazzo, Giovanni Paolo. *Scritti sulle arti.* Ed. Roberto P. Ciardi. 2 vols. Florence: Centro Di, 1973–76.

Longo, Pier Giorgio. "Alle origini del Sacro Monte di Varallo: la proposta religiosa di Bernardino Caimi." *Novarien* 14 (1984), 19–98.

MacCormack, Sabine. *Art and Ceremony in Late Antiquity.* Berkeley and Los Angeles: University of California Press, 1981.

MacCormack, Sabine. "Change and Continuity in Late Antiquity: the Ceremony of Adventus." *Historia* 21 (1972), 721–752.

Machiavelli, Nicolò. *Lettere*, ed. Franco Gaeta. Milan: Feltrinelli, 1961.

Maguire, Pauline. "Poussin in France: Chantelou's Collection." Ph.D. dissertation. Columbia University, 1994.

Mahon, Denis. *Studies in Seicento Art and Theory.* London: Warburg Institute, 1947.

Malvasia, Carlo Cesare. *Felsina pittrice: vite de' pittori bolognesi.* Bologna: Forni, 1974.

Mancinelli, Fabrizio. *A Masterpiece Close-Up: the Transfiguration by Raphael.* Vatican: Libreria Editrice Vaticana, n.d. [1979?]

Mancinelli, Fabrizio. "Raffaello e l'Incoronazione di Carlo Magno (1516)." *Tecnica e Stile, esempi di pittura murale del rinascimento italiano*, ed. Eve Borsook and Fiorella Superbi Gioffredi, 111–123. The Harvard University Center for Italian Renaissance Studies, Villa I Tatti. Florence: Silvana, 1986.

Mancini, Giulio. *Considerazione sulla pittura.* Ed. A. Marucchi, intro. Luigi Salerno. Rome: Accademia dei Lincei, 1956.

Martin, John Rupert. *Baroque.* New York: Harper and Row, 1977.

Mason, Rainer Michael, and Mauro Natale. *Raphael et la seconde main.* Exhibition catalogue. Geneva: Cabinet des Estampes et Musée d'Art et d'Histoire, 1984.

Maza, Francisco de la. "Fray Diego Valadés Escritor y Gradador Franciscano del Siglo XVI." *Francisco de la Maza: Obras Escogidas*, 97–159. México: UNAM (1945), 1992.

Mazzini, Franco. "La pittura del primo Cinquecento." *Storia di Milano*, VIII, *Tra Francia e Spagna (1500–1535)*, 565–655. Milan: Fondazione Treccani degli Alfieri, 1957.

McCormick, Michael. *Eternal Victory: Triumphal Rulership in Late Antiquity, Byzantium and the Early Medieval West.* Cambridge: Cambridge University Press, 1989.

McGinness, Frederick. "Rhetoric and Counter-Reformation Rome: Sacred Oratory and the Construction of the Catholic World View 1563–1621." Ph.D. dissertation. University of California, Berkeley, 1982.

Meditations on the Life of Christ. An Illustrated Manuscript of the Fourteenth Century, ed. Isa Ragusa and Rosalie B. Green. Princeton: Princeton University Press, 1961.

Meiss, Millard. "Some Remarkably Early Shadows in a Rare Type of Threnos." *Festschrift Ulrich Middeldorf*, 112–118. Berlin: De Gruyter, 1968.

Melfi, Eduardo. "Curti (Corte, Corti, Curtius), Lancino." *Dizionario biografico degli italiani* 31, 487–488. Rome: Istituto della Enciclopedia Italiana, 1985.

Meneghin, Vittorino P. *I Monti di Pietà in Italia dal 1462 al 1562.* Vicenza: L.I.E.F. Edizioni, 1986.

Meseguer Fernández, Juan. "Contenido misionológico de la *Obediencia* e *Instrucción* de Fray Francisco de los Angeles a los doce apóstoles de México." *The Americas* 11 (1955), 473–500.

Migne, J.-P., ed. *Patrologia Latina.* vol. 34. Paris: J.-P. Migne, 1861.

Mignolo, Walter. "On the Colonization of Amerindian Languages and Memories: Renaissance Theories of Writing and the Discontinuity of the Classical Tradition." *Comparative Studies in Society and History* 34:2 (1992), 301–330.

Montagu, Jennifer. *Alessandro Algardi.* 2 vols. New Haven: Yale University Press, 1985.

Moorman, John. *A History of the Franciscan Order from its Origins to the Year 1517.* Oxford: Oxford University Press, 1968.

Mosini, Giovanni Atanasio. *Diverse figure al numero di ottanta, disegnate di . . . Annibale Carracci . . . e cavate dagli originali da Simone Guilino Parigino.* Rome: L. Grignani, 1646.

Motolinía (Fray Toribio de Benavente). *Memoriales o Historia de los Indios de la Nueva España y de los Naturales de Ella (1541).* Ed.

Edmundo O'Gorman. México: UNAM, 1971.

Müntz, M. Eugène. *Les historiens et les critiques de Raphael, 1483–1883, essai bibliographique.* Paris: Librairie de l'Art, 1883.

Murúa, Martín de. *Historia del Origen y Genealogía Real de los Reyes Incas del Perú* (*c.*1590). Ed. Constantino Bayle. Madrid: Consejo Superior de Investigaciones Cientifizas, 1946.

Nesselrath, A. "Art-historical Findings During the Restoration of the Stanza dell' Incendio." *Master Drawings* 30 (1992), 31–60.

Nesselrath, A. "La Progettazione della 'Incoronazione di Carlomagno.'" *Raffaello a Roma*, 173–181. Rome: Edizioni dell' Elefante, 1986.

Niçaise, Claude. "L'Ecole d'Athènes et le Parnasse de Raphaël d'Urbin. Tableaux du Vatican expliqués en françois sur l'italien de Mr. Bellori . . ." MS 180, Bibliothèque Municipale de Beaune (Côte d'Or), 1698.

Nova, Alessandro. "I tramezzi in Lombardia fra XV e XVI secolo: scene della Passione e devozione francescana." *Il Francescanesimo in Lombardia. Storia e arte*, 197–215. Milan: Silvana Editoriale, 1983.

O'Gorman, Edmundo. "Estudio Analítico de los Escritos Históricos de Motolinía." 1541. Motolinía, *Memoriales o Historia de los indios de la Nueva España y de los Naturales de Ella*, ed. Edmundo O'Gorman. México: UNAM, 1971.

O'Malley, John. *Praise and Blame in Renaissance Rome. Rhetoric, Doctrine, and Reform in the Sacred Oratory of the Papal Court.* Durham, N.C.: Duke University Press, 1979.

Oberhuber, Konrad. *Raffaello.* Trans. Maria Magrini. Milan: Mondadori, 1982.

Ocaranza, Fernando. *Capítulos de la historia franciscana.* Second series. Mexico: [n.p.], 1934.

Ossola, Carlo. "8. 'Ut pictora poesis': Paleotti." In *Autumno del Rinascimento, "Idea del Tempio" dell' arte nell' ultimo Cinquecento*, 63–75. Florence: L. S. Olschki, 1971.

Othón, Arróniz. *Teatro de evangelización en Nueva España.* Mexico: Universidad Nacional Autonoma de Mexico, 1979.

Pagden, Anthony. *Hernán Cortés: Letters From Mexico.* New Haven: Yale University Press, 1986.

Paleotti, Gabriele. *Discorso intorno alle imagini sacre e profane.* Bologna, 1582. Reprint edn. Paola Barocchi in *Trattati d'arte del Cinquecento*, vol. 2, 117–509. Bari: Giuseppe Laterza e Figli, 1961.

Paleotti, Gabriele. *Instruttioni di Monsignore Illustrissimo et Reverendissimo Cardinale Gabriele Paleotti, Arcivescovo di Bologna Per Tutti quelli, che havranno licenza di Predicare nelle Ville, & altri luoghi della Diocese di sua Signore Illustrissimo.* Vatican, Biblioteca Apostolica Vaticana, Ferraioli 4, 9833 (7).

Palomera, Esteban. *Fray Diego Valadés* O.F.M.: *Evangelizador Humanista de la Nueva España*, México: Editorial Jus, 1962.

Palomera, Esteban. "Introduccíon." Valadés, *Rhetórica Christiana*, vii–xlviii.

Parry, John H. and Robert G. Keith, eds. *New Iberian World: A Documentary History of the Discovery and Settlement of Latin America to the Early Seventeenth Century.* 5 vols. New York: Times Books. Hector & Rose, 1984.

Pedretti, Carlo. "The Zaccolini Manuscripts." *Bibliothèque d'Humanisme et Renaissance* 35 (1972), 39–53.

Pelikan, Jaroslav. *Imago Dei. The Byzantine Apologia for Icons.* Princeton: Princeton University Press, 1990.

Perini, Giovanna. "Il lessico tecnico del Malvasia." In *Convegno Nazionale Sui Lessici Tecnici del Sei e Settecento*, 221–53. Pisa: Scuola Normale Superiore, 1980.

Pezzini, Grazia Bernini, Stefania Massari, and Prosperi Valenti Rodinò. *Raphael invenit: stampe da Raffaello nelle collezioni dell' Istituto Nazionale per la Grafica.* Rome: Edizioni Quasar di Severino Tognon, 1985.

Phelan, John Leddy. *The Millennial Kingdom of the Franciscans in New Spain.* 2nd edn. Berkeley and Los Angeles: University of California Press, 1970.

Picciafuoco, Umberto. *Fr. Nicolò da Osimo (1370?–1453). Vita, Opere. Spiritualità.* Monteprandone: Officine grafiche Axanum, 1980.

Pigman, G. W., III. "Versions of Imitation in the Renaissance." *Renaissance Quarterly* 33 (1980), 1–32.

Pinto, Giuliano. "I costi del pellegrinaggio in Terrasanta nei secoli XIV e XV (dai resoconti dei viaggiatori italiani)." *Toscana e Terrasanta nel Medioevo*, ed. Franco Cardini,

257–284. Florence: Alinea Editrice, 1982.

Podro, Michael. *The Critical Historians of Art.* New Haven and London: Yale University Press, 1982.

Poirier, Maurice. "Studies on the Concepts of *Disegno, Invenzione,* and *Colore.*" Ph.D. dissertation. New York University, 1976.

Poirier, Maurice. "The Disegno–Colore Controversy Reconsidered." *Explorations in Renaissance Culture* 13 (1979), 52–86.

Posner, Donald. *Annibale Carracci: a Study in the Reform of Painting around 1590.* 2 vols. London and New York: Phaidon, 1971.

Prodi, Paolo. *Il Cardinale Gabriele Paleotti (1522–1596).* 2 vols. Rome: Edizioni di Storia e letteratura, 1959–1967.

Promis, Domenico, and Müller, Giuseppe. *Lettere ed orazioni latine di Girolamo Morone.* Miscellanea di Storia Italiana edita per cura della Regia Deputazione di Storia Patria, no. 2. Turin: 1863.

Puttfarken, Thomas. *Roger de Piles' Theory of Art.* New Haven: Yale University Press, 1985.

Quintilian. *Institutio oratoria.* New York: G. P. Putnam's Sons, 1921.

Raffaello: Elementi di un mito. Florence: Centro Di, 1984.

Ravicz, Marilyn Ekdahl. *Early Colonial Religious Drama in Mexico: From Tzompantli to Golgotha.* Washington, D.C.: Catholic University of America Press, 1970.

Reeves, Marjorie, ed. *Prophetic Rome in the High Renaissance Period: Essays.* Oxford: Oxford University Press, 1992.

Reeves, Marjorie. *The Influence of Prophecy in the Later Middle Ages: A Study in Joachimism.* Oxford: Clarenden Press, 1969.

Reilly, Patricia. "Writing Out Color in Renaissance Theory." *Genders* 12 (1991), 77–99.

Richard, Jean. *La Papauté et les missions d'orient au Moyen Âge (XIIIè–Xvè siècles).* Rome: Ecole Française de Rome, 1977.

Rojas Garciadueñas, José J. "El teatro franciscano en Méjico durante el siglo XVI." *Archivo Ibero–americano,* 11 (1951), 129–189.

Rosenberg, Martin. *Raphael and France: The Artist as Paradigm and Symbol.* University Park, P.A.: The Pennsylvania State University Press, 1995.

Rosenberg, Marvin Israel. "Raphael and the Florentine *Istoria.*" *Raphael Before Rome,* ed.

J. Beck, 175–87. Washington D.C.: National Gallery of Art, 1986.

Rubin, Patricia. *Giorgio Vasari, Art and History.* New Haven: Yale University Press, 1994.

Rusconi, Roberto. "'Confessio generalis.' Opuscoli per la pratica penitenziale nei primi cinquanta anni della introduzione della stampa." *I Frati Minori fra '400 e '500,* 189–227. Assisi: Università di Perugia. Centro di Studi Francescani, 1986.

Rusconi, Roberto. "Carcano, Michele." *Dizionario biografico degli italiani.* 19. Rome: Istituto della Enciclopedia Italiana, 1976, 742–744.

Rusconi, Roberto. "Dal pulpito alla confessione. Modelli di comportamento religioso in Italia tra 1470 circa e 1520 circa." *Strutture ecclesiastiche in Italia e in Germania prima della Riforma,* ed. Paolo Prodi and Peter Johanek, 259–315. Bologna: Società editrice il Mulino, 1984.

Rusconi, Roberto. "La predicazione francescana sulla penitenza alla fine del Quattrocento nel 'Rosarium sermonum' di Bernardino Busti." *Studia Patavina* 22 (1975), 68–95.

Rusconi, Roberto. "Manuali milanesi di confessione editi tra il 1474 ed il 1523." *Archivum Franciscanum Historicum* 65 (1972), 107–156.

Rusconi, Roberto. "Michele Carcano da Milano e le caratteristiche della sua predicazione." *Picenum Seraphicum* 10 (1973), 196–218.

Sahagún, Bernardino de *Códice florentino.* 1569. Facsimile edition issued by the Biblioteca Medicea Laurenziana and Archivo General de la Nación, 1979.

Scavizzi, Giuseppe. "La teologia cattolica e le immagini durante il XVI secolo." *Storia dell'Arte* 21 (1974), 171–213.

Schmitt, Jean-Claude. "Gestas-Gesticulatio. Contribution à l'Étude du vocabulaire latin médiéval des gestes." *La lexicographie du latin médiéval et ses rapports avec les recherches actuelle sur la civilization du moyen Âge,* 377–390. Paris, 1981.

Schmitt, Jean-Claude. *La raison des gestes dans l'occident médiéval.* Paris: Gallimard, 1990.

Schwoebel, Robert H. *The Shadow of the Crescent: the Renaissance Image of the Turk (1453–1517).* New York: St Martin's Press, 1967.

Shearman, John and Marcia Hall, eds. *The*

Princeton Raphael Symposium. Princeton: Princeton University Press, 1990.

Shearman, John. "Leonardo's Color and Chiaroscuro." *Zeitschrift für Kunstgeschichte* 25 (1962), 13–47.

Shell, Janice, and Venturoli, Paolo. "De Donati." *Dizionario biografico degli italiani*, 33, 650–656. Rome: Istituto della Enciclopedia Italiana, 1987.

Simonut, Noe. *Metodo d'evangelizzazione dei francescani tra musulmani e mongoli nei secoli XIII–XIV*. Milan: Pontificio Istituto Missioni Estere, 1947.

Southern, R. W. *Western Views of Islam in the Middle Ages*. Cambridge, Ma.: Harvard University Press, 1962.

Spear, Richard E. *Domenichino*. 2 vols. New Haven and London: Yale University Press, 1982.

Spear, Richard. "Leonardo, Raphael, and Caravaggio." *Light on the Eternal City: Observations and Discoveries in the Art and Architecture of Rome*, 59–90. Papers in Art History from the Pennsylvania State University. University Park: Penn State University Press, 1987.

Spence, Jonathan. *The Memory Palace of Matteo Ricci*. New York: Viking Penguin, 1984.

Stafford, Barbara Maria. "Beauty of the Invisible: Winckelmann and the Aesthetics of Imperceptibility." *Zeitschrift für Kunstgeschichte* 43 (1980), 65–78.

Steck, Francis Borgia, trans. *Toribio de Benavente (Motolinía). History of the Indians of New Spain*. Washington, D.C.: Academy of American Franciscan History Documentary Series, 1951.

Steer, John. "Art History and Direct Perception: a General View." *Art History* 12, no. 1 (1989), 93–107.

Stefani Perrone, Stefania. "La 'Gerusalemme' delle origini nella secolare vicenda edificatoria del Sacro Monte di Varallo." *Sacri Monti. Devozione, arte e cultura della Controriforma*, ed. Luciano Vaccaro and Francesca Riccardi, 27–57. Milan: Jaca Book, 1992.

Stefani Perrone, Stefania. *Questi sono li Misteri che sono sopra el Monte de Varalle (in una "Guida" poetica del 1514)*. Borgosesia: Società per la conservazione delle opere d'arte e dei monumenti in Valsesia, 1987.

Stettiner, Richard. *Die illustrierten Prudentius-handschriften* (Berlin, 1895). Berlin: Grote, 1905.

Stone, David M. *Guercino, Master Draftsman: Works from North American Collections*. Cambridge, Ma.: Harvard University Art Museums, 1991.

Stone, David M. *Guercino: Catalogo Completo del Dipinti*. Gigli dell'Arte, 21. Florence: Cantini, 1992.

Stone, David M. "Theory and Practice in Seicento Art: the Example of Guercino." Ph.D. dissertation. Harvard University, 1989.

Stridbeck, Carl Gustaf. *Raphael Studies*, 2 vols. Acta Universitatis Stockholmiensis, Stockholm Studies in the History of Art, 8. Stockholm: Almqvist & Wiksell, 1960–63.

Suárez de Figueroa, Miguel. *Templo de N. grande Patriarca San Francisco de la provincia de los doze apostoles de el Perú*. Lima, 1675.

Sumption, Jonathan. *Pilgrimage: An Image of Medieval Religion*. Totowa, N.J.: Rowman and Littlefield, 1975.

Taylor, René. "El Arte de la Memoria en ee Nuevo Mundo," 45–76. *Iconología y Sociedad: Arte Colonia Hispanoamencano*. México: UNAM, 1987.

Testelin, Henri. *Sentiments des plus habiles peintres sur la pratique de la peinture et sculpture, mis en tables de preceptes avec plusieurs discours academiques temps*. Paris: Mabre-Cramoisy, 1696.

Testori, Giovanni, and Stefania Stefani Perrone. *Artisti del legno. La scultura in Valsesia dal XV al XVIII secolo*. Borgosesia: Valsesia Editrice, 1985.

Teyssèdre, Bernard. *L'histoire de l'art vue du grand siècle. Recherches sur l'Abrégé de la Vie des Peintres, par Roger de Piles (1699) et ses sources*. Paris: René Julliard, 1964.

Teyssèdre, Bernard. *Roger de Piles et les débats sur le coloris au siècle de Louis XIV*. Paris: La Bibliothèque des Arts, La Fondation Wildenstein et du Centre National de la Recherche Scientifique, 1957.

Thode, Henry. *Franz von Assisi und die Anfänge der Kunst der Renaissance in Italien*. Berlin: Grote, 1926.

Thuillier, Jacques. "Polémiques Autour de Michel-Ange an XVIIè Siècle." *XVIIè Siècle* 36–37 (1957), 353–391.

Thuillier, Jacques. "Pour un 'Corpus Pussinianum.'" *Nicolas Poussin. Conference Proceedings 19–21 Sept. 1958*, ed. André

Chastel, II, 49–238. Centres National de la Recherche Scientifique, colloques internationaux. Paris: Centre National de la Recherche Scientifique, 1960.

Todorov, Tzvetan. *The Conquest of America.* New York: Harper & Row, 1984.

Torquemada, Juan de. *Monarquía Indiana.* Mexico City: Editorial Porrúa, 1986; reprint of the Seville, 1615 edition.

Trexler, Richard. "We Think, They Act: Clerical Readings of Missionary Theatre in 16th Century New Spain." *Understanding Popular Culture: Europe from the Middle Ages to the Nineteenth Century,* ed. Steven L. Kaplan. 189–227. Berlin and New York: Mouton, 1984.

Urbano, Henrique. "Syncretismo y Sentimiento Religioso en Los Andes. Apuntes sobre sus Origenes y Desarrollo." Unpublished paper presented at the Andean History Workshop, University of Chicago, February 1992.

Vaccaro, Luciano, and Francesca Riccardi. *Sacri Monti. Devozione, arte e cultura della Controriforma.* Milan: Jaca Book, 1992.

Val Julian, Carmen. "Danses de La Conquête: une Mémoire Indienne de L'Histoire?", 253–66, in *Vingt Études sur le Mexique et le Guatemala Réunies à la Memoire de Nicole Percheron,* ed. A. Breton, J.-P. Berthe, and S. Lecoin. Toulouse: Presses Universitaires du Mirail, 1991.

Valadés, Diego. *Rhetórica christiana ad concionandi et orandi usum.* Perugia: Petrumiacobum Petrutium, 1579. Facsimile ed. México: Fondo de Cultura Económica, 1989.

Vauchez, André. *Ordini mendicanti e società italiana XIII–XV secolo.* Milan: Il Saggiatore, 1990.

Verbraeken, René. *Clair-obscur, histoire d'un mot.* Librairie des Arts et Métiers. Nogent-le-Roi: Éditions Jacques Laget, 1979.

Waddell, Helen. *The Wandering Scholars.* Garden City: Doubleday, 1955.

Waterworth, J., trans. *Canons and Decrees of the Sacred Oecumenical Council of Trent Celebrated Under the Sovereign Pontiffs Paul III, Julius III, and Pius IV.* Chicago: The Christian Symbolic Publication Society [n.d.].

Watts, Pauline Moffitt. "Hieroglyphs of Conversion: Alien Discourses in Diego Valadés's *Rhetorica Christiana.*" *Memorie Domenicae,* Nuova serie, no. 22 (1991), 405–433.

Watts, Pauline Moffitt. "Prophecy and Discovery: on the Spiritual Origins of Christopher Columbus's 'Enterprise of The Indies.'" *The American Historical Review* 90: 1 (1985), 73–102.

Watts, Pauline Moffitt. "Talking to Spiritual Others: Ramon Llull, Nicholas of Cusa, Diego Valadés." *Nicholas of Cusa in Search of God and Wisdom,* ed. J. Christianson and T. Izbicki, 203–218. Leiden: E. J. Brill, 1991.

Watts, Pauline Moffitt. "The New World and the End of the World: Evangelizing Sixteenth-Century Mexico." *Imagining the New World: Columbian Iconography,* ed. Irma B. Jaffe, Gianni Eugenio Viola, Franca Rovigatti, 29–39. Rome and New York: Istituto della Encyclopedia italiana, 1991.

Weil-Garris Posner, Kathleen. *Leonardo and Central-Italian Art 1515–1550.* CAA Monograph Series, vol. 28. New York: Institute of Fine Arts, 1974.

Winckelmann, Johann Joachim. *Winckelmann: Writings on Art,* ed. and trans. David Irwin. London: Phaidon, 1972.

Winner, Matthias. "L'Autoritratto di Raffaello e la misura per il nostro occhio: appunti sulla costruzione prospettica della Scuola di Atene (c. 1510–11)." *Tecnica e Stile, Esempi di Pittura Murale del Rinascimento Italiano,* ed. Eve Borsook and Fiorella Superbi Gioffredi, 83–94. The Harvard University Center for Italian Renaissance Studies, Villa I Tatti. Florence: Silvana, 1986.

Witkowski, Gustave Joseph. *L'Art profane à l'Église, ses licences symboliques, satiriques et fantaisistes. Contribution à l'Étude archéologique et artistique des édifices religieux.* Paris: J. Schemit, 1908.

Wölfflin, Heinrich. *Classic Art: an Introduction to the Renaissance,* trans. Peter and Linda Murray. London: Phaidon, 1968.

Wölfflin, Heinrich. *Principles of Art History,* trans. M. D. Hottinger. New York: Dover, 1950.

Wyngaert, Anastasius van den and Georgius Mensaert. *Sinica Franciscana.* 5 vols. Florence, 1929–54.

Zaccolini, Matteo. "Prospettiva del Colore" (1618–22). Florence, Biblioteca Laurenziana, Laurentian Ashburnham 1212 (2).

III EARLY COLLECTING PRACTICES

Acidini Luchinat, Christina, and Giorgio Galletti. *Le ville e i giardini di Castello e Petraia a Firenze*. Florence: Pacini Editore, 1992.

Ackerman, James S. "Early Renaissance 'Naturalism' and Scientific Illustration." *Natural Sciences and the Arts*.

Ackerman, James S. "The Involvement of Artists in Renaissance Science." *Science and the Arts*.

Actas de los capítulos provinciales de la provincia de Santiago de México, Orden de Predicatores, siglo XVI. Colección Gómez de Orozco 11. Archivo Histórico, Biblioteca Nacional de Antropología e Historia, INAH, Mexico.

Actas provinciales de la provincia de Santiago de México del Orden de Predicatores, México, 1540–1590. M-M 142. Bancroft Library, Berkeley.

Allegri, E., and A. Cecchi. *Palazzo Vecchio e i Medici, guida storica*. Florence: S.P.E.S., 1980.

America: Bride of the Sun. Ghent: Imschoot, 1992.

Amico, L. "Les céramiques rustiques authentiques de Bernard Palissy." *Revue de l'Art*, 78 (1987), 61–69.

Andres, Glenn M. *The Villa Medici in Rome*. 2 vols. New York and London: Garland, 1976.

Ashworth, William B., Jr. "Marcus Gheeraerts and the Aesopic Connection in Seventeenth-Century Scientific Illustration." *Art Journal* 44 (1984), 132–138.

Ashworth, William B., Jr. "Natural History and the Emblematic World View." *Reappraisals of the Scientific Revolution*, ed. David C. Lindberg and Robert S. Westman. Cambridge: Cambridge University Press, 1990.

Ashworth, William B., Jr. "The Persistent Beast: Recurring Images in Early Zoological Illustration." *Natural Sciences and the Arts*, 46–66.

Avery, Charles, and Anthony Radcliffe, eds., *Giambologna 1529–1608: Sculptor to the Medici*. London: Arts Council of Great Britain, 1978.

Avery, Charles. *Giambologna: The Complete Sculpture*. Mt. Kisco, N.Y.: Moyer Bell, 1987.

Bacci, Andrea. *L'alicorno*, Florence: Giorgio Marescotti, 1573.

Bacci, Mina. *L'opera completa di Piero di Cosimo*.

Milan: Rizzoli, 1976.

Bacon, F. *Gesta Grayorum*, London, 1594. *Works*, ed. J. Spedding, R. Ellis, and D. Heath, London: Longman, vol. 7, 1862.

Bakhtin, Mikhail. *Rabelais and His World*, trans. H. Iswolsky. Cambridge, Ma.: MIT Press, 1968.

Balsiger, B. "The Kunst- und Wunderkammern: a Catalogue Raisonné of Collecting in Germany, France and England, 1565–1750." Ph.D. dissertation. University of Pittsburg, 1970 (University Microfilms, Ann Arbor, 1971).

Baltrusaitis, J. *Aberrations: an Essay on the Legend of Forms*, trans. R. Miller. Cambridge, Ma.: MIT Press, 1989.

Baltrusaitis, J. *Anamorphic Art*, trans. W. Strachan. Cambridge: Chadwick-Healey, 1976.

Bardazzi, Silvestro, and Eugenio Castellani. *La Villa Medicea di Poggio a Caiano*. 2 vols. Parma: Edizioni del Palazzo, 1981.

Bedini, Silvio A. "The Papal Pachyderms." *Proceedings of the American Philosophical Society* 125 (1981), 75–90.

Benesch, Otto. "The Orient as a Source of Inspiration of the Graphic Arts of the Renaissance." *Festschrift Friedrich Winkler*. Berlin: Gbr. Mann, 1959.

Berner, Samuel. "Florentine Society in the Late Sixteenth and Early Seventeenth Centuries." *Studies in the Renaissance* 18 (1971), 177–199.

Bober, Phyllis Pray, and Ruth Rubinstein. *Renaissance Artists and Antique Sculpture*. London: Harvey Miller Publishers, 1986.

Borghini, Raffaele. *Il Riposo*. Florence: Giorgio Marescotti, 1584.

Bott, G., ed. *Wenzel Jamnitzer und die Nürnberger Goldsmiedekunst, 1500–1700*. Exhibition catalogue. Munich: Klinkhardt and Biermann, 1985.

Burkhart, Louise. *The Slippery Earth: Nahua-Christian Moral Dialogue in Sixteenth-Century Mexico*. Tucson: University of Arizona Press, 1989.

Campbell, Malcolm. "Observations on Ammannati's *Neptune Fountain*: 1565 and 1575." *Renaissance Studies in Honor of Craig Hugh Smyth*. 2 vols. Florence: Giunti Barbéra, 1985.

Cellini, B. *Vita*, ed. E. Camesasca. Milan: Rizzoli, 1954.

Châtelet-Lange, Liliane. "The Grotto of the Unicorn and the Garden of the Villa di Castello." *Art Bulletin* 50 (1968), 51–62.

Chiapelli, Fredi, ed. *First Images of America.* 2 vols. Berkeley: University of California, 1976.

Christensen, Stephen Olaf Turk. "The Image of Europe in Anglo–German Travel Literature." *Voyager à la Renaissance Actes du Colloque de Tours, 1983,* ed. Jean Céard and Jean-Claude Margolin, 257–280. Paris: Maisonneuve et Larose, 1987.

Clarke, T. H. *The Rhinoceros from Dürer to Stubbs, 1515–1799.* London: Sotheby's Publications, 1986.

Clarke, T. "I am the Horn of a Rhinoceros." *Apollo* 125: 303 (May 1987), 344–349.

Codex Vaticanus A. *Codex Vaticanus 3738 ("Cod Vat. A," "Cod. Ríos") der Biblioteca Apostolica Vaticana.* Introduction by Hans Biedermann. Graz: Akademische Druck-u. Verlagsanstalt, 1979.

Codex Vaticanus A. *Il manoscritto messicano Vaticano 3738, detto il Códice Ríos.* Commentary by Franz Ehrle. Rome: Danesi, 1900.

Codex Vaticanus B. *Codex Vaticanus 3773 (Codex Vaticanus B) der Biblioteca Apostolica Vaticana.* Introduction and summaries by F. Anders. Graz: Akademische Druck-u. Verlagsanstalt, 1972.

Coffin, David R. *The Villa in the Life of Renaissance Rome.* Princeton: Princeton University Press, 1979.

Cole, F. J. "The History of Albrecht Dürer's Rhinoceros in Zoological Literature." *Science, Medicine and History. Essays in honour of Charles Singer,* ed. E. A. Underwood, 337–356. 2 vols. London and New York: Oxford University Press, 1953.

Cole, Richard G. "Sixteenth-Century Travel Books as a Source of European Attitudes toward Non-White and Non-Western Culture." *Proceedings of the American Philosophical Society* 116 (1972), 59–67.

Conforti, Claudia. "La grotta 'degli animali' o 'del diluvio' nel giardino di Villa Medici a Castello." *Quaderni di Palazzo Te* 6 (1987), 71–80.

Corti, Laura. *Vasari: Catalogo completo dei dipinti.* Florence: Cantini, 1989.

Cox-Rearick, Janet. *Dynasty and Destiny in Medici Art: Pontormo, Leo X, and the Two Cosimos.* Princeton: Princeton University Press, 1984.

Cuttler, Charles D. "Exotics in Post-Medieval European Art: Giraffes and Centaurs," *Artibus et Historiae* 23 (1991), 161–179.

Dacos, Nicole, and Caterina Furlan. *Giovanni da Udine 1487–1561.* Udine: Casamassima, 1987.

Dacos, Nicole. "Présents américains à la Renaissance: l'assimilation de l'exotisme." *Gazette des beaux-arts* 73 (1969), 57–62.

Danforth, Susan. *Encountering the New World, 1493 to 1800.* Exhibition catalogue. Providence: John Carter Brown Library, 1991.

Davis, Margaret Daly. "La galleria di sculture antiche di Cosimo I a Palazzo Pitti." *Le arti del principato mediceo.* Florence: S.P.E.S., 1980.

de Boodt, A. *Gemmarum et lapidum historia,* Hanau: Wechel ianis apud C. Marnium & heredes J. Auaril, 1609.

Dickerman, S. "Some Stock Illustrations of Animal Intelligence in Greek Psychology," *Transactions of the American Philological Association* 42 (1911), 123–130.

Dimier, L. "Bernard Palissy Rocailleur, Fontenier et Décorateur de Jardins." *Gazette des beaux-arts* 76: 12 (1943), 8–29.

Doering, O. "Des Augsberger Patriziers Philipp Hainhofer Bezeihungen zum Herzog Philipp II von Pomern-Stettin." *Quellenschriften für Kunstgeschichte* 6 (1894), 8–9.

Doggett, Rachel, et al. See *New World of Wonders.*

Donati, Lamberto. "La Giraffa." *Maso Finiguerra* 3 (1938), 247–268.

Durandus, *Rationale divinorum officiorum,* as *The Symbolism of Churches and Church Objects,* ed. J. Neale and B. Webb. Leeds: T. W. Green, 1843.

E. Hackenbroch. "A Set of Knife, Fork and Spoon with Coral Handles." *Metropolitan Museum Journal* 15 (1981), 183–184.

Eisler, Colin. *The Genius of Jacopo Bellini: the Complete Paintings and Drawings.* New York: Harry N. Abrams, 1988.

Elliott, J. H. *The Old World and the New 1492–1650.* Cambridge: Cambridge University Press, 1970.

Fader, Martha Alice Agnew. "Sculpture in the Piazza della Signoria as Emblem of the Florentine Republic." Ph.D. dissertation. University of Michigan, 1977.

Feest, Christian. "Koloniale Federkunst aus Mexiko," in *Gold und Macht: Spanien in der Neuen Welt*, ed. Christian Feest and Peter Kann, 173–178. Vienna: Verlag Kremayr & Scheriau, 1986.

Findlen, Paula. "Jokes of Nature and Jokes of Knowledge: the Playfulness of Scientific Discourse in Early Modern Europe." *Renaissance Quarterly* 43 (1990), 292–331.

Fock, C. W. "Pietre Dure work at the Court of Prague and Florence: Some Relations." *Prag um 1600*, ed. Fucíková, 51–59.

Foucault, Michel. *The Order of Things: an Archaeology of the Human Sciences*. New York: Pantheon Books, 1970.

Friedmann, Herbert. "Bacchiacca's Gathering of Manna in the National Gallery." *Gazette des beaux-arts* 32 (1947), 151–158.

Friedmann, Herbert. "Cornaro's Gazelle and Bellini's *Orpheus*." *Gazette des beaux-arts* 32 (1947), 15–22.

Fritz, J. *Goldsmiedekunst der Gotik in Mitteleuropa*. Munich: C. H. Beck, 1982.

Fritz, R. *Die Gefässe aus Kokonuss in Mitteleuropa, 1250–1800*. Mainz am Rhein: P. von Zabern, 1983.

Fucíková, E., ed. *Prag um 1600. Beiträge zur Kunst und Kultur am Hofe Rudolfs II.* Freren: Luca Verlag, 1988.

Fuson, Robert H., trans. *The Log of Christopher Columbus*. Camden: International Marine Publishing Company, 1987.

George, Wilma, and Brunsdon Yapp. *The Naming of the Beasts: Natural History in the Medieval Bestiary*. London: Duckworth, 1991.

George, Wilma. *Animals and Maps*. London: Secker and Warburg, 1969.

Gilbert, C. "The Egg Reopened Again." *Art Bulletin* 56 (1974), 252–258.

Giovio, Paolo. *Ragionamenti sopra i motti, et disegni d'arme, et d'amore*. Venice: Giordano Ziletti, 1556.

Glanville, P. *Silver in Tudor and Early Stuart England. A Social History and Catalogue of the National Collection, 1480–1660*, London: Victoria and Albert Museum, 1990.

Glass, John B., in collaboration with Donald Robertson. "A Census of Native Middle American Pictorial Manuscripts." *Guide to Ethnohistorical Sources*. Part 3. Ed. Howard F. Cline, 14: 81–252. *Handbook of Middle American Indians*. Robert Wauchope, general editor. Austin: University of Texas Press, 1975.

Grafton, Anthony, with April Shelford and Nancy Siraisi. *New Worlds, Ancient Texts: the Power of Tradition and the Shock of Discovery*. Cambridge, Ma., and London: Belknap Press, 1992.

Greenblatt, Stephen. *Marvelous Possessions: The Wonder of the New World*. Chicago: University of Chicago Press, 1991.

Harms, Wolfgang. "On Natural History and Emblematics in the 16th Century." *Natural Sciences and the Arts*.

Haskell, Francis, and Nicholas Penny. *Taste and the Antique*. New Haven and London: Yale University Press, 1981.

Hatfield, Rab. "Some Unknown Descriptions of the Medici Palace in 1459." *Art Bulletin* 52 (1970), 232–249.

Hay, Denis. *Europe: the Emergence of an Idea*. Edinburgh: Edinburgh University Press, 1968.

Hay, Denys. "The Italian View of Renaissance Italy." *Renaissance Essays*. London and Ronceverte: The Hambledon Press, 1988.

Hayward, J. *Virtuoso Goldsmiths and the Triumph of Mannerism*. London: Sotheby Parke Bernet, 1976.

Heikamp, Detlef. "Agostino del Riccio, 'Del giardino di un re.'" *Il giardino storico italiano*, ed. G. Ragionieri. Florence: Leo S. Olschki, 1981.

Heikamp, Detlef. *Mexico and the Medici*. Florence: Editrice Edam, 1972.

Hind, Arthur M. *Early Italian Engraving*. 7 vols. London: B. Quaritch for Knoedler, 1938–48.

Hoefnagel, G. and J. *Archetypa studiaque patris Georgi Hoefnagelii*. Frankfurt: Francofurti ad Meonum, 1592.

Hoeniger, F. David. "How Plants and Animals Were Studied in the Mid-Sixteenth Century." *Science and the Arts*.

Honour, Hugh. *The European Vision of America*. Cleveland: The Cleveland Museum of Art, 1975.

Honour, Hugh. *The New Golden Land: European Images of America from the Discoveries to the Present Time*. New York: Pantheon Books, 1975.

The Illustrated Bartsch 24, Early Italian Masters, ed. Mark Zucker. New York: Abaris, 1980.

Impey, O. and A. MacGregor, eds. *The Origins of Museums: the Cabinet of Curiosities in Sixteenth- and Seventeenth-Century Europe*.

Oxford: Clarendon Press, 1985.

Inventarium manuscriptorium latinorum Bibliothecae Vaticanae. Sala Cons. MS. 304. 4 vols. Vatican City: Biblioteca Apostolica Vaticana, 1596–1600.

Janson, Horst W. *Apes and Ape Lore in the Middle Ages and the Renaissance*. London: The Warburg Institute, University of London, 1952.

Joost-Gaugier, Christiane L. "Lorenzo the Magnificent and the Giraffe as a Symbol of Power." *Artibus et Historiae* 16 (1987), 91–99.

Kaufmann, T. DaCosta. "Remarks on the Collections of Rudolf II: the *Kunstkammer* as a Form of *Representatio*." *The Art Journal* 38 (1978), 22–28.

Kaufmann, T. DaCosta. *The Mastery of Nature. Aspects of Art, Science and Humanism in the Renaissance*. Princeton: Princeton University Press, 1993.

Kaufmann, T. DaCosta. *The School of Prague. Painting at the Court of Rudolf II*. Chicago: University of Chicago Press, 1988.

Kemp, Martin. "From 'Mimesis' to 'Fantasia': the Quattrocento Vocabulary of Creation, Inspiration and Genius in the Visual Arts." *Viator* 8 (1977), 347–398.

Kemp, Martin. "Palissy's Philosophical Pots." In *Architectura del Pensiero*, ed. W. Tega. Bologna, forthcoming.

Kemp, Martin. "Style and Society in Some Instruments of Art," *Interpretation and Cultural History*, ed. J. Pittock and A. Wear, 135–152. London: Macmillan, 1991.

Kemp, Martin. "Temples of the Body and Temple of the Cosmos: Vision and Visualisation in the Vesalian and Copernican Revolutions." *Picturing Knowledge*, ed. B. Baigrie, Toronto: University of Toronto Press, 1995.

Kemp, Martin. *The Science of Art. Optical Themes in Western Art from Brunellesschi to Seurat*. London and New Haven: Yale University Press, 1991.

Kenseth, Joy, ed. *The Age of the Marvelous*. Exhibition catalogue. Hanover: Hood Museum of Art, Dartmouth College, 1991.

Kliemann, Julian-Matthias. *Politische und humanistische Ideen der Medici in der Villa Poggio a Caiano: Untersuchungen zu den Fresken der Sala Grande*. Bamberg: Bamberger Fotodruck Schadel & Wehle, 1976.

Knight, David. *Zoological Illustration*. Folkstone, England: Dawson, 1977.

Kolhaussen, H. *Nürnberger Goldschmiedekunst des Mittelalters und der Dürerzeit, 1240 bis 1540*. Berlin: Deutscher Verlag für Kunstwissenschaft, 1968.

Kris, E. "Der Stil 'rustique': die Verwendung des Naturabgusses bei Wenzel Jamnitzer und Barnard Palissy." *Jahrbuch der Kunstsammlungen in Wien* 1 (1926), 137–208.

Kruse, Jeremy. "The Spectacle of Slaughter: Hunting and the Papal Court in the Renaissance." *Melbourne Historical Journal* 20 (1990), 45–64.

Lach, Donald F. *Asia in the Making of Europe*. 2 vols. Chicago and London: The University of Chicago Press, 1970.

Landucci, Luca. *Diario fiorentino dal 1450 al 1516*, ed. I. del Badia. Florence: G. C. Sansoni, 1883.

Lang, S. "Bomarzo." *Architectural Review* 121 (1957), 427–430.

Langedijk, Karla. *Portraits of the Medici, 15th to 18th Centuries*. 3 vols. Florence: Studio per edizioni scelte, 1981–87.

Lapini, Agostino. *Diario fiorentino dal 1252 al 1596*, ed. Giuseppe Odoardo Corazzini. Florence: G. C. Sansoni, 1900.

Lazzaro, Claudia. *The Italian Renaissance Garden: from the Conventions of Planting, Design, and Ornament to the Grand Gardens of Sixteenth- Century Central Italy*. New Haven and London: Yale University Press, 1990.

Le Corbeiller, Claire. "Miss America and Her Sisters: Personifications of the Four Parts of the World." *The Metropolitan Museum of Art Bulletin* 19 (1961), 207–223.

Legner, A. *Die Parler und der Schöne Stil 1350–1400. Europaische Kunst unter den Luxenburgern*. Exhibition catalog. Cologne: Museen del Stadt Köhn, 1978–80.

Lehmann, Phyllis Williams. *Cyriacus of Ancona's Egyptian Visit and its Reflections in Gentile Bellini and Hieronymus Bosch*. Locust Valley, N.Y.: J. J. Augustin, 1977.

Leithe-Jasper, Manfred. *Renaissance Master Bronzes from the Collection of the Kunsthistorisches Museum, Vienna*. Washington, D.C.: Smithsonian Institution, 1986.

Levenson, Jay A., ed. *Circa 1492. Art in the Age of Exploration*. Exhibition catalogue. Washington, D.C.: National Gallery of Art, 1991.

Levenson, Jay A., Konrad Oberhuber, and

Jacquelyn L. Sheehan. *Early Italian Engravings from the National Gallery.* Washington, D.C.: National Gallery of Art, 1973.

Ley, Willy. *Dawn of Zoology.* Englewood Cliffs, N.J.: Prentice-Hall, 1968.

Lhotsky, A. *Die Geschichte der Sammlungen. Festschrift des Kunsthistorischen Museums zur Feier des 50 jährigen Bestandes*, II.1. 3 vols. Vienna: Verlag Ferdinand Bergen, 1941–1945.

Lightbown, Ronald. *Mantegna.* Berkeley: University of California Press, 1986.

Livorno e Pisa: due città e un territorio nella politica dei Medici. Exhibition catalog. Pisa: Nistri-Lischi e Pacini Editori, 1980.

Lloyd, Joan Barclay. *African Animals in Renaissance Literature and Art.* Oxford: Clarendon Press, 1971.

Loehr, George. "The Medici and China." *Art and Archaeology Research Papers* 6 (1974), 68–77.

Masi, Bartolomeo. *Ricordanze di Bartolomeo Masi, Calderaio Fiorentino dal 1478 al 1526*, ed. G. Corazzini. Florence: Sansoni, 1906.

Mason, Peter. *Deconstructing America: Representations of the Other.* London and New York: Routledge, 1990.

Massinelli, Anna Maria. *Bronzetti e anticaglie dalla Guardaroba di Cosimo I.* Florence: S.P.E.S., 1991.

Massing, Jean-Michel. "Early European Images of America: The Ethnographic Approach." In *Circa 1492: Art in the Age of Exploration*, ed. Jay A. Levenson, 515–520. Exhibition catalogue. Washington, D.C.: National Gallery of Art, 1991.

McCulloch, Florence. *Medieval Latin and French Bestiaries.* Rev. edn. Chapel Hill: The University of North Carolina Press, 1962.

Micheletti, Emma. "I 'Ritratti di Uccelli' del Giambologna per la grotta di Castello." *Scritti di storia dell'arte in onore di Ugo Procacci.* 2 vols. Milan: Electa, 1977.

Miller, N. "Domain of Illusion: the Grotto in France," In *Fons sapientiae: Renaissance Garden Fountains*, ed. B. Macdougall, 177–205. Washington, D.C.: Dumbarton Oaks, 1978.

Montaigne's Travel Journal, trans. D. M. Frame. San Francisco: North Point Press, 1983.

Morrogh, Andrew. "Vasari and Coloured Stones." *Giorgio Vasari: tra decorazione ambientale e storiografia artistica*, ed. G. C. Garfagnini.

Florence: Leo S. Olschki, 1985.

Moryson, Fynes. *An Itinerary Containing his Ten Yeeres Travell.* 4 vols. Glasgow: James Machehose and Sons, 1907.

Mourlot, E. "'Artifice naturel' ou 'nature artificielle': les grottes Médicéennes dans la Florence du XVIᵉ siécle." In *Ville et campagne dans la littérature italienne de la Renaissance.* 2 vols. Paris: Université de la Sorbonne nouvelle, 1976–77.

Münster, Sebastian. *Cosmographei.* 1550. Facsimile edn. Amsterdam: Theatrum Orbis Terrarum, 1968.

Natura viva in Casa Medici. Florence: Centro Di, 1985.

The Natural Sciences and the Arts: Aspects of Interaction from the Renaissance to the 20th Century, ed. Allan Ellenius. Stockholm: Almqvist & Wiksell, 1985.

New World of Wonders: European Images of the Americas 1492–1700, ed. Rachel Doggett with Monique Hulvey and Julie Ainsworth. Washington, D.C.: The Folger Shakespeare Library, 1992.

Nicholson, H. B. with Eloise Quiñones Keber. *Art of Aztec Mexico: Treasures of Tenochtitlan.* Exhibition catalogue. Washington, D.C.: National Gallery of Art, 1983.

Nikolenko, Lada. *Francesco Ubertini called Il Bacchiacca.* Locust Valley, New York: J. J. Augustin, 1966.

Nowotny, Karl A. *Mexikanische Kostbarkeiten aus Kunstkammern der Renaissance im Museum für Völkerkunde Wien und in der Nationalbibliothek Wien.* Vienna: Museum für Völkerkunde, 1960.

Oakley, K. *Decorative and Symbolic Uses of Vertebrate Fossils*, Oxford: Oxford University Press, 1975.

Ong, Walter. *Ramus, Method, and the Decay of Logic.* Cambridge, Ma: Harvard University Press, 1958.

Origo, I. *The Merchant of Prato*, London: Jonathan Cape, 1960.

Pagden, Anthony. *European Encounters with the New World. From Renaissance to Romanticism.* New Haven and London: Yale University Press, 1993.

Pagden, Anthony, trans. and ed. *Hernán Cortés: Letters from Mexico.* New Haven: Yale University Press, 1986.

Pagden, Anthony. *The Fall of Natural Man. The American Indian and the Origins of Comparative*

Ethnology. Cambridge and London: Cambridge University Press, 1986.

Palissy, B. *Discours Admirables*. Paris: Martin le jeune, 1580. Trans. A. la Roque, *The Admirable Discourses of Bernard Palissy*. Urbana: University of Illinois Press, 1957.

Palissy, B. *Recepte véritable*, La Rochelle: Berton, 1563. Ed. K. Cameron. Geneva: Droz, 1988.

Panofsky, Erwin. "The Early History of Man in Two Cycles of Paintings by Piero di Cosimo." *Studies in Iconology*, 33–67. New York: Harper and Row, 1962.

Pechstein, K. et al. *Deutsche Goldsmiedekunst vom 15 bis 20 Jahrhundert aus dem Germanischen Nationalmuseum*. Berlin: Verlag Willmuth Arenhövel, 1987.

Plaisance, Michel. "La Politique culturelle de Côme Ier et les fêtes annuelles à Florence de 1541 à 1550." *Les Fêtes de la Renaissance*, ed. Jean Jacquot and Elie Konigson, 133–152. 3 vols. Paris: Éditions du Centre National de la Recherche Scientifique, 1975.

Pliny, *Natural History*.

Prag um 1600. Kunst und Kultur am Hofs Rudolfs II. Exhibition catalogue. Villa Hügel, Essen, Freren: Luca Verlag, 1988.

Quiccheberg, S. *Inscriptiones vel tituli theatri amplissimi*. Munich: Adam Berg, 1565.

Quiñones Keber, Eloise. *Codex Telleriano-Remensis: Ritual, Divination, and History in a Pictorial Aztec Manuscript*. Austin: University of Texas Press, 1995.

Rasmussen, J. "Mittelalterliche Nautilusgefaesse." *Studien zum europaeischen Kunsthandwerk: Festschrift Yvonne Hackenbroch*, ed. J. Rasmussen. Munich: Klinkhardt and Biermann, 1983.

Ripa, Cesare. *Iconologia*. 1603. Facsimile edn. Hildesheim: Georg Olms Verlag, 1984.

Robertson, Clare. *"Il Gran Cardinale": Alessandro Farnese, Patron of the Arts*. New Haven and London: Yale University Press, 1992.

Rossacher, K. *Der Schatz des Erzstiftes Salzburg*. Salzburg: Residenz Verlag, 1966.

Ryan, Michael T. "Assimilating New Worlds in the Sixteenth and Seventeenth Centuries." *Comparative Studies in Society and History* 23 (1981), 519–538.

Sahagún, Bernardino de. *Códice florentino*. 1569. Facsimile edition issued by the Biblioteca Medicea Laurenziana and Archivo General de la Nación. 3 vols. México: Secretaria de Gobernación, 1979.

Saville, Marshall H. *The Goldsmith's Art in Ancient Mexico*. New York: Museum of the American Indian, Heye Foundation, 1920.

Schaefer, Scott J. "The Studiolo of Francesco I de' Medici in the Palazzo Vecchio in Florence." 2 vols. Ph.D. dissertation. Bryn Mawr College, 1976.

Scheicher, E. "Korallen in fürstlichen Kunstkammern des 16 Jahrhunderts." *Weltkunst* 52: 23 (Dec. 1982), 3447–3450.

Schiavo, Armando. *Il palazzo della Cancelleria*. Rome: Staderini, 1964.

Schönherr, D. "Wenzel Jamnitzers Arbeiten für Erzhog Ferdinand." *Mitteilungen des Instituts für Oesterreichische Geschichtsforschungen*. 9 (1888), 289.

Schürer, R. "Wenzel Jamnitzers Brunnen für Maximilian II: überlegungen zu Ikonographie und Zweck." *Anzeiger des Germanischen Nationalmuseums* (1986), 55–59.

Science and the Arts in the Renaissance, ed. J. W. Shirley and F. D. Hoeniger. Washington, London and Toronto: Associated University Presses, 1985.

Shapley, Fern Rusk. "Giovanni Bellini & Cornaro's Gazelle." *Gazette des beaux-arts* 28 (1945), 27–30.

Shearman, John. *Andrea del Sarto*. 2 vols. Oxford: Clarendon Press, 1965.

Shearman, John. "The Collections of the Younger Branch of the Medici." *Burlington Magazine* 117 (1975), 12–27.

Soderini, Giovanvettorio. *Il trattato degli animali domestici*, ed. A. Bacchi della Lega. Bologna: Romagnoli dall' acqua, 1907.

Spallanzani, Marco. "Saluki alla Corte dei Medici nei Secoli XV–XVI." *Mitteilungen des Kunsthistorischen Institutes in Florenz* 27 (1985), 360–366.

Spivak, Gayatri Chakravorti. "Can the Subaltern Speak?" *Marxism and the Interpretation of Culture*, ed. C. Nelson and L. Grossberg, 271–313. Urbana and Chicago: University of Illinois Press, 1988.

The Splendor of Dresden: Five Centuries of Art Collecting. Exhibition catalogue. New York: Metropolitan Museum of Art, 1978.

Strauss, Walter L. *The German Single-Leaf Woodcut 1550–1600*. 3 vols. New York: Abaris, 1975.

Sturtevant, William C. "The Sources for European Imagery of Native Americans." *New World of Wonders*, ed. R. Doggett et al., 25–33.

Tait, H. *Catalogue of the Waddesdon Bequest in the British Museum II. The Silver Plate.* London: British Museum, 1989.

Tescione, G. *Il corallo nella storia e nell'arte.* Naples: Montanino Editore, 1965.

Thomas, Keith. *Man and the Natural World: a History of the Modern Sensibility.* New York: Pantheon, 1983.

Tongiorgi Tomasi, Lucia. See *Livorno e Pisa.*

Toynbee, J. M. C. *Animals in Roman Life and Art.* Ithaca: Cornell University Press, 1973.

Trexler, Richard C. *Public Life in Renaissance Florence.* 2nd edn. Ithaca and London: Cornell University Press, 1991.

Tuan, Yi-Fu. *Dominance and Affection: the Making of Pets.* New Haven and London: Yale University Press, 1984.

Vasari, Giorgio. *Le vite de' più eccellenti pittori scultori ed architetti*, ed. G. Milanesi. 8 vols. Florence: G. C. Sansoni, 1906.

van den Velde, J. *Spieghel der Schrijfkonste.* Rotterdam: Coopstadt, 1605.

Vaughan, Alden T. "People of Wonder: England Encounters the New World's Natives." *New World of Wonders*, ed. R. Doggett et al., 11–23.

Vignau-Schuurman, T. *Die emblematischen Elemente im Werke Joris Hoefnagels.* 2 vols. Leiden: University of Leiden Press, 1969.

Virgil. *The Eclogues*, trans. Guy Lee. New York: Penguin Books, 1984.

Vocabolario degli Accademici della Crusca. 12 vols. Florence: Galileiana di M. Cellini & C., 1886.

Volpi, Guglielmo. *Le feste di Firenze del 1459: notizia di un poemetto del sec. XV.* Pistoia: Libreria Pagnini, 1902.

von Schlosser, J. *Die Kunst- und Wunderkammern der Spätrenaissance.* Leipzig: Klinkhardt and Biermann, 1908.

Ward-Jackson, P. "Some Main Streams and Tributaries in Europen Ornament", 1500–1750, Part 3, *Victoria and Albert Museum Bulletin* 3: 4 (1967).

Weirauch, H. "Vortstufen eines Nautiluspokals." *Anzeiger des Germanischenm Nationalmuseums* (1976), 105–112.

Wenley, R. "Robert Paston and the Yarmouth Collection." *Norfolk Archeology* 41: 2 (1991), 113–144.

Whalley, J. and V. Kaden. *The Universal Penman. A Survey of Western Calligraphy from the Roman Period to 1980.* Exhibition catalogue. London: Victoria and Albert Museum, 1980.

White, Hayden. "The Forms of Wildness: Archaeology of an Idea." *Tropics of Discourse: Essays in Cultural Criticism*, 150–182. Baltimore and London: The Johns Hopkins University Press, 1978.

Winner, Matthias. "Raffael malt einem Elefanten." *Mitteilungen des Kunsthistorischen Institutes in Florenz* 11 (1964), 71–109.

Woldbye, V. and B. von Meyenburg, eds. *Konkylien og mennesket.* Exhibition catalogue. Copenhagen: Danske Kunstindustrumuseum, 1984.

Wright, David R. "The Medici Villa at Olmo a Castello: Its History and Iconography." Ph.D. dissertation. Princeton University, 1976.

Zammit-Maempel, G. "Fossil Shark's Teeth: a Medieval Safeguard against Poisoning." *Melita Historica* 6: 4 (1975), 391–410.

IV   MEDIATING IMAGES

Acosta, José de. *The Natural and Moral History of the Indies.* Vol. 2, *The Moral History*, ed. Clements R. Markham, trans. Edward Grimston. 1604. Reprint. London: Hakluyt Society, 1880.

Acuña, R., ed. *Relaciones geográficas del siglo XVI.* Mexico: UNAM, 1984.

Adams, Richard, and Arthur J. Rubel. "Sickness and Social Relations." *Handbook of Middle American Indians*, gen. ed. Robert Wauchope, vol. 6, 333–356. Austin: University of Texas Press, 1967.

Adso Dervensis. *De ortu et tempore Antichristi*, ed. D. Verhelst. Corpus Christianorum, Continuatio Mediaevalis, vol. 45. Turnholt: Brepols, 1976.

Alba, Ramon, ed. *Del Anticristo.* Madrid: Editora Nacional, 1982.

Alexander, Paul J. "Byzantium and the Migration of Literary Works and Motifs: The Legend of the Last World Emperor," in *Medievalia et Humanistica.* N.S. 2, 47–68. Cleveland and London, 1971.

Alvarado Tezozomoc, Fernando. *Crónica mexicáyotl.* Translated by Adrián León. 2nd edn. Mexico: Universidad Nacional Autónoma de México, Instituto de Investigaciones Históricas, 1975.

Anderson, Benedict. *Imagined Communities: Reflections on the Origin and Spread of Nationalism*. London: Verso Editions, 1983.

Anderson, Ruth M. *Hispanic Costume, 1480–1530*. New York: Hispanic Society of America, 1979.

Annio da Viterbo. *Ad beatissimum papam sixtum et reges ac senatus christianos de futuris Christianorum triumphis in Saracenos Epistola magistri Ionnis Viterbiensis incipit*. Gouda: Gerard Leeu, 1481.

Annio da Viterbo. *Questiones super multo Iudaico et civili et divino; Pro monte pietatis*, Viterbo, 1497. (Biblioteca Vaticano, 1131).

Archivo General de la Nación. *Catálogo de ilustraciones*. Mexico City: Centro de Información Gráfica del Archivo General de la Nación, 1979.

Arvey, Margaret Campbell. "Sex, Lies, and Colonial Manuscripts." M.A. thesis. University of California, Los Angeles, 1993.

Arvey, Margaret Campbell. "Women of Ill-repute in the Florentine Codex." *The Role of Gender in Pre-Columbian Art and Architecture*, ed. Virginia E. Miller, 179–204. Lanham: University Press of Maryland, 1988.

Bailey, Joyce Waddell. "Map of Texúpa (Oaxaca, 1579): a Study of Form and Meaning." *Art Bulletin* 54 (1972), 452–479.

Baird, Ellen Taylor. "Sahagún's *Primeros Memoriales* and *Codex Florentino*: European Elements in the Illustrations." *Smoke and Mist: Middle American Studies in Memory of Thelma D. Sullivan*, Part 1, ed. J. Kathryn Josserand and Karen Dakin, 15–40. Oxford: B.A.R., 1986.

Baird, Ellen Taylor. "The Artists of Sahagún's *Primeros Memoriales*: a Question of Identity. *The Work of Bernardino de Sahagún*, 211–228.

Baird, Ellen Taylor. *The Drawings of Sahagún's Primeros Memoriales: Structure and Style*. Norman: University of Oklahoma Press, 1993.

Bernheimer, Richard. *Wild Men in the Middle Ages: a Study in Art, Sentiment, and Demonology*. Cambridge, Ma.: Harvard University Press, 1952.

Blaffer, Sarah C. *The Black Man of Zinacantan: a Central American Legend*. Austin: University of Texas Press, 1972.

Blumenkranz, B. *Le Juif médiéval au miroir de l'art chrétien*. Paris: Étude Augustiniennes, 1966.

Boone, Elizabeth Hill. *The Codex Magliabechiano and the Lost Prototype of the Magliabechiano Group*. Berkeley: University of California Press, 1983.

Boone, Elizabeth Hill. "Glorious Imperium: Understanding Land and Community in Moctezuma's Mexico." *Moctezuma's Mexico*, ed. David Carrasco and Eduardo Matos Moctezuma, with essays by Anthony Aveni and Elizabeth Hill Boone, 159–176. Niwot: University Press of Colorado, 1992.

Boone, Elizabeth Hill. *Incarnations of the Aztec Supernatural: the Image of Huitzilopochtli in Mexico and Europe*. Philadelphia: Transactions of the American Philosophical Society, vol. 79, part 2, 1989.

Boone, Elizabeth Hill. "Mapping the Aztec World," paper presented at "Maps and America: J. B. Harley Memorial Lecture," University of Wisconsin–Milwaukee, April, 1992.

Boone, Elizabeth Hill. "Pictorial Documents and Visual Thinking in Postconquest Mexico." *Native Traditions in the Postconquest World*, ed. Elizabeth Hill Boone and Thomas B. F. Cummins. Washington, D.C.: Dumbarton Oaks, forthcoming.

Bousset, Wilhelm. *The Antichrist Legend*, trans. A. H. Keane. London: Hutchinson, 1896.

Brettle, S. *San Vincente und sein literarischer Nachlass*. Munster: Aschendorff, 1924.

Brinton, Daniel G. "Nagualism: a Study in Native American Folk-lore and History." *Proceedings of the American Philosophical Society* 33 (1894), 11–73.

Browe, Peter. *Die Eucharistischen wunder der Mittelalters*. Breslau: Muller and Seiffert, 1938.

Bruhn, W. and M. Tilke. *A Pictorial History of Costume*. New York: Arch Cape Press, 1988.

Bucher, Bernadette. *Icon and Conquest: a Structural Analysis of the Illustrations of de Bry's Great Voyages*. Translated by Basia Miller Gulati. Chicago: University of Chicago Press, 1981.

Burkhart, Louise. *The Slippery Earth: Nahua–Christian Moral Dialogue in Sixteenth Century Mexico*, Tucson: University of Arizona Press, 1989.

Burton, Jeffrey Russell. *Lucifer: the Devil in the*

Middle Ages. Ithaca and London: Cornell University Press, 1984.

Burton, Jeffrey Russell. *The Devil: Perceptions of Evil from Antiquity to Primitive Christianity*. Ithaca and London: Cornell University Press, 1977.

Campbell, Tony. "Portolan Charts from the Late Thirteenth Century to 1500." *The History of Cartography. Volume I: Cartography in Prehistoric, Ancient and Medieval Europe and the Mediterranean*, ed. J. B. Harley and D. Woodward, 371–463. Chicago: University of Chicago Press, 1987.

Caporali, G. B., ed. *Annio da Viterbo, documenti e ricerche*, Consiglio Nazionale delle Ricerche, Centro di studi per l'archeologia etrusco-italica. Contributi alla storia degli studi etrusci e italici, 1. Rome, 1981.

Caro Baroja, Julio. *The World of the Witches*. Chicago: University of Chicago Press, 1965.

Caso, Alfonso. *Los calendarios prehispánicos*. Mexico: Universidad Nacional Autónoma de México/Instituto de Investigaciones Históricas, 1967.

Certeau, Michel de. *The Practice of Everyday Life*, trans. Steven Rendall. Berkeley and Los Angeles: University of California Press, 1984.

Cervantes, Fernando. *The Idea of the Devil and the Problem of the Indian: The Case of Mexico in the Sixteenth Century*. Institute of Latin American Studies Research Papers No. 24. London: University of London, 1991.

Chastel, André. "L'Antechrist à la Renaissance." *Cristianismo e Ragion di stato. L'Umanesimo e il demonico nell'arte*, Atti del II Congresso Interazionale di studi Umanistici, ed. E. Castelli. 177–186. Rome: Fratelli: Bocca Editori, 1952.

Chastel, André. "L'Apocalypse de 1500: la fresque de l'antechrist à la Saint Brice Orvieto," *Bibliothèque de l'Humanisme et Renaissance*. 14 (1952), 122–140.

Cline, H. "Civil Congregations of the Indians in New Spain, 1598–1606." *Hispanic American Historical Review* 29 (1949), 349–369.

Codex Mendoza. Codex Mendoza, ed. Frances Berdan and Patricia Anawalt. Berkeley and Los Angeles: University of California Press, 1992.

Codex Nuttall. The Codex Nuttall: a Picture Manuscript from Ancient Mexico, ed. Zelia Nuttall. New York: Dover Publications, 1975.

Códice Vaticano Latino 3738 or *Códice Vaticanus Rios*. Antiguedades de México basadas en la recopilación de Lord Kingsborough, vol. 3, ed. José Corona Núñez. Mexico: Secretaria de Hacienda y Crédito Público, 1964.

Cohen, Gerson D. "Esau as Symbol in Early Medieval Thought," in *Jewish Medieval and Renaissance Studies*, ed. A. Altman et al., Brandeis University Studies and Texts, vol. 4. 35–49. Cambridge, Ma.: Harvard University Press, 1967.

Cohn, Norman. *The Pursuit of the Millennium: Revolutionary Millenarians and Mystical Anarchists of the Middle Ages*. 1957. 2nd edn. New York: Harper, 1970.

Colin, Susi. "The Wild Man and the Indian in Early 16th Century Book Illustration. *Indians and Europe: an Interdisciplinary Collection of Essays*, ed. Christian F. Feest, 5–36. Göttingen/Aachen: Edition Herodot/Radar Verlag, 1987.

Consenza, M. E. *Biographical and Bibliographical Dictionary of the Italian Humanists and of the World of Classical Scholarship in Italy, 1300–1800*, vol. 1. 2nd edn. Boston: G. K. Hall, 1962.

Coronil, Fernando. "Discovering America Again: the Politics of Selfhood in the Age of Post-Colonial Empires." Review of *The Conquest of America* by Tzvetan Todorov and "The Game of Critical Arrival," *Diacritics*, Spring 1989, 34–61. *Dispositio* 14: 36–38 (1989), 315–331.

Cruttwell, Maud. *Luca Signorelli*. London: George Bell, 1907.

Damisch, Hubert. "La Grille Comme Volonté et Comme Representation." *Cartes et Figures de la Terre*, 30–40. Paris: Centre Georges Pompidou, 1980.

Damisch, Hubert. *The Origin of Perspective*, trans. John Goodman. Cambridge: Massachusetts Institute of Technology, 1994.

Didron, Adolphe Napoléon. *Christian Iconography: the History of Christian Art in the Middle Ages*. Trans. E. J. Millington. 2 vols. New York: F. Ungar, 1965.

Durán, Diego. *Historia de las Indias de Nueva España e Islas de la Tierra Firme*. Ed. Angel Ma. Garibay Kintana. 2 vols. Mexico: Editorial Porrúa, 1967.

Echeagary, José Ignacio, ed. *Códice Mendocino. Colección de Mendoza: Manuscrito mexicano del siglo XVI que se conserva en la Biblioteca*

Bodleiana de Oxford. Preface by Ernesto de la Torre Villar. Mexico: San Angel Ediciones, 1979.

Edwards, John. *The Jews in Christian Europe, 1400–1700.* London and New York: Routledge, 1988.

Ehrenreich, Barbara, and Deirdre English. *Witches, Midwives, and Nurses: a History of Woman Healers.* Old Westbury, N.Y.: Feminist Press, 1973.

Emmerson, Richard K. *Antichrist in the Middle Ages: a Study in Medieval Apocalypticism, Art and Literature.* Seattle: University of Washington Press, 1991.

Fages, H. D. *Histoire de Saint Vincent Ferrier.* 2 vols. Louvain and Paris: A. Uystpruyst, 1901.

Ferares, S. "Le medaille dite de Fourvières et sa légende hébraïque." *Revue Numismatique* 14 (1910), 196–227.

Foster, Elizabeth Andros, trans. and ed. *Motolinía's History of the Indians of New Spain.* Westport, Cn.: Greenwood Press, 1950.

Fuchs, Eduard. *Die Juden in der Karikatur.* Munich: A. Langen, 1921.

Fumi, L. *Il Duomo di Orvieto e i suoi restauri. Monografie storiche condotte sopra i documenti.* Rome: Societa laziale tipografico-editrice, 1891.

Fumi, L. *San Bernardino da Siena in Orvieto e in Porano.* Siena: Accademia "La Nuova Fenice," 1888.

Furst, Jill Leslie. "Mexica–Aztec Conceptions of Disrupting the Flesh." Paper presented at the 1993 College Art Association Annual Meeting, Seattle, February 4, 1993.

Geiger, Gail L. *Filippino Lippi's Carafa Chapel; Renaissance Art in Rome.* Sixteenth Century Essays and Studies, 5. Kirksville, Mo.: Sixteenth Century Journal Publishers, 1986.

Gerber, Jane S. *The Jews of Spain: a History of the Sephardic Experience.* New York: Free Press, 1992.

Gerhard, Peter. *A Guide to the Historical Geography of New Spain.* Cambridge: Cambridge University Press, 1972.

Gerhard, Peter. "Congregaciones de indios en la Nueva España antes de 1570." *Historia Mexicana* 103 (1977), 347–395.

Gibson, Charles. *The Aztecs Under Spanish Rule.* Stanford: Stanford University Press, 1964.

Gibson, Charles. *Tlaxcala in the Sixteenth Century.* New Haven: Yale University Press, 1952.

Gorce, M. M. "Vincent Ferrier (Saint)." *Dictionnaire de théologie catholique,* vol. 15.2, cols. 3033–3045 Paris: Letouzey et Ane, 1946.

Greenblatt, Stephen. *Marvelous Possessions.* Chicago: University of Chicago Press, 1991.

Greenleaf, Richard E. *Zumárraga and the Mexican Inquisition, 1536–1543.* Washington, D.C.: Academy of American Franciscan History, 1961.

Gruzinski, Serge. "Colonial Maps in Sixteenth-Century Mexico." *RES* 13 (1987), 46–61.

Gruzinski, Serge. *La Colonisation de l'Imaginaire: Sociétés indigènes et occidentalisation dans le Mexique espagnol XVI–XVII siècle.* Paris: Editions Gallimard, 1988.

Hain, L. *Repertorium Bibliographicum,* vol. 1. Milan: Gorlich, 1966.

Haney, Kristine Edmondson. *The Winchester Psalter: an Iconographic Study.* Leicester: Leicester University Press, 1986.

Harley, J. Brian. "The Map and the Development of the History of Cartography." *The History of Cartography, Volume I: Cartography in Prehistoric, Ancient and Medieval Europe and the Mediterranean,* ed. J. Brian Harley and David Woodward. Chicago: University of Chicago Press, 1987.

Harner, Michael J. "The Supernatural World of the Jívaro Shaman." *Peoples and Cultures of Native South America,* ed. Daniel R. Gross, 347–356. Garden City, N.Y.: Doubleday/NHP, 1973.

Hartley, Dorothy. *Medieval Costume and Life: a Review of their Social Aspects,* London: Scribner's, 1931.

Harvey, P. D. A. *The History of Topographical Maps: Symbols, Pictures and Surveys.* London: Thames and Hudson, 1980.

Herrera y Tordesillas, Antonio de. *Historia general de los hechos de los castellanos en las islas y tierrafirme del mar oceano.* 17 vols. Madrid: Tipografía de Archivos, 1934–1957.

Hevesy, André de. "Portraits of the Borgias: Cesare." *Burlington Magazine,* 61 (1932), 70–75.

Hevesy, André de. "Une *Histoire Turque* enluminée provenant de la Bibliothèque de Wladislaw II, Roi de Hongrie et de Polonie." *Gazette des beaux-arts,* 8 (1923), 286–296.

Hockers, Joseph. "New Chronicles on the

Expulsion of the Jews from Spain, its Causes and Consequences" (in Hebrew). *Zion* 44 (1979), 201–228.

Holtved, Erik. "Eskimo Shamanism." In *Studies in Shamanism*, ed. Carl-Martin Edsman, 22–31. Stockholm: Almgvist & Wiksell, 1967.

Honour, Hugh. *The New Golden Land: European Images of America from the Discoveries to the Present Time*. New York: Pantheon Books, 1975.

Husband, Timothy, with the assistance of Gloria Gilmore-House. *The Wild Man: Medieval Myth and Symbolism*. New York: The Metropolitan Museum of Art, 1980.

Irizarry, Estelle. "Echoes of the Amazon Myth in Medieval Spanish Literature." *Women in Hispanic Literture: Icons and Fallen Idols*, ed. Beth Miller, 53–66. Berkeley: University of California Press, 1983.

Johnson, Julie Greer. "Women in Early Historical Writings." *Women in Colonial Spanish American Literature*, 9–59. Westport, Cn.: Greenwood Press, 1983.

Kagan, Richard. "The Spain of Ferdinand and Isabella." *Circa 1492: Art in the Age of Exploration*, ed. Jay A. Levenson, 55–61. Washington, D.C.: National Gallery of Art, 1991.

Kamen, Henry. *Inquisition and Society in Spain in the Sixteenth and Seventeenth Centuries*. London: Weidenfeld and Nicolson, 1985.

Kelchner, Ernst, ed. *Der Enndkrist der Stadt-Bibliothek zu Frankfurt am Main*. Frankfurt: Frankfurter Lichtdruckanstalt Wiesbaden, 1891.

Keuning, J. "The History of Geographical Map Projections until 1600." *Imago Mundi* 12 (1955), 1–24.

Kirchhoff, Paul, Lena Odena Güemes, and Luis Reyes García. Introduction. *Historia Tolteca-Chichimeca*. Mexico City: INAH-CIESAS, 1976.

Kisch, Guido. "The Yellow Badge in History." In *Historia Judaica* 4 (1942), 95–144.

Klein, Cecelia F. "Rethinking Cihuacoatl: Aztec Political Imagery of the Conquered Woman." *Smoke and Mist: Mesoamerican Studies in Memory of Thelma D. Sullivan*, Part 1, ed. J. Kathryn Josserand and Karen Dakin, 237–277. Oxford: B.A.R. Press, 1988.

Klein, Cecelia F. "Snares and Entrails: Mesoamerican Symbols of Sin and Punishment." *Res* 19/20 (1990/1991), 81–103.

Klein, Cecelia F. "Woven Heaven, Tangled Earth: a Weaver's Paradigm of the Mesoamerican Cosmos." *Ethnoastronomy and Archaeoastronomy in the American Tropics*, ed. Anthony F. Aveni and Gary Urton, 1–35. Annals of the New York Academy of Sciences 385, 1982.

Klor de Alva, J. Jorge. "Colonizing Souls: The Failure of the Indian Inquisition and the Rise of Penitential Discipline." *Cultural Encounters: the Impact of the Inquisition in Spain and the New World*, ed. Mary Elizabeth Perry and Anne J. Cruz, 3–22. Berkeley: University of California Press, 1991.

Klor de Alva, Jorge. "Language, Politics and Translation: Colonial Discourse and Classical Nahuatl in New Spain." *The Art of Translation: Voices from the Field*, ed. Roseanna Warren, 143–162. Boston: Northeastern University Press, 1989.

Klor de Alva, J. Jorge, H. B. Nicholson, and Eloise Quiñones Keber, eds. *The Work of Bernardino de Sahagún: Pioneer Ethnographer of Sixteenth-Century Aztec Mexico*. Albany: Institute of Mesoamerican Studies, State University of New York, 1988.

Krinsky, Carol H. "Representations of the Temple of Jerusalem Before 1500." *Journal of the Warburg and Courtauld Institutes* 33 (1970), 1–20.

Kubler, George. "The Colonial Plan of Cholula." *Studies in Ancient American and European Art: the Collected Essays of George Kubler*, ed. Thomas Reese, 92–101. New Haven: Yale University Press, 1985.

Kubler, George. *Mexican Architecture of the Sixteenth Century*. New Haven: Yale University Press, 1948.

Lea, Charles Henry. *A History of the Inquisition of Spain*, 4 vols. New York and London: Macmillan, 1906–1907.

Leff, Gordon. *Heresy in the Later Middle Ages: the Relation of Heterodoxy to Dissent, c.1250–c.1450*, 2 vols. New York: Barnes and Noble, 1967.

Leibsohn, Dana. "Primers for Memory: Cartographic Histories and Nahua Identity." *Writing Without Words: Alternate Literacies in Mesoamerica and the Andes*, ed. Elizabeth Hill Boone and Walter Mignolo, 161–187. Durham: Duke University Press, 1994.

Leonard, Irving. *Books of the Brave*. Cambridge: Harvard University Press, 1949.

Lewis, Suzanne. "*Tractatus adverous Judaeos* in the Gulbenkian Apocalypse." *Art Bulletin*, 68 (1986), 543–566.

Lipp, Frank J. *The Mixe of Oaxaca: Religion, Ritual, and Healing*. Austin: University of Texas Press, 1991.

Little, Lester K. *Religious Poverty and the Profit Economy in Medieval Europe*. Ithaca: Cornell University Press, 1978.

Llorentes, Jean-Antoine. *Histoire critique de l'Inquisition d'Espagne depuis l'époque de son établissement par Ferdinand V jusqu'au règne de Ferdinand VIII*. Trans. A. Pellier. 2 vols. 2nd edn. Paris: Truettel, 1818.

Lockhart, James. *The Nahuas After the Conquest: a Social and Cultural History of the Indians of Central Mexico, Sixteenth Through Eighteenth Centuries*. Stanford: Stanford University Press, 1992.

López Austin, Alfredo. "Cuarenta clases de magos del mundo náhuatl." *Estudios de Cultura Náhuatl* (1967) 7, 87–117.

Mallet, Allain Manesson. *Description de l'Univers, contenant les Différants Systèmes du Monde. . . .* 5 vols. Paris: Chez D. Thierry, 1983.

Malleus Maleficarum. Written by Henry Institor (Kraemer) and Jacob Sprenger. Trans. and ed. Rev. Montague Summers. New York: Benjamin Blom, 1970. First published 1486.

Markman, Sidney D. "The Gridiron Town Plan and the Caste System in Colonial Central America." *Urbanization in the Americas from its Beginnings to the Present*, ed. Richard Schaedel et al., 471–490. The Hague and Paris: Mouton Press, 1978.

Mason, Peter. *Deconstructing America: Representations of the Other*. London: Routledge, Chapman and Hall, 1990.

Matos Moctezuma, Eduardo. *The Great Temple of the Aztecs: Treasures of Tenochtitlan*. London: Thames and Hudson, 1988.

Mendieta, Gerónimo. *Historia eclesiástica indiana: obra escrita a fines del siglo XVI*. 2nd edn. Mexico: Editorial Porrúa, 1971.

Mignolo, Walter. "Colonial Situations, Geographical Discourses and Territorial Representations: Toward a Diatopical Understanding of Colonial Semiosis." *Dispositio* 14 (1989), 93–140.

Mignolo, Walter. "Literacy and Colonization: the New World Experience." *1492–1992: Re/Discovering Colonial Writing*, ed. René Jara and Nicholas Spadaccini, 51–96. Minnesota: The Prima Institute, 1989.

Miller, Arthur. "Transformations of Time and Space: Oaxaca, Mexico, circa 1500–1700." *Images of Memory: On Remembering and Representation*, ed. Susan Küchler and Walter Melion, 141–175. Washington: Smithsonian Institution Press, 1991.

Moreno de los Arcos, Roberto. "New Spain's Inquisition for Indians from the Sixteenth to the Nineteenth Century." *Cultural Encounters: The Impact of the Inquisition in Spain and the New World*, ed. Mary Elizabeth Perry and Anne J. Cruz, 23–36. Berkeley: University of California Press, 1991.

Mundy, Barbara. "The Maps of the Relaciones Geográficas 1759–1584: Native Mapping in the Conquered Land." Ph.D. dissertation. Yale University, 1993.

Newton, S. M. *Renaissance Theatre Costume and the Sense of the Historic Past*. London: Rappa and Whiting, 1975.

Nuttall, Zelia. "Royal Ordinances Concerning the Laying Out of New Towns." *The Hispanic American Historical Review* 5 (1922), 249–254.

Nuttall, Zelia. *The Book and the Life of the Ancient Mexicans Containing an Account of their Rites and Superstitions*. Part 1: Introduction and Facsimile, 1903. Reprint. Berkeley: University of California Press, 1978.

O'Callaghan, James F. *A History of Medieval Spain*. Ithaca and London: Cornell University Press, 1975.

O'Malley, John W. *Giles of Viterbo on Church and Reform: a Study in Renaissance Thought*. Studies in Medieval and Renaissance Thought, 5. Leiden: E. J. Brill, 1968.

Oakley, Francis. *The Western Church in the Later Middle Ages*. Ithaca and London: Cornell University Press, 1979.

Oettinger, Marion. *Lienzos coloniales: una exposición de pinturas de terreños communales de México (siglos XVII–XIX)*. Mexico City: UNAM, 1983.

Olmos, Andrés de. *Tratado de hechicerías y sortilegios*. Ed. Georges Baudot. Mexico: Mision Arqueologica y Etnológica Francesa en México, 1979.

Patrides, C. A. "'The Bloody and Cruell Turke': The Background of a Renaissance

Commonplace." *Studies in the Renaissance*, 10 (1963), 126–135.

Perali, Pericale. *Orvieto: note storiche di topografia e d'arte dalle origini al 1800*. Rome: Multigrafica Editrice, 1979.

Peterson, Jeanette F. "Sacrificial Earth: the Iconography and Function of Malinalli Grass in Aztec Culture." *Flora and Fauna Imagery in Precolumbian Cultures: Iconography and Function*, ed. Jeanette F. Peterson, 113–148. Oxford: B.A.R. Press, 1983.

Peterson, Jeanette F. "The *Florentine Codex* Imagery and the Colonial Tlacuilo. *The Work of Bernardino de Sahagún*, 273–293.

Peterson, Jeanette F. *The Paradise Garden Murals of Malinalco: Utopia and Empire in Sixteenth-Century Mexico*. Austin: University of Texas Press, 1993.

Phelan, John. *The Millennial Kingdom of the Franciscans in the New World*. Berkeley: University of California, 1970.

Phillips, Henry, Jr., trans. "Historia de los mexicanos por sus pinturas." *Proceedings of the American Philosophical Society* 21 (1883), 616–651.

Prosperi, Adriano. "New Heaven and New Earth: Prophecy and Propaganda at the Time of the Discovery and Conquest of the Americas." *Prophetic Rome in the High Renaissance Period*, ed. Marjorie Reeves, 279–303. Oxford: Clarendon Press, 1992.

Quezada, Noemí. "The Inquisition's Repression of Curanderos." *Cultural Encounters: the Impact of the Inquisition in Spain and the New World*, ed. Mary Elizabeth Perry and Anne J. Cruz, 37–57. Berkeley: University of California Press, 1991.

Reeves, Marjorie. *The Influence of Prophecy in the Later Middle Ages: a Study of Joachimism*. Oxford: Clarendon Press, 1969.

Reeves, Marjorie. *Joachim of Fiore and the Prophetic Future*. London: SPCK, 1976.

Rieger, Paul and H. Vogelstein. *Geschichte des Juden in Rom*. 2 vols. Berlin: Mayer and Muller, 1895–1896.

Riess, Jonathan. "Republicanism and Tyranny in Signorelli's *Rule of the Antichrist*," in *Art and Politics in Late Medieval and Early Renaissance Italy, 1250–1500*, ed. Charles M. Rosenberg, Notre Dame Conferences in Medieval Studies, No. 2, 157–185. Notre Dame and London: University of Notre Dame, 1991.

Ripa, Cesare. *Baroque and Rococo Pictorial Imagery*. Ed. and trans. E. A. Masur. New York: Dover, 1971.

Robe, Stanley L. "Wild Men and Spain's Brave New World." *The Wild Man Within: an Image in Western Thought from the Renaissance to Romanticism*, ed. Edward Dudley and Maximillian E. Novak, 39–53. Pittsburgh: University of Pittsburgh Press, 1972.

Robertson, Donald. *Mexican Manuscript Painting of the Early Colonial Period*. New Haven: Yale University Press, 1959.

Robertson, Donald. "The Pinturas (Maps) of the Relaciones Geográficas." *Handbook of Middle American Indians*, ed. Robert Wauchope and Howard F. Cline, volume 12, 243–278. Austin: University of Texas Press, 1975.

Roth, Cecil. *A History of the Jews of Italy*. Rev. edn. New York: Schocken Books, 1961.

Roth, Cecil. *The Jews in the Renaissance*. Philadelphia: Jewish Publications of America, 1959.

Rubens, Alfred. *A History of Jewish Costume*. 2nd edn. New York: Funk and Wagnalls, 1973.

Russell, Jeffrey Burton. *Lucifer: the Devil in the Middle Ages*. Ithaca: Cornell University Press, 1984.

Sahagún, Bernardino de. *Florentine Codex: General History of the Things of New Spain*, trans. Arthur J. O. Anderson and Charles E. Dibble. 13 vols. Monographs of the School of American Research, No. 14. Santa Fe: The School of American Research and the University of Utah, 1953–1982.

Sánchez Ortega, María Helena. "Sorcery and Erotism in Love Magic." *Cultural Encounters: the Impact of the Inquisition in Spain and the New World*, ed. Mary Elizabeth Perry and Anne J. Cruz, 58–92. Berkeley: University of California Press, 1991.

Sandstrom, Alan R. *Corn is Our Blood: Culture and Ethnic Identity in a Contemporary Aztec Indian Village*. Norman: University of Oklahoma Press, 1991.

Schulz, J. "Jacopo de' Barbari's View of Venice: Map Making, City Views, and Moralized Geography Before the Year 1500." *Art Bulletin*, 60 (1978), 425–474.

Setton, Kenneth M. *The Papacy and the Levant (1204–1571)*, vol. 2, *The Fifteenth Century*. Memoirs of the American Philosophical

Society, 114. Philadelphia, 1976–1984.

Sherman, William L. *Forced Native Labor in Sixteenth-century Central America*. Lincoln: University of Nebraska Press, 1979.

Silverblatt, Irene. *Moon, Sun, and Witches: Gender Ideologies and Class in Inca and Colonial Peru*. Princeton: Princeton University Press, 1987.

Simpson, L. *Studies in the Administration of the Indians of New Spain*. vol. 1–2 (The Laws of Burgos and Congregations). Berkeley and Los Angeles: Iberoamericana, 1934.

Smith, Mary Elizabeth. *Picture Writing from Ancient Southern Mexico: Mixtec Place Signs and Maps*. Norman: University of Oklahoma Press, 1973.

Solís, Felipe. *Gloria y fama mexica*. Mexico: Smurfit Cartón y Papel de México, 1991.

Southern, R. W. *Western Views of Islam in the Middle Ages*. Cambridge, Ma: Harvard University Press, 1962.

Stewart, Kenneth M. "Witchcraft Among the Mohave Indians." *Ethnology* 12(3) (1973), 315–324.

Sweet, Leonard I. "Christopher Columbus and the Millennial Vision of the New World." *The Catholic Historical Review* 72 (1986), 369–383.

Synan, E. A. *The Popes and Jews in the Middle Ages*. New York and London: Macmillan, 1965.

Thorndike, Lynn. *A History of Magic and Experimental Science*. Vol. III and IV. *Fourteenth and Fifteenth Centuries*. New York and London: Columbia University Press, 1934.

Todorov, Tzvetan. *The Conquest of America: the Question of the Other*, trans. Richard Howard. New York: Harper and Row, 1984.

Torquemada, Juan de. *Monarquía Indiana*. 3 vols. 5th edition. Mexico: Editorial Porrúa, 1975.

Trachtenberg, Joshua. *The Devil and the Jews: the Medieval Conception of the Jew and its Relation to Modern Anti-Semitism*. New Haven: Yale University Press, 1943.

Underhill, Ruth Murray. *Red Man's Religion: Beliefs and Practices of the Indians North of Mexico*. Chicago: University of Chicago Press, 1965.

Vecellio, Cesare. *Habiti antichi e moderni di tutto il mondo*. Venice and Paris: Firmin Didot, 1860.

Velázquez, Primo Feliciano, trans. *Códice Chimalpopoca: Anales de Cuauhtitlan y Leyenda de los soles*. Mexico: Instituto de Investigaciones de Históricas, Universidad Nacional Autónoma de México, 1975.

Watts, Pauline Moffitt. "Prophecy and Discovery: On the Spiritual Origins of Christopher Columbus's 'Enterprise of the Indies.'" *American Historical Review*, 90 (1985), 73–102.

Weiss, Roberto. "Traccia per una biografia di Annio da Viterbo." *Italia medievale ed umanistica*, 5 (1962), 425–441.

Weyer, Edward M. *The Eskimos: Their Environment and Folkways*. New Haven: Yale University Press, 1978.

White, Hayden. "The Forms of Wildness: Archaeology of an Idea." *Tropics of Discourse: Essays in Cultural Criticism*, 150–182. Baltimore: The Johns Hopkins University Press, 1978.

Williams, Barbara. "Mexican Pictorial Cadastral Registers." *Explorations in Ethnohistory: Indians of Central Mexico in the Sixteenth Century*, ed. H. R. Harvey and Hanns Prem, 103–126. Albuquerque: University of New Mexico Press, 1983.

Williams, Barbara. "The Lands and Political Organization of a Rural Tlaxilacalli in Tepetlaoztoc, c. AD 1540." *Land and Politics in the Valley of Mexico*, ed. H. R. Harvey, 187–208. Albuquerque: University of New Mexico Press, 1991.

Wisdom, Charles. *The Chorti Indians of Guatemala*. Chicago: University of Chicago Press, 1940.

Wistrich, Robert S. *Antisemitism, the Longest Hatred*. New York: Pantheon, 1991.

The Work of Bernardino de Sahagún. See J. Jorge Klor de Alva, et al., eds.

Wright, J. *The Play of Antichrist*. Toronto: The Pontifical Institute of Mediaeval Studies, 1967.

Yoneda, Keiko. *Los mapas de Cuauhtinchan y la historia cartográfica prehispánica*. Mexico City: Archivo General de la Nación, 1981.

Zafron, Eric M. "The Iconography of Antisemitism: a Study in the Representation of Jews in the Visual Arts of Europe, 1400–1600." Ph.D. dissertation. New York University, 1973.

PHOTOGRAPHIC CREDITS

INDEX

2-21-96, Coutts, 45(40.50), 62801

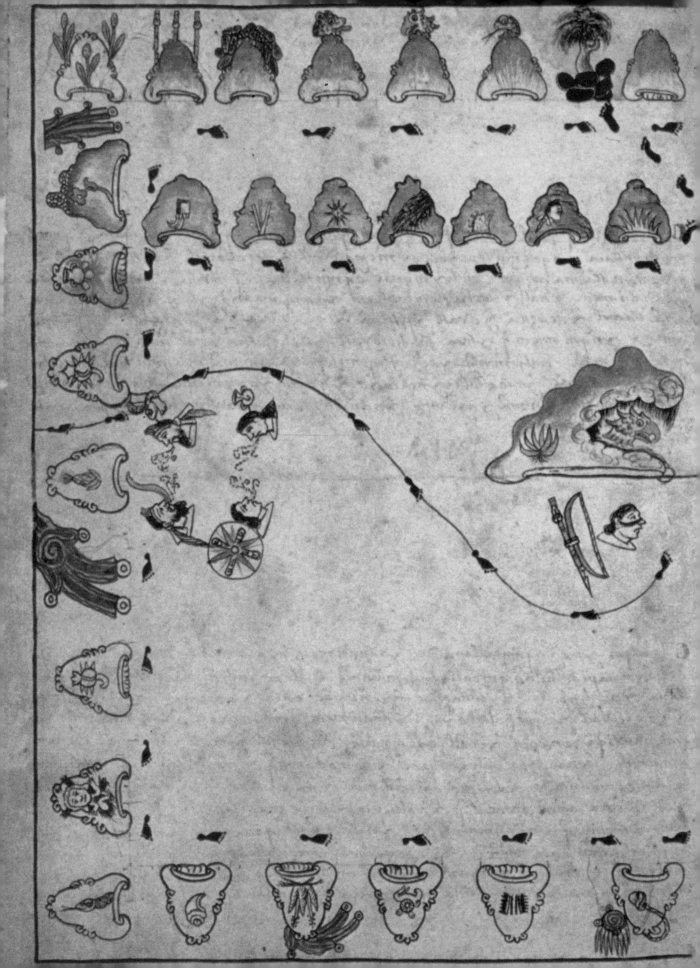